He was convinced that government investment and regulation at home and the export of democracy abroad would ensure domestic stability and pave the way to global peace. He had the ear of presidents in times of crisis, and he held the attention of the nation's intellectuals as his prolific writings articulated liberal ideas for an era. Schwarz boldly examines not only Berle's principles, but those seeming contradictions that allowed him to distinguish between British colonialism and America's "economic imperialism" in Latin America. He explores as well Berle's eventual rift with such liberal friends as John Kenneth Galbraith, Arthur Schlesinger, Jr., and ACLU founder Roger Baldwin over American policy in Vietnam.

A truly comprehensive work that looks into political back rooms, "brain-trusting," and informal networks among the most powerful men of the century, *Liberal* clarifies and revises our understanding of the vision that stoked a half-century of American idealism and well being.

JORDAN A. SCHWARZ, author of the critically acclaimed *The Speculator: Bernard M. Baruch in Washington,* is Presidential Research Professor at Northern Illinois University. He received his M.A. and Ph.D. in history from Columbia University.

LIBERAL

Adolf A. Berle
and the
Vision of an American Era

Jordan A. Schwarz

THE FREE PRESS
A Division of Macmillan, Inc.
NEW YORK

Collier Macmillan Publishers
LONDON

The Free Press
A Division of Macmillan, Inc.
866 Third Avenue, New York, N.Y. 10022

Collier Macmillan Canada, Inc.

Printed in the United States of America

printing number

1   2   3   4   5   6   7   8   9   10

Library of Congress Cataloging-in-Publication Data

Schwarz, Jordan A.
  Liberal.

  Bibliography: p.
  Includes index.
  1. Berle, Adolf Augustus, 1895-1971. 2. Statesmen—
United States—Biography. 3. Economists—United
States—Biography. 4. New Deal, 1933-1945. 5. United
States—Politics and government—1933-1945. 6. United
States—Politics and government—1945-   . I. Title.
E748.B47.S38 1987   973.9′092′4   87-15147
ISBN 0-02-929170-4

IN LOVING MEMORY

Samuel Leibowitz
(1909–1985)

Helen Schwarz
(1900–1986)

Oscar Schwarz
(1900–1946)

Contents

Preface

This is a book about Adolf A. Berle, who transcended careers as a corporation lawyer, legal scholar, and writer on current affairs to become a braintruster for two dynamic twentieth-century American politicians, Franklin D. Roosevelt and Fiorello H. La Guardia. Had the improbable happened and Berle died suddenly or retired from public life in 1933 at the age of thirty-eight, many Americans would have mourned the loss of the most brilliant of the New Dealers. History might then have wondered how different the course of Franklin D. Roosevelt's presidency might have been. In Berle's own lexicon, his life already deserved his greatest encomium of importance: "causative"—it had had an impact on the course of men's thought and actions. Entranced with power and how ideas shaped it, Berle already had written an influential book and helped shape the thoughts and words of a great president. True to his credo as a liberal, only his own personal limitations could prevent the rest of his life from being even more causative. Yet most men live lives of disappointment, and Berle had his share. He was never causative enough.

Ever ambitious—although taught by his Calvinist mother to fear his own ambitions—Berle's quest was to shape the history of ideas. For most men that would have been too tall an order, but Berle, assured at an early age that he was brilliant, set no modest goals for himself. An ordained moral order existed in the universe, and it was his spiritual mission to reveal it. He made the law his vehicle. Aspiring to be the Marx of the shareholding class, a great social critic who rallied people to corporate liberalism, he sought to transform the system rather than abolish it—a task he considered as revolutionary as uprooting capitalism itself. He had studied history well enough to recognize its lessons, uses, paradoxes, irony, and romance. He tried to live a hero's life—making it an adventure or a series of adventures in which he influenced his times and posterity through powerful political patrons and through his writings and ideas. He wanted to be Marx *and* Machiavelli. Power and order were worthy goals and Berle made himself expert on the nature and sources of both.

Indeed, his place in the history of the New Deal is secure. As a historian once remarked, Berle is worth a book about him if only because of *that* book: *The Modern Corporation and Private Property*. Written with the assistance of economist Gardiner Means, it was published in 1932 and became the most acclaimed book of the depression decade, if not of the first half of the twentieth century. With it, Berle and Means converted a dry, almost academic study of economics and law into a manifesto for augmenting a system of private planning with a system of public planning. Berle's original intent in writing the book had been to reveal how the corporation in America transferred control over property from the owner (the stockholder) to management. For most of the 1920s he had relentlessly pursued in law journals the relatively mundane theme that corporations violated the fiduciary trust of stockholders. By itself, the point was not enough to shake the earth; but combined with Means' evidence that a subtle concentration of most national wealth in the hands of only 200 corporations threatened to dominate markets, their studies uncovered a pattern of concentrating corporation wealth in the hands of a relatively few managers. Even that was not new, but their timing coincident with the Great Depression helped explain that crisis by attributing it to economic concentration. There still remained the question of what to do. Bigness might not be goodness, but it was nature's way—a divine order in the cosmos. Big corporations should be regulated by a supreme national power in Washington that liberated Americans from economic oligarchy and broadened wealth without altering the essentials of American individualism. Berle was an effective advocate of "collectivist" capitalist planning and one of the more heralded radicals of the depression decade.

A scholar of power and sometime practitioner of its black arts, Berle's varied careers are important for what they tell us about the ideas and policies that underlay the economics and foreign affairs of his time and how they became the ideas and policies of our time. Words were the tools of Berle's several trades and he chose them carefully. Although Berle did not invent the term "braintruster," he applied it to his advisory work for important political patrons. That work included developing and promoting strategies for the exercise of America's global economic and political power during the New Deal, World War II, and the epoch between the Age of Roosevelt and the Age of Reagan. Berle correctly considered his half century the heyday of the American "empire," another term he did not use capriciously; as a student of history he knew that Americans did not like empires, and that America's adversaries liked to accuse her of imperialism, but that no other term better described a great power system—even if the

American empire was unlike any other empire that preceded it. As a brain-truster Berle had few peers in interpreting the forces of history or in advancing his ideas through ingenious economic and political arrangements consistent with the liberal and democratic precepts of his time. He called himself a "liberal" because he viewed Washington's augmented role in markets everywhere as liberating America and other nations from the restricting clutches of opportunity-stifling corporations and hegemonous colonialism. He did not use the term "state capitalism," but he was among its strongest advocates. Public capital sometimes had to augment and extend the activities of private capital, if only because it was in the national interest. State capitalism, liberalism, and imperialism all were in the best interests of "order," a necessary objective for any ideal society. Daring to define and determine the future of state capitalism, and liberalism, imperialism, Berle set a great course for himself—thereby giving any book about him a large scope.

Berle was one of the most significant of the New Dealers and now is the least written about. This oversight is perhaps explained by observing that he was not likeable to most people. He carried enough inner contradictions about himself to confuse historians who prefer their pigeonholes easily labeled "liberal" and "conservative." Berle was a New Deal liberal intellectual who frequently detested other liberal intellectuals enamored of Marxism and the Soviets; the appellation "cold war liberal" best describes his post–New Deal career. One New Dealer recalled that Berle was the first person he heard use the term "Soviet Empire." Had he lived another decade, he might have been a model study in "neoconservatism." I suspect that he would have detested and rejected both "cold war liberal" and "neoconservative" as essentially meaningless "cartooning," but that does not prevent others from categorizing him. Certainly Berle gave enough of himself for historians to chew over—writing prolifically about law, economics, and foreign affairs, but mostly relegating his writings about himself to a useful diary he kept for history. This book, then, while not aspiring to be definitive, is more a measure of a man's life than the measure of the man.

Berle's career tells us much about policymaking in a democratic epoch: the New Deal's state capitalism; its "Good Neighbor" diplomacy; and the ideological politics of World War II, Roosevelt, La Guardia, and liberalism. As a braintruster, Berle referred to himself as an "intellectual broker"—a technical advisor and speechwriter to select politicians and a polemicist to an informed public. In a pluralist society he sought the ultimate corporatist role. The role took Berle from the relatively exclusive realm of ideas into a secular political arena where he interpreted the crises of their times for men of action and developed schemes and words with which they moved the masses. Timing is important in all marketplaces, even the marketplace of ideas, and Berle always sought to defeat the revolutionary alternative during a time of crisis with a stabilizing alternative. In the 1930s and 1940s, he played a key role in fashioning, implementing, and explaining the imperial system known as the Good Neighbor Policy. He was an assistant secretary of state during World War II, a time when such a secondary position carried considerable prominence and authority in the councils of foreign affairs. During the 1950s Berle pursued his own hemispheric policy through personal relations with Latin American leaders; by 1961 it was evident that, as Dean Rusk put it, in Latin American affairs all roads led to Berle. That entitled him to a place in the unhappy history of the New Frontier's Cuban policy. By then he seemed out of step politically with the 1960s and even with his friends, perhaps because he and his times lost a true fix on the world.

Always a peculiar personality (who else could have whimsically addressed Roosevelt as "Dear Caesar"?), Berle did not mellow with age. His friends and family knew his warmth and generosity, and it is a measure of their respect and admiration for him that they urged me to write a book about a man who, because he "did not suffer fools gladly," came across to the world as difficult, irascible, prickly, obnoxious, and arrogant. He was that—and so much more. Whatever his paradoxes, he has interested and enlightened me ever since Arthur Schlesinger, Jr., first challenged me in 1981 to investigate Berle's historical worthiness. I am grateful to Professor Schlesinger for his unfailing courtesy, kindness, and generosity. He and Berle's colleagues at The Twentieth Century Fund placed enough value upon the project to confer an extraordinary grant upon Northern Illinois University, thus facilitating the book's research and writing. However, this is not a Twentieth Century Fund book. Its grant was given without any conditions other than those normally placed upon accounting for the expenditure of research grants. Moreover, as he promised, M. J. Rossant, Director of The Twentieth Century Fund, graciously gave me the freedom of the Fund's files and duplicating machines. I talked with Dr. Beatrice Bishop Berle for many hours at Konkapot and on East 19th Street about her life with Adolf Berle. Her husband and Berle's friend, Dr. Andre Cournand, contributed several unexpected insights during that time. Also, I have profited from conversations with the following members of the Berle family: Lina Berle, Peter A. A. Berle, Beatrice Meyerson, Frederick Meyerson, and Alice and Clan Crawford. William Emerson, Director of the Franklin D. Roosevelt Library, and his staff gave me their usual expert cooperation. Ernest Cuneo distinguished himself by giving me so much of his time and his knowledge of an old friend. I am also grateful to these other people who talked with me about Berle: the late James Rowe, John Kenneth Galbraith, August Heckscher, Frances Grant, Fletcher Warren, Harvey Goldschmid, Luke Battle, Robert Alexander, Gardiner Means, and Caroline Ware.

Along the way friends and acquaintances of mine sharpened my thoughts of Berle. Frank Freidel warmly assured me that Berle was more than worth my time. Ted Morgan picked apart FDR et al. with the scrutinizing eye of an experienced biographer. Priscilla Roberts contributed certain foreign policy dimensions to my study. Bruce Murphy put Berle in the context of other New Deal lawyers, and Dan Reynolds placed Berle in the context of corporation lawyers and lawyers in general. Leonard Baker thoughtfully brought a Brandeis letter to my attention. North of the border, Robert Cuff set me on the fruitful trail of Escott Reid, and Duane Freer of the International Civil Aviation Organization in Montreal called Edward Warner to my attention. James Divine added to my knowledge of "prodigies." Jonathan Brown gave me the benefit of his considerable knowledge on Latin America. Trumbull Higgins put U.S. policy toward Latin America in another light. Albert Berger steered me through the Rockefeller Papers. Jim Smith filled me in on the doings of foundations. Henry Berger, Gary Glenn, Jeff Mirel, Elliot Rosen, and Blythe Stason provided me with useful tidbits. Joe Burchfield enlightened me on the importance of being G. Frederick Wright. Stanley Horst was indispensable in solving the mysteries of the NIU Law Library. Otis L. Graham and Lloyd C. Gardner read most of the manuscript; I have taken their valuable comments to heart. Joyce Seltzer cajoled and provoked, as an outstanding editor should. Certain officials at Northern Illinois University facilitated my leave of absence and other important matters: John La Tourette, William Monat, Carroll Moody, James Norris, Lawrence Sallberg, Jerrold Zar, Caroline Wood, Elaine Kittleson, Carol Grehn, Joan Biebel, and Linda Schwarz; however, the latter reserved for me special favors that nobody else would or could give me: home, hearth, love, Orrin, and Jessica. Who could ask for anything more?

1

A Causative Life

Yesterday, January 24, was the 100th birthday of my father, born 1865, a few months before the assassination of Abraham Lincoln. He died six years ago. He spanned a century of American history, world history, covering about the greatest changes since the Renaissance.

The immigrant, my grandfather, Protas, established a bridge-head enough to enable his son, my father to get an education and enter the causative processes of the United States. The third generation—mine—is the one that can enter the causative group to the extent of its capacity. I did—and if I was not more causative, it was my fault and not anyone else's.

—Diary, January 25, 1965

THE SCHOOL IN THE HOME

Adolf Augustus Berle, Jr., believed that part of his dynastic mission was to perpetuate the Berles' place in America's political and intellectual heritage. The Berle heritage was what Adolf and his father before him chose to make it; after all, they were the first two Berle males born on these shores. They chose to make the Berles part of an aristocracy of intellect; if a Berle was of modest means, he would still be among the first families in brainpower. Ideas were power, and the Berles asserted the progressivism of theirs during America's progressive era at the beginning of the twentieth century. They carefully put distance between themselves and reactionary plutocrats and political bosses who misled the masses—as well as alienated socialists. The Berles foreswore a monolithic economic determinism and asserted the superiority of spirituality in guiding the affairs of nations. Adolf Berle, Sr., knowing the importance of place to any dynastic enterprise, planted his family in Massachusetts, a state whose dominant old families, Calvinism, and higher education were congenial to his notions of aristocratic liberalism.

The Berles could create their own history because they did not know the particulars of theirs. They were free to imagine that their ancestors had been local aristocrats in a small town called Berleburg in Germany, even if they had no real evidence of that. All they knew for certain was that Protas, the first Berle in America, was hardly a New England Calvinist. Protas had been a German Catholic liberal, a "forty-eighter," who migrated in the wake of the failed revolution of 1848 to Missouri. He served with St. Louis Germans on the Union side of the Civil War and married a fairly well-to-do German woman with whom he had two sons, Theodore and Adolf Augustus. He died suddenly in his thirties. His widow spoke little English, remarried, favored Theodore, and alienated Adolf. Estranged from his mother, brother, and stepfather, the fatherless Adolf was free to develop his own ideas and history. In so doing he cut himself off from his real family; his children did not know of their uncle until they were almost teenagers. As a youth he turned away from Catholicism and explored the liberal romanticism of nineteeth-century German St. Louis.[1]

German St. Louis was a hotbed of ideas and learning. Its immigrants brought with them a love of disciplined study and debate, as well as a conviction that reading the philosopher Hegel made substantive argument possible. Adolf Berle read Hegel as a student at the Polytechnic High School as preparation for oratorical combat at the Philosophical Club and the Liberal Club. Taught by a Yale-trained Hegelian, William T. Harris, the young Adolf Berle discovered the joys of philosophy, and Mozart and Beethoven. More than sixty years later he could recall his secondary education vividly.

Barely five feet tall, Adolf, Sr., sought stature in the world of ideas. At Liberal Club meetings on Sunday afternoons, Berle heard religion declaimed as obsolete by the findings of science. Debates about religion in the Liberal Club inspired him to study the Bible. An apostate from Catholicism, Berle sought another order for the world that harmonized religion and science. At the suggestion of a teacher, he attended services at the United Presbyterian Church where the minister befriended him. Recognizing a streak of romantic idealism in Berle, the minister urged him to study Congregationalism at Oberlin College because the New England faith had a strong intellectual appeal and comparatively few adherents in the West. Berle enrolled at Oberlin and it gave his life direction. In 1887 he graduated Oberlin with a divinity degree and a wife, Mary Augusta Wright, the daughter of his mentor, George Frederick Wright, Oberlin's distinguished professor of the Harmony of Science and Religion. On Wright's advice, Berle furthered his divinity studies at Harvard where he would ever after identify himself with its class of '91. Oberlin gave him an intellectual home and Harvard gave him an aristocratic home. Through marriage, Harvard, and a series of Massachusetts ministerial posts, Berle nearly forgot Catholicism and German St. Louis. He became a staunchly Calvinistic New Englander.[2]

But wherever Adolf Berle, Sr., located, his debt to his father-in-law multiplied and overshadowed his own ambitions. Berle hankered to be an intellectual and political power, but fame and influence in the measure he sought mostly eluded him. He sought to write momentous articles, but what mostly came from his pen were ponderous tidbits for *Bibliotheca Sacra,* Oberlin's theological journal, edited by Wright. As a leader of men from the pulpit, he was beholden to Wright's great prestige and extensive contacts for gaining Massachusetts congregations. More than once his temper alienated his parishioners and compelled Berle to turn to his father-in-law for another church.

The driven Berle found greatest appreciation for his efforts among reform movements in need of both numbers and a righteous spokesman of the cloth; they made him a remarkably well-connected minister whose approval was sought for social legislation and nominees for the U.S. Supreme Court; they also opened doors for his children. The family liked to think that Berle possessed influence that was his "power," but he knew that his greatest success was in producing children who achieved public acclaim he did not enjoy. Adolf Augustus and Mary Augusta Wright Berle began their dynasty with four children: Lina Wright, Adolf, Jr. (born January 29, 1895 in Brighton, Massachusetts), Miriam Blossom, and Rudolf Protas.

Dr. Berle made his family as comfortable as a minister's salary could make it, supplementing congregation salaries with speakers' fees on the Boston lecture circuit. In demand as an orator, Berle employed the talents he had developed in the German clubs of St. Louis and at Oberlin to earn a local reputation for eloquence. Although his inspiring rhetoric lost something on paper, he also wrote editorials occasionally for a Boston newspaper to add a bit to his income. He held a Brighton, Massachusetts, church until 1903 when he briefly took a Chicago pulpit. The democratic West was not to Berle's liking and he pleaded with his father-in-law to find him a New England church in need of a minister. That brought him an offer of a Salem, Massachusetts, pulpit. However, when the Salem schools refused to admit the Berle children to the grade levels their father believed they had attained, he enrolled them in neighboring Beverley's schools. Berle soon found a Boston congregation and moved the family to suburban Brookline and, later, Cambridge. In 1912 Berle lost the Boston pulpit when he stubbornly refused to brook congregational interference with his pastoral independence. He then obtained a professorship of Applied Christianity at Tufts College's theological school and, as he assured his father-in-law Wright, with income from his lectures and editorials, "I shall earn this year with half the labor and a fourth of the responsibility as much as I received at Shawmut Church."[3]

What George Frederick Wright thought of his son-in-law's struggles is not known, but it is likely he was too busy to be concerned. Wright was the intellectual giant that Berle yearned to be. Born in 1838 on the Homestead Farm in Whitehall, New York, close to the Vermont state line, Wright had gone west to earn three degrees at Oberlin before returning for parsonages at Bakersfield, Vermont, and Andover, Massachusetts. Ministers had a lot of time on their hands and Wright made himself a man of many parts. He read the Bible in Hebrew and Greek and devoted his time beyond parish obligations to careful study of how the glacier had affected farming in Vermont, New Hampshire, and Massachusetts. Before long he achieved considerable recognition among natural scientists. Embarked upon two careers, Wright moved to Oberlin in 1881 where he became one of the earliest champions of a Christian Darwinist theology, while as a geologist he traced the drift margin from the Atlantic Ocean to the Mississippi River. Moreover, he traveled widely and wrote prolifically. Beginning in 1901, he toured the world for fourteen months, studying the geology of Siberia and the archaeology of the Middle East. In 1902 his two-volume study of Asiatic Russia found a large audience. More trips to Europe and the Middle East neatly combined his expertise in glaciology and theology. Locally, he wrote about Ohio geology and history, including a biography of the antebellum antislavery Oberlin preacher Charles Grandison Finney. Wright was one of those rare individuals who translate their experiences into engrossing articles or books marked by graceful prose. Many of his scientific, religious, and historical articles appeared in prestigious and popular journals such as *The Nation* and *The Independent.* In a given year he produced two dozen highly readable articles on science, religion, history, and travel. Yet today he is best remembered as a pioneer in glaciology—*Man in the Glacial Period* (1892) and *The Ice Age in North America* (1911) being works of enduring importance as well as readable science. More than 40,000 copies of his books were sold in his time. A founder of the Geological Society of America and active in several other organizations promoting natural history and science, Wright set quite a standard of intellectual fame for his son-in-law and grandchildren.[4]

Wright's direct influence on his Berle grandchildren was limited to only occasional visits, but it was communicated through his daughter, even after he had died in 1921. Mary Augusta Wright Berle taught her children to combine Calvinistic work habits with scientific rationality and Congregationalist spirituality in their eclectic intellectual quests. She took seriously her Calvinistic duty to succor the poor, teaching for a time on a Sioux reservation in South Dakota. She also adhered to her father's faith in a natural order in the universe that harmonized science and religion. He had written:

> I believe that, in the beginning, God created the elements out of which evolved, under his direction, the heavens and the earth; in other words, that he gave the ultimate particles of matter the qualities of inertia which permit them to be segregated into various masses in the universe; that he imparted to these particles and masses the motions appearing in infinite of combinations incident to a progressive universe, and, over all, imposed the mysterious power of gravitation. How these things were done, I have no idea. They belong to the mysteries, no less of science than of theology.

Wright's science enhanced his spirituality. He averred that God had created order in the universe and in the lives of men, repeating these words of Sir Thomas Browne: "Surely there are in every man's life certain rubs, doubtings, and wrenches, which pass awhile under the effects of chance, but, at the last, well examined, prove the mere hand of God." His grandson, Adolf Augustus Berle, Jr., also espoused an order in the world that largely owed itself to spiritual convictions. Even his great-grandchildren repeated his faith of an order in the universe that could not be defied, although they did not know the source of their beliefs.[5]

What science was to Wright, politics and social reform were to Dr. Berle. In "the golden age of Massachusetts aristocratic liberalism," Dr. Berle assailed industrial America's materialism and aligned himself with reformers of working conditions, politics, and the corporation system that threatened to disrupt middle-class America with wars between proletariat and plutocracy. Enlightened professionals and aristocrats had to save the nation from being torn apart by the extremes by siding with the underclasses. Dr. Berle lectured his flock and even other clergy not to encourage the rich in their acquisitiveness. But he was not happy or satisfied as a minister. He wanted his sons to commit themselves to social uplift, but to use other professions to attain it. Taking a page out of William James, whom he intensely admired, Adolf, Sr., labeled the ministry "a pragmatic calling" that combined spiritual and public service in equal parts. However, he righteously denounced the "moral inertia" of the schools of theology that prepared future religious leaders to be indifferent to monopoly capitalism, unemployment, political corruption, and other social ills. He concluded that law school better prepared a young man for preaching the Social Gospel than any divinity school. He envisioned his sons championing great causes with thundering rhetorical bursts in behalf of social justice such as those of the famed lawyer Clarence Darrow. But their immediate model would be the scholarly Louis D. Brandeis—lawyer, writer, social critic, and millionaire. Brandeis was a model of how a life at the bar, wealth, and social standing need not preclude social idealism and intellectuality. And a client's remuneration could easily surpass that of a congregation. When Dr. Berle's namesake briefly considered a career as a history professor, the senior Berle hastened to counsel against its genteel poverty.[6]

He did not want his sons to teach history when they could make history. In part, that was what he sought to do through his political activities. "We live in an era of reform," he trumpeted in 1907. "The ethical and spiritual interests of to-day call for some kind of public activity. The spirit of the age is social and socialistic." He quoted approvingly a philosopher who had written, "As the oak springs from an acorn, so may Socialism be traced to Christianity. In every Christian there is a germ of Socialism, and every Socialist is unwittingly a Christian." But he left no doubt as to which came

first. "The church is the natural asylum from persecution for all social revolutionaries by reason of its teachings and the example of its Founder. A
democracy that is genuine, and not itself a form of tyranny, must coincide
with the fundamental law of Christ." His double-edged sword of reform
slashed against both monopoly capitalism and the dictatorship of the proletariat.[7]

The reformer brought the world into his home. Politically active in
causes ranging from antimonopoly to anti-imperialism, Dr. Berle invited
the intellectual giants of Boston and Harvard to his pulpit to discourse on
matters beyond the spiritual realm, following which he brought them home
to dinner and freewheeling conversations about the world of ideas which
entertained and enthralled the Berle children. Decades later his firstborn
recalled guests that included a zoologist who had studied marine life in Japan, a curator at Harvard's museum, Frank Sanborn, "the leading social
worker of the day," and the progressive lawyer Louis D. Brandeis. They
were intellectually eclectic—Darwinists and others who had "lost faith"
and embraced agnosticism—but engaged the Congregationalist minister in
fierce discussions concerning the compatibility of science and religion. He
encouraged his children to assert themselves in debate and argument on
matters of knowledge.[8]

Dr. Berle preached a gospel of public service, but it did not need to
take the form of government service. Private humanitarian activity through
education or just succoring workers—as Berle did for the unemployed during the depression of 1903 when he and Mrs. Berle brought striking transit
workers hot coffee while they manned picket lines in the snow—were "practical kinds of social action." But it was not enough. He went to the legislature to demand laws that ameliorated working conditions or facilitated
state-sponsored savings banks for the working poor and middle classes. He
joined or created civic organizations that promoted great social causes. "My
father was one of the recognized progressive men of the community," his
son remembered, "and he was a good hot campaigner, and he had his
friendships, although he was hardly regular as a politician, and had very
little to do with the formal organization of politics." Indeed, Dr. Berle had
an aristocratic disdain for mass political parties. Issue politics was his mé-
tier. At the behest of Brandeis the antitruster, he joined the Massachusetts
Anti-Merger League in 1908 and invited the Jewish lawyer to carry the cause
to his congregation. Brandeis respected Berle as an orator and Berle's admiration of Brandeis sent him to Washington in 1916 to testify before the
Senate Judiciary Committee on why a Protestant minister wanted a Jew on
the Supreme Court. Brandeis, retailer Edward A. Filene, Senator Murray
Crane of Massachusetts, and other well-to-do reformers constituted Berle's
network of reformers. What he actually accomplished through these activities is uncertain; but they enhanced his sense of personal power and self-

importance and gave him access to powerful patrons who might benefit his sons.[9]

Of all his reform activities, the one dearest to Dr. Berle's heart was educational reform. He hoped to create a model educational system in his home. A visit to the old country had left Berle resolved to apply German methods of educational discipline to American children, beginning with his own. Adding a dash of Montessori methodology, the Berles set strict rules for their children—acceptable rules which pragmatically stressed individuality and freedom within the confines of family law. While the rules left the young Berle minds free to pursue most inquiry, they also disciplined their habits. Thus, the Berle children learned that freedom and discipline were compatible. When his firstborn was three Dr. Berle taught Lina to recite the Lord's Prayer in English, Latin, Greek, and Hebrew, because, he said, "We believed that by training her to speak correctly and fluently in different languages we would at the same time be training her in habits of attention, concentration, observation, and quick and correct thinking." By the time she was six Lina had learned the rudiments of the ancient languages, mathematics, reading, writing, and spelling in English. The education of Adolf, Jr., Miriam, and Rudolf followed this pattern. While the Berle children attended the public schools, their father always stressed that learning continued at home. Dr. Berle trained his children to absorb information and, more importantly, to seek it out. At early ages the Berle children made games out of the study of classical languages, and history and literature. This did not deprive them of conventional youthful fun—although they lacked ordinary playmates their ages. And perhaps their early attainments made them arrogant toward peers they had eclipsed in learning. Although somewhat isolated, they enjoyed pastoral summers amid the forest and ponds of rural New Hampshire after their parents bought a vacation home there in 1899. Still, it was a childhood that passed quickly: Lina and Miriam entered Radcliffe at 16; Adolf, Jr., and Rudolf entered Harvard at 14. Their accelerated learning made them known as child prodigies. It would be said that acclaim for them made them haughty, an accusation that led them to strive to know and love the common man.[10]

Dr. Berle seized upon great public interest in prodigies that had been stirred by two other prodigies, William James Sidis and Norbert Weiner. (Sidis enrolled at Harvard at age 11 and Weiner gave a lecture to the Harvard Mathematical Club while a 15-year-old graduate student.) He encouraged a magazine article in 1911 that breathlessly treated the Berle children's normal behavior as remarkable: "The two boys take kindly to the roughest forms of exercise, and frequently box together. The girls are vivacious and exceptionally attractive." In it Dr. Berle challenged anyone "to find anything 'freakish' in their appearance or manner; the only difference between them and other boys and girls of the same age is that they are more advanced intellectually." He savored the acclaim for his educational concepts that came with "the hundreds of letters I have received since the publication of the magazine article about the children."[11]

It encouraged him to write a book setting forth his educational methods and philosophy. Published in 1914, *The School in the Home* is a verbose work that celebrates the example of German methods for "breeding intellectual ambition" which he practiced on his children and others. Like his other writings, it is didactic and hortatory, partly intending to promote a venture the minister called "The Berle Home-School," a school in Litchfield, Connecticut, that appealed to ambitious parents intent upon following the example of the Berle children. Although Dr. Berle denied that his intensive training would produce prodigies, he nevertheless sold it as something intended to "secure the highest possibilities of each child." However, if he sought to remake the American educational system in the image of the German, his timing was bad. For the year *The School in the Home* was published was the year the Germans marched into Belgium and stigmatized German culture in New England as anti-Christ.

Dr. Berle exploited his exceptional children and they brought him the only real fame he ever enjoyed. He had intended to make them intellectually competitive, and they were; but he also wanted glory and acclaim for their intellects. "You may see your grandson before you die a man of national fame," Dr. Berle had bragged to his father-in-law. Justifiably proud of his children and himself, Dr. Berle assailed the prodigy tag as "brutal" and decried publicity that treated prodigies as freaks rather than accomplished youths. But a prodigy was one for life. When Adolf, Jr., won the fame his father had predicted, news profiles seldom failed to mention that he had been a prodigy. And when young Berle was arrogant to his adversaries in politics, they relished labeling him an "infant prodigy who never ceased to be an infant."[12]

An accelerated and extensive education was not intended to inculcate humility in the Berle children. Early on they were told they were brilliant and every encounter thereafter confirmed it. Dr. Berle bred confidence in them toward their peers, courtesy to their elders, and kindliness to all less fortunate than they. They were also schooled to make sport in matching wits in brilliant conversation. This did not disadvantage them socially, but it left them feeling so superior that a quest for an intellectual equal was nearly impossible. Lina never married, Adolf married at thirty-two when he discovered that Beatrice Bishop was brilliant enough for him, and both Miriam and Rudolf married late. Few people were made to feel good enough for them. As aristocrats of the intellect, their circles precluded those less gifted.

Aside from his children's accomplishments and his efforts to peddle his methods through *The School in the Home,* Dr. Berle's only other noteworthy product was a forty-seven-page pamphlet, *The World Significance of a Jewish State* (1918). Sensitive to charges of "Prussianism" in his educational schemes during the Great War of 1914–1918, and eager to assert that "we are Americans to the core," Berle dedicated the work "To Louis D. Brandeis, Associate Justice United States Supreme Court, exemplar and leader of the liberating influence of the Jew in American life, with memories of our struggles in the public service." Its diffuse argument for the triumph of Zionism in Palestine appealed to enlightened Christians. A Jewish state in the Near East would bring peace to the world, unleash the material and spiritual genius of Jews, expel the Turks who fought with the Central Powers, stand as a rebuke to imperialism, and forward the principle of self-determination of small states. Twenty and thirty years later Jews remembered Berle's pamphlet as prophetic.

Berle's writings sought enduring fame and his competitive children pushed him to write more. Only the previous year his oldest child, Lina, had a book published, *George Eliot and Thomas Hardy,* a work of literary criticism heavily tinged with Victorian moral judgment and dedicated to her parents—"The first fruits of their love and toil." In it she contrasted "rational idealism" in literature with the "mistaken effort to democratize literature and thought [that] fastened our attention upon our social and intellectual inferiors." The "new humanitarianism" was "disquieting." She celebrated George Eliot's recognition of "the relation of the spiritual elements in life to the grosser material forces," preferring it to an "understanding of commonplaces and brutalities" that marked the new realism. She desired a "sound radicalism" that sought a "law which controls the liberties." It was a plea for an aristocracy of intellect and it surely pleased her father. However, it also drove him to write to fulfill his own ego. Alas, writing did not come easily to him. In 1918 he reported to "Ado," "I am plugging hard on the new book and it goes well pretty easy tho the labor is trying." Indeed, his wife confirmed that he was "busier than ever" writing a book on moral education and was complaining how hard it was "to write such an obviously moral book!"[13]

Maturity made his children materially independent of him, another disquieting part of his aging process. With his children either at college or pursuing careers in New York City during the 1920s, the elder Berle sometimes tended to be a tyrannical patriarch. While Lina boasted to "Ado" that, with both of them self-supporting, "the family savings are more and more accumulating. . . . I think we shall finally reach the capitalist class if things keep on as they are," Dr. Berle's book on moral education was never published. Because he was intellectually a force in their lives, their physical independence of the Berle home-school was not something he accepted gracefully. When Lina, Miriam, and Adolf together set up their own apartment in New York in 1923, Dr. Berle resented their separation from him although they were all over twenty-five. There followed an outburst "like a thunderstorm," as his son later recalled it. Fits of temper that passed quickly were remembered even by his grandchildren, and they left his loving wife and daughters with very deep hurts. "But I always left the door open," his eldest son said.[14]

At sixty-one he called himself an old man whose battles were behind him while not being old enough to write his memoirs. Now his own writings were mostly cranky and rambling missives to newspapers and magazines. His mind still nimbly followed current events and he rendered opinions that sought an audience. Having always railed against social evils—monopoly, imperialism, and corrupt government—he considered himself a progressive man, but his rational idealism was increasingly out of fashion with a new liberalism. His aristocratic liberalism patronized the emerging masses of the cities. A longtime fan of *The Nation* magazine, he was appalled when it published "that wretched drivel of Heywood Broun," even though its publisher assured Dr. Berle that Broun added considerably to the journal's circulation and survival. Al Smith also incited Dr. Berle's wrath in 1928 because he was the advance agent of Tammany Hall's corruption and the Catholic church's illiberality. When his son worked closely with Mayor Fiorello La Guardia in the 1930s, Dr. Berle counseled him not to trust that "cynical" and "treacherous" New Yorker. He was not a democratic man.[15]

Rational idealism was being ground under by interest group liberalism. It made his behavior more erratic with age. Known to American Jews as an old friend of Zionism because of *The World Significance of a Jewish State* and his old association with Justice Brandeis, Dr. Berle privately turned against Jewish activism during the late 1930s. "The whole liberal movement is so cluttered up with the 'political Jews' like [Rabbi Stephen] Wise and his American [Jewish] Congress of humbugs and every liberal movement is made to seem like a Jewish movement!" he fulminated. "Just as the Jews' grievances are their insistence that everybody and everything should be made to hinge on them has made it odious to many people who naturally sympathize with them. I have fought their battles for fifty years, but I am frankly tired of having to subordinate every other interest to theirs."[16]

Jewish activism during the 1930s contradicted one of Dr. Berle's tenets: that American society could assimilate its minorities through equal opportunity and eradicate any causes for social discontent. But Jewish crusaders suggested an unwillingness to become homogenized Yankees in order to achieve tolerance. At a time when Rabbi Wise and other "professional Jews" believed Dr. Berle was a "lifelong friend," he denounced them as "bunk and a treacherous lot." Dr. Berle was not an ordinary Jew-hater, but he liked his Jews to be either very religious or genteel—certainly not prehensile Jews or Jews who espoused peculiarly Jewish political causes like Zionism. He liked a Jew who was "not visibly one." In particular, he liked Bernard Baruch because "unlike the Northern Jew he has what I have noted in most of the high class Southern Jews, a certain maturity and practical *Angriff.*"[17]

His rage against interest group liberalism increased with his own obscurity and his son's emerging fame. He had urged his son to seek power and influence and when he attained a measure of that, the old man felt diminished. Adolf, Jr., and his mother did all they could to extol him and acclaim his past accomplishments. Much of his own success his son happily and hyperbolically attributed to his father, as when he suitably dedicated his first book, "To Adolf Augustus Berle, A.M., D.D. a student of the laws of an older civilization a recognized influence on the laws of our own time whose adventure into corporation finance in New England safeguarded the savings banks of Massachusetts in an evil time." But what Augusta Berle called "his intense temperament" would not be assuaged by flattery. In the winter of 1932 Dr. Berle went off to live by himself before acceding to a reconciliation with his wife. "After forty two years of life together, I do not understand him any more than I did when I married him," his wife wrote his son. "Only I know that the very intensity and force which made him the power he was for so many years has to cast a black shadow. He could not be so great if he were not so human. . . . I know it does him a world of good to feel that he still is a power in public affairs. How much of a power I don't know, but the attitude of mind makes for health."[18]

On the other hand, Augusta Wright Berle was self-effacing, a gentle counterpoint to her husband's intensity. She deferred to his need to dominate the family, but it is possible she was more of a "causative" force upon her children than they acknowledged, so overwhelmed were they by their father's hegemony. "My Mother was one of the last of the pioneer Christians, whose faith in life was great in its quiet and simplicity," Berle wrote upon her death in 1940. "There was so much of the building of America in her life: the pioneering of the Western Reserve prairie in her father's life, the opening of South Dakota in her own; the intense insistence on a spiritual synthesis and the refusal to accept any hatred, which has kept this country clear of the decay which seems to have characterized this century elsewhere."[19]

Berle perhaps exaggerated her pioneering role, but not her tolerance. She taught her son to value spirituality over materialism, public service without power, recreation for relaxation, and kindliness to all. Through her, her son came to believe that the "order of the universe" depended upon the providence of God and excluded evil. If good men persevered, they could rid that universe of disorder. Within young Adolf the demanding and brusque father seemed to duel the reflective and mannered mother. "In temperament she was very different from her husband," her daughter-in-law recalled. "There was a serenity about her bearing that never ceased to impress me." It sharply contrasted with his father's petulance. At times, in an action-oriented world, her son remembered her counsel to take time for retreat and contemplation. "Wisdom can only come by taking time to marshal the throng of ideas and events which are pouring in upon us at all times, and evaluating them as best you can and drawing from them the wisest conclusions possible to us in our human judgement," she told him once during a crisis in his State Department years. Like his father, she tended to homilies, although hers were so much more succinctly and gracefully stated. Another time she wrote: "This is the time for taking stock, so to speak, and considering your spiritual and mental development, and upon the result of that to determine the course which will lead to your greatest happiness and service. It is very easy to be blinded by many affairs so that you miss the deepest meaning of life." She appealed to the better angels of her son's nature, a side of him that did not easily reveal itself.[20]

Unlike her husband, Mrs. Berle was indifferent toward political power. When her son mulled over an offer of assistant secretary of state, she counseled him to treat it as an obligation to the community because "we are going to need strong, wise men to lead us safely through the international chaos we are in and you can define a policy and get a hearing for the deeper aspects of peace, which may check somewhat the tendency to hysterical jingoism. If only spiritual forces can be brought to bear upon our political life!" She was the Calvinistic New Englander her husband and her son aspired to be. When her son asserted that politics was a service to humanity rather than a private quest for power and material gain, it was Augusta Berle speaking. As she told him, "But whatever you do, I believe you are being guided by the ambition to be of service to God and man, purged of personal desires for self advancement." Power corrupted men. Indeed, when Berle vowed to leave the State Department after only six months there, his mother warmly applauded it because "I believe you can do more outside than in, and be much freer in your mind."[21]

Her emphasis upon spirituality and personal freedom did not remove her from secular concerns or intellectual interests. Late in her life she discussed with her eldest son the theme of a gap between an ideal and its performance, which she drew from reading a book about the Soviet Union, wondering, "After all, is there any nation that isn't backward, only they won't admit it about themselves." She wanted justice and charity for all peoples, even those who did not share her Christian spiritualism. "The Italian anti-semitism was a great surprise—where are all these dispossessed people to go?" she asked her son. "No one seems to want them and we think ourselves too civilized to massacre them though we blithely drive them out, homeless and moneyless, and then wash our hands of them." She communicated an absence of hubris, an inner peace with herself and with nature when she urged her children to discover within themselves "sources of tolerance and forebearance that preclude bitterness." Hers was a liberalism in tune with twentieth-century America and did Berle honor during his crusades in the New Deal.[22]

HARVARD PRODIGY

Dr. Berle's point in accelerating his children's education was that it need not be extraordinary. Nevertheless, it was. Adolf Berle, Jr.,was academically prepared for Harvard at thirteen, but he did not enroll until a year later in order to allow for more social maturity. That he entered Harvard at such a tender age formed a major part of the Berle legend a quarter century later. All the world knew that Berle was brilliant, so it always was assumed that he performed brilliantly at Harvard; yet, years later Berle counseled his son Peter, then a freshman following in his father's footsteps—albeit at sixteen—not to be "buffaloed by the myth of your father's alleged brilliance which the record in the Dean's office would not substantiate." He correctly remembered that as a freshman he got 4 Bs and 2 Cs, hardly an extraordinary achievement. The following year he got his first A in comparative literature; his other courses were all Bs, including economics and history. In his junior year he got an A in German and government, and he was recommended by the Division of History, Government, and Economics for a cum laude degree in history.

In fact, the fourteen-year-old freshman made a noteworthy adjustment to Harvard. A group of seniors, led by John Reed, who won fame by supporting the Bolshevik Revolution in Russia and being entombed in the Kremlin Wall (the class of 1910 also included columnist Walter Lippmann, congressman Hamilton Fish, poet T. S. Eliot, and writer Heywood Broun) gave this particular freshman unusual attention and smoothed his adjustment. They seemed to enjoy this precocious youngster whose verbal abilities belied his age. Socially, Berle had neither the money nor the social status to make him acceptable with the clubs, but he quickly found a niche in dramatics and debate and wrote a piece that was published in the Harvard *Lampoon*. He majored in history and excelled in debate. To help pay his way, he wrote for the *Boston American* and the *Boston Globe*—congratulating himself when he earned $15 a week. He could have graduated in 1912, but he decided to take more history courses and earned in 1913 both a bachelor's and a master's in history, writing an essay under Edward Channing. Lippmann may have been influenced by the philosophers William James and George Santayana, but Berle preferred the historians Channing and Wilbur Cortez Abbott, in whose names he later gave a gift to Harvard. Berle was in thrall with the study of history, his intended place in history, and his command of its lessons. Certain that he possessed an enormous store of information, he deemed a philosophy of history as more important. Later, he liked to claim that he would have sought a career as a historian but for his father's wishes that he enroll in the Harvard Law School. "More than once," he declared when he was nearly sixty, "I have wished that fate had slated me for a lifetime of history."[1]

He never attempted to write any history except that which pertained to his legal studies or his own involvements. But he early on wanted to make history through politics. From his later life, one might have assumed that Berle always had been a Democrat, or at least a Theodore Roosevelt Republican. In 1912, while he was at Harvard, two candidates for president had firm progressive reputations that appealed to reformers such as Berle's father: the Democratic governor of New Jersey, Woodrow Wilson, and the former president, the trust-buster, Theodore Roosevelt. Surprisingly, young Berle became chairman of the executive committee of the "Taft for President" Club in 1912. Perhaps he merely reflected his father's "aristocratic liberalism" and a preference for a patrician as opposed to a demagogue. Or perhaps it reflected his father's friendship with U.S. Senator Murray Crane, a patron who arranged for young Berle to visit the lame-duck President Taft in the White House in January 1913. The admirable Brandeis had endorsed Wilson, but it would not be the last time that young Berle and "old Isaiah" disagreed on issues of great importance.[2]

Upon graduation in 1913 Berle entered the Harvard Law School and encountered Professor Felix Frankfurter. Frankfurter had just returned to Harvard from Washington to begin a career as a teacher. Both men were anxious to succeed and there developed between them a strong animus that would ripen into the bitterest and most ideological of New Deal rivalries— although almost nobody knew for certain just how it came about. At times the hostility was articulated along New Freedom–New Nationalism lines, the issue between them being whether the antitrust laws should be used to break up big corporations and restore competition or whether big corporations were the products of natural economic forces and should be controlled through federal regulation. But it was really a more personal antagonism which alienated Berle from Frankfurter.

As a first-year law student Berle enrolled in the thirty-two-year-old Professor Felix Frankfurter's class, determined to flaunt his brilliance. The Berle family later liked to tell the story of how Professor Frankfurter was a dinner guest at the Berle house and found himself constantly upstaged by the brilliance of the family's conversation. "Conversation at the Berle table is a marathon," he is alleged to have told others peevishly, it being suggested that he was either unaccustomed to the competition or no match for them. Later in life neither man cared to discuss the other, and there are only snippets of stories concerning their Harvard years. Yet, what emerges is an arrogant young Berle bent on cutting others down to size. The young Adolf relentlessly challenged Frankfurter in class, thereby making himself an unforgivable embarrassment to the professor. According to William O. Douglas, later a Columbia Law School and New Deal colleague, in the year following Berle's enrollment in Frankfurter's course Berle began attending it for a second year in a row. Frankfurter was puzzled and asked Berle if he had taken the course the previous year. Berle replied affirmatively and Frankfurter asked, "Then why are you back?" "Oh," Berle responded, "I wanted to see if you had learned anything since last year." Another story has a vengeful Frankfurter blocking the young Berle from making the *Law Review*. Berle himself explained how he failed to make the *Law Review* in this way:

> Now, as to getting on with the students, I can't say I did very well. The first year I had a B record which was not good enough for the LAW RE-VIEW, and the second year I had a straight A record which normally would have called for election to the LAW REVIEW. For various reasons which I can only guess about, and don't here transmit the guesses, a couple of men of lower rank than I went onto the LAW REVIEW. I did not, and I was very unhappy. A LAW REVIEW election of course was a passport to a career. I didn't have one now.

Actually, the first year he had two As, lacking an A average by one point. His second year average was an A. Over a half century later it still rankled him that he did not make the *Law Review*, although he did not attribute his failure to lack of academic achievement; he just did not "get on" with his fellow students. Significantly, he omitted any mention of Frankfurter, even when discussing the great teachers who inhabited Harvard Law School then.[3]

Frankfurter had been something of a prodigy himself. He came to this country from Austria as a twelve-year-old who spoke no English; seven years later he graduated from the City College of New York. Following a brilliant record at Harvard Law School, he worked as an assistant in the U.S. attorney's office of Henry L. Stimson. He was a Jew in a world of Yankees. Yet, skilled in debate and exceptionally articulate, Frankfurter quickly learned social skills that made his brilliance all the more useful to establishmentarians such as Stimson. Frankfurter had just joined the Harvard Law School faculty when Adolf Berle enrolled in his class. Both professor and student had something to prove and Harvard was the arena for that. Classroom confrontations did not endear Berle to Frankfurter, who later was known for cultivating adoring acolytes. Moreover, in the words of a Frankfurter biographer, "the key aspect of Frankfurter's personality as it affected his public behavior was his attitude toward public opposition. Because his self-image was inflated, and because his psychological peace rested upon that self-image, Frankfurter could not accept serious, sustained opposition in fields he considered his domain of expertise; he reacted to his opponents with vindictive hostility." Berle gave offense and would enjoy his hostility for the rest of their lives. Their ambitions seemed to need each other's enmity.[4]

Neither Harvard College nor the Law School launched Berle's career. The abrasive young man had not made lifelong friends there. He was a Harvard man, but ambivalent about it. At various times in his life he identified with it until an appearance before an alumni gathering in 1941 provoked an outburst against him because he was a New Dealer. That embittered him; if he had to choose between Franklin Roosevelt and Harvard, the former earned Berle's loyalty. He identified himself with the institutions of his maturity.

In 1916 Berle left Harvard at twenty-one, the Law School's youngest graduate in its history. Hearing that the Boston law firm of Brandeis, Dunbar, & Nutter had a vacancy for a beginning lawyer, Berle "told my father about it and he telephoned Louis Brandeis and I got the job." It was a tribute to his father's "power" that Berle obtained a very desirable position with Brandeis' firm. Several candidates for the opening were passed over and Berle suspected that "there was some resentment in the Brandeis firm" of him because he had gotten the job through his father's influence with Brandeis. (It was the year that Adolf, Sr., had lobbied for the Brandeis appointment to the Supreme Court.) The Brandeis firm mixed corporation law with social service cases and young Berle apprenticed by mostly writing briefs for senior partners like George Nutter; in this way, and by occasionally trying a minor case, he gained "a thorough training in the detailed law." He was paid $50 a month until his salary was doubled after eight months, most of which he saved by living at home. Berle made no durable contacts there. Except for inviting the young lawyer to lunch, Brandeis ignored Berle during that year. Berle would never be a Brandeisian like Frankfurter.[5]

All these men belonged to that early twentieth-century middle class identified by historians Richard Hofstadter and Robert Wiebe as standing aloof from the bourgeoisie and critical of it. It was a hate-love relationship. They were aristocratic liberals who earned their fame by preaching spiritual, moral values to a commercial society they perceived as devoid of anything but materialism. In morally superior tones, they lectured revolutionizing corporations on the iniquity of indifference to poverty, the exploitation of labor, middle-class insecurity, and nationalist expansion overseas in the Philippines and the Caribbean. The Berles, father and son, admired William James' pragmatic tolerance of the big corporation as well as Louis Brandeis' courage in demanding that corporation leaders live up to a higher standard of law. Their beau ideals were the aristocratic lawyers who both served the corporations and admonished them with lofty noblesse oblige.

Commerce itself was not immoral—if it did not greedily forget the public interest that esteemed fair wages and hours for workers and savings banks for the lower middle class that sought entry into the system. The middle class interposed itself between exploiting corporations and the exploited workers. Amelioration-minded lawyers were "intellectual brokers" who wrote laws that humanized the system. But these same lofty-minded lawyers also dreaded the incipient political power of "prehensile" ethnic groups—Russian Jews, Irishmen, and Italians. They sought to "Americanize" them and demand accountability before they became commercial creatures without spirituality. Yet the aristocratic liberals divided over how to come to terms with the corporations. Did the leviathans have to be destroyed or disciplined? Pragmatism and history taught Berle that the corporation structure was the product of a natural revolution that consolidated national power. This revolution would not recede nor could it be diverted. For the time being he had to join it and guide the corporation on a more spiritually humane course. Eschewing economic determinism, the Berles could not consign the collectivity to a historical hell. The Great War had signaled national greatness and now America looked to its corporations to do the job.

2

Old Empires and New

*Liberals must seek allies in other parts of the world, for the job cannot
be done alone. . . . We must girdle the earth with the idea that peace is as
possible as war, though its links must be forged through a period of many
years. We must sedulously refuse to be persuaded by the voices here which
would lead us to an infinite foreign-trade expansion in the Far East, sad-
dling us at length with an Asiatic problem not unlike that which our British
friends are facing with anxious eyes in India and Egypt. We must forego
the lust of dominion over palm and pine.*

—"Bread and Guns," *The Survey,*
February 11, 1922, p. 756.

*At the time it looked to me as though self-determination was being sac-
rificed and I was unhappy about it. . . . It was then that I learned the
practice of foreign affairs was essentially a damnable profession.*

—COHC, pp. 59, 41

SELF-DETERMINATION FOR THE DOMINICAN REPUBLIC

Adolf A. Berle, Jr., enlisted in the army during the Great War, but not
out of enthusiasm for the war, patriotism, or a spirit of public service. "I
didn't like the idea of being in the Army," he recalled more than a half
century after the "war to end all wars." "Most of all I didn't like this war.
I didn't see any particular reason why the United States had to put all its
energies into settling whether the Hohenzollerns dominated Europe or
whether the French entrenched interests behind Clemenceau and so forth
were to be the masters of Europe." He enlisted because of the anti-German
sentiment attendant to the war and his father's desire to demonstrate Berle
loyalty to America. And so Berle joined the Army Signal Corps which was
then, in his words, "a *corps d'elite* and sounded to me like rather fun."[1]

New Englanders from good schools were treated as an American elite
then. Two weeks after it made him a private, the Army offered the young
lawyer from Harvard a commission as a second lieutenant. Berle accepted
with alacrity and soon found himself en route to Plattsburg in New York's

Adirondack Mountains, then known as a preparatory camp for well-bred young men who sought opportunities for military command. There he befriended a bright young man from Maine who shared his double bunk, Gardiner Means, and was introduced to the craft of intelligence. Berle was then sent to the Army War College in Washington. He did not see Europe until the end of hostilities.

In February 1918, the army assigned him to the Dominican Republic, then under occupation by the United States military. It was a turning point in Berle's life both because the episode gave him a firsthand view of errant American imperialism and because it introduced him to the sugar trade, the Caribbean area, and Latin America—where he devoted himself professionally as a lawyer for sugar producers, and to his advocacy of public policy. The Caribbean and the Americas ever after had a special appeal for Berle.

The decision to send Berle to the American-occupied Dominican Republic was inspired by world shortages of sugar during the war that sent prices soaring. With sugar in tight supply and rationed in the United States, Washington had an interest in the Dominican Republic's expanded production of sugar, "an essential industry in war time." A request by the South Puerto Rico Sugar Company and its Dominican Republic subsidiary, Central Romana, for legal aid in untangling a web of landholding laws that inhibited sugar production in the Dominican Republic went to the army. The company was represented by a New York law firm—Rounds, Hatch, Dillingham & Debevoise—and its senior partner, Ralph S. Rounds. Rounds specifically asked for Berle because Rounds and Berle's father had soldiered together in various reform movements. In fact, the Dominican Republic assignment actually was the second army furlough Berle enjoyed courtesy of Rounds—the first being special work for a New York state legislative commission of which Rounds was a member. Although Rounds' law firm was small, as New York firms went, Rounds was a millionaire and a force in Caribbean sugar ventures. The army put the twenty-three-year-old Berle on inactive duty and Rounds gave him a retainer of $250 a month plus travel expenses, along with accelerated lessons in Spanish.[2]

On March 8, the day before Berle sailed on the SS *Brazos* for Puerto Rico and the Dominican Republic, Rounds offered Berle in writing a post-war position in his New York law firm at not less than $3,000 a year. Rounds assured young Berle that for a considerable time he had been looking for a partner with whom he could develop a practice along the line of "legal ideals" and that following the war he would be used in public interest law like that practiced by Brandeis. Visions of becoming "a Brandeis raised to the nth power by the driving force of social development" filled Berle's mind. Like "the young Jewish group" of lawyers who specialized in progressive causes, he too would battle for social settlements in the slums of American cities, fight for improved working conditions in the factories, and advance the causes of consumers against the rapaciousness of monopolies.

It was, he exuberantly told his mother, "a strange thing. . . . A thing at least to meditate over—and God is great." But first he had to negotiate new land laws in a strange country to facilitate expanded sugar production.[3]

It was Berle's initial encounter with American imperialism. The military governor of the Dominican Republic was an American admiral, H. S. Knapp, and the Dominican cabinet served as his staff—"A dictatorship, full, complete, absolute and total, no doubt about it," Berle noted. In 1916, the Dominican Republic had been deemed by the United States as too unstable economically and politically to maintain itself. Moreover, as victims of imperialism are wont to be, it was strategically important to a great power; its location on European routes to the Panama Canal attracted Washington's interest. (Indeed, that was a prime motivation for the U.S. purchase of the Danish West Indies—the Virgin Islands—in 1914). If Washington did not intervene militarily, it reasoned, this valuable island would be easy prey to German militarism and imperialism. Instability elsewhere in the region also was used to justify U.S. military occupations of Nicaragua in 1909 and 1912, Mexico in 1914, and Haiti in 1915. In 1916, American marines were landed in the Dominican Republic on a mission to reform the economic and political structure of a poor country of less than a million people, 85 percent of whom were engaged in agriculture. Since much of its sugar production had been purchased by Germany, it now became the task of the occupying marines and Adolf Berle to deny the Germans Dominican sugar and deliver its expanded production to the Unites States.[4]

Berle's legal assignment called for developing a theory of land titles for a land court which cleared titles to land and enhanced sugar production. The land title system of the Dominican Republic was an antiquated and confused relic of three centuries of Spanish colonialism. But history was the young lawyer's tool of understanding. As Berle later recalled, "suddenly my frustrated studies in Roman Law began to be singularly useful." Under pressure from Washington, the Dominicans had been trying to liberalize the system for several years without success. Uncertainty about the titles was seen by the Americans as an obstacle to the large American sugar companies' development of the country. Moreover, the American military government moved cautiously because it lacked familiarity with the problem. Confusion multiplied and in September 1917, the American minister to the Dominican Republic pleaded with the State Department to act. Acceding to the wishes of the sugar companies and their New York attorney, Rounds, the army sent a youthful Adolf Berle to begin clearing titles.[5]

His base in a marine camp at Seybo, in the foothills of the mountainous island country, was a three-hour horseback ride from Santo Domingo City, and amid a tedious legal process Berle found other adventures to distract him. He traveled alone around the island, frequently reporting to military intelligence on what he observed among the natives. He disdained the American occupation. Around him raged a sporadic guerrilla war between

Dominican insurgents and the American marines; it gave Berle a thrilling sense of danger. As Berle recalled wartime Seybo: "I had lived under the Occupation; had heard marine officers gossiping about prisoners 'shot while attempting to escape' after being hammered over the head with a revolver-butt to make them run; had seen something of the defense of the guardia lieutenant who had shot eleven hostages in Seybo after a marine was sniped in the bush; I had seen, too, a lot of marines laughingly pull his stalled Ford out of a ditch. I had seen leathernecks light their cigarettes at the candles which burn eternally before the shrine before which all Dominicans uncover or cross themselves, and I had seen them playing with the mulatto children in the bush." On one occasion a marine captain was killed in an ambush and in retaliation the marines executed ten Dominican hostages. At Berle's insistence, the Americans investigated the incident and punished those parties responsible for the brutality. While many Americans believed that Dominicans welcomed the occupation because American funds and equipment built roads, schools, and hospitals they had not enjoyed before, Berle did not. He knew that Dominicans still preferred self-government to the American imperial beneficence.[6]

After three months, Berle reported to Rounds that his legal work was nearly complete. However, the military governor of the Dominican Republic and the chief of military intelligence in Washington pressed Berle to continue his ostensible legal assignment in order to "feel the pulse a bit"—to report on how the natives felt about their American overlords. Berle found that the Dominicans he met resignedly considered their military rulers "a stable fact . . . a necessary evil." Tradesmen and small landholders appreciated the order which the military regime imposed. Workers were somewhat indifferent to the American presence, except when food was scarce. The ordinary people of Latin America did not hate American civilians. Through casual contact among peoples, Americans had "a real opportunity to annex a vast territory of good feeling" among the Dominicans or other Caribbean peoples. However, in the Dominican capital, most of Berle's acquaintances were "of the educated class" and happy with American law and order, even as they complained how the Americans colonized them. While Berle romanticized the ordinary Latin American, most of his associations were with the elites of the Americas.[7]

He liked to tell a story of a Dominican Republic experience that buttressed his confidence in the courtesies and kindliness of the common peoples of the Americas:

> My work took me into the back country. One day I got lost in the hills.
> . . . A great storm blew up. Torrential rain, in the tropics, pours down as if every hydrant in the world had opened up. It can be quite frightening. Night falls quickly here—there is no prolonged twilight. . . . Then I saw a small, isolated house by the side of the trail. Fighting the driving wind and rain, I went up to the door and knocked. A man came to the door,

and I asked for shelter. Leaving the door ajar, the man turned to people whom I could not see, and there was a whispered conversation.

"Entre, Senor," The door was opened, and I went in. Three men and a woman were sitting around a table. The house had a dirt floor and adobe walls, one window in the rear, an oil lamp.

We spoke of the weather and the crops. I was invited to share rice and beans with them. The storm abated. I rose to leave, expressing my appreciation. They looked from one to another. The father stood in front of the door. *"Un momento, senor; hay peligro. Mi hijo van con usted."* His son would pilot me down the mountains' circuitous trail.

. . . Only later did I learn that in the recent shooting of hostages by the American occupation forces, a relative of the boy who guided me had been killed. The population was prepared to shoot any American who ventured into the neighborhood. But the boy's presence had shown them that I had broken bread with the uncle of the victim. I was safe. Such is the meaning of friendship.[8]

Berle's affection for the ordinary people of Latin America may have been patronizing; nevertheless, he genuinely disdained military "colonialism." When, in late 1920, the United States announced that it would withdraw troops from the island, Berle wrote an assessment of the occupation for an American magazine. While it had not been all bad because new roads, hospitals, and schools built by the United States were an "adventure in social missionarying," more significant was the moral cost to the United States and the political cost to the Dominicans:

On the debit side we have to record some slight damage to our national honor . . . and a considerable loss of confidence in our ability as national social-welfare missionaries, owing to the various atrocities of the marines on the field, persistent injustice of the courts-martial which were set up throughout the island, and the shocking invasion of rights of free speech and conduct. . . . Worst of all, there has been absolute destruction of the Dominican permanent administration and consequent loss of officials capable of picking up the tasks of reconstruction. . . . [Reconstruction] will probably demonstrate the essential mistake of depriving a country of the chance to give governmental and administrative experience to the men who in time must run its affairs.

"Rarely has a friendly government been so thoroughly destroyed and a friendly country so completely submerged," Berle concluded. Washington could not justify military intervention and occupation of a country on the grounds of national interest. No matter what Americans did for others, "the worst is the effect on Americans. We lose something of our honor, and we blunt our national sensibilities in permitting it. The numbing of moral sense which is the inevitable effect of militarist occupation is a danger which no thoughtful American dares overlook." Nevertheless, United States economic development of the Americas was salutary as an asset in improving the economic welfare of the host country and expanding both countries' trade.

Still, no matter how beneficient to others, it was American imperialism. When Berle returned in 1922 to the Dominican Republic, he marveled at the roads built by the American occupation: "Somehow straight, paved roads are the symbol of colonial power—Rome, Spain, England, now the United States (though we don't call this a colony). It will be interesting to see whether the peace (in Santo Domingo) lasts, and the roads are kept up. But—someone cursed me in the street this morning and it developed that his father had been shot without trial in the last marine operation hereabouts. I suppose the answer is that warfare is most deadly against the maker of it." He preferred an imperialism of trade and aid to one of force. In 1918 Berle left the Dominican Republic a firm advocate of self-determination for all countries. His work for Rounds was not inconsistent with his anticolonialism if Americans obeyed the laws of host countries in which they worked.

Self-determination allowed for foreign investment. What he opposed was military intervention, occupation, colonialism, and hegemony. These beliefs were principal articles of his liberal faith. Ironically, there came a time four decades hence when he remembered them wryly and endorsed American military interventions in the Dominican Republic and in Vietnam.[9]

THE RUSSIAN SECTION IN PARIS

Berle had a gift for acquiring expertise quickly. His father had trained him how to learn what he needed to know before others discovered his ignorance. New fields and tasks did not overwhelm him. Thus, without much background in the language, he confidently took on an assignment in a Spanish-speaking country. What others correctly saw as arrogance was also Berle's confidence that he could master what he could learn and apply. It enabled him to give others the benefits of his eclectic knowledge. Without superficiality, he was an insightful observer and a voluble reporter. A clever man bent upon capturing the ears of men of power, Berle inevitably would be somebody's "braintruster."

Returning from the Caribbean in the fall of 1918, Berle checked in at the adjutant general's office and was directed to the War College for an intelligence assignment. On his own without his father to find a Brandeis or Rounds to advance his career, in a room filled with officers awaiting reassignment, Berle found himself standing next to a desk at which sat a Lieutenant Cushing. Suddenly Cushing was paged and given orders for Siberia; Berle took his seat. Presently an orderly appeared in search of an expert on Russian economics and Berle told him that if he wanted Cushing he was on his way to Siberia. The nonplussed orderly wondered what to do with the paper in his hand; Berle, with great assurance, commanded him, "What is it? Give it here." It was a query from a colonel concerning the current rate of exchange on Finnish marks. Remembering that he had just finished reading *The New York Times,* Berle retrieved it from a wastebasket and found the answer in its financial pages. Subsequently, other questions came from the colonel concerning "Russian economics," all of them requiring little more than rudimentary knowledge of sources and an inquisitive intelligence. Finally the colonel appeared, curious to meet his "expert of Russian economics." Thus did the youthful Berle become one.

Destined for Siberia, he spent the next couple of months gleaning information from a variety of sources on Russia in the library and one personal source—his own grandfather, the author of two impressive volumes on Asiatic Russia. Grandfather Wright provided a foundation; "the rest of it I naturally studied as best I could," he recalled decades later. "Nobody challenged it."

But he never went to Russia. Its last offensive a failure, Imperial Germany sought a cessation of hostilities and peace discussions with the West. The November Armistice made stateside generals eager to get to Paris for the Peace Conference before the State Department could get there with its "experts." The army assigned Berle to Paris as one of its authorities on Russia. With much of Washington hankering for such a historic assignment, he was overjoyed with the opportunity. In late November 1918, Adolf Berle and other officers shipped out across a gale-tossed Atlantic. They landed in Southampton on December 5 and boarded a converted cattle boat for the overnight channel crossing to Le Havre, during which Berle slept as best he could on a cold wooden shelf wrapped in his overcoat. It was worth enduring, for the next night they would be in Paris![1]

His initial Paris accommodations made up for any discomfort suffered in the channel crossing. Finding that their orders for the Supreme War Council (a ruse to get army intelligence officers to Paris) had them headed for suburban Versailles, and that officials assigned to the conference were lodged at Paris' Hotel Crillon, they struck out for the Crillon and through bluff got the rooms they sought—"A palatial palace with Marie Antoinette furnishings!" an awed Lieutenant Berle exclaimed. The Crillon was headquarters for the American delegation to the Peace Conference and already "a rather unchoate mass" of various diplomatic and military officers and "gold-plated secretaries swaggering in splendid and unused uniforms." A bureaucracy was organizing and with it came an atmosphere of intrigue. Amid the hotel's luxury moved all sorts of European servants, inspiring suspicions among the young Americans that many of them were spies for various powers. For a few days Berle had all the exhilaration of a young man discovering the City of Lights for the first time—strolling on the boulevards and along the Seine, and the shock of expensive dining at the Crillon in wartime inflation—his idyll "tempered only by a wonder (on the part of the poorer members like myself) whether we are to be presented shortly with an enormous bill." Alas, President Wilson and his advisers were en route to Paris and on December 11 Berle and his companions were evicted from the Crillon. He spent a day searching the Left Bank for a room and turned up one in an old palace on the rue de Varennes. The tempo of Paris accelerated.[2]

Paris in 1919 seethed with the famous and the would-be famous, everyone with an eye on the main chance. Young Berle was not in the same league with notables such as the president's confidant Colonel Edward M. House, Secretary of State Robert Lansing, General Tasker Bliss and the other American commissioners, or the president's economic advisors—Bernard M. Baruch, Herbert Hoover, and Vance McCormick. But a future generation of presidential advisors prowled the halls of the Crillon and other makeshift offices. Among Berle's lower-echelon cohorts were future notables such as Joseph C. Grew, Walter Lippmann, William Bullitt, John Foster Dulles and brother Allen, and the historian Samuel Eliot Morison. It did not require much imagination to sense history in the making and many of them, including Berle, kept a diary as a token of their self-importance. In it Berle attempted this description of "Wilson's triumphal entry":

> Place de la Concorde was solidly packed with thousands upon thousands—we could look down from our window in the Hotel Crillon opposite the Obelisque. A lane was cut from the Pont Alexandre III, and edged with blue soldiers in double line—there were mobs everywhere, even on the quai. I went to work about 9, and there had been crowds for hours. At half-past ten the guns saluted, and a little time later the Republican guards galloped down the lane, and then came a couple of automobiles; and then open carriages, Wilson, Poincaré, Mrs. Wilson, Bliss, Pichon, Castelnau, Jusserand, Pershing, etc.—amid cheers. Then the blue lines folded inward and the lane was lost in a seething mass. I thought there was not much enthusiasm; but it may have been that the crowd was not noisy.[3]

On Sundays the Americans in Paris adopted a pattern of mixing recreation with negotiation. On the morning of December 15 Berle attended mass at Notre Dame. "St. Paul's in London was so much grander," he sniffed. "Perhaps it was the effect of boardings and sandbags etc." He spent the afternoon working and the evening enjoying the beautiful costumes and settings of a performance of *Daphnis and Chloe* at the luxurious Théâtre Edward VII. But there would be fewer moments of relaxation in the busy days ahead.

The absence of any clear lines of authority among the Americans was ready-made for instant experts such as Berle. A chance meeting with Robert Lord, chief of the East European Divisions and one of his professors at

Harvard, brought Berle an invitation to be his aide while organizing the Russian Section's office above Maxim's restaurant and across from the Crillon. Samuel Eliot Morison "drifted in [wearing], of all things, striped pants and a cutaway coat. . . . When we saw him in striped pants we thought, 'Oh my God.'" A cluster of young Harvard aristocrats ran Western relief efforts for a Russia torn by civil war and Western invasions. The cocky Berle soon found himself making life-and-death decisions such as to which Russian port to send a 10,000 ton ship with desperately needed American food: "I finally sent it to Riga . . . , largely on the basis of the fact that there was a population there with somewhat higher literacy, higher education, somewhat more organized, more likely to make good use of it there than in Odessa, which was in full tide of the Russian Revolution." In the wake of the Bolshevik Revolution and amid the civil war between Reds and reactionary Whites aided by the expeditionary forces of Japan, Great Britain, France, and the United States, the American intelligence officers endeavored to prevent a conference policy that, as Berle expressed it, simply isolated Russia, "into the Deep Freeze."

They were not sympathetic to the Bolshevists, but the young liberals believed that Russia had a right to self-determination. They preferred to save the Russians by sending them food stores instead of sending Western armies to intervene in behalf of reactionaries in the Russian civil war. They criticized the conference's League of Nations proposals of mid-February for virtually excluding Germany and Russia as outlaw nations. Nor did they care for proposals to liberate the nations of Eastern Europe from their beaten empires and impose antirevolutionary arrangements better designed to contain the Red virus than to create viable states. Berle was concerned not merely for ideals but for consequences as well. "The result," he forecast, "is to put an irresistible pressure, military, economic, moral, on these races to ally, unite, smash the buffer states of Poland and Bohemia [sic], and with the greatest resources of manpower, raw material, and technical, organizing ability in the world, defy the whole league. They would have the power to do this." Another war was inevitable unless the West adhered to a true principle of self-determination and did not oppose revolutions that brought radical regimes. To avert another war, Berle said, "The remedy would be a rapprochement with the one or the other [Russia or Germany]; and it is manifestly a political impossibility at the present time to get any sympathy for a rapprochement with the Germans. Personally I should think a German rapprochement would be preferable to a Russian one, but it can't be done. On the other hand the Russian rapprochement might be reached with goodwill and careful negotiation at Prinkipo."

Prinkipo was an island in the Sea of Marmora where Wilson invited all parties to the Russian civil war to negotiate a peaceful settlement of the conflict. Berle had great hopes for the Prinkipo conference, notwithstanding vehement hostility to it by conservatives in the entente countries and in

Russia—as well as the wariness of the Bolsheviks. He conceded that "the whole thing may be smashed up by the refusal of all hands to go on with the Prinkipo conference—which would leave us in a very bad diplomatic hole, with the honors all to Lenine. . . . " Still, in February, with the president back in Washington and Colonel House acting as "viceroy" of the American delegation, Berle fired off a memorandum that argued for Prinkipo. He was proud of it: "I pointed out that we must be prepared to reach a real understanding with the Bolshevists!"

However, what did Western diplomats in Paris really know about Russia? Robert Lord, a good interpreter of events in Russia, went to Poland on special assignment. In his place as chief of the Russian Section was Captain Walter W. Pettit of military intelligence. Pettit had traveled and lived in Russia, spoke and wrote the language, and Lord respected his grasp of the situation. And now the second in command of the Russian Section was Adolf Berle, Jr., an irony that tickled Berle: "There is no one in Government Service, except ourselves, who has followed the [Russian] situation closely. It is all wrong of course; no youngster of twenty-four ought to be making policy. But the simple fact is that there is no one else to make it." Berle flattered himself; he soon learned that he was not making policy— that his memoranda on Russia were routinely ignored by policymakers who knew less about Russian developments than he did.[4]

Nevertheless, Berle was determined and arrogant. He brashly expanded his memos from the single page he sent Colonel House to the several pages he directed to Christian Herter. He intruded himself in other ways—such as arranging a luncheon to discuss Russia with William Allen White, the American negotiator chosen for Prinkipo. And when he learned that an informal committee had been formed to debate policy toward Russia, "though not invited myself I called up D., & wandered in. . . . " There he encountered several military intelligence and State Department officers, including Colonel Van Deman, who had given Berle orders for the Dominican Republic, Herter, Joseph C. Grew, and others. With a cockiness that was his hallmark in later years, the committee's youngest member asserted that he was its best-informed; he was not surprised when it selected him to write a memorandum on the Russian anti-Bolshevists that would form the basis for their discussion at another meeting, thereby giving this minor researcher an opportunity to initiate Russian policy.

Wanting Russia to determine democratically its own destiny, Berle was contemptuous of White Russian autocracy: "The Kolchak administration is a dictatorship, assumed without election or other manifestation of popular will. . . . Kolchak himself is reactionary. . . . His regime has been guilty of a certain amount of oppression." He concluded that "no anti-Bolshevist government is the result of a popular choice." Russia had a right to self-determination and other Eastern European peoples had rights to self-determination from Russia. A consensus developed within the committee for self-determination of the Baltic states independent of Russia, a cause to which Berle adhered two decades later when the Soviet Union swallowed them. But the liberal Berle was consistent in pressing for the protection of all small nations. At times the committee's sessions became heated between "Bolshevists & Bourgeois" factions, Berle counting himself among the anomalous "Bolshevists." In one meeting a "scion of the right wing" startled Berle by agreeing to send food to Bolshevist Russia, although Berle suspected that the effort would founder upon haggling over payments, distribution, and other technical details. "Some hope that by refusing [food] the Russians will furnish the great argument for intervention," he observed; "the army officers know that if we don't have [an] armistice, there will be a military disaster; but we, who are still young and who abide in hope, see the possiblity of illumining a stormy night with one blazing deed of international idealism. And now to work."[5]

With revolution in the air throughout all of Central and Eastern Europe, Berle and other self-styled liberal idealists in Paris demanded of American leaders that Washington disassociate itself from Allied military expeditions in Russia: "The attitude of Japan, Great Britain and France has entailed the constant danger of our becoming involved in an apparently imperialistic policy. . . . Our own purposes toward Russia are not identical with those of the other Associated Governments." At the same time, self-determination for Russia did not license its export of bolshevism. The United States should contain bolshevism, but not endorse counterrevolution: "Failure to isolate the Russian Revolution may involve us in the disastrous policy of having to fight the European Revolution (a thing we neither can nor should do)." Anyway, the Russian Section believed that the Bolshevists sincerely desired ("however insolently expressed") and needed peace. The Soviets could not absorb the Baltic states, but the principle of self-determination countenanced their "eventual federal union with Russia." Berle argued that Washington should recognize the Russian Revolution, declare friendship for its ideals, cease the Western blockade of its ports, and implement these policies, if need be, independent of associated European imperialists. But it was not to be.[6]

In Paris Berle showed an awesome capacity for hard work, seeming to thrive on meetings that sometimes went on all night. However, like many Americans visiting Europe for the first time in 1919, Berle also found time one Sunday to tour the Marne, Chateau-Thierry, and other battlefields, names that had become part of the American vocabulary. On April 6 he and a colleague took a staff car and drove 250 miles, returning so exhausted and depressed by what he saw of the battlefields that he ended the day by downing a half bottle of heavy wine. The countryside was desolate and pacified, but inflation or influenza made Paris hazardous. The commission's librarian caught the flu (1918 saw a worldwide influenza epidemic) followed by a bout with measles; it was feared she would contract pneumonia. Her immediate superior, Professor James T. Shotwell of Columbia, having lost an assistant to the flu only days before, was nearly frantic. An American doctor recommended the U.S. army hospital, but Berle found it "crammed to the doors with venereal" and hastily decided, "after a brief interval of raving" at Americans at the army hospital and at the YMCA, to get her admitted to the Pasteur Institute. At five in the morning he left the librarian there with a temperature of 105 and then spent the rest of that harrowing day in a "fourth-rate" hotel sitting on a trunk in intense conversation with Russian social revolutionaries.

April in Paris boiled with socialist activity. Red flags hung everywhere, houses with the tricolor were stoned, and much gossip anticipated a coming May Day march of 100,000 people—"all the evidence of a coming upheaval," Berle wrote. "Meanwhile Bavaria has become Bolshevist. The game is on; the next move will be to win it or lose it." Berle envisioned a life or death struggle at hand, a cataclysmic expectation he revealed in almost every public crisis during his lifetime.[7]

Most of the time, however, radicals worried him less than did reactionaries. A critical moment for Berle came when journalist William Bullitt arrived in Paris carrying a proposal for peace in Russia from Lenin. But British and French leaders ridiculed or ignored it. Negotiating only with the exiled White Russians, American and European conservatives wanted to ship more guns to anti-Bolshevist forces in Russia, prompting a sharp warning from the American delegation's Russian Section that "to continue supplying munitions to the Russian opponents of the Bolshevist government on the theory that it is necessary to aid the Czecho-slovaks, scarcely conforms to the requirements of a straightforward, consistent and defensible policy." Bullitt, not yet twenty-six, was in disgrace. Even so, Berle found Bullitt's determination to launch a new drive for rapprochement with Russia attractive—if only because "it would be better to tie to a man who was at least trying to get something done than to a bunch who consider that 'watchful waiting' is slowly letting the matter straighten itself out." Thus was born the self-proclaimed *Jeunesse Radicale*.[8]

In the spring of 1919 a group of young Americans in Paris, including Berle and Bullitt, fancied themselves radicals in rebellion against the obtuseness of their leaders. Disappointment—nay, disillusionment—was rife among them. The liberalism of Woodrow Wilson's Fourteen Points, calling for self-determination of Eastern European nations, seemed about to be suffused under a welter of anti-Bolshevism and Western European revenge against Germany. Paris abounded with stories of secret European understandings that would impose imperial spheres of influence upon Eastern Europe. Young liberals felt unhappy and betrayed. In May, British Treasury official John Maynard Keynes resigned from his delegation to write a scorching indictment of the treaty's follies. But there was no American of similar stature to resign in protest—just the *Jeunesse Radicale*: Bullitt, Berle,

Morison, and a few other lower-echelon Americans who endeavored to show their disgust with the turn of events. Never mind, it was a "time when brilliant young men had their innings." They were brilliant—and impudent enough to think they could defy the leaders of the world.

At dinner on Friday, May 23, around a table set with yellow jonquils and red roses in a private room in the Crillon and presided over by journalist Lincoln Steffens—who had accompanied Bullitt on his mission to Lenin—the *Jeunesse Radicale* gathered with sympathizers who dared not go public and resign in protest from the commission. Over coffee, Bullitt, in a foul mood, tossed jonquils at those who had not resigned and roses at those who had, declaring that he would go to the Riviera to lie on the sand and watch the world go to hell. ("He had a great deal of ego in his cosmos," Berle later thought of a man who often accused him of the same.) The conversation was mostly about how they had been sold out. One of the women present asked if anything would be accomplished by a few resignations that had all "the futile gallantry of several mosquitos charging a battleship." This touched off a debate over whether idealism had any place in the affairs of states, Berle vigorously asserting that in the long run force mattered less because morality and ideals determined history. Her democracy was "America's sharpest sword." They all signed the menu (which Berle kept as a souvenir) and the party broke up late in the evening. Berle strolled dramatically alone through the Place de la Concorde's blue fog, recalling Oxenstiern's [*sic*][9] advice to his son, "Go forth, my son and see with how little intelligence the affairs of the world are governed."[10]

In his letter requesting reassignment Berle protested that the spirit of the treaty neither served "the idealistic or material interests of America, or, indeed, of humanity." House's secretary, Joe Grew, assured Berle that his judgment had been brought to the attention of the commissioners. When the socialist newspaper *L'Humanité* printed Bullitt's letter of resignation, Berle relished "the quiet intoxication of a really big row." In mid-June, a month after he had determined to "resign," Berle sent the commissioners a five-page memorandum on American policy toward Russia. It recommended no American relations with either the Kolchak or Lenin governments and pleaded for withdrawal of all foreign forces from Russia. In conclusion, he wrote, "*In no event ought we to conceal from ourselves or from the American public the fact that we are about to participate in a Russian civil war, of at least two years duration, potentially as great as the world war just finished, ultimately involving, in all probability, our men as well as our money and moral standing.*" It was as vigorous a plea for nonintervention as still could be heard in Paris, London, or Washington.

But Berle could not depart as easily as a Keynes or a Bullitt. He was still a second lieutenant in the army and his determination to leave his assigned post in Paris was a violation of his orders. Although he bitterly complained that he found himself "in the peculiar difficulty of whole-heartedly disagreeing with a proposed line of action, and completely unable to secure its alteration,'' Christian Herter directed Berle to stay at his post until the army decided on his case. At a meeting in the commanding general's office there was strong sentiment for court-martialing Berle for refusing to execute orders, but General Tasker Bliss quashed it. If nothing else, the memorandum brought Berle on June 25 his release from the commission and a ticket home.[11]

GLOBAL SELF-DETERMINATION

The conference altered the lives of its participants. Being with Wilson in Paris made many of them statesmen. Herbert Hoover became president, John Foster Dulles and Christian Herter became President Eisenhower's secretaries of state, William Bullitt became the first U.S. ambassador to the Soviet Union, and Joseph C. Grew became a distinguished ambassador under Franklin Roosevelt. Of the young men in the Russian Section, however, Samuel Eliot Morison became a venerable professor of history at Harvard University; Robert Lord left intelligence and academic work to become a Catholic priest; Walter Pettit returned to a social worker's career; and Adolf Berle laid the groundwork for a career in diplomacy.[1]

Berle knew that diplomacy relies upon intelligence, but the United States did not then maintain a foreign intelligence service apart from the military and foreign services. In 1919 Washington was intent upon demobilizing its military intelligence. The Military Intelligence Division (MID) of the War Department reluctantly reduced its wartime staff by discharging, among others, second lieutenant Adolf Augustus Berle, Jr., infantry.

Nevertheless, MID secretly sought to maintain an informal intelligence network. "It is suggested that you keep this division in mind," wrote the director of military intelligence, "so that as time goes on you will help and aid us by contributing anything that may come to your notice that you know would be useful in our work." Berle saw nothing sinister in the request. Indeed, he was eager to "render a real service" to his country without a uniform or compensation, telling a government official, "I have never thought that the only time the Government had a right to call a man was in time of war." To Berle, foreign intelligence was public interest idealism. Working again for Ralph Rounds' law firm, Berle used MID to discover if its Latin American clients had records favorable to the United States; and he probably shared with MID information he obtained on his Caribbean travels for Rounds. He was a patriot. He became a reserve officer for MID and in 1922 even inquired if he could go on active service for limited periods of time. But a parsimonious Congress reduced federal spending and would not spend on a superfluous intelligence apparatus.[2]

Intelligence was deemed vital to a world power, but an unofficial network of volunteers—a reserve intelligence corps composed of New York and Boston elitists—could not fill the need. MID defined intelligence for its reservists as the collection and dissemination of positive information about almost anything relating to "an international movement"—i.e., "Anarchism, Bolshevism, Christendom, Islam, Jewry, etc." That excluded nothing. MID wanted to compile a systematic index from its mass of information in order to make a "very conservative prediction as to the future" of military, political, economic, or psychological activity in every country of the world and to keep Congress and all the departments of the government informed of what to anticipate. Berle eagerly volunteered his knowledge of the West Indies, Central America, and Russia to MID. However, he did not share the enthusiasm of some MID people for spying on American radicals. And when some of Berle's fellow reserve intelligence gatherers were caught zealously spying upon American labor unions or radical groups, Berle agreed with the adjutant general's stern admonition that "such activities have caused embarrassment to the War Department. A secret military police operating in time of peace is most obnoxious to the American people."[3]

Civil liberties and domestic intelligence are at odds with each other. Berle was a committed civil libertarian who did not need to be told what was not foreign intelligence. Moreover, he knew that much of intelligence depends upon research in published sources available to anyone who bothered to read them. Therefore, wanting to inform both those charged with intelligence gathering and an informed public, Berle turned to writing articles for journals of opinion that interpreted foreign affairs. He understood that a thin line separated journalism from intelligence and diplomacy. Several writers such as Bullitt, Steffens, and Lippmann had eagerly served Wilson and House by reporting on the activities of foreigners. They eschewed the myth that journalists were impartial witnesses in service to the truth for the chance to be impassioned servants of policymakers. As a lawyer and a writer, whenever Berle traveled and gained special information concerning foreign affairs, he too sought to share his intelligence in order to shape policy.

One policy he attempted to influence was the Senate's rejection of the Paris Peace Treaty. The quick fury of John Maynard Keynes' book, *The Economic Consequences of the Peace,* had launched a war of words over the treaty and the conference that wrote it. Numerous articles, histories, and memoirs attacked and defended Wilson. Certain that his experiences in Paris bestowed upon him unique credentials, Berle could not resist making his contribution to public debates on the treaty. "The thing is not a Peace but a truce," he prophetically told Senator Philander C. Knox:

> It does not mean less war but more; it aims at humiliating Germany and crippling her without providing either for her reconstruction or for any

advantage to her late enemies by permitting them to disarm. In the Far East it achieves a plainly immoral settlement. The policy of mandates is the merest concealment of colonial annexation. It is more than probable that four fifths of the Treaty relate to some sort of accords of which we know nothing; just as our troops were landed at Archangel under the terms of a Franco-British agreement for "zones of action" in Russia, which was not and has never been disclosed to us.

In *The Nation* magazine Berle denounced the treaty as a "betrayal" of war ideals and cautioned the League for Political Education that the United States needed to pursue generous policies that "acquire [the] friendship of the Russian people, free access to Russian markets on our own terms, . . . and at the same time we could avoid supporting either Russian governments whose ideas we cannot accept, or imperialist ambitions of other countries." He was neither an internationalist nor an interventionist. His study of history had taught him the value of careful definition of long-range national interests based upon generous principles. It was important to adhere to those interests and principles whatever the consequences.[4]

High among his liberal principles was anti-imperialism, an inheritance from his father. He came by his opposition to the American presence in Santo Domingo and Murmansk naturally; the elder Berle had thundered against the American occupation in Manila less than two decades earlier. "I protest against the lowering of the American ideal from one of character to one of power," Dr. Berle had told an Oberlin audience at the turn of the century. (However, his son did not believe that the exercise of global power was incompatible with character or ideals.) Active in the New England Anti-Imperialist League, Dr. Berle maintained that any abridgment of Filipino liberties foreshadowed a curtailment of American liberties: the United States could not "persist half-democratic and half-imperialist." A government despotic in the Philippines would be despotic in America. Adolf, Jr., held similar anti-imperialist principles through most of his career. But he steadily modified them as circumstances overseas seemed to warrant.[5]

As a commentator on foreign affairs, young Berle was incisive, eloquent, even elegant—comparing favorably with Walter Lippmann at his best. Writing with gravity and grace about what he witnessed firsthand or about what he knew best, Berle's foreign affairs analyses blended morality with realism. He deplored American military intervention anywhere, particularly in Russia and in the Dominican Republic, as "a terrible mistake." The American expedition to Russia served no good purpose because "upsetting other people's governments is bad business," especially since Americans there were in league with British and French imperialists. In 1920, when many American boys returned home from Russia in flag-draped coffins, Berle movingly wrote in *The New Republic* how he stood before passing coffins "meditating on many things. Intervention had failed; intrigue

had failed; . . . half Europe and half Asia was still in flames; and the plen-
ipotentiaries [of Paris] had made fools of themselves." Americans had
"nothing to show for our adventure save an unnecessary hate of us in the
Russian people." He did not advocate a pro-Soviet policy; "the Soviets
have many sins on their hands." But he wanted Washington to come to
terms with the Russian people and extend to them the humanitarianism they
deserved and which our ideals expressed. A year later he was hopeful that
the Soviets were "fast approaching the end of [their] revolutionary phase"
and that they were ready to welcome good relations with America: "One
touch of simplicity; one moment of plain speaking without afterthought,
and we may be able to come together. Both Russia and America would
profit thereby."[6]

A decade later he would repeat the theme that modern problems of
government and foreign affairs were technical in nature requiring political
adaptation to bureaucratic realities; state and private institutions, whether
Communist or capitalist, shared similar concerns—as did the people they
served. Twentieth-century technocracy signaled an end to ideology, if we
and the Soviets were wise enough to realize it. Until the mid-1930s he would
be confident that Moscow and Washington were on political courses that
intersected somewhere down the road. The young Berle made himself a
spokesman for a sophisticated tough-minded liberalism that blended idealism with realism in foreign policy. In a dozen years he would have the
ear of a president during a world crisis. While opposed to overseas military
adventures, he was neither an isolationist nor a pacifist. His writings appealed to both radical and conservative sensibilities with his astute understanding of complex international political and economic relationships. *The
Survey* magazine asked him to write a series of articles in 1921 about the
Washington Disarmament Conference.

"The war educated us in sociological cause and effect," Berle wrote.
"We know now that a military campaign in Hungary means starving children in Vienna and [charity] collections on American street corners." No
modern country could isolate itself from the consequences of a remote war.
And certainly no country involved itself more in the world's difficulties
than the United States: "As America is the world's banker she bears not
only her own burden but those of nations abroad. A French expenditure
for arms means added French credits here—because France is living on
American credit—which means higher interest rates to every American mer-
chant and higher prices to every American consumer, and poorer families
in American cities. Every charity must reckon the cost of past or future war
into its budget." No market was immune from the ravages of somebody
else's war. He had learned such lessons firsthand in Santo Domingo and
Paris. Isolation from famines or wars anywhere was rendered impossible
by global geopolitics and modern communications: "There is no such thing
as neutrality in war. Every gunshot means an appeal for charity; every pur-

chase of American munitions means higher rent." Ironically, he would be an assistant secretary of state during the next episode of American neutrality.

All politics had to reckon with the fact that the twentieth century was a democratic age. "As never before," Berle observed, "foreign relations and policies depend on the view of the mass of men as distinct from their governments, and the extreme responsibility of the press is once more violently illustrated." He did not suggest that the masses made policy, but he did insist that if not properly educated or manipulated they would unmake governmental policies not in their best interests. Where imperialism was the issue, he welcomed democratization of foreign affairs. For instance, the West could not impose itself contemptuously upon China; as in Russia, self-determination ultimately would prevail in China. He quoted approvingly a Chinese delegate to the Washington conference: "We do not mind the open door, but it is our door."

The Washington conference forged a treaty limiting arms among four powers. For Berle, it was "a beginning, nothing more." Peace societies throughout the world would have to work with their governments and with each other to assure an end to wars. He feared that the world still sought an elusive peace. Berle recalled a Paris evening in June 1919 when it was announced that the Germans had acceded reluctantly to the terms of the treaty. Guns boomed throughout the city in celebration and milling throngs of Parisians exulted. A Frenchman spontaneously embraced Berle. *"Enfin, c'est la paix,"* said Berle. *"Mais non!"* the Frenchman cried. *"C'est la victoire!"* Given the grievances that lingered throughout Europe in 1919, it was unreasonable to anticipate a durable peace. Now, two years later, another document for peace had been signed "without victory this time" and only time would tell whether it could "replace outworn swords with ploughshares."[7]

A decade later Berle knew that the Washington conference had attained merely an "interval of rest." Only self-determination was assured by the Paris and Washington treaties. He blamed "British intrigues for economic monopoly" for adding discord to global politics. But British imperialism alone did not threaten the world with conflict. He conceded that the United States also had imperial propensities, although he liked to think that American economic imperialism, by disavowing the sword in favor of the dollar, was less of a danger to ourselves and others than British colonialism. Americans did not need to see the Stars and Stripes flown in faraway lands; their imperialism was not "an end in itself" but a drive to share material benefits and idealism with others.[8]

Berle temporarily abandoned writing about foreign affairs during the late 1920s to devote himself to a career in law. But the liberal principles of foreign affairs he enunciated as a young man remained with him. Paramount among them was self-determination of all peoples and freedom of small countries from the rapaciousness of imperial powers—especially arrogant British imperialism. Imperialism bred war and war was seldom in any nation's self-interest. America always had to determine its best interests independently of the policies pursued by European imperialists. At the same time he came to grips with the fact that the United States through its historical circumstances was a great power; he knew that a great power could not be anything but imperial. But to be liberal it has to be imperial without being hegemonic. The task of statesmen was to pursue policies that assured peace and the greatest equity among all peoples. The time would come when foreign affairs occupied Berle again, but for the time being Adolf Berle, like most Americans in the 1920s, pursued a career. Characteristically, he also found time for local public service where he applied principles of self-determination and fairness for the emerging masses. Those principles were the hope of an aristocratic liberalism. Time and events beyond his control would test their success.

CHAPTER

3

Social and Legal Reformer

We are moving out of a state which was primarily political *and into a state which is primarily* economic. *The corporation struggles today with the government as in older day political governments struggled with the Catholic Church. If power is ceasing to be a function of political sovereignty and is transferring itself to industrial principalities, we may be writing, dimly, part of the constitutional law of tomorrow. Even a tyro at statistics knows that the economic situation reflected in the world of corporation finance betrays, not a settled result, but transition: a society in terrific flux. Concentration of power over property has reached a point literally unknown in the world's history. . . . Accordingly, it behooves us to be slow in our going, careful in our thinking and call to aid . . . a law which may well become of paramount importance during the next century.*

—"The Organization of the Law
of Corporation Finance,"
Tennessee Law Review
(April 1931), pp. 144–45

SELF-DETERMINATION ON HENRY STREET AND IN SANTA FE

During the early 1920s, while he worked in corporate law at the Rounds firm in Wall Street, Adolf Berle, Jr., lived among the urban poor of the Lower East Side of New York for two years and, in 1923, assisted the American Indian Aid Association's efforts to restore lands to New Mexico's Navajos. These two episodes in young Berle's career contributed to a reputation for putting himself on the line for liberal causes—thereby identifying him with social workers, labor leaders, and others who sought to organize the poor both to enhance opportunity and to ameliorate their lot. The aspiring attorney exhibited social conscience and noblesse oblige, at the same time developing a useful network of wealthy liberal friends and associates.[1]

Until October 1922, when he moved to an apartment he shared with his sisters at 45 West 11th Street, off Fifth Avenue, home on the Lower East Side of New York was a tenement flat at 265 Henry Street next door to the Henry Street Settlement. The settlement was administered by the nurse and social worker Lillian D. Wald—who, not incidentally, was an old friend of Berle's father.

He made himself a favorite of Lillian Wald, addressing her affectionately as "Madonna." To some people that name might have suggested Berle's obsequiousness to New York's liberal heroine, but she recognized it as Berle's way of bestowing pet names upon people he liked. (His sister Lina was "Starlight," Beatrice Bishop would be his "Playmate," and Franklin Roosevelt would be "Caesar.") Besides, the name suggested her matriarchical saintliness. She had much about her for Berle to admire, for "Miss Wald was the ideal Fabian. Shrewd, practical, dry-eyed, she had a genius for the concrete, seeing life as it was and wanting to make it better. There was no shrinking, no condescension, no idolizing, no sentimentalism, no preening, little theorizing, nothing but work, hard and endless and free from contaminations of self." This German-Jewish woman could have been more Calvinistic than a Berle.[2]

Theirs was a friendship that surprised those who adored her and found him an imperious, brusque, and arrogant snob. He revealed himself to different people in different ways. When some of her friends questioned how she tolerated his manner, she deflected his detractors, saying, "You don't understand him." She did; she was grateful for his "rare quality of . . . precious loyalty and friendship." When he left Henry Street she assured him, "You belong to us and we to you and three years of such comradeship and fellowship spiritually unite us. . . . Please be with us a great deal." And he was in all sorts of ways. He gave the settlement nonremunerative legal assistance when it sought the closing of a disorderly saloon during prohibition on the corner of Henry and Montgomery Streets. Or there was the time when he was called from his dinner to dash uptown to a Harlem community center in emergency need of a young lawyer known for his "devotion to Henry Street."[3]

Berle lived among the poor but he was not one of them. The experience ennobled him, earned him valuable credentials and friends, and kept faith with the Social Gospel of his father, mother, and grandfather. He fulfilled a mission to succor the disadvantaged and Americanize them through education so that they could enjoy this country's economic and social opportunities. And for his own reasons Berle wanted to be in touch with the reality of squalid lives in the ghetto while he negotiated the reality of corporation problems in the nation and in the world. Hopefully, he could benefit the poor through an amelioration of their harsh conditions and possibly demonstrate through education the fluidity of America's class structure. Finally, it was not at all unusual for young people of his status to volunteer service to the poor. Most social workers came from the middle class or the well-to-do and among the volunteer workers in the settlement houses of New York one frequently could find a Lehman, Morgenthau, Warburg, or Harriman. When Berle was elected to Henry Street Settlement's board of governors, his cogovernors included the likes of George Gordon Battle, Hamlin Garland, Lyttleton B. P. Gould, Norma Hapgood, Sam A. Lewisohn, Alton B. Parker, Albert Shaw, Cornelius Vanderbilt, Jr., Virginia C. Gildersleeve, Mrs. Emil Goldmark, Mrs. Simon Guggenheim, Mary K. Simkhovitch, Mrs. William Howard Taft II, and Mrs. Frank A. Vanderlip. Few organizations had New Yorkers more prominent in finance or civic affairs. In fact, a cynic could argue that the settlement house was as good a place as any for an ambitous young middle-class lawyer to make contact among the eleemosynary elements of the upper classes.[4]

Self-determination not only applied to nations abroad but to the nations of New York City. Well-to-do liberals wanted to teach ghetto dwellers democracy and Americanize them. "Results will not come in this generation," he suspected, partly because politicians exploited them, well-intentioned charitable organizations could not decide upon a unified strategy of help, and the immigrants themselves were an "undeveloped people" hindered by their alien cultures. Berle wondered how the poor could learn about American democracy, improve their living and working conditions, and attain assimilation and absorption into American society when the volunteers and government workers who came among them lacked a cohesive organization and strategy for effective action. He particularly found Catholics hindered by a "a religion still in the stage of absolute dictatorship." Inspired by the chaos of life as he witnessed it, Berle articulated a theme that was central to his liberal credo: the need for efficient government to organize the self-improvement of disadvantaged peoples. As he wrote in *The New Republic,* "We spend a [great] deal of time talking about self-determination of subject peoples, and about helping them to help themselves, and so forth. Insofar as that talk means anything, it means teaching such people to liberate themselves from their own conditions. This is what we must some time begin doing at home." Somehow the liberal elites and parvenus like himself had to educate the immigrant and his children for self-determination.

But he did not see himself as patronizing or engaging in a form of domestic missionary imperialism. He hoped to improve conditions among poor immigrants and their offspring through teaching new habits, attitudes, and ideas without depriving them of their self-esteem. "Having someone come around to tell him to learn, or having a social worker enter his home unasked to prescribe hygenic standards puts him in the position of a delinquent who must be watched, and involves all kinds of degrading connotations," he wrote with the sort of sensitive acuity that endeared him to Lillian Wald and others who considered themselves enlightened. "You cannot give away ideas any more than you can give away money, without running a fair chance of pauperizing the recipient." Patronizing the poor was not uplifting.[5]

The Henry Street Settlement experience provided Berle with insights for thoughtful articles, many of which appeared in *The Nation, The New Republic,* and *The Survey,* the principal journals where the progressives of the 1920s talked to each other. "Moved by the faith that an elite of professional persons and community leaders, if well informed, could move the nation along the paths of welfare and progress," these journals of opinion dedicated themselves "to sound reporting of social facts and to the elaboration of policies and programs designed to ameliorate social evils and reconstruct a more just America."[6] In particular, Berle wrote for the social service journal *The Survey* beginning in 1920 a three-decade relationship with its editor, Paul U. Kellogg, in which he proved to be a friend, contributor, neighbor, benefactor, and advisor. He performed legal services for Kellogg, turned back to *The Survey* the modest honorariums he received from it for his articles, and always found there an eager audience for his ideas.[7]

New York liberals in the 1920s were a village unto themselves. It seemed that everyone knew everyone else worth knowing through elite reform organizations to which they all belonged—the Civic Club, the Foreign Policy Association (organized by Ralph Rounds), the National Child Labor Committee, the Women's Trade Union League, the National Consumers League, and the American Association of Labor Legislation. The myriad of organizational titles suggested the various causes that attracted them: efficient, corruption-free government; U.S. participation in world affairs; maximum hour workweeks, collective bargaining for workers, better wages and working conditions, including an end to child labor; and consumer protection in a time of higher prices and increasing corporation power. Adolf Berle either belonged to or subscribed to the principles and purposes of these organizations.

Beginning in May 1923, a new organization found Berle: the American Indian Defense Association (AIDA). Led by John Collier, it sought to protect Indians from the Bursum bill, introduced on July 20, 1922, by Senator Holm O. Bursum, at the behest of his predecessor in that seat, Secretary of the Interior Albert B. Fall. The Bursum bill threatened to deprive New Mexico pueblos of titles to their lands. A longtime New York reformer, Collier knew that New York's liberals would support the Indians' cause. *The Survey* had published his articles on Indians, and when he organized AIDA, its national advisory board and board of directors listed numerous names from Henry Street Settlement's board of governors, including that of Adolf Berle.[8]

But reformers could not agree among themselves as to how to give the Indian pueblos self-determination; even the U.S. Senate could not decide, and on February 28, 1923, the Senate Subcommittee on Public Lands and Surveys reported a substitute proposed by Senator Irvine Lenroot of Wisconsin for the feared Bursum bill. The Lenroot bill made one concession to the pueblos, thereby dividing friends of the Indians. Collier formed AIDA to unify support for American Indians and to serve as an umbrella organization for four existing groups—the Eastern Association on Indian Affairs, the Chicago Indian Rights Association, the New Mexico Association on Indian Affairs, and the Indian Welfare Committee of the General Federation of Women's Clubs—all endeavoring to defend American Indians from anyone who would deprive them of their heritage.

Collier, who was "research agent" for the General Federation, took AIDA's important executive secretary position. He was not a harmonizing influence. In the words of his biographer, Collier was "a ruthless and hyperbolic propagandist who consistently maligned the motives of his opponents and who left behind him a trail of broken friendships and bitter estrangements." He was obsessed with protecting all alien groups from assimilation into American society. According to Mabel Dodge Luhan, in New York Collier had used "pageants, parades, and prizes to persuade Italians, Russians, Germans and all the others to keep their national dress, their customs, their diets, their religion, and all their folk ways." He sought no less for New Mexico's Indians. An experienced polemicist, Collier proclaimed his intent to protect the American Indian from being "swiftly denatured, stripped naked of his personality and turned into an Anglo Saxon." Of course, Collier too patronized the Indians. D. H. Lawrence, the English novelist, met Collier in New Mexico and observed that Collier was likely to destroy the Indians by "setting the claws of his own white egotistic benevolent volition into them."

All of the Indians' friends opposed the Bursum bill; some of them accepted the Lenroot alternative; Collier steadfastly opposed both. He was not one to seek compromise among factions when only his could be correct. Given the task of raising funds and recruits for AIDA's letterhead organization, for which he would be paid $5,000, Collier vowed, "There's method in any madness found herein. A certain minimum of information—a point of view—the setting for our necessary policies—and the emotional or 'moral' appeal. I believe the latter must be made in the effort to get members and money."[9]

Trouble loomed when the New Mexico Association favored the Lenroot bill. Anticipating that Collier would come to AIDA's first executive committee meeting on May 25 looking to do battle with Francis Wilson, attorney for the New Mexico Association, five interested lawyers met at the Harvard Club to head off a clash. The lawyers were Wilson; Roberts Walker, attorney for the Eastern Association and a well-known corporation lawyer; Herbert Stockton, an inactive member of the Eastern Association; Howard Gans, described as "a Jew, but a very fine and distinguished person";[10] and Berle, "a brilliant young fellow" who was brought in when Collier sought *pro bono* assistance from Rounds, Hatch, Dillingham & Debevois, "a firm with a reputation for interest in 'causes.'" Berle was the logical person for the case, not only because of his *pro bono* inclinations, but also because "this again was the old Spanish colonial law and in the Dominican

Republic I'd become quite familiar with it.'' The lawyers at the Harvard Club thought they had "calmed down" Collier, but when he went to California to devote himself to fund-raising for AIDA, he told reformers there that Wilson and the New Mexico Association were not true reformers.[11]

As AIDA's general counsel, Berle decided he should go to New Mexico in August to discover what the Indians themselves wanted. Collier concurred; his fund-raising among California and New York liberals (most of the money coming from *New Republic* publisher Dorothy Whitney Straight and Dr. John R. Haynes of Los Angeles) would cover Berle's expenses and a $500 fee.[12]

Privately, Berle doubted that the best interests of the Indians were served by the Lenroot bill, the reformers, or the Indians themselves. While some liberals wanted to abolish the government's Indian Bureau, Berle feared that without any government protection the result would be "mass exploitation of the worst kind." Nor did he believe that ownership of property would protect the Indians from land speculators. He also wondered if reformers realized that Indian interests and tribal social development varied from region to region. Finally, he was wary of tying up too closely with the mercurial Collier while intent upon doing the right thing for the Indians without patronizing them.[13]

Berle was eager for the journey—an exhilarating adventure that would enable him to view parts of the United States unfamiliar to him, deal with poverty-stricken natives like those he knew in the Dominican Republic, put his knowledge of Spanish and Spanish land titles to work again, harmonize well-intentioned reformers at odds with each other, and establish his reputation with the Indians' liberal New York constituency. Additionally, having come to the conclusion that he should leave the Rounds firm, his legal career was at a crossroads as Berle discussed partnerships with other young lawyers. The trip would afford him time to think and even the boredom of train travel could not diminish his anticipation of it (he took a good supply of the best novels of the day with him to maintain his habit of reading before he slept). In deference to the importance of his mission, both for himself and for his fellow liberals, he decided to keep a diary. At the end of his first day of travel he wrote: "Good to be roving again."

The journey was uneventful except that the second night out was broken by the sudden news that President Harding had died. Shocked, Berle lay awake thinking of the dead president—"Big, flundering, boneleg, as he was, one somehow felt that Harding was human and safe." And he thought of his successor, "the ineffably dumb Cal Coolidge standing on Boston Common; and of the tangle to come. . . . " Somehow politics did not bring out the best men, but so certain was Berle of his "destiny" that he wondered what these remote events had in store for him. He arrived in Santa Fe on August 3 amidst a thunderstorm so heavy that it obscured Berle's initial view of the town. But it passed quickly, as storms in the mountains do at that time of the year, and soon Berle was admiring Santa Fe's Spanish flavor and comparing it to San Juan, Puerto Rico.

The members of the New Mexico Association were a strange mixture: symbolically, Margaret McKittrick, its chairman, gave Berle the initial impression of being a wide-eyed idealist, which he soon decided was errant. Then there was the shrewd lawyer Wilson, who also published Santa Fe's newspaper; artists like Alice Corbin Henderson; and the leader of the Taos artists colony, the fabled Mabel Dodge Luhan, and her Indian husband, Antonio Luhan, "silent, huge, amiable, with burnous slung about this waist." Berle quickly learned that the reformers were split by numerous personal ambitions and feuds, except that one thing united them—"these people hate Collier like poison."[14]

While Collier treated the Indians as noble savages whose primitivism must be preserved, the New Mexico reformers saw the peublos as ineluctably trampled by white civilization. Berle toured the peublos with Luhan. ("A splendid Indian with a fine sense of humor, good judgment, and excellent company. He advised me not to buy cigarettes with which to treat councils. 'They smoke too much anyhow,' he said." Even an educated Indian patronized Indians.) Berle loved the Rio Grande country, zestfully climbing its mountains and fishing its waters between conferences with Indians and Mexicans. He put his experiences in the Dominican Republic to work in New Mexico, spending hours poring over ancient titles and grants of land, some more than 200 years old. In certain instances towns had been built on Indian lands in flagrant violation of titles—but since then people innocent of that injustice had settled in them. Would justice be served by removing the Mexican-American settler? Berle spent one evening with Franciscan priests debating the problem of "the honest squatter" and learned that self-determination in New Mexico had to victimize either Hispanics or Indians.[15]

Many New Mexican reformers were more interested in protecting the rights of Spanish-Americans against exploitation by Anglos than giving lands back to the indians. (Among them was Bronson Cutting, owner of the *New Mexican* and a Harvard man from Long Island who had gone west for his health; politically ambitious, he later became a U.S. senator.) Berle knowingly embroiled himself in a politically hot local issue. Believing stories of how Francis Wilson had allegedly defrauded Indians, Berle came to distrust the New Mexico Association. Like Collier, he suspected the New Mexicans of supporting the Lenroot bill and opposing Indian consent and compensation in order to deprive Indians of self-determination—even as they sought to increase Spanish self-determination. On the other hand, the New Mexicans distrusted the New Yorkers and the Californians as "visionary and idealistic" troublemakers.

At a climactic gathering of the Indian pueblos, the New Mexicans turned out in full force—Berle calling it a "raid" on the meeting. Berle and his reform friends pushed a resolution to give the Indians self-determination over their lands while the New Mexicans accused them of misleading the Indians to anticipate white evacuation of certain lands. The New Mexicans fought for support of the Lenroot bill and, when they failed, withdrew from the meeting rather than "fighting it out before the Indians." As expected, the Indians sided with the outsiders and the New Mexico Association made the voluble Berle out to be the villain of the piece. In late August Berle departed New Mexico for New York knowing that his trip had resolved nothing.[16]

Yet the episode proved instructive for Berle. He learned that social rights and wrongs were not nearly as obvious as John Collier painted them. "There is no villain in the play. The Indian enemy is no single man or group. It is the whole drive of the white materialistic political and economic organism," he thought. Two very different cultures were in conflict—the Indians, with "their spiritual, idealist civilization fares ill in competition with our more grasping ideas of life." However, the reformers still girded for an all-out fight against the Lenroot bill. The General Federation of Women's Clubs ("the Federated Females Feudatories," Roberts Walker dubbed them) and John Collier vowed to drive the New Mexicans out of AIDA. Nonetheless, their counsel, Berle, began to look for conciliation.[17]

The scene shifted back to Congress—which could either pass the Bursum bill (unacceptable to all who spoke for the Indians), the Lenroot bill (acceptable with certain modifications to the New Mexico Association), or something else yet to be determined. The lawyers, including Berle, descended upon Washington looking for a deal. Although a rhetorical duel erupted between Berle and the sharp-tongued Roberts Walker, counsel for the Eastern Association (Walker charged that "the latest Berle tweedledees" were slight modifications of the Lenroot bill; Berle accused Walker of a "malversion of the truth"), they were close to an agreement. In early February 1924, Berle conferred with senators in Washington and eventually wrote a substitute bill satisfactory to all sides. In the eyes of fellow lawyer Howard Gans, the substitute bill was "a distinctive achievement for the Indians, and a feather in Mr. Berle's cap. He certainly has been a brick."

The episode revealed in Berle a streak of amelioration that relished the rhetoric of radicalism. Also, as he had in Paris, he showed himself to be a lawyer able enough to write drafts that won the support of lawyers senior to him in age and experience. In 1924 he put distance between himself and John Collier and AIDA's California patrons; a young New York lawyer on the make was not about to align himself with the wild-eyed Collier—even if a $500 monthly retainer from AIDA enabled him to go into private practice on January 1. Berle helped write and defend the compromise Pueblos Act of 1924, disavowing Collier who continued his fight against it and the New Mexico social system. Significantly, when Berle resigned in June as AIDA's counsel, he was commended by its directors for "your tact, and above all, your patience in the un-knotting of the legal tangle." Symbolically, he closed the episode over a harmonious lunch with Francis Wilson of the New Mexico Association. He was twenty-nine, and it was time to get along with his legal career and turn his attention to reforms of corporation law.[18]

A CORPORATION LAWYER

Aside from the Indians of New Mexico, the restless Berle had spent much of 1920–1923 tending to Rounds' legal affairs in the Caribbean sugar trade. But his work in the Rounds office at 62 Cedar Street was unsatisfying and in 1922 he wondered if he should remain in Wall Street or return to Boston to find work on State Street. He briefly explored the Boston market for a position as a corporation lawyer, contacting Reginald Heber Smith— a partner in the Boston firm of Hale and Dorr and, of course, an old friend of his father's in various reform movements. Smith advised Berle that only three Boston firms engaged in the sort of practice for which Rounds had trained him and that it was unlikely he would find an opening in them.[1]

Nevertheless, he could not long subordinate himself in a large firm. He scorned the "legal factories" of New York and Chicago with their thirty or forty partners and their two hundred or more associates who were chiefly "financial experts and draftsmen of financial papers [who have] contributed little to legal literature, social responsibility or public leadership." Through an independent practice Berle obviously sought to broaden his horizons as a legal scholar, social reformer, and civic leader.[2]

He opened an office at 67 Wall Street with Guy Lippitt whom he had met in the Dominican Republic, launching their practice on January 1, 1924, "chiefly on our nerve" (a third declined partnership with them) and their contacts in the sugar trade. They did well, Berle's 1923 income of $4,845.96 from the Rounds firm being nearly matched by the $4,480.17 he took home from Lippitt & Berle in 1924. However, it was still a modest practice: the 1925 average income for a Harvard Law graduate in an individual practice was $10,000—a figure Berle would not attain for several years.[3]

"Corporations are worth studying and worth respecting," he wrote somewhat apologetically for *The New Republic* in 1921. A career in corporation law appealed to Berle's realism without tarnishing his romantic idealism. He wanted to combine a corporation practice with legal scholarship that incorporated social realism. Moreover, a causative life certain of its own destiny knew that the law "remained one of the careers through which a man could attain influence and wealth even without having capital at the start." Corporation law was a vehicle to obtaining both influence and wealth—although Berle might have insisted that the money was desired not for its own sake but as a means for attaining influence for good works.[4]

Berle planned to be one corporation lawyer who put the interests of the community on a par with those of his clients by pursuing simultaneous careers as a legal scholar and a civic leader. He did not expect that such diffuse careers would make him as rich as Rounds. "The law is primarily a curative profession," he insisted. "It was never intended to be primarily a money-making profession." This did not mean that Berle disapproved of rich lawyers. His ideal was "the lawyer who is also a scholar, who understands both legal history and legal theory and who can dovetail with the sister sciences of economics and government. For, after all, law is merely one of the frames of life; it must change, expand and develop as life develops; and it can be used to guide developments toward a sounder and more gracious civilization." Louis Brandeis was graciously civilized, liberal, intellectual, socially responsible, and rich. Like Brandeis, Berle believed that private accumulations had to be balanced by public service.[5]

For that matter, public service could be enhanced by a private accumulation. Berle's quest for gracious living led him to seek a wife from the milieu into which he had moved. The reform and legal circles of New York teemed with wealthy young women, but few of them were compatible with his liberal or intellectual inclinations—or his modest means. Then he met Beatrice Bend Bishop. A mutual friend introduced them under Washington Square Arch on a lovely May evening in 1925. Like Berle, she was a student of history; unlike Berle, she was a *born* aristocrat—yet in touch with twentieth-century democracy. They spent the evening in intellectual sparring, impressing each other with their historical knowledge. Years later a reporter wrote, "It is possible that there was never a more cerebral courtship than the Berles'."[6]

Beatrice Bend Bishop's life was either the stuff of psychological novels or poor-little-rich-girl potboilers. The opening paragraph of her autobiography well suggests the former:

> I was born in Lenox, Massachusetts, on August 6, 1902, an only child. My parents had wanted a boy; sometimes they called me by Father's name— Cortlandt. I often wondered why I was born. It is hard to imagine that my mother, the beautiful Amy Bend, ever wished to become pregnant. She used to tell me that pregnancy spoiled her figure. In her eyes all matters female—menstruation, pregnancy, childbirth—were disgusting. Femaleness was so abhorrent to her that she insisted on having a hysterectomy before the age of forty, declaring that the pain of menstruation was intolerable.

Beatrice's father was an American aristocrat, a descendent of the Van Cortlandts and de Peysters who settled seventeenth-century New Amsterdam. By his daughter's standards, Cortlandt Field Bishop was "a charming dilettante" who never applied either his law degree or his doctorate in political science because gentlemen of independent means at the turn of the century did not seek employment that denied less fortunate people an income. Also, Bishop was a pioneer in aviation and in "automobiling." He applied his considerable intellectual curiosity and investment capital to sponsoring projects like those of the Wright Brothers, as well as collecting valuable rare books and prints, and Manhattan real estate.

To his daughter Bishop was an anachronism, but others considered him either a talented intellectual or an astute businessman-collector. His published dissertation, *History of Elections in the American Colonies* (1893), is a standard reference work on the subject. However, abandoning the academy he applied himself to purchasing art, rare books, stamps, furniture, and innumerable antique items of value for his American Art Association–Anderson Galleries, Inc., having put together two galleries in the 1920s that became known as one of the most successful operations in New York. Bishop's only business failure was *The Paris Times,* a paper that catered to American tourists and expatriates in Paris in the 1920s. "He was so secretive about what he bought that very few people had any idea of the magnitude of his purchases," declared one who did. Following his death in 1935 his collections were liquidated and created quite a stir among collectors. Masters from the fifteenth to the twentieth centuries were sold, including French eighteenth-century color prints, "said to be the finest and most extensive ever offered at public sale in this country." They brought his estate $276,145, "one of the highest totals ever brought here by etchings, engravings and color prints." That was minor compared with what Bishop's books brought. In "one of the leading rare book sales of several years here," Bishop's books too were auctioned off in 1938. That included everything from a tenth-century Anglo-Saxon manuscript to Dickens' own copy of *A Christmas Carol.* Like his art, his books showed "a predilection of the romantic, as opposed to the classic tradition," with emphasis on French works without exclusion of English masterpieces. Bishop's "fabulous riches" went under the hammer to the tune of $616,597 in several "historic sessions." And still New York had not seen the last of Bishop's collections. His stamp collection sold for $19,547. His coins and watches fetched $7,481. Furniture, including a Chippendale-carved piece, sold for another $14,091. From time to time more paintings and assorted antiques were sold for thousands. As late as 1948 Bishop's rare books drew over $300,000 in sales.[7]

The Bishops spent six months of every year on the Continent and divided the rest of the year between New York and the Berkshires. They were Francophiles: they spoke French at home (a Frenchman could not believe that Beatrice was American), Bishop drove only French automobiles, a French-trained architect designed his New York home, and Beatrice "had a French governess, Mother had a French lady's maid, Father had a French valet, and the search for a French chef was neverending." Bishop did not collect for money alone; he considered himself an aristocrat and looked down upon nouveaux riches Vanderbilts and Rockefellers. The Bishops attended fashionable Grace Church and sent Beatrice for a lady's education at the Brearley School and the best schools of Paris. Beatrice knew she was bright and her rebellious decision to go to college provoked a family crisis: "Nonsense," declared her mother. "You will become a bluestocking and no man will look at you. Men can't bear women who think they know everything." In spite of her mother's injunction, "*celà ne se fait pas*—it is not done," she went off to Vassar. She took a bachelor's degree in history and over her father's pleas that she should marry a gentleman, enrolled for a master's in history at Columbia. Mrs. Bishop was right: Beatrice's bright intellect shone and some men came to dislike her—except for a few admirers and a thirty-year-old lawyer, Adolf Berle.[8]

He called her "Playmate," appropriately wearing a top hat to dinner at her parents' house (because her father had decreed a gentleman "always wears a top hat when he comes to dine with a lady"), and invited her to Shabbos dinner with his Jewish friends at Henry Street Settlement, a gesture that appealed to her liberalism and her defiance of her anti-Semitic parents. They never forgave him for encouraging her independence. A top hat did not make Berle a gentleman and her mother forbade her from seeing Berle, a challenge Beatrice could not ignore. They spent a summer apart from one another when she took a social worker's position in Labrador, but constantly they wrote poetic letters to each other. They enjoyed each other too much to be apart. She may have been Berle's only real "playmate" aside from his brother and sisters. But when Beatrice disobeyed her parents by seeing him, they removed her from their lives. By their choice she would never again see them. Without them present, she married Adolf Berle in December 1927, vowing to make their marriage a work of art.

A great marriage took carefully planning. They wanted independent careers (in defiance of her father's dilettantism), a family (a Berle dynasty), and to be very much a part of each other's lives. They shared so much together—their love for the arts, history, ideas, idealism, liberalism, and New England. Prior to their wedding they bought a rustic farmhouse in the rural Berkshires between Great Barrington and Stockbridge, where they found recreation, refuge, and relaxation amid their books; to the right of the door of their "Konkapot" home they nailed a Portuguese tile that bore the liberal creed,

> *My house has the most noble coat of arms.*
> *To receive without distinction both rich and poor.*

Nevertheless, the Berles were rich because Beatrice was a Bishop. In 1928 Bishop vindictively disinherited his daughter. As late as 1933 he specifically excluded her from his will and named his widow and their housekeeper its executors and beneficiaries. Beatrice fought it in court in a 1936 complaint that accused her father of "reckless speculation" for individual benefit with an aunt's estate Beatrice would have inherited upon his death.

It is not clear what legal role Berle played in the case of *Berle* v. *Bishop;* even before Bishop's death he was asked to take over the argument in behalf of Beatrice, declining to do so because it was "bad psychology" and Beatrice wished not to involve him. In any event, in 1938 Beatrice won a settlement of $515,000. Berle benefited because, Beatrice said, "we were independently wealthy, and it freed Adolf from the necessity of practicing law primarily for financial gain. He could afford to work for the government or to be a full-time professor if he chose to do so." Beatrice gave him the means for a causative life.[9]

Independent wealth also enabled Beatrice to choose a life different from her father's. For a brief while she taught at Sarah Lawrence College and then took a degree in social work from Columbia and worked as a psychiatric social worker. These experiences only whet her appetite for something more fulfilling—a degree in medicine, which she obtained in 1938, and a career in public health. By then the Berles had three children, daughters Alice and Beatrice Van Cortlandt, born in 1929 and 1931, and a son, Peter Adolf Augustus Berle, born in 1937—the dynasty was intact for another generation. Except for the first year of their married lives ("We are still without a maid and Beatrice is getting to be a noble cook," reported Berle), in their townhouse at 142 East 19th Street in fashionable Gramercy Park they were seldom without servants who cared for the children or helped entertain guests from all over the world and from all the milieus they entered. Her father's money enabled the Berles to be whatever they chose to be. They could take on a multitude of democratic and bourgeois pretensions or they could be the aristocratic, snobbish Francophiles the Bishops had been.

After more than ten years of their marriage, Berle's mother told him, "I admire and love Beatrice more and more every time I am with her." In the eyes of many people who met her, loving Beatrice Bend Bishop Berle was no facile accomplishment. She was *not* the sort of woman then admired by men or women. Extraordinary for her times, she had both a family and a career. Of course her wealth afforded her those luxuries, but how many wealthy women sought both? Vowing in the 1930s "I will not be a committee woman," she left her children with nannies while she went to medical school and then practiced public health. After that, she was rightfully *Dr.* Berle to her acquaintances and demanded to be addressed with her title. She loved the poor and wanted to succor them, but there was no mistaking her for anything but the aristocrat she was. Franklin Delano Roosevelt's aristocratic mother, Sara Delano, immediately perceived her as one of her own kind and, as Beatrice recalled, "took me under her wing. She soon discovered she had known both my grandmothers and could trace their lineage as far back as her own." Like her husband, Beatrice did not suffer fools gladly. She did not have to flaunt her lineage; it was evident about her. However, she did flaunt her intellectuality and her liberalism, both not often displayed by the women she knew. She frequently terrorized people—at least those people who could be awed or put off by an intensely exceptional woman. She was an opinionated woman whose aristocratic bearing contrasted oddly with her egalitarian judgments. At a time when wives of public officials were expected to give teas for each other and dinners for their husband's colleagues, Dr. Berle did those things with magnificent style; at her parties well-known musicians performed classical music and she herself, in Grecian costume, recited poetry. Yet she never dared to upstage her husband; on the contrary, she put him on a pedestal and frequently bored or irritated an audience by celebrating his brilliant accomplishments in a manner that expected them to follow suit.[10]

Undoubtedly Berle's talents as a lawyer commanded exceptional fees, but Beatrice's estate permitted him to enjoy a multitude of other careers—all of which benefited his practice. While others, including his brother Rudolf, tended to the details of a practice, Berle was free to write, to pursue an ostensibly nonremunerative law professor's career, and to play at politics. Fame in 1932 rewarded Berle financially. His taxable income from his law partnership swelled from $5821.55 in 1925 and $9813.53 in 1930 to $21,277.93 in 1933. It was still not the sort of income that could simultaneously support a great career in legal scholarship, public service, and Beatrice Berle. But the Berles were candid about how the Bishop largesse had made possible the extraordinary public career of Adolf Berle by freeing him from the mundane world of corporation law.

Berle Without Means

Even before Berle achieved fame as the coauthor of *The Modern Corporation and Private Property* he enjoyed considerable standing as a published scholar of corporation law. He was a recent law graduate in 1917 when the *Harvard Law Review* published his first article, "The Expansion of American Administrative Law"—a prescient piece inasmuch as law schools did not yet offer courses on administrative law. This initial article celebrated regulatory bodies such as the Interstate Commerce Commission for combining legislative, judicial, and executive functions. It also anticipated greater national economic regulation.[1]

In 1921 the *Harvard Law Review* rejected his first submission on corporation law because of Berle's "looseness of thought" and careless writing. Seldom, if ever, would anyone complain again about his unusually vigorous writing in law journals or elsewhere. Almost two years later the *Columbia Law Review* published his first article on the corporation, which released a flood of sixteen law articles in nine years from Berle, including four in the *Harvard Law Review*. He shrewdly focused on corporation finance in a time of much financial inventiveness and little scholarly attention to it. Soon he could boast of being the originator of what he dubbed the law of corporation finance. The best law reviews in America solicited his articles and the states of Ohio, California, and Wisconsin sought his counsel on regulating corporations. The young scholar on the make never forgot an appreciation or forgave a slight; *Columbia Law Review* had "the first right [to an article] because they gave me house room ten years ago when my stuff was considered too dangerous by the *Harvard Law Review.*"[2]

The scholar was not a professor when he began to publish. Berle yearned for a law school appointment but, beginning in 1925, he taught corporation finance part-time at the Harvard Graduate School of Business, commuting once a week from New York to Boston for the next three years. Meanwhile, he sounded out Yale Law for an appointment, but its dean was not interested in his services. By his own account, in 1927 he approached Columbia Law, brashly telling Dean Harlan Fiske Stone that corporation law as taught at Columbia did not conform to modern realities. Stone was not put off by Berle's impudence; he agreed that the course, taught by Stone's law partner, was thirty years out of date but could not be changed because the man was close to retirement. So they arranged for Berle to teach a seminar in corporation finance temporarily in the business school. However, Berle's story of how he came to teach at Columbia loses something when we learn that Columbia's law dean in 1927 was Huger W. Jervey and Stone had been on the Supreme Court since January 1925. Nevertheless, the story is consistent with Berle's personality and Columbia's situation.[3]

In 1927, through his friendship with William Zebulon Ripley at Harvard Business School, he obtained a grant from the Laura Spelman Rockefeller Foundation to study corporations with an economist. The grant was in turn contingent upon his having an academic appointment. Thus, Berle got a Columbia appointment by giving Columbia the opportunity to house him and the grant. Temporarily he taught a course in corporation finance until a law school vacancy was available for him. To assist in the research he hired a Columbia graduate student in economics, Gardiner Means, his old friend from Plattsburg Camp days.[4] A year younger than Berle, Means had had a business career in textiles before he decided to become an economist. Means had just completed a master's degree in economics at Columbia when Berle was awarded the Rockefeller grant for an interdisciplinary study of corporations and went searching for a collaborator. Their interests neatly dovetailed and they set out to demonstrate the harmony of scholarship in the law and in economics.[5]

Along with Yale, Columbia Law then was a leader in "legal realism." While the traditional legal education satisfied a law student for life at the bar, legal "realists" insisted that such training had little relevance to society unless it utilized research in the social sciences and involved the law in society. Columbia's faculty included realists Herman Oliphant, William O. Douglas, and others. However, following what came to be called the Columbia Law School's "battle of 1928" between realists and traditionalists, Oliphant left Columbia for the Institute for the Study of Law at Johns Hopkins University and Douglas moved to Yale. Berle was a natural ally of the legal realists but, in 1929, he declined a position at Johns Hopkins, deciding to make Columbia his "intellectual home" and Wall Street his laboratory.[6]

The man who figured most importantly in Berle's work was W. Z. Ripley. Sixty years old in 1927, the genial Ripley had had many careers—first as a civil engineer and then as an anthropologist before becoming professor of political economy at Harvard in 1902. Theirs was an odd alliance of disparate personalities, Ripley having a bantering sense of humor that enjoyed playing with the seemingly humorless Berle's name. (Ripley addressed him "A squared," perhaps for reasons other than his initials.) Although nearly three decades his senior, Ripley intensely admired Berle's scholarship. Ripley's book *Main Street and Wall Street* (1927) created a minor sensation as a popularized study of corporation financing. Serialized in *The Atlantic Monthly,* it stirred enormous controversy in the financial community. Years later critics of *The Modern Corporation and Private Property* accused Berle of plagiarizing from Ripley. In fact, Ripley cited or mentioned Berle's legal scholarship seven times in his book. In turn, Berle later acknowledged Ripley's influence in the preface to *The Modern Corporation and Private Property.* Indeed, Ripley and Berle mutually influenced one another and enjoyed a most congenial collaboration. Ripley strongly advocated the regulation and concentration of the railroads, as did Berle. In January 1927, when Ripley came to New York to speak before the State Bar Association on corporations, he was seriously injured in a taxicab accident; Berle delivered the paper as if the words were his own.[7]

Berle's legal articles during the 1920s fastened on the theme of the corporation's separation of ownership and management. (The issue of the corporation's *control* would be contributed later by Means.) In theory, the corporation's owners were its stockholders; in practice, stockholders were nominal owners with little say concerning corporation policies and actions. The directors legally could deny stockholders a fair division of profits and property, regardless of their stock privileges. Berle zeroed in on the stockholder's lack of defined rights in an unregulated securities market. However, later generations of readers of Berle might have been surprised to learn that Berle avoided federal regulation of securities markets as a stockholder remedy. In the conservative 1920s Berle favored stockholder action through courts of equity or self-regulation by the exchanges.

In 1923 Berle accused corporations of diluting the value of existing shares by issuing non-par stock. Although aggrieved stockholders had recourse to courts of equity, Berle knew that litigation would be fruitless unless it proved that the corporation intended fraud in issuing the additional stock. That was most unlikely. But he went on to show that issuing stock below par was only one of several corporation practices that diminished the stockholders' power over management and their investment. For instance, many corporations issued "bankers' shares" of class B common stock without par value that enabled a minority of financiers to own a majority of voting rights. While Berle demonstrated the flagrant absence of equity, he noted that courts routinely assumed the absence of conspiracy and venality by management.[8]

This revolution in corporation financing increased the concentration of power in corporation management. Each new instrument of increased capitalization—e.g., convertible bonds and stock purchase warrants—reduced shareholder influence over the corporation and raised again the matter of good faith between management and an unprotected investing public. Moreover, managers, directors, and investment bankers were themselves stockholders—"inside traders"—who possessed privileged information not available to individual investors. Was it fair to individual investors when insiders manipulated equity prices? Berle urged that the courts "review" practices that jeopardized the presumed fiduciary trust between individual investors and the corporations.[9] All of Berle's articles published between 1923 and 1928 spotlighted how managers and directors frequently subverted any public accountability and thereby converted democracy in American capitalism into a corporate oligarchy.[10] In the 1980s, amid "junk bonds" and other devices, Berle's arguments of six decades earlier attain a new relevance.

Despite a pattern of financial gimmicks to extend management power over corporations, and the absence of protection for individual investors, Berle held to voluntarism instead of federal regulation. Concluding in 1928 that the "courts are not in a position to assume large responsibilities in the conduct of business," Berle hypothesized three other potential safeguards for unprotected investors: an association of interested investment bankers, stock exchange regulation of markets, and the organized market power of institutional stockholders whose interests coincided with individual stockholders. Berle's first book, *Studies in the Law of Corporation Finance* (1928), a compilation of his law articles, emphasized the voluntarism theme. Considering that all his research pointed to the corporation's genius for evading market checks, Berle's proposals for remedy seem conservative and even disingenuous. If neither the courts nor the markets could or would protect investors, who then? His essay on the historical role of government hinted vaguely that Washington could be a regulator. After all, did not the corporation, as a free association, owe its charter to the state? But the man who would become famous for his collectivist solutions to economic problems in the 1930s still sounded like Herbert Hoover singing the praises of voluntarism in 1928.[11]

Even so, we must remember the atmosphere of Wall Street in the 1920s and that, as Berle said, much of the book "must seem radical to the New

York practitioners." He was buoyed by the fact that his articles stirred great controversy in Wall Street and he expected that his analysis would find favor among the more "liberal" lawyers inside and outside of New York. Although a couple of reviews were mildly negative, at the age of thirty-four Berle considered himself "far too old a hand at this business [of criticism] to be particularly bothered" by them; "some time I may want to hit hard myself." He professed to enjoy the academic give-and-take as long as it never became personal: "Otherwise all academic life would become a mutual admiration society. My own work has been roughly treated at various times, often by my best friends; and I have never resented it." When a hostile review brought an admiring letter from David E. Lilienthal deploring its "injustice," Berle shrugged and magnanimously declared, "a man who writes gives hostages to fortune."[12]

Berle's articles had attracted considerable attention among corporation lawyers across the country. A Wall Street admirer applauded them as "not only readable but of great value in helping to visualize present-day problems of corporation law." Many corporation lawyers—fearing they would lose business if they publicly approved of Berle and fearing an impending debacle if nobody said anything about the abuses he spotlighted—quietly encouraged Berle. In 1927–1928 Ohio and California state officials requested his assistance in drafting new corporation laws. He relished his license for power. "I have always suspected that the legislature did not make the law, and my experiences in the last two years make me certain of it," he later wrote excitedly. Meanwhile, his publisher boasted that his book's sales were "unprecedented" and coming "from so many different quarters and such varied sources, that we find it impossible to make any estimate of the probable demand."[13]

There were two Berles—an uptown Berle and a downtown Berle, a Morningside Heights academic and a Wall Street practitioner. The Wall Street Berle was not hurt financially by the writings of the Morningside Heights Berle. Although many Wall Streeters disliked his articles, Berle noted with satisfaction that "business continues good and since none of it comes from these people, I can afford their dislike." Still, he wondered if the publication of a particular article "was altogether wise . . . because my life lies rather down-town than at Columbia." At Columbia his academic career flourished. In 1927 he was an instructor in law; in 1928 he was an assistant professor; in 1929 he was an associate professor. In 1930 he published a casebook in the law of corporation finance. Law reviews now breathlessly solicited his articles. In the spring of 1929 he declined certain invitations because he feared "overwriting" and becoming a tiresome "hardy annual whose name appears in print with rather more frequency than force." And he so much wanted his writings to have the force of influence.[14]

While the uptown Berle advanced swiftly in academic recognition, the downtown Berle moved in circles of civic power. The Corporation Trust Company organized a committee of prominent Wall Street lawyers to redraft Delaware's permissive law on corporations and it invited him to participate because the Trust Company "had begun to fear that the process had gone entirely too far, and they hoped, I think, that I could persuade the committee to produce a law which gave the investor a reasonable degree of safety." To make certain that the Delaware legislature would get its message, the Trust Company retained the secretary of the Delaware Bar Association as its Wilmington counsel and, as Berle confided to *New York World* editor Walter Lippmann, "he arranges to have anything sent down from New York passed through the Delaware legislature without discussion or debate." Berle, the individual investor's friend in Wall Street, helped draft the Delaware corporation laws of 1928 and 1929, but he could muster only an ineffectual minority in the committee for provisions that would protect the interests of small stockholders. The experience made him realize that corporation financing was becoming even riskier: "Compared to this, the non-voting stock provisions of a few years ago are child's play."[15*]

Yet he still clung to the increasingly fragile belief that only the New York Stock Exchange, not Washington, could police the corporations. Berle hoped to attract a wide audience for his writings without appearing to be a muckraking crusader. In law reviews he detailed dispassionately how corporations schemed to benefit bankers and promoters. Yet he pulled no punches. "These corporations are parasitic in nature," he asserted; "the law of finance has ceased to be either common sense or good conscience, and has become mere mystification." But the only remedy he prescribed was a court of equity inquiry into questionable stock issues to decide if there was "goodwill." If the court established that a corporation deliberately sought to profit an unscrupulous few at the expense of the investing public, then outraged stockholders could explore a redress of grievances in the courts. Still, few lawyers were outspokenly concerned that corporations diluted individual investors' holdings. At this point he still seemed too academically focused to make his mark as a reform-minded corporation lawyer.[16]

THE MAKING OF *THE MODERN CORPORATION*

By the spring of 1929, Berle discerned a significant trend in Means' research and his attitude toward government intervention changed.

---

*Was Berle a stockholder? Yes. On his tax return for 1923 he reported $196 earned on stock dividends, $227 in 1924, $276 in 1925, and $98.04 in 1934. In the late 1920s he accumulated a portfolio consisting mostly of par value bonds and preferred stock at a cost of $9,315.50 and adding $607 annually to his income. Moreover, in 1935 his wife's trust had bonds totaling $100,000 that paid $4,273.75 in interest.

The economist working with me has produced statistics indicating that presently something over one-third of the national wealth of the country will be administered by some two hundred corporations who in turn are dominated by less than eighteen hundred men. This small group in connection with their bankers thus has a power over a very large proportion of the savings of the country; likewise over the lives of the men who work in the industries; and, in a less direct sense, over the public served by them. *This is a problem of government rather than finance.* And the common law acting through equity is apparently the only instrument preventing this situation from turning itself in process of time into a more or less futile absolutism. We thus are really groping for a kind of constitutional law of *economic government* permitting the flexibility and freedom of action required for successful business operations on the one hand; and at the same time, having sufficient rigidity of principle to protect the very large, unrepresented interests implicit in public security markets.

It was a powerful thesis: American capitalism headed toward an oligarchical concentration of economic power unless Washington's regulation of the marketplace protected a liberal economy from a dictatorship of unscrupulous corporation interests. Congress would have to regulate corporations with laws consistent with financial practices.[1]

In December, sixty days after the Wall Street crash, Berle summarized their findings in a paper at the American Economic Association meeting in Washington. Quoting economist Thorstein Veblen's description of the corporation as "the master instrument of civilization," he argued that government had abdicated its responsibility to protect individuals from corporation power. "A major shift in civilization" akin to the struggle for liberal democracy from political absolutism had occurred. Now, however, instead of diffusing power into many hands, the corporate revolution threatened to concentrate economic power in a comparatively few corporations. The corporations were becoming the absolutists the church had been centuries before. "A Machiavelli writing today would have very little interest in princes, and every interest in the Standard Oil Company of Indiana," Berle declared. "And he would be right; because the prince of today is the president or dominant interest in a great corporation." Unless a "statesman" intervened to rectify the situation, he warned, a future generation would witness an "adjustment of interests . . . tantamount to revolution." Endeavoring to be sanguine, Berle tentatively forecast that "the economic organisms of today will bring forth the legal and economic statesmen of tomorrow, who in turn may bring these instruments to a balance which will more nearly serve the state in which we live."[2]

A year later he took Means' projections of economic concentration to the National Association of American Law Schools in Chicago where he again characterized modern economic organization as "industrial feudalism." Asserting that "Concentration of power over property has reached a point literally unknown in the world's history," he forecast that "We are moving out of a state which was primarily *political* and into a state which is primarily *economic*."[3]

The depression crisis ended his infatuation with market self-regulation. The depression did not diminish his personal or professional fortunes— indeed, his legal services were in greater demand—but it surely influenced his social prescriptions. Like most Americans obsessed with social insecurity, he turned to Washington for palliatives. Keeping in mind that his father was a Social Gospel minister who had helped bring about savings bank life insurance in Massachusetts, Berle dwelled upon how Wall Street unnecessarily risked the personal savings of individual investors. He maintained that, "paradoxically, the stock market serves a function analogous to that of a savings bank." A person should be able to save for retirement by investing in the stock market, he believed. "I still want to get some bunch of responsible economists working on the project of making the stock exchange more like a savings bank and less like a roulette wheel," he advised Ripley in 1931. Such a notion must have seemed preposterous in Wall Street; markets required risk, not the safety of savings. Yet Berle insisted that investor risk could be minimized and security maximized simply by "curtail[ing] the range of action of certain individuals." In other words, if he could restrain the asocial behavior of corporate manipulators who diluted values out of venality, an organic market could be made to work to the benefit of ordinary investors. Of course, the only way he could expect to curtail anyone's range of action was by invoking the powers of Washington. The time for redress in the courts of equity and exchange self-regulation had passed; the time for federal control was at hand.[4]

In the fall of 1931, millions of American workers were without the security of a job; about 500 banks failed each month with the loss of deposits because there was no deposit insurance—thereby suggesting that banks were as risky as stocks for savings. The failure of banks heightened feelings of insecurity. Increasingly politicians demanded federal relief for the unemployed, farmers, the banks, and state and local governments. As American values turned from the absolute freedoms that placed workers and individual investors at the mercies and vagaries of a marketplace fettered only by a comparatively few corporation conspirators, Berle too wanted Washington to intervene in the marketplace. Growth mattered less than integrity of control. In words similar to those he wrote for Franklin D. Roosevelt's Commonwealth Club Address a year later, he told a friend,

> Today with a finished plant the job is to shift from promoting into administration. A depression like this is pretty expensive education. But it does educate. For the first time in my conscious life, pretty much everyone is endeavoring to think out where we are going with all of this and what we really want out of life. As nearly as I can see it, people want safety; a

reasonable amount of subsistence; and a chance to develop the better things of life out of their own heads rather than out of a tremendous collection of material things.

Washington would have to organize collective action by putting controls upon the corporation. "My friends say that this is socialism," he conceded. "But it does not seem to matter very much. As between a system run by somebody and a system run by nobody, I am all for the former no matter what name you tack on it; as between the Government and the National City Bank, the bets are in favor of the Government every time. . . . The great question is whether the American people prefer to have a set of lottery tickets which may make them rich . . . or whether they would rather have a safe life. I cannot see that the lottery ticket means much even if you win." Safety and security were more important than speculation in a mature economy. Compelled to choose between corporate collectivism and that represented by the government, Berle took the latter.[5]

On the subject of collectivism and economic planning, attentions inevitably turned to the Soviet Union. Having parted company with voluntarism, Berle was by no means intent upon embracing socialism or communism. But corporate concentration had brought about a collectivist capitalism, even though the number of its beneficiaries was low. With government planning of the economy, power would be substantially broadened. Of course, to diehard free market advocates, that was tantamount to socialism or even communism. Berle suspected that a middle way existed between pure capitalism and socialism. Returning to a theme he had played with a decade before, he suggested that capitalist planning would obscure differences with communism. While corporate capitalism would necessarily discipline a free market, Moscow in turn would liberalize its society. As he told a friend engaged in trade with the Soviets,

> Whether we arrive at [collectivization] by a communist road or by a process of corporate mergers does not seem to be particularly material; the result is the same. If your communist friends knew it, the big corporation executive in America probably talks their language more nearly than anyone else. For the first time too, I think they realize that they are talking a form of modified communism. Faced with the economic depression here, they do not have many illusions about strictly private enterprise anymore.[6]

As Berle wrote the concluding section of *The Modern Corporation and Private Property,* the nation seemed to anticipate greater federal intervention in a capitalist economy. Although Means supplied data that gave the book its controversial thesis of corporation concentration and control, its dynamic writing and thesis that the power of the corporation had been separated from its stockholders was Berle's. In other ways too, the book was uniquely Berle's. He had initiated the project, obtained a grant for its research (Means was then a doctoral student in economics at Columbia while Berle taught the law of corporation finance in the Columbia Law School) and, as project director, was not obliged to put Means on the title page as coauthor. However, he not only gave Means equal billing, but he gave him one-third of the royalties. And while they went their separate ways following its publication (for which Means would be awarded his doctorate from Columbia in 1933), they remained friends who were linked inextricably through history.[7]

THE MODERN CORPORATION IN HISTORY

On the fiftieth anniversary of the publication of *The Modern Corporation and Private Property* by Adolf A. Berle, Jr., and Gardiner C. Means in 1982, the conservative Hoover Institution sponsored a conference on the book. It did so out of conviction that *The Modern Corporation* is "one of the most influential books of the twentieth century" and "is still widely cited, considered a classic and the intellectual grandfather of much criticism of large-scale corporate capitalism." However, what made the conference so extraordinary was that its originators sought to condemn its subject rather than celebrate it. Even so, in excoriating the book fifty years after its initial appearance, the conference reaffirmed the significance of what Berle and Means had accomplished a half century before.

The conferees, as market-oriented economists hostile to planning, assailed the book's themes that the corporations tended toward concentration of wealth and power, and that managers' and bankers' control of corporations deprived stockholders of the ownership; the themes were either wrong or insignificant. They had to respect the book's success—albeit wrongheaded and undeserving—in the marketplace of ideas. Economist George Stigler explained its popularity as a matter of timing: "There was no better date in modern history to launch an attack on large corporations than 1932, and no better place than New York City." He suggested that Berle and Means satisfied malcontents who sought to explain the Great Depression's origins with something sinister such as the undemocratic concentration of economic power in 200 big corporations. Moreover, their conclusion, prescribing federal economic planning as a cure for devious private plans, was wrongheadedness that satisfied only socialists. Fifty years later the conferees were certain that Berle and Means had been wrong in their argument and data. Berle had died nearly a dozen years before, but octogenarian Gardiner Means was there to defend his work. However, perhaps the book's best advocate was economic historian Douglass C. North, who commented that "the fact that the book is worth a conference fifty years later and is still widely known suggests that its influence on the ideological perspective of subsequent generations was not negligible. After all, if economists have rightly ignored it, and its main conclusions are found wanting, what are we doing here?" What indeed![1]

The convenors of the conference had already answered the question. More than a half century after its publication, economists, lawyers, historians, business writers, and social scientists still return to *The Modern Corporation* because it consciously defined contemporary and classical social problems concerning wealth and power. Berle and Means were among the pioneers in modern historical and social science literature in arguing that the big corporations had abridged the fundamentals of liberal capitalism and that "the traditional logic of property and profits" no longer applied; "In modern industry, individual liberty is necessarily curbed" and those outside of the "power" had to consider cooperative action to redress community grievances. Entrepreneurial competition had given way to depersonalized monopoly. The modern corporation could be understood "not in terms of business enterprise but in terms of social organization."

> On the one hand, it involves a concentration of power in the economic field comparable to the concentration of religious power in the mediaeval church or of political power in the national state. On the other hand, it involves the interrelation of a wide diversity of economic interests—those of the "owners" who supply capital, those of the workers who "create," those of the consumers who give value to the products of the enterprise, and above all those of the control who wield power.

Power is what the book is about. The depression 1930s were obsessed with it. A revolution in corporation size, "a modification of the principle of private property," seemed to ineluctably foreshadow a struggle for social and political control in which "power shall be used for the benefit of all concerned." It was a gradual revolution in which the economic power of corporations rewrote the Constitution to usurp the political power of all the people. As the bourgeoisie once usurped the power of the aristocracy and the Church, so now the corporate-financial elite threatened to impose an economic government. Not content with analysis and interpretation of the legal and economic revolution, lawyer Berle and economist Means concluded with advocacy, demanding that "the modern corporation serve not alone the owners or the control but all the society." Washington represented that needed rein on unbridled corporation managers and financiers.

The Modern Corporation excited readers and inspired hyperboles as no other book of the times had. On the front page of the New York *Herald Tribune*'s book review, historian Charles A. Beard applauded it as a "masterly achievement of research and contemplation" and wondered if it could be "the most important work bearing on American statecraft" since the Federalist Papers. Likewise, liberal lawyer Jerome Frank wrote, "This book will perhaps rank with Adam Smith's *Wealth of Nations* as the first detailed description in admirably clear terms of the existence of a new economic epoch." The authors, Frank privately told Felix Frankfurter, "have done a beautiful job of presenting in very sharp terms what may well be the vital problem of our times."[2] Others thought so too. Ernest Gruening called it "epoch-making" in *The Nation* and Stuart Chase in *The New Republic* acclaimed it as the most significant book of 1932. Harry W. Laidler in *Survey Graphic,* asserted that it should be required reading for every student of economics because *The Modern Corporation* was "bound to make economic history."[3]

In fact, it already had made history. Justice Louis D. Brandeis, in a notable March 13, 1932, dissent on corporation law that presaged the New Deal in *Liggett* v. *Lee,* cited the work of "able, discerning scholars" Berle and Means, the first of numerous such citations in federal court decisions involving corporations. The book also made New Deal history, *Time* magazine dubbing it in the spring of 1933 "the economic Bible of the Roosevelt administration." Berle and Means laid the ideological foundations for much of the New Deal's industrial, banking, and finance legislation, especially the Securities Exchange Act and the sensational Temporary National Economic Committee hearings late in the decade. *The Modern Corporation* became required reading for bright undergraduates in the social sciences and in law schools for two decades. Although it would seem dated or dull to students following the 1960s, as recently as 1982 a U.S. Court of Appeals decision noted that "the intellectual patrimony of the Securities Exchange Act includes Berle and Means' influential book" and that although their distinction of the separation of ownership and control was controversial, "the distinction itself . . . is accepted even by their critics." *The Modern Corporation* defined many of the economic issues of modern capitalism: "Whatever the authors' original intent, their ideas were continually cited as evidence that capitalism had to be replaced by a more collectivist economic system," a modern historian has written.[4]

While it never enjoyed spectacular sales, in its first twenty years the book sold about 35,000 copies. But sales can never measure a classic. *The Modern Corporation* launched the literature on the social concentration of wealth and power that led to C. Wright Mills' *The Power Elite* and beyond. Every study of the distribution of wealth in America begins where Means' data on the concentration of capital among 200 corporations left off. John Kenneth Galbraith's *The Affluent Society* and *The New Industrial State* are the intellectual heirs to Berle's vision of industrial government. The *Fortune* 500 picks up from Means' 200. Since 1932 any book about corporations is obliged to cite it, although not necessarily approvingly. After all, as legal scholar Walter Werner reminds us, most big industrial corporations were barely thirty years old when the book was published and Berle's analysis of the shareholder's role "was a radical departure from earlier views." Also, the book "dominated thinking about the nature of the business firm and its place in society for two generations" and initiated a continuing debate concerning the nature of corporate goals.[5]

Berle and Means had their imitators, but the prolific Berle himself was among the best. He re-examined his themes repeatedly in the light of developments since the original publication.[6] For years almost every symposium on the corporation included Berle. Moreover, perhaps most suggestive of the book's place in intellectual history, its detractors flourished on both the left and right. Socialists either assert that Marx wrote Berle's thesis fifty years before him or disapprove of its thesis that managers control what capitalists cannot. More than one new leftist in the 1970s found in Berle an example of "corporate liberalism's" discreet apologia for the corporation.[7] Long before then, however, renascent conservatives scored Berle for his evident disbelief in a properly functioning market system.[8]

Did Berle and Means intend to be too conservative for collectivists and too radical for free enterprisers?

The Marx of the Shareholder Class

Adolf Berle intended *The Modern Corporation* to become a classic. He wanted to be an opinion maker for America's intelligentsia. During one heady moment in the 1930s he exclaimed to Beatrice "that his real ambition in life is to be the American Karl Marx—a social prophet." Like Marx, he wanted to arrest the flow of history and redirect it through his writings. Marx had proletarian revolution in mind, but Berle's point was that, caught between the proletariat and plutocracy the middle class needed a revolution against corporate concentration. Berle sought to redirect the flow of power from corporate managers and financiers in Wall Street toward popular control in Washington. Between the proletarian revolution and monopoly capitalism lay a middle way of which he was the prophet: corporate liberalism.

A career in corporation law, teaching the law of corporation finance, and writing for the audience that read journals of law and economics were unorthodox vehicles for achieving recognition beyond legal and academic circles. But Berle discovered that a writer of specialized pieces could generate an audience because journals "buy names—people sufficiently known to the public so that their work will be read; in part, people who have investigated certain rather dramatic aspects. Getting an audience in a technical field is itself the work of some years. . . . You begin with the technical journals, which are hospitable to work by younger men who have made technical studies. Gradually, as the circle widens, it becomes possible to approach the general public, and by that time you will find that almost anybody is willing to publish anything you have to say. But it does take time."[1]

It took Berle about a decade to establish credentials in law journals by fastening upon the "dramatic aspect" of corporation finance. His concern was not original; before Berle, Thorstein Veblen, John Maynard Keynes, Ripley, and others had characterized the corporation as a burgeoning economic state unto itself. Berle himself denied that the book was wholly original—and he was not given to false modesty. A quarter century after its publication, he confessed that "It seemed to me that it in no way broke new ground. For at least twenty years prior to that study, corporations and their bigness had been the subject of discussion and controversy. I thought we were merely describing a phenomenon with which everyone was familiar, and still think so. But the phenomenon had not, apparently, received academic attention." A social scientist documents and generalizes concerning social behavior. Berle and Means eschewed Veblen's and Keynes' sardonic essays in favor of systematic analysis that blessed the idea with greater credibility. They targeted *The Modern Corporation* "for economists, lawyers, bankers and serious students of financial problems." In other words, they sought to take the study of big corporations from the hands of muckraking popularizers and give it the authenticity of serious modern scholarship.[2]

Nevertheless, it was Berle's experience in writing for journals of opinion and his skill as a polemicist that enabled the book to rise above the academy to become a manifesto. If the ideas were fresh in 1932, they nevertheless already had been rehearsed and tested in law and economics journals as early as 1930. They were refined until the classic's preface dramatized the theme of a silent, sinister revolution of political relationships in which business challenged the supreme power of government. Also, he shrewdly wrote the last section of the book for general readers who might be "too lazy, busy or uninterested to read three hundred pages of academic argument," but curious enough to read a rousing conclusion of a widely discussed book. "The academic form consists of a requirement of about three hundred pages in pure shop talk to prove to the academic mind that you know what you are talking about, and then you are allowed about thirty pages to say what you really think," he told a friend. "Some day I hope to be able to write a book in say seventy-five pages flat, with a note at the end that all of the shop talk is deposited in the Columbia Library where anybody who wishes can consult it. Most people are interested not in how you got that way, but in where you finally got." He provided the "shop talk" for those who cared, but that only buttressed the conclusions so startlingly laid out; he knew that any significant book had to include an exposition of a grand synthesis: "The scholarly work of providing the facts is useful precisely as it permits this sort of generalization. But, absent the generalization, presentation of the facts is likely to be only of transitory value—and if no target is hit, may be of no value at all."[3]

The Modern Corporation has the enduring value Berle sought for it. He could write elegantly—although sometimes when he reached for eloquence he sounded florid and/or obscure. However, his scholarly work not only examined recent developments in corporate finance afresh, but did so with a literary stylishness remarkable in legal journals. "In the desert of sloppy economic and legal writing you are a real oasis!" a fellow Wall Street lawyer once exclaimed. He had a journalistic sense of what the public wanted to read, "an amazing way of re-stating familiar things and making them new," a magazine editor remarked.[4] But the book's stirring conclusion calling for greater federal intervention in the markets ironically owed something to an episode that hints at Berle's reluctance to embrace the radical corporate collectivism for which he would become famous.

During the penultimate stage of *The Modern Corporation*'s creation, Berle became involved in an academic controversy hereafter to be known in the law schools of America as the "Berle-Dodd debate." Put concisely, the issue between Berle and Professor E. Merrick Dodd of Harvard Law School concerned corporation powers—Berle holding that they were held in trust for shareholders while Dodd asserted that corporation powers were held in trust for society. Berle instigated the debate in a "forceful" 1931 article in the *Harvard Law Review* where he reiterated that all powers granted to the management of a corporation are necessarily for the benefit of all the *shareholders*.[5]

Dodd's rebuttal perhaps surprised Berle because it was not the usual lawyerly defense of the corporation managers' freedoms of action that one would have anticipated in a law review. Instead, Dodd took a position to the *left* of Berle. Characterizing Berle's case as a mundane concern for "a legal control" which protected stockholders from the corporation managers who diverted profits, Dodd loftily contended that the corporation belonged neither to the stockholders nor the managers: it was "private property only in a qualified sense, and *society may properly demand that it be carried on in such a way as to safeguard the interests of those who deal with it either as employees or consumers even if the proprietary rights of its owners are thereby curtailed.*" Thus, exploited workers and customers held greater claims upon the corporation than Berle's deprived shareholders or the usurping managers.

Berle struck back by reconnoitering to the high ground of idealism. In a published reply, he assured readers that he too had made the argument that the corporation served the needs of society in a 1930 article and would repeat it in his forthcoming book, *The Modern Corporation and Private Property* (which he mentioned four times in eight pages). So where did Berle and Dodd disagree? Berle maintained that Dodd dangerously confused the issue with a socialist abstraction while American practice fastened upon who owned the corporation's profit: "Either you have a system based upon individual ownership or you do not. If not—and there are at the moment plenty of reasons why capitalism does not seem ideal—it becomes necessary to present a system of law (none has been presented) or government, or both, by which responsibility for control of national wealth and income is so apportioned and enforced that the community as a whole, or at least the great bulk of it, is properly taken care of." Until workers socialized the corporation, Berle insisted that lawyers could deal with it only as property which lay at the center of a dispute between stockholders and managers. If society intervened in that dispute, the only thing that can come out of it, in any long view, is the massing of group after group to assert their private claims by force or threat—to take what each can get, just as corporate management do. The laborer is invited to organize and strike, the security holder is invited either to jettison his corporate securities and demand relief from the state, or to decline to save money at all under a system which grants to someone else power to take his savings at will. The consumer or patron is left nowhere, unless he learns the dubious art of boycott. This is an invitation not to law and orderly government, but to a process of economic civil war.

Berle insisted that Dodd had changed the rules by introducing either alien socialism or a tumultuous interest group pluralism; the former made intellectual sense, but Dodd did not advocate it; rather, Berle interpreted Dodd as advocating the latter, which ineluctably converted society into a battleground pitting bankers and promoters against small stockholders, managers against workers, consumers against producers, etc. To Berle, socialism was impossible and pluralism was chaos. Both thrived on social warfare. Although Berle and Dodd agreed that the public interest should prevail, Berle accused Dodd of excessive idealism. Berle maintained that an ethical public interest could be attained and group conflict averted only by broadening wealth to expand the shareholding class; the middle and working classes should entrust their savings, through organizations such as savings banks or pension funds, to the security—rather than the risk—of the stock exchanges. Of course, Berle's "people's capitalism" was as utopian in 1931–1932 as Dodd's worker and consumer utopia. However, a people's capitalism more closely resembled the existing system and, according to an opportunistic Berle, it behooved them "as lawyers [to] best be protecting the interests we know, being no less swift to provide for new interests as they successively appear."[6]

It was not the first time Berle espoused corporate liberalism as an alternative to socialism. A decade before when he had been writing for liberal journals such as *the Nation, the New Republic,* and *the Survey,* he already had attracted attention in New York as "a crusader, an adventurer of the spirit" for a compassionate capitalism as opposed to the early 1920s' materialism. Then he had played with the vision of an evolutionary capitalism where the means of production would be controlled by workers and shareholders because capitalists would voluntarily "abandon the stockholding field to the workers"—buying bonds in worker-owned and worker-managed enterprises. Since it mattered not which class managed the corporation so long as it was done efficiently, the old investors would yield their power peacefully to a workers' capitalism. This American-style middle-class revolution presented a stark counterpoint to the Bolshevik Revolution. But who were the revolutionaries? He puckishly envisioned a corporate body composed of a banker, a manufacturer, and a corporation lawyer meeting in the vicinity of Wall and William Streets to initiate a new system of social organization which would make capitalism safe for a plant-managing proletariat that shared ownership and control with the plant's old stockholders. Their initial investment secure, the old capitalists would accede to the bloodless American revolution and divide profits with the workers.

Rhetoric is important, and Berle loved his radical. Yet he did not hide the caution of his ideas. In the early 1920s the time for a social revolution was at hand, Berle argued: "Five years ago we thought [capitalists] were impregnable. We know now they are not." Revolution stalked Europe and in America "nothing is permanent. . . . But the more thoughtful business men are looking about for a chance to make a system which shall be deluge proof." Capitalism could be stabilized by democratically broadening its base. Moreover, a corporate liberalism appealed to Americans more than Marxism because it better suited their preference for a peaceful transition. His capitalist revolution, he conceded, was "nothing radical or new. On the contrary it is the logical working out of our own system." It extended ownership and control of the corporation to the middle and working classes by giving them equity with managers and bankers. "We can have that kind of revolution or we can have the other kind. So far we have been content to leave it to the red who had a simple dramatic, coordinated program. He knew where he was going. What we need is a program of our own."[7]

Now, a decade later in 1931–1932, the American revolution was in earnest. Although most of his writings had been confined to defining the usurpation of traditional stockholders' rights by unscrupulous managers and promoters, the intervening years had not diminished Berle's interest in workers' capitalism. The depression had shaken him and the articulation of "a simple, dramatic coordination program" such as those of socialistic intellectuals such as John Dewey, Paul Douglas, and others made Berle's nostrums seem like palliatives. When Berle accused Dodd of neglecting his capitalist base, Dodd's real crime was making Berle seem like a Tory in the midst of an American revolution. *The Modern Corporation* intended to move the debate away from socialist planning to corporate planning.

One scholar of corporation law speculates that the Berle-Dodd dialogue "may well have been the source of the 'social responsibility' paragraph" in *The Modern Corporation*'s conclusion. That part of the book excited the most comment in 1932–1933. In it Berle powerfully asserted that "neither the claims of ownership nor those of control can stand against the paramount interests of the community."

> It remains only for the claims of the community to be put forward with clarity and force. Rigid enforcement of property right as a temporary protection against plundering by control would not stand in the way of the modification of these rights in the interest of other groups. When a convincing system of community obligations is worked out and is generally accepted, in that moment the passive property right of today must yield

before the larger interest of society. Should the corporate leaders, for example, set forth a program comprising fair wages, security to employees, reasonable service to their public, and stabilization of business, all of which would divert a portion of the profits from the owners of passive property, and should the community generally accept such a scheme as a logical humane solution of industrial difficulties, the interests of the passive property owners would have to give way. Courts would almost of necessity be forced to recognize the result, justifying it by whatever of the many legal theories they would choose. It is conceivable—indeed it seems almost essential if the corporate system is to survive—that the "control" of the great corporations should develop into a purely neutral technocracy, balancing a variety of claims by various groups in the community and assigning to each a portion of the income stream on the basis of public policy rather than private cupidity.

Berle did not propose any system, program, or policy; he did not have to do so then. He had defined the problem and suggested remedies that lay within the existing system. But what if a scheme for apportioning community obligations did not emerge and prevail? Then Berle saw the corporations tending toward increasingly oligarchic behavior, "not only on an equal plane with the state, but possibly even superseding it as the dominant form of social organization." Big business would organize the society and its state along economic lines: corporate dictatorship, perhaps even fascism.

This apocalyptic vision of an impending corporation hegemony for the future aroused intellectuals. Berle knew that a great many people were prepared to accept criticism of the system that perhaps they might not have been prepared to accept earlier. Indeed, the time was ripe for certain liberals, but not for others in Wall Street. The original publisher of *The Modern Corporation* was the Corporation Clearing House, then owned by the Corporation Trust Company; shortly after publication it decided that it "could not handle the book properly" and arrangements were made to transfer the book to Macmillan and Company. Fifteen years later Berle learned that a client of Corporation Trust, probably General Motors, had complained and caused the Clearing House decision not to handle it. Criticism of corporations was not conservatism.

Berle's gloomy perspective of an impending corporation hegemony suggested an unimaginably oppressive future which nobody dared to articulate before. (Berle freely expressed the most apocalyptic visions in private, always exciting the imaginations of intellectuals. But he also translated his cataclysmic visions into action; in 1931 he confided to David Lilienthal that he anticipated food riots and had stored barrels of sugar in the basement of his New York home.) The dismal vision stimulated fascinating discussions among liberals who sought to throw off the corporation hegemony and substitute democratic collective planning. As Jerome Frank excitedly told Felix Frankfurter, Berle's vision of society's confrontation with tyranny or chaos was too gloomy: "With the present drift of events, we may soon come to *state capitalism* (via the R.F.C. or something like it) as an alternative to break-down. If so, then their predictions may be wrong."[8]

Frank was correct: Berle sought a state capitalism to preserve the essentials of the existing system by dramatizing the "silent revolution" of a creeping concentration of plutocratic wealth in order to rally those who would demand a "workers' capitalism" administered by Washington. Thus, as Frank and others suggested, *The Modern Corporation* intentionally pointed to the New Deal's state capitalism (and Berle became a counsel to the Reconstruction Finance Corporation [RFC] in 1933). Fifty years later what the book said still mattered as the beginning of any analysis of wealth and power in America leading to a modification and broadening of the system. Although principally concerned at the time with the shareholders' deprivation of power, Berle's adroit exposition of Means' data and advocacy of increased federal intervention made him the Marx of the "New Deal Revolution." As he intended, what he wrote then still says something about the condition of twentieth-century capitalism. Perhaps this is the definition of a classic. And perhaps no other social thinker so much enhanced the fruition of state capitalism and corporate liberalism.

4

Roosevelt and La Guardia

Our problem is to maintain individualism by balancing economic concentration—specifically, big banks, big corporations, big industrial units—with enough State police power to make them our servants instead of our masters.

—Berle in *The New York Times,*
March 4, 1934

ADVENTUROUS MINDS

In March 1932, Governor Franklin D. Roosevelt of New York sought the Democratic nomination for president. With unemployment visible on the streets of New York and throughout the industrial heartland that circled the Great Lakes to Chicago, Roosevelt had to address himself to the problems of an accelerating industrial depression. Symptoms of the economic conditions included the shanty towns in public areas like New York's Central Park, derisively called "Hoovervilles" by their homeless occupants, who had come to mock President Herbert Hoover for his apparent indifference to the crisis. Beyond the mill towns and into the corn fields of the prairie and the wheat fields of the plains, farmers helplessly watched commodity prices and their own incomes dwindle to the point where the value of their assets was in doubt, as was the very existence of life itself. In Washington the Reconstruction Finance Corporation organized to augment depleted credit resources with loans to troubled banks and railroads from the federal treasury—action that encouraged a popular fear that the administration would preserve the rich while America's other classes "went through the ringer." Meanwhile, in Congress bills were prepared for federal public works projects to provide job relief for the unemployed and representative Fiorello H. La Guardia from New York City's East Harlem organized fellow progressive Republicans and sympathetic Democrats for an assault upon the leadership's proposal for a national sales tax to balance the federal budget upon the backs of the poor. For the time being Governor Roosevelt kept silent about these national concerns and dealt mostly with state issues, but his quest for the presidency demanded that he address national concerns.

The national issues troubled Sam Rosenman, the governor's thirty-six-year-old counsel. Accustomed to writing speeches about New York matters for Roosevelt, Rosenman felt inadequately prepared for advising the governor in his upcoming presidential pursuit. With spring speaking engagements across the country crowding in on them, the governor needed outside help. And so it was that one March evening as they discussed state business, Rosenman cautiously suggested to Roosevelt that he consider seeking advice elsewhere on national issues and in writing campaign speeches.

"Do you have anyone in mind?" Roosevelt asked. Rosenman recommended that Roosevelt turn to university professors for expert assistance. It was probably not an unexpected suggestion. Who else presumably had the time and the qualifications? Industrialists and financiers had been tainted by the depression or were too busy with their struggling enterprises to give time to an ambitious politician in need of ideas and words. Political activity in America, especially for Democrats, was usually profitless—requiring civic-minded souls who worked for decency, glory, and incipient power. With the rise of the social sciences, politicians increasingly turned to professors for advice on the complexity of governmental affairs. The use of professors in government had its roots early in the century with the popularization of the "Wisconsin idea"—when the governor of that state, Robert M. La Follette, ventured a mile from the state capitol in Madison to the state university to borrow the expertise of its professors in fashioning a reform program. Roosevelt too had employed various Columbia University professors in advisory and minor administrative capacities. Rosenman knew that the governor enjoyed contact with them. Unlike cautious lawyers and the businessmen, the academics were "adventurous minds"—people who were fertile with ideas, as well as the words that made ideas comprehensible to an informed public. Thus, Rosenman responded to Roosevelt's query by saying, "The first one I thought I would talk with is Ray Moley."[1]

Moley was no stranger to Roosevelt. The Columbia University professor of government, a specialist in the political administration of criminal justice, had known Roosevelt since 1928 when the incoming governor had drawn on his expertise. In 1928 and 1930 Moley published books on criminal justice and in 1931 Roosevelt asked him to sit on the state's commission on the administration of justice. Also, Moley assisted Judge Samuel Seabury in investigating New York County's corrupt court system and as recently as January, Roosevelt had invited Moley to Albany for consultation on that portion of the governor's annual message pertaining to judicial reform. Inevitably the discussion had shifted to politics and the ambitious Moley volunteered his assistance in the coming campaign. In later years Rosenman and Moley disagreed over whether Rosenman was responsible for Moley's inclusion in the 1932 campaign—the testy Moley dating the beginning of his involvement in January, Rosenman dating it in March. In any case, they agreed that it was Moley who organized Roosevelt's "Brains Trust."[2]

Moley assembled his experts by listing the issues Roosevelt needed to confront. Agriculture headed the list and Moley readily identified his first recruit—Rexford Guy Tugwell, professor of economics at Columbia. A neighbor in Morningside Heights, Moley first approached Tugwell one frigid March day on Claremont Avenue. He knew Tugwell well enough to believe he would be congenial with Roosevelt and astute enough not to embarrass Moley in his initial recruiting effort. The handsome and affable Tugwell was an agricultural economist from an upstate rural community and had written broadly about economics and government. In 1928 he had made a short-lived effort to advise Al Smith on agricultural policy in the presidential campaign. It was well for Tugwell that Smith had been indifferent to him, for it disassociated Tugwell from Smith's ignominious defeat. But Roosevelt was a very different political animal and Tugwell's first meeting with him went well, thereby confirming Moley's judgment. That was fortunate for Moley, for his next choice as an advisor on tariff matters, Lindsay Rogers, gave Roosevelt a memo that duplicated one Rogers had given Roosevelt's rival for the Democratic nomination, Al Smith. Both Roosevelt and Smith used it and both discovered the duplication only when a New York newspaper compared their speeches. Roosevelt swallowed his embarrassment, but not Rogers. Moley would have to be more circumspect about future advisors. So, on the issue of credit and corporations, Moley turned to Adolf A. Berle, Jr.[3]

Moley knew him only by campus reputation. *The Modern Corporation* had not yet been published and, while Moley spent most of his time across Broadway at Barnard College where he headed the government department, Berle was downtown much of the time at his law practice. But Berle had a reputation as the most knowledgeable man at Columbia on corporation finance. Moley went to Berle's campus office one April day and asked if he was interested in helping Roosevelt. Berle bluntly answered that he had another candidate for president. Moley persisted, explaining that "it was his technical assistance that was wanted, not his political support, which carried not the slightest weight." Berle "nodded energetically, laughed, and enlisted."[4]

Berle's candidate was the Cleveland corporation lawyer, Newton D. Baker. Baker had been a reform mayor of Cleveland before the war, succeeding Tom Johnson (who had been Moley's political hero in his native Ohio). Known as a progressive, Baker served as secretary of war under Wilson and ardently supported the League of Nations in the 1920s. Perhaps this mugwump internationalism was what attracted Berle to Baker's undeclared candidacy—that and Berle's suspicion that any New York Democrat, even Roosevelt, was tainted by association with Tammany Hall corruption. Berle esteemed Baker as a man of "character and courage" who would be "a great pilot" to steer the nation through the depression crisis. Berle had been circulating a petitition for Baker through the law school when Moley arrived to ask Berle to work for Roosevelt and he remained very "lukewarm" about Roosevelt even after he won the nomination, considering Baker "the much finer and more precise intelligence."[5]

Politically, Berle was not even a Democrat. New York Democrats were dominated by the Irish and notorious for graft and corruption. Berle was a mugwump reformer who early in the 1920s had looked to Wall Street Republicans for his political associations.[6] But Berle's public interest Republicanism had been alienated in the 1920s by the party's crass preference for the likes of Harding, Coolidge, and Hoover. He fancied himself a reform-minded political realist. When queried in 1928 by *The New Republic* as to how he would vote in the Hoover-Smith presidential election, Berle boasted that he had met all the major candidates, but they troubled him. Intellectually he preferred the socialist Norman Thomas, who, "of course, is a gesture only." Berle rated Smith as capable, but was bothered by "the group represented by Smith"; he did not say who they were. But "groups" were on Berle's mind. He believed that Smith had been "forced to draft Franklin Roosevelt [for governor in 1928], who might have been a Republican for all practical purposes, except that he happens to be a Democrat. He represents the same group that the Republicans do." While he did not define Smith's and Roosevelt's "groups," it seems that Berle preferred a public interest Hudson River aristocrat with a Harvard education to a Lower East Side Irishman. So in 1928 he reluctantly concluded that, "the answer seems to be Hoover. Not that I think his administration would be enjoyable, but that it probably will bring to the fore an abler and more responsible group than that supporting Smith. . . . In the Democratic Party generally the ablest men are again men who might as well be Republicans as not. The rest of them are men one would not care to see running a national government." In his heart Berle was neither a democrat nor a Democrat.[7]

When Moley sounded him out about becoming a Roosevelt braintruster, Berle was already braintrusting for the state of Wisconsin and David E. Lilienthal. Another Harvard Law School product, Lilienthal had assisted Chicago labor lawyer Donald Richberg, before going off on his own to become a recognized expert on public utility law. In 1931 he gave up a lucrative Chicago practice to accept Governor Philip F. La Follette's offer of a seat on the Wisconsin Public Service Commission. For years he and Berle had exchanged reprints of law review articles and flattering letters. In February 1932, Lilienthal asked Berle to assist him in revising the state's "Blue Sky" laws, which protected investors from unscrupulous hawkers of securities. Berle eagerly accepted; he had worked on the Ohio corporation law and envisioned the states as laboratories for developing "some federal or interstate machinery which might make the financial system a little sounder.''[8]

In March Berle gave Lilienthal a memorandum that characterized corporation securities as unregulated public savings. Later that month Lilienthal persuaded Governor Philip La Follette to bring the New York lawyer to Madison for a modest $1,000 fee to attempt a redraft of the laws affecting corporate securities. Savoring the opportunity, Berle eagerly went to Madison "to try to fix something there even if I have to combine the several techniques of Queen Elizabeth, Calvin Coolidge and Karl Marx all rolled into one." By July, draft revisions of the Wisconsin statutes were in the works.[9]

Berle served Lilienthal mostly as a legal technician; but when he went to work for Roosevelt he expected to be that as well as a financial technician, a word technician, and an intellectual factotum. At a time when the economic crisis seemed to call for new departures, Berle was easily a most persuasive thinker of breathtaking schemes for economic planning which he buttressed with the technical vocabulary of corporation and public finance as well as historical precedents others had forgotten. He came to be seen as the Roosevelt brain trust's crafty lawyer, financial genius, and historian par excellence. In conferences he gave virtuoso performances by presenting several alternative gambits while discounting the ideas of others as wholly inadequate. And he was the brain trust's best advocate of state capitalism. He dismissed Hoover's Reconstruction Finance Corporation as inadequate—as akin to "bailing out Lake Erie with a teaspoon."

> The central fund idea is right; but it has to revolve; and the only way you can do that is to have the holder of the fund issue currency or something which acts like it—for instance, bank deposits. What I want to do is, concisely, to get up a central organization; pool the funds; permit loans against good but frozen assets; but the funds have to be deposited in the central organization, to be drawn only in case of necessity; and all transactions affecting such securities would have to be cleared through this organization and left on deposit. In other words, the cash and the frozen assets together would be a base for bank credit perhaps twice the amount of the cash fund.[10]

The brain trust sessions before the Chicago convention were intellectually exciting and Roosevelt obviously enjoyed them. Good conversation always stimulated Roosevelt and Moley, Tugwell, and Berle gave him that. They gave assured performances that demonstrated quick and creative minds; Moley was the governmental technician, Tugwell the economic theorist, and Berle the scholar of finance who buttressed his remarks with a confident grasp of precedent. Disagreement with Berle had its perils, but harmony reigned in the group because a consensus developed among them on the need for more positive government intervention in the market to organize it collectively while preserving the principles of individualism. Roosevelt was comfortable with them. They sharpened his thoughts and enhanced his expression of them. But they actually contributed little toward winning the nomination for Roosevelt. They were speechwriters, and the most notable preconvention brain trust contribution to his winning the nomination was Moley's draft of the ten-minute "forgotten man" radio speech. It vaguely called for more public works and expanded credit, decried the RFC as biased in behalf of those at the top, and coined a phrase that added to Roosevelt's image as a progressive. His only other noteworthy pre-convention speech, a commencement address at Oglethorpe University that urged more economic planning, had been drafted by reporter Ernest K. Lindley. Otherwise, the professors contributed memos suggesting alternatives to Hoover's policies on agriculture and finance. Meanwhile, Berle kept his lines open to the Baker camp.

As Berle said, he was capable of the guile of Elizabeth, the Virgin Queen, the caution of Coolidge, the New England politician, and the revolutionary rhetoric of Marx, the radical philosopher. Like many thoughtful people in 1932, this corporation lawyer encouraged everyone to study the Soviet experiment; it "becomes increasingly important . . . as the great alternative to our own system of capitalism." He entertained radical thoughts, calling Lawrence Dennis' book *Is Capitalism Doomed?* "probably the best contribution to economic thinking since John Maynard Keynes' *Economic Consequences of the Peace.*" Dennis's book, he told the editor of the New York *Herald Tribune,* "happens to be the first book indicating that an uncontrolled system, like our own, in the long run is headed for a smashup." Importantly, Berle wanted people to give more thought to government planning as an alternative to corporation planning. It made him sound radical about concepts and plans that were quite conservative.

The depression compelled Americans to question whether planning was incompatible with individual rights, he told a friend who sought to create a tourist business in Moscow. Liberal Democrats had to forsake Wilson and Brandeis' New Freedom legacy of enforced competition. Rereading Brandeis' essays of 1915, Berle concluded that their antitrust theme was outdated. Corporate concentration had gone too far, he advised the justice: "I can see nothing at the moment but to take this trend as it stands endeavoring to mold it so as to be useful. If the next phase is to be virtually a non-political economic government by mass industrial forces, possibly something can be done to make such government responsible, sensitive and actuated primarily by the necessity of serving the millions of little people whose lives it employs, whose savings it takes in guard, and whose materials of life it apparently has to provide." The next phase, according to Berle, would see government planning that used big economic units rather than attacking them.[11]

However, his government planning would not annihilate traditional liberal individualism with collectivism. In a memorandum, "The Nature of the Difficulty," written with the assistance of bank economist Louis M. Faulkner, and discussed with Roosevelt and the brain trust in late May, Berle maintained that "fundamentally, the entire system can only rest on the individual." Still, capitalism was a collective enterprise: "The true antithesis just now is not, as commonly stated, between the American system and the Russian system. At the present rate of trend, the American and the Russian systems will look very much alike within a comparatively short period—say twenty years. There is no great difference between having all industry run by a committee of Commissars and by a small group of Directors." Of course, in twenty years Berle would know that his notion of the Soviets was based upon a misperception of Stalinism. But in 1932 he envisioned state capitalist planning and he proudly noted that the memorandum's theme of planning, control, and management of the economy "formed the general outline of the Democratic campaign."[12]

Roosevelt's nomination catapulted the professors into the public arena. In September, James Kieran of *The New York Times* dubbed them "the brains trust" and the title took hold—albeit used in the singular, "brain trust." Roosevelt, with regal grace, called them his privy council. Although the team of Moley, Tugwell, and Berle remained intact, before Chicago and after the convention names were expediently added and subtracted according to the Democratic patron and the issue at hand. Thus, Bernard Baruch, known for his generous gifts to poverty-stricken Democratic campaigns, exacted from Roosevelt a place in the brain trust for his acolyte, Hugh Johnson—a general in the army, lawyer, and businessman verbal enough to hold his own in any group of intellectuals. Although pained by the thought that they had to share their influence, Moley and Berle adapted to political realities posed by Baruch and Johnson. After all, Johnson had his own extraordinary flair with words and concepts, and Baruch's largesse was more persuasive than anything they brought to the campaign.

The New Deal was *not* the creation of the brain trust. The brain trust espoused economic planning during the campaign, but they were speech writers who aspired to be policymakers. In the words of a latter-day braintruster, J. K. Galbraith, "In the American culture there is no institution with such a high potential for pure comedy as a presidential campaign staff. It is recruited hurriedly, ad hoc, and extensively by self-selection. Many are prima donnas; more are self-identified saviors of the Republic." This was true of Roosevelt's 1932 entourage. But it also should be added that these Machiavellians survived the campaign because their principles were compatible with those of their prince. As Ernest Lindley, himself an occasional braintruster, wrote of Moley, Roosevelt "wanted a high-grade research assistant and literary secretary, an intelligent, reliable man who knew where to get facts and ideas, and how to analyze them and put them in usable form." That neatly defined how Roosevelt used and limited them. Their adventurous minds ventured as far as Roosevelt allowed them.[13]

Yet policy was on their minds—which made Felix Frankfurter's intrusion into the campaign intolerable. Aside from his old personal animus to the Harvard law professor, Berle saw in Frankfurter an ideological adversary—a Brandeisian "atomist" who opposed the brain trust consensus on large economic units for industrial planning. Their careers diverged after Harvard, but in 1932 they came together in the Roosevelt campaign. Massachusetts politics in the early twentieth century had made them both "aristocratic liberals" and Berle conceded that there was much in Frankfurter's career since then to admire—e.g., his brilliance in defending Sacco and Vanzetti. Still, in writing about Frankfurter for a Jewish encyclopedia some years later, Berle carefully associated Frankfurter with the Hoover administration through his friendship with Secretary of State Henry L. Stimson. Frankfurter followed Stimson's practice "of placing his students in positions in government departments; and it was his habit to maintain an elaborate correspondence with these men, so that he could make suggestions at various times to them as opportunity arose. He had some contact, though only in passing, with Franklin D. Roosevelt. . . . "[14]

Frankfurter wanted his man included in the brain trust to counteract their schemes for a corporate collectivism—ideologically at odds with Brandeisian antitrust prescriptions. At Frankfurter's behest and with the permission of Roosevelt, on August 5 labor lawyer Max Lowenthal joined a brain trust session devoted to critiquing Hugh Johnson's draft of a speech on currency. Lowenthal quickly found himself the target of only slightly veiled animosity. The braintrusters were all sound money advocates and they attacked Lowenthal as the advance agent of inflation. Berle, insisting that the brain trust should be above interest group politics, lambasted Lowenthal as a secret agent for both the Amalgamated Clothing Workers Union and Jewish financiers. Lowenthal, he sneered, was "the typical 'liberal on the make,' with some sincerity, some good ideas, considerable ability, and no loyalty—except to F. F. and the particular little group that revolves around him."

Not one to suffer somebody else's fool, the next day Berle fired off a letter to Frankfurter expressing his outrage over Lowenthal's interruption of "the usual conference with Governor Roosevelt." In turn, Frankfurter denied that Lowenthal was his agent, although he had mentioned to Roosevelt that Lowenthal had "unusual equipment for certain contributions to his campaign." He especially took exception to Berle's assertion that further policy debate within the Roosevelt camp had been foreclosed, pronouncing himself "troubled that the judgment of a man so wise, so experienced in financial matters and so seasoned in affairs of government as is

Lowenthal, should be deemed irrelevant simply because the issue had been previously discussed by your group."[15]

The real issue here was policy. During the campaign Berle deluged Roosevelt with memoranda that stressed the importance of railroad consolidation for economic stabilization under government supervision. Berle's messages stressed that nineteenth-century competition and individualism were anachronistic. Berle now had a retainer from Bernard Baruch to work with a group called the National Transportation Committee, which put him in league with a man whose ambition it was to effect rail consolidations in defiance of the antitrust laws. "B.M.B. [Bernard M. Baruch] poses the essential issue between the two wings of the party," Berle observed. While he thought that Baruch philosophically wanted too much freedom for businessmen, Berle believed that agreement on specific measures was possible. His advocacy of railroad consolidation was not missed in the Frankfurter camp. At a dinner with writer Edmund Wilson, Frankfurter's English friend, Harold Laski discoursed on how "Frankfurter thought that the thing to aim at was to tax the money away from the rich and that it was all wrong to talk against the Sherman [Antitrust] Act—it ought to be applied—the concentration of wealth in a few hands ought to be impeded. Berle was all wrong."

And Berle thought that Frankfurter was all wrong. Berle warned Roosevelt against any "New Freedom" speech such as Brandeis had inspired for Woodrow Wilson and Frankfurter wanted to outline for FDR. "Individualism" such as that prescribed by the Brandeisians was a Hoover euphemism for Washington's inaction: "Whatever the economic system does permit, it is not individualism," Berle argued. He sardonically ridiculed pleas for individualism and offered an alternative industrial policy:

> When nearly seventy per cent of American industry is concentrated in the hands of six hundred corporations; when not more than four or five thousand directors dominate this same block; when more than half of the population of the industrial east live or starve, depending on what this group does; when their lives, while they are working, are dominated by this group; when more than half the savings of the country are dominated by this same group; and when the flow of capital within the system is largely directed by not more than twenty great banks and banking houses—the individual man or woman has, in cold statistics, less than no chance at all. The President's stricture on "regimentation," accompanied by a willingness to let the centralized industrial scheme dominating things run loose, is merely ironic; there is not regimentation in work, in savings, and even in unemployment and starvation. . . .
>
> What Mr. Hoover means by individualism is letting economic units do about what they please.
>
> I can see the opposite view, which is a far truer individualism, and might be a policy by which the government acted as a regulating and unifying

agency, so that within the framework of this industrial system, individual men and women could survive, have homes, educate their children, and so forth.

He defined the issue as one of control which could only be attained when Washington exercised power on a par with Wall Street. Specifically, Berle prescribed revision of the antitrust law, coordination of transportation, and expansion of credit. "In a word," he advised Roosevelt, "it is necessary to do for this system what Bismarck did for the German system in 1880, as result of conditions not unlike these. . . . Otherwise only one of two results can occur. Either these handful of people who run the economic system now will get together making an economic government which far outweighs in importance the federal government; or in their struggles they will tear the system to pieces. Neither alternative is sound national policy." Roosevelt as president would be confronted with either private corporatism or chaos. Berle urged him to make a "pronouncement" on the need for public collective planning during a forthcoming swing through the West. He compellingly predicted that it "would probably make at once your place in history and [have] a political significance vastly beyond the significance of this campaign." Roosevelt did not respond to this memorandum, but in thanking Berle for a recent series of messages, he handwrote, "You are a wonderful help." Five weeks later he gave the Commonwealth Club Address in San Francisco.[16]

Berle called it his "new individualism" speech, to contrast his ideas from Frankfurter's "old individualism" and to usurp Frankfurter's efforts to make individualism a sole theme of the campaign. He wrote the Commonwealth Club speech with an assist from Beatrice Berle and editing by Moley, Tugwell, and Baruch's friend Senator Key Pittman. With Roosevelt then campaigning in the West, Berle airmailed a draft memorandum on individualism to Moley in Portland, Oregon. In San Francisco Roosevelt read the edited version.[17]

It was vintage Berle. Historical in its tone, it was too historical for Roosevelt and Moley, who excised Beatrice Berle's contributions, prompting her to exclaim, "What is Louis XIV to San Franciscans, what indeed?" Its focus was the American individual's relations with government from Alexander Hamilton through Woodrow Wilson. Its theme was that an active government need not portend the destruction of the individual: "In many instances the victory of the central Government, was a haven of refuge to the individual," Roosevelt asserted. Government under Hoover had benefited the few at the expense of the many through a protective tariff on industry and RFC loans to big banks. Concentration of wealth was much greater in 1932 than in 1912, thereby suggesting that Wilson's New Freedom had been ineffective. He invoked Berle and Means, although not by name, to argue that concentration of business proceeded apace and that "we are steering a steady course toward economic oligarchy, if we are not there already." Growth had to give way to sane economic management for security and stability.

> Our task now is not discovery or exploitation of natural resources, or necessarily producing more goods. It is the soberer, less dramatic business of administering resources and plants already in hand, of seeking to reestablish foreign markets for our surplus production, of meeting the problem of underconsumption, of adjusting production to consumption, of distributing wealth and products more equitably, or adapting existing economic organizations to the service of the people. The day of enlightened administration has come.

The time for planning had arrived. Insisting that Americans could not "abandon the principle of strong economic units, merely because their power is susceptible of easy abuse," Roosevelt proclaimed that "today we are modifying and controlling our economic units." Brandeisian trustbusting was not the order of the day. The chaos of the marketplace had to be disciplined by "an economic constitutional order." It was time to curb speculators, "not to hamper individualism but to protect it." After all, certain individuals had "undertaken to be, not business men, but princes of property." (The alliteration thrilled Beatrice Berle: it was her phrase.)[18]

It was the most radical speech of the 1932 campaign; it became "the manifesto of the New Deal." In the words of historian Richard Hofstadter, "the speech was considered the most momentous of the campaign because it was the one indication Roosevelt gave of the drastic innovations he would make." After the Commonwealth Club Address few skeptics could argue that Roosevelt was cut from the same cloth as Hoover. "None of Roosevelt's speeches caught up more poignantly the intellectual moods of the depression than this one," Arthur Schlesinger, Jr., has written. When Tugwell later turned historian he insisted that Roosevelt delivered the speech without his own editorial touch and that it reflected Berle's dour pessimism more than Roosevelt's own bouyant optimism. Its tone was Berle's, but FDR unmistakably subscribed to its theme: even Tugwell acknowledged that "we all agreed well enough that collectivism was by now a commitment." Although Berle downplayed economic growth as part of that commitment, he also stressed that the New Deal would bring production into balance with consumption and expand foreign markets.[19]

Through October the Roosevelt campaign and the brain trust were confident of victory. The administration could not escape the fact that it was a Hoover depression. The brain trust, isolated from the rest of the campaign in its fourth-floor headquarters in Manhattan's Hotel Roosevelt, chiefly tended to maintaining the ideological purity of Roosevelt's positions. However, despite the radicalism of the San Francisco speech, Wall Street had to be reassured: the tariff, the veterans' bonus, and inflation were to be disdained. Only the gold standard was expendable. Tammany Hall was kept at a distance. So was Felix Frankfurter. But the braintrusters were exultant that the intellectual had his day in national politics, that ideas and words seemed to matter in public affairs more than ever. Writing a speech for vice-presidential nominee John Nance Garner, Adolf and Beatrice Berle chortled over how they limited its vocabulary to words of three or four syllables.

But Berle's respect for Roosevelt grew. Here was a rare intelligence— one formed, not by reading, but by voracious contact with people. Berle never forgot whose intellectual jobber he was. He was Roosevelt's lawyer, a source for ideas, a speechwriter. He did not then make political suggestions, although he certainly possessed his own ideas on politics. He was content to articulate a policy consensus framed in brain trust discussions for Roosevelt and with which Roosevelt concurred. Cavalier toward most politicians, Berle dared not doubt FDR's courage or concentration; and he learned that a challenger for the presidency was not a champion of lost causes. As Berle told an opponent of the veterans' bonus, "You and I, from the outside, can wave a banner for principle and go down with our consciences saved, even though the result is not attained. I gather the Governor considers that his business is to get the result." Roosevelt possessed principles worth defending, but he did not fasten unalterably upon them—as Berle learned when the gold standard issue arose and Roosevelt declared emphatically, "I do not want to be committed to the gold standard. I haven't the faintest idea whether we will be on the gold standard on March 4th or not; nobody can foresee where we shall be." Berle, the intellectual aristocrat, learned from Roosevelt, the landed aristocrat, what democratic politics was about.[20]

By the first week of November the brain trust had been eclipsed; the politicians were in control of the campaign. "We estimate that by Saturday night there will be nothing left of the Brain Trust but the secretary," Berle gloomily observed. Senators Key Pittman and Jimmy Byrnes had taken over speechwriting duties—when Byrnes was not playing nurse to a drunken Pittman or protecting the hotel's taxicab starter from assault by Pittman. Berle had anticipated displacement by the politicians and had given some thought to his public career after November. He had Baruch's retainer on the Coolidge Transportation Committee, a position Roosevelt approved with an encouraging, "More power to your arm!" But that was a temporary and part-time assignment. He felt that Roosevelt's victory would not entitle him to "a big Washington job" and any lesser position would not be worth a financial sacrifice. However, his interest in local politics had been kindled by Roosevelt's troubles with Tammany Hall and the forthcoming mayoralty election in 1933. Always able to sustain simultaneously several involvements, Berle was certain there would be something for a former braintruster after FDR became president.[21]

New Dealer

Victorious politicians are rich with debts. In 1933 Franklin Roosevelt had more than his share, but Adolf Berle disavowed any immediate collection on his credit. His service in the campaign was not enough to entitle him to a cabinet appointment and anything less was not worth his time. He was nearly unknown in Congress, had not been a Democrat, had no political constituency such as Henry Wallace's farmers or Harold Ickes' Senate progressives. What could a braintruster expect? Moley became assistant secretary of state and Tugwell assistant secretary of agriculture, but Berle bided his time. The assumption of power called for soul-searching by braintrusters. They were introspective intellectuals who disliked bureaucracy; they simultaneously feared and craved power. They viewed electoral politics as necessarily corrupting. Yet they believed that government and politics needed their apolitical expertise—and they were not above desiring an appreciative reward for service in the campaign. However, the aftermath left them feeling superfluous to Roosevelt's election. Berle did not think that the brain trust had made a difference: "My candid conviction is that the result of the election would have been about the same if we had all sat on the banks of the river and angled for cat fish. That, however, may be ascribed rather to a lack of sleep than to a lack of egotism."[1]

It surprised many people when Berle became assistant secretary of nothing in 1933. His widely acknowledged brilliance, the rewards given the other braintrusters, and his growing reputation for vanity all suggested that he had to be offered a job which he could not possibly refuse. Could he walk away from public office? Berle insisted he could—especially if the office proferred was not commensurate with his interests or abilities. He had had no hint from Roosevelt that he would receive any. On the Saturday afternoon before the election Roosevelt and Berle had discussed positions and policies in the next administration, the governor dismissing the cabinet expectations of party elders such as Owen D. Young, John W. Davis, and Newton D. Baker because, with the possible exception of Young, they lacked "adventurous minds." However, he did not want to commit anything to anyone then because events in the interregnum might alter those plans. So uncertain was the depression crisis that Roosevelt envisioned the possibility of becoming president before March should his majority be substantial enough to move Hoover to appoint him secretary of state and then resign along with Vice-President Curtis; but that was improbable. In any case, he told Berle, he did not want to say or do anything that might excite public anticipation.

Roosevelt enjoyed "adventurous minds" but preferred cautious politics. He had grown in Berle's estimation from an unknown lightweight to a "open-minded and intelligent" leader with "a tremendous intuitive grasp of situations, and an absolute refusal to assume that they can be settled by shibboleth.'' Berle particularly savored Roosevelt's penchant for unconventional ideas, of which Berle had his share. He could imagine Roosevelt institutionalizing a White House brain trust, if it were only possible to translate concepts into political realities. Significantly, Berle and Roosevelt easily found much common ground when they discussed public finance and foreign affairs. Yet FDR never mentioned what Berle might do in the New Deal, even if their discussions augured an assignment.[2]

In the interim Berle performed several various tasks as Roosevelt's representative. During November and December he drafted a bill on federal incorporation for the House Committee on Interstate Commerce, met with the influential National Industrial Conference Board to explain the domestic allotment plan for agriculture, drew up a railroad receivership bill for the Coolidge Committee on Transportation, collaborated with Congressman Fiorello La Guardia on revisions of the 1898 Bankruptcy Act, and recommended to Moley that a job in the Administration be found for his friend David E. Lilienthal. However, he confounded even his fellow braintrusters by refusing any long-term Washington position. In February, when the allocation of jobs was in earnest and rumor slated Berle for the Federal Trade Commission, Rexford Tugwell thought he detected a Berle change of heart: ''His reasons for not going are that he has assembled a whole group of his family around him in his law office and that they are dependent upon him for their productivity, but I imagine this resistance may break down and March 4 may see the whole group [of brainstrusters] assembled in Washington in some way or other.''[3]

It was true that he disdained bureaucracy and had personal obligations to a burgeoning law practice in New York that employed his brother Rudolf and his sister Lina, but he also felt no need to hold a title or an office to have influence as a policymaker; he already possessed access to Roosevelt's receptive mind, an enviable position that no government appointment would enhance. To be sure, Berle would be seen in New Deal Washington frequently, but by choice he took no prominent post. He was content to commute to a temporary job in the Reconstruction Finance Corporation or other ephemeral assignments. If access to power bestowed power, Berle felt he gained nothing by taking an obscure post in the new administration. He considered himself ''one of those rare people who happens to have in life the thing he most wants—the position of an *intellectual free lance,* with a moderate living, the gracious gift of friendship, and no lack either of color or work. Short of some peculiar set of circumstances imposing a real obligation, I should be merely foolish to trade this for the mazes of official life in Washington.'' In November Berle asserted, ''I shall choose merely that [position] of being *an intellectual jobber and contractor from time to time when jobs come forward.*'' He meant it. He wanted to remain in New York. And he wanted to make policy without implementing it. ''I do hope to have a relationship which will permit my going to the White House occasionally to delve in when various discussions are forward; and that, in all conscience, is responsibility enough."[4]

He did not consider himself too intellectual for government service; he had been angling to get into politics ever since he joined Republican clubs shortly after returning to New York in 1919. Politics translated ideas into programs and he had ideas and programs. A scant two days after the election he outlined his own version of the New Deal. It included general proposals for agricultural and jobless relief, industrial stabilization, and taxation ("whether by sales tax or otherwise, the budget has to be balanced"). He prescribed centralized industrial planning—federal regulation of security issues, a federal incorporation act, a branch banking act, coordination of all federal credit agencies such as home loan banks, and revision of federal receivership laws and the Interstate Commerce Act to allow "additional unification of railway facilities to eliminate unnecessary competition"— concluding, "It must be remembered that by March 4 next we may have anything on our hands from a recovery to a revolution. The chance is about even either way. My impression is that the country wants and would gladly support a rather daring program."[5]

He liked catering to a market that wanted a daring program. His letters, his widely disseminated memoranda, and his now famous book *The Modern Corporation and Private Property* identified him with the relatively radical idea of planning and collectivization of American life. He shared this distinction with other braintrusters, but Berle was more artful in promoting it. "The thing that counts here is the steady intellectual drive which at long last must condition every political change," he assured a Columbia colleague. It was time for "men who can think straight and be vocal in their thinking." And that was how he projected himself.[6]

Berle did not embrace big corporations and big government as much as he realistically accepted them as part of a historical trend: "I am afraid we are doomed to an era of big business, and possibly even State socialism. The line that I am working on is a vague dream that the commercial organizations which we have built up may be used, more or less as they stand, without being destroyed, in the public interest. This means seriously cutting into the profit motive." In an age of burgeoning great organizations, he conspicuously defined a happy medium between Hoover's anarchistic individualism and that of corporate liberalism: "It cannot be individualism, pure and simple, as we used to know it. It must not be either regimented socialism or fascism as we ordinarily think of it. Surely there must be the middle ground which permits individuals to fulfill themselves in their lives, without leaving the bulk of the population merely the sport or prey of passing economic ambition."[7]

He endeavored to define that middle ground. Carefully distinguishing his views from Roosevelt's New Deal, he nevertheless was among a select group which sought to combine existing business organizations with innovative government regulation to obtain what he called "four major desiderata . . . in any stabilization plans":

(1)   There must be a supply of the commodity manufactured at a fair price.
(2)   As many men as possible must be put to work, consistent with a living wage for the lot.
(3)   So far as possible (this is far more difficult and therefore must be more elastic) the price in the labor cost structure ought to provide for a fair return on capital—but we can't assume responsibility for the excesses.
     . . .
(4)   At least initially, the plan must be open to everyone.

These objectives he told a businessman, required government controls such as:

(1)   Government regulation of accounting.
(2)   Some control of accumulations and surplus and investment in additional and possibly unnecessary productive capacity. This is a terrific problem.
(3)   Some legally imposed responsibility for labor—conceivably, a properly drawn unemployment insurance scheme might cover this, but it would be preferable if these schemes could be worked out within the industry. What I am vaguely driving at is that you cannot allow an individual [business] to save money by an improved process or machine, scrapping labor, when the community is asked to bear the cost of readjusting that labor— a cost which may far exceed the savings of the individual [business]. The individual [business] makes money; on aggregate balance, however, there is a net loss which ultimately we all pay for.
(4)   A close statistical review of the industry. . . . Properly used, this might even result in assisting the banks to pursue an enlightened policy in not financing, when financing is foolish, and in financing, when the obvious result is constructive, though the temporary outlook may be unhappy.[8]

In retrospect, much of the economic planning Berle prescribed came to pass in the next decade and a half: stabilized industrial prices through the National Recovery Administration (NRA), financing of new industry through the Reconstruction Finance Corporation, reemployment of workers through successive public works agencies, taxation of undistributed profits, federal unemployment insurance, collective bargaining for unions, minimum wage laws, and the possibility of a government-coordinated industrial policy through the Employment Act of 1946. While he did not anticipate all of the New Deal—and Berle's ideas were not peculiar to him alone—his was a great vision of state capitalism.

To bring it all about he had to duel intellectually such unbelievers as conservative businessmen and competition-minded liberals—Brandeis and Frankfurter, and their acolytes—while rallying believers in New Deal capitalist planning. Berle was up to those tasks. For much of the previous decade he had written for arcane law journals, but now—famed as a brain-truster and coauthor of "the most important contribution to economic theory published in 1932"—he sought to inform a larger audience on the need for planning and community control of business. Thus, reviewing *Recent Social Trends,* a social science survey of developments promoted by the Hoover administration, Berle lauded the book's efforts to achieve understanding even as he faulted its perspective. Its chief problem, Berle wrote, was that the study had been commissioned in the halcyon days of 1929; the turmoil since then made it outdated. Sounding the themes of *The Modern Corporation*'s conclusion and the Commonwealth Club Address, Berle insisted that the election of Roosevelt marked a new spirit in the nation: "That men must work for ideals and service rather than for money, sufficiently illustrates the clean turn-around." FDR had awakened Americans to a greater consciousness of the community's relation to the individual: "We are insisting that the government shall evolve machinery for the purpose of guiding economic life so that it shall serve the individual." Whether they called it a "new individualism" or "collectivism," responsible bankers, industrialists, and farmers "have agreed among themselves that there must be a nucleus of directed activity; that they have been unable to evolve, privately, the machinery to achieve this; and they have appealed to the paramount authority for assistance in solving the problem." Thus, government became the vehicle for cooperation among producers intent upon results, rather than "techniques" that promoted individualism. And he asserted that a public bureaucracy would not intimidate individualism. "Let us concede that this [collectivism] abandons the traditional theory that the government should not mix in business, and substitutes a government-economic nucleus in place of a private nucleus. But does the nucleus differ for all of that?" In other words, the New Deal would employ government to conserve the fundamentals of capitalism. He did not employ the term "state capitalism," as Jerome Frank had, but that was what he advanced.[9]

In 1933 Berle worried less about Hoover's discredited individualism than that of Brandeis. Previous efforts to moderate Brandeis' intolerance for bigness had failed. Berle's corporate collectivism and Brandeis' individualism defined the debate within the New Deal. "Brandeis dreams of turning the clock backward," Berle warned. "His constant phrase is 'the curse of bigness'—who shall say he is not right?—but from the puzzled position of mid-career, I cannot see how the tide can be turned back." Brandeis and Frankfurter, Berle noted, believe "the small unit is more efficient." Berle's work with Baruch on the Coolidge Transportation Committee, where he and Baruch pushed for consolidation of the railroads, the antithesis of Brandeis' war against big business, threatened to bring him into additional conflict with Brandeis and Frankfurter.

He expected a war with Frankfurter and he was not disappointed. In January, Frankfurter began phoning people connected with the transportation committee, interrupting Berle during a conference with Moley. A heated shouting match erupted between them and Berle hung up, petulantly complaining that Frankfurter wanted to "ruin" him. The next day, confessing to "an intense personal desire" to see Frankfurter shot, Berle made certain that Roosevelt heard about the incident and shrewdly thanked Baruch for his "vigorous support . . . when the shooting started in my direction."[10]

As the inauguration drew near, Berle principally dealt with problems of money and credit. In 1933 the banking system was disintegrating and talk about planned inflation abounded. Talk was about all anyone could do. Hoover was immobilized by his repudiation at the polls and Roosevelt was without authority until March 4. The braintrusters adamantly opposed inflation, as did most of Roosevelt's political advisors. Yet Roosevelt cannily refused to commit himself either way, hinting that a small dose of inflation might be needed. Many of his advisors wondered if he could rebuff congressional demands for inflation in March and April.

On the issue of inflation Berle was no populist. He liked credit inflation through selective loans to "the 'white collar' and intelligentsia classes," because "something like this will have to be done to head off a pure inflation program in the next Congress." He would use loans to industry to head off more radical inflation proposals. Meanwhile, he was among those representing Roosevelt in discussions with America's financial elite that sought a strategy against the financial crisis. The transportation committee was one avenue of communication. Another was a February meeting at the Century Club with the Federal Reserve Bank of New York, at which it was hinted that the banking system would "be in a bad jam within the next few weeks." For Berle it was the first indication of the magnitude of the banking crisis.[11]

The day after the inauguration Berle and others designated by Roosevelt met at the Treasury with Federal Reserve officials, bankers, and holdovers from the Hoover administration to plot a way out of the banking crisis. How could they save the banks other than to close them down to prevent withdrawals? The more than twenty-five participants wrangled through the morning—Will Woodin, Roosevelt's secretary of the treasury, and George L. Harrison of the New York Federal Reserve Bank pressing for a bank holiday, to which there seemed general agreement. As adjournment for lunch approached, Berle disdainfully noted to himself that "it is now obvious that this bunch *cannot* develop a program. All that can be done is to get the lay of the land." Notwithstanding his haughty pessimism, following lunch the conference adopted unanimously Berle's motion for the bank holiday. Another unanimously approved proposal called for a special session of Congress. However, the conferees could not agree upon a plan to be recommended to Congress for reopening the banks. A subgroup of five (a corporate body of a corporate body) was formed, with Berle added to act as its secretary, to develop a specific scheme for Congress. In it debate centered around guaranteeing a percentage of bank deposits on hand and urging upon the Congress that it give Roosevelt war powers. (Roosevelt opposed any guarantees; in April, Berle thought that was a mistake, but in August he tacked, certain that "in the long run, guarantees are unsound and do not work." By October he knew that Congress would not eliminate deposit insurance.)[12]

The tensions of the banking crisis augmented Berle's reputation for being brilliant; now he was both brilliant and difficult. His slight stature and boyish face suggested to others a man younger than thirty-eight. According to one description,

> His narrow-shouldered body had a somewhat unfinished look, as if its growth had been arrested in midadolescence, and his head appeared, by contrast with his torso, abnormally large, which augmented the general impression he gave of physical immaturity, though his general health was excellent and he was physically far stronger than he looked. His face was sharp-featured, sharp eyed. His mouth, closed, wore a slightly smug, self-satisfied look, and it had in it an exceedingly sharp tongue, one that could pierce and slash sensitive psyches during his moments of irritation, though he seldom raised his voice. Not a few dealing with him were highly irritated by him. They deemed his manner arrogant and supercilious and looked upon him as a brash, cocky, obviously very bright schoolboy who had never quite grown up—a case of arrested emotional as well as physical development.[13]

During those critical days he was an acerbic Cassandra. Fatigued from seemingly always being in transit between Washington and New York, he exhibited morbidity and a volatile temper. His scorn for established reputations was never more evident than when he left others aghast by sharply challenging Secretary of the Treasury Will Woodin's judgment during one conference. On the Sunday morning following the inauguration, Berle met with Moley at his hotel to discuss the Treasury conferences and, annoyed that Moley had invited journalist Ralph Robey to participate, snapped "there is too much Colonel House business going on here." Affronted, Moley turned on his heel and left. Later that day, shortly before Moley was to retire, Berle burst into his room "in a state of great agitation," exclaiming that they would not be able to reopen the banks within three days. A few days later, at breakfast with his friend Charles Taussig, Moley, and James P. Warburg, "Berle was in a highly excited state, . . . two jumps ahead of a fit, but apparently doing excellent work on the railroad problem, [and] exploded ideas all over the place," Warburg wrote. "He takes a very pessimistic view of the future and talks about complete collapse—whatever he means by that—by July 1st and general hell to pay unless all sorts of things are done." Even Beatrice Berle, who seldom saw her husband during those frenetic days, noted that he was "very uneasy in his mind about the future," talked about how the banking collapse was only the beginning, and apocalyptically forecast that the ultimate smashup would come in September. That behavior and talk became a Berle trademark in Washington, along with his arrogant certainty that he, if anyone could, would "think a way through" a crisis.[14]

Yet his acknowledged talents and forceful advocacy of industrial planning appealed to many in Washington. Without portfolio and ambivalent about needing any, the peripatetic Berle on April 12 became special assistant on railroad matters to the new head of the Reconstruction Finance Corporation, Texas banker Jesse Jones. Roosevelt had been disappointed that the railroads did not reorganize under the bankruptcy law designed by Berle to facilitate railroad mergers. Instead of combining, the roads sought RFC loans to avert bankruptcy. Jones chose Berle to deliver the administration's merger message to the roads. Six weeks later Berle announced that roads desiring RFC loans would have to consolidate or look elsewhere for financing. But, as carloadings swelled through 1933, railroad interest in consolidation waned.

The RFC appointment entitled Berle to a place in the New Deal's inner councils, which he used to seek positions for allies such as David E. Lilienthal and others, just as Frankfurter pushed his friends and former students for administration jobs. Also, he participated in White House conferences such as the one where Roosevelt announced that the United States would leave the gold standard, a move endorsed by Moley, Taussig, and Director of the Budget Lewis Douglas, who declared dramatically that it marked the end of Western civilization. Berle was not alone in his crisis theatrics.[15]

But Roosevelt gave few advisors the privilege of being an exclusive insider; he enjoyed dividing authority among competitors. It disconcerted Berle when Roosevelt gave the task of writing a new securities law to Frankfurter and three of his students, James M. Landis, Thomas G. Corcoran, and Benjamin V. Cohen. Berle beseeched Will Woodin to consult Congressman Sam Rayburn and a few others "for practical comment" on a draft bill. "Felix is a brilliant man with excellent ideas," he wrote condescendingly, "but some experience sometimes helps in these matters." Frozen out of its writing, Berle deprecated the securities law, insisting that he would have "preferred a rather different variety of act" because "it leaves unsolved the major questions." Toward the end of the year Berle smugly informed Roosevelt that brokerages were boycotting new issues in protest against the securities law and suggested that the RFC enter the investment banking business, a proposal Jesse Jones endorsed and Roosevelt quashed.[16]

Berle was a minor actor in the New Deal's Hundred Days of dramatic legislating for recovery. He took no direct part in the development of major cooporative institutions such as the National Recovery Administration and the Agricultural Adjustment Administration for which he had laid the ground intellectually in *The Modern Corporation* and elsewhere. He was the New Deal's ardent advocate, explaining it in enthusiastic speeches and writings to academic and business audiences, exhorting businessmen to behave as "a thoroughly responsible, organized business community," accusing big business leaders of failing to organize against the disaster and turning the masses to Washington for leadership against the crisis, and reassuring Americans that the New Deal was not fascism, communism, or socialism, but a middle way collectivism that preserved individualism. "The real difference between fascism and the New Deal," he wrote, "lies not in the form of organization, but what goes on inside of the heads of the men forming the organization, and where the residuum of ultimate control lies." The New Deal had not altered American values and American government. "To the contrary, it would seem that the last few months have been almost the heyday of individualism; certainly there never was a time when an idea which was at once intelligent and practical got swifter recognition, irrespective of its source."

In print Berle always treated Brandeis with deferential courtesy, even conceding that "Isaiah"—"who informs his economics with a certain quality of mysticism without which economics is worth very little"—might be correct that "bigness" had gone too far. Like Brandeis, Berle too informed his economics with mysticism. "The great desideratum," he once told Brandeis, is "that life is dominantly spiritual and not economic. I have got myself the reputation for sentimentality by insisting on this at Columbia; but I think it is sound." Against the Marxist intellectual grain of the Great Depression, Berle disavowed economic determination. Industry, he firmly asserted, was "a tool of life and not the end and aim of life itself." Intellect was more important in determining economic or political behavior than the social system itself. While aspiring to analyze and to interpret social and political power in the most realistic terms possible, Berle rejected the ascendant materialism of his times.

> [Laws, finance and commerce] are nothing save in the hands of men and women of vision, of courage, of faith, proceeding from an inner spiritual strength and discipline. This is why the now much-despised Puritans contributed the greatest single force in American life; it is, perhaps, why in the last decade our economic institutions grew fragile as our life grew meaningless. A credo of some kind is as necessary to keep an economic civilization going as it is a political or religious civilization.

More than anything else in his public life, Berle hungered to define that credo. Ideas gave a man immortality. As discussed earlier, he burned to become an "American Karl Marx—a social prophet." A Machiavelli to his Prince, Roosevelt, he wanted to be both *éminence grise* and the Prince's philosopher—a lord temporal, a lord spiritual. State capitalism was his vehicle for undercutting the extremes of the right and the left and defining himself as the prophet of a mixed system. But he could not discover his vehicle for implementing it. Even his passionately loyal wife, Beatrice, doubted that he could be both the man of ideas and the man of action: "He has shown a surprising agility in business and politics so that I expect he will be condemned to tight rope walking all his life. Even the most skilled tight rope walkers eventually fall off and break a neck or a leg but do they then become philosophers?" In 1933 Berle walked the tightrope with bankers and labor leaders, encouraged in part by the fact that Roosevelt himself was a Christian spiritualist and a pragmatist too.[17]

Roosevelt also appreciated Berle for some of the enemies his words made. That autumn a Berle article, asserting that the New Deal had not ignored the laws of economics but had merely used levers and controls available to government to fulfill human needs, created a stir in Lombard and Wall Streets. The "historic" experiments of the Roosevelt administration would succeed, Berle predicted, because "complicated and difficult as it may seem to manipulate private industry and private economic processes this is still preferable to attempting a wholesale solution, so long as there is any hope of success." American values determined any social system the people wanted. He believed they wanted a mixed system. As he had said privately, were Americans "to adopt the Russian Soviet system entire, it would look a good deal more like the Rotary club or the four railway brotherhoods than like the Moscow Soviet." The New Deal only modified American civilization to meet changed conditions; "In a world in which revolutions just now are coming easily, the New Deal chose the more difficult course of moderation and rebuilding." Yet, in London, this essentially conservative interpretation of the New Deal was labeled the "most surprising" utterance to "have emanated from the United States since 1776." In lower Manhattan, it moved one Morgan partner to tell another, "Brought up as a follower of [William Graham] Sumner I find it difficult to adjust myself to the theory that somebody owes me a living or that I owe somebody a living." In certain quarters his defense of the New Deal made Berle a radical. It would be decades before a New Dealer would be viewed as a corporate liberal who helped save a rotting capitalism.[18]

Among certain liberals, Berle's ideas and energy had admirers. With a Puritan work ethic engrained in Berle's eclecticism, no single obligation monopolized his attention. In his private life he was devoted to a growing family, his parents, sisters, and a law practice he shared with his brother. In his public life his only official attachment was to the RFC in 1933—but he entertained a multitude of competing interests and involvements. Jerome Frank, counsel to the Agricultural Adjustment Administration, wanted Berle as special counsel to the AAA on sugar—but legally Berle could not serve simultaneously both the RFC and AAA and ethically his dual employment by the Molasses Company and the AAA constituted a conflict of interests. Anyway, Berle resigned from the RFC on September 1, when

Roosevelt sent him with Sumner Welles on a special mission to Havana to deal with Cuba's instability.[19]

Then the Commerce Department asked him to serve on a special committee studying proposed laws regulating the conduct of the stock exchanges. Also, he became heavily involved in New York City's mayoralty race—advising Fiorello La Guardia on his Fusion candidacy and Roosevelt on how to be neutral between his party and the progressive La Guardia. In 1933 Berle happily began work on his second brain trust—this time for La Guardia in his Fusion campaign for mayor of New York. In this he had the tacit support of FDR, who was not adverse to a maverick Republican trimming the Tammany Hall Democrats. Moreover, they saw it as part of a national strategy enhancing national economic recovery through good management and fiscal stability in New York City. In 1934 Berle would hold two positions: official braintruster to La Guardia and unofficial braintruster to Roosevelt, a New Deal portfolio Berle invented for himself. All this activity was enough for one lawyer to exclaim to Berle, "How you can find time in an ordinary day of twenty-four hours to do what you have to do and, at the same time, write the numerous articles that seem to flow incessantly from your facile pen, is a mystery I hope to be able to penetrate some day."[20]

THE LAST CHAMBERLAIN

La Guardia designed the scene. At five minutes into 1934 he was sworn in as mayor of the City of New York in the library of Judge Samuel Seabury's town house on East 63rd Street with Berle and other supporters looking on with great pride. In the pause that followed the taking of the oath, Seabury said what was on many minds: "Now we have a Mayor of New York." But what sort of mayor? Again it was Fiorello La Guardia who set the tone: "We are embarked on an experiment to try to show that a nonpartisan, nonpolitical government is possible, and, if we succeed, I am sure that success in other cities is possible." Then he gave orders to the police to move against suspected racketeers.

La Guardia. "His career is not over by a long shot and I think he ought to be annexed," Berle had told Moley in late November 1932. But Roosevelt did not want a progressive Republican congressman from East Harlem who had gone down to defeat in the Democratic landslide in his administration. A congressman for all but two years since 1918, La Guardia was an anomaly in New York—a progressive Republican who fought monopoly interests, favored government ownership of public power or strict regulation of natural resources and railroads, and espoused public works for relief and recovery from the Great Depression. In 1926 his fellow Republicans had labeled La Guardia a socialist. On the other hand, Roosevelt saw progressive Republicans as kindred spirits—as long as they were Westerners who inhabited traditional Republican states and not New Yorkers who fought Democrats like La Guardia.

Anyway, La Guardia would never be somebody else's annex. Berle's recommendation was doubly naive: Roosevelt did not want La Guardia and he could not have had him. The tempestuous La Guardia burned with political ambition, even if defeat was no stranger to him. He had been running for all sorts of offices since 1914, aided in part by his fluent Italian and Yiddish, the languages of New York's East Side neighborhoods. Important for Berle, he hated Tammany Hall. He made an abortive race against Tammany's James J. Walker for Mayor of New York in 1929. In 1932 he lost the House seat from East Harlem he had held since 1926 because he ran as a Republican in a Democratic year. In the winter of 1933, La Guardia was a lame-duck congressman with his eye on New York City where the corrupt Tammany was in trouble. And he had made a new friend in Adolf Berle.[1]

In May 1932, Paul H. Kern, a law student working for the Legislative Drafting Bureau at Columbia University, suggested that Congressman La Guardia seek legal assistance from his professor, Adolf Berle. Berle was considerably interested in this good government Republican whose political career had reached a crossroads. In November Berle invited the charismatic maverick to dinner and La Guardia expressed his eagerness to shepherd Roosevelt's legislation through the lame-duck session. Berle assisted La Guardia in the revision of the National Bankruptcy Act of 1898 that permitted more orderly liquidation and reorganization. Hoover signed the bill on his last day as president.[2]

Berle and La Guardia already had New York City politics on their minds. In the summer of 1932 revelations concerning Tammany graft had come to a head in an investigation conducted by Judge Samuel Seabury, a staunchly anti-Tammany Democrat. The climax came on September 1 when Mayor Walker resigned. In the midst of Roosevelt's campaign for the presidency, New York City's attention was on its mayor. So was Berle's. "Sick" about Tammany's shenanigans, Berle sounded off about putting a third party in the field for the upcoming 1933 mayoralty contest. In an overwhelmingly Democratic city, Berle wanted an alliance between good-government Democrats and "silk stocking" Republicans. "How in the hell are you out for O'Brien?" he demanded curtly of a law school colleague, Harold R. Medina, who supported a Tammany man for mayor a year before the election. Not about to back any New York Democrat, Berle cast about for an alternative candidate. By the spring of 1933 it was apparent that his man was La Guardia. But the key figure in New York City's reform politics was the aristocratic and arrogant Samuel Seabury.[3]

Seabury was both a patrician and a Democrat. His great-great-grandfather had been the first Episcopal bishop in the United States. In his youth Seabury belonged to Henry George's Single-Tax Club, the Good-Government Club, and advocated public ownership of utilities and the city transit system. He lost his first political race for a judgeship on the Independent Labor ticket in 1899, but between 1900 and 1914, backed by labor unions and reform groups, he was elected judge of New York City's courts, appointed a justice of the State Supreme Court of New York, and elected to the Court of Appeals as a Progressive. In 1916 the Democrats nominated him for governor, but he went down to defeat when Tammany and Republican progressives defected. Judge Seabury remained active in the Democratic party until the summer of 1930, when Roosevelt appointed him referee in an investigation of magistrate courts in New York City. The investigation turned up "little tin boxes" of money stashed in the sheriff's office, evidence of graft that implicated Mayor Walker and the Tammany organization. Bipartisan good-government forces organized a Fusion party intent upon ridding the city of partisan vices. But they lacked a candidate for mayor who could win. The 60-year-old Seabury had the visibility needed to win (it was said that he was too ambitious to be Mayor—he wanted to be president), but, although he maintained a town house on East 63rd Street he also had a voting residence outside of the city at East Hampton, Long Island (it also assured his "nonpartisan" involvement in the city's politics). Still, he was formidable enough to choose New York's next mayor.

That was why Adolf Berle called him one day to arrange a meeting. Seabury invited him to his office. They did not know each other, but they had a lot in common. Berle's father, like Seabury's, had been a clergyman and a professor of theology; both hated Tammany Hall and had passed their passions along to their sons. Now Berle sought to convince Seabury that La Guardia was right for good-government reformers. He left with Seabury's assurances that La Guardia would be considered.

But other Fusionists wanted Robert Moses—a Yale man, a Jew who wore it unobtrusively, a Republican who ran nonpartisan public works administrations for Tammany politicians, a former secretary of state under Al Smith, and Smith's State Park Authority head. When Seabury first heard of their preference for Moses over lunch at the Bankers Club, his face reddened, his fist hit the table, and he righteously denounced his fellow Fusionists for consorting with Tammany. Seabury preferred purity to power, even if he had to fight Fusionists as well as Tammany. In La Guardia he had a man of instincts similar to his own—purity in quest of power. On August 3, 1933, the octogenarian C. C. Burlingham convened a caucus of Fusionists at the Bar Association where Berle made an eloquent appeal for La Guardia for mayor. An argument broke out and Seabury rose to La Guardia's defense. It was then that Burlingham startled the assembled Fusionists by telling the august Judge Seabury, "Sit down, Sam! Sit down."

No one could recall hearing the Judge called by his first name in public before. Nevertheless, Seabury bent the Fusionists to his will: La Guardia became their candidate for mayor.[4]

Was the populistic La Guardia an unlikely candidate for these blue-blooded mugwumps? Certainly the pugnacious and fiery La Guardia at five-foot-two seemed to have little in common with the likes of a cool Ivy Leaguer like Newbold Morris at six-foot-five. La Guardia was a vituperative fighter and immigrant son who spoke to New Yorkers in their European languages; the Fusionists were genteel aristocrats who hoped to obliterate overseas origins in the melting pot. Yet, in his way, La Guardia was the melting pot. His father had been an agnostic Catholic, his mother had been an Italian Jew, his wife was Lutheran, and La Guardia joined the Episcopal church. He had fought Tammany Hall up and down Manhattan's streets for two decades—and still some of these Protestant goo-goos in a city of Catholics and Jews doubted he was good enough for them. Would the "nice people" ever accept him? During the big meeting a Fusionist had shouted, "If it's La Guardia or bust, I say bust!" To them, he was a demagogue. "If he was a demagogue," Berle said some years later, "then he was a demagogue in the right direction." Berle saw him as a street-wise "gut-fighter" who knew how to get honorable results in Congress or in City Hall. (An old friend believed La Guardia capable of violence or even murder in order to obtain justice.) That was how Berle sold him that August evening— as the man who would clean up New York and restore its political integrity.[5]

Was New York ready for reform? Tammany seemed to have a death wish when it renominated John Patrick O'Brien, Walker's blundering replacement and an undeniably weak candidate. But Roosevelt prevailed upon anti-Tammany Democrat Joseph V. McKee, president of the Board of Aldermen since 1925, to run on a newly created "Recovery" party ticket. McKee was the man to beat. La Guardia promised efficiency, honesty, economy, and a balanced budget in city government. He would reform assessment rates, restore the city's credit rating, unify the transit system, and give jobs only to real workers rather than the parasites who drew paychecks under Tammany. That reassured Fusion and Republican voters, but would Democrats follow him? Would Roosevelt back McKee, La Guardia, or keep his counsel?

Berle hoped to keep Roosevelt out of the New York contest while bestowing the aura of the New Deal upon La Guardia with his own well-publicized support for La Guardia. He tried to neutralize Roosevelt's vague commitment to McKee with a campaign to show the city that Roosevelt's braintruster was La Guardia's too. He lined up New Dealers and the Columbia faculty behind La Guardia, always insisting that Roosevelt would be neutral in the New York race. But Berle knew that the claim needed reinforcement. In August, he explained his enthusiasm for La Guardia to Roosevelt and tied it to New York City's financial plight. Of the four major financial crises confronting the administration, Berle told Roosevelt, two of them were under control, a third was manageable, but the city's could "only be settled by winning an election" and "independent Democrats walked out on us so we do what we can." Six weeks later, amid rumors that McKee sought Roosevelt's full blessings, Berle sent a telegram pleading with the president not to abandon "a premier moral position" by endorsing McKee. In October, Ogden Mills—Hoover's secretary of the treasury and a New York Republican whom Roosevelt personally detested—endorsed La Guardia. An agitated Berle hastened to remind Roosevelt that La Guardia and Mills were old foes too and suggested that Mills' support was intended to hang Roosevelt with McKee at a time when La Guardia was pulling ahead. He beseeched Roosevelt to reaffirm his neutrality and assured him that La Guardia, "as the left progressive," appealed to the same voters who had elected the president: "Don't deliver us into the hands of your (and our) enemies." Roosevelt said nothing—to La Guardia's tacit advantage. In November, La Guardia won by a quarter of a million votes over the runner-up McKee.[6]

La Guardia's triumph gave Berle a political debt that demanded prompt repayment. In this election he had been a prominent operative, rather than a backroom technician who developed ideas and words for the candidate. Berle had successfully reassured both Roosevelt and Republican blue bloods that a La Guardia mayoralty did not threaten them. When La Guardia offered him the post of chamberlain of the City of New York and an opportunity to mastermind Gotham's financial recovery, Berle accepted. Rejecting Bernard Baruch's advice "that a public office was a good place to keep out of if possible," Berle declared he could not "honestly stay out" because "unlike the Federal Government, the City of New York has not the whole country to draw from."[7]

Besides, a city post allowed him to remain in his New York home near his law practice and his teaching duties at Columbia, as well as corroborating the wisdom of his refusal to take a secondary position in Washington; he would be a prime mover in New York and a power in his own right. With La Guardia he established a political base, something no other brain-truster could boast of. Moreover, he demonstrated political sagacity in going with La Guardia while maintaining his loyalty to FDR. Berle had ended 1931 a lawyer and a scholar, 1932 an advisor to the president-elect of the United States, and 1933 an advisor to the mayor of New York.

La Guardia was a Puritan revolutionary in quest of his City upon a Hill, an incorruptible municipal government; but that is not how he is best remembered. Mayor for twelve years, the La Guardia of memory is the La Guardia of a multitude of scenes he designed. There is La Guardia wielding a sledgehammer against slot machines because he was a crime fighter and gambling is a vice that takes money from the poor; operating a crane at a construction site because he was a builder; in fireman's garb because it was a city service of which he was proud; wielding a baton at a band concert because he loved music enough to create city cultural institutions such as the High School of Music and Art; shaking hands with President Roosevelt or his representative because this mayor was one of the important political figures of his time and a liberal friend of the New Deal; reading the Sunday comics on the radio to the children of New York City during a newspaper strike because he was enough of a child to know there is a bit of a child in all of us. But those who worked with him knew that he also defined himself best: "I'm an inconsiderate, arbitrary, authoritative, difficult, complicated, intolerant—and somewhat theatrical person."[8]

He was also moralistic. In the puritan administration in which Adolf Berle served as city chamberlain, La Guardia made war against mobsters and pornography without discrimination. He was a prude and a taskmaster. His pursuit of virtue and efficiency had few limits. For instance, he admonished city employees to use city letterheads only for official business, use of stationery for political purposes being "subject to immediate dismissal." At Christmastime city workers were forbidden to exchange gifts. During the city's noise abatement campaign, in which La Guardia eliminated organ grinders from New York's streets, he asked city employees to sign pledges of cooperation and to secure signatures from their families and friends. A magnanimous gesture for La Guardia was to allow city employees to begin work an hour later than usual the day after Christmas. Department reports for the municipal year book had to stress that "this administration is one of vision, imagination, progress, plans and hopes for the future . . . in the cause of honest, efficient and non-partisan City government." La Guardia, Berle, and other Fusionists believed that they were chosen to lead the City of New York in order to liberate it from the clutches of politicians and gangsters. As liberals they defended freethinkers and fought totalitarians like Nazis and Communists. No evil was too big or too small for them to fight. They would restore New York to self-determination.[9]

As chamberlain, Berle's principal foe was the bankruptcy which threatened the city. It was an anachronistic position from which to restore the city's finances, the city controller being more directly involved with budgets and taxes. But both Berles relished the irony that among the economy reforms Berle vowed to initiate was the abolition of his own office—apt because Beatrice's ancestor, a de Peyster, had been the city's first chamberlain, and Beatrice's husband would be the city's last chamberlain.

Beyond that, the position gave Berle the freewheeling opportunity to delve into anything he and La Guardia considered fair game. As La Guardia's braintruster he was intent upon demonstrating that every great leader in government needed a braintruster. He was "a brilliant prime minister without portfolio," recalled Robert Moses, a man given to accumulating multiple portfolios. "This is a sinecure office," Berle wrote in describing what he had done for three years, "and has really been used to cover a good deal of general brain trusting for the administration on a wide variety of subjects including elevator strikes, transit unification, the rehabilitation of the credit of the City of New York, salvaging the real estate mortgage bond situation, and so forth." The office was administered by Deputy Chamberlain Louis Faulkner of the Bank of New York and Trust Company's security research department, who had previously collaborated with Berle on financial studies and the writing of memoranda for Roosevelt's brain trust.[10]

To resolve the city's financial crisis, La Guardia and Berle made self-determination of the city's budget from state authority their first objective. Having favored war powers for Roosevelt the previous March, Berle favored near-dictatorial financial powers for La Guardia's "Hundred Days." Reasoning that New York's budget desperately needed pruning which only "dictatorial" powers would allow, La Guardia sought the state legislature's permission to deal with the city's budget over a two-year period without Charter restrictions upon him. But the Democrats in Albany distrusted this maverick without a party. Governor Herbert Lehman assailed the mayor for seeking dictatorial authority and for months Tammany Democrats fought La Guardia's economy bill before enough compromises could be wrung from the recalcitrant mayor.[11]

A key to resolving New York's financial dilemma was federal aid, an area where Berle's influence with Roosevelt and with agencies such as the Reconstruction Finance Corporation was important. Thus, in the middle of the La Guardia–Lehman war of words in January, Berle reminded Roosevelt that La Guardia was an ally and accused Republicans of backing the Democratic governor because they wanted "to take a poke" at Roosevelt. "What I want to do is to navigate New York City into a friendly cooperative basis with both the State and National Administrations, and if there is any line to take here, I should be glad of a steer." "You are right about navigating New York City," Roosevelt responded. "I will talk with you about it when next you come down." City Hall took care to keep its tie to the White House strong. On January 29, the indefatigable mayor, who normally begrudged city workers time off for lunch, gave permission for city offices to close an hour earlier if workers attended celebrations in honor of Roosevelt's birthday.[12]

But navigating New York City in concert with Washington was difficult in 1934 if it did not tack alongside Albany. As in the mayoral campaign, Postmaster General Jim Farley was a behind-the-scenes captain of city Democrats, as was Bronx boss Ed Flynn, Berle's predecessor as chamberlain. In February Berle raised Democratic hackles during a four-hour appearance before a legislative committee by accusing his Democratic predecessors of leaving city coffers with a $31 million budget deficit and obligations of about $82 million payable that year. Berle insisted that city obligations could no longer be met through the sale of bonds. Exchanges with the Democrats were sharp, Berle taunting a Democrat to "be as accurate as you can within the limits of your capacity." When their cross-examination apparently nettled him, Berle insinuated that the legislators shirked their responsibilities to the city, thereby drawing a Democratic rebuke that the legislature would not approve unconstitutional bills "drafted by the so-called 'brain trust.'" Because the city's economy bill sought to reduce the deficit by furloughing civil service employees whom Democrats sought to protect, Berle charged Democrats with trying to save "political sinecures" by reducing salaries instead of positions; "I would rather furlough people than given them a reduction in salary which I might not be able to return," he said. In the next breath he announced a reduction of his own salary from $13,300 per year to $10,000 by refunding the difference to the controller. (In May he offered to work for a dollar a year, an example city workers who lacked wealthy wives could not afford to follow.) He kept up the attack on Democrats by announcing the discovery of a police fund begun in 1921 totaling $338,000 for a war memorial and not collecting any interest. (Berle and Parks Commissioner Robert Moses decided to use it for playgrounds in each of the five boroughs.) Also, he accused Flynn of benefiting from a trust fund invested in a title concern of which he was counsel. Politicians shook their heads; Flynn was too powerful a man to alienate. Nonetheless, Berle persisted in assailing his predecessors for mismanagement, declaring with mixed metaphors that "we are up against the muzzle of perhaps as difficult a financial situation as any government of this size has ever been in, short of acknowledging the inability to navigate."[13]

La Guardia got a watered-down Economy Act by compromising on other measures deemed less desirable. In loan negotiations with an "angry, weary" Berle and the city's controller, the bankers agreed to loans at the lowest interest rate possible without burdening future generations—a key element in the city's rescue. Berle made a couple of trips to Washington to woo aid from Harold Ickes at the Public Works Administration for expansion of city-owned subways and other projects. Higher real estate taxes and a city sales tax (La Guardia had distinguished himself in the 1932 Congress by opposing a national sales tax) were adopted because the nickel subway fare was sacrosanct for another generation: Berle decried the bankers for compelling the city to choose between a sales tax or increasing subway fares, thereby making a sales tax "the less of several evils." Also, in keeping with themes of public ownership, La Guardia sought to buy the private subway lines and consolidate them without doubling the fare. By the end of July, Berle told Roosevelt that "the New York City financing is over . . . , and, incidentally, finishes what I set out to do in this New York adventure. Now all we have to do is to govern this town."[14]

He preferred to be a "nonpolitical" braintruster, but the only way to govern the city was politically, and 1934 was another election year. The economy battles had verified that governing New York required power in Albany. In August Berle pledged his support to Judge Seabury for governor, but Lehman wanted another term and the GOP disdained Seabury's nonpartisanship in favor of a real Republican nonpartisan candidate, Robert Moses.[15]

Roosevelt loved Berle's sobriquet for Moses, the "duc d'Enghien"— for the French general Napoleon executed for exceeding his authority. Between Roosevelt and the imperious Moses there was nothing but mutual contempt. Because Moses simultaneously held two state jobs, the president was determined to force Moses from one of them as the price for federal aid to New York. However, Berle knew his history: the execution of d'Enghien had caused Napoleon great grief, and Berle suggested to Roosevelt that a frontal assault against Moses might unwittingly martyr him. Berle addressed Roosevelt in his letters as "Dear Caesar," and, in a rare acknowledgment of Berle's name for him, Roosevelt said, "though I do not mind your calling me Caesar, I hate your suggestion about Napoleon!" Berle apologized for the reference to Napoleon, saying, "Caesar, of course, is historically accurate. A supreme power, elective, subject to Senate and people." Thus, "duc d'Enghien" Moses continued to frustrate "Caesar" Roosevelt.[16]

In the fall New York politics was an inchoate mess. As Berle told "Caesar," "between Bob Moses and the reactionaries on one ticket, and Lehman, flanked by Al Smith and by Tammany on the other, there is not much of any place to go in New York State just now." What were liberals to do? Why, form a Liberal party, of course. And that is what Berle did on October 3 at a National Democratic Club conference, with liberal Democrats Nathan Straus and Langdon Post and about thirty political and civic "leaders." They prepared a party emblem (the bison) and a declaration of principles written by Berle. Espousing the liberalism of Roosevelt and La Guardia, the "party" proclaimed that "in local government, which is predominantly technical in character, party lines have no place." A brain trust of experts should manage the city. Yet the "Liberals" endorsed Democrat Herbert Lehman for governor and Joseph McGoldrick for city controller, thereby giving Democrats another line on which to win votes. Two weeks later, before 1,200 liberals at the Cooper Union, Berle explained that they must give Lehman support as an alternative to the Tammany "gang" of "the Currys, the Doolings, and the Farleys."

But, as Berle confessed to Roosevelt, "we made a political failure in the attempt to work La Guardia and Lehman into the same boat." The mayor and the governor ran different candidates for city controller, leaving La Guardia "to support the duc d'Enghien *pro forma* without attacking Lehman." The mayor and his chamberlain supported different candidates for governor! The Democrats swept to victory in November, Berle's liberals working with Roosevelt's Democrats. "Oddly enough," Berle observed, La

Guardia was the only effective opposition to Democrats in New York and he pleaded with Roosevelt to "fix it so we are not the opposition, when you can!"[17]

As the La Guardia administration entered its second year, Berle was chipper and almost smug, boasting that New York was "pretty well out of the woods financially." A year later Berle crowed that "not only is the budget balanced, but there is probably a concealed surplus" and that the Fusion government was the "strongest in the East today," respected even by "those who hate us most." He predicted that Fusion would rule New York for years to come because "the bulk of the voters are no longer steadfastly in the Republican and Democratic parties. Both old parties are merely fighting skeletons." He blamed any financial problems that still plagued the city on state legislators who engaged in "horseplay" and "monkey business." La Guardia, said his chamberlain, was "an Andrew Jackson of the cities" with an unlimited political future: "I myself rather dream of a La Guardia nomination in 1938 for Governor of New York on the rejuvenated Republican ticket." He did not say that a La Guardia presidency would follow, but he did not have to.[18]

However, in 1935 the administration was troubled by its inability to achieve unification of the subway system. The mayor commissioned Berle and Judge Seabury to devise a plan for unification and on February 19 they recommended city purchase of the BMT lines. The proposal triggered a flurry of Wall Street speculation in BMT and IRT stocks, thereby raising the specter of a more costly buyout of the private operators. Berle immediately charged that "stock-rigging" was afoot, but the Stock Exchange investigated and found no evidence of manipulation, a judgment in which Berle concurred. In fact, Berle himself may have inadvertantly encouraged the speculation by recommending that the city pay a price some observers considered "grossly excessive." Although the city completed the purchase of the subways, approval for their unification still faced several political hurdles and was not achieved until 1940.[19]

"Things do move along in this city government though ever so slowly," Berle commented early in 1936. He was ambivalent about his work. He enjoyed being an intellectual free-lancer, solving modern urban problems, not only those of finance and transit, but also labor strikes and involving himself in labor politics. And the post gave him an opportunity to push pet causes such as a municipal arts center. He was a braintruster with power— escorting visiting New Deal friends such as David E. Lilienthal to meet the mayor, "the second most responsible job in the United States," in a manner suggesting both La Guardia's accessibility and Berle's power. As he told his father, "In many ventures, the happiest outfit I have found yet is the government of the City of New York under Fiorello, and if I can end the incident honorably and with good reputation I am quite happy."

Berle was restless and looking forward to a second Roosevelt campaign and possibly a brief State Department assignment because "eventually the empire is going to need men who are honest and experienced." In mid-1936 he handwrote a letter to La Guardia suggesting that although the city was far from solvent, his "usefulness to the administration" was about at an end; he begged La Guardia to "permit me to resign." The City's economy program had taken its toll of efficiency, a fatigued Berle complained.

> I cannot very well fight half the day with a set of transit lawyers: and the other half with a staff which is unpaid, a printer who is unpaid and a stenographer who is unpaid, knowing that they are not going to be paid. . . . I shall of course defend anything done in the past, and support you in anything you undertake in the future, either in public or private. I merely cannot continue in a position which has become personally impossible almost to the point of dishonesty in my relations to . . . subordinates. Were you in my place, you would take the same position.[20]

Perhaps too he was bothered by the fact that reform of the chamberlain's office had not been free from scandal. An assistant in his office, Hiram C. Connor, whom Berle made head of his office's real estate division with considerable financial discretion, had been forging checks and falsifying book entries to cover his thefts. An audit showed that the deception began in 1935 and totaled $80,000, Connor using his stolen money for bets on horse races. Although Connor was sentenced later to three and a half years in Sing Sing Prison, Berle was held legally liable for a portion of the stolen funds. He repaid $18,000. *The New York Times* twitted Berle as to how he could have promoted Connor to a position of financial trust while failing to notice that Connor was living high on a $3,000 per year salary and that he was "unscrupulous and selfish to an inordinate degree." Berle detractors attributed the oversight to Berle's susceptibility to Connor's sycophancy.[21]

La Guardia's impulsive solution to Berle's weariness was to run him for president of the Board of Aldermen without even consulting the vacationing Berle. Unhappy with the Republicans' nomination of Newbold Morris, the mayor announced that he preferred Berle for that post. La Guardia, believing himself above parties, called the White House to ask if Roosevelt would use his influence to have the Democrats nominate Berle instead of the Queens County sheriff, telling presidential secretary Stephen Early that he could not broach the matter with Jim Farley because "he and Farley speak different languages." But the White House killed the gambit by responding that any such move had to be cleared through Ed Flynn—who had no more use for Berle than he for Flynn.[22]

Significantly, in 1936 La Guardia had political value to the Democrats.

Eager to win reform votes for Roosevelt in the presidential election, Jim Farley joined forces with La Guardia and union leaders David Dubinsky and Jacob Potofsky to organize the American Labor party, thereby giving Roosevelt two places on the New York ballot. Also, the ALP served as a party for the maverick La Guardia. Nonpartisan government had left the mayor without a party as reelection time approached in 1937. He was a Democratic adversary, a Republican pariah, and a Fusion party of one. At its first convention in August, Berle "unexpectedly" attended to signal La Guardia's participation in the ALP. The ALP had arrived in time to give La Guardia a political home.[23]

Following Roosevelt's reelection, Berle took a two-month leave of absence as chamberlain to serve as United States commissioner to the Pan American Peace Conference in Buenos Aires. When he returned, New York City politics was heating up for La Guardia's reelection bid, which Berle also envisioned as a springboard for a La Guardia race for governor and, at the end of Roosevelt's second term, a La Guardia race for president. He imagined that "New York City Government will then become the beginning of a larger national movement somewhat analogous to the Free Soil Party"; the ALP would be a national vehicle for La Guardia and once more Berle would brain trust for a president.[24]

But first they had to reelect the mayor in 1937. Berle now spent almost as much time lambasting Republican reactionaries as he did slashing at Tammany. The braintruster had developed into a good stump speaker who knew what political audiences wanted to hear. "Shall we at this time turn the city back to the people who wrecked it four years ago?" he asked a New York luncheon of La Guardia admirers amid anticipated shouts of "*No!*" The choice, he assured them, was between independents "who believe in honest, non-political government" and "groups which are prepared to swallow graft and rotten politics, and the reactionaries, opposed to free speech, freedom of the press and other liberties in the interests of preserving the profit motive." At a meeting of 1,500 members of the International Ladies Garment Workers Union, Berle ripped into La Guardia's Democratic opponent: "Mahoney! He is the Charlie McCarthy of the Democratic party. When you think of [him] you have to think of the Kellys, Sheridans and Marinellis who pull the strings." A Berle speech, carrying with it his braintruster credentials, plus a growing reputation for rough political oratory, had become an organizational drawing card.

But Berle did not want to run for any office. He much preferred politics as a free-lancer for Roosevelt and La Guardia without accountability to the voters. He could be tough, as when the GOP hesitated about putting La Guardia on its ticket, Berle got the ALP leaders to agree not to endorse any Republican if the Republicans did not nominate La Guardia. He had become a prime operator for the mayor at political—both Democratic and Republican—meetings. La Guardia talked a great deal in 1937 about running Berle for governor on an ALP ticket, but Berle insisted he wanted only to make "a graceful exit" from New York politics and resume private life. He suspected that city politics had expended his political viability, "that, except for my Labor Party friends, neither the Republicans nor the Democrats will care to have me around for some time." Indeed, rumors had it that Roosevelt had agreed to take him into the New Deal to relieve the New York Democratic party of a thorn in its side. He never would run for electoral office.[25]

"I hate these infernal politics," he told Lillian Wald and anyone else who would listen. He was happiest as a braintruster. Whatever ambitions La Guardia had for him, he always refused public offices that required election. Years later he discouraged any gossip of a Berle for mayor or a Berle for governor race, confiding to his father, "the only reason for refusing is that I don't like that kind of life. . . . If there is any one political job I have never wanted it is being Mayor of New York. . . . I don't want to get tied down in the city when there may be more interesting and important things to do later on. Politics is a kaleidoscope and nobody can see the end." What did he want? Early in 1937 he had served Roosevelt in a mission to Buenos Aires, bouyantly telling an acquaintance, "life seems to be one succession of adventures after another." That was what he desired: a succession of adventures of six months' duration as Roosevelt's "intellectual jobber," not a four-year sentence in a political job.[26]

A month after La Guardia's reelection in 1937, Berle submitted his resignation as chamberlain. "He won't be out of official life very long," La Guardia predicted. National matters, never far from Berle's thoughts, now occupied most of his thoughts. He wanted to brain trust on foreign affairs and national economics. The Roosevelt administration had brought him in on Latin American concerns before; now Nazi Germany's designs upon Europe and Latin America vied for American attentions. Also, the recovering economy had suffered a setback. Berle did not like the direction of economic policy in 1937. The national planning of 1933, the National Recovery Administration and the Agricultural Adjustment Administration, had been ruled unconstitutional by Brandeis and the Supreme Court in 1935–1936. To pay for agricultural parity benefits, the administration had adopted an undistributed profits tax which business considered punitive. Frankfurter and the Brandeisians waged a pointless war against big business and Berle entertained overtures from Jesse Jones to rejoin the Reconstruction Finance Corporation. However, more certain than ever of his own worth, he was still unwilling to assume a subordinate position such as RFC counsel. Perhaps a post in the State Department would enable him to advise Roosevelt on foreign affairs and economic policy. But it would have to be temporary, for he still had little stomach for Washington bureaucracy. At forty-two, he was a braintruster without portfolio and professing indifference to one.[27]

A Cabin in Washington

"Brandeis, besides being a great man in action, is above all a philosopher," Berle wrote on the occasion of the Justice's eightieth birthday. He admired—intensely, always—Brandeis for his dual role and for demonstrating "a passionate faith in man." Many could be men of action, but few could be a philosopher. However, in Brandeis he admired the man more than his public philosophy. Most commendable in Berle's eyes was Brandeis' exposition on individual freedom, "his passionate belief in the doctrine that men are entitled to fulfill themselves; hence democracy." Berle's biographical portrait of Brandeis was a not-so-covert exercise in self-definition. Brandeis, Berle declared, retained "a purely spiritual and mystic quality" in an age of materialism: "the sense that men must commune with the Infinite and with the best in themselves; that out of this communion there comes the strength to act and the insight to act wisely. In the years to come, this philosophical phase will stand as a far greater attribute perhaps than the political and economic battles." He shared with Brandeis a conviction that economics involved more than a science of society, that economists had "to be just as interested in intellectual or spiritual forces as [they are] in the statistics of production and consumption, since any one of these forces may change either the supply or the demand or both."[1]

It would have been discourteous of him on Brandeis' anniversary to suggest that Brandeis' vision of the American political economy was errant and anachronistic—which is what Berle believed. Instead, Berle targeted Frankfurter and his acolytes—"the would-be Brandeis follower of today" who lacked the great man's admirable genius for being both radical and practical—rather than attack Brandeis directly. If not for Frankfurter, Brandeis would be isolated in Washington—a great dissenting justice whose notions of political economy had greater relevance a quarter century ago. In the mid-1930s Brandeis and Frankfurter refought the battles of 1912 and 1932–1933: how to dissolve or punish big business and atavistically restore competition, thereby thwarting the industrial planners who sought to channel big business' hegemonic tendencies in the public interest. At a time when Marxism also appealed to believers in economic planning, capitalist planners such as Berle fought a rearguard war against Brandeisian social reactionaries who were neither for business nor against capitalism.

Berle's writings of the 1930s naturally focused on economics, but he also believed that all problems were interrelated. Political, economic, legal, social, and foreign affairs questions failed the test of any monocausal materialist explanation which did not admit philosophical, psychological, or spiritual causation. Like many New York intellectuals of the 1930s, Berle read Marx and he was impressed—but not persuaded. He thought Marx showed "some really first-rate economic thinking . . . buried under a mess of political talk." Marx the economist fascinated Berle as much as Marx the polemicist of class war appalled him. Marx's elucidation of capitalist overproduction and cyclical crises in escalating frequency and intensity enthralled Berle and had him nodding in agreement. But Berle opted for American exceptionalism when anyone applied Marxist theories of class war to American society, labeling them "merely absurd." Like Brandeis, Berle's paramount concern was for individualism; unlike Brandeis, he sounded both radical and practical when he defined the task of government as the liberation of individuals from the tyrannies of corporate empires in the marketplace. To bring about a "new individualism," governments—without bureaucratic arrogance—should encourage organization of individuals into countervailing forces. It was not a radical's credo. It was the interest group politics he once feared.[2]

Socialism in the New Deal was not an issue. "Of course there has been nothing in the government program thus far which even remotely tends to deny the profit system," Berle wrote in 1934. The Roosevelt administration had "probably gone farther than any government in the world to protect a profit economy [and] to provide a market." The New Deal had modified private capitalism with state capitalism, investing public funds and organizing producers to bring output in balance with consumption. "A question has been asked," he wrote, "why, in a civilization over-full of material things, more than able to supply every human need, the organization of economics leaves millions upon millions of people in squalor and misery?" State capitalism organized private capital to "erect a form of law so changing the machinery of production and distribution that human needs throughout the country will be approximately satisfied."[3]

Berle combined a radical diagnosis with a liberal palliative, a technique that confused conservatives. ("Socialized Banks Favored By Berle," screamed *The New York Times* headline; what he actually proposed was "mutualizing our banking system" through a two-tiered system that allowed community control.) His analysis of social ills always sounded original, as did his prescient prescriptions. For example, in 1933 he projected the need for sickness and unemployment compensation, other working-place improvements, and, an idea at least three decades ahead of its time, "*women performing equal tasks receive an equal income* . . . a field we have not yet entered but it is plainly foreshadowed by the modifications going on." Arguing that government already performed a myriad of economic functions constitutionally—such as the postal service or the construction and maintenance of roads—that private enterprise could not perform profitably, government activity had a popular mandate to enhance the mixed economy.[4]

"Remember always that you are a conservative. So are we all!" Moley wrote Tugwell following his departure from the administration. But they were all conservative *planners* at a time when, in 1935–1936, New Deal planners were under siege from different directions—those who accused it of being too radical or too conservative. The gathering forces of Marxists, Huey Long, Dr. Townsend, and Father Coughlin posed a radicalism that suggested the New Deal's caution; on the other hand, Brandeis and the Supreme Court suggested a wrongheaded collectivist radicalism. When the administration was a year old, a troubled Justice Brandeis told Jerome Frank that he wished to see Berle and Tugwell. Their meeting was a harbinger of escalating intra–New Deal warfare. As Berle told FDR,

> His idea was that we were steadily creating organisms of big business which were growing in power, wiping out the middle class, eliminating small business and putting themselves in a place in which they rather than the government were controlling the nation's destinies. He added that he had gone along with the legislation up to now; but that unless he could see some reversal of the big business trend, he was disposed to hold the government control legislation unconstitutional from now on. I think also he regretted not having had a chance to talk to you about it. He, of course, wants drastic taxation of big business units, accompanied by leaving small business, via the N.R.A., strictly alone.
>
> His view, if ever stated, would command wide popular support. But as long as people want Ford cars they are likely to have Ford factories and finance to match.

Roosevelt replied that he expected to "have a good long talk" with Brandeis soon. He had been warned through Berle that Brandeis the reformer was prepared to strike down Roosevelt's wrongheaded reform program.[5]

In the summer of 1934 Brandeis, while vacationing on Cape Cod, again summoned Berle concerning "the great problem of whether the policy is directed toward allowing concentration [of industry] and balancing it by government, or trying to decentralize altogether." Later Berle learned that NRA's days were numbered—if only because of its internal disintegration under Hugh Johnson's erratic leadership. He feared that the adminstration was "in very bad shape indeed." Conferring with Charles Taussig, Sumner Welles, and Tugwell, Berle agreed to seek an audience with Roosevelt to "simply attack the situation on all phases." At Roosevelt's invitation, Berle lunched with the president at Hyde Park on September 4 along with an Eastern railroad president and SEC Chairman Joseph P. Kennedy. Financial matters dominated their discussion. Cordell Hull, a former leader in the lower House on tax matters, recommended that fiscal concerns be coordinated by the old brain trust, a proposal heartily seconded by Berle. But Roosevelt was then satisfied to solicit Berle's advice without giving him formal power. Aside from the question of sharing power, Roosevelt rejected a chief of staff arrangement, preferring a philosophical void in administration leadership that brought about a collision between the Treasury's orthodox finance and the New Deal's spending for relief and recovery. With the NRA's days numbered and the tax battles of 1935–1936 at hand, the New Deal lacked ideological and political direction.[6]

Like Roosevelt, Berle believed that the Schecter decision declaring NRA unconstitutional imposed a theory upon a fact; a national economic system existed outside the purview of Washington. Roosevelt's greatest problem, as Berle saw it, was Brandeis, who stubbornly refused to recognize "Hugh Johnson's remark that all this business was collectivising the United States faster than any form of government is literally true." Brandeis wanted both his government and his business small, even if it defied history. "Life under a small unit society would satisfy both you and me a great deal better than life under the present system does," Berle told a friend. "As someone said in discussing Mr. Brandeis' views: I feel sympathy for decentralization and will support it wherever I can with the hopeless feeling that all bets are the other way."[7]

The Brandeisian attack on state capitalism, rather than "recognize the existence of integrated business and deal with it," took the form of tax proposals designed to "smash" big business. Berle simplified the conflict as one of "social control" of big business versus "redistributing business units." While the Brandeisian punitive taxes were morally defensible, Berle feared that they would not gather the great quantities of revenue needed for modern government. The income tax, then constituted to exclude a great majority of incomes, was ill-suited as a revenue device. Berle reasoned that a tax upon estates would collect more revenue than one upon incomes—an unexpected argument from one whose wife just benefited through the legacy of a sizable estate. He suspected that the sales tax was the best revenue gatherer of all and it left income intact for investment purposes. However, in 1936, Congress adopted the undistributed profits tax, a law Berle considered "hastily drawn." Articulating a theme he repeated many times again, Berle insisted that wealth was not necessarily power and that corporation influence would not be diminished by compelling a redistribution of its profits. Rather, government should enhance consumer organizations (or producer groups such as labor unions) that countervailed the corporation's power. While the Brandeisian taxes discouraged the growth of capital, "The real object [of taxation] must be increase in national income," Berle asserted. "Distribution is one problem. But if the ultimate goal is to be reached, there must be a great deal more to distribute." In the year that John Maynard Keynes published his famous opus on growth, Berle sounded downright Keynesian.[8]

The tax fights of 1936 further divided the Berle-Tugwell planners from the Brandeis-Frankfurter antitrusters. Friends of both, like Jerome Frank, wished "to reconcile those differences as far as possible," but the issue was too critical for compromise. Frankfurter had warned Frank in 1935 that "the Administration plainly has reached a new stage. From now on it must be to a large extent trench warfare." Berle scored the Brandeisians for their "lust for battle in mere punitive expeditions" and ignoring the importance of achieving "a socially workable result." As it became evident that the tax bill would be hard on big corporations, Senator Robert La Follette, Jr., without consulting Berle, handwrote a letter to Roosevelt requesting that Berle "be put in some useful position where his experience and excellent mind could be available to your administration. . . . I do know that he wants to be of service to you." The Wisconsin senator hoped a place could be found for Berle at the Treasury. But it was an election year and, as Berle knew, Brandeisian atomism made better politics than business collectivism.[9]

Moreover, Berle was useful to Roosevelt through his ties to Wall Street. In August 1934, Richard Whitney, president of the New York Stock Exchange, asked Berle to serve on its advisory board. Afraid to "seem to be crossing from the public side to some supposedly private group," Berle sought Roosevelt's advice. "I think it is absolutely all right to go on that stock exchange board," the President assured him. "As a matter of fact, as you and I know, the fundamental trouble with this whole stock exchange crowd is their complete lack of elementary education. I do not mean lack of college diplomas, etc., but just inability to understand the country or the public or their obligation to their fellow men. Perhaps you can help them to acquire a kindergarten knowledge of those subjects. More power to you!" Stipulating that he would have absolute freedom to speak out and to resign at any time, Berle took seat 55 on the quasi-public governing committee.[10]

Wanting to regulate capital, Berle boosted his old friend from early Columbia days, William O. Douglas, as a candidate to succeed Jim Landis as chairman of the SEC. Yet he shared with Wall Street the fear that SEC rules were too complex and, as he complained to Roosevelt, "I cannot convince anybody that in government as in mechanics simplicity is essential." Securities regulation ironically enriched the bigger law firms in Wall Street who could promise to guide clients through "the mazes of administrative rulings." "I suppose I am hopelessly old fashioned in some things," he told Douglas; "but the more I see of government, the more I believe there is a good deal in the Massachusetts formula that a government should be a government of laws and not of men." When a dramatic decline in market prices sharpened the "perpetual warfare" between business and Washington in late 1937, Berle advocated either "clean-cut" nationalization of certain industries or understandings with them—but the Brandeis-Frankfurter style of "merely perpetuating a political advantage based on having a running row [with business] eventually doesn't work."[11] Significantly, the Exchange met an administration demand that it "clean house" by appointing a committee of nine that included Berle and excluded its old guard to consider internal reforms.[12]

Berle was also in demand for posts in Washington. He rebuffed Tugwell's plea to join the National Emergency Council, but Hugh Johnson's offer in 1934 "to do plain and fancy thinking" for NRA tempted him enough for him to touch base with Roosevelt. "Your old Uncle Franklin thinks that you ought to stick by the pretty good ship you are now voyaging on—at least until you abolish your own job!'' the president advised New York City's chamberlain. ''When that time comes, and perhaps sooner, there is a cabin with hot and cold running water ready for you in Washington. We will decide on its location later!'' Perhaps Roosevelt, assailed for New Deal radicalism, thought one braintruster in the administration was enough. More than two years later, on the eve of his landslide victory and reelection, Roosevelt told Harold Ickes that a place would be found for Berle in the second-term administration.[13]

On at least two occasions in 1935 the president commented that he missed Berle, but he evidently had misgivings about the political value of Berle's economic planning. He mirrored a popular distrust of any brain trust. ''I like . . . your friend in California,'' Roosevelt revealingly told Berle, ''because he has some realization—first, of the importance of public support if the Democratic procedure is to continue; and, secondly, of the fact that no two or two hundred or two thousand economists, businessmen or politicians could possibly agree on a definite policy of permanent reconstruction for more than one year in the future!'' Still, lest Berle take this personally, Roosevelt concluded with the wish, ''I do hope you will run down to Washington sometime soon. I have not had a chance to talk with you for ages.'' More than a quarter century later Berle would write, ''friendship (it was real between Roosevelt and his Brain Trust) never can and never should control the statesman. Roosevelt knew and appreciated Tugwell's quality. He also knew that Tugwell's ideas were not generally held, let alone likely to attract votes either at the ballot box or in Congress.'' So might it have been said of Berle, too.[14]

As Roosevelt scanned the administrative horizon for a suitable location for Berle's ''cabin,'' it must have occurred to him that foreign affairs better suited Berle's corporate approach. In 1936 Roosevelt sent Under Secretary of State William Phillips to Rome as ambassador and Berle pleaded that Sumner Welles should be given the vacancy. In December, Welles and Berle went with Roosevelt and Hull to the Buenos Aires Pan American Peace Conference. Although Berle was close to receiving an appointment to the State Department, it politically required the sacrifice of another braintruster and planner—Tugwell. A temporary place for Tugwell was found in Charles Taussig's American Molasses Company.[15]

Seldom was Roosevelt politically insensitive. Although the president ventured to ''pack'' the Supreme Court in 1937, he was not indifferent to accusations of an impending dictatorship. Thus, a letter from Berle in February with its familiar ''Dear Caesar'' salutation ignited a small furor in the White House. Berle's salutations ''are highly indiscreet,'' Missy LeHand told FDR; ''Can we not ask him to bear in mind that he is writing to the President of the United States?'' For four years Berle had begun his letters that way without comment, except for the time in 1934 Roosevelt said he preferred Caesar to Napoleon because the former was elected by the Senate. But now Roosevelt told Marvin McIntyre, "Get hold of Berle and tell him to be darn careful in what he writes me because the Staff sees his letters and they are highly indiscreet. Tell him a little later on I want him to come down and lunch with me." On March 3 McIntyre called Berle and, "after a little fencing" it dawned on Berle that the jocularity of "Caesar" had been lost in the New Deal's second term. A world with Hitler, Mussolini, and Franco was certain to take these things less lightly.[16]

In April 1937, Hull informed Berle that Welles would be made under secretary and that they wanted Berle to be assistant secretary upon the conclusion of La Guardia's current term. Having declined offers of other Washington posts, Berle instinctively thought of declining, but said nothing. In August Hull and Welles again invited Berle to come into the State Department. "I am frank to confess I should hardly go across the road to get that appointment," he wrote pompously. "My feeling, however, is that fate opens the way and that one cannot indefinitely struggle against fate." The La Guardia reelection campaign monopolized Berle's attention until early September when Roosevelt suggested that, although a visit from Berle during the mayoral campaign would be construed as political, "If, however, while I am in Hyde Park next week, you happened to be motoring past, you could drop in to say 'howdy' it would be grand."

On September 9 Berle drove to Hyde Park and found the president in bed with a cold. They talked politics for a while and then Roosevelt said that he had been discussing Berle with Welles and Hull. Should he take their State Department offer seriously, Berle inquired. "Yes," Roosevelt answered; the Department needed new blood. Then they discussed how the United States might keep out of war despite Japanese ambitions in East Asia. A week later Berle met with Hull and discussed the price of isolation or war in Asia and Europe. In October he conferred with Welles just prior to the Nine Power Conference in Brussels. On November 29 Welles advised Berle that "the way is now cleared in a manner, I hope, agreeable to you for you to come to Washington." With the resignation of William E. Dodd as ambassador to Germany, Hugh Wilson would go to Berlin and leave the assistant secretary post vacant for Berle. Berle's "fate" was at hand and he quoted for the benefit of Beatrice the duc de Rohan's proud motto: "*Roi je ne puis; ministre ne veux pas—Rohan je suis.*" ("I cannot be king; I don't wish to be minister—I am Rohan!") Nevertheless, his ego was flattered. Although he had "no sense of the joy of adventure as Assistant Secretary of State," Berle took the post rather "than leave it to some second-rate intriguer picked from the political basket who will get us in a British alliance and a European Asiatic war."

Welles wanted Berle to be a braintruster serving both Roosevelt and the State Department—patiently explaining that Roosevelt lacked advisors except for Morgenthau on domestic matters and himself on foreign. While it tickled Berle's fancy that Welles described what amounted to a chancellorship for Roosevelt's regency, he shrewdly recalled Moley's firing after he took on that role from the same comparatively minor post of assistant secretary of state. Moreover, Roosevelt told him that it was the State Department that needed a braintruster! Describing Hull as timid in action and Welles hampered by being a career man, Roosevelt suggested that the Department needed an adventurous mind. Berle protested that he would be more useful in New York where "the situation would probably run loose" without him. Roosevelt said he thought not and noted that a declining economy needed help, to which Berle could only say that the State Department "is the world's worst place" from which to brain trust, especially on economic matters.[17]

Roosevelt knew that the opportunity to brain trust on the economy appealed to Berle. The economic decline of 1937 had confirmed Berle's certainty of the Brandeisian tax program's wrongheadedness. In a debate with the English eocnomist Harold Laski (a friend of Frankfurter), Berle asked, "If the major difficulty is concentration of property, why not deal with concentration of property, instead of insisting that the philosophy of the individual has to be re-created?" Power to regulate the big corporation lay with the federal government. Organized labor, too, possessed the power of numbers at the ballot box and, in 1937, through sit-down strikes in the automobile industry. Although sympathetic to labor's quest for fairness from big capital, the sit-down strikes frightened middle-class America and Berle too. The depression of 1937 made Washington's intervention in defense of the public interest more imperative. "The government budget must be so handled that it will fill up the valleys and level off the peaks," Berle wrote in agreement with Vermont businessman Ralph Flanders. "A flexible budget would go a long way towards determining whether there was prosperity or not."[18]

It was becoming known as the concept of the compensatory federal budget. Many critics thought that Roosevelt's budget favored deflation. But Roosevelt would not change economic course without external political pressure for it. That was the subject of a December 12 casual conversation over lunch in Washington among Tugwell, Taussig, John L. Lewis of the CIO (Congress of Industrial Organizations), and CIO counsel Lee Pressman. The next day Tugwell conveyed their thoughts to Roosevelt, who tacitly agreed that "perhaps a message addressed to him by a mixed group of labor and business leaders would be one way in which he could find means for retreat and a change of policy." Tugwell's assignment was to compose a corporate body of differing interests and bring Roosevelt a set of economic proposals they agreed upon.

On December 22 eight men met in the afternoon at the Century Club in New York: Tugwell, Taussig, Lewis, Pressman, steelworkers' leader Philip Murray, industrialist Owen D. Young of General Electric, investment banker

Thomas Lamont of the House of Morgan, and Berle. Berle immediately defined their purpose and established himself as their informal chairman. Berle did not know the representatives of labor or Young, but he had had a recent exchange of letters with Lamont in which they agreed that "there is something fundamentally erroneous certainly in the *methods* now being pursued at Washington." The eight men concurred on the need for federal spending, even if it necessitated an unbalanced budget, but differed over taxes. Lamont and Young were irate on the subject of the undistributed profits and capital gains taxes; Berle too attacked the Brandeisian undistributed profits tax as wrong in theory and unproductive of revenue. Tugwell halfheartedly defended its theory. Lewis and Murray were less concerned with theory than in assuring that any cut in capital taxes did not shift tax burdens to labor. Thus, a consensus prevailed on more federal spending and tax revisions. On other economic matters, industry and finance wanted government to keep out of the utility business, labor wanted it to get into the housing business, and everyone wanted railroad consolidation and relaxation of antitrust prosecution. They completed their discussions the next morning at Taussig's Wall Street office, and Tugwell brought a summary to Roosevelt on December 28. The president added his own concerns with crop control, wages, and hours, and in what sounded like a refrain of the NRA, "some method of balancing prices, if not by the use of the anti-trust laws, then by substantial agreement among industries, which would result in something other than merely continuing raised prices." Tugwell viewed these price issues as divisive and pressed Roosevelt to meet with the group prior to their next meeting. Then he returned to New York and in the evening of December 30 met with Taussig and Berle.

Berle was in a foul mood. On December 26, Robert Jackson, the active chief of the Justice Department's antitrust division, delivered a vitriolic speech blaming monopolies for the depression. Lamont sent Berle a long letter of protest. Berle interpreted Jackson's Brandeisian speech as a bid for the governorship of New York. Privately, Taussig attributed Berle's irritation to ambitions to be governor of New York and fears that Jackson would get there ahead of him. On December 29 Jackson again raised the threat of antitrust action. That evening, while Tugwell met with Berle and Taussig, Secretary of the Interior Harold Ickes gave a nationwide radio speech in which he proclaimed that America was in the clutches of a plutocracy of sixty families, an idea borrowed from Ferdinand Lundberg's recent book, *America's Sixty Families*—which Berle wryly guessed had been taken from *The Modern Corporation and Private Property.*[19]

Did Berle lust after the governorship—his claims to the contrary notwithstanding? If he did, it would explain La Guardia's endorsement and Berle's apparent reluctance to take the State Department post. Did Roosevelt want Berle out of New York during a Jackson bid for the governorship? Berle certainly did not doubt Welles' sincerity in wanting him in

Washington where he might coordinate economic policy with foreign policy; the matter of Berle's going to Washington had been discussed for years. As for Roosevelt, he was capable of anything politically.

Roosevelt insisted that he had nothing to do with the Jackson-Ickes speeches, and that denial cleared the way for the corporate group, *sans* Murray and Pressman, to go to the White House on January 13 and 14, 1938, for conferences with the president. What was to have been a low-key meeting was covered by hordes of reporters and photographers and made the front pages. The conferees agreed that broadened purchasing power through federal spending was more desirable than any curtailment of prices through wage restraints or expanded output. Roosevelt encouraged them to continue their conferences, but elsewhere there was derision, Arthur Krock suggesting in *The New York Times* that Congress would be unhappy with the proposals of "Mr. Berle's economic zoo." Late in January Lamont and Young grumbled to Berle that their sincere efforts to cooperate with the administration "had been used to make third rate politics." In February the automobile industry told Lamont that it would not hold back production. The corporate group was dead, a victim of pluralist politics. Yet Berle insisted that "it demonstrated that opposing interests can get together . . . an attitude which I wish were more general in the United States just now."[20]

However, Berle went to Washington in early 1938 to reconstitute a corporate group—a brain trust—that would deal with economic problems even as he held down a post in a department concerned with foreign affairs. For if big business was a natural product of American history, then, Berle believed, so was America's imperial role in the world. And that imperial role also required state capitalism. Whether they could be satisfactorily integrated remained to be seen, but that is what Berle attempted at the State Department that momentous year.

CHAPTER

5

Imperial Visions, 1938-1941

Students know that capital in the modern age is supplied as often as not by the state; and that this in no way prevents private capital from doing the work if the owners have the courage and vision to use it so.

—*New Directions in the New World*
(1940), p. ix

We have no need to seek a new international order. We have achieved an American order. . . .
The cooperative peace in the Western Hemisphere was not created by wishing; and it will require more than words to maintain it. In this co-operative group, whoever touches any of us touches all of us.

—draft of FDR's Pan American
Day speech, April 17, 1940

SIX MONTHS IN 1938

Robert Moses recalled that when Berle left New York for the post of assistant secretary of state, he told the master builder, "Bob, it's all very well for you to fuss with street openings. As for me, I'm off to settle the Chinese question." Berle may have been ribbing Moses, whose own ego seldom deferred to anyone else's—but as Moses admiringly remembered it, the haughtiness and arrogance was pure Berle.[1]

Berle possessed a profound faith in his own intellect which success did not humble. Fond of saying that what counts most is what goes on in a man's head, he told an interviewer in 1934 that his "most important work is done in solitude. The time that counts is the time I pass meditating and fairly praying over money problems. Such thinking even goes on in the bathtub." (He wasn't kidding about the last; twin baths had been installed in his East 19th Street home to allow Berle to share his thoughts with his soul mate Beatrice while he bathed. When the bath arrangement became known, the lower echelons of the State Department took to referring to him as "two-bathtubs Berle" behind his back.) The "one-man brain trust" fairly reveled in his own brilliance. In moments of such unfortunate candor, he cowed some people and alienated others. Few persons had Moses' sang-froid that allowed them to laugh with Berle's brainy contemptuousness. When he told reform Democrats in 1934 that Jim Farley "is not a partic-ularly brilliant politician"— a comment that suggested Berle was—*The New York Times* deplored "his shying of brickbats at an honored head from an irreverent youth." (Farley was forgiving; later Berle would write "brilliant" speeches for him.) Friends and admirers considered his ratings of intellect benign; others considered them unforgivable arrogance. It seemed that everyone had a Berle story. One New York official recalled the time he and Berle visited the White House and he overheard the chamberlain saying, "I have to get back to New York. You know, if I stay away, Fiorello gets into trouble." A similar story reported in 1938 had Berle discussing with New York friends a La Guardia speech in Albany that uncharacteristically fell flat. "How do you explain that?" someone asked. "Well," Berle re-sponded, "I can't be in New York and Albany at the same time."[2]

His reputation for vanity preceded Berle in Washington. Drew Pearson welcomed him to the capital with a column depicting an "egotistical" Berle "high-hatting" Secretary of State Cordell Hull at the Buenos Aires con-ference, "as if he, not the secretary of State, were running the show." Other Pearson columns portrayed Berle as haughtily telling friends, "They want me to come down and prevent the world from massacring a lot of women and children. I don't want to go but I suppose some one has to go to save them." Berle considered such articles "nasty," but many who knew him found them quite believable. We know from his diary that he considered Washington his "destiny." Pretenses of modesty were a waste of time for him. One profile of Berle began, "Surveying a world that is patently out of joint, Adolf Augustus Berle, Jr., never doubts that he was born to set it right."[3]

As a columnist wrote, "Upper Washington is divided between those awed by the Berle brain in operation and those driven to fury by Berle's vociferous hero-worship of A. A. Berle. . . . The widespread conviction that Berle is just as good as he says he is doesn't make him any easier to take. . . . Although numerous harpoons, javelins and daggers are being sharpened for use on Berle, this energetic genius has a remarkable record which suggests that history may come to know him as one of the major statesman of his time. He does manage to put things over." That Berle was as good as he said he was made him useful and tolerable. Rumors were rife that Hull did not want Berle and, when questioned by reporters as to whether Berle would be working on a special peace project, Hull told them to ask Berle. Yet the secretary assured Roosevelt that Berle had impressed him during their Buenos Aires mission "as being a person of splendid abil-ity and excellent practical judgment."[4]

Berle was upset. He suspected Frankfurter and his friends of badly wanting to keep him out of Washington. Reminding Roosevelt that he had not sought any Washington position, Berle deplored the fact that "taking office means assuming the risk of what our political enemies do to us." To himself Berle commented that "the prospect of spending any considerable amount of time in the poisonous atmosphere of Washington is appalling."[5]

Still, on March 4 the Senate confirmed him as assistant secretary of state. Determined to stay only about six months, he assumed his post during *Anschluss,* Germany's absorption of Austria, and he attempted to leave it on the eve of the Munich conference that discussed the fate of Czechoslovakia. The impending crisis was part of a "destiny" that kept him in Washington.

Although he gave the impression that modesty was for people of modest abilities, Berle was a man of paradoxes. He was a gracious person who valued courtesy toward his fellow human beings as the greatest social quality. At a dinner party in 1937, he told a lawyer that the prohibition amendment had granted Congress the power to define intoxicating liquor. The next day the lawyer read the Constitution and sent off a letter cautiously telling Berle he was wrong. "I have been wrong so many times that it would hardly surprise me to find myself wrong again; and in any case your opinion is probably a great deal better than mine," Berle replied. "One of the great regrets about dinner table conversation is that one is tempted to express views without very great previous consideration. The likelihood increases with the interest of the dinner." The surprised lawyer found Berle's response unexpectedly "magnanimous."[6]

Now in his early forties, Berle could afford to be magnanimous, gracious, and loyal in his personal relations. Life had been good to him. Coming from a modest home, he had married a rich woman who shared his enthusiasms and who loved him—the word is not used lightly—passionately. The Berles had noblesse oblige. When her inheritance was complete, it was devoted in large measure toward enabling him to pursue his destiny. No longer could Berle refuse government positions on the spurious grounds that his practice required his presence in New York. Indeed, without giving up their New York and Berkshire homes, her wealth allowed him to live magnificently in rented Washington estates such as Henry Stimson's "Woodley." Berle was a happy man—made happier by the arrival of his only son, Peter Adolf Augustus Berle, in December 1937, to perpetuate the dynasty he and his father envisioned.

The reality of Berle was his contradictoriness. For all his evident absorption with self, he also prided himself on loyalty to beliefs and to friends. Thus, upon the death of a Yale University Law School professor who had fought for civil liberties during the Red Scare of 1919–1920, Berle wrote a letter to the New York *Herald Tribune* recalling the man's integrity in a time of fear: "Liberals have cropped up aplenty since 1932; but in the early twenties it took real courage." A staunch defender of civil liberties, in the

mid-1930s he encouraged liberal congressmen like Maury Maverick to oppose sedition legislation that would "cut into freedom of speech and freedom of the press." His fame had not made him forget old friends who
never saw the inside of the White House or City Hall. He had time for
former associates from Toledo or New York to "drop in and discuss the
state of the nation" or to remind an old intellectual hero like the ailing
William Z. Ripley that the New Deal had its roots in his earlier writings.[7]
"I am never too busy to see old friends," he told David E. Lilienthal. He
wrote strong letters of reference to advance the career of an old law school
friend less fortunate than he. When Jerome Frank found himself persona
non grata in certain quarters of Washington and looked to old friends for
aid, Berle went all out to lobby for a federal judgeship for him at a time
when others found Frank too controversial.[8]

He was remarkably faithful to his academic responsibilities. As chamberlain he continued to meet his Columbia Law School classes on Tuesday
and Thursday evenings, and, one Friday evening in March 1936, he responded to James Harvey Rogers' request to talk with some promising
young economists at Yale. He enjoyed teaching and considered it a sacred
duty. Obliged to report on his activities for the academic year 1933–1934,
Berle gave Dean Young B. Smith of the Columbia Law School two pages
that summarized his work for the RFC and devising financial schemes to
save New York City from bankruptcy, concluding pointedly, "Unlike the
other New Dealers around here, I have taken some pleasure in the fact that
instead of abandoning my academic work, I kept it up both on the research
and the instruction side." Indeed, he kept his hand in scholarship. Along
with his frequent articles in journals of opinion, he published in 1934 with
the aid of a student, Victoria J. Pederson, *Liquid Claims and National
Wealth,* which he characterized as "the first study in the English language
of the economics of liquidity with an indication of a parallel in legal machinery."[9]

His legendary arrogance suggested an absence of humor. His habit of
talking melodramatically in a low voice out of a corner of his mouth hinted
at the importance of his words and his chain-smoking suggested an almost
intolerable intensity. He seemed to lack patience for levity. He either did
not understand or did not appreciate the dirty jokes politicians and lawyers
often told. Yet, even the cerebral Berle was not totally humorless. William
O. Douglas recounted a story of Berle dramatically exercising his "mighty
ego" with startling good humor:

> At Yale one night he spoke at a dinner. The dining room was at the street
> level, and because it was a warm evening the windows were open. Berle
> was explaining the banking crisis of the early thirties and his role in it. He
> described a meeting of the experts in Washington that lasted way into the
> night. According to the story the advice he tendered was not accepted, and
> the meeting broke up. When everyone else had left, he said, he stepped

onto the balcony of the Treasury Building and watched a golden moon rise over the city.

"As I stood there," he said, "the words of Goethe came back to me."

At that point in his speech to us at Yale a drunk on the street stuck his head into a window and let loose a rather vulgar "Phooey."

Berle paused a half-minute, then continued, "Perhaps the gentleman is right." And then he went on to explain the Keynesian theory that ultimately prevailed in Washington.

Many people despised Berle, but few gainsaid his brilliance. Although not fond of him, Douglas found him "creative, and the essence of integrity." "Adolf Berle," Alvin Johnson wrote, "do you know what a profound satisfaction it is . . . to see in the world a man who handles action and intelligence with equal sureness and facility, like you?" Such flattery could be disingenuous, but nobody questioned the intellectual excitement he engendered. "He is the best brains we have," Rexford Tugwell told his diary. "His mind ranges over a great variety of subjects in a most fertile way." R. Walton Moore mixed admiration with disdain in his observation that Berle "is certainly brilliant, but I often think that a very brilliant man is more of a shooting star than a steady planet."[10]

Only under Roosevelt was Berle's brain-trusting possible. In an era when the White House staff had few assistants with undefined roles (an executive reorganization bill was then making its way through Congress), braintrusters made the federal payroll through second-level department assignments. Moley and Tugwell had gone into State and Agriculture in 1933 with unhappy consequences: Moley upstaged Secretary Hull at the London Economic Conference and was banished from the department and eventually from Washington; Tugwell ran afoul of bureaucratic quarrels and undeservedly earned the tag of "radical," rendering him a political liability. Now Berle navigated Hull's hostile waters.

Berle could avoid the political sharks that beset braintrusters because in 1938 he enjoyed several advantages unavailable to Moley and Tugwell in 1933. He went to the State Department with a political base in New York among La Guardia liberals, with a lawyer's skills and training well suited to the work he would perform, and with a nearly six-year-old personal relationship with Roosevelt made stronger by Berle's physical absence from Washington. Moreover, he had learned from Moley's and Tugwell's mistakes. Finally, he went to Washington without a commitment to stay. "My understanding is that the particular job which the department has in mind for me may not last more than a few months," Berle told the press. "I am accordingly retaining my professorship at the Columbia Law School." That spring he pointedly asserted his independence of Roosevelt and Washington by commuting once a week to Columbia to teach a seminar.[11]

Berle went to Washington as Roosevelt's braintruster, officially a second-level State Department official, and acted as a free-lancer with special access to the president. For bureaucrats accustomed to strict definition of assignments and relationships, Berle's license to free-lance took more than a little getting used to. The British ambassador noted that Berle took it upon himself to "co-ordinate political and economic affairs in general without concerning himself with any questions of routine." Moreover, contrary to what was expected of a Foreign Service official, domestic economic policies and politics headed Berle's calendar. While the depression asserted itself at home and Hitler asserted himself abroad, Berle's primary mission was to focus Roosevelt's and Washington's economic thinking, through discussion and speechwriting, on recovery schemes consistent with business realities and America's place in the world.[12]

Berle was intent upon becoming "the Hjalmar Schacht" of the administration. He admired the German financier who devised the Third Reich's financial schemes until 1937, telling people "that only a man trained in complete financial orthodoxy could so successfully have violated all the rules of financial orthodoxy." Berle's esteem for the Nazis' financier is not surprising. Schacht confirmed Berle's faith in the workability of state capitalism. For the same reason, Berle admired British economist John Maynard Keynes or anyone who used government capital to enhance private capital. Thus, he admired Robert Moses' genius at building roads and other projects in New York, even if Moses was a political enemy of Berle's patron. His New Deal hero, aside from FDR, was Jesse Jones, the Texas banker whose Reconstruction Finance Corporation bankrolled so much of the New Deal that he already was the Schacht of Roosevelt's Washington.[13]

But Jones had been on the skids for a few years, and Roosevelt had threatened to accede to Brandeisians by phasing out the RFC. However, the resurgence of the depression in 1937–1938 put an end to those plans. Now Berle devised plans for enhancing the RFC and rescuing the nation from the Roosevelt depression of 1937–1938. He discussed with Roosevelt a proposal for regional capital credit banks to facilitate borrowing and stimulate recovery from the nagging depression, an idea he had first proposed without success in 1934. But now Berle enhanced the scheme with ideas he and his *éminence grise* on finance, Louis Faulkner, borrowed from Keynes and his book *A General Theory of Employment, Interest and Money.* His ardor for innovative capital schemes distinguished Berle as probably the highest ranking official in Washington conversant with Keynes' ideas in 1938. Berle advocated increasing America's national wealth through "pump priming," a Keynesian term for the effect government expenditures could have in multiplying the national income. As Berle told a State Department colleague in August, government spending was preferable to "a deflation which would destroy the great cities of Detroit, Cleveland et cetera." Still, the capital credit banks that would have augmented public works spending were not developed; the Brandeisians wanted a war against big business.[14]

The Brandeisians were "working on the progressive thesis of the 90's, which was old in the time of McKinley," Berle warned Roosevelt. Nothing could change the fact that fifty million people lived "from the proceeds of a large scale industrial system." Their living standards would not improve by breaking up big corporations into smaller units or taxing them to death. Nor could their jobs and wages be increased by calling Berle "Morgan's man" and a "defender of monopoly."

As Roosevelt described his economic advisors in 1938, there were three schools of thought: one that forecast recovery in May or June but had been wrong about it in February; one that forecast a sideways movement with an eventual upturn; and a third that forecast a sideways movement to worse levels. "In either of the latter cases," the president said, "we lose the Fall elections." For political reasons Roosevelt decided upon "rapid fire" federal spending. It would not be the last time Keynesian economics rationalized political expediency.

Why not also expand private spending through RFC expansion, Berle asked? Roosevelt sent Berle's memo to the cautious Henry Morgenthau. Amid this flurry of initiatives, in June the antitrusters in Congress created a twelve-member Temporary National Economic Committee, composed of three members from the House, three from the Senate, and one each from the SEC (Securities and Exchange Commission), the FTC (Federal Trade Commission), and the Departments of Justice, Commerce, Labor, and the Treasury. In TNEC a three-way battle of economic ideas among the planners, the antitrusters, and the industrial self-government advocates was joined.

Anticipating the last great intellectual battle of the 1930s, Berle circulated a memorandum deriding the "loose thinking" that labeled small enterprise competitive or big units efficient. The test of any good economic theory, he asserted, was "to provide more goods, better goods and cheaper goods: to provide more jobs, better paying jobs and steadier jobs; and to provide continuous ready access to capital financing needed to create and maintain additional plants and provide for the continuous development of the arts." To achieve all this, competition, cartelization, or even public ownership may be needed as the situation required. Berle's message struck responsive chords among those seeking less dogmatic nostrums. "If it does nothing else," said *The New York Times,* "it should help to break up many preconceptions that might otherwise stand in the way of a full and impartial factual study and the adoption of sound policies." At a time when Brandeisians and others appeared unyielding in support of a pet theory, Berle represented himself as a practical liberal eschewing all doctrines.[15]

Berle's schemes for state capitalism complemented his vision of America's world role. He had the ability to fit a local project of no apparent great consequence into his grander imperial scheme of things. In 1938 he made the development of a St. Lawrence seaway his pet State Department project for enhancing both state capitalism and American hemispheric ambitions. Roosevelt gave him the special assignment of negotiating with Ottawa a treaty for development of the St. Lawrence. It was "a T.V.A. experiment in New York . . . really a domestic program, which comes into the orbit of the State Department because of the accident of the frontier."[16]

Berle and Roosevelt attached great significance to it. Roosevelt considered it potentially a major public works project for economic recovery. The Canadian power negotiations had lingered since 1929 and Roosevelt was now eager to move them ahead. In 1937 he mentioned the St. Lawrence project to Prime Minister Mackenzie King, who wanted time to prepare Canadian public opinion. Berle and Roosevelt conferred twice about it in March and decided to press the Canadians. By June 1 Berle reported that a draft treaty with Ottawa was in the works. In August, in preparation for Roosevelt's meeting with Mackenzie King at the dedication of the Thousand Islands Bridge, Berle urged "that you talk to him like a Dutch Uncle" about the proposed St. Lawrence treaty. However, the political situation on the Ontario side of the river proved too hazardous for Mackenzie King and it would be another couple of years before the moment would be right. By then the project would loom even larger in Berle's vision of a hemispheric empire.[17]

And then it was facilitated by the expedience of defense. For the world was headed for war. Europe was the center of State Department attention in 1938, even if Washington could not influence events there. The United States had no way of blocking Austria's annexation to Germany. Berle feared that too pusillanimous a recognition of *Anschluss* would "simply strengthen the military party in Germany." Europe was victim of great power imperialism. French and British efforts to have the Czechs demobilize in May was more evidence to Berle of how European imperialists cynically manipulated the lesser states. It made Berle vow that "We may have to go to war, but if we do, it will be our own decision and not someone else's."[18]

America's self-determination of its foreign policy was a principal goal for Berle in the State Department. Obsessed with the lessons he drew from the Great War and determined not to allow the United States to be manipulated into a European conflict again by cynical British and French imperialists, Berle made it his duty in the State Department to thwart "any Colonel House or Walter Hines Page"—Woodrow Wilson's advisor and ambassador to Great Britain, respectively. As Berle interpreted 1914–1917, House and Page had used their positions to involve America in the war, had subordinated American interests to British imperial interests and, ultimately, had assured the Paris Peace Conference debacle by permitting secret Allied deals to prevail. Berle did not discount the likelihood that Fascist regimes would draw the United States again into a world war; but this time it would be for American interests and without illusions.

Berle had strong credentials for foreign affairs. He had been at the Paris Peace Conference and an advisor on the Good Neighbor Policy since

1932. In the midst of a September 1933 Cuban revolution, Welles and Berle found themselves one night sitting on a long divan in a Havana hotel lobby in direct line of hostile rows of machine guns while they calmly smoked cigarettes and discussed the merits of Emily Dickinson's poetry and the beauty of the Berkshire hills. The apparent bravado was real, he later said, because in Havana "there is order without law because the Cubans are friendly people." Ultimately calm was restored to Havana, only after Welles and Berle assured young Cubans that Franklin Roosevelt would never intervene in Havana because he espoused the principle of self-determination. The Roosevelt administration abrogated the Platt Amendment to the Cuban Constitution and ended U.S. military intervention in Cuban affairs. In 1936 Berle lobbied with newspaper publisher Roy Howard for editorial endorsement of an administration bill to give Puerto Rico independence. He was proud of the New Deal's anticolonialism and its Good Neighbor Policy.[19]

Roosevelt had invited Berle to be a delegate to the 1936 Buenos Aires conference on peace in the hemisphere. The brainchild of Sumner Welles, the conference was deemed significant enough to be attended by both the president and Hull. Its purpose was to knit the countries of the western hemisphere together under American leadership and to exclude antidemocratic European influences from the Americas. Berle envisioned it as part of a larger design to create "what might be called a civilized island in the world composed of this hemisphere, possibly Great Britain and a considerable part of western Europe" while quarantining the totalitarian powers. While en route to Argentina the Americans heard that Germany and Japan had signed the Anti-Comintern Pact, making peace more fragile throughout the world. In Buenos Aires Roosevelt delivered a stirring speech written by himself, Hull, Welles, and Berle. It was, Berle said, "addressed to Europe more than the Americas." However, although the conference called for mutual consultation among hemispheric countries, it rejected Berle's proposal for a permanent body for consultation. Also, while the conference asserted the principle of hemispheric neutrality in European wars, it left the American states free to align themselves if they chose to; Berle blamed this on the British influence in Argentina. Peace in Europe could not be made in Buenos Aires. Nevertheless, Berle and Welles remained certain that their North-South strategy would keep the Americas free from Europe's imperial wars.[20]

The Buenos Aires conference tied Berle more closely to Roosevelt, Hull, and Welles. His views on the maintenance of peace were consonant with theirs. Hitler's threats to Austria and Czechoslovakia in 1938 and Western acquiescence to his promises of peace earned such peace factions in the democracies the epithet "appeasers." But Berle was not an appeaser.[21]

He was suspicious of British imperial designs and British handling of its Continental interests. Although he mistakenly hoped that a European conference might bring peace, he was an anti-Fascist liberal. He considered Hitler a racist madman who distorted Continental politics. However, he argued, "Our emotion is obscuring the fact that were the actor anyone but Hitler, with his cruelty and anti-Semitic feeling, we should regard this [German foreign policy] as merely reconstituting the old system, undoing the obviously unsound work of Versailles and generally following the line of historical logic," he told Roosevelt. In his "colder analysis" of 1938's crises, Berle found historical analogues in the mistakes of 1914–1919. It made him isolationist, anti-imperialist, and antiwar. He was fearful again, he told a liberal friend, of British "falsity of propaganda . . . [and] the entirely cynical use made of the decent humanitarian instincts of the American people."[22]

Nearly a month before the Munich conference that settled Czechoslovakia's fate, Berle forecast "that the denouement of the German situation will be a move by Hitler, followed by the virtual absorption of some, if not all, of Czechoslovakia. This will be successful and the rest of Europe will back down." Then what? "A reconstituted great Germany," he assured Roosevelt on September 1, would require a vaster organization than Hitler could sustain in polyglot middle Europe. While the Nazis exhausted themselves in Europe, U.S. strategy should concentrate upon the western hemisphere, develop "a north-south axis, and not be swung off base by either diplomacy or emotion." He would organize resistance in the Americas to Nazi or British imperialism while encouraging peace discussions in Europe. American policy should not be seduced by developments in 1938 but should keep events a quarter century ago in mind and anticipate events a quarter century to come. Historically, the Czech crisis was "the birth pains of a new eastern empire, a German succession to the old Austro-Hungarian empire." The United States was powerless to prevent it. "Summarized," he wrote, "I doubt if what is happening will precipitate a general war; but if it does, I doubt that Europe will disappear; or that even a successful great Germany will be forever the hideous picture that it is today; and I reject the thesis that our intervention would have any results other than those achieved last time."[23]

Berle did not intend to be around the State Department for the denouement. In July he offered Roosevelt his resignation, but the president told him to hold it until August. FDR complimented Berle on his work on economic recovery and reminded him that the State Department had "too many careerists and too little thinking." Still, Berle wondered aloud how he alone could energize its bureaucracy. His role as a free-lance braintruster was a handicap in the department because he "was not in the chain of command to get things cleared." Berle found State Department work "anything but heavy" and expected to leave the department untouched by his presence. So did others. "Neither I nor anyone else that I know of, has any idea of why Mr. Berle was appointed or what he did in office," a puzzled

British foreign officer reported to Whitehall. "I have looked in on him two or three times, and he has told me that he was engaged in economic work, and was attending to no routine matters at all."[24]

In mid-August he sent Roosevelt a letter of resignation, but some State Department staffers wanted him to stay. Pierrepont Moffat, who shared Berle's isolationism, believed Berle "could be of tremendous usefulness. . . . He has a real understanding of foreign affairs. He has a mind fertile in expedience [experience?], he is a remarkable draftsman, and he has played the game 100% with the Secretary." Also, because Berle was "immensely interested" in the St. Lawrence negotiations, "Mr. Roosevelt's pet child, with his going there will be no one to push [Canadian] matters." In early September a column by Joseph Alsop and Robert Kintner defended Berle and assailed his enemies as "left-wingers." Tellingly, it concluded, "throughout the spring barrage of insinuation against Hull's management of foreign policy, Berle stood at Hull's elbow and joined in determining the Secretary to stick by his guns."

The much maligned Hull needed Berle's loyalty. Derided as excessively cautious and only trade-minded, the secretary made the best of a department whose organization belonged to the elitest Foreign Service and whose hierarchy belonged to the president. On September 13, during the Czechoslovakian crisis, following his usual relaxation with aides in a game of croquet, Hull invited Berle to a private dinner at his apartment. At nine o'clock he called the president to report on the day's events in Europe; "The Secretary also asked the President if he would hold up my resignation until we saw where this came out, which the President promptly agreed to do."[25]

"I thought I was going to be clear here, but I am not, at least for the time being," Berle told friends. "The President withdrew his acceptance of my resignation until things cool down." He could not know he would be there for six years. For with the Czech crisis and the Munich conference the State Department had begun what "might almost be called the 'death watch' of Europe."[26]

DEATH WATCH

"Mr. Berle's position in the State Department is rather curious," the British ambassador to Washington, R. C. Lindsay, commented in March 1939; "he resigned in the autumn but his resignation was not accepted, and he was asked to stay on. . . . he still has a room in the Department but I believe he only goes there about once in ten days." It was a curious situation. In the wake of the Munich crisis, Berle took a leave from the Department in order, as a headline piquantly put it, "TO TAKE REST TO PONDER NATION'S FUTURE." Berle would teach at Columbia, write, and do "some serious thinking"—according to his conviction that in the daily rush of events there "is too much practice and not enough theory in Washington." But the assistant secretary of state did not take his leave to contemplate foreign affairs; rather, he meditated on panaceas for the economic crisis he anticipated in 1941.[1]

The leave was his compromise between severance from the Department altogether or plunging immediately into its daily routine. In December he attended a Pan American conference in Lima as Hull's second in command, expecting then to return "home to New York to stay." But somehow his resignation became a leave of absence. He began it on February 15 and by April he was back at work in the crisis-ridden, understaffed, State Department. In September Europe would be at war and in 1940, in a change of heart, Berle decided, "there is no more fascinating place in the world than the State Department, just now."[2]

His "destiny" brought him to this place at this moment in history. He continued his peculiar brain-trusting ways because Berle could not imagine that his tenure in the State Department would exceed the two years remaining to the Roosevelt presidency or that he would be integrated into the bureaucracy and given routine foreign affairs tasks. History taught him that he was serving in the lame-duck years of the Roosevelt presidency. More than ever the administration required a braintruster whose mission was to define the issues and concerns that transcended the New Deal. Abroad that meant directing American interests toward a western hemisphere free from European imperialism and war. At home it meant expanded state capitalism for growth and stability that complemented a great power's role abroad.

With Hitler determining events in Europe, Washington grew more concerned that the Nazi revolution was being exported to the New World. German penetration of Latin America was increasingly evident in Berlin's diplomacy and propaganda. The Munich crisis had demonstrated that Britain and France were too weak and uncertain to be relied upon in Europe. "We shall stand alone," wrote Assistant Secretary of State George Messersmith, "and retire to this hemisphere. . . . We must concentrate on the defense of the Western Hemisphere and on consolidating our relations with the American States." The threat of European imperialism required a North-South counterimperial strategy.

In November 1938, Washington sought to devise an American system, as Berle defined it, "to associate some South American countries with us; and if possible, make it a unanimous act of the Lima conference." Washington hoped to make the peace of the hemisphere a model for Europe and Asia. It was "not the peace of empire. It is the peace of cooperation." While Europeans pursued empire by conquest, Americans were imperial through other means. Indeed, seven peace organizations understood this point well enough to condemn Berle for plotting a Latin American "overlordship." Although some people later denounced this strategy for an

American system of cooperation as "American appeasement" of Nazi designs in Europe, in 1938 peace groups assailed it as "American aggression" in Latin America.[3]

The Eighth International Conference of American States at Lima was important enough to the American strategy to call for a rather unusual delegation. Although Sumner Welles had performed the diplomatic spadework for the meeting, he was not included in the American delegation. Hull headed it and was seconded by Berle and the Minister to the Dominican Republic, R. Henry Norweb. Its other members were an eclectic bunch that included the radical daughter of labor leader John L. Lewis, Kathryn Lewis, several representatives of feminist organizations, the leader of the electrical workers union, the president of Notre Dame University, State Department economics affairs adviser Herbert Feis, and Alfred M. Landon, the former Republican governor of Kansas and ignominiously defeated Republican candidate for president in 1936. En route to Lima aboard the liner *Santa Clara,* the group indulged in shuffleboard games which Hull usually won, and in Panama the feminists took time to rally a luncheon of 100 women.

Had the State Department's intent for it not been so serious, the conference might have been comic. The strange behavior of the Peruvian telephone system suggested to the Americans that their wires were tapped, which Berle diplomatically discounted. Landon had never visited a Latin American country, knew no Spanish, and mostly contented himself with a role supporting American bipartisanship. The electricians union leader busied himself with labor contacts. Kathryn Lewis, whom Berle called "the problem of the party," called for revolution against the bourgeois Peruvian government; "aghast" at her undiplomatic behavior, his loud complaints about it ignited a feud between himself and her daddy.[4]

The work of the conference was initially handled by Hull, who seemed relieved not to have Welles around. However, after three days Berle began drafting agreements on resisting European intervention in Latin American affairs through mutual consultation. Argentina, encouraged by Germany, resisted the agreements. But Washington's friends in the hemisphere adopted them and Hull personally considered the conference a triumph.[5]

Berle rated the Lima conference a great success because it established the principle of mutual consultation in case of totalitarian penetration of the hemisphere, thereby enabling the democratic American republics to organize for their collective security. "The Latin American policy is really the foundation of pretty much everything we are doing," Berle confided to friends. Thus, in case of a greater Nazi threat to the hemisphere, Washington would be able to mobilize the Americas. As Berle put it, in the shadow of Munich, Lima was "the first Pan-American conference to feel the impact of European diplomacy." Washington could not influence events in Europe, but it was determined to do so in the Americas. Insisting publically that Pan American conferences should not be taken "as merely expressions of general platitude," Berle vowed that the United States would follow up the rhetoric of cooperation in Lima with low-interest credits for its southern neighbors' economic development—overseas state capitalism—"our substitution for imperialism." The British foreign office saw this thrust as American opportunism and "masked imperialism" that intended to displace it in Latin American markets while London was distracted by Europe. It could only wonder "whether this machinery will be as efficacious . . . as Mr. Berle hopes."[6]

Lima also was important to the United States because Mexico earlier had challenged American "imperialism" when it expropriated foreign-owned oil holdings on March 18, 1938. The oil companies had been beset by labor troubles and, failing to win the Mexican government's support against the unions, had begun to withdraw capital from the country. The government reacted by nationalizing the industry. In retaliation the British broke off diplomatic relations and applied economic sanctions. U.S. Ambassador Josephus Daniels argued that Washington should not follow London's example, but rather seek nothing more than compensation of our nationals. On March 28 Hull urged oil company officials to negotiate with Mexico for compensation. The oil companies insisted that the Mexicans could not compensate them adequately. They wanted the State Department to demand a return of their properties. Berle preferred Mexican compensation, fearing that any punitive government action—such as limiting silver purchases—would foment social unrest south of the border, although he too wondered if they were being "simply soft about it." Two days later the Mexican ambassador informed Berle that his government would compensate the oil companies, but was "unshakably" opposed to returning the properties. The oil companies were intransigent: property rights were inviolable and the Mexicans had to return their oil fields. But the State Department would have been content to contain "the tide toward expropriation without compensation" and "definitely eliminating again this dangerous doctrine."[7]

All Washington sought from the Mexicans, Berle said, was "negotiation in good faith in connection with oil properties—not that we love the oil companies, but that we have to preserve some sort of norm. . . ." When some of the oil companies sought to finance an insurrection against the Mexican government, Berle admonished them that the United States "had a pledge not to intervene in the internal affairs of other countries and that we meant it."[8]

The principle that the United States applied at Lima, in Mexico, and throughout Latin America was that intervention was inadmissible when the opportunity for negotiation was available. It had to be applied universally, for its real intent was to apply moral restraint against Germany in Europe and Japan in Asia. Until Munich the United States had been a spectator, but now it involved itself as a party of peace who, by bringing disputes to conference tables, set examples for international cooperation. Through its exemplary behavior in Latin America, Washington hoped to maintain self-determination and peace in Europe and Asia. It salutarily demonstrated for European imperialists that a great power could accomplish its goals through peaceful alternatives to hegemony and war. Failing that, if Europe went to war, then Washington needed to assert its own imperial interests more forcefully in the hemisphere. That would come through repeal of the neutrality act's arms embargo provision and a blunt warning that the western hemisphere was off-limits to European imperialism—which would, Berle believed, "really change the status of the New World; a kind of *pax Americana.*"

Alas, it was too late for negotiation in Europe. Surrounded by expansionist powers, the new states carved out of the prewar European empires were, Berle said, in "the unfortunate position of an old-fashioned general store in a town full of hard-bitten chains." On the occasion of the Italian seizure of Albania, Roosevelt and the State Department decided that the time was right to assert Washington's interest in the fate of small states through letters to Berlin and Rome. Berle, the braintruster, drafted them for Roosevelt, and Hull, Welles, and Norman Davis contributed revisions and additions. Mostly it was Roosevelt's message, especially those portions asking if the Germans intended to invade any of about thirty listed independent nations—which was received with great laughter when Hitler read it aloud in the Reichstag. But Roosevelt was not about to go as far in pursuing peace as Ambassador to Great Britain Joe Kennedy, who attempted to call upon the British not to support war—a "dangerous" move Berle brought to Roosevelt's attention and squelched.[9]

Averting war in Europe was unlikely, Berle thought; "We have now neither peace nor war—only an indefinite armistice, with all armies pretty well mobilized." Yet, he knew that "Americans want two inconsistent things at once: to stay out of war and to damn the side they disagree with." A policy of peace was popular, whatever its improbability. Tensions in Europe built toward a climax. Latin America, Berle believed, would never see that climax if Washington was vigilant: "the hemispheric line must never be crossed by any non-American power." Moreover, the hemispheric strategy was set back when its proposal for loans to Latin America ran into a storm of congressional Republican outrage; and, an adminstration effort to repeal an embargo upon arms sales met a similar fate. The administration could do little before Europe exploded.[10]

In August 1939, the State Department had an air of helpless anticipation of war. No one was prepared for the startling August 21 announcement that Germany and the Soviet Union had signed a nonaggression pact; the suddenness of the Molotov-Ribbentrop Pact suggested to Berle that "the Russians were double-dealing right along." Berle saw the Nazi-Soviet alliance creating "a [totalitarian] bloc running from the Pacific clear to the

Rhine." On the periphery of that Eurasian alliance was Germany's uncertain relationship with its anti-Comintern allies—Japan and Italy. Now that the Comintern had cynically embraced Berlin, would Japan and Italy join with the West as they did in the First World War? Since the mid-1930s when Stalin staged the Moscow purge trials, Berle had grown increasingly anti-Communist and now, although furious, he found humor in the thought that "the Marxoid group" would find it ideologically difficult to explain Stalin's "moral bankruptcy." But what did it mean for Poland? The British threatened to fight if Poland was invaded and Hitler warned them to get out of the way. Cutting his vacation short, Roosevelt sent messages to Berlin and Warsaw requesting negotiation, arbitration, or conciliation—all of which Berle saw as having "about the same effect as a valentine sent to somebody's mother-in-law out of season." Communication with Eastern Europe was difficult as anticipation of war mounted. Berle wrote in his diary on August 26: "Yesterday a rather shattering day; . . . the nerve ganglia of Europe began to decay [and] I have a feeling of seeing . . . a civilization dying before its actual death."

The death watch ended at 2:50 A.M. on September 1 when the American ambassador to Poland telephoned Roosevelt to report that German bombs were falling on Warsaw. Fifty minutes later the State Department summoned Berle from an uneasy sleep. In two days Britain and France declared war on Germany, but the United States did not go to war for Poland. Instead, Roosevelt and the State Department confined their collective security arrangements to the western hemisphere. Roosevelt decided to tell the nation that as long as Germany limited its aggression to the Old World he did not envision American entry into the war. The initial draft of the speech was written by Berle, "always more literary, more formally eloquent, and less guarded than the President." Roosevelt usually reworked Berle's frequently purple prose into a "more usable" speech. Significantly, however, they concurred on policies, if not styles of expression. "Now that force is opposed to force," Berle wrote, "at long last you will probably find that there are ranged on one side people who believe in an ordered world, based on principle, and on the other groups who believe in little save cynical force. It is always dangerous to prophesy, but I hold the faith that the world will then resume its age-old endeavor to re-establish the principles of justice, of equity, and of law. So it has always been; and so, I think, it will be again."[11]

By the next day the State Department had a draft of the speech that defined U.S. geopolitical interests in this hemisphere and its determination not to intervene outside in Europe. As Berle wrote in his diary, "A very gloomy meeting in the Secretary's office on Sunday morning; it was really the last meeting of the deathwatch over Europe. There was really not very much to be done, save to watch the game play itself out."[12]

Years later Berle insisted that the diplomacy of 1937–1939 had been basically correct in its pursuit of collective security in the hemisphere. The principle that the democratic countries of the Americas had to cooperate against totalitarianism animated his activities south of the Rio Grande for the rest of his life. In time, however, he came to believe that in the absence of cooperation the United States had a duty to intervene unilaterally against totalitarian intervention. The memory of these years eventually caused him to change his mind concerning the limiting of intervention against totalitarianism to the western hemisphere. What had begun at Lima in 1938 would be recalled as justification of anti-Communist intervention globally twenty years later.

But, in 1939–1941, the United States was committed to a policy of nonintervention in Europe while guarding the Americas against Nazi intrusions. American public opinion enthusiastically endorsed this policy which justified a mobilization of arms and men for defense of the Americas while incrementally sending arms to European democracies and embargoing materials against Japan's Asian aggressions. Gradually Washington expanded its *Pax Americana.*

THE *PAX AMERICANA* IN 1940

"We should stay neutral and stay out of the war," Berle wrote in September 1939. He was not alone in official Washington in thinking that. Cordell Hull told the president that the United States should declare that it would never go to war. Roosevelt stared at him for some seconds and then asked, "Can you guarantee that? Can I guarantee it?" Nobody could.

American policy increased the likelihood of war with Germany by attempting to exclude Europeans from the Americas. The administration toyed with the idea of drawing an imaginary North-South line through the Atlantic and daring Berlin to extend its power beyond that line. However, isolation and neutrality, Berle recognized, were impossible if Washington asserted its "national interest in not having an imperialist power in the Atlantic [and] Germany has made no bones about her intention to establish imperialist connections in this Hemisphere." Sooner or later the Monroe Doctrine would be tested by a European power.

Collective security in the hemisphere was the key to American foreign policy in 1940. "An attempt to disrupt or dominate any American nation means necessarily an attack on all American nations and would be met with a response of solidarity by all American nations," Berle told a Washington audience. Isolationism was not realistic, he wrote in *The New York Times Magazine;* it was morally wrong and economically impossible. But this did not compel the United States to enter the European war. Whether America went to war depended upon German intentions in the hemisphere. The New Dealers wanted to make the Americas free from totalitarian trespass, preferably with the cooperation of other American republics. If Pan American cooperation could not be freely attained, Berle advised Henry Wallace, then the United States might have to resort to unilateral action to prevent German encroachments in the hemisphere. Berle also imagined that a 1940 German spring offensive in Europe might inspire "fantastic" diplomacy—a British deal for peace in Europe in exchange for German freedom in the Atlantic: "It would be just like some bright Englishman to concede them a sphere of influence in South America, leaving it up to us to meet the situation."[1]

Berle was an ardent Pan Americanist. "The British have made the mistake of living next to the French for several hundred years and not understanding them," he told a journalist. "I see no reason why we need to make the same mistake about Latin America." Berle once gleefully goaded Europeanist Walter Lippmann into an argument at a dinner party by commenting that South America was a fascinating place—to which Lippmann predictably retorted that he had no interest in it. Berle gave Latin American countries importance that few others assigned them. A visit from the president of Costa Rica occasioned a memorandum to Roosevelt reminding him that it was a democratic country: "free press and speech, good education, anti-totalitarian." Unfortunately, he could not say the same for corrupt Cuba, but he had faith that "when a group of people arise in Cuba who are prepared to put the public service ahead of graft or profit, that island will get somewhere."[2]

Berle wanted to rid the hemisphere of poverty through judicious loans from an inter-American bank. In 1939–1940 he asserted that cheap U.S. credits for economic development would enable the American republics to withstand totalitarianism. With little more preparation than a casual conversation with Jesse Jones, Berle brought to the Inter-American Financial and Economic Advisory Committee on November 17 a proposal for an inter-American bank to finance development in Latin America in a manner similar to the Export-Import Bank's financing of overseas trade. But Secretary of the Treasury Morgenthau resented State's meddling in international finance and Berle accordingly deferred to the Treasury. However, his idea found support with Morgenthau's aide, Harry Dexter White, who shaped it into a more workable scheme. Aside from bureaucratic jealousies, another obstacle to credits for Latin America was Treasury's fear that capital might not be safe south of the border; Mexico's expropriation of oil was very much on American minds. When Berle insisted "that the rights of capital had to be so handled that they did not come into conflict with the social development of the country," White "did some first-class missionary work" at Treasury to gradually win Morgenthau over to the Inter-American Bank. Jones mitigated banker resistance to the proposal, Roosevelt gave it his backing, and in February it appeared that, pending congressional and Pan American approval, the Inter-American Bank would be launched. However, when Congress and several American republics refused to subscribe their shares of the capital, the Inter-American Bank's debut was delayed until after the war.[3]

The State Department's attention to Latin America during the winter of 1939–1940 was enhanced by Europe's "phony war," a period of German and Russian consolidation in Poland while the West awaited a blow that never seemed to come. But the phony war had to end in the spring of 1940. At a diplomatic reception in May, Berle was informed that Germany had invaded the Low Countries. "The word slowly circulated," he later wrote in his diary. "The Belgian Ambassador, who has a son and a son-in-law at the front, merely lifted an eyebrow and continued, suavely, to flirt a little with the ladies." Berle hurried to the State Department to monitor German movements and Allied responses through the night. Several nights later Germany launched a blitzkrieg against France. Without arms or the authority to deliver them to the French and British, Americans felt helpless.[4]

Germany's swift triumphs in Europe echoed through Latin America, Berle and Welles fretting that if its large German populations were impressed by the fatherland's success, "the hemisphere would be split up." They decided to test collective security in Latin America. On June 15 Hull announced the convening of a special Pan American conference to consider hemispheric political and economic action. Berle, in a Charlottesville, Virginia, speech, proposed that—to counter the German barter system in Latin America—the republics should store their raw materials until such time that a free market could find buyers for them. It was not a new idea, nor was it uniquely Berle's. Roosevelt had suggested stockpiling raw materials to Berle back in December as a device for intimidating have-not belligerents. The Americas would organize a pool of raw materials that would operate like a cartel. In January Roosevelt conceded that it amounted to risky economic warfare: "I do not know that any of us have minds big enough to comprehend this kind of situation, but we have to work at it, just the same." Nor was it the sort of proposition to be expected from an administration whose secretary of state preached free trade for achieving peace and railed against British monopolies of trade. Indeed, because it also challenged British markets in the Americas, the plan caused some consternation in London. The British Ambassador to Washington, Lord Lothian, erroneously attributed it to Berle, but correctly forecast little support for a cartel in Congress (Berle wished that the word "cartel" had never been used to describe the pool), adding that "in some quarters it has been dismissed as fantastic."[5]

In June of 1940 the whole world seemed fantastic. The swastika flew in Paris, Amsterdam, Copenhagen, and Oslo, surpassing in six weeks German military accomplishments in all of 1914–1918. Britain stood alone in Europe. And the United States claimed to pursue a peace that few believed it could obtain without resorting to war. In Washington an apparently lame-duck adminstration considered all aid to Britain short of war, hoping, along with London, that circumstances would compel the Russians to change sides as suddenly as they had divided Poland with the Nazis. Although Roosevelt resolved to arm the United States to defend its hemisphere, the State Department was in confusion on issues of war and peace.

The problem of the State Department was dramatized by the publication of two books on foreign affairs in 1940 in which Berle was a featured actor. One was a book of six pieces by Berle, *New Directions in the New World,* some of them written during his sabbatical from the State Department. It reprinted an essay on the significance for Latin American cooperation of the Lima conference of 1938, a memorandum Berle wrote at the inception of the TNEC, and an exposition for capital credit banks. The other three were new and endeavored to be prophetic—forecasting a postwar world in which spiritual values would assert themselves, liberal capitalism would enrich America and the world, and the Good Neighbor principles of cooperation and free trade would prevail. The prose was uneven, ranging from the eloquence of his speeches, to the floridity of his spiritual exhortations, to the flatneess of a government memorandum. But, in the words of an anti–New Deal columnist, as a glimpse at American policy then and possibly for the future, it was "significant as well as interesting [and] just seethes with ideas." Berle believed it contained some of his most important writings.[6]

The other book also endeavored to instruct Americans on the making of U.S. foreign policy in a troubling time. Written by two young newspapermen Joseph Alsop and Robert Kintner, *American White Paper: The Story of American Diplomacy and the Second World War* looked inside the State Department since the Munich crisis. It relied heavily upon interviews with participants and a reading of the diary of Adolf Berle. "I think it's a really important story; I want to get an audience for it," Alsop had told a friend. The isolationist *Saturday Evening Post* commissioned the work as a series of articles, but when Alsop and Kintner came in with pieces that suggested Americans would be drawn into war in spite of a popular preference for nonintervention—and its timeliness was enhanced by the fall of France—it became a book so important that a second edition with a postscript was published only a few months after the first. Aside from its unhappy theme, the book excited talk in Washington diplomatic circles because it so obviously depended upon Berle's unpublished diary. "It indeed does almost seem like an autobiography of Berle," a former State Department hand muttered with hyperbole. Berle, without admitting the role his diary played in it, liked the book and told Alsop so. But it was not favorably received by the secretary of state.[7]

Cordell Hull viewed it as the latest insult to his leadership of the department. Earlier he had had to contend with Moley's insubordination and George Peek's competition as foreign trade advisor for control of export policies. Hull could tolerate constant press gossip that American foreign policy was Roosevelt's, not his, because he was loyal to the president and satisfied that his direction of trade policies furthered American interests and the cause of peace. But Hull was disturbed by the president's penchant for surrounding him with subordinates loyal only to Roosevelt. Welles and Berle had carefully deferred to Hull at all times and Hull in turn gave them great latitude, as when Berle negotiated the Lima agreement and Welles embarked upon a quixotic peace mission to the capitals of Europe. Hull suffered unintended slights and accumulated indignities in silence. But he deeply resented the Alsop and Kintner book, which recalled for him the Moley incident. He was irate over the book's "unintentional portrayal of him in the light of a simple country boy with a certain limited amount of common sense but who needed guidance" in making decisions. According to his friend, Breckinridge Long, Hull "thought that books like that should not be published but that if something had to be published that it ought be somewhat more general in scope and not so personal in its glorification [of Berle]." Suspicious of Berle's "motives, ambitions and judgment," Hull later scrutinized press leaks for evidence of Berle's responsibility for them because "Berle advertized himself out of all proportion by turning over his diary and talking out of turn to Alsop."[8]

The State Department in 1940 was overwhelmed by intrigue and fatigue. Hull was then sixty-nine and, although he was revered in Congress as an astute political manager, he precluded a race for president (some thought because his wife was Jewish) and considered his wife's pleas to take a retirement he had so richly earned through six decades of public service. He did not have to put up with malicious gossip within the administration and his own Department. He may not have known the intricacies of foreign policy, but he certainly knew the levers of power better than any member of Roosevelt's cabinet and his high esteem in Congress made him valuable to the president. He was determined to outlast and destroy Welles, Berle, or any other man who may have coveted his portfolio.

Early in the year Hull replaced George Messersmith with Breckinridge Long as an assistant secretary of state—ostensibly to facilitate trade legislation, even though Long admitted to himself that "finance and economics are strangers to my mind." It was Long's second tour of duty in that post, the first being in 1917–1920. Hailing from an aristocratic border state background, Long had distinguished himself in the 1920s through party loyalty that frequently took the form of sizable contributions to the Democratic National Committee. For part of that time it had been Hull's onerous duty as national chairman to raise funds at a time when few Democrats were sound political investments. Made ambassador to Italy during 1933–1935, Long went into semiretirement in 1936 until Hull asked him to return. Hull valued Long for his party loyalty, political savvy, and as a rare State Department crony whom he could trust. Dean Acheson later noted that "like Mr. Hull, he was a gentleman of the old school—spare, courteous, and soft-spoken." (Although Paul Appleby later insisted that Acheson was Hull's favorite, Acheson himself observed, "It was pretty plain that Long was Mr. Hull's principal confidant and emissary.")[9]

Hull complained openly and often about the prima donnas of the Department. Berle ranked high on that list because he showed "extreme egotism and ambition," worked almost exclusively for the president, and covered too much ground in the Department. Hull also distrusted Welles. When Welles undertook his peace mission to Europe, he reported directly to the president in a cipher for which Hull lacked a key, leaving him dependent upon Roosevelt for what Welles reported. Additionally, their styles contrasted sharply: Hull liked to mull things over and in more than one instance Welles acted while the secretary contemplated. Welles increasingly acted independently of Hull in 1940 because he anticipated that in 1941 either Hull would be president and sack him or Roosevelt would be president and sack Hull. It seemed inconceivable that Hull, Welles, and Berle would be around for a third Roosevelt term.[10]

BRAINTRUSTER FOR A THIRD TERM

At a Washington garden party in the summer of 1939, a young White House aide James H. Rowe, Jr., found himself unexpectedly drawn into an intense conversation with Assistant Secretary of State Adolf Berle. The New Deal needed to leave America an intellectual legacy, Berle told him, his low voice hinting at the importance of his words. Having just been introduced to Berle, Rowe was unprepared for his invitation to brain trust the New Deal's legacy.[1]

Berle feared that the Roosevelt presidency was marking time, bogged down in the inertia of a second term; it needed an agenda. He did not expect enactment of any program—but he wanted to secure the philosophical basis of a future administration. Someone other than Roosevelt, hopefully a liberal like La Guardia or a moderate like Hull, would become president in 1941. In 1939 and early 1940 Berle tended to discount a third-term movement for Roosevelt as selfishly promoted by the politically bankrupt Frankfurter group. It was still unimaginable, even for the imaginative Berle, that the Germans and the Russians would conquer and divide Europe—crisis events that would justify Roosevelt's rupture of the third-term tradition. In 1939 New Dealers like himself still fastened upon the lingering depression and debated programs for recovery.

The Temporary National Economic Committee was liberalism's testing ground in the late New Deal. Goaded by antitrusters who blamed the depression on big business, Congress had created TNEC—a twelve-man directorate representing a wide variety of governmental bodies and economic interests. TNEC may have been, as Raymond Moley suggested, the "final expression of Roosevelt's personal indecision, an inquiry that would relieve the President from the nagging of his subordinates, put off adoption of a definite program, and free his mind for consideration of other matters.'' Amid distracting foreign affairs, he was keenly aware that the economic concerns that brought him to the White House had not been resolved. He approved TNEC to be "designed . . . as a means of setting up the issues for the 1940 campaign, particularly in the hope of furnishing a good springboard for a liberal president.'' Berle knew that Roosevelt was unwilling to lead the debate out of fear of alienating somebody in his administration, or perhaps unable to lead because he was uncertain of his own mind. The president "tacitly and cynically" encouraged policy conflicts among advisors that produced either consensus or exhaustion—peace in any case. Thus, TNEC became the New Deal's last ideological arena in which nobody could win and nobody could afford to lose.[2]

It was an opportunity to educate the public on economic planning that might be translated into a program in the unforseeable future. Besides Berle, numerous economists, politicians, bureaucrats, and businessmen took TNEC's mission quite seriously. Marxist theorists too envisioned TNEC as an opportunity to invoke socialist planning and achieve political viability amid a mushrooming consensus for state control. In the atmosphere of 1939 the Left also found the state capitalism of Berle and the punitive taxation of the Brandeisians appealing. Not a few Marxists then considered Keynesian "compensatory fiscal policy" a reasonable way station on the road to socialism in America. Thus, antitrusters, capitalistic planners, and Marxists would all make TNEC in part "a showcase for Keynesian economics."[3]

Berle saw big business as a historically necessary evil. Although certain big corporations were unnecessarily evil, he argued that taxing them would not improve their morals and busting them would not improve their efficiency. However, he portrayed himself as less dogmatic on the matter of competition than the Brandeisians. "Why in the world do people insist that the whole spectrum of economic activity, running all the way from a violinist to a utility company, has to be tackled on the same basis?" he rhetorically inquired of Jerome Frank. "You might equally say that all disease ought to be treated with exactly the same medicine." As he would not espouse monopoly, so he would not espouse indiscriminate antitrust. In certain industries, he reasoned, competition was preferable; Berle fought Pan American Airways' quest for monopoly in international air travel in the State Department. A consensus was possible if only Brandeisians pragmatically recognized that big was not always bad. At dinner with Alf Landon in 1939, he listened to all the familiar arguments for smaller enterprise because the former Kansas governor had spent the afternoon with Frankfurter. But, "when I asked him how small he would make railroads, telephone systems and so forth there was no answer." In rebuttal Berle asserted that "few air-tight monopolies" existed and "some concentration of industry is obviously necessary.'' Besides, private monopolies were administered by the Interstate Commerce Commission or similar public regulatory bodies. Of greater concern to Berle was the absence of adequate investment capital for the massive requirements of transportation and utility development. State capitalism had made possible great projects such as the Tennessee Valley Authority or the Rural Electrification Administration and state capitalism would build the great projects that were still needed.[4]

As he had earlier in the New Deal, Berle espoused government-organized credit banks for economic expansion. He envisioned ''the conflict in the next decade'' as ''between a reorganization of our credit system or a reorganization of the social system.'' If credit was not liberalized, the system could stagnate and 1940 could see 8–10 million unemployed workers, many of whom might turn to socialism. Sharp swings in the business cycle would leave an upper third or half of the nation prosperous at the expense of the rest. ''Credit is one way of stimulating the organization of men and materials to create wealth,'' he wrote. ''We happen to have a laboratory experiment in doing just that, carried on by [former German finance minister] Schacht; and some of the mechanics could be used without involving us in the German dictatorship.'' The Schacht experiments were useful precedents in state capitalism and confirmed the ''Keynes multiplier'' theories. To finance the further creation of wealth, public works needed additional credit institutions modeled on the RFC. Having circulated in Washington his memos on the need for credit banks since 1933, Berle anticipated using the TNEC as a forum for his schemes.[5]

But he did not leave it to chance. Two former colleagues William O. Douglas and Jerome Frank were then chairman and commissioner respectively of the SEC, the agency charged with investigating investment banking for the TNEC. In February 1939, Berle sent Peter Nehemkis of the SEC staff a six-page memorandum and attempted to get his own economist, Louis Faulkner, appointed as a TNEC aide. A Berle speech calling for a semipublic credit body was summarized prominently in the business pages of *The New York Times*. At the same time he increased Frank's political debt by lobbying Roosevelt to nominate him for a federal judgeship. However, Southern congressmen did not want a Jew sitting on the District of Columbia Circuit Court bench and Frank believed that Roosevelt knuckled under to congressional anti-Semitism. Berle then pushed him for chairman of the SEC, which got the president's nod after Douglas went to the Supreme Court. In the spring Frank agreed that Berle would testify on investment at a TNEC hearing.[6]

''The public hearing route is not a good way of developing clear cut intellectual conclusions,'' Berle asserted. He feared that he would come across as dogmatic, rather than sounding like the voice of pragmatism and sweet moderation. A week before the hearing, TNEC's staff held ''a dress rehearsal, so to speak'' in order ''to see how each part of the testimony fits into the larger whole." To make investment banking comprehendable to the layman, Berle was adjured to use nonacademic terms; "Instead of talking about 'durable goods' we want to talk about brick and mortar." A ten-page description of desirable and undesirable vocabulary, along with definitions of terms and their connotations, followed from Nehemkis. Witnesses were earnestly advised that in discussing the economy, "*mature* means the end of growth, if not indeed senility. Horrors! the end of progress. . . . Impossible! The witness is crazy. It might be better to use two relatives: *A rapidly expanding economy. A slowly expanding economy.*"[7]

Also, Nehemkis and Frank edited a draft of Berle's testimony and Federal Reserve Board economist Lauchlin Currie furnished statistical research. Berle himself asked Roosevelt to give the investment banking investigation "a send-off" with advance publicity. He would not allow the public to guess as to his message; as Berle told Henry Dennison, "This business of collecting facts and letting other people try to draw conclusions if they can has been carried to the point of cowardice." Leaving nothing to spontaneity, Berle, Nehemkis, and Frank orchestrated some "startling" conclusions that led one reporter to conclude the Berle proposals were "a segment of an Administration plan to revise the banking system" and increase federal spending prior to the 1940 election.[8]

Berle made three proposals. First, he prescribed the creation of a comprehensive "Public Works Finance Corporation," a bank where governmental agencies could go for public works funds without reference to legislation—an RFC that would make agency administrators as autonomous as Robert Moses was in New York. Second, an agency that would make federal loans available to small businesses that could not finance internally. Third, his favorite, Congress would create capital credit banks for public or private enterprises in need of financing not available from private lenders. As intended, the proposals were provocative. Ernest Lindley, a long-time Berle-watcher, forecast that they would "stimulate intelligent discussion, not only in the New Deal but in quarters in which any idea which emanates from the Roosevelt Administration is usually summarily dismissed."

Lindley was correct, but the discussion was not always intelligent or flattering of Berle. Stuart Chase and Lincoln Filene were predictably enthusiastic since both likewise advocated liberalized credit. But other reactions ranged from respect to outrage. The *Chicago Tribune* distorted Berle's testimony to make it appear that Berle wanted government ownership of most of America's productive plants. Predictably, bankers saw his proposals as threats to their interests, one banker urging his fellow lenders to fight for the "preservation of our inherent rights which as . . . men of the banking fraternity we hold so dear." If a credit shortage existed, the Illinois Bankers Association denied the accusation that bankers withheld legitimate credit from businesses and blamed Washington for a lack of confidence that restricted capital for expansion. A letter to *The New York Times* condemned the capital banks' scheme as "dangerous" and "as obnoxious and un-American as any subversive movement designed to uproot our tree of liberty." Nevertheless, Senator Mead of New York introduced a bill for a capital credit bank and Marriner Eccles, chairman of the Federal Reserve Board, endorsed it; the American Banking Association opposed it.[9]

A young economist for the Federal Deposit Insurance Corporation, Herbert Stein, offered this thoughtful analysis:

> Since Mr. Berle's plan confers so much power and leaves so many problems for administrative decision, the nature of the capital credit banks is of great importance. On this question only one thing is clear. The banks are to be quasi-public, quasi-private, non-profit, non-political institutions. It contributes to clarity, but not to hope, to translate this to mean that the managers are to be unselfish and honest. How anyone becomes, or ceases to be, the manager of a capital credit bank we are not told. It does not seem an unduly cynical interpretation of recent history to see danger in "entrusting" any important measure of discretionary power to philosopher-king "professionals."

Stein's argument hit home. Berle sought a corporatist economy that ostensibly divorced credit from both politics and the marketplace. "I wonder," Stein wrote, "whether the *technician,* rather than the politician, is not needed." Could a Schacht-like financial technician succeed in America without abridging its social and governmental systems? "As far as I can see," Berle retorted, "we have now a situation in which a good many of those decisions are made by a group who are neither philosophers nor kings, and the natural checks which one might expect do not seem to work." He preferred the planning in Washington's hands rather than in Wall Street's. But nearly three decades later Stein believed that Berle's "argument seemed to frighten more people than it persuaded, because it suggested no limits to either the direction or the amount of the federally-stimulated investments." Berle, Raymond Moley said, was preaching "economic totalitarianism."[10]

Stein, Moley, and other critics had a point while the United States was at peace, but within a matter of months the whole issue would be subsumed by the war and then, ironically, Berle's concepts came closer to fulfillment under defense exigencies. Berle's prescription became the economic agenda of the 1940s when the RFC effectively operated as America's capital bank, creating subordinate capital credit agencies such as the Defense Plants Corporation, the Rubber Reserve Corporation, and the Smaller War Plants Corporation. Jesse Jones in the RFC already was Berle's technician, his Schacht! Beginning in 1940 the RFC's state capitalism liberated American output in World War II enormously by loaning billions of dollars to industry without resort to the economic totalitarianism forecast by Stein and Moley.

Berle sensed that only in war would he triumph. The antitrusters always had the better of it politically because they pleaded the case of David against Goliath. Berle viewed their attacks as opportunism. It was never a question of "what is to be done, but whether our crowd, as contrasted with somebody else's crowd, is to keep control of the situation." As anticipated, TNEC yielded "a glorious indefiniteness" because the Brandeisians preached antitrust, although "no one had the courage to formulate a measure designed to that end." Assessing the New Deal in 1940, Berle thought that "the most significant social experiment to be tried was probably the TVA" (Tennessee Valley Authority). The major problem, "providing full employment," he told columnist Marquis Childs, "was dealt with only at odd intervals." Gains were made in public power and housing, "but there was not any real attempt to tackle the rural problem [or] the banking problem; and there has not been any real attempt to expand municipal services." After two terms of the New Deal, America was not yet committed to national planning. Noting how the concept of Keynesian compensatory fiscal policy had taken hold among policymakers, "the war is as likely to accelerate the process as not," he prophesied.[11]

Ever the aristocrat distrustful of the electorate and Congress, Berle hoped to give national economic planning a fillip through a reconstituted brain trust. A plethora of brain trusts permeated Washington in 1939, "more a jig-saw puzzle than a blueprint . . . a reflection of every conceivable school of thought on economics, politics and finance extant"—unlike the dominant Moley-Tugwell-Berle triad of 1932. In part Berle tried to recruit Jim Rowe and Ben Cohen because he was so bereft of allies and could not command Roosevelt's ear alone. When Rexford Tugwell initiated correspondence, Berle eagerly responded that only recently the president had spoken of how he missed him, how he valued his loyalty and wanted him back in Washington. A surprised Tugwell thought this "strange" and "queer." Why, he wondered, did the president use Berle and not call him direct? Was Berle indulging in nostalgia? Tugwell admitted that he wanted to return to the administration, but honestly "can't imagine what the President would want me to do." In Washington during November 1939, Tugwell lunched with Berle *en famille*.

> Afterward—it was a warm, sunny day with falling leaves very beautiful on the long south slope—we sat on the hillside and talked. We did not stay long and he came to the point. I ought to be in Washington. Something like the old brains trust ought to be at work again. I did not mention the differences nor the fact that one *was* at work though we were not included. [This was a reference to the Frankfurter alliance with Harry Hopkins, Robert Jackson and Harold Ickes.] But he was very full of the present

confusion, etc. I said not much would be done in the next year and that F.D.R. would be unlikely to run again. So where would we be? He said yes, but we ought to leave an "intellectual heritage." I did not demur too much . . . ; so he said F.D.R. was quite serious about wanting me back.

But where? Berle suggested the RFC and Tugwell allowed that they should think about that. They parted, Tugwell "saying that I would do nothing to follow up the suggestion and he saying that I might leave it all to him." It was recruitment of an old associate with whom he agreed on a planners' brain trust to rival the influence of the antitrusters. In July 1940, Tugwell learned that Roosevelt really wanted him back in government, but Tugwell's next federal service would be as governor of Puerto Rico.[12]

With less than a year before the next presidential election, the demise of the New Deal and the drive for a successor to Roosevelt were uppermost in Berle's mind. The Democratic party and the administration were torn into factions that vied for leadership and the power to determine Roosevelt's successor, without even being certain that Roosevelt would not decide the matter himself—or even anoint himself for a third term. The game had been going on since the 1936 election and was in full tilt when Berle arrived at the State Department in March 1938. Cabals swirled around Roosevelt, struggling to promote his successor. Early booms for Robert Jackson and Harold Ickes went nowhere. Berle's new political vehicle, La Guardia, was in truth a man without a party. Jim Farley desperately wanted to be the first Catholic president, but he was seen as too much the party hack. A consensus candidate—a staunch party man, admired by Congress, moderate enough to attract liberals and conservatives, with experience in foreign affairs and politics to command respect if not adoration—was Cordell Hull. He was, Berle said in 1938, "the symbol of what the Democratic Party ought to be like." Or, as others put it, "Hull would be the easiest man to elect."[13]

The Frankfurter faction feared Hull enough to launch the third term movement. Hull was too conservative, too unsympathetic to the British cause, and too little in control of the State Department to control the government. On the other hand, Berle feared that the third term was a "singularly sterile issue" that would subordinate the intellectual heritage of the New Deal. Not wanting to believe that the New Deal "rested solely on the shoulders of a single man," Berle hoped that Roosevelt would resist the temptation to run again. Still, given their friendship, should FDR want it, Berle remarked, "a third term would suit me, personally, very well." Even for Berle, who fervently believed that issues mattered more in politics than personalities, Roosevelt was the indispensable man. If Berle desired to retain influence in Washington, Roosevelt was a better vehicle for him than Hull. Following a trip to Colorado in August, Berle reported to Roosevelt that Democrats there believed that it came down to a third term or Hull. Sumner Welles would observe later that Roosevelt knew that either he or Hull would be the 1940 Democratic nominee. Hull kept his counsel and FDR chose not to discourage the third-term movement. "Knowing the President well," Berle thought, "I know that anyone who acts in his name is permitted to go right ahead. He never disavows anybody. As matters go along he will eventually take a stand. We will therefore simply watch events."[14]

Roosevelt held all the cards in 1940 and Berle eagerly deferred to him. Hull never doubted that Roosevelt would be renominated and told supporters that he did not want to be vice-president; he wanted to be a third-term secretary of state. Loyalty was a strong suit among politicians and Berle too wanted the president to know that he was a Roosevelt man—"if you wish to run." When he planned to go to Houston for a Jefferson Day dinner speech to Jesse Jones' Democrats, Berle discussed it with Roosevelt, "principally for the purpose of giving you a chance to give me a steer if you think the line is wrong." He told the Texans, "frankly, I do not think the President wants a third term" but he would accept a draft. Of course FDR got that draft.[15]

Berle did not betray any disappointment. As far as his own fortunes were concerned, it was a standoff. A Hull presidency would not have benefited Berle politically unless the ticket was balanced with La Guardia—a long shot at best. A Hull presidency would have had Norman Davis leading the State Department, with Breckenridge Long playing a more prominent administration role. Welles and Berle, the Roosevelt men, would have been out. Berle insisted that he expected to return to private life in 1941, and no doubt he did. But in the fall of 1940 he enthusiastically busied himself as braintruster by writing speeches for the third-term campaign.

Three weeks before election day Berle was summoned to the White House for campaign speechwriting duties. "It was the old Brain Trust back again, except that the scene was the Cabinet Room instead of the Hotel Roosevelt." Again he worked with Sam Rosenman, while Grace Tully typed their drafts of Roosevelt's speeches. However, Tugwell and Moley were absent and Harry Hopkins filled the latter's role. Roosevelt preyed upon Berle's sentimentality for those days when he instructed Hopkins to tell Berle that he needed "a new 'Commonwealth Club' speech on the future of America." On election night, 1940, Berle went to the Stork Club with Ernest Cuneo and, in the company of gossip columnist Walter Winchell and the legendary Charlie Chaplin, listened to the returns come in. Although registered in the American Labor party, Berle had voted Democratic, except for a vote for a bluestocking Republican congressman, Fritz Coudert. He had much reason for satisfaction that night.[16]

The election had little to do with the New Deal and its legacy. The war controlled events. War in Europe returned FDR to the presidency and kept Berle in the State Department. However, the war also assured a greater experiment in state capitalism than Berle could expect in peacetime. No war could be fought without capital planning. Had not Woodrow Wilson, the apostle of the New Freedom, resorted to state capitalism in 1917–1918? Frankfurter might win some political battles, but atomistic competition in the twentieth century was atavistic. Rather, the issue involved assuring a fair availability of capital and a fair distribution of benefits under a leviathan state ineluctably charged with imperial responsibilities abroad.

"NEUTRALITY DOES NOT IMPLY IMPARTIALITY"

Roosevelt made a few changes at the start of his third term, the most important being State's circumvention in relations with London. Harry Hopkins became his liaison to Churchill and John Winant replaced Joe Kennedy as ambassador—taking along Ben Cohen as an aide, moves that, together with the appointment of Dean Acheson as an assistant secretary of state, revealed the hand of Felix Frankfurter. State tolerated Winant because, as Norman Davis told Pierrepont Moffat, there simply was "no logical man to send in his place." A "sombre" Cordell Hull pondered his Department's "diminished influence." Berle ruefully agreed. At the start of Roosevelt's third term it appeared that the State Department was exhausted, demoralized, and disintegrating.[1]

State's problems were fair game for critics of its noninterventionist policies. Columnists Drew Pearson and Robert Allen, who drew a lot of their gossip from Ickes, Corcoran, and Bullitt, were likely to print anything which suggested friction and division in the Department. In October, they reported that Welles wanted Hull's job and Berle wanted Welles' job and Hull wanted to spite them both by not quitting. Berle attributed the story to Bullitt (who frequently feuded with either Messersmith, Long, Kennedy, or Berle and maintained a private pipeline to Roosevelt—and wanted Hull's job). When Pearson and Allen reported an instance of Welles going around Hull, the under secretary demanded and won a retraction. Yet such gossip had believers in Washington. "S.W. has been tactless and [has] given the Secretary the impression that he thought the latter was on his way out," Moffat wrote. Consequently, with Roosevelt committed to Hull, in 1941 Welles' influence appeared to wane. And yet, Moffat shrewdly observed, the real extent of intra-Departmental hostility "has not come to the surface"![2]

Some of the bickering was blamed on Berle. "He works in every direction, with or without instructions," R. Walton Moore had heard. His role as a factotum for Roosevelt and a free lance in the Department had not changed much in two years. "Berle's sphere of activity is still more or less of an enigma," Long told his diary.

He does the liason [*sic*] with the F.B.I., Army and Navy on some of the intelligence matters (Welles does some—the major policy matters), is often in consultation on general matters, does drafting for the President from time to time, but I do not know what he does though he works long hours and is always available. . . . I do not exclude Berle from the load, but I do not know just what his share is, though I do know he has a propensity for getting into all manner of things which are not in his bailiwick—often to the consternation of Hull who is not one of Berle's staunchest admirers and from time to time is frankly critical.

According to Long, when Hull offered him the post of counselor, Berle blew up and threatened to leave the Department if he was not offered it. Hull compromised by leaving the post vacant. (Strangely, Berle had turned down the counselorship in 1937.)[3]

With the arrival of Acheson in February 1941, the Department had its first bona fide Frankfurter man, Anglophile, and interventionist. Economic advisor Herbert Feis had played that role before, but Feis was not as close to Frankfurter nor as enthusiastic for the British. Because Acheson had been lobbying for the British before he signed on, his arrival added to departmental tensions. "Dean Acheson is in a state of mind where all the world is out of step but himself," Moffat wrote. "He feels that we should be in the war." Acheson the "bellicist" told Long that the United States ought to get into the war in order to speed up the defense program and control labor—to which Long tartly replied that Acheson had the cart before the horse. Acheson was Frankfurter's agent and the Supreme Court Justice fought the Department's noninterventionism. "Anyone who didn't follow his line of reasoning was branded an appeaser," Moffat noted. Yet Acheson probably strengthened Berle's loyalty to Hull, especially when he heard gossip that Frankfurter intrigued to have the secretary replaced with Acheson. Frankfurter was "getting a little out of scale," Berle growled.[4]

Policy and personalities were seldom in separate spheres. The Frankfurter factor loomed again during the fund freezing controversy of early 1941 although it pitted Morgenthau and the Treasury against Hull and the State Department. Morgenthau was as dubious of British designs as was State, but he sometimes was more concerned with Treasury's territorial imperative than good policy. A complainer, Morgenthau always defended Treasury turf against alleged encroachments. Welles called him a psychopathic case and Berle called him infantile. In early 1941 they clashed over the freezing of foreign assets, an issue Berle preferred to see handled by a special body such as 1917's War Trade Board. But Roosevelt then opposed all emergency bodies, preferring to see his Department Heads squabble over wartime authority. Morgenthau wanted the freeze while Berle insisted that it would endanger American neutrality and subject American companies abroad to retaliation; "it is a war measure" for which America was unprepared, Berle argued. Anglophiles in the Treasury immediately branded opponents of fund freezing "appeasers." At a meeting between the two Departments, Hull rebuffed Morgenthau, who flew into "a fit of rage . . . , a child-like performance." Directing State's strategy, Berle guilefully decided "to navigate the Frankfurter boys [Acheson and Feis] into the picture and let them stand the brunt of opposition from the Treasury." That would test Acheson's willingness to defend State's position and America's economic interests: "Acheson seems to me like a decent chap, and he just may not lend himself to all this. We shall know later." When the Justice Department lined up with State, Morgenthau angrily sought the advice of Frankfurter—who counseled a White House showdown. But Roosevelt upheld State's veto on all freeze orders. State won the battle, not because funds freezing was wrong; Morgenthau was too early. In June Berle and the Department decided that German military strikes against Eastern Europe now justified freeze orders.[5]

At issue was whether the foreign policy of 1940 would prevail in 1941. German successes in Western Europe prompted Washington to accelerate its Latin American defenses and diplomacy. Another Pan American conference was held in Havana and there American delegates confronted intense German propaganda concerning American economic imperialism. Despite a feckless delegation, the Americans obtained an "Act of Havana" that recognized the right of intervention by any American nation to protect hemispheric peace and security. Berle hoped that the United States could use this diplomatic triumph to compel the Germans to abandon their Latin American intrigues and buy peace with Washington. Peace would give Washington more time to arm and play a larger role in Europe. With a larger role in Europe, U.S. trade and ideas would become a greater economic and cultural factor in a reconstituted postwar continent. Far from being isolationist, Washington's strategy in Latin America portended greater prominence in Europe.

Berle thought that America "had not quite adjusted itself to the fact that the British Empire was dead" and that the United States "was supposed to inherit that empire." That required patience instead of precipitate action. The Roosevelt-Hull-Welles-Berle strategy called for Washington to decide upon the place and timing of American initiatives and responses. Thus, the fall of France did not necessitate an immediate American entry into the war at Britain's side. Rather, Washington wanted time to fashion a new relationship with Britain and its Dominions and Commonwealth nations. The State Department first had to determine what leadership remained in Britain. Neville Chamberlain had resigned as prime minister and Winston Churchill became his successor. What the State Department knew of Churchill it did not like—Welles reporting that during his visit to London he saw Churchill drunk on two different occasions. Berle asked him if he saw any evidence of leadership in Churchill and Welles responded that he saw none. Suppose England collapses, went the State Department considerations during the summer months of 1940: "The blunt fact is that Britain cannot now reconquer the Continent—and we are not going to do so," Berle wrote.[6]

Nevertheless, the destroyers for bases deal of 1940 took America a long way toward displacing a British imperial presence in the western hemisphere, as well as toward military involvement in Europe. In it London agreed to give Washington two bases in Canada and to lease eight others in the hemisphere in return for fifty overage American destroyers. "The value of the destroyers is inconsequential when compared to that of ten bases," Long exulted. "In a single gulp we have acquired the raw material for the first true continental defense we have had since the sailing ship days," Berle cheered. The British agreed to the lopsided exchange because, not only did they desperately need the ships for defense (which arrived in Britain requiring repair and refitting that took many months), they also needed to involve the United States in the war in any way they could. The deal dispelled any American doubts concerning Britain's and Churchill's determination to fight. As Berle confided to Moffat, Washington now was "fast moving into war" and relations with the British were "incredibly close." All that remained was for the British to concede that their empire could not survive the war intact, that "the salvation of the world will be the building of a system more nearly like that which we have in this hemisphere than anything which the British are likely to produce with their experience. . . . " In other words, an American-style liberal empire of trade and credits would replace British hegemony and power. But that would require American intervention before Britain succumbed to German terror bombings or invasion. "We ourselves will be in difficulties if they go under," Berle declared. "I don't take wars very lightly." If only Washington could obtain a peaceful resolution without an "ocean of anarchy and blood."[7]

Lend-lease in 1941 brought the United States closer to war. Fearing an enormous American outpouring of sentiment and sympathy encouraged by and for the British, Berle urged that Washington's aid be predicated upon self-interest. "I doubt if the present British feeling toward us is as friendly as ours toward Britain," he declared in a memo to Hull he decided to hold. "I think they rather resent our apparent safety. . . . We have also to assume as a dead certainty, that in handling matters the British will take care of their own interest; and should they fail, that we shall be expected to take care of ourselves. Hence, I think that our weapons and our production should at all times be in our own hands." State knew that its distrust of the British had fallen out of step with the emerging national mood. "The emotional pitch in Washington is very strong, with the interventionists in the saddle," Moffat noted. The swing of American sympathy toward London increased British haughtiness toward the State Department. In the wake of "a snooty note" from Whitehall, Berle fumed that the British "cannot easily get over the idea that no foreign government is entitled to a foreign policy without their OK, they of course reserving complete freedom." However, when the British ambassador in Washington, Lord Lothian, died, Lord Halifax replaced him and brought with him an appreciation that this time Americans had imperial concerns as well as Wilsonian ideals. Britain would have to cater to American interests in order to justify its acquisition of American arms.[8]

The State Department made the end of the British imperial preference system and the transfer of islands in the Pacific desired for "strategic considerations" its price for lend-lease. It had toyed with demanding transfer of British investments in Latin America in payment for American arms, but the Department's Latin Americanists demurred on the grounds that those investments were mostly in utilities and that the local trend toward expropriation made them possessions "we were better off without." On the price Britain would pay for lend-lease, Moffat noted, "for a wonder Welles, Acheson and Berle agreed completely." With lend-lease the United States crossed over into a shadowy area of semibelligerency—confident that Germany was unprepared to contest another front and the American people still preferred not to fight. Legally, the Justice Department assured State, lend-lease did not abrogate neutrality: " 'neutrality' does not imply impartiality when somebody else starts an unjustified war."[9]

But it was a fragile neutrality. In March Berle interpreted State Department intelligence from Eastern Europe as signalling that Germany would attack Russia that summer. The British-Soviet relationship since the Hitler-Stalin Pact of August 1939 had angered him. The British granted the Soviets a free hand in the east, hoping that Moscow's opportunism would inspire them to switch sides in order to gain territory at the expense of Berlin. London's ploy recognized the Soviet conquest and absorption of the Baltic countries—revealing British indifference to the Treaty of 1919 and the fate of small nations. To Berle it confirmed the British as immoral opportunists. And so it was that when Germany attacked Russia as Berle predicted it would, that old anti-Communist Winston Churchill swiftly pledged support to the Soviets. Berle was in Ottawa at the time and noted Canadian consternation at not having been consulted by the British foreign office, additional evidence that London had not changed its old imperial habits. Yet London had gained an ally in Moscow and was closer to gaining one in Washington.[10]

CANADIAN CAPERS

In 1941 Canada was important to the administration's hemispheric scheme. A primary objective of the scheme was economic cooperation with Ottawa as a vital partner. And central to the partnership was an agreement to develop the St. Lawrence waterway. As Moffat noted in 1938, Berle alone in the State Department shared Roosevelt's commitment to build a St. Lawrence waterway. The St. Lawrence project would have many purposes. Through state capitalist planning on an international scale, it would stabilize industrial economies to avert either totalitarianism or economic chaos. The eruption of war had increased the need for the waterway's power and trade facilities. Cooperation in developing the waterway would facilitate the economic integration of Canadian and American industry, and diplomatically woo the Canadians from the British Empire. It was not a unilateral American policy. Through negotiations with Canada Berle found that these hemispheric ambitions had some well-placed sympathizers in Ottawa, where the war was seen as an opportunity for Canada to define its interests independently of the British Empire. Canada's assertion of its diplomatic independence would enhance American manipulation of Allied diplomacy during the war. Thus, Berle sought a larger role for Canada in wartime Allied diplomacy.

Canada did not enthusiastically second Britain's declaration of war upon Germany in 1939. Poland's fate did not provoke the concern in Canada that it did in Britain. In the words of a Canadian historian, "what is striking about the first few days of the war is the coolness of the Canadian response." Unlike 1914, "there were no crowds around newspaper offices, no bands in the streets, no impassioned singing of *God Save the King* or *La Marseillaise*." The Canadian mood might best be described as resignation that its blood and political ties committed it to a needless war, a high official in the Ministry of External Affairs observing that "there is a widespread feeling that this is not our war, that the British government which blundered into it, should have been allowed to blunder out."

Nonetheless, Canadian neutrality was impossible, a fact discussed in Washington. While considering U.S. neutrality proclamations in that fateful first week of September 1939, Roosevelt raised the question of "the formula about the British Empire." By law Canada was at war when Britain was at war, for "Canadian neutrality was equivalent to secession" from the empire. But nothing was official until the Canadian Parliament made it so. Perplexed State Department officials debated the matter in Roosevelt's White House bedroom on September 5, Berle noting that if they labeled Canada a neutral the British would accuse them of trying to break up the empire. On the other hand, they did not want to take Canada's involvement for granted lest they offend Ottawa's sense of independence, Roosevelt declaring "that if he had to choose between going along with London and going along with Ottawa, he would rather go along with Ottawa; it was nearer." That was a double entendre: aside from its geographical proximity, Canada was nearer the U.S. political and economic interests than Britain.

To resolve the matter of Canada's belligerency right away without any hard feelings in Ottawa or London, Hull telephoned Prime Minister Mack-

Lina and Adolf Augustus Berle, Jr., perched here on the knees of grandfather G. Frederick Wright (a Congregationalist minister and pioneer geologist) in 1896, owed much of their intellectual inclinations to him and to their parents, Adolf and Mary Augusta Wright Berle, shown *(at left)* in the 1930s. The "school in the home" taught the young Berles to combine the rationalism and spiritualism of their grandfather. *(Courtesy Dr. Beatrice Bishop Berle and Beatrice Berle Meyerson)*

For Berle, a prodigy, the "school in the home" was not his only school. Here he sits in the front row of a public school third grade class in Beverly, Mass. (*Courtesy Dr. Beatrice Bishop Berle and Beatrice Berle Meyerson*)

Berle volunteered for service in 1917 at age twenty-two. He was sent to Paris in 1918 to participate in the peacemaking process. In the company of fellow army intelligence officers, Berle became a part of the U.S. delegation's Russian Section. Their evident youth and assurance belies a heavy responsibility to advise on policies toward a leviathan Russia in the grip of civil war and hunger. (*Courtesy Franklin D. Roosevelt Library*)

Berle's "playmate," his wife Beatrice, shown at about the time Berle met her in 1925, was the object of both his heart and his intellect. Friends considered them inseparable. Beatrice Bishop Berle was his lifelong intellectual companion as well as the mother of two girls shown below at their Konkapot home in the 1930s. (*Courtesy Dr. Beatrice Bishop Berle*)

No known photos of Roosevelt and the brain trust exist except for the picture shown above of the president-elect en route to his inauguration with Admiral Cary Grayson, Norman H. Davis, Raymond Moley, Rex Tugwell, and William H. Woodin. Berle unfortunately missed this singular picture-taking. However, there is a still from a newsreel made by *Pathe News* of him with Tugwell, Moley, and Louis Howe, in which Berle explains his role in the new administration: he looks into the camera and intones, "A lawyer is an intellectual broker. . . ." (*Courtesy The Bettman Archive and Sherman Grinberg Film Labs*)

The banking crisis of the New Deal's first month brought Berle, the author of the pathbreaking *The Modern Corporation and Private Property*, to the White House frequently, here in the company of his good friend, businessman Charles Taussig. The intensity of the crisis, as always, found Berle with cigarette in hand. (*Courtesy The Bettman Archive*)

Berle, sworn in by La Guardia as New York City's last Chamberlain in 1934 *(above)*, enjoyed that position as much as any he held in public life. In part that was because he viewed his administration of the city's financial affairs as testimony to his genius for devising fiscal schemes. Even before the swearing-in ceremony he had brought Mayor-elect La Guardia together with Federal Relief Administrator Harry Hopkins *(below)* to plan for an infusion of state capitalism for New York's beleaguered budget. (*Courtesy The Bettman Archive*)

In New York City, Berle was both a technician and a politician. He played a prominent role in liberal politics by developing an informal coalition of Roosevelt and La Guardia supporters that probably reached its zenith with La Guardia's election to a third term in 1941. (*Courtesy Franklin D. Roosevelt Library*)

During World War II the United States became a superpower, and Berle envisioned a postwar *Pax Americana*. In November 1944, at the International Civil Aviation Conference at Chicago, Berle endeavored to compel British acquiescence to American demands for freedom of the air. Lord Swinton *(on the left)* resisted him while Clarence Howe was among those Canadians who mediated Anglo-American differences. (*Courtesy Franklin D. Roosevelt Library*)

enzie King and advised him of their conundrum; whereupon King suggested that nothing be said about Canada until its Parliament acted. Australia, New Zealand, and the Union of South Africa immediately announced their declarations of war, but Canada delayed until September 10. Only then did Washington include Canada in its embargo of belligerents—restraint that suggested greater respect for Canadian independence than for its place in the British Empire.[1]

Notwithstanding that one country was at war and the other at peace, the war encouraged Canadian-American cooperation for a St. Lawrence waterway project. Before the war both governments had feared that development threatened state or provincial interests or those of private power companies. North of the border, Ontario Premier Mitchell Hepburn had argued that Canada was "neither in need of a new avenue of transportation nor additional electrical power." Yet three weeks after Canada entered the war Hepburn informed Ottawa that Ontario "was prepared to reverse, completely," its opposition to development of the St. Lawrence's power with the United States. In New York the power companies had fought development of the St. Lawrence project, but when word of Ontario's change of heart reached Leland Olds of the Federal Power Commission, he asked the president about "getting forward with the St. Lawrence waterway pact as a part of our necessary power defense plans." Roosevelt sent Olds' memorandum to Berle, writing on it, "Adolfo: Seems to be the time to throw in the clutch. FDR."[2]

In October 1939, Loring Christie, Canadian minister to the United States, Berle, and Olds mapped their joint plans. In December King formally requested the State Department to resume negotiations on the proposed waterway. It was decided that Berle, Olds, and John Hickerson, the State Department's expert on Canada, should go to Ottawa in January. As *The New York Times* noted, "success would mean the achievement of one of President Roosevelt's chief power projects."[3]

As eager as both sides were for agreement, they were also aware that defense necessities had not completely eliminated local opposition to the proposed St. Lawrence project. Its cost, the diversion of freight traffic, and the sharing of water were live issues in both countries. The American and the Canadian peoples would have to be educated to the wartime need for the project. Indeed, fearing that Southern and Western senators would block ratification of a St. Lawrence waterway treaty, FDR postponed further negotiations until after the 1940 elections.[4] Assuring the Canadians that delay did not mean any diminution of U.S. interest in the St. Lawrence's total development, Washington encouraged Ottawa to proceed with engineering surveys in the rapids area of the river, and to draw power and to divert water from existing projects—the United States to pay for up to a million dollars of the cost of Canadian engineering surveys.[5]

"In the last analysis," a Canadian official wrote, "it is going to be the

President's personal interest in the St. Lawrence project which will be controlling." The election did not clear the way for the proposed waterway treaty. Because Hull thought that the waterway would make more political trouble in the Senate than it was worth, Roosevelt decided to find a way to get it without submitting a treaty to the Senate. At Roosevelt's bidding early in 1941, Berle went to Ottawa to seek an *agreement* with the Canadians rather than a *treaty;* in this way he and Roosevelt hoped to win approval from a *simple majority* of *both* houses of Congress and thereby prevent a minority of the Senate from blocking a treaty. When some Canadians professed skepticism that an agreement would be as binding as a treaty, Berle assured them that adequate precedent for this went back to the Rush-Bagot agreement of 1817. Mincing few words, Berle reminded the Canadians that Roosevelt had gladly "gone out on a limb" to help Canada by looking the other way when it tapped the Niagara River and now he expected Canadian help with the administration's problem. The Canadians resignedly assented to the agreement strategy.[6]

Neither was Canadian support for the project a settled issue. Montreal chafed that the waterway would diminish its status as a port, the *Montreal Gazette* hoping that the project would be defeated in Congress. King feared that the waterway issue would topple the government of Quebec and possibly his own. Although King agreed that national defense in 1941 was a powerful argument for it, he seemed to prefer postponement of the project until after the war. Roosevelt understood King: "I have never been didactic about method: if it is politically easier to sign up for the seaway, let's do that. If Canada can't accept the seaway at the moment, let it go; . . . once the Dam is constructed, the completion of the seaway will follow as surely as day follows night. . . . But there's no point in forcing the issue now. We can't ask King to risk his Cabinet and it wouldn't be in our interest to do so."[7]

Although the prime minister was "most appreciative of the President's understanding of his difficulties," King found other excuses for procrastination. When a week passed without the Canadian cabinet authorizing approval, Moffat advised King that "Washington was growing terribly impatient," that it had accomodated him to get this far so that valuable construction time would not be lost to any further delays. King's procrastination disgusted Berle and other Americans, but in March the Canadians assented to signing the proposed agreement and Moffat hurriedly telephoned Washington before they changed their minds.[8]

Prior to departing for Ottawa for the signing of the agreement, Berle and Olds went to the White House on Sunday, March 16, and found the president working in bed. Roosevelt, Berle observed, "was in excellent form."

> He reminisced a little about the St. Lawrence waterway; pointed out that he, as a youngster in the New York Senate had had a good deal to do with

blocking the aluminum company's attempt to take all the water in the river. The man who had got the grant, and who opposed the repealer legislation, was Leighton McCarthy, now Canadian Minister to Washington, who subsequently has been an old friend of the President. The President jollied McCarthy about it when he came in to present his credentials as Minister.[9]

Roosevelt's equanimity contrasted sharply with King's "new set of jitters," but upon arrival in an Ottawa that had ten degrees below zero on March 18, Berle was warmed by the fact that Moffat had the agreement "pretty well in hand, and there is not much for me to do." That evening the Americans hosted a grand dinner for the Canadians at the American Legation, Berle observing approvingly that "Pierrepont Moffat does it up to the nines." At 2:30 the next afternoon, Berle, as the ranking American, put his name on the agreement, the first such document he had signed for the United States. "I found myself too excited to hold the pen properly and therefore blamed it on the Canadian pen—which was merely discourteous," he later recalled. Then they all went to the Canadian House of Commons to hear King announce that the agreement had been signed and the notes exchanged. Berle watched while seated next to "a plain but intelligent girl" who was introduced as Princess Juliana of the Netherlands. Later, King, "in good spirits," told Berle that he looked forward to visiting Roosevelt soon.[10]

Berle still anticipated "a first-class fight in Congress" against the project. In the weeks that followed he made a national radio speech praising the project as "a magnificent undertaking in a great time" and spent "five mortal hours on the griddle" in Senate hearings on the bill. When Democratic congressional leaders proved unenthusiastic about pushing the project, the president gave them "some help" by warning that if the Americans bailed out of the St. Lawrence seaway, the Canadians might build their half and charge us tolls. (That was a scare tactic; Roosevelt knew that the Canadians could not build it without U.S. funds.) Out of desperation, the administration in August combined it with the omnibus rivers and harbors bill. Once that was done it cleared the House committee with votes to spare. Admittedly the administration had yielded to pork barrel politics, but Berle rationalized the expediency on the grounds that the United States needed power development for defense at any price.[11]

Berle believed that cooperation between Canada and the United States was imperative—that "the accident of a frontier" divided two English-speaking nations of similar cultures—and that they could use their mutual defense needs to bring them closer economically. Some Canadians were neither innocent of Berle's "imperial" intentions nor indifferent to them. In fact, with European markets increasingly closed to Canada and its Treasury coffers draining under war obligations, some Canadians almost welcomed Berle's interest.

An incident sharpened Canadian awareness of Berle's interests and designs. As Berle told it, on June 12, 1940, shortly after the fall of France, Bruce Hutchison, a Canadian reporter, "came in wondering about the course of things." Having been told that he "must see" Berle if he "wanted to know the inside of the situation," Hutchison asked what Berle expected to happen if the British Empire should come to an end. It was the sort of question that revealed two sides of Berle: the diplomat betrayed no information and probed others ceaselessly for useful intelligence; the intellectual enjoyed speculating on the unimaginable and could be disarmingly candid, almost savoring their shock when others heard his blunt analysis. In both instances he was anything but sympathetic to the British Empire. First denying that he could give an answer, Berle, by his own account, "said that of course were England to drop out of the picture (she had not done so yet; we hoped she would not do so), the relations between Canada and the United States would become even closer, and the only problem would be economic." To read his version of the conversation, Berle was prescient, but not sensationally interesting.

However, Ottawa stamped Hutchison's version of it "absolute secret," and considered it to be "the inside picture" of a "remarkably frank" conversation. Berle had told his Canadian visitor that he had been studying how the hemisphere might reorganize to make it economically self-contained. South America's dependence upon European capital made it "spiritually" fertile for nazism. To counter Nazi economic penetration in Latin America, Berle was advising the president to develop an economic plan for the hemisphere. "This is the great project they are working on now," Hutchison wrote breathlessly, "and which I call the new American Imperialism. It is not a dream, but the subject of the most detailed official plans." Where did Canada "fit into this new hemispheric economy?" Hutchison had asked. The war economy would make Canada prosperous and destroy the last vestiges of its market economy because the government would have to control the economy for war, Berle replied. When Hutchison suggested a familiar Canadian fear that the United States would use economic pressures to absorb Canada politically, Berle scoffed at it. Hutchison concluded that Berle's "whole assumption was that Canada's economy would be merged with that of the U.S., but he did not foresee political union." He was certain that "Berle is working now actively for the President on a vast plan of hemispheric re-organization which will entail the end of capitalism as we know it; or rather a complete extension of the whole New Deal, totalitarian theory." The result would be "the new American Empire."[12]

Berle was indiscreet—not in revealing a confidence, but in trusting a journalist lacking background, sophistication, or insight to appreciate that his conjectures were neither novel nor part of some vast, sinister plan. Accustomed to brainstorming in a low voice that suggested the importance and confidentiality of what he was saying, Berle could not know that the

Vancouver correspondent mistook his dreams for blueprints. Impressed with gossip that Berle as "the President's very closest adviser and brain man," Hutchison did not know that Berle propagandized for a grander vision of his Latin American "cartel" plan—which most of Washington rejected as unworkable. Hutchison was unprepared for weighing Berle's imagination with political realities.

Fortunately, Ottawa did not read Hutchison's interview as a revelation. "It is rather extraordinary that Berle would speak so freely but that is in keeping with the expedients adopted in the preparation of the American White Paper," observed O. D. Skelton, then head of the Department of External Affairs. Thus, Skelton saw the interview as Berle's bid to prepare public opinion "for some of the developments to come." What were those anticipated developments? According to a Skelton aide, H. L. Keenleyside, "Washington is likely to require Canadian co-operation. If the United States is forced to defend the Americas, Canada will be expected to participate; thus the negotiation of a specific offensive-defensive alliance is likely to become inevitable." A military agreement would have to precede any economic arrangement. In fact, two months later at Ogdensburg, New York, Roosevelt and King almost casually agreed, at Roosevelt's suggestion, to create a Permanent Joint Board on Defence. It was America's first defense pact with a belligerent and signaled that Canada no longer relied upon the British Empire for its defense, but its powerful neighbor.[13]

Berle wanted economic cooperation that complemented a defense alliance. With Britain crying poverty and turning to the Canadians and the Americans for credit on its war expenses, Berle maintained that Washington had a right to set terms for the English-speaking belligerents. The Canadians bought so heavily from the Americans that Ottawa's trade deficit threatened to grow out of all proportion—Moffat advising Berle and others that the Canadians "were getting towards the end of their economic resources." Already spending 45 percent of their national income on armaments, the Canadians desperately tried to restrict imports from the United States. Complicating the situation was the fact that lend-lease compelled the British to take their war trade to the United States; London demanded more favorable terms from Ottawa, if it expected continued British trade. By the end of 1940 Keenleyside quietly called for a Department of External Affairs study of Canadian-American economic cooperation to prevent "duplication and mutually injurious competition" through the "establishment of stock piles of all strategic, critical and essential war materials."[14]

Keenleyside liked Berle's multinational state capitalism. When Berle came to Ottawa in January 1941, Keenleyside gave him a memorandum which Berle read with delight. In it Berle concisely saw "two fairly distinct problems": short-term U.S.-Canadian coordination of military production and long-range coordination of industrial activities. Through Escott Reid, a young Canadian diplomat stationed in Washington, Berle suggested to

Keenleyside that a joint committee be appointed to study the first problem as a step toward the second.[15]

At the March signing of the St. Lawrence agreement, Berle and Keenleyside discussed economic pooling. Berle already knew that the war committee of the Canadian Cabinet had approved Keenleyside's memorandum, declaring that "the Canadian Government attaches great importance to the proposal." Although the Canadians wanted to discuss only its short-term implications, Berle fairly rhapsodized that "the rest of it goes much farther." "Keenleyside realizes that this is now one continent and one economy, that we shall have to be integrated as to finance, trade routes, and pretty much everything else; and in this I so thoroughly agree with him that it is refreshing," he told himself. "We talked long and happily about it—though much lies in the realm of dreams. This at least is a new order which can exist without hatred and can be created without bloodshed, and ought to lead to production without slavery." Listening to Berle go on "full of enthusiasm and drive," Keenleyside had to remind him that all they discussed was a possible wartime study and report. Still, Berle's zeal did not seem excessive; at the same time, Mackenzie King was telling Moffat that the Permanent Joint Defence Board was "among the great developments of recent times," and "grew quite lyrical and pointed out how the face of the entire continent would be changed." If this was American imperialism, its appeal certainly surpassed the British version.

The British inadvertently contributed greatly to Canada's enthusiasm for Berle's vision. The Canadians felt exploited by British demands that Ottawa build fuselages for British planes while British factories built the engines. They were convinced that this would leave them economically and technologically dependent upon Britain after the war. So they played their American hand—suggesting economic union with the United States—and even informed London that they sought industrial integration with the Americans.[16]

When that news made no visible impression upon London and the British threatened to shift war orders to the United States unless the Canadians matched the cheap American credits, Mackenzie King decided to visit Roosevelt. Ottawa was in a bind: it could not compete with American lend-lease and it did not qualify for it. Thus, on what King called "a grand Sunday," April 20, he met with the president at Hyde Park; from that came the Hyde Park Declaration, stipulating, in part, "Insofar as Canada's defence purchases in the United States consist of component parts to be used in equipment and munitions which Canada is producing for Great Britain, it was also agreed that Great Britain will obtain these parts under the Lease-Lend Act and forward them to Canada for inclusion in the finished article." For King it was a coup! Caught between London and Washington in a trade conflict that left Ottawa with a spiralling debt, he persuaded Roosevelt to indirectly subsidize London's lend-lease purchases from Canada to the tune of 200–300 million dollars in the next year. Thus, Ottawa traded with Washington and London while London borrowed from Washington for that trade. King had a right to be jubilant.

But, while the Hyde Park Declaration surprised many Canadians and Americans, it miffed Berle. Aside from its vague recognition of the need for the "most prompt and effective utilization . . . of the productive facilties of North America," it did not discuss economic integration of the two nations. King's new external affairs minister, Norman Robertson, "felt that the Canadian proposals now under consideration by Mr. Berle were too rigid and had to be revised. . . . The Berle-Keenleyside project might lead to planning for a much longer range and a much broader extent than that provided for in the Hyde Park Declaration." John Hickerson noted that Berle was "very much upset over the Hyde Park Declaration in as much as he had not had a chance to discuss the matter with the President in as much detail as he wanted." Lacking Berle's perspective of Canadian eagerness to pool war production, Roosevelt had given Ottawa financing for its output without strings that tied it to joint defense production with the United States.

Not surprisingly, the Canadians lost interest in Berle's grand design after the Hyde Park Declaration. Escott Reid, who shared many of Berle's state capitalist visions, told Moffat in June that he was "surprised at how little importance [Canadians] attached to the idea of setting up a long-term economic planning board between the United States and Canada." Although the two governments created a Joint Economic Committee on June 17, which heartened Berle, it proved ineffective. All joint economic planning between the two countries would be based upon wartime expedients such as the need for price stabilization. An opportunity to use the war to develop bilateral economic planning and possibly extend it to the rest of the hemisphere had been lost. "It is a trick proposition," Berle sighed, "partly educating the public, and partly doing some real planning." He worked at the former and dared to hope for the latter.[17]

IDEOLOGICAL POLITICS

The years 1938–1941 were an unforgettable period. A quarter century later those who remembered it would employ the "Munich Metaphor" to justify their determination that never again shall totalitarians anywhere be emboldened to aggression by the acquiescence of democracies. Berle was among those Americans who drew significance, not only from Chamberlain's misguided understanding with Hitler at Munich in 1938, but from Molotov's nonaggression pact with Ribbentrop at Berlin in August 1939; he applied it in both foreign affairs and domestic politics. Because the Nazi-Soviet Pact came at a time when the Soviets were negotiating a mutual defense treaty with Britain and France, it suggested that liberals could not trust any totalitarian regime. All totalitarian ideologies sought to destroy liberalism. Moreover, the pact proved that American Communists were capable of any deception where the interests of the Soviets were at stake. Also, recognizing the opportunism of the totalitarians, he accurately forecast the Nazi invasion of the Soviet Union, which he considered an eastern war for the right to rule Europe and to confront liberalism in Britain and in the Americas.

He had not been overtly anti-Soviet before 1939. Bolshevik savagery in the revolution had sickened him, but did not turn him against the Soviets. Like many Americans who espoused economic planning in the depths of the depression, Berle admired Soviet planning and expected it to teach capitalists to be less doctrinaire toward unregulated markets. Likewise, he anticipated that Soviet rigidity in planning would turn pragmatic and liberal. Soviet planning and American liberalism would find common ground some day and grow to resemble each other in fact, if not in theory. Big corporations and big governments were still inevitable, but his perspective of the Soviet system was changing. Stalin's peremptory trials and executions of opponents sickened him and it became evident to him that American Communist politics and policies were influenced, if not determined, by Moscow's totalitarianism. "The fact is slowly emerging that the Russian and the German points of view are moving closer together and are finding common enemies," Berle wrote in 1939. "Bluntly, they are both fighting what they conceive to be a capitalist civilization; and they will both wind up together."

He considered the united front against fascism a sham. "Under the tactic of the united front," he told Luigi Antonini, a Social Democratic refugee from Italy's fascism, "a good many parties, Communist, Marxist revolutionary, and others, join under the name of 'democracy,' that, of course, [are] no more democratic in ultimate outlook than the parties who are frequently actually in power." A united front that included the Soviets expediently ignored "that huge majority of people in the Western world who see little practical difference between living under a Russian or Nazi tyranny. Nor could any conceivable Russian government be expected to treat such an understanding as anything other than an opportunity to forward their own type of political penetration." He was unmoved by Max Lerner's "wholly unconvincing differentiation of the Nazi's from the Communist's point of view." He scorned liberals who advocated Soviet-American understanding: "We have no reason to suppose the Russian government has ever interested itself in the matter." The Soviets were dedicated to revolutionary intervention against all non-Communist governments around the globe. They respected no country's right to national self-determination.[1]

His darkest suspicions of the Soviets were confirmed by the Molotov-Ribbentrop Pact of August 1939, the Nazi invasion of Poland, and the Soviet seizure of the Baltic states. Now he saw a "Russo-German Europe bent on dominating the world." However, given the opportunism of both partners, and drawing from his reading of Hitler's *Mein Kampf,* Berle believed that it was a temporary arrangement and within a few years the world would "see this tremendous combination tear itself to pieces internally. . . . But they will be ghastly years." In September he wrote, "the Western world as we know it ends at the Rhine River; and for the time being, Europe is gone." Only his reading of history comforted him: Europe had endured dark times before and would revive following this cataclysmic age. He tended to exaggerate Russian ambitions, interpreting the Russo-Japanese Nonaggression Treaty as a bid to divide China, thereby leaving the Rhine and the Himalayas as the only frontiers against totalitarianism. Conversations with State Department colleagues such as Breckinridge Long—who was convinced that Russia would be "the only winner in a prolonged war and America's eventual enemy"—reinforced his pessimism.[2]

The Russian invasion of Finland in late 1939 verified to Berle that Soviet designs were as sinister as those of the Nazis.[3] When the Soviets bombed Helsinki, Welles wanted to break relations with Moscow, but Hull, as usual, was cautious, and Berle reasoned that "these emotional moral gestures do not get very far in the long run." The State Department declined to proclaim a state of war existed in the Baltic, lest it be bound under the neutrality law from aiding the beleaguered Finns; aid to Finland was a straight business deal with a good creditor. On the other hand, Roosevelt wanted to curtail gasoline and scrap iron shipments to Russia; Berle assured him that neither had gone there for two months. It did not help relations when Soviet propaganda accused the United States of instigating the Finnish war. Furious, Roosevelt and Berle wanted to embargo all shipments to Moscow even if it meant breaching contracts to build Russian plants for the manufacture of aviation fuel. Moffat and Berle argued over the contracts, Moffat finding himself "in the strange position of advocating decent commercial treatment with the U.S.S.R."; Berle, "the ultra-Protestant, out-Jesuited the Jesuits, and I, an Anglo-Catholic, out-Calvined Calvin for a rigid respect of the signed word." For Berle, a contract with the Russians no longer had much sanctity.[4]

As party members later confirmed, Berle was correct in asserting that American Communists in the 1930s were under orders from the Comintern to conceal their party affiliations and endorse liberal causes. Thus, the popular front for democracy and the united front against fascism confused many liberals who mistook Communists for Social Democrats like themselves. The Hitler-Stalin pact changed all that. For eighteen months it revealed them as Berle identified them—expedient totalitarians. The months following the Hitler-Stalin Pact held some strange ideological twists and turns. The State Department facilitated the escape of Spanish loyalists from Spanish fascism who then gave Berle "a rather rude shock" by endorsing

Russia's war against Finland. Further evidence of how Communists cynically viewed the united front against fascism came in April 1940, when Moscow blamed the Nazi seizure of Denmark on British and French breaches of Danish neutrality and almost every Soviet argument defending its alliance with Hitler was parroted by American Communists. Before long the State Department had intelligence that Soviet and Nazi spies in the United States were collaborating and Berle warned Roosevelt against the appointment of Communists to government posts where they could sabotage the defense program. (Berle gloated that State Department intelligence was so good that he often knew Moscow's orders for American Communists before they did; civil liberties did not extend to foreign agents.) The former anti-Fascists now fought against the defense preparedness program and espoused American isolationism. Berle branded the Communists as "foreign stowaways" and needled leftists like Max Lerner who "had believed in collective security until last August" and now were isolationists![5]

Anti-Communists and ex-Communists sought Berle out. The winter war had stirred their hopes for a Soviet collapse—journalist Isaac Don Levine proposing that Washington send Alexander Kerensky back into Russia to restore 1917's brief liberal democracy. Kerensky himself visited Berle, claiming knowledge of an abortive coup in Russia. But Berle concluded that "somehow, I doubt if Kerensky represents very much." The House Un-American Activities Committee under chairman Martin Dies wanted Bolshevist Leon Trotsky to visit Washington from his Mexican exile to expose Communist activities in the United States. But Berle tried to dissuade the Dies committee because he felt that Trotsky would turn the propaganda to his advantage or be assassinated in the United States by a Stalinite.[6]

Berle found that the Nazi-Soviet alliance defined New York's politics like nothing else—especially in the American Labor party. He had committed himself to the ALP in the belief that it offered an evolutionary redistribution of power free from Tammany's corruption and Republican reaction. In 1936 he had forecast that the 1940s would see a shift in political strength "from the entrenched capitalist group to a group composed of labor and enlightened citizens" and he considered the ALP to be a principal beneficiary of that shift. He cultivated his ties with New York's union leaders—especially David Dubinsky, president of the International Ladies Garment Workers Union (ILGWU), ALP leader, and a militant labor liberal. The ALP—originally founded to give Roosevelt another line to run on in 1936, thereby taking advantage of the Communist commitment to the popular front—was especially important to La Guardia and Berle, both of whom were estranged from the two major parties.

But they were outsiders even in the ALP. In the 1939 race for Kings County district attorney, Berle advised ALP leaders to support a Republican because "a separate race [would be] solely for the purpose of making a record" and the Democratic candidate, William O'Dwyer, was a Tammany hack. Dubinsky retorted that Berle was out of touch with the ALP's worker constituency and that the ALP needed to boost its morale and prestige through an independent, if abortive, race. Dubinsky was not about to allow Berle and La Guardia to guide the ALP's fortunes according to their political conveniences. He knew that they needed the ALP more than it needed them. Indeed, in 1939 Berle and La Guardia opportunistically decided to go on registering in the American Labor Party.[7]

But the Communists in the ALP troubled Berle. "If there is even a shadow of Communist influence in there, I want nothing to do with it," he told Dubinsky. Fearing that "the pinks" would dominate the ALP leadership, he hoped Dubinsky would lead his workers into the Democratic party before that happened. In the "popular front" days, the Communists supported La Guardia's 1937 reelection and made themselves a significant minority in the ALP's coalition. Not until the Nazi-Soviet Pact did Dubinsky and other ALP leaders move to oust the Communists, only to discover then that the Reds were too entrenched. In April 1940, Berle urged Dubinsky to withdraw the ILGWU from the ALP to avoid electing "Communist-dominated candidates." Dubinsky listened to him principally because of Berle's influence in obtaining, among other things, RFC loans to small dress manufacturers that sustained needle trade employment. Also, well-to-do liberals like Berle made timely contributions that carried liberal labor groups through their financial difficulties. But Dubinsky and his friends then valued their political independence too highly to accept subordination in the Democratic coalition. The needle trade unions continued to battle the Communists in the ALP until 1943, when they bolted to form the anti-Communist Liberal party.[8]

Following the Hitler-Stalin Pact Berle feared Communist subversion of any social democratic organization. In 1939 he had supported the American Youth Congress; a year later he fretted that several of their leaders were "pretty close to the Communist line, if not actually over it." He was relieved when the pact prompted the Reds to abandon the Spanish Refugee Relief Campaign to the liberals. "These damned Communists are everywhere," he exclaimed when, in April 1940, he joined in a campaign to rid the National Lawyers Guild of them.[9]

Actually, the fight to rid the National Lawyers Guild of Communists antedated the Hitler-Stalin pact. Founded in 1936–1937 by New Deal liberals alienated from the conservative American Bar Association (ABA), the Lawyers Guild espoused civil liberties, minority rights, and the rights of labor above that of property. Among its early leaders were liberals such as Morris Ernst, Frank P. Walsh, and Jerome Frank. Its membership read like a who's who of liberalism in Washington, the states, and the law schools. From its beginnings, however, some lawyers refused to join because its membership included radicals; a struggle erupted between members who insisted on supporting the united front against fascism in Spain and those who focused only upon domestic legal issues. Nevertheless, it always was a professional organization that openly embraced politics. A frequent critic of the ABA, Berle joined the Guild and served as a contributing editor to the *National Lawyers Guild Quarterly.*

The Communist issue emerged at a Chicago meeting of its executive board in February 1939. Berle's friends Ernest Cuneo and Morris Ernst proposed an amendment to its bylaws and constitution "making clear once and for all that we are for democracy, the bill of rights and we are opposed to Communism, Fascism, Nazism." However, too few liberals then lumped Communists with Fascists as totalitarians. A substitute motion, declaring that, "One of our avowed objectives is the maintenance of democracy. . . . That means that we oppose any and all ideologies which challenge [our democratic institutions], whether from the right or from the left. Communism, Fascism, Naziism—any *Ism,* be it of native or alien origin—which seeks to supplant our democracy, is a target for our attack" was adopted, eighteen to nine. Ernst and Cuneo voted in the minority.[10]

But that was before the Hitler-Stalin Pact. The pact crystallized the liberal attack. In the words of a radical guild official, the liberals "founded us in 1937 and dumbfounded us in 1939." In an effort to win control of the Washington chapter and send an anti-Communist delegation to the national convention, the liberals ran a slate of officers in 1940 and lost fourteen of the twenty contested seats. That triggered an exodus of government officials from the Guild led by Tommy Corcoran, Robert Jackson, Jerome Frank, and Nathan Margold. Berle soon followed, declaring in a letter released to the press that "it is now obvious that the present management of the Guild is not prepared to take any stand which conflicts with the Communist Party line." The incoming president of the guild, Robert Kenney, a state legislator from California, pleaded with Berle, Frank, and Jackson to stay in the Guild as a gesture of solidarity with its avowed democratic principles. After all, Kenney argued, hadn't the guild condemned the Russian invasion of Finland? According to Kenney, Frank and Jackson were willing to listen, but told him, "You've got to clear this with Berle." Kenney went to Berle, who said, "You're clean, but I'll have to check further about those executive board members that have just been elected." Later Berle hinted to Kenney that if certain members of the board resigned he would consider withdrawing his resignation. Kenney went home to California and the Lawyers Guild never recovered its liberals. Explaining his stand on the Guild, Berle declared, "my father used to say that there were times when a man did not have a right to all his rights." In the cold war of 1940, Berle did not believe that liberals had to protect the rights of antilibertarian Communists.[11]

Sometimes it was easier for a liberal to oppose totalitarianism than to explain liberalism. It troubled Berle that politics in America was usually based upon expedience and self-interest without the leavening of ideals and ideas. Politics should be a crusade for programs that expanded the economy, improved working conditions, and broadened the welfare state—all within the framework of democratic collective planning that enhanced individual opportunity. The 1940 election was a case in point. It disturbed Berle even as it benefited him. The third term suggested that Roosevelt's personality, not issues of peace and prosperity, was the liberal's standard. Berle loftily noted that the people around the president were not program-oriented: Rosenman, Hopkins, and others were good and honest men, but "as unscrupulous a crew as ever put together." They were principally devoted to FDR, loyal to the extent they "would commit murder for the President." With a patrician's eye he assayed the president's party for "any of the saving grace of solidity of character" and concluded that "we shall get one of these clever, progressive administrations in which the end always justifies the means, as a result of which nobody has confidence in the outcome. But that is secondary." To Berle, nobody better represented the self-serving element of Washington liberalism than Frankfurter's fixer, Tommy Corcoran, "the symbol now of a rather corrupt progressivism which has no scruples." But, when Ernest Cuneo brought Berle a message that Corcoran wanted to get together with him, Berle did not refuse the fixer's olive branch: "I hope I have the reputation for being courteous, fair, and willing to listen to all sides," he told himself. On election night 1940, at La Guardia headquarters where Berle went following the Stork Club, Corcoran sought him out. Could he talk with Berle sometime soon? "Certainly," Berle replied.[12]

"I feel nothing but a vast sense of disillusionment and a huge desire to go home and stay there," he confided to David Dubinsky in the heady days that followed Roosevelt's third-term victory. "The country as a whole is, I think, going to be better off; and that, I take it, is the major justification for our work." Publically he proclaimed the triumph of liberalism over the Communists' "tragic illusion that progress could be made through dictatorship, and the still more dangerous idea that American progressive thought had to be tested by some foreign standard." He celebrated "the repatriation of American liberals, and the liberation of American liberalism from the shackles of sterile European revolutionary thought."[13]

American liberals in 1941 needed the labor movement. The news that Roosevelt planned to reorganize the Democratic party to lean more heavily upon irregular labor groups elated Berle. "The fact is that in perhaps a dozen key states the irregulars mean more in the way of votes than do the regulars—but the nominations and the patronage always reflect the regulars," he commented. Labor liberals should destroy the "obsolescent" Tammany machine. He did not speak out of disinterestedness. Berle had his own personal vehicle ready to replace it in New York—the Affiliated Young Democrats—and he toyed with the idea of using it as a springboard to the governorship.

The Affiliated Young Democrats (AYD)—claiming a membership of 125,000 in New York State, 65,000 in the city alone—were led by an ambitious, 35-year-old Brooklyn lawyer, Harold R. Moskovit, who hoped to take the Democratic party away from the likes of Jim Farley and Ed Flynn. Moskovit sought to build a counterorganization to "bore into" the regular Democrats. Although AYD's letterhead sported a formidable list of officers and honorary members that read like a who's who of liberal Democrats, Moskovit was the organization. A graduate of St. John's University Law School and an active organizer of liberal groups since his college days there, he ran the AYD from the Hotel Piccadilly on West 45th Street, leaning heavily upon Berle's advice and influence. Moskovit followed instructions; Berle assured Judge Seabury, "at least he has always followed mine." Berle described Moskovit as a man with "limitations," albeit "energetic and honest."[14]

But the patronized Moskovit wanted patronage. He was not Berle's fool. He wanted Berle to deliver federal jobs for members of the AYD. With letters and phone calls Moskovit politely badgered Berle to secure positions for his friends in federal agencies such as the SEC, the Federal Power Commission, and the Office of Civilian Defense, while promoting others for judgeships and Democratic nominations for Congress and the state legislature. At the same time, Moskovit built alliances with established Democratic aspirants and officeholders, looking to the day when the liberals would take over the New York party. AYD rallies or dinners usually featured Berle's good political rhetoric. In May 1941, Moskovit boasted that, "no one in the City who is a candidate for an office in the City election or leadership, makes his plans known until he has talked with me, thus enabling me to have control and final word in the coming Democratic primaries." Likewise, he expected Berle to take care of "my matter"—regional director of Civilian Defense, a patronage plum "most necessary at this time"—to demonstrate that the leader of AYD "is in a position of prestige and power." Berle got La Guardia the national Civilian Defense leadership but he evidently was either unwilling or unable to satisfy Moskovit's local ambitions.[15]

Berle used Moskovit and the AYD to sustain La Guardia's floundering political career. As his second term wound down in 1941, the Little Flower, "confused and tired," found himself at still another political crossroads. The job of mayor was enervating and his interest in it was waning. In vain Berle tried to get him a Cabinet-level job in 1940, but only the part-time Civil Defense post was to be had. La Guardia considered running for governor in 1942, but he was still a politician without a party or even the sort of reform movement that had propelled him into the mayoralty in 1933. Without an effective GOP ally in New York County and having run too often against Democrats to have any friends in its organization, La Guardia's only vehicle was the American Labor party. In February 1941, Berle beseeched La Guardia to run for mayor again, reasoning that a cabinet appointment would rescue him from City Hall before the third term was completed.[16]

For a while La Guardia bided his time, watching Democrats fight among themselves for the honor of running to succeed him. Also, he floated trial balloons that Berle considered a race for mayor—reports that drew the ire of Tammany Democrats who had "as little use for Mr. Berle . . . as for Mr. La Guardia." Berle himself disdained even the thought of the mayoralty and advised the AYD to consider La Guardia for another term, unless "he should be called to some more important job." To that end Berle launched a draft La Guardia movement, telling a gathering of AYD faithful that Roosevelt preferred La Guardia and it would be "absurd" for the Democratic party not to nominate him. Moskovit, "following my direction in the matter," Berle said, dutifully echoed him while Democratic leaders in the five boroughs screamed that neither the White House nor the AYD spoke for them. The ALP's left wing likewise denounced a La Guardia candidacy, accusing the mayor of conspiring to drag the country into war. In a last effort to get Democratic backing for La Guardia, Berle sent Moskovit to Bronx boss Ed Flynn; Flynn responded by nominating Brooklyn District Attorney William O'Dwyer for mayor. A battle for third term was launched.[17]

It was not a campaign that defined liberalism. La Guardia narrowly won the Republican primary and compelled the old guard to fall in line. By this time Germany had invaded Russia and the ALP's left wing dutifully abandoned its opposition to both the war and La Guardia. La Guardia even revived the goo-goo Fusionists to secure a third line on the ballot. Finally, Berle and the Affiliated Young Democrats manufactured the United City party in a bid to draw Democratic votes from O'Dwyer—although it failed in its purpose when La Guardia alienated thousands of Democrats late in the campaign by petulantly calling Governor Herbert Lehman a "goniff," Yiddish for thief. Morris Ernst tried, through Berle, to get La Guardia to renounce Communist support in the ALP, but La Guardia resisted Red-baiting now that they were on the same side of the war issue. Besides, he valued even a Red's vote if it helped him win. To Berle's surprise, La Guardia won with only 53 percent of the vote in the closest mayoralty election since 1909.[18]

As in 1940, liberals in 1941 had won on the basis of a great personality and the war issue. What would New York liberals do when Roosevelt, La Guardia, and the war were gone? After the election Berle profusely thanked Roosevelt for his support for La Guardia, certain that the third terms of both Roosevelt and La Guardia made for a stronger liberal coalition in the face of resurgent conservatives. Ideological politics went out the window when Hitler marched east. All that politics in 1940–1941 proved was that great personalities could command the vote of a nascent labor coalition and that politics overseas made strange bedfellows at home.[19]

A Temporary Confluence of Interest

Berle anticipated the Nazi invasion of Russia, but he did not welcome it as the British did. He knew it brought the United States closer to war and meant the end of Eastern Europe's small states. Churchill's courtship of the Soviets and his recognition of their conquest of the Baltic states disgusted Berle—who thought it typically unprincipled of the British in dealing with small countries. More than ever, Berle feared British cunning and Russian treachery. If America had to fight, would it fight for Britain's imperial hegemony and an economic system of imperial preference and/or a Soviet–Pan Slavic eastern empire that obliterated the national promises of 1919?

The United States, Berle averred, had to define its interests before it went to war. It must not repeat the mistakes of 1918–1919. American policymakers must know British and Russian interests before they committed soldiers to fight. In July 1941, while others planned for war, Berle planned for the postwar peace in the firm belief that the British and the Russians had postwar designs and that America needed to know them and plan its own according to its defined interests. "It is now evident that preliminary commitments for the post-war settlement of Europe are being made, chiefly in London," he warned Roosevelt. Americans were not informed of those understandings and he reminded the president that "at Versailles President Wilson was seriously handicapped by commitments made to which he was not a party and of which he was not always informed." He suggested that Washington issue a general caveat that it would not be bound by any British-Russian agreements to which it was not a party. The United States should demand a postponement of all discussions of postwar settlements which might at best yield "cooperative machinery . . . and at its worst might be the type of British economic system as violently opposed to our own as the German system was"—a preferential system that violated liberal U.S. trade policies. At times it seemed to Berle that Americans, moved by compassion for the besieged Allies, were united "in wanting to give all help to Britain: the division is between those who want to draw Britain a blank check and those who want in return to have a say in the future." Among the latter were most of Berle's State Department colleagues. Unfortunately, the former, Berle told columnist Raymond Clapper, had the "sentimentalized idea that we musn't annoy the British . . . while they are fighting for their lives."[1]

Others in the State Department shared Berle's trepidations that "the

Frankfurter group" and Harry Hopkins were willing to allow London and Moscow what they wanted in Europe without other interests represented. Berle wanted to ask rude questions now in order to spare the United States embarrassment later. If the British and the Russians had postwar arrangements, then they ought not to hide them from the Americans. Washington must have a say concerning the future of all Europe. Even when the British denied Berle's allegations that they already had territorial agreements concerning Eastern Europe, he persisted. On July 11 he learned that Roosevelt was considering a note to the British along the lines Berle had suggested—disavowing all Allied postwar agreements to which he was not a party. In fact, Hopkins delivered that message to Churchill when he visited the British prime minister and a Roosevelt telegram on July 14 hammered home the point that Washington disapproved of any commitments to a postwar division of power. Berle continued to press Roosevelt to have Hopkins put questions concerning a British-Soviet understanding on Slavic Europe to the British. On July 17 the British acknowledged that there were indeed agreements with the Russians concerning Czechoslovakia. By the end of July 1941, Welles decided to organize a departmental committee on American postwar goals.[2]

At stake was America's pursuit of self-determination for all nations and its vision of a world without political barriers to trade. Believing as he had two decades earlier that Britain disregarded the rights of small nations, Berle used the occasion of a speech at a Washington dinner given by the Grand Duchess of Luxembourg to proclaim his expectation that in the postwar world small nations would "live in freedom and peace, in a family of nations ruled by law which recognizes the right of the weak as well as the strong." It was not a mere homily; the Nazi blitzkrieg against the Low Countries in the spring of 1940 had brought home the point again that small countries had no guarantees in a world where the might of great powers made national rights. Moreover, Berle believed that the rights of small countries were consistent with America's liberal interests. In essence, that had been the message inherent in the Good Neighbor Policy and cooperation with Latin America. The United States was the protector of small states who could not resist totalitarianism and greater military power.[3]

The plight of Denmark in 1940 gave Berle an opportunity to marry the principle of self-determination to American interests in Europe. Following the fall of his country, the Danish ambassador, Henrik Kauffmann, sought Berle's advice as to whether he still represented Denmark or had to accept status as a German puppet. Berle responded that Denmark lived, "even though its government was temporarily submerged," and Kauffman was its representative in Washington. That raised the problem of Denmark's possession of Greenland, an uninhabited land except for strategically significant air and naval bases. Berle maintained that since Greenland was in the western hemisphere, it was subject to the same doctrine of nonintervention by Europeans that applied to Latin America. Not everyone in Washington agreed with Berle's interpretation. Breckinridge Long and Norman Davis objected to extending the Monroe Doctrine to Greenland and sending a consular agent there. But, in the words of Moffat, "it was agreed that Berle should concentrate in his own hands matters relating to Greenland, but that he should keep the European Division informed." (A decade later Washington insisted that China "lived" on Taiwan.)

Berle was a vigilant protector of Danish and Greenland's interests. When he heard that Canadian and British warships were en route to Greenland, Berle summoned the diplomatic officials of both countries and demanded to know if the ships carried landing parties for an occupation, indignantly telling them "that Cecil Rhodes has been dead a long time and even if he was alive, Greenland was hardly a place for his talents." In his diary Berle wrote, "this is plain grand imperialism, on a miniature scale. If there is any more monkey business, we are going to have a destroyer sent up there and stop it. I hope the Canadians and English accept my not too diplomatic invitation to have a drink on the Governor of Greenland and go home." Roosevelt approved of Berle's actions: the British and Canadians were advised that Greenland was a part of the western hemisphere and that Washington could not "acquiesce in any operations which constituted a permanent occupation or change in the status of the territory." When Berle informed Roosevelt that the Canadians had requested landing rights in Greenland, "the President's only comment was that he was sorry they had raised the question."

Nevertheless, in early 1941 the British requested American assent to establish an air field in Greenland. Berle opposed any base there, but the U.S. Army and Navy also wanted bases there. Instead of maintaining Greenland's demilitarization, Berle now pressed for an American advantage. On April 9, he and Kauffmann signed an agreement that permitted the United States to build landing fields in Greenland. It "raised some interesting questions in international law," Berle conceded. Kauffmann no longer represented occupied Denmark, but Berle insisted that he legally represented Greenland; of course, Greenland was still under occupied Denmark's jurisdiction—which Berle dismissed as a government "acting under duress and . . . is in no sense a free agent." In this way, Washington got its bases in Greenland from a theoretically free Denmark. When occupied Copenhagen sent three Danish consuls to Washington, Berle, acting at Kauffmann's insistence, had them expelled. As he wrote in late 1941, "we can choose a representative in case we do not happen to recognize the full sovereignty or existence of another government."[4]

But he would not allow London to decide the fate of small nations. At a dinner party in July 1941, with British diplomat A. D. Marris as guest and attended by State Department official Loy Henderson and his Estonian wife, Berle accused His Majesty's Government of endeavoring "to sell the

Baltic States down the river." In what Marris called an "extremely frank" discussion, Berle was "extremely insistent that it would be the greatest mistake" for London to acquiesce to Soviet absorption of the Baltic states without consulting Washington. He reminded Marris that in 1919 Britain had endorsed the independence of these states, and any action which contravened that sovereignty now was an act of betrayal. Berle and Henderson warned Marris that the American public needed to believe "that [British] foreign policy was based upon principle and not upon opportunism." Although his tough talk irritated London, it conceded that, in T. North Whitehead's words, Berle's opinions *"are* widely held, especially by the more thoughtful amongst our friends in America."[5]

Three months later Berle discussed postwar planning with Ralph C. S. Stevenson, formerly principal private secretary in the Foreign Office and British minister to Uruguay. Knowing that the Russians had sought certain assurances concerning Eastern Europe in 1939, Berle asked if the British had given them in 1941. "Stevenson fished around a bit" and replied that Washington already knew about Russian negotiations with Eastern European governments in exile in London. Dissatisfied with that answer, Berle demanded to know if the Russians wanted hegemony over Eastern Europe. "Speaking frankly," Stevenson allowed that his government "had given a half promise to that effect." When Berle commented "that this would necessarily bring the Russian system considerably east of Vienna," Stevenson tried to reassure him that "there was no longer any real problem of a world revolution; they were merely dealing with the old imperialist Russia" and Stevenson hinted that at the war's end "the British half promise in regard to this area might not be brought to fruition" unless the Russians had the power to enforce it. In the words of a British historian, Berle, "suspicious as ever of Britain, kept a *justifiably* close watch" on London.[6]

Along with two of Frankfurter's friends, Dean Acheson and Herbert Feis, Berle then sat on the Department's Board of Economic Operations. In the fall of 1941, as the British negotiated financing for lend-lease and other purchases with the Americans, the board debated American foreign economic policies. Anxious not to appear as an Anglophobic obstructionist, Berle accepted arguments for Anglo-American cooperation, nonetheless vigorously pursuing tough terms for America's largesse. At various times he reminded colleagues that a basic conflict of interests existed between the United States and "the sterling bloc" (a reference to the empire's alleged hoard of precious metals); that a British-proposed, London-based buying pool could dictate prices to American sellers; that economic decisions which impinged upon the interests of countries not represented in the Anglo-American discussions should not be made; that pleas for food shipments to countries such as Greece should be granted even if London wanted the cargoes to go elsewhere. "Everyone in town suddenly yearns to run the economic foreign policy of the United States," he remarked in November;

"and I propose to have a word or two to say about it." He bristled over the British determination to control North Atlantic shipping lanes, which meant practically reducing Iceland to colonial status through "some very oppressive arrangements." After one heated argument over Iceland, he unhappily admitted, "I am afraid I was unpleasant."[7]

He had to be unpleasant because "the British are pushing the Russian interests all over the lot now." Additionally, American left-wingers were allied with Frankfurter's Anglophiles in pursuit of all aid to Russia. "The extreme Anglophile view is that we should turn over everything to the Russians at once," Berle wrote. "They seem to think that the Russians now love them and will be in all respects a part of their train. Knowing that the Russians have almost as great antagonism to the British as the Germans have to the Jews, I am in no way sanguine." The Anglophiles accused Berle and the State Department of blocking aid to Russia at this critical time, but he did not. In fact, shortly after the German invasion of Russia, Berle urged Jesse Jones of the RFC to extend credits to the Russians for purchases of American supplies. However, when the Anglophiles demanded that the Americans share their military secrets with the Russians, Berle treated that as more naive than sinister or cynical. He expected to be accused of "sabotaging" aid to Moscow—"which God knows we are not," but, as he told Harry Hopkins, "Having had my fingers burned in Russian affairs several times in my life," he believed that American interests required that they treat "The Russian denoument [as] unpredictable." After all, what if Russia sought a "Peace of Brest-Litovsk" and thereby pulled out of the war? What if Hitler was overthrown by generals seeking alliance with Russia? How could Americans trust the Soviets if as late as June 21 the Soviet ambassador in Washington regularly exchanged intelligence with the Germans? "For God's sake," Berle wrote to Hopkins, "tell the sentimentalists to watch themselves." It should be an American rule of diplomacy, Berle believed, that "we are much better off if we treat the Russian situation for what it is, namely, a temporary confluence of interest."

He favored giving Russia money, guns, planes, and machinery, "but she ought not have anything she can sell or turn over to someone else should there be a violent change in party line." He had witnessed too many changes in party line to value altruism that was not based upon self-interest. "Eastern Europe is looking out for itself: not for the British or for us," he concluded. "We can be of help to each other now and will do so. But we cannot bet our whole shirt on the continuance of the relationship." He expected a German defeat in Russia; on July 31, fragmentary news from the East convinced him "that the German adventure is already a failure." But he did not join the Russophiles out of opportunism. He remained suspicious of all foreign interests and their special pleaders. "I think the formula is: every aid to Russia and no nonsense from the Communist party here," he told Morris Ernst. In other words, the temporary confluence of interest would not tolerate American Communists who spied for the Soviet Union. He would not forget the Soviet pact with the Nazis.[8]

Berle knew what American Communists were up to because among his State Department duties was the coordination of intelligence with the FBI. Two days after the 1940 election, the State Department launched its own intelligence division. "Intelligence is beginning to be interesting in the Department now, so everybody wants in on it," Berle commented. "The surprising thing is that what they say rarely, if ever, reveals any great knowledge of what it is all about." Obviously Berle thought that he knew what intelligence was about. He had been at it in 1917–1919 and, in a sense, never left the game. It was an elitest, intellectual extension of foreign policy and he enjoyed its information gathering and the matching of wits. In this country the military, especially naval intelligence, kept tabs on the military activities of the great powers. Domestic intelligence was the responsibility of the FBI, as long as it did not interfere with the civil liberties of American citizens. But between the wars no agency in the U.S. government had the responsibility of assembling information gleaned by the military and diplomats abroad. Roosevelt was aware of the need for it, but he treated it as a casual governmental function that required no formal bureaucracy. Roosevelt always wanted to know what others were up to, either for legitimate national purposes or merely because he was an extraordinary gossip with an insatiable curiosity.[9]

"All governments resort to it," Assistant Secretary of State George Messersmith later wrote with some justification. "It may be a dirty business but there are dirty governments and dirty people and one must know how to deal with them." Diplomats understood that a part of their responsibilities entailed observation and reporting of activities in the countries in which they served. The totalitarian regimes, however, Nazi Germany and the Soviet Union, broadened the scope of intelligence and the range of its gatherers to where it seemed to Americans that nearly every German diplomat or businessman abroad was a part of the Berlin intelligence apparatus. In mid-1939, Cordell Hull told Messersmith that the president wanted to end the duplication of investigations by various governmental agencies and charged Messersmith with coordinating them. Hull knew from experience that intelligence gatherers were very protective of their turf and were even loath to share information with each other. Messersmith did as he was bidden, even hosting dinner meetings for rival agency heads at his Georgetown home, but that ended when he was made ambassador to Cuba. The outbreak of war in 1939 made cooperation among intelligence agency heads even less likely by raising the bureaucratic stakes.[10]

Roosevelt wanted Berle to assume Messersmith's task of coordination with J. Edgar Hoover and the FBI. Aside from normal diplomatic intelligence, the State Department and the FBI operated defensively so as not to suggest the possibility of American intervention in the European war—the

FBI keeping tabs on Nazi and Soviet spies in the United States and elsewhere in the western hemisphere. Edward Tamm of the FBI informed Berle of what Nazi and Soviet agents were up to—the Bureau's job being made easier by the fact that Nazi and Soviet spies coordinated their activities better than did the agencies of the U.S. government. Although secrecy was crucial, the FBI found its counterespionage and countersabotage plans in the newspapers because Justice Department employees feared—"not without justice," Berle conceded—that counterintelligence might obstruct legitimate civil liberties. During the Hitler-Stalin Pact, the FBI frequently encountered trouble with civil libertarians, especially, Berle thought, when the FBI "begins to come close to the Communist machine." From FBI evidence Berle knew that Communists had spied or sabotaged in alliance with the Nazis while "soft-headed liberals" worried about their civil rights. He tended to agree with Morris Ernst that J. Edgar Hoover "has run a secret police with a minimum of collision with civil liberties, and that is all you can expect of any chief of secret police." Freedom and national security often clashed; at a May 16, 1940, meeting of army, navy, FBI, and State Department intelligence officers it was decided to reduce the number of accredited press representatives, some of whom undoubtedly were spies, and Berle "met the story in the hands of the newspapermen exactly thirty minutes after the meeting was over. We killed it, pointing out that we were merely trying to conform to regulations generally. But it did not make one feel happy."[11]

The FBI had no mandate to operate overseas until 1940, but that did not prevent it from doing so, with State Department encouragement, in Colombia and elsewhere in Latin America during the 1930s. If the United States pursued a hemispheric collective security policy, it needed an expanded intelligence apparatus with which to organize the defense of the hemisphere. In May and June, Berle, the FBI, and military intelligence decided to create a Special Intelligence Service (SIS) for operations in South America.[12]

"The time has come," Berle wrote, "when we would have to consider setting up a secret intelligence service—which I suppose every great foreign office in the world has, but we have never touched." In late June FDR decided that in foreign intelligence, "he wished that the field should be divided"—the FBI covering the western hemisphere and the military intelligences covering the rest of the world. A forerunner of the Office of Strategic Services set up under New York lawyer William Donovan a year later, the SIS did little as the FBI and military intelligence could not even agree on which office to meet in, much less on how to coordinate their activities. In February 1941, Berle had to negotiate "an armistice" between the FBI and military intelligence—"harder diplomacy than negotiating an inter-American agreement." In the State Department Breckinridge Long challenged Berle for leadership of its intelligence activities to no avail. "This work is singularly disagreeable,'' Berle grumbled, "but it has to be done, especially in these times.''[13]

Part of the problem was Roosevelt himself. He enjoyed muddling authority. Military mobilization and economic stablization had been confused for two years and would remain that way through 1941, mostly because Roosevelt did not want to grant power to any one agency. Mobilization and stabilization were visible problems; much less evident was the matter of intelligence. In one instance he did not muddle authority; in fact, early in 1941 he created his *personal* intelligence service! He commissioned New Deal newsman John Franklin Carter, who wrote under the name of Jay Franklin, to set up an intelligence operation with an initial budget of $10,000 for three months that came from the military authorization of 1940. Although Carter reported to Roosevelt, he did so through Berle.

"This is the President's idea,'' Berle wrote. "He knows what he is doing; I don't, in this case; but I don't have to.'' The Carter operation disturbed Berle. He knew full well that Carter's mission was to spy upon Americans for political reasons, which offended Berle's sense of civil liberties. Moreover, Carter's charge extended beyond national security. As Berle uncomfortably explained to Welles, "I endeavored to make it clear that the Department here is primarily a post office—that is, that the unit is a part of the personal staff of its creator. . . . I am not, of course, familiar with what the President has asked him to do, nor do I wish to be.''[14]

However, as Carter's "paymaster,'' Berle knew the range of Carter's activities and those of his agents. In May the three-month arrangement was renewed, although Carter was still in the process of recruiting agents—having a particularly difficult time finding a British agent in this country who was not already in the employ of Whitehall. By the end of 1941 the Carter spy unit had a staff of eleven and its leader requested permission to expand operations. It filled Roosevelt's mind and files with amateurish, bizarre, and gossipy reports on the wives of State Department officials, Japanese-Americans on the West Coast, the activities of businessmen at home and abroad, isolationist leader Charles Lindbergh, and so forth.[15]

Roosevelt relished the competition of agencies and individuals with overlapping functions and responsibilities, but intelligence in 1941 demanded definition. William Donovan, another private spy for Roosevelt, was made Coordinator of Information (COI) in July. Donovan wanted to run intelligence everywhere, but was admonished that the State Department and the FBI considered him a poacher in the western hemisphere. Berle and Hoover had little use for the New York lawyer, Berle's complaint being that the British were running Donovan's intelligence service. Thus, instead of solving it, Donovan added to the intelligence problem by seeking to become the intelligence czar and allowing the British intelligence to shape his own. Because British intelligence knew no continental boundaries, in late 1940 it requested permission to operate in the United States. However, Hoover knew that since April 1940, William Stephenson had operated in the United States as the British security coordinator.[16]

Berle's assistant, Fletcher Warren, ran the State Department intelligence operation, the "Foreign Activities Correlation," but it was principally concerned with Latin America. As long as Donovan and the British stayed out of his way, Berle said nothing. Alas, that was seldom the case. When British intelligence obtained the president's permission to use State Department radios for transmissions to London, Berle complained to Roosevelt that the British used their own code "and the F.B.I. accordingly has no knowledge of the matter they are sending." Hoover also accused British intelligence of tapping the telephones of Frenchmen in the United States, leaking stories to the press that suited British purposes, and carrying out surveillance and wiretapping operations against Americans. Confronted with Hoover's evidence, the British offered to share their spies with him; at a time when civil libertarians wanted his scalp for other alleged FBI activities, Hoover said "no, thanks."[17]

A pattern was established in which Donovan enlarged his intelligence empire while Berle, Hoover, and Nelson Rockefeller, coordinator for Latin American affairs, protected the hemisphere as an FBI preserve. The State Department could never surrender intelligence, for what was foreign policy without it? But, in late 1941, Roosevelt told Berle that he believed Donovan "was doing a pretty good job on propaganda and something of a job on intelligence." Berle was never removed from intelligence completely, but he became a minor, albeit important, actor in the American intelligence saga of World War II.[18]

Berle easily confined his intelligence gathering to Europe and Latin America, his principal theaters of interest, and was not much involved with events in Asia or with Japanese aggression. Seldom did Berle write memoranda concerning Asian affairs. In July he noted that the Japanese had demanded Vichy France's bases in Indochina. Also, he endorsed the Department's suggestion that the British raise India to Dominion status. But in his eyes these were really problems involving European imperialism in its decline. On principle, he warmly approved of administration demands that the Japanese clear out of China and open its markets. The Department was so united against all hegemonies and for free trade everywhere that Raymond Clapper was startled when Welles "used almost the same words [as Berle] in saying that what we wanted was simply that every nation have [the] same rights to trade—and take its chances in the market." As talks between Hull and Japanese diplomat Saburo Kurusu began in November, Berle was optimistic that Japan would not resort to war: "But this rests in abler hands than mine, and my ignorance of the Far Eastern situation is so profound that I hesitate to make any comment."[19]

Nonetheless, to his surprise, Berle "got into the Far Eastern business by a curious side door" and only later did he realize that he had been intimate to the climax that brought the United States into the war. On November 27, 1941, Welles asked Berle to use his expertise on finance in consultation with the Department's Asian advisors Stanley Hornbeck and Max Hamilton concerning U.S. plans to make a ten million dollar loan to Thailand to stiffen its resistance to Japan. The Asian experts were aghast; Welles plans made no sense unless Washington was "prepared to fight Japan if Thailand was attacked." Otherwise, the loan signaled that the United States would help defend Thailand. At the same, Japan agreed not to take any aggressive actions for ninety days if the United States would relax certain trade restrictions. However, Roosevelt suggested that he might discuss the Asian situation with Congress and asked Hornbeck to draft a message. Hornbeck was among Berle's closest friends in the Department and Berle, ever eager to play the draftsman, volunteered to assist him; Hull "somewhat wearily" agreed. At Berle's house that weekend they went over Hornbeck's notes and on Monday morning brought a draft to Hull. As Berle left the secretary's office, the Japanese negotiators arrived. Later, Hull told Berle that he "talked to them with a good deal of bark" and assailed Japan's actions in Indochina. "He had told them that he had done his level best to hold things in line here so as to give them a chance to get something done with their own public opinion, but he could not hold things very much longer."[20]

Berle spent December 6 working on the president's Asian message to Congress and anticipating that the Japanese would break off discussions. It was Saturday and at about 1:30 in the afternoon he took a break to meet his daughters Alice and Beatrice at the Hay-Adams Hotel for lunch and then on to a performance of *The Student Prince*. Upon his return to the State Department late in the afternoon, Hull asked him to complete the draft that evening: "There were fresh reports indicating Japanese naval and military activity in various directions." An attack against Thailand was anticipated. Berle resumed working that evening and at 7:30 army intelligence reported an interception of a Japanese reply to the last American message.

> It was not only a flat turn-down, but a coarse and gratuitous and insulting message as well. Bad as this was, the accompanying message, likewise intercepted, was worse. The Japanese envoys were to keep this message locked up in their safe and present it only on receipt of a signal. . . . In other words, they were to hold up delivering the answer until certain military dispositions were completed.

By one in the morning Berle completed the speech and retired. Returning to the Department later that December 7 morning, Berle and Hull "fussed a little more with the message" and were discussing it when the Japanese ambassador asked to see Hull at 1 P.M.; "The secretary fixed the time for 1:45." As the Japanese arrived, Berle and Welles went to lunch at the Mayflower and returned at 2:45. By then the Japanese had attacked

Pearl Harbor. For that matter, reports of Japanese attacks throughout the Pacific flooded the State Department; Berle anticipated a German attack on Greenland and Iceland: "It was a bad day all around; and if there is anyone I would not like to be, it is the Chief of Naval Intelligence." During the rest of that Sunday of infamy, the Department and the FBI tried to paralyze overseas communications and transportation to prevent enemy movement, cabled South American countries to freeze Japanese assets there ("If ever a policy paid dividends, the Good Neighbor Policy has."), and resumed work on a presidential message to Congress that now asked for a declaration of war. After three years of anticipating that the United States might be drawn into a war, the time had arrived. For once Berle did not enjoy his role as draftsman: "I must say that the task of a logothete [*sic*?] is not very satisfactory when the guns are actually moving."

A few days later Berle thanked his assistant, Fletcher Warren, for his hard work during those "difficult and trying days." In the words of Warren's aide, Frederick B. Lyon, "the Chief also rates an extra palm on his decoration for the way he has carried on." Another person thanked Berle twenty years later for his performance in those days following Pearl Harbor: Ambassador Nomura had requested a Samurai sword, but Berle turned it down lest his suicide endanger Ambassador Joe Grew in Tokyo. When they met again in Japan in 1961, Nomura thanked Berle for that decision during the awful days of December 1941.[21]

6

A Liberal's War

To the limited extent that new forms of empire may be inevitable, must not American policy, and that of other superpowers, be translation of nineteenth-century conceptions of empire into co-operative arrangments in which a minimum of control and a maximum of co-operative effort are achieved for all the inhabitants of the region?

That was the conception of Roosevelt's Good Neighbor Policy as it evolved during his regime. . . . If empire cannot be avoided, it can be made fruitful. It may even be made to move toward an effective system of world order.

—*Power,* pp. 504-5

Closed areas are not merely closed in economics. They tend to become closed in politics and in culture, as well.

—*New Directions in the New World,* p. 7

EMPIRES

Escott Reid was angry and bitter. Critical negotiations during the war between Adolf Berle and his British counterpart were floundering, hindered in part by mutual distrust and dislike. Reid knew that shadowing all relations between Berle and any Englishman was widespread gossip that Berle was an Anglophobe. A young Canadian diplomat, Reid knew Berle both informally and officially during service in Canada's Washington Ministry in 1940. Now he expected that Berle would be wrongly faulted for the impending diplomatic debacle. He liked and admired Berle and only wished that the British could know him as he did, although Reid suspected that Berle at times almost preferred to be their adversary. But as a go-between in the negotiations Reid was frustrated because he knew that Berle's complex personality had been reduced to a caricature that could sour relations between two countries. Reid believed that the real Berle had "peculiar qualities" and his notorious Anglophobia "is only a partial truth." Yes, Reid reported to Ottawa, "Berle dislikes most Englishmen, but my guess is that there are probably not more than a half-dozen Americans who recognize as full as he does that the continued existence of Great Britain as a first-class power is essential to the national interest of the United States.''

A Canadian liberal intent upon his country's economic and diplomatic emancipation from Britain's imperial hegemony, Reid appreciated that Berle's liberalism shared a common goal with his own—the end of all nineteenth-century empires. Should the war end in a *status quo ante bellum,* only the Nazi, Italian, and Japanese empires would be destroyed while the United States sought a postwar world that peacefully dismantled the British, Belgian, Dutch, Portuguese, French, and the developing Soviet empires. In the democratic twentieth century, a nineteenth-century empire could not be justified ethically, economically, or politically; statesmen were compelled to plan rationally to avert postwar chaos. Spheres of influence were preferable only as ephemeral systems of stabilization in the postwar political vacuums. However, American liberals believed that all colonial areas would be opened to free trade in which America's economic power ineluctably would assert itself. Call it a *Pax Americana,* as some might describe American imperialism—but it would be a bloodless imperialism that would bring the world a more durable peace and a greater prosperity than it had known under British imperialism. The American business suit would replace British khaki. Nevertheless, the transition to political independence by colonial countries would be turbulent without the cooperation of old imperial powers such as Britain. If the British accepted a transition role in the new world order—and only unreconstructed imperialists wanted to thwart it—then Berle was no more anti-British than other Americans were anticolonialist.

On reflection, even Reid's characterization of Berle as a cold-blooded realist intent upon furthering America's own imperial ambitions did not satisfy him. While it did justice to his intellect, it did not describe Berle's complex humanity. In relaxed moments Reid had come to appreciate a different man from that brusquely intense and arrogant snob depicted in written profiles and gossip. He wished Berle had revealed himself to the British

in those hours of release of tension which can follow a small pleasant dinner between people who have wrangled with each other, . . . not as a bitter anglophobe and a devious combination of Machiavelli, Talleyrand and Fouche, but as a man with the virtues and faults of a great renaissance statesman, a man with encyclopedic knowledge, with a lucid, fertile and an inquisitive mind, a man who can see visions and dream dreams of a better world and try to make those visions and dreams come true. . . . While Mr. Berle finds most Englishmen unsympathetic, his policy towards the United Kingdom is rooted in a firm conviction—driven deep into his soul in the dark months of the summer of 1940—that the national interests of the United States demand that there be a powerful Great Britain. [An Englishman] and Mr. Berle might even have discovered a common bond in their suspicions of the Soviet Union and in the dogged devotion with which each of them serves his prime minister or president.[1]

But Reid knew that reputation made reality—especially if the owner of the reputation did not refute it. When Berle haughtily declared, "there is nothing more second-rate than a second-rate Englishman," in a manner that left listeners wondering if any first-rate Englishman existed, it was hard to conclude that Berle was a closet Anglophile. He was contemptuous of the British Foreign Office, believing it inept, deceitful, and arrogant. Had he seen Foreign Office profiles of himself, Berle's contempt for London would have been enhanced. Six years after Berle entered the State Department—more than a dozen years after he became an advisor to Franklin Roosevelt—the Foreign Office was still uncertain about his family background, information available in a reference library; it could have asked him, instead of listening to gossip. "I naturally blamed the inaccuracies on the strain under which the Foreign Office is operating," he commented about a British diplomatic note in early 1941 while Britain stood alone against totalitarianism; "This was not insincere. If I was drafting notes with bombs falling all around, the notes would be pretty bad." A year later Berle's sympathy for the British was good politics. Assailed for impeding the war effort with his Anglophobia, he acknowledged that since "I already have my troubles with the British Intelligence, I do not think that it is advisable to get into any more trouble at the moment than is absolutely essential." On the other hand, a sympathetic Berle confirmed British impressions of a diabolical Berle. In truth, however, while he disapproved of many of its policies, he privately held Britain in great respect. "I am not so clear that I am sure that England is a declining empire," he wrote in 1944.

> By every standard of arithmetic and economics it ought to be—but then by all those standards England never had the base for being a world power—despite which she achieved and held that position for 300 years. I could fire a salvo for the proposition that it is not the essential strength of a country, but the moral and intellectual quality which the country contributes, which are the real bases of empire. A few hundred men could not possibly hold India were it not for the fact that they put something into the Indian picture that the Indians want sufficiently badly so that they do not quite dare to throw it over—or, at least, have not cared to do so up to now.

The point buttressed a favorite argument of his that ethical and intellectual values surpassed economic materialism, but it is significant that he credited the English with them.[2]

State Department "realists" distrusted "perfidious Albion." While Frankfurter, Ickes, Morgenthau, Norman Davis, Ambassador to France William Bullitt and State Department economic advisor Herbert Feis had made themselves a "war party" by insisting that the fate of Western civilization required an American alignment with Britain, State Department realists insisted that Anglo-American national interests were not necessarily identical. Their practical idealism nearly embraced the sin of cynicism. Moved by what they interpreted as a failure by President Wilson in 1919 to disavow British and French manipulations, their innate distrust of Whitehall was augmented when Colonel House's published diary suggested that American interests were compromised by British imperialism. When Berle entered the State Department, the European political affairs desk was headed by J. Pierrepont Moffat, whose suspicions of Britain nearly exceeded Berle's. Roosevelt, Hull, Welles, and Long likewise suspected secret British ploys for imperial preference arrangements that propped up a declining empire. The realists believed that Britain and America shared many common interests, but when their interests were at cross purposes, they would not tolerate either British indifference to American interests or condescension. The British might accuse the Americans of economic imperialism—and Berle might not quarrel with that—but at least American imperialism was modified by American idealism.

Less than two weeks after the Nazis invaded Poland, a visit by Sir William Wiseman, who then served as an aide to the new ambassador to Washington, Lord Lothian, made Berle's historical wheels spin.

> Well, I thought, under cover of some courteous remarks, this approaches the fantastic. For Lothian, in an earlier incarnation, was Sir Philip Kerr, [Prime Minister] Lloyd George's secretary. As young men, he and Wiseman were the brain trusters; Wiseman arranged many of the meetings between Colonel House, Lloyd George's private emissaries and the British Ambassador . . . and of all things, they took place at a house which [American ambassador to Italy] Billy Phillips then had, called Woodley, and which I have now. The history of our past English "interpretations" was a history of half truths, broken faith, intrigue behind the back of the State Department, and even the President, and everything which goes with it.

Affably sounding out a State Department official considered hostile by the British Foreign Office, Wiseman inquired how the British could "do their purchasing so that it should square with political developments" in Washington. Could Wiseman "feel free to drop in for occasional 'steers?'" Berle was gracious and cordial, but when Wiseman left he fired off a departmental memorandum describing the "ghost's" visit and recalling Wiseman's role of more than two decades ago, concluding, "caution is urged."[3]

Sometimes Berle threw "caution" to the winds. Invited by Lothian to a dinner, Berle was annoyed when a British naval attaché's wife imperially referred to the United States as "out here." Berle turned "disagreeable," and began to mimic her with "out in London," using it six times before he exasperatedly reprimanded her: "you should not say 'out here' when you are in the American capital." At another point he challenged Lothian's memory of events at the Peace Conference. "I like Lothian," he told himself, "but the conviction rose in me that these English have learned nothing and forgotten nothing."[4]

Perhaps Berle remembered too much. The British at war needed money, food, and ships—all of which required sympathetic American minds and more. In 1939–1940 Roosevelt sought revisions of the Neutrality Act, but the administration's quest of free trade ran afoul of the British blockade of the Baltic and other sea lanes. Berle admonished London to respect American trade rights lest "the principal sufferers [of the blockade] will be neutral countries with whom we do have a common interest, friendship and understanding." (Anglophiles would have been aghast at Berle's hint that Americans did not have a common interest, friendship, and understanding with Britain.) Additionally nettled by the British practice of detaining American vessels at Gibraltar in 1940, Berle admonished Lothian that "instances of this sort gave rise to the feeling that the British government presumed on our friendship, and sacrificed our legitimate interests." He blamed the commercial sections of His Majesty's Government for attempting to create a closed European trading area—"another illustration of the classic fact that in war each side promptly takes over the worst qualities of its opponent." In early 1940, a joint British-French mission was sent to Washington to soothe America's bruised feelings: Berle considered the French representative "first-rate" but the man from London was "one of these fat, pudgy, ever so slow voiced Englishmen, with rapt expression and a soft tone and an air of injured innocence. . . . He began by pulling out the *vox humana* stop and saying Britain was fighting for her life, which he remembered all day and all night, and every night. This is interesting, but not relevant to most of the problems. . . . He made a distinctly unfavorable impression."[5]

Because he had drafted and delivered the American protests against British contraband control, Berle knew that the British Embassy was "gunning for my scalp." That was true, and in March 1940, the Foreign Office thought it had it. An officer in the Ministry of Information exulted with the news that Berle, who "infused into the Notes of the U.S. Government as much acerbity as he could induce the Secretary of State to accept," had "thrown off the mask" and resigned from the State Department to join the new German-American Trade Corporation! "His departure is a great relief to us," the official wrote; "Now . . . we may look for milder phraseology, if not a more accommodating attitude on our measures." Alas, a week later the official confessed that he was mistaken: "The person referred to was BERT HUNT, Assistant Legal Adviser, and not ADOLF BERLE. Therefore you can put my original note in the waste paper basket."[6]

The comedy of errors had a serious point: "During the winter of 1939–40, . . . relations between HMG and the State Department became particularly strained, largely because of British economic warfare." According to a definitive British study of British-American relations in this period, "most of the Administration found Britain's policy exasperating to some degree. However, there was a widespread feeling that State had lost its sense of proportion." Hull himself lamented departmental divisions over the British blockade in which twisters of the British lion's tail got it to roar. Bullitt accused "Little Adolf" of showing off to the British "what a good note writer he was." Henry Morgenthau needlessly flattered Berle as he darkly whispered that Berle was the architect of neutrality—"He's the final word and the whole policy is in his hands." When Welles and Moffat toured European capitals as a show of America's neutrality, Bullitt sniped that Welles had "sold the President on the trip by saying that it would make a hit with the ladies' peace societies."[7]*

The Americans correctly saw much of the problem between capitals as rooted in London's patronizing of Washington as a recalcitrant Dominion, one observer in the Foreign Office commenting, "it is a fact—of which most people are unaware—that Americans are the most difficult people on earth to deal with. That is very likely due to their political system." It was "no good expecting logical reactions from a nation like the United States." Such condescension was not shared by all Britons, but nearly all of them considered Berle to be evil incarnate.

Much of London's view of Berle stemmed from intelligence reports drafted by a young philosopher stationed in the British Embassy in Washington, Isaiah Berlin. His dispatches were important "for their contribution to the shaping of British official thinking in wartime" and it is not wrong to say that Berlin detested Berle:

> I should say about Berle that he is a very clever man with a very torturous mind, whose early academic success went to his head for good and all. He is a queer combination with atypical German passion (he is only half German in fact—through his father) for the most ingenious methods of doing things. . . . At the same time he hates capitalism, imperialism, liberalism, and the entire heritage of the 19th century, and has a nostalgia for pre-industrial civilisation and the Middle Ages . . . with the result that he has a horror of cartels and corporations. A pupil of Brandeis, he hates all forms of "bigness" in private hands, and inclines towards a sort of R. Catholic ideal of small owners under general State control (which in his case replaces the church). . . . He is very vain, likes elaborately constructed intellectual patterns which he weaves ingeniously, and falls easily for the flattery of foreigners for whose intellect he has respect. He likes to think of himself as half dreamer, half *éminence grise,* a Holstein due one day to become modern Talleyrand, fighting, however, always for the

---

*British intelligence on Americans was often hilariously wrong. Prior to the war it called William Bullitt "unscrupulous" and "no friend of Great Britain." Yet in the winter of 1939–1940, Britain had no better friend than Bullitt.[8]

highest good but inevitably misunderstood. . . . He is in fact a megalo-
maniac, who has to be humored.

At best this description is a partial truth. Perhaps it was inspired by Berle's
cocktail party chatter, which could boomerang on him, perhaps partly by
Berle's published essays and speeches; but it certainly was different from
Escott Reid's sympathetic dispatches to Ottawa! Unfortunately, London
did not have time to discern fact from impression and Berlin's caricature
helps explain why London believed that Berle was converting to Catholicism and helped spread that tale in Washington.[9]

Felix Frankfurter, to be sure, adored Berlin's "usual whimsical and
wise comments on the universe"; we can only wonder how Frankfurter influenced Berlin on Berle and thereby influenced British-American diplomacy. After America's entry into the war, Berlin noted that Berle showed
Whitehall a new face. "The British Empire *used to be* for him the symbol
of all he hated—industrialism, imperialist exploitation, 19th century liberalism, an obstacle to a united Christian Europe, etc., and in 1940–41 he
believed that it was disintegrating and a good thing too, and wished to speed
it on its way," Berlin wrote. "He now believes that it will probably survive
and remain quite strong and, being *a complete opportunist,* wishes to get
on terms with it and has, therefore, been *unusually civil* to its representatives. He is, so far as is known, prepared to co-operate with us on quite
sensible lines provided that we curb our imperialist greed and offer him
support against the excessive demands by American big business which hates
Berle and is hated by him in return." The British did not know what to
make of a pleasant Berle. In a February 1942 speech in Iowa, Berle unexpectedly praised London: "It is to the everlasting credit of Great Britain
that when in 1939 Hitler attacked Poland, she, with her ally France, refused
to stand idly by." Had Isaiah Berlin relied on his own senses, his characterization of Berle might have read like that of a British businessman: "In
speaking of Anglo-American collaboration he said that the time was past
for words and had come for deeds. Both the U.K. and the U.S.A. wanted
definite things and we should in his opinion each state our requirements."
This Berle was hardly odious; he was gracious but firmly direct while expecting the British to reciprocate with candor.[10]

Felix Frankfurter once wrote in his diary, "There is not one iota of
doubt that Berle is almost pathologically anti-British and anti-Russian, and
his anti-Semitism is thrown in, as it were, for good measure, though probably derived through certain personal hostilities and jealousies."

Beyond a doubt Berle was hostile to British and Soviet interests. But,
not even a Berle-hater like Frankfurter could reduce Berle to the level of a
Jew-hater. The accusation tells us something about the accuser. Frankfurter
"was a genuine Anglomaniac," Isaiah Berlin wrote many years later. "The
English, whatever he thought of their public policies, individually they could

do little wrong in his eyes." He possessed a "touching and enjoyable Anglomania—the childlike passion for England, English institutions, Englishmen—for all that was sane, refined, not shoddy, civilised, moderate, peaceful, the opposite of brutal, decent—for the liberal and constitutional traditions that before 1914 were so dear to the hearts and imaginations especially to those brought up in eastern and central Europe, more particularly to members of oppressed minorities, . . . for all that ensured the dignity and liberty of human beings." His Anglophilia, which probably had its origins in Frankfurter's youth, was given support by the 1918 Balfour Declaration's recognition of Zionist aspirations for a Jewish homeland in Palestine, and received its greatest confirmation when Frankfurter went to Oxford for a sabbatical year in 1934—"perhaps the happiest year of his life," Berle accurately observed. In 1939 Frankfurter went to the Supreme Court and became an ardent lobbyist for British interests because Americans just did not appreciate "the notion of the so-called British Empire, not as an exploiting force but as scattered members throughout the world of a cohesive whole expressing and making possible a democratic society"; in Berle's words, "to one steeped in English folklore there is nothing unusual about finding a judge in active political life."[11]

Berle's Anglophobia should neither surprise nor appall us. He did not see the war as one to preserve the British Empire; it was for a world free from hegemonies. Much of the American sloganeering that came out of this period had anti-British connotations. Henry Luce's "American Century," Henry Wallace's "People's Century," and Wendell Willkie's "One World" all carried liberal or nationalistic suggestions that the postwar world had no place for the old British Empire. To Amereicans like Berle, Britain represented "an imperialist system which had done great things in its time but seems now to be merely in the nature of a preparation for something else." A less formal American empire would succeed it. American liberals and nationalists, the British observed, "see the world as a vast market for the American producer, industrialist and trader. They are believers in the American Century, energetic technicians and businessmen filled with romantic, equally self-confident, economic imperialism, eager to convert the world to the American pattern." American anti-imperialism, warned British officials in Washington, was "subtly anti-British." Churchill visited Washington in 1942 to cement the alliance against the Axis with the Declaration of the United Nations, but he rubbed some Americans the wrong way when he presumed to speak for the Commonwealth as well as the empire. "I was quite shocked by the degree of anti-British feeling I found in Washington," Moffat noted, following one of his frequent visits from Ottawa. Americans were alienated by London's "chronic tactlessness." Politely but firmly Berle told the British to understand that a "small group of Americans who are thoroughly saturated with British thought were [sic] the worst possible guide to American thinking as a whole." In other words,

London should dismiss both the Anglophobic Colonel McCormick of the *Chicago Tribune* and Felix Frankfurter as reflecting accurately American public opinion.[12]

A major region of conflict between the old and the new empires was the Americas. Aside from colonies such as British Honduras in Central America and Guyana on the north coast of South America, and several Caribbean islands, the British political presence to the south was insignificant. But British investments and trade were substantial nearly everywhere. The British viewed the Good Neighbor Policy as a thinly disguised invasion of their western hemisphere markets; American talk of hemispheric cooperation was economic imperialism. Berle conceded that American ambitions were ineluctably imperial, but at least Washington's imperialism respected national self-determination. Thus, when the British in early 1942 proposed coups to replace neutralist governments in Argentina and Chile, Roosevelt indignantly vetoed the scheme. A British diplomat visited "the redoubtable Berle" in May to sound him our about hemispheric policy (and found Berle, "rather contrary to my expectations, according to all previous information, was both very pleasant and encouraging"). Berle assured his visitor that the United States had no design for exclusivity in Latin American markets. But the British Ministry of Economic Warfare insisted that American trade expansion formed a pattern of American "aggression" against British interests south of the Rio Grande. Over a "most friendly" lunch, Berle reassured British officials "that American war policy in Latin America was not intended to cramp [London's] legitimate trade interests." Berle further dumbfounded them on three different occasions by mollifying British fears that Americans intended to drive them out of the Latin American trade.[13]

"The present war is definitely a 'people's war,'" Berle wrote. "I think if I were an Englishman, after realistically adding up the factors I should take the view that Britain's position as a world power no longer depended upon her control of the empire, [but] . . . on her moral and intellectual ability to bring about common action among a great number of nations. . . . In this respect her position is analogous to the position held by the United States among the nations of the Western Hemisphere." He was disturbed by London's quest for postwar understandings in Europe which gave it preeminence in the Mediterranean and a clear path to its eastern empire. If only the British took heart from the realization that the world was too big to be policed by one, two, or three powers. A world organization and international law, not the United States, would have to supplant the British Empire. "This country never was an empire," he told British official Richard Law, "and is quite unable to understand why anyone else should be attached to the idea. [It does] understand the general outline of the British Commonwealth and thinks it is a magnificent and civilized development."[14]

While such talk was meant to reassure the British, it only disturbed true imperialists. Nonetheless, the British in 1943 invited Berle to London. But

Hull—in a truculently insecure mood—found excuses to keep Berle home and prevent him from representing the State Department abroad. When Law visited Washington in June, he discussed affairs of state with Berle for two hours. What did Berle think of a British "Good Neighbor" Policy for Europe, Law asked? Berle confessed that Law "had touched me on a sympathetic point, because it seemed to me that at bottom the Good Neighbor policy was the only safe policy to follow." Did the United States contemplate the possible exclusion of British interests from South America, Law asked? Berle said that he "could see no problem there at all. Our policy had never been exclusive, and was not now." He reminded Law that the United States in 1940 could have taken British investments in Argentina as security or part payment for loans to Britain, but the State Department vetoed the idea because it did not want to cripple British trade.[15]

Berle was at pains to distance himself from the "baroque" Anglophobic notions of Henry Luce's "American Century." "While I am no great friend of imperialism, British or otherwise, I think people ought to be pretty cautious before they start hammering away at the British Empire for the fun of it," he wrote. "One of things I am afraid of is that this anti-British movement masks a kind of trend towards imperialism in this country." An American imitation of British imperialism would justify both. Thus, during a May 1943 luncheon hosted by Churchill at the British Embassy and attended by a half dozen high-ranking Americans (not Berle), the prime minister elaborated upon his vision of a postwar Europe divided into spheres of influence in which the United States might share with Britain and France the task of policing the peace. Several months later Berle responded in a speech that it was "absurd" that the United States should engage in military adventures abroad or intervene in other peoples' affairs. He assailed Churchill by name for quoting Edmund Burke to the effect that the idealist is always the enemy of the statesman: "The dreamer will always be ahead of the diplomat." At a conference of Latin Americans in New York, Berle called for a global "Good Neighbor" Policy—which inspired a British foreign officer to comment curiously that Berle was "always an intellectual chameleon."[16]

London still depicted Berle's concept of a global Good Neighbor Policy as American "economic aggression," an endeavor to muscle in on Britain's world trade. Unimpressed by his idealistic baggage of political self-determination for weaker nations, some Britons wanted a quid pro quo—an American sphere of influence in Latin America for recognized British spheres elsewhere. London could not understand Washington's opposition to spheres of influence when Moscow eagerly sought its eastern sphere.

The British-Soviet accord, conceding Moscow's 1941 conquest of the Baltic states, boggled minds in Washington. The old anti-Communist Churchill, partly out of an unreasonable fear that Russia would conclude a separate peace with Germany and partly in quest of understandings that preserved the British Empire and its other global economic interests, sent Foreign Minister Anthony Eden to Moscow to reassure the Soviets of London's military support and to endorse their territorial ambitions. Eden sought commitments from Stalin upholding the principles of the Atlantic Charter, the eventual disarmament of Germany, and the creation of Eastern European confederations. To Berle the last point amounted to British betrayal of the Baltic states. Washington had refused to make any postwar commitments, but Berle realistically knew that "the smaller countries in Eastern Europe cannot exist as isolated units. They will be dominated [militarily] by someone." If Berle could be certain that absorption of the Baltic states and a sphere of influence on its borders would satisfy the Soviets, he could accept an abridgement of Atlantic Charter principles. Besides, a spheres of influence policy would preserve United States interests in the Americas. Although he knew that the Soviets exported espionage and encouraged revolution in the Americas, he hoped that wartime cooperation would assuage Soviet paranoia and discourage its global designs. "Experience in the present war ought to prove to the U.S.S.R. that the idea that all parts of the world are at war with her is so much rot," he wrote. If the Soviets could cease to be revolutionaries, then spheres of influence might contribute to the peace of the world.[17]

The Anglo-Soviet understanding divided the State Department between those for it and those against it. Roosevelt told Welles that any endorsement of an Anglo-Russian territorial understanding "would mean that I tear up the Atlantic Charter before the ink is dry on it. I will not do that." Reaffirming the charter's commitment to national self-determination, Roosevelt implicitly rebuked Churchill's contention that "the principles of the Atlantic Charter ought not to be construed so as to deny Russia the frontiers which she occupied when Germany attacked her." Churchill wanted Stalin to keep the profits of his pact with Hitler. The politics of war dumbfounded Americans. As one State Department man put it, "it was curious to see the alliance between the old British Tories on the one hand and the pro-Russian groups on the other."[18]

Pondering the triangular dilemma, Berle wondered if economic hegemonies would satisfy Churchill's quest for confederations in Eastern Europe, Stalin's quest for friendly frontiers, and Roosevelt's quest for national self-determination. Although Churchill declared at Quebec that he would not be a party to setting up left-wing governments all over Europe, Berle made the point in State Department conferences that British policy gave the West "nothing to do east of the Adriatic." Moreover, satisfying Stalin in the Baltic put the United States in "a dangerous position, both morally and realistically, and I may add, in terms of American politics." Berle wanted to avoid a "Baltic Munich" and Welles attacked the British position as "extraordinarily stupid [and] indefensible from every moral standpoint." Not only had the British abandoned three million people in the Baltic states, but they probably encouraged additional Soviet territorial demands in Eastern Europe. Washington wanted no part of any proposed Anglo-Soviet Pact, but it seemed to Berle that Churchill and Stalin determined events which Roosevelt accepted fait accompli; fatigued and exasperated by his struggle to maintain the self-determination of the Baltic states, Berle wrote, "if I have contributed anything to history I should have difficulty in knowing what it is."[19]

He was marked as anti-Soviet and "not progressive" during the war years because he reminded Americans that our Great Soviet Allies were Hitler's former allies. In September, a *PM* story by I. F. Stone accused State Department and War Production Board officials of blocking shipments of aviation fuel and explosives to the Soviet Union—Berle heading the list of "the men to blame." Few officials connected with the State Department or the Petroleum Administration escaped blame—not even the "much more progressive" Dean Acheson. Berle branded the story as "false and misleading in every material respect" because the United States at the time in question barely had had enough aviation fuel for itself and since then had filled Russia's requirements. "A great many of us have no interest whatever in introducing Communism into the United States," Berle wrote. "But that does not blind any of us to the fact that Soviet Russia has made, and is making, the greatest contribution thus far to beating the Axis." It made no sense to hinder the Russians' war effort. He had wanted shipments of supplies sent to the Russians "before, instead of after the attack." "The Russians are keeping up the agitation for a second front," he noted in July. "I think they are right—and do not know the military considerations which have prevented its being established already." Yet Harold Ickes, head of the Petroleum Administration, and blessed by I. F. Stone as "outstandingly friendly to the Soviets," told the Soviet ambassador that Berle had prevented the acquisition by Russia of refining machinery "*before Russia found herself at war.*" Indeed, Berle had opposed shipments to the Soviets at a time when they "opposed by all possible means our own rearmament."[20]

"We are fighting really an anti-imperialistic war," Berle reaffirmed in late 1942. "This cannot merely serve Russian imperialist interests." After the war a few friends such as David E. Lilienthal recalled that Berle had dared to talk about "Soviet imperialism" long before it became fashionable. Into 1943 he pushed for an understanding with the Russians before American troops landed on the Continent, although he knew that diplomatic understandings upholding the Atlantic Charter would be impotent against the Red Army. Moreover, Berle had to be careful not to bring down upon his head a torrent of accusations that he sought to disrupt the Allied war effort with anti-Soviet talk. In a clever, well-publicized speech to the Reading Rotary Club in April, he declared that there would be no *cordon sanitaire* following the war because buffer states were impractical in the air age and unprincipled in a world of liberalized trade—the British noting, "Berle went out of his way to condemn various views which have been not without cause commonly attributed to him." In one stroke he aligned himself with friends of the Soviets and against Churchill's spheres of influence policies. In the words of *The New York Times'* influential columnist Anne O'Hare McCormick, "What is needed, Mr. Berle intimated, is a new conception of the relations between nations, a conception that supersedes Russia's fear that the western border States . . . will be used against her by others, and that substitutes a limited but less illusory independence for the trembling insecurity of little nations."[21]

Without any U.S. understanding with the Soviets, Berle forecast that at the close of the war the Soviets could dominate the Eurasian continent— although "a capability does not by any means imply the will to do this." He saw evidence of the spread of Soviet influence as far away as Norway, Spain, and France, in addition to its likely dominance over Eastern Europe: "The whole of this very vast machinery is more or less protected by her agreements with Britain." He reminded others of Soviet operations in the western hemisphere and the vulnerability of a corrupt Cuba. American security needed European stability (not "a mere alliance with the British Empire"), a worldwide liberal trade policy ("hemispheric exclusion is not required and probably not desirable, . . . provided at the same time the policy of hemispheric solidarity is continuously stressed"), and a rising standard of living in the Soviet Union that made it dependent upon trade with Western Europe and deterred the Europeans from flooding the United States with their cheaper goods ("while we like to have foreign markets, we dislike to import").[22]

Berle's sober definition of American interests brought Drew Pearson's accusations that a "reactionary State department" sought to disrupt the Grand Alliance by restoring the *cordon sanitaire*. Berle hit back: "Mr. Pearson has been characterized by the President as a chronic liar. [This article] merely lives up to his settled reputation." The State Department was annoyed and disgusted by the absurd stories that it sought buffer states in Eastern Europe. In early 1944 the State Department sent intelligence operatives into Bulgaria and Hungary when it received hints that those two Nazi satellites sought to change sides. Although it expected Soviet objections to such an adventure, it was the British who complained. To Berle this was additional evidence that the British Empire had acceded to the creation of a Soviet empire. American liberalism at the end of the war would confront something more dangerous than the British Empire.[23]

THE RIDDLE OF THE STATE DEPARTMENT

"The Secretary was a thoroughly angry man," Berle noted on the evening of January 23, 1942. Berle had been dining with a Canadian diplomat when Cordell Hull called: "He was almost heart-broken, and I left the dinner table and went forthwith to his apartment." Hull had just heard a radio broadcast describing the text of a new compromise proposal submitted by Under Secretary of State Sumner Welles to delegates from American republics at a Rio de Janeiro conference. News commentators described the resolution as *recommending* that the Republics break relations with the Axis, instead of Hull's demand *requiring* a rupture of diplomatic relations; Hull concluded that Welles had undercut him. When Berle arrived at his apartment, Hull was vowing "that a lot of things were going to change." They already had.

Berle agreed that the revised resolution was "disastrous" because "our moral leadership at the conference has been lost." The fabric of Pan American collective security woven at the Lima and Havana conferences would be torn when Argentina and possibly other countries chose to maintain relations with our enemies and belligerent hemispheric countries could not demand "cooperation." Argentine ships plied the Atlantic with trade that fueled the Nazi war effort because Buenos Aires disdained that American system's "recommendation." It demonstrated how fragile was the New Deal's American system.

Hull phoned Welles on the White House's wires and, according to Berle, there ensued a "violent conversation" in which the secretary scolded the under secretary for "giving away the whole thing"—thereby suffering "a terrific diplomatic beating, with incalculable loss to our diplomatic position." Welles attempted to explain his side to Hull, and Roosevelt was called to the phone; the president listened to both men and was inclined "to let well enough alone." Hull wasn't. He put in another call to Rio to get Ambassador Jefferson Caffery's judgment that the nations supporting the original resolution felt abandoned by Welles' apparent turnabout.

Berle was dismayed. He left Hull's apartment with Welles' assistant, Larry Duggan, and went "to get a stiff drink, which represented my sole remaining idea of a tangible approach to the situation." It sounded to him as though Welles, "one of my best friends," indeed had blundered in softening Hull's resolution. Listening to Hull's end of these conversations, Berle "felt that several careers were ending that night—quite likely including my own. . . . For it is obvious that now there is a breach between the Secretary and Sumner which will never be healed—though the Secretary will keep it below hatches to some extent. Life in this Department under those circumstances will be about as difficult as anything I can think of."[1]

But it had long been difficult. Through his direct contact with Welles, the president encouraged Washington gossip that the under secretary was more important than the secretary. Roosevelt saw nothing wrong in circumventing Hull. As assistant secretary of the Navy under Wilson, Roosevelt had gone around Secretary Josephus Daniels with assorted initiatives. Like Daniels, Hull was patient, self-effacing, and loyal. He did not mind if he read everywhere that the president made foreign policy, but it galled him to read that Welles was its chief instrument. Almost two years before the Rio blowup Berle had observed that "the press stories about Welles having a more intimate contact in the White House than the Secretary have not been helpful."[2]

Berle thought of himself as loyal to Hull. He admired Welles who was both a colleague and a drinking buddy—one of the few people in Washington who could match Berle for intellectual arrogance. Welles properly deferred to Hull, but Hull was very different from Welles and Berle. He was a pure politician, having spent decades laboring in the lower House of Congress and for the Democratic National Committee. At seventy he was bound to Roosevelt through codes of loyalty and duty. However, in the mountains of Tennessee from which Hull sprang, men were also bound by codes that included feuding. He knew Welles' weakness—that when Welles worked hard and was fatigued, he tended to drink in excess. That was forgivable in Washington, if the toper did not make a spectacle of himself. Roosevelt and Hull were moralists, but they were men with vices too who could overlook those of their loyalists. The greatest sins could be forgiven or ignored if they remained discreetly in the closet. However, Hull was not above exploiting an adversary's indiscretions—and one of Welles' mistakes surprised even him.

Welles' downfall began when Speaker of the House William Bankhead died on September 15, 1940, and Roosevelt decreed that the entire cabinet ought to go to his funeral in Alabama. At lunch with Berle that day Welles was "furious" because Hull wanted Welles to go in his place. Hull had served with Bankhead in the House for many years, but for some reason he pulled rank on Welles. Welles would spend two days on trains: "Going to funerals just for the ride is not Sumner's idea of sport," Berle commented. The first night on the train Welles retired to his sleeping car compartment, drank heavily, and began summoning porters. Several answered his calls to find the statesman drunk and propositioning them. All refused his advances, but not all remained quiet about it.

It became a gossip item. Less than four months later presidential assistant "Pa" Watson directed J. Edgar Hoover to have the FBI make a thorough but discreet inquiry. Within a month two special agents confirmed the worst. Roosevelt assigned a bodyguard to Welles to protect him from further indiscretions and further embarrassment, but he did not lose trust in his under secretary. Still, Roosevelt could not protect Welles from his enemies—especially former Ambassador to France William Bullitt who wanted Welles', or Hull's, job. In Paris Bullitt had sometimes run his own foreign policy, but the arrival of the Nazis brought a presidential order to return to Washington pending reassignment. Soon he picked up the story of Welles' homosexual escapade and before Roosevelt had the FBI report Bullitt had an affidavit from one of the porters. In April 1941, he took it to Roosevelt who insisted that no harm had been done or would be done. Nevertheless, Bullitt warned the president that he would accept no other diplomatic assignment while Welles was in the Department. And then he began to gossip with, among others, veteran gossip Harold Ickes.[3]

Ickes too did not like Welles and he had heard "those stories about Welles' personal habits." He could not restrain himself when Rexford Tugwell visited him in June. "His personal conduct has been such that he could be blackmailed by a foreign government," exclaimed Ickes, who knew something about blackmail. Tugwell was incredulous: "Welles seemed too stiff and proper, if nothing else, for such stories to be true," Tugwell thought. Now the story went beyond Bullitt and Ickes; by the time Bullitt reached Henry Wallace with the Welles story in March 1942, the vice-president had already heard it the day before from a *New York Times* reporter! Breckinridge Long too heard the story from Welles himself who labeled it a malicious lie invented by Bullitt. Thus, when Long heard it again from Arthur Krock of the *Times,* he dismissed it as "malicious, improbable and incredible." But Hull heard it from a "trustworthy, accurate and informed" source and the secretary was "very much inclined to believe it"; he eagerly cast about for evidence to support the gossip. However, discretion was still in order because the story was known to the White House and its suppression could involve the president in scandal. Hull went to J. Edgar Hoover on October 24 and demanded to see the FBI report on Welles; Hoover refused to let him see it without presidential approval.[4]

If Berle knew about it he was not even telling his diary. (Those who told their diary usually did so obliquely; it was not something a gentleman put in writing; nor did one put down information that would help the enemy if the diary fell into wrong hands. During the war Berle kept many things from his diary, mostly matters having to do with military operations.) But Berle probably did not wish to discuss it because of his friendship with Welles and his awareness that Welles could be the victim of blackmail if his diary fell into enemy hands. But Department turmoil over the "lurid story," as Hull put it, worried Berle. Following the Department reorganization of early 1941, few people expected the frail Hull to remain for much longer. Speculation concerning a successor inevitably centered on Welles, whom State Department insiders now knew was vulnerable. On the other hand, Bullitt's candidacy was not helped by his performance in the Welles matter. Much as Pierrepont Moffat too respected Berle's talents and shared his aristocratic liberal views, he thought it unlikely Berle would replace Hull: "Very few people can work with Adolf Berle and most of them accuse him of playing a personal game"; Frankfurter's pet, Acheson, "too works as an individual and turns over to other agencies problems that essentially belong to the State Department." The only logical choice for secretary of state in the age of Roosevelt was Cordell Hull.

Hull remained as secretary and continued to be, in Long's words, "a little put out by the intimate association of Welles and the Chief." Hull's testiness showed more and more. He resented so many people—Welles,

Berle, Acheson, Ickes, Churchill, Wallace, etc. The brooding atmosphere of the Department was oppressive; "the top six men are pulling in six different directions," Moffat said. Good men left the government, a salary of $9,000 per year being insufficient for most of them. Berle, living on his wife's legacy, compared himself to the Abbé Sieyes, "who was asked what he did during the French Revolution, and answered: 'I have survived.'"[5]

But surviving Hull was not easy. Everybody wanted to run foreign policy, Hull once groused to Berle; "They all come at me with knives and hatchets." Berle obsequiously tried to cheer Hull a week after Pearl Harbor with a six-page letter effusively celebrating his "wise and statesmanlike" leadership in dealing with Japan through 1940–1941 for which "the country owes you individually a very great debt of gratitude." Disheartened and more estranged from Roosevelt than ever, Hull suspected that Roosevelt wanted to "sacrifice" him. In January 1942, he began to clean out his desk in anticipation of the ultimate ignominious blow. Following the Rio conference, when Roosevelt took Welles' side, Berle noted that Hull "was nervously and spiritually torn to pieces, to a point where his doctor kept him in bed." Hull returned within a few days and began a Department meeting with an old Tennessee story about "a darky" who claimed to be the best mule trainer in the country but kept being thrown, picking himself up and saying, "Boys, you see how it is done. When it looks as though you were going to be thrown, you just get off." Health permitting, Hull was determined to outlast Welles and all his detractors.[6]

"These wars within wars!" Long expostulated. "They may ruin us yet." It was bad enough that State fought for turf against Morgenthau's Treasury Department and Wallace's Board of Economic Warfare without its secretaries fighting among themselves. Egos blossomed everywhere. Welles endeavored to match Wallace's "Century of the Common Man" speech with a great progressive statement of his own, but, Berle observed, "he committed the fatal mistake of speaking as though he were the Secretary of State, when there is alive a very active Secretary of State in the immediate vicinity." Hull too tried his hand at a great speech, however much he "distrust[ed] dramatics"; Berle found it "was far more practical than Welles' speech" because it appealed to a more conservative audience. Tired and irritated, Hull remained tenacious—a feudist; Welles, "my fairy," Hull jocularly called him, would leave before he did. Hamilton Fish Armstrong told Hull "that at a time when the greatest country in the world is engaged in the greatest war in the history of the world, it is too awful to have the head of the premier Department of the Government suspect disloyalty on the part of his subordinates." Hull responded that he believed "in giving people enough rope to hang themselves." In early 1943 the Department headed for an unknown climax. An intradepartmental battle broke out over who should control postwar policy—the Frankfurter boys Feis and Acheson making a bid for power against Berle and Leo Pasvolsky. "Things naturally go at 6's and 7's," Berle commented. "But there is not much to be done about it." Hull kept aloof, sitting in February to have his portrait painted and muttering to Long that they would have to keep an eye on "the radical boys" working for Wallace—"the post-war spreaders of peace, plenty, and pulchritude," Long called them. Ever the loner, Berle observed, "this bodes no good for anybody concerned, and least of all for me."[7]

Four different State Departments really operated under Hull, Welles, Berle, and Acheson, Bullitt told Wallace—and Harry Hopkins really ran FDR's foreign policy; he may have been correct. However, if Bullitt had had his way, he would fire all but Hull. Deciding to try to get his way, Bullitt went to Republican Senator Ralph Owen Brewster of Maine with his evidence on Welles; Brewster went to Hoover demanding to see what the FBI had. Of course, Hoover refused Brewster, but acknowledged the existence of a Welles file. So Brewster went to Hull and asked why Welles remained on the job; Hull pointed to the White House. Brewster went to the Justice Department and threatened Attorney General Biddle with a Senate investigation. Biddle informed Roosevelt. The White House could no longer ignore the fact that Welles' indiscretion was known to much of Washington, even if it never appeared in the newspapers. When Long told Welles that the Republicans had the story, Welles assailed it as a pack of lies which he would not dignify. Welles' friends mobilized to save him by planting stories in *The New York Times* that portrayed Welles as a victim of a crotchety Hull and others intent upon defaming a great progressive and internationalist. But Department insiders knew why that would backfire: not even loyalty and a sense of duty, or the support of United Front partisans, could save Welles from his vulnerability to unspeakable rumor and blackmail. Finally, in August, Roosevelt offered Welles a roving ambassadorship and a special mission to Moscow. Welles refused it all, emptied his desk, and took off for his summer home in Bar Harbor, Maine. It had taken three years for the 1940 incident to seal his fate. On September 26 the White House announced Welles' departure due to his wife's poor health. The real reason awaited another age.[8]

Welles' resignation created quite a stir. Newspaper columnists divided according to their loyalties—Arthur Krock using Hull's argument that Welles "had become, and would remain a disorganizing force" and Drew Pearson depicting Welles as the State Department's "liberal pillar" victimized by a bitter and vindictive Hull. Pearson also suggested that Welles had been Red-baited because he had recently met with Communist chieftain Earl Browder and had made other overtures to the Russians. It was true that Berle and others in the Department were peeved by Welles' sudden courting of Russophiles. But, as Long declared elliptically, Welles "knew the real reason" for his departure.

Ironically, Welles' departure came while Hull was in Quebec and it made Berle acting secretary of state for two days. Berle had tried to convince

Welles to take the Russian assignment, but Welles insisted that Hull would not like it. On a Sunday morning Berle theatrically "said farewell and left [Welles] in a dusty, sunlit office, in an empty building, finishing as he believed, his stormy but brilliant career." Later, when gossip surfaced that he would follow Welles into retirement, Berle scurried to Long to make sure that his rival knew he had no such intentions. Everyone in the State Department now struggled to be on his best correct behavior.[9]

By the end of September the State Department learned via a radio broadcast that Edward R. Stettinius, Jr., had been appointed under secretary of state. Roosevelt, who had vowed in 1933 not to tie up with 23 Wall Street, J. P. Morgan & Company, did so in 1943 because Stettinius was Harry Hopkins' choice. Stettinius brought in efficiency experts from New York and reorganized the Department in January 1944. "Advisors" became "offices," "desks" became "divisions" and certain egos swelled as rapidly as stationery orders. Cynics wisecracked, "Every desk, a division, every officer, a chief." "The precise purpose of it is unclear and the plan is a sloppy, botched job," Berle thought; "I do not fare too well myself." The hated Acheson obtained a mandate in foreign economic matters and Berle was concerned.

Nevertheless, Berle knew that "events have a way of transcending organization charts." Ever a free-lancer who did not fear to antagonize others with intrusive forays into Latin American or other affairs, Berle was no respecter of Department flow charts. The British hoped that since Berle's job had a "closer definition, he no longer has any excuse for intervening in Latin American affairs." But Welles' departure made Berle the senior man in hemisphere matters and this worried the British. Also, they were unhappy that "Berle has emerged as controller of the *crucial* policies relating to international services," namely commercial aviation and other matters relating to postwar policy. The British ambassador, who would have liked to see Berle expelled from the Department, reported to London that *"Berle thus emerges as in charge of all technical operations in the international field. [He has been] confirmed in his control of a number of divisions which are likely to assume increasing importance in the near future."*[10]

The Welles affair may have had portentous consequences for Berle and American foreign policy. It eliminated a strong veteran of foreign policy committed to advancing the American empire, distrustful of the British Empire, and (despite his wartime reputation) suspicious of the emerging Soviet empire. It advanced the influence of Harry Hopkins—who put his man Stettinius into the State Department—and Acheson, who was there to comfort the weak Stettinius when he was no match for the machinations of Berle and others. Unlike FDR, they were Anglophiles prepared to defer to London's leadership and experience in the world. Paradoxically, Roosevelt had a worldview more closely resembling that of Hull, Welles, and Berle.

For the time being Berle remained, his power enhanced. Welles' departure might have aided that ambition by making Berle the most experienced hand in the Department's upper echelons. And the emergence of the Anglophiles made his presence all the more important. Who else better understood the global significance of the Good Neighbor Policy or even cared about Latin America? Who else saw the looming threat of the Soviets and the expedience of the British imperialists? He hungered to fulfill his "destiny," to help write the peace of the world following this war.

AN AMERICAN LIBERAL AND THE JEWS

In February 1941, the left-wing New York newspaper *PM* ran a series on the State Department. As its publisher, Ralph Ingersoll, told Felix Frankfurter, "It was you who inspired the series—or rather, you set off the fuse to a charge that had been building up." The charge was that the State Department was isolationist at a time when Britain stood alone against the Nazis and their Soviet allies. Only the State Department was isolationist, Ingersoll and Frankfurter carefully placing Franklin Roosevelt above criticism. Ingersoll assigned two young reporters from his foreign news department to the task of investigating State's leadership. In episode six of the series they tackled Assistant Secretary Adolf A. Berle. "He has almost more enemies than any man in the Government," they assured *PM*'s readers in the second paragraph. "Some of them charge that he's the 'trickiest' person they've ever known, that he employs unsavory characters in other government departments as spies, that he is the 'most dangerous man' in the Government. A common charge is that he is anti-Semitic."

To their credit, the reporters found Berle's reputation more infamous than the man. If Berle had "so many supreme ambitions" as legend had it, "he'd be busier than Superman," they wrote. "We didn't uncover Mr. Berle's espionage system—if it exists—nor can we say definitely that Mr. Berle is or is not anti-Semitic. His manner of speaking of 'wealthy Jewish reactionaries' seemed to confirm the charge, but we know that he has employed Jewish lawyers. We did not find Mr. Berle a particularly sinister figure."[1]

The article outraged Berle's friend Morris Ernst. "When your experts say, in effect, that they cannot make up their minds whether or not a man is an anti-Semite," he told Ingersoll, "newspaper reporting is at its lowest stage. By admitting their doubt or ignorance they smear their subject. This is far worse than any direct verbal assault." Ernst accused the paper of creating an "intentional haze" through which the reader could imagine that Berle was an anti-Semite. An assistant to Ingersoll responded to Ernst that "the responsibility of all *PM* writers is to seek the truth, [and] report it fearlessly." Ingersoll himself ignored Ernst. Berle thanked Ernst for writing

Ingersoll, reminding him about "the famous advice about not fighting with a skunk." The series, Berle thought, "was as nearly libelous as it dared to be."[2]

However, Ingersoll did not ignore at least one letter concerning the series; that was from Felix Frankfurter and it concerned an article on his friend, State Department economic advisor Herbert Feis. Feis was furious and labeled the article about him as "*dirty, smart, sneaky, unreliable, inaccurate, irresponsible* journalism." Frankfurter accordingly screamed at Ingersoll that the Feis article was "ignorant, inaccurate, misinforming and tawdry," although he reserved comment on the rest of the series. Ingersoll conceded that he had had "a very bad report on the way the two youngsters . . . had handled themselves in Washington. And then I got a second piece on Wells [sic] from them which turned my hair because its authors were obviously sitting in judgment of the Under Secretary's belief in democracy and using as evidence the record of his attitude towards Soviet Russia. . . . This piece has not been printed and will not be." Thus, Ingersoll rated Roosevelt's good friend Sumner Welles untouchable, and about Feis he was apologetic—but we may assume that the Berle piece had found its mark. Not mollified, Feis accused Ingersoll of being "perfectly willing to risk anyone else's skin and reputation in order to protect his own." Under that heading, the world still could assume that because *PM*'s reporters could not find evidence to the contrary, Adolf Berle was an anti-Semite.[3]

"The charge of anti-Semitism," Berle wrote, "is so silly that one is ashamed to have to refute it." But he nevertheless endeavored to do so.

> At Harvard, I resigned from my principal club (The Speakers Club) because they declined to admit Jews. On coming to New York, three of us had a tenement top floor together, next to the Henry Street Settlement, and one of them was Hyman Schroeder, a Jew, and one of the finest men I have ever known. When I set up my own office in New York, the first man we hired was Irving Mischkind, and he was a junior partner in the office at the time when I left to come to Washington. I could multiply the list of personal, professional and public relations through several columns of close type.
>
> I do not recall using the phrase "wealthy reactionary Jews," but it is perfectly possible to use it and I might have. For your private information, that phrase could accurately be used as describing the opposition in various foreign countries to a generous policy in taking care of Jewish refugees. I have used similar phrases in dealing with wealthy reactionary groups of other faiths or race, whenever there was a known nucleus of opposition to some humane or progressive measure to hammer at.[4]

The question of how Berle and the State Department felt toward Jews would not go away. Jews and Catholics ranked the State Department along with the local country club as the epitome of discrimination. At a time of when Nazis attacked Jews and synagogues in Germany, some Americans strongly suspected that the State Department did not disapprove. In particular, the evident reluctance of Breckinridge Long to facilitate the entry of refugees was attributed to anti-Semitism. "Direct proof of anti-Semitism in the department is limited," a historian has written, but evidence of nativism and indifference to the plight of Europe's Jews is substantial. As a participant in and as a defender of State Department decision making, Berle could not avoid taint by association.[5]

In fact, Berle opposed all forms of discrimination, preferring to assimilate all groups into American society. In this respect he was not too different from other liberals—even Jewish liberals. Many New Dealers viewed Jerome Frank as a quintessential liberal, but in 1941 he wrote an article for the *Saturday Evening Post* that essentially declared it was no affair of American Jews what happened to their European brethren; besides, Jews in America ought to be Americans first and to Frank, that called for noninvolvement in Europe's wars. Like presidential counsel Sam Rosenman, Frank feared that bringing Jewish refugees to America would convert it to a "World Ghetto."[6]

Many American liberals resisted intervention in Europe, opposed allowing more Jews into America (especially those from Eastern Europe), and hoped that American Jews would assimilate to achieve fairness as Americans rather than as Jews. Berle too subscribed to the concept of an American melting pot. As he told Walter A. White of the National Association for the Advancement of Colored People, "the United States does not recognize discrimination among its citizens, and there is no more reason for having a Bureau of Negro Affairs than there is for having a Bureau of Jewish Affairs, a Bureau of Italian-American Affairs, or a Bureau of Anglo-American Affairs. To adopt the principle would be to fragmentize the United States." If blacks did not deserve special status, then Jews certainly did not. Liberal America did not discriminate and therefore there was no discrimination.

Berle was not a Jew-hater. He was against "fragmentation" and advocated great tolerance of group differences that allowed everyone to share in equality of opportunity. He always advanced the opportunities of young Jewish lawyers. Quite literally, some of his best friends were Jews (Taussig, Ernst, etc.); also, some of his best enemies were Jews (Frankfurter, etc.). Jews neither warranted his affection nor his alienation simply because they were Jews. However, he obtusely could not sympathize with victims of discrimination if they resisted assimilation. Jews had to surrender their identities to the ideology of liberalism. (A Congregationalist did not have to surrender his identity; he already was an American.) Militance or even a strong self-consciousness among racial, religious, or ethnic groups defied his vision of Americanism. As he would eradicate all hatred based upon such differences, so he would eradicate the differences themselves. "I hope that never will Jewish problems be considered apart from American problems and that the element of segregation will never creep into our national thinking," he told Jewish social workers in 1944. The hope defied reality.[7]

His name and his appearance caused Berle to be frequently taken for a Jew, and to this day there are many people, including Jews, who believe he was an assimilated Jew. Until it could get its facts straight, British intelligence described him as Jewish, then "part-Jewish." He was the target of anti-Semitic crank letters. He professed to be wryly amused that "In one day I was listed in a Nazi sheet appearing in Brooklyn as one of the Jewish enemies of the republic working for Mr. Roosevelt; and the same day in another sheet as a leading anti-Semite."

"If I were a Jew myself," Berle wrote in 1939, he would have been a very Americanized one. He might have avoided association with most Jews, preferring those Jews who were, like his friend Charles Taussig, "cultivated, . . . liberated from the usual prehensile quality of Jewish life." He did not like an "aggressive Jew." He was of two minds on the common practice of religious quotas that limited the number of Jews in an organization or institution. Berle saw the function of education as Americanization of Jews. On the one hand, he instinctively resented any discrimination. "On the other hand, a school which does not do this, and becomes predomiantly Jewish, ceases to give the precise service which most Jews want— namely, the education of their children in a society comprising Jews and Gentiles alike, on terms of complete equality. . . . Instead of resisting a percentage limitation I should insist on it, in the hope of avoiding schools which became distinctly Jewish and thereby ceased to serve that function." Thus, Berle would have discriminated against a Jew when he judged it in the interests of other Jews to limit their numbers and their visibility, thereby not inviting Gentile hatred of Jews by Jewish numerical dominance. He once recommended that Mayor La Guardia appoint a certain lawyer to the City Treasurer's Office because "a Gentile or two on that staff would be a good idea."[8]

Again, such thinking was not unusual for New Dealers or even Jewish New Dealers. Protestants who worked with Jews, such as Adlai Stevenson, constantly raised questions as to whether particular Jews had notably Jewish "racial" characteristics, preferring those who did not and as few Jews in an office as possible. Jerome Frank was not only "embarrassed" by the noticeably large number of his coreligionists on his AAA legal staff, but actually reproved Gentile staff members who recommended hiring good lawyers who were also Jews. Among liberals Berle's attitude toward Jews was commonplace and perhaps even comparatively generous.[9]

To his credit, Berle did not believe that the United States had its quota of Jews. "The additional fear that refugees have added to the anti-Semitic feeling in this country is also very much exaggerated," he told a conference of Jewish leaders. At a time when some Jews such as Jerome Frank were fearful that a major influx of their persecuted European coreligionists would fan the flames of domestic anti-Semitism, Berle maintained that "it would be more than unfair to limit the admission of refugees to America because of this particular prejudice." But the Jews of Europe now lacked the freedom of migration. Reports that Polish Jews were being deported to concentration camps moved Berle. "We should register a protest," he pleaded with the cautious Hull. "I see no reason why we should not make our feelings known regarding a policy of seemingly calculated cruelty." He admonished a representative of the Finnish government not to turn over any Jewish refugees in his country to the Germans—"the equivalent in most cases of condemnation to a horrible death." He opposed Breckinridge Long's stringent interpretation of visa regulations, favoring more liberal admission policies. The news that Jews were being exterminated in the camps was "horrible" and he told Frances Perkins that it required one action—"smash the Germans" as soon as possible. Threats of retaliation against Nazis would accomplish little: "Talking Christianity to cobras is not much fun."[10]

Although he and Welles were the State Department officials most sympathetic toward Jews, Berle opened himself to accusations that he was anti-Semitic by endorsing the Department's policy toward Palestine. The Department's "Arabists" opposed a Jewish state there and Berle agreed with them. Yet, was not Berle the son of Adolf Berle, the author of the tract *The World Significance of a Jewish State,* which proclaimed that the concept of a Jewish homeland in Palestine stirred the idealism of Christendom? (Few people knew that his father privately denounced American Zionists like Rabbi Stephen Wise as "political gangsters.") But the elderly Berle's idealism of 1918 seemed only remotely relevant to Middle Eastern problems in the 1940s. Confronting a conundrum involving the militancy of American Zionists, British oil interests, and neutralist Arabs, the State Department argued that American and Zionist interests did not coincide. For that matter, the Department correctly pointed out that in the early 1940s, many—perhaps most—American Jews did not subscribe to Zionist aspirations; indeed, assimilationist Jews accused Zionists of being "fanatic Jewish nationalists" and "Jewish sojourners in America." And among Zionists there was disagreement on a satisfactory American policy.[11]

Early in 1939 a rabbi and Justice Brandeis complained to Berle that the Department prevented Jews from displaying the Star of David flag along with the flags of other nations at the New York World's Fair. Berle explained that the World's Fair Committee decided not to allow the Star of David because it represented no existing state and Palestine was a British mandate. However, Berle patronizingly expressed his "personal feeling" that display of the flag at the fair "would not be a good idea" because it was not in the best interests of Zionists. The Zionists of course did not agree with him and through persistence finally won permission to display the Star of David in the parade that opened the fair. But the issue of Palestine went beyond flags. Roosevelt himself did not think that Zionist pressures in 1939 were significant and did not share State's trepidations that Zionist agitation would incite anti-American feelings among Arabs.[12]

The Department's Near Eastern division was run by Wallace Murray, a man believed to be anti-Semitic, in a manner calculated to enhance American oil interests by currying favor with Arab sheiks. He reported to Berle and Berle agreed with Murray that Roosevelt should curry favor with King Ibn Saud of Saudi Arabia. He also agreed with Murray's evenhanded approach toward Arab and Jewish needs in Palestine, lest anything "be taken as putting us squarely on the Jewish side and against the Arab side—and this at a time when the Arab feeling in the Near East may easily prove crucial." Berle discouraged Roosevelt from sending a friendly message to the American Palestine Committee's dinner out of fear that Arabs would interpret it as an endorsement of its Zionist speaker, Dr. Chaim Weizmann. Berle worried that Zionists might sacrifice American interests in the Near East as interpreted by the State Department.[13]

Zionist concerns were part of America's geopolitical interests. The eastern Mediterranean had been crucial in the First World War and increasingly the matter of oil in the Near East bulked large in Berle's thinking; he feared both a German and a British advantage there. Therefore, although he wished to save the Jews of Europe, he saw "dangers" should they be allowed to find haven in Palestine and generate Arab hostility toward the United States. He shrewdly distinguished among Zionists, moderates being those willing to live with Arabs as opposed to those waging war aginst them. When Princes Feisal and Khalid of Saudi Arabia visited Washington in 1943, Berle greeted them on behalf of the Department. The warmth of his greeting did not endear him to Zionists. A Zionist wrote Berle inquiring directly as to how his attitude toward Zionism differed from that of his father's in 1918. "I am and continually have been interested in the erection of a Zionist organization which, founded upon the Palestine tradition, might keep alive the intellectual and cultural traditions of the Jews," he responded.

> A Zionist state established by force which becomes a symbol of force operation to surrounding millions is not likely to realize the values which my father and I both wish to protect, nor is it likely to have success which most of its protagonists, including Mr. Brandeis, wished for it. A Zionist state based ultimately on consent and good will is likely to be a glorious addition to the spiritual values of the world.

Berle was his father's son. He wished the political and military leaders of Britain and America had the good sense to create a Jewish state and thereby steal the thunder of radical Zionists prepared to fight the British or the Arabs who stood in their way. But the majority of Zionists were coming to believe that a fight for the homeland was inevitable and that Berle's hope was tantamount to opposition to their cause.[14]

The time for American liberals to save Europe's Jews was passing; the time for them to choose a Jewish state was at hand. Sadly, in both instances, the sweet reason which liberals sought was not to be found. Berle appreciated that the Jews would be saved by force, yet wished that the Jewish state would not owe its existence to force. His father's Christian spiritualism endorsed a Zionist state; his father's Christian liberalism did not. In a world at arms idealists with guns would triumph.

A GANGLION OF COMPLEXES

Neither politics nor gossip was adjourned during the war. Washington must have bewildered foreign observers, for it gave them too much information—too much intelligence about developments and personalities—thereby making it difficult to sort truth from partial truth. The wartime expansion of bureaucracy increased the normal political chatter of this great imperial capital. Although unity against the Axis was the watchword, that did not prevent many Democrats and bureaucrats from conspiring against their political or ideological antagonists. At issue sometimes was who was more militantly anti-fascist and the shape of postwar America and the postwar world. No stranger to controversy nor shy about it, Adolf Berle immersed himself in wartime Washington's politics and gossip.

During the war Broadway columnist Walter Winchell took many of his ellipses to Pennsylvania Avenue because its personalities achieved a celebrity status usually reserved for those of the stage or screen. Of course, Washington characters were consciously on stage or before cameras in newsreels around the nation and around the globe. Mixing the news and show business did not await the advent of postwar television. Numerous "one-day stories" on personalities ephemerally dominated the newspapers and entertained a nation hungry for news of the war's progress. Drew Pearson had institutionalized the Washington gossip column during the New Deal, and the war prompted Walter Winchell to go after the Nazis. Both had favorites whose tips colored the Washington scene. Pearson was entrenched as a New Deal columnist with lines to such politically diverse people as Frankfurter, Welles, Ickes, and a multitude of other tipsters. Berle detested Pearson and welcomed the opportunity to feed gossip to Winchell through his former law student and now Democratic party counsel, Ernest Cuneo, Winchell's Washington "legman" (a word Cuneo detested).

Gossip about Berle competed with wartime gossip about all sorts of New Dealers and temporary bureaucrats. After all, Harry Hopkins, the president's sickly former chief of relief, moved into the White House, even married Louise Macy in the White House, and assumed duties that ranged from secretary of commerce to special missions to London and Moscow, thereby earning him the press sobriquet of "assistant president." Vice-

President Henry Wallace took an office that had been "not worth a pitcher of warm spit" and created a formidable bureaucratic empire that included the Board of Economic Warfare (BEW), and made himself a spokesman for the liberal left and "the people's century." Democratic financier Bernard Baruch (who paid for Hopkins' wedding reception) gave unwelcome advice concerning economic stabilization to assembled reporters in his Lafayette Square "office" and achieved durable fame as "the park bench statesman." Clare Boothe Luce, Baruch's former girlfriend and now wife of publisher Henry Luce (who celebrated the war as the fulfillment of "the American century"), took her beauty and talents as an actress to the Congress where she became an instant expert on world affairs ("globaloney"). Leon Henderson, a pugnacious New Dealer, ran the Office of Price Administration (with Baruch's unwanted advice) and brought upon himself the obloquy of a host of newly minted wartime free enterprisers intent upon federal dollars without federal restraints. Jimmie Byrnes, a Southern conservative, went from the Senate to the Supreme Court to chief economic "czar" and competed with Hopkins in the press for FDR's "assistant president" title. Harry Truman, a previously unheralded senator, following a renomination battle against the Missouri Democratic governor, decided that a headline-grabbing investigation of war mobilization waste was the route to reelection in 1946. A host of other Washingtonians also achieved fleeting fame in a tumultuous time by encouraging alliances and antipathies that made better gossip than coherent ideological alignments.

But ideology was in the eye of the contemporary beholder. Subjected to scathing journalistic profiles in *Time* and *The New Yorker* magazines and the left-wing New York newspaper *PM,* Berle's fame made it evident that he had more than his share of enemies—even if many of the stories raised questions in the "when did you stop beating your wife?" category. The German invasion of Russia had swung Washington's liberal politics sharply leftward, leaving a liberal anti-Nazi *and* anti-Communist such as Berle looking conservative and isolationist. In the words of a 1942 book about the State Department, he had failed "to live up to [the] expectations . . . [of] socialistically minded liberals who rejoiced when Berle was appointed to the Department [and] have long since ceased to regard him as a champion."[1]

During the war, British and Soviet sympathizers charged that Berle, not the times, had changed—that he had betrayed the united front against fascism to become an anti-Communist, a Fascist sympathizer, an anti-Semite, an Anglophobe, a Russophobe, a European monarchist, a reactionary, an appeaser, an anti-anti-Fascist, and a secret Catholic convert. Of course, Berle either was none of these things or had been one all along. Even so, shibboleths swirled about Berle because his enemies gossiped well and his outspoken liberalism now made him appear out of sympathy with the war's Grand Alliance with the Soviets.

"These fellows hated you," Berle was told several years after the war. He did not need to be told that he had had enemies in Washington during the war. His enemies frequently gave muddled ideological reasons for their antipathy, but they seldom conspired against him for those reasons. More often than not their hate was personal or based upon their own ambitions for bureaucratic turf. Who were they? Sometimes Henry Wallace hated Berle because the State Department obstructed the Board of Economic Warfare's plans. Sometimes Henry Morgenthau hated Berle because foreign economic policy involved both Treasury and State. Sometimes Harold Ickes hated Berle because it was personal or because the petroleum administrator wanted freedom to make foreign oil policy. A young administrator in the Office of War Information's foreign language division, Alan Cranston (long before he became rich in California real estate and went to the Senate), hated Berle for the "misguided" reason that Berle sought to impose "fascists" upon the leadership of European refugee groups by not forcing them to accept the Communists Cranston favored. Prominent among Berle-haters was the Frankfurter network and its allies. Within the State Department, his principal enemy was fellow assistant secretary of state Dean Acheson, Frankfurter crony and employer of Frankfurter students such as the Hiss brothers, who wrote of Berle many years later, "The fact that we disliked one another is too well known to attempt to disguise. Its causes are irrelevant—and useless to discuss. . . . " Yet the animus animated their "wary coexistence" then and endured the rest of their lives. Acheson's son told how he spurred the writing of his father's memoirs by saying, "If you don't write it, someone else will. Do you want to wait until Adolf Berle does?"[2]

"Two-bathtubs Berle" was not easily liked in the labyrinths of Washington politics. When Norman Davis once complained bitterly about Berle, Pierrepont Moffat, who had learned to be an admirer, conceded that Berle suffered from "too much ego, too much public speaking, and dealing with too many problems." Making it all the more difficult for Berle was the fact that after four years in the State Department, he still free-lanced with a direct and personal access to Roosevelt that could be matched only by Welles. Although his responsibilities—the western hemisphere, financial matters, intelligence matters, the passport office, and other units—were better defined than previously, detractors tended to focus upon his encroachments in other areas. His abrasive personality rubbed many people the wrong way and it did not help his popularity that he had unusual political visibility for an assistant secretary of state. His widespread activities nettled traditionalists: "Is there nothing we can do to rid the Capitol city of A. A. B.?" an irate Charles C. Burlingham asked Frankfurter. An eighty-five-year-old Wall Street lawyer who knew Berle from their patrician collaborations on behalf of La Guardia, Burlingham loathed and feared him.

> He is anti-British and anti-Semitic. . . . But he is as smart as [Harold] Laski and if Father Hull sent a colored messenger over to wake him in the

middle of the night he would write a speech on any subject in fifteen minutes. I am told that . . . a plan was submitted [by him] for investigation
and discrimination among an estimated million aliens. . . . These things
may not be true, but nothing is to be said for A.A.B.; of that I am certain.
. . . He will misuse and abuse [any given power]. He is smart as Satan
but absolutely devoid of common sense. He knows nothing of men and is
a ganglion of complexes. How can we get him out?

Others merely raised the question of how in the first instance Berle came
to Washington. "I distrust Berle," declared Secretary of War Henry L.
Stimson, perhaps reflecting the animus of his one-time protégé, Frankfurter. "I don't know who is responsible for Adolf being in that Department. Is that the Chief [FDR] also?"[3]

Only Roosevelt could explain the presence and power of Adolf Berle.
"He had a curious relationship with Mr. Roosevelt, which I never understood," James P. Warburg commented many years later. The Roosevelt-
Berle relationship baffled many supposedly knowledgeable people. Could
it be explained merely by the fact that Roosevelt found him loyal and useful
for his ideas and his skills as a draftsman? Such reasons explain the professional relationship, but they tell us nothing about how the president felt
personally about him—although that may be relatively unimportant. After
a friendship of more than a decade, it is significant that Berle enjoyed access
to Roosevelt. "Caesar" could have banished his scribe to New York or a
far part of the empire, had he been displeased with Berle's reputation or
his enemies. He had known of the Berle-Frankfurter animus since 1932;
there was little that Roosevelt did not know about the people in his court.
Roosevelt gossiped about them all, including Berle. Henry Wallace later
recalled that "the President used to look on Berle as being abnormal and
he used to make cracks at Berle's expense. . . . I didn't even see any particular fun in it. Anyhow the President liked to tell stories on Berle. I think
he respected his intellect but questioned his judgment. . . . My guess is that
some enemy of Berle's was continually feeding him material against Berle."
One such enemy was William Bullitt, who delighted in using his family name
as a code word for Adolf Hitler. "Whenever I get the time, I will punch
Bullitt's head," Berle threatened. "Why not punch your namesake's head
instead of Bullitt's?" counseled an unsympathetic president.[4]

As Burlingham said, Berle was a ganglion of complexes. Known to be
short-tempered, difficult, abusive, snobbish, and elitist, Berle was unexpectedly genial and generous with his time with strangers who dared to seek
him out in spite of his forbidding reputation. Even a somewhat hostile journalist surprisingly observed, "He is accessible, cordial, and free with his
time, and his wide-ranging conversation is fascinating as an intellectual exercise." Berle could be moved to remorse by his own unforgivable rude-
ness—even when he felt justifiably provoked by unctuousness or ignorance.
He was confident that certain people deserved his wrath, although its display disturbed him. His favorite virtue among strangers was courtesy and

with his subordinates he could be a model of kindliness and consideration. Four decades later he was remembered by his aides with affection and loyalty, in addition to considerable awe.

But he gave no quarter to his peers. High on his list of bêtes noires was Secretary of the Interior Harold Ickes, whom Berle once described as "a neurotic who is very good at his best and unspeakable at his worst." That may have been the kindest word Berle ever said about Ickes. Ickes was a self-righteous moralist who condemned anyone who disagreed with him. In February 1940, they clashed over the State Department's prerogative to name a delegation to a conference on Indian affairs to be held in Mexico in April, Ickes firing off a letter of protest to Roosevelt that brought a phone call from Berle who accused Ickes of not getting "his information direct, instead of from the town gossip." Temporarily at a loss for words, Ickes saved them for his diary where he called Berle "arrogant and distasteful." Shortly afterwards Berle heard that Ickes "is pretty bitter at me, which I regret." However, he was outraged when Ickes' former assistant, Oscar Chapman, informed Berle that Ickes was wiretapping other members of the adminstration. Later that year at a dinner at the British Embassy, Berle was cool to Ickes: "God forgive me, I didn't even shake hands with him. My conviction remains unchanged—that while he has values in a world in which God has use for every one, fundamentally he is a louse." Berle wrote off "Howling Harold" as a "jumping jackass of the first order." About a year later Archibald MacLeish unwittingly invited the Ickes and the Berle couples to dinner. All went well until after the dinner when the women retired to another room. An apparently innocent comment by Jane Ickes brought an "acid" remark from Beatrice Berle that the lady ought to be a better judge of political invective. Jane Ickes glared and retorted, "It happens that my husband is a master of invective." "Jane is not quick at repartee," Ickes later commented and he vowed that all of Washington would hear how Beatrice Berle "outraged the hospitality" of the MacLeish home.[5]

Dr. Beatrice Berle often outraged Washington. Few capital wives were as intellectual, outspoken, or career-minded as Beatrice Berle, M.D. She minced few words in expecting deference to her degree. "I know enough now to say Dr. Berle," wrote a properly instructed Sam Rosenman. Although this proud Van Cortlandt descendant had three children at home, she was on the staffs of the Gallinger Hospital and the George Washington University Medical School. Beatrice and Adolf were nearly inseparable and he valued her judgment and needed to discuss most matters with her. While most wives retired to quiet obscurity in Washington, Dr. Berle seldom kept her peace. She loved good French cuisine, great literature, classical music, and holding sit-down dinner parties for forty or fifty people. Tales of her aristocratic snobbishness abounded. "That story of yours about Mrs. B. and the Junior in the British Embassy is almost too good to be true," Burlingham chortled to Frankfurter. "Is my remembrance correct that you said to her 'You are on the fringe of a democratic administration. Perhaps it would be well for you to get to know the Juniors as well as the heads'?"[6]

She might have been a lonely woman. Women felt threatened by her professional attainments and her outspoken opinions on politics and everything intellectual. Obviously certain men preferred a woman who knew her place. Once, following a Cabinet meeting, Henry Wallace stayed behind to tell the president another Berle story, which he concluded with the observation that while "Berle was animated by profound religious conviction, . . . his soul was a tortured one." Roosevelt, in one of his petulant moods, shot back, "Living with Mrs. Berle was enough to torture one." Recalling that unkind remark years later, Wallace commented, "I suppose maybe it was her rather aristocratic atmosphere [*sic*] that annoyed Roosevelt. She was a very earnest and serious person. She was a doctor who worked hard at her profession and at home. Sometimes people who are so exceedingly serious annoy other people. . . . I always liked her myself."[7]

The Berles did not make a sympathetic duo, but the vicious Washington gossip mill also victimized them. A prime example is the story alleging Berle's conversion to Catholicism. Morris Ernst gave a party in October 1943, to which he mostly invited journalists, and, as he told Berle, "in the chit-chat I was greatly disturbed and impressed by the number of people who raised the question about your joining the Catholic church." Ernst's party was not an isolated instance. A newsman told Henry Wallace in 1944 that Berle had "strong instincts pulling him toward Roman Catholicism and that he has a picture of the Madonna in his room." (Was it Lillian Wald?) A British report to London in 1943 declared, "He is often rumoured to be about to become a Roman Catholic, but nothing has happened so far." Even Berle knew that "the rumor of my alleged conversion to Catholicism has been travelled widely and pushed so heavily that it almost looks like a propaganda stunt." Although the liberal Ernst believed that a man's religion was a private matter, knowing what gossip could do in Washington, he told Berle that "from your point of view, it is less than wholesome to have so many people running to the assumption that you have joined the Catholic Church but have been disinclined to admit it." Of course, it was also less than wholesome for Berle to proclaim publicly that he was *not* taking instruction to become a Catholic.[8]

In part, Berle was inadvertently responsible for the rumor himself—his friend Ernst suggesting that he believed it and only wanted to hear definitively from Berle himself. Affronted by the rationalism or materialism that dominated public thought in his time, Berle made himself one intellectual who asserted the superiority of spiritualism. At dinner parties he liked to be a contrarian and overstate his case in order to score points in the discussion. While the combination of "the spiritual and the rational . . . comforts me," he would declare, the "spiritual" and the "moral" were superior to other values. Of course, world affairs were governed by realpolitik, but he maintained that the United States had to perpetuate "the myth of President Roosevelt" as a man of his word because it sharply contrasted with the evil Hitler and "we should lose a moral strength" should it be shown otherwise. Also, in intellectual discourse he delighted in downplaying modernity while invoking the spiritual and moral superiority of the pre-industrial world: "On balance, I am prepared to think that the industrial revolution was one of the greatest mistakes the human mind ever committed." He applauded the Middle Ages for its social harmony, discipline, and spiritualism, all of which were enhanced by a strong Church. He claimed to find it comforting that the Church, with its values mostly intact, was still strong, particularly in Latin America, and when liberals attacked its conservatism he defended it as a force for social solidarity and professed to admire its faith. In a 1940 speech to the Association of American Universities, Berle confronted academic rationalism by asserting that "in older times . . . the quality of goodness and the quality of faith" were paramount; "I think our fathers knew something in this field which we have forgotten. I think they knew that all truth involves of necessity an act of faith." Former generations had known that some things had to be taken on faith: "The controlling conceptions had to do with values—which they believed to be universal and which by faith they considered eternal."[9]

At times Berle sounded like a religious mystic and perhaps he was that or at least a spiritualist. The passing of his mother in early 1940 inspired a fear in Berle that morality and religion in American life had passed with her generation. She had always stressed spiritual values to strengthen her son's serenity of mind. Shortly after her death he wrote, "Even today I find myself resolving to ask my Mother what she thinks of this or that problem we are working on; and suddenly realize that consultation has to be done through memory and spiritual interpretation." Believing that even after a person had passed away it was possible through recalling their values to remain in touch with the departed, he sought flashes of spiritual communication with her. Later he met a "wise old Mohammedan Imam" and found himself comparing his "devoutness" to his mother's: "Somehow the two merged in a fantastic moment of realization that a great faith in a kindly God produces characters that are much alike. Even the voice and the face, for half a second, seemed the same." In the spring of 1942 he recorded in his diary "an odd incident. I seemed to get a telephone message from my mother and to see her quite clearly. I asked when she was coming. She said in about ten days. Nothing my mother was ever connected with could be aligned with the events of today nor did this seem to be."[10]

This Christian "spiritualism," which Roosevelt shared to a degree, gave Berle a loyalty to the president that others did not perceive. But it did not signal his turn to Roman Catholicism. In fact, during this period he found a job in the State Department for a former La Guardia administration colleague, Paul Blanshard, who later won notoriety for his anti-Church writings. Also, Catholicism would have gone against his mother's spiritual heritage. Hence, as he wrote Ernst,

> I am not a Catholic, never have been a Catholic, and never expect to be. I have never contemplated it, studied for it, come within miles of it. Several generations of New England ancestors would turn in their graves if it happened, and to arrive at that conclusion would involve reversing pretty nearly every cell in my head.
>
> I have many friends in the Church, and great respect for the people who sincerely hold that faith, or, for that matter, any honorable faith. But such Christianity as I profess—and I happen to think Christianity still has a great deal to say—has got to be worked out as best it can through the Protestant Congregationalism in which I was born.

Years later Henry Wallace would recall the wartime rumors about Berle's imminent conversion and merely observe, "He didn't finally go through with it." Old gossip would survive them all.[11]

In the words of a State Department colleague, "Berle is too complex to explain." But, diplomats, news reporters, and intelligence operatives were in the business of explaining personages such as Berle. Some people were more easily perceived than explained and Berle was, as the British ambassador stated the consensus, "a 100 per cent intellectual" and "an acute case of the inferiority complex." Sam Rosenman felt that Berle "was quite snobbish intellectually and very intolerant intellectually."[12]

Moreover, Berle apparently enjoyed his reputation to the extent that it was his Achilles' heel. A British intelligence report put it another way: "He is extremely vain of his intellectual attainments and is susceptible of being flattered." Lord Halifax's aide in Washington, Michael Wright, frequently met with Berle and informed the Foreign Office that compliments would make an irascible Berle "purr."[13]

Few descriptions of Berle flattered either his behavior or his appearance. The standard profile of Berle noted his brilliance, intensity, earnestness—his "pleasant, smooth manner, and a vanity which likes to be appeased," as Isaiah Berlin put it. Jim Farley thought Berle "had an air about him. He's a short fellow . . . and a superior type." Berle took himself seriously to the point that it was part of his mission; he once told a *Survey* magazine editor that he wished a book was "a little more serious—but the American fetish for not taking yourself too seriously is well expounded in it." Although small in stature he styled himself to be perceived as a giant among intellects. James P. Warburg complained that "he mumbles everything so that you can't hear half of what he says," in a low voice that suggested the importance of his words.[14]

But while a consensus could agree on his braininess, few people saw the man as others did. Did his "intensity" suggest a nervous man? "His eyes are clear, alert, thoughtful," declared one respectful newspaper account. "He has a boyish look, too, and his mobile face and quick gestures indicate nervous energy, but not nervousness." A British banker found Berle "very friendly"—but "he gave me the impression of being highly strung, and he smoked cigarettes incessantly during our interview. He spoke very fast and in a very low voice. His conversation was full of literary quotations." Less charitable was the Englishwoman who sat next to him at a dinner and thought "he looks like a hunchback, but isn't one." Some people focused on his worst mannerisms. "While I talked to him," Jonathan Daniels wrote, "Berle picked his nose and rolled the damp results of his picking into little balls, which he disposed of with his fingers. I told Lucy. 'Why,' she said, 'he did it at the dinner table when we were at his house.'" As charming as he could be, his rude moments were most remembered. On the pronounciation of his last name, *Time* once wrote that it "rhymes with surly."[15]

Berle expected to make some enemies with his manner and his ideas—almost as a consequence of being a person to be taken seriously. He seemed to make little effort to ingratiate himself with those whom he did not expect to convert to his way of thinking. He liked directness, although it clearly mattered who showed it. Thus, one day he met Alice Roosevelt Longworth, the pugnacious daughter of Theodore, reputed to have the most acerbic tongue in Washington: "There is only one way to deal with Alice: kick her shins once and keep on kicking them. If you ever stop, she kicks yours." He had "a pleasant time" with her. After a decade in politics Berle's intensity was still more memorable than his appreciation of wit. He relaxed with few people other than old friends like Roosevelt, La Guardia, and Charles Taussig who could bring out frivolity in him. He appreciated irony, as when he commented of Gandhi and the British in India, "I have always wondered why rulers finally shot saints—and I am beginning to find out." Never a modest man, he could still tell a story at his own expense:

> Many years ago when first in London, I perceived a large gray building with an iron fence around it, and asked an English friend what it was. With the hesitation of courteous reserve (indicating that he did not wish to hurt my feelings but had to answer the question) he stated that it was Buckingham Palace. I carried the ego bruise for more than twenty years. Then a Foreign Office man who had been sent to Washington to consult us during the War walked across Lafayette Square with me. He indicated a pillared white building with an iron fence around it and asked what it was. I recognized him at once as a healing angel, and was comforted.

In 1944 he sent the under secretary a memorandum that demonstrated how he could leaven his infamous and intense moral outrage with wry humor:

> They are moving the Visa Division to a building at 916 G Street, which is in the longitude of Tenth Street. This is in the middle of the red-light dis-

trict. The Visa Division is naturally unhappy, having been moved five times in three years; but we might get over that. A bowling alley is not a perfect advertisement for the State Department, but I suppose we could worry along with that, too. The adjacent Burlesque show might be an attraction. But when prospective and putative immigrants and their families have to come to prove their stainless moral character in the middle of a low-priced brothel district, these hapless immigrants might be pardoned for wondering if something was not screwy somewhere.[16]

Indeed, something was screwy about the way some people characterized Berle. Undeniably Berle was vain concerning his intellectual worth, but Washington at war brimmed with arrogant people. At least he was vain about how well he performed without apparently worrying about his titles or how one spelled his name (not Adolph). Mumbling, smoking, and perspiring nervously were not peculiar to him. People who fastened upon his size (5 foot 7) and rapid stride may inadvertently reveal more about themselves than about Berle. Instead of making him grotesque they could have noted that he was unusually prescient, articulate, and concerned about attainments of the mind. In an age where reputations are made on the basis of journalistic superficiality and a complex personality defies explanations limited to a thousand words, parts of Berle were better left unseen and unknown lest they confuse. Who cared that on short notice he made himself available for all sorts of causes that marked him as a liberal and concerned person? He was compassionate, worrying about laws and bureaucracies that denied "common decency to illegitimate children" by depriving them of citizenship if born abroad to American parents. His company stimulated creative people. Rexford Tugwell later wrote volumes about Roosevelt, urging Berle to also write because "I know that you are at once more fluent and more lucid than I am." He was an elitest, more concerned with the plight of Europe's intellectuals than that of its ordinary refugees from oppression. But, in a world where oppression extended to the burning of books, he conspired with economist Jacob Viner and others to bring a multivolume edition of the works of David Ricardo to the safety of these shores for the duration of the war. He was too complex to explain, but he had qualities simple enough to be appreciated.[17]

"And What Shall We Do Then?"

As Henry Wallace told the story, he had lingered with the president following a cabinet meeting in December 1942, to show Roosevelt a speech he would be delivering on foreign policy and their conversation then turned to Latin America and the Soviet Union. Wallace—smarting from recent bureaucratic disagreements between his Board of Economic Warfare and the State Department, and especially Berle's criticisms of his speech on Latin

America seven months before—fussed that State wanted to keep him out of Latin America, that conservatives there had marked the Soviet Union as the real enemy, and that Berle endeavored to destroy friends of his who were pro-Soviet. None of this gossip and rumor was news to Roosevelt, but the president latched on to Wallace's mention of Berle and there ensued some rambling chatter about the personalities of Berle and his wife; then, Roosevelt suddenly shifted gears in his monologue and "indicated that Berle and others who were trying to control the peace need not worry too much, that if every department of this government were represented at the peace and other governments had each department represented, there would be at least 40,000 people at the peace conference. . . . The President said there were just going to be three folks making the peace conference."[1]

The president was at war, but he was thinking of peace. And he remembered the making of the peace in 1917–1919. Roosevelt had been assistant secretary of the navy when peace erupted in 1918 and could remember the rush of major and minor bureaucrats in the regular and emergency departments of the government to be part of the Peace Conference in Paris. This time it would be different. Wallace and others in the emergency departments might want to get in on foreign policy, but they were not the Baruchs and Hoovers of this war and were doomed to disappointment if they thought they would make the peace. This time the blueprints of the peace would not await events overseas. This time it would be made through almost personal understandings at conferences among the Big Three—Roosevelt, Churchill, and Stalin—aided by technicians in the regular departments who would hammer out preliminary agreements concerning the details of the peace. This time Roosevelt would see to it that there was no "Colonel House" role in postwar planning. Berle always had been on guard against a Colonel House in the administration; now Roosevelt suspected him of wanting to be just that. Roosevelt could not single-handedly reach agreements with Churchill and Stalin on everything, but he would not allow Berle or anyone else to upstage him or take policy from him. This time the mob scenes of Paris would not be repeated.

If Wallace was looking to get in on the making of the peace, he was a Johnny-come-lately; American discussions of the postwar international system had begun even before the United States became a belligerent. At a time when most men barely could envision the shape of wartime organizations, Adolf Berle had pontificated on the shape of postwar economics. In 1940 he described a postwar international financial system marked by American leadership, liberalism, and generosity:

> It seems fantastic today to suggest handing over some of our accumulated gold as a free gift to re-establish international currency, to let other nations set their houses, and thereby re-establish trade and normal life. But this may not seem nearly so fantastic a few years hence. It seems impossible today to think of using the enormous resources of the Federal Reserve

System as a means of rebuilding the shattered life of another continent, but when the time actually comes, and we are faced with that contingency, we may find that the idea looks more like an immediate necessity than a fairy tale.

Also, in a magazine article entitled "And What Shall We Do Then?" he forecast that the United States would emerge from the war as the richest country on the planet with an altruistic policy justified by the fact that in the natural order of things "any economics is moral." Berle too had 1919 in mind—how could he forget it? He had protested then and there the Allies' faulty ethics and logic when they took revenge upon their defeated enemies. Instead of restoring the vanquished to a trading partner status where everyone prospered, the British and the French—with the acquiescence of tight-fisted Americans—"squeezed the pips until they squeeked" through illiberal reparations and war debts. Berle's point was that good economics was good morals and a moral policy made good economics.[2]

In numerous conversations concerning economics and foreign affairs that went back to 1932, Roosevelt and Berle had agreed on the outlines of a policy they now pursued, with Berle once more the brain trust technician. They shared a conviction that the time for making peace was during war. Roosevelt knew that Berle lusted for a greater role and the president was not about to exclude his best draftsman and one of his most knowledgeable advisors simply because his personality offended certain individuals. Although a more affable Harry Hopkins would handle the personal touches with Churchill and Stalin, Roosevelt channeled Berle into technical areas where his legal guile and genius for adaptation would do the most good. Berle might antagonize useful people, but Roosevelt could not yet discard a Machiavelli who explicated so well on his princely conception of a postwar international system.

Berle believed that the liberalization of the international system was inevitable because the old imperialism had been subsumed in "a people 's war" a quarter century ago. The United States could no more maintain its protectionist isolationism of the 1930s than Britain could maintain imperial preference or France its Maginot Line. Britain must realize that her postwar world influence did not rely upon empire, but rather "on her moral and intellectual ability to bring about common action among a great number of nations, notably the Dominions." If it substituted a "good neighbor" Commonwealth of nations for colonialism, London stood a good chance of remaining a force in the world. A poorer Britain could not afford a great world role, but the gradual relaxation of its imperialism would encourage American generosity that surpassed even lend-lease. The Federal Reserve System and the Reconstruction Finance Corporation were great engines of American state capitalism that would pull a tired train of European imperialists. Foreign aid to Europe and the undeveloped countries made sense in Washington: "The United States, to keep its own people employed and happy, has actually yearned to give away goods and services, and to manufacture for internal purposes the money necessary to pay for them." Having manufactured wartime abundance, Washington needed "a [postwar] system of open finance so that no country shall find itself short of supplies because it is short of exchange. I am clear that this can be worked technically if anyone really want to do it—and I think we shall want to do it."[3]

Berle's ideas were not original. In 1918–1919 British and American liberals had recognized that the United States was now the world's creditor nation and the principal arbiter of capitalism's destiny. In the British Treasury, John Maynard Keynes had devised a plan for employing America's wealth in the reconstruction of Europe—only to be frustrated by imperial nationalists in his own government. Berle and American liberals had shared that sense of frustration, particularly when the corporatist planners were overcome by party politics. In the intervening years his admiration for Keynes' iconoclastic economics grew; the Great Depression made Keynes even more timely. Keynes' vision of 1919, albeit without British political leadership and even more dependent upon American interests, continued to inspire liberals. In Berle's mind, the reconstruction of Europe rationalized the RFC and his schemes for a great domestic credit mechanism and the inter-American development bank. However, it remained to be seen whether he and others in the State Department could restrain American and British nationalism to obtain a more rational settlement than that of their predecessors of 1919. In 1942 Berle was both Keynes' collaborator and competitor, paradoxes he also shared with Herbert Feis in State and Harry Dexter White in the Treasury.

While Berle's design for postwar relief and reconstruction was "substantially similar in its essentials" to British proposals, State Department economists pointed to a multitude of obstacles that still blocked agreement to an international scheme. For example, responsibility for detailed economic planning in the State Department was divided between two adversaries, Berle and Acheson. Additionally, Morgenthau in the Treasury jealously guarded its role in international finance. At the same time American sloganeers consciously antagonized British imperialists with reminders of their imperial poverty. Henry Luce propagandized an imperial vision of the "American Century" which Henry Wallace nebulously rebutted with an imperial celebration of the "People's Century"—neither of which had much of a role for London. Berle ignored Luce, but Wallace's courtship of leftwingers and liberals irritated him. "There is not a great deal new in it," Berle testily remarked, "but it has made Henry temporarily the hero of the Left—I suppose because he saluted all revolutions, including the Russian." As Roosevelt once said, the vice-president overgeneralized and overidealized in a manner that defied political reality; and Berle approvingly quoted Cordell Hull, "It's all right to recite the Beatitudes, but the tussle is coming when you lay out new methods." Wallace sensed Berle's disapproval and "a very definite rift developed between me and Berle," even if Berle had insisted his "People's Century" speech was first-rate. They agreed on a vision of state capitalism, but Berle despaired of Wallace's rhetorical flourishes. And he was irate that the bureaucratic politics of planning for reconstruction began with the war relief of Europe, which Wallace's Board of Economic Warfare bid to control.[4]

But Wallace was less of an obstacle to Berle's ambition to be the architect of the world's postwar recovery than similarly ambitious men in the Treasury. Berle especially respected Morgenthau's under secretary, Harry White, a brilliant financial strategist who had played a very constructive role in planning an inter-American bank that would finance development south of the border to make the Latin Americans more useful trading partners. When adoption of the inter-American bank was postponed, White proposed a "Stabilization Fund and Development Bank" that would extend the hemispheric design to the world. The inter-American bank would have put financial muscle into the Good Neighbor Policy; now White proposed, as Berle had intended, to globalize the Good Neighbor Policy. At July meetings chaired by White and attended by representatives of the BEW, the Federal Reserve Board, and Leo Pasvolsky and Berle from the State Department, it was decided to forward planning at an early stage by bilateral discussions of memoranda with the British, rather than "anything spectacular" such as an international conference. Berle pushed discussion of White's plan—which achieved even greater significance when the British submitted Keynes' scheme for a "Clearing Union" that resembled White's Stabilization Fund. Thus, a consensus formed in 1942 that lead to the Dumbarton Oaks conference and the creation of the International Monetary Fund and the World Bank.[5]

Much as he respected both White and Keynes, it was not in his destiny for Berle to submit to their leadership. In August 1942, he aggressively promoted his own United Nations Bank intended to eliminate politics from the economic reconstruction of Europe—a ploy State Department economist Louis Bean rightly called "bold." However, to insure a capitalist reconstruction of Eastern Europe, he specifically subordinated any Soviet-dominated Eastern European regional federation in his world bank. Implicit in any American scheme was the understanding that British or other economic spheres of influence were incompatible with liberal financial aid. While Herbert Feis doubted the bank's feasibility, Berle used it as a ploy to compel State Department economists to "go out on the end of a plank as he did" by submitting their own proposals. At least Berle set the agenda, Bean finding it "important to observe that there is emerging from the Berle committee—with Berle doing the leading—the assumption that there will be United Nations Economic Council" after the war. Of course, American wealth would dominate it.[6] In late 1942 it seemed to the British and the Canadians that Berle was calling the shots "for the financial aspects of post-war planning." Nevertheless, as a September 10 meeting with the British in his office, Berle conceded that the White and the Keynes plans still had priority.[7]

Berle stressed that he not only wanted to win the war in progress "but also the 'war' which may emerge after victory in efforts to create the right kind of peace."[8] America had to determine the peace this time and in the developing contest between the British Keynes plan and the American White plan, Berle insisted that "White's is obviously better." Operating on a premise that some sort of postwar West European economic organization would be imperative, Berle argued that the White plan could better accomplish that multilateralism than the Anglo-American bilateralism in the Keynes plan. After all, why should the American largesse be reserved exclusively for the use of the British Empire and Commonwealth? To underscore that point, in January 1943 Berle initiated financial discussions with the Chinese.[9] The British grumbled that Berle acted hastily, and they insisted that an Anglo-American accord should precede multilateral discussions, but Berle retorted that he wanted to avoid the appearance of "an Anglo-Saxon gang-up."[10]

The Americans perplexed the British by their reluctance to dictate Anglo-American terms to the rest of the world; also by dividing responsibilities for postwar planning among so many different strategists and departments. Of course, the latter was due to Roosevelt's manner of dealing with his subordinates. The president parceled responsibilities according to topics of Allied concern. In that way the White House retained ultimate authority for making the peace. Berle understood this and even explained it to Escott Reid of the Canadian Office of External Affairs and a puzzled Redvers Opie, the British Embassy counselor, who observed that "coordination of this would be a real task." Berle agreed, intimating that "the [State] Department staff would have a good deal to do with it." However, he knew that responsibility for economic discussions was being divided in ways that involved too many hands for any single person or group to control all of American economic postwar planning.[11]

The British attempted to take advantage of uncertain American lines of authority with diplomatic ploys that compelled the Americans to undertake discussions of monetary stabilization plans on their terms and turf. In March 1943, the British leaked the Keynes plan to an American correspondent in London and then insisted that its publication called for publication of the American plan and British discussion of both plans with European governments in exile in London. However, White and Berle demurred—insisting that any initial explanation of the American plan ought to come from Washington, not London. But then, lo and behold, one of the London governments in exile leaked the White plan, thereby threatening to embarrass the administration in the eyes of Congress.

However, the contest over the monetary stabilization plans involved

Berle less and less. When Keynes visited Washington in September, Berle sat in on conferences with him, but he deferred to Treasury's leadership. A year later the Dumbarton Oaks conference shaped the postwar stabilization of capitalism without Berle, who privately confessed that he was "sorry about that." Later that year he lead his own conference—on postwar international civil aviation, a major foreign policy problem that belonged to Berle alone. But no one person made policy. Negotiations reflected a consensus among American planners that American power would not restore British imperialism, that the United States would demand freedom for European spheres of influence and developing colonial areas. In Berle's mind Washington should assert its power in Latin America—not to claim it as an exclusive American preserve for trade, but to free it from British dominance of markets. He wanted Latin America to become a model of the free trade that awaited the colonial areas of the world after the war. Against the American effort to mobilize Latin American "cooperation" came word via Canadian Minister Lester Pearson that the British were endeavoring to build empire solidarity on economic questions. The wartime ally remained an imperial adversary, determined to confront American power around the globe. As long as he controlled one phase of Roosevelt's segmented postwar planning, Berle was assured of a role in extending America's state capitalism and its imperial mission against the dying British Empire and the ascendant Soviet empire.[12]

7

Air Power

American interests [would be] short-sighted as not to see that the doctrine of free air is their plainest road to superiority.

> —Diary, Memorandum, "International Aviation Conference," September 16, 1944

"INTERNATIONALIZATION OR AMERICANIZATION"

Discovering a neglected cause, or letting it find him, was part of Berle's art. He hunted for underinvested public issues, whether it was the Caribbean, Indians in New Mexico, individual shareholders in large corporations, or the candidacy of Newton Baker for president. Fortunately for Berle, Franklin Roosevelt was avoided by most intellectuals when Raymond Moley brought them together. Shrewdly, Berle attached himself to the ambitions of Fiorello La Guardia at a time when the Little Flower seemed to have come to the end of his career. Events in the 1930s vindicated Berle's advocacy of state capitalism and Latin America. So it was that during 1942 Berle asserted himself on postwar planning in international finance—only to find the field crowded with the redoubtable Keynes, the able Harry White, and a host of State Department hands, including the odious (to Berle) Acheson, all lusting for their piece of the peace. Had Berle been as abrasive as his reputation suggested, he might have fought for turf—instead he took up an unheralded concern, international civil aviation.

Incredibly, in a war largely decided by air power, Berle noted that, "thanks to the dunderheadedness of this Department," almost nobody in Washington understood the diplomatic ramifications of international civil aviation. The Civil Aeronautics Board (CAB), the Commerce Department, the navy, and the War Department all had experts on aviation in peace and war, but they lacked an overview of foreign affairs. Berle saw the vacuum and filled it. With Hull's permission, at the onset of 1943 he formed an interdepartmental board with himself as chairman to develop American policies on postwar international civil aviation. "I think we will get a good deal done that way," he observed with no little satisfaction. At the same time, he excluded others from aviation "matters which they don't very well understand; we shall see what we can do about it."[1]

Berle's own ignorance of aviation mattered less than his mastery of economic foreign affairs. All he had to do was make the diplomacy of international civil aviation consistent with the administration's foreign policy goals. Roosevelt's policies asserted an international liberalism that did not countenance monopoly of markets, the dominance of the British pound in world markets, or imperial spheres of influence that strangled smaller countries. Put positively, the postwar world must be governed by freedom of opportunity in the air—an appealing slogan that enabled America to wield the power of her wealth and her cornucopia of airplanes. A pattern of diplomacy had been set in developing an international economic stabilization scheme; Berle repeated it in creating a system of international civil aviation: American discussions, followed by bilateral discussions with the British, and then a multilateral conference. As White's and Keynes' ideas dominated postwar stabilization policies, so did Berle's proposals in the postwar system of international civil aviation.

The issue was made to order for Berle. In international civil aviation several governments had launched the practice of "the chosen instrument"—selecting one airline, either private or public, to exclusively represent the country in overseas civil aviation. Only in America was there enough capital to allow extended private development of civil aviation and even then it was inadequate for the markets to be developed. Planes were expensive and the amount of capital required to develop, build, and maintain them was the equivalent of a public works project in need of government financing; state capitalism in civil aviation was logical. Moreover, state security and the military uses of aviation, established since 1918, required the investment. No country could tolerate an unregulated breach of its air space. The rules governing air travel between countries were still somewhat primitive, mostly depending upon airline negotiation with governments to penetrate their air spaces and to secure permission to land at certain airports.

In Washington, the wily, manipulative Juan Trippe sought nothing less for his Pan American Airways than it should be the American chosen instrument. Trippe—debonair, aristocratic, and well-connected through marriage to the sister of Edward R. Stettinius, Jr., and the Morgan investment interests—adeptly used his connections to secure landing rights throughout the world. When the American Export Lines employed its wealth from shipping to build a competing airline, Trippe tried to block it from operating on transatlantic routes. Roosevelt took a dim view of Trippe's machinations. Berle shared that hostility. Although the administration promoted the state capitalism of the Tennessee Valley Authority and insisted upon regulated monopolies in the generation of electric power, it looked askance at both government ownership and private monopoly in international civil aviation. It confronted a choice between either Pan American or American Export as a chosen instrument. "I have no great love for either," Berle commented in 1940; "I want some competition."[2]

By no means had Berle joined the Brandeisians. It was his way of being undogmatic and choosing his enemies well. Early in the war Trippe pursued a cartel arrangement with the British Overseas Airways Corporation (BOAC), London's chosen instrument for Britannia's ruling the air as it had previously ruled the waves. That partnership further excited Berle's opposition because it linked Trippe to the British Empire. Berle wanted air competition with Britain because American airplane manufacturers led the world in the 1930s and the war's diversion of British sources to weapons increased the likelihood that American aviation would dominate postwar markets. But the sun had not yet set upon the British Empire and London counted its bases around the world as bargaining chips in negotiating the American advantage in planes. As its bases in the hemisphere had purchased American destroyers in 1940, so its air fields around the globe would buy either American planes or time for Britain to build its own. Supremely aware of the importance of bases in any imperial scheme, the British were confident that the Americans wanted and needed their bases. They had not yet gauged the peculiar nature of the American empire.

Britain's global strategy required that it control the diplomacy of its Commonwealth nations, but the Canadians did not want to be anyone's trump card. They resented British efforts to dominate their trade and diplomacy; they also feared industrial and military dependence upon the United States. Soon after the United States entered the war the Canadian Ministry of External Affairs plotted a course politically independent of both London and Washington. To Berle's amusement, Ottawa rebuked London's claim to represent all the British Commonwealth nations' economic interests. However, the Canadians also told Washington bluntly that they resented the way United States lend-lease replaced Canada as a British trading partner. What did Canada seek? Simply to use its "marginal position" to become a North Atlantic balance of power that mediated U.S.-U.K. disputes. It was a successful diplomatic strategy that endured from 1940 through the Canadian proposal that set up the United Nations organization at the San Francisco conference in 1945. And perhaps in no other area of wartime diplomacy did Canadians command such a respectful hearing as in international civil aviation.[3]

In international civil aviation location made some countries terminals while others were significant for their air space. Thus, Australia and New Zealand were too remote to be anything but terminals dependent upon British determination to develop their markets with its chosen instrument. On the other hand, transit between London and New York compelled planes to pass over and through Canada, bestowing upon the Canadians a strategic importance that commanded attention elsewhere. The Canadians had their own aviation ambitions, but their plans depended upon America's decision on a chosen instrument.

Washington opposed mercantilism in the skies. In 1942 the chairman of the CAB, L. Welch Pogue, advanced an American doctrine of freedom of the air. It really was not new and had been discussed since 1919. Nevertheless, in an age of increasing state capitalism, it required restatement. Besides, freedom of the air was in America's interests. "In view of the technical and business proficiency of the United States," Pogue wrote, "supremacy in the field of international air transport can surely be gained by [freedom]." National security would not permit unrestricted freedom. "Cabotage"—flights within a country restricted to that country's carriers—would prevail ineluctably. But the rules regarding flight between countries were largely unwritten. Pogue proposed an international conference to draft international flight codes consistent with the "freedoms" demanded by most Americans except for Trippe (who conducted his own foreign policy). At the same time the State Department circulated a summary section of a Council on Foreign Relations study by Oliver James Lissitzyn arguing that American supremacy in the western hemisphere and freedom of the skies elsewhere were compatible diplomatic goals.[4]

Toward those ends Berle sought a "crystallization" of State Department policy that gave America postwar access to airports around the world on a nonexclusive basis. In that way Americans could increase their commerce and confront British imperial preference. Without a policy of freedom of the postwar skies, Pan American and British Airways could form a cartel and divide the world between them, thereby limiting American trade abroad. With these considerations in mind, Berle pressed Cordell Hull, the old "Tennessee free-trader," to establish an interdepartmental group under State's leadership.[5]

Berle sought to create an international system where practices had been helter-skelter and governed largely by private arrangements such as Trippe's. "At present we have a system of what is called 'reciprocity'—which means that if another country allows some American line to land there, with a certain number of landings per week, we will allow the same privileges to them," Berle explained to his diary. "But this strikes me as being too frail and artificial a channel to handle the enormous amount of aviation traffic which will come in the future." Bilateral arrangements had to yield to universal rules that permitted freedom of international skies and free access to airports, consistent with national security requirements. On January 8, 1943, Berle convened an interdepartmental committee on international aviation consisting of Wayne Coy of the Budget Bureau, Robert Lovett of the War Department, Artemus Gates of the Navy Department, Wayne Taylor of the Commerce Department, and Pogue of the CAB. Thomas Burke—the State

Department's advisor on aviation matters, alleged to be disappointed that he was not chairman of the group, leaked word of its activity to the magazine *Aviation*. The story tipped off the British that a policy for freedom of the skies was in the works. The British responded with a call for "internationalization" of aviation, through which the British Commonwealth of Nations would use its numbers in an international organization to command American planes and forestall an American air hegemony.[6]

However, if the British thought they could arrest American air nationalism, they were rudely disabused of that notion on February 9 by a beautiful American lady. The occasion was the maiden speech of the newly elected Republican congresswoman from Connecticut, Clare Boothe Luce—actress, playwright, and an outspoken American nationalist. Entitled "America's Destiny in the Air," her speech followed her Henry Luce's "American Century" theme in attacking internationalism as "globaloney," and asserting, "We want to fly everywhere. Period." While she did not differ much with State Department demands for freedom of the air, she made Berle sound like sweet reason to British ears. For a change London noted approvingly that Berle was "doing his best to calm down the somewhat imperialistic and anti-British agitation now going on in the U.S.A. as regard aviation" and that it was "obviously in our interest to strengthen Mr. Berle's hand." To soothe British fears that Mrs. Luce struck responsive chords in American hearts, the president told Berle to soften the State Department's line. Accordingly Berle told the House Foreign Affairs Committee to eschew "narrow nationalism" in aviation and pursue international cooperation that would enable American planes to land anywhere.[7]

London was gratified that "Berle has rebutted the agitator in fair and just words." But it still noted that American lawmakers coveted postwar American use of overseas airfields being built with American lend-lease. "If plans for internationalisation come to naught, we must expect severe U.S. pressure on this point," it was observed in the Foreign Office. However, internationalization of aviation was not seriously considered by Pogue or Berle.[8]

The United States and Britain had understandings that they would hold aviation talks "at an opportune time" and that the British would build fighter planes with which to repel Nazi bombers while the Americans would manufacture cargo planes and bombers to be shared with their Allies. While America's promised generosity gratified them, British imperialists were paranoid concerning America's overwhelming advantage in aviation. American planes would command access to British bases around the world, a harbinger of the empire's doom. American "freedom of the skies" struck terror in British imperial hearts. Yet internationalization, through which the numbers advantage of Commonwealth nations and Dominions would prevail, had only one influential friend in Washington, Vice-President Henry Wallace; and even the Foreign Office's aviation expert, Michael Le Rougetel, ruefully judged that "Mr. Wallace's influence is waning & with it the support for general internationalization."[9] The British monitored American debate on aviation for hopeful signs that the Americans weakened in their commitment to freedom of the air, but reluctantly admitted to themselves that internationalization was "clearly unacceptable to the United States, the Dominions and probably Russia." Perhaps, they hoped, the Americans would be amenable to spheres of influence in international civil aviation.[10]

As the Canadians put it, the British feared it was "internationalization or Americanization." The Canadians did their best to convince London that "the concept of internationalization . . . appears so revolutionary to most people on this continent that it could not get a respectful hearing." After all, the world was not ready for a world government of the skies to be dominated by the British Empire. Although London wistfully wished that Berle would employ "his broad and generous outlook on world affairs to favor internationalisation," it hoped to settle for spheres of influence that gave Britain air dominance in the Commonwealth and in Europe too. Ironically, Canadian liberals concurred with British imperialists that internationalization offered the fairest solution; they feared that "freedom of the air" would develop "national rivalries, duplication of services, pressure for subsidies, and distrust among the nations concerned." However, any British proposal to discard internationalization in favor of "a new imperial preference system in air transport" was ignored in Ottawa. London had to find an alternative to imperialism or internationalization of the air—or accept the American freedoms. Moreover, time was not on the side of the British. If they could not agree on an aviation policy in 1943, they would be less likely to get satisfaction in 1944 when an American election would make the administration "unwilling to tackle such a thorny subject."[11]

For his part, Berle sought to isolate the British by persuading Canada that it had two choices: "she can either endeavor to pool her interests with us on a fair basis, or she can pool her interests with BOAC. If we are thinking of commercial rivalry . . . , our obvious interest is to bring Canada into an American system."[12] He knew that economic integration of the two nations encountered a stone wall of Canadian nationalism. He had to mollify Canadian fears that because of America's ability to subsidize its airlines and overwhelm any competition, freedom of the skies was "freedom in name only." Since nobody in Ottawa expected the Americans to surrender their advantages in aviation to internationalization, the Canadians prepared to broker nineteenth-century British imperialism against America's twentieth-century imperialism.[13]

Without cartels, imperialism, or internationalization, the British in 1943 lacked room to maneuver against American demands for free enterprise in aviation. When Berle informed London that the United States would be prepared in June to discuss aviation affairs, he created consternation in

Whitehall. In conversations with British representatives, Berle insisted that he sought "a very considerable ground of common judgment" on aviation, but warned that internationalization was "unrealizable at this time." That left the British with either imperialism or the American freedoms. How, Le Rougetel wondered, could Britain and the Dominions discuss aviation problems with the Americans when "we are not yet in agreement among ourselves"? Berle knew that the British could not count upon Canada's support because Lester Pearson had told him that the Canadians "preferred to talk with us first, or with the British and ourselves together, when the time came." Ottawa would sooner offend London than Washington. Berle might have bearded the Foreign Office in London that summer and spotlighted the importance of international civil aviation had Hull not used the economic talks with Britain as an excuse to keep him in Washington. That gave the British more time to find an international civil aviation policy.[14]

Knowing that Britain wanted to exclude American planes from much of Europe and Asia after the war, the Americans asserted "the widest generalization of air rights." With American air nationalism growing in Congress and in the American public, Berle and his interdepartmental committee ruled out any American chosen instrument. "While all of us hope for world harmony," Berle told one of the most outspoken air chauvinists in the Senate, Pat McCarren of Nevada, "it has to be recognized that at the close of war nationalism is commonly ascendant; and that our national welfare must never be lost sight of." The United States would muster its money, materials, and manufacturing to get its way in the postwar race for aviation markets.[15]

Britain's best hope for deflecting America from its course was in marshalling the Commonwealth's support. Prime Minister Winston Churchill visited Washington on September 19, 1943, and conferred with the heads of Commonwealth missions to the United States at the British Embassy. Lester Pearson raised the touchy subject of aviation. As he described it,

> The great man faced me squarely, waved his cigar at me, and told me that he knew our worries in this regard, but he must emphasize that there was going to be a family discussion of this matter within the Commonwealth before we talked outside, whether we wished to attend or not. He did not feel that the possible annoyances of other Powers could be allowed at any time to interfere with such discussions. . . . They in the United Kingdom had no intention of attempting to compete on an equal basis with the U.S.A. in this field. They could not do so; they had neither the population nor the resources. All they wished was an air transport fleet adequate for their needs. In working out policies in this regard, he felt sure that the Commonwealth could present a united front. At any rate, they were going to try. With an admonitory final wagging of the cigar in my direction, the Prime Minister left.

Stung by Churchill's words, the Canadians decided that it would be politic to attend an October Commonwealth conference in London. However, Pearson assured Berle, Ottawa would not be a party to "ganging up" on the United States. Nevertheless, at the London meeting the British rammed through approval of their scheme for imperial preference in aviation, waiving aside Canadian misgivings that it violated the Atlantic Charter. Moreover, Churchill's insistence upon the Commonwealth and British Empire talking *"en famille"* with the Americans made Ottawa fearful that "imperial centralization" would prevail at the expense of its own developing special relationship with Washington.[16]

Although the British wished Roosevelt viewed aviation their way, the president warmly supported freedom of the air. He adamantly opposed an American chosen instrument. Certain international routes might require only one carrier because they were commercially unprofitable, but heavily traveled routes needed competition. While aviation was a private business that might need public start-up funds, once it attained maturity the government would retire from the field. As a free enterprise it did not allow for internationalization or spheres of influence. Believing that Roosevelt's "own thinking has gone very far in the matter," Berle wanted to strike for an international aviation conference "that would be mainly educational and preparatory in character." To the relief of London, FDR decided that it was not yet an "opportune time" for an international conference. Roosevelt discussed a conference with Churchill at Quebec but told Berle that it would best serve American purposes to take some time to firm its own policy while conducting bilateral, informal discussions.[17]

The British obtusely interpreted Roosevelt's decision to delay bilateral discussions as a defeat for Berle. Sir Ronald Campbell, who had endured several tongue-lashings by the choleric Berle, rejoiced that "Mr. Berle appears to have been unable to maintain his position." Also, for the time being the British were heartened by the abrupt departure of Sumner Welles and his replacement by Stettinius, Juan Trippe's brother-in-law. However, Stettinius assured Berle that he "wants to stay away from the subject" and avoid any appearance of conflict of interest. American aviation policy was firmer than the British wished to acknowledge.[18]

By late 1943 London decided for talks and inadvertently revealed a Commonwealth in confusion. C. D. Howe, a Canadian friend of the Lord Privy Seal, Lord Beaverbrook, and a member of the Commonwealth negotiating team on air, prodded Berle in December for an early aviation conference in London. Berle was a bit taken aback when Howe hinted at a British-Canadian agreement. But when Berle checked with Ottawa, he was quickly reassured that if Howe attended aviation talks, he would be Canada's man, and not represent any "British group of countries."[19]

In January 1944, Hull officially assigned the responsibility of negotiating that problem to Berle. This guaranteed that he would have a say in the construction of the postwar world and made him eager to go to London. He had found his destiny and would have a say in the making of the peace. "One way or another, it is quite a proposition," he told his diary, "and in a sense it tends to delimit what might be called the 'American Empire'—except that we do not propose to make it an empire." Persuading the British that the Americans were not a rival empire would be a tall order for the man who would negotiate a postwar civil aviation agreement.[20]

MR. BERLE GOES TO LONDON

Lord Beaverbrook rose in the House of Lords on January 19, 1944, to discuss His Majesty's Government's civil aviation policy. Beaverbrook—born Max Aitken in Canada—had made himself a wealthy man in his native country before the Great War, following which he left for London and "took an influential sector of British society by storm, for his charm, exuberant good humor and eagerness to bestow financial benefits on new-found friends opened important doors with a speed that has never been equaled." Among the beneficiaries of a largesse that expanded through shrewd investments in automobiles and in the press was Winston Churchill. When Churchill became prime minister in 1940, despite the misgivings of many who saw Beaverbrook as devious and mercurial, he asked Beaverbrook to become minister of aircraft production. It was said of the affable Beaver that he "had few principles, only a limited number of convictions, no respect for the truth and loyalties restricted to a few old friends and employees and, above all, to Winston Churchill himself." But he performed heroically in those days of the Battle of Britain. Deciding that Britain's defense depended upon the Spitfire fighter—even if it meant denying the Air Ministry its bombers and the army its tanks—he became "Lord Spitfire" and waged incessant bureaucratic warfare against the Air Ministry while petulantly bedeviling Churchill with frequent resignations. Eventually Churchill accepted the Beaver's resignation from that post, but Churchill enjoyed his good company too much to let the chimerical Beaverbrook leave his government.[1]

Now without a department as the government's Lord Privy Seal, Beaverbrook had Churchill's commission to advance Britain's cause in international civil aviation. They shared a conviction that Britain's future greatness depended upon her control of the skies throughout much of the world. Also, they intensely felt a rivalry with the upstart Americans. Late one night, Churchill, in a black mood, declared that "Far more important than India or the Colonies or solvency is *the Air*. We live in a world of wolves—and *bears*." Churchill and Beaverbrook hoped Britannia could rule the skies through its control of bases around the globe. That was Beaverbrook's theme as he addressed the Lords: Britain's empire "was in every respect suited to the use" of civil aviation, one way of saying that its very future depended upon control of the skies and bases. "Where aviation is concerned, the Third British Empire gives high hope and high promise," he told the Lords. The airplane was the galleon of empire in the twentieth century. But its fullest development required the empire's "solidarity and single purpose," another hint to Ottawa that London demanded a united Commonwealth front behind its imperial aviation policy. If North America did not like such a policy, it could opt only for internationalization. Under no circumstances would Britain surrender to American dominance in aircraft production. The empire would prevail in the air. "And in all our plans and schemes the youths who fought our battles must be our mainstay," Beaverbrook declared grandiloquently. "The development of the airways of the Empire must be their instrument."[2]

But Roosevelt and Berle were intent upon frustrating Churchill and Beaverbrook with demands for freedom of the skies. London obsessively watched Washington for any sign of its air policy. Although "anxious to avoid excessive competition," Roosevelt told Lord Halifax that he also disdained a chosen instrument in the air; London knew that the president was giving the matter "considerable thought." The British too had given aviation policy considerable thought and still could not decide among their few alternatives. How could they exploit suspected American uncertainties when they differed over their own policy and who would make and implement it? For instance, Foreign Minister Anthony Eden and Beaverbrook squabbled—Eden urging consultations with the Dominions and Beaverbrook impatiently insisting upon an imperial policy dictated from London. Washington's declaration in late January 1944, that it desired political talks, caused Beaverbrook to peevishly tell Eden to lead them because "you do not wish to contest the ground with the United States to the extent that I am prepared to go." Eden demurred, insisting that his job only called for advising on the international aspects of the aviation problem. As would be evident throughout these critical negotiations, everyone in the War Cabinet wanted to be a kibitzer on policy but nobody wanted leadership of a venture likely to fail.[3]

Meanwhile, Berle exploited British differences with the Canadians with a timely call for an early exchange of views. In quest of undisputed leadership of international civil aviation policy, he disingenuously urged Roosevelt and Hull to appoint an experienced diplomat such as George Messersmith or Joe Grew for the task, a ploy that only confirmed Berle's control. Then Berle told London that Ottawa must be included in aviation talks and that the Soviets must be kept informed of their progress. The British responded that if the Canadians participated, so must Australia, New Zealand, and South Africa—three Dominions more attuned to London on imperial cartels. Berle, meeting almost daily with Michael Wright of the British Embassy during early March, balked at that and demanded tripartite discussions with Canada that would not isolate the United States.[4]

Of course, Ottawa appreciated Berle's efforts to demonstrate that "Canada has her own policies and viewpoints quite independent of those of the United Kingdom." In London Berle's tactic further divided British policymakers between those who wanted a tough line with the Canadians and those who would "humour" them. Moreover, as Halifax commented, if Britain wanted the inclusion of Dominions other than Canada, Berle might demand the inclusion of Mexico, Brazil, and other Latin American governments—and that would "present awkward problems for His Majesty's Government." The Latin Americans might support "predatory" American designs on British bases. Finally, where should the discussions be held? Berle suggested Ottawa or Washington as a site for a trilateral aviation conference; Beaverbrook wanted bilateral talks and held out for London, lest "we should be venturing into the Lion's Den."[5]

To their surprise, Berle quickly replied that he would meet the British anywhere, with or without the Canadians! The startled British had "to get on with the affair, whether we start with a modest bridal couch or with the great bed of Ware." So they formally invited Berle to London for exploratory talks. With Roosevelt's blessing and his admonition to keep the Soviets informed, Berle accepted and said he would come in about three weeks, stipulating that he would consult with the Canadians en route to London. To create an impression of "American inferiority" on aviation policy, someone in London—probably Beaverbrook—leaked the British "aviation agenda" to the *American Aviation Daily* while British propaganda trumpeted "past and present achievements of British aviation."[6]

The British hastened to define a strategy for the talks: They would stand firm against any American demand for American-built bases on British territory while conceding the American demand for four freedoms—innocent passage over territory, to refuel, to land, and to discharge passengers flown from country of origin. The imperialists demanded and won colonial cabotage, the exclusive right to fly between non-Dominion points of the empire. But there was sharp disagreement in London concerning the division of European routes—the Foreign Office favoring internationalization of all continental transport while Beaverbrook considered "an international agency to be impossible of attainment"; he wanted a British sphere of influence over European markets—while the Americans would have dominance over the western hemisphere. The Foreign Office expected Berle to reject any sphere of influence proposed by Britain and to demand U.S. rights to British air bases. As the day of Berle's arrival approached, Whitehall ruefully observed that "we are prepared to give more & ask more in return. As we have more to give this is not unpromising."[7]

Berle believed that American air power afforded him the luxury of a firm but accommodating position with the Canadians and the British. For the sake of harmony and his reputation, he could make magnanimous compromises, certain that as long as he obtained the four freedoms, American air power would prevail. He had been eager to go to London a year before when Hull squelched his plans and now any bartering over location was simply designed to give an appearance of a concession. The trip also gave him the opportunity to consult with Ottawa, much to British displeasure.

Because Stettinius was due in London for talks April 6 or 7, Berle decided, with Roosevelt's approval, to go about a week before him, stopping en route in Montreal for brief consultations. He took aviation expert Edward Warner of the CAB with him and in London an aviation aide in the American Embassy also would assist him. The Canadian stop had at least two purposes: Washington gave its recognition of Ottawa's independence of London and Berle had a chance to achieve understandings with the Canadians. Berle knew that some Canadians favored internationalization and deplored Washington's "unwillingness to entrust an international body with real power" and pursuit of greater American air power. While other Canadians favored freedom of the skies, they feared that unfettered freedoms benefited the Americans most. Given its location, the freedoms of overflight and landing were de facto concessions by Canada. In Montreal on March 29, a conciliatory Berle pleaded that while nationalism prevented effective internationalization of civil aviation, he could agree to an international air authority with powers limited to regulating air worthiness and eventually other aviation matters. Also, Berle and the Canadians agreed to oppose "discriminatory measures and preferential systems," an intended blow to British cartel schemes. In these ways he attempted to put the internationalization issue to rest while reaffirming a tacit North American alliance against British imperialism.[8]

And he was successful. The Ministry of External Affairs found Berle "genuinely anxious to find acceptable international solutions and ready to consider alternative methods." Its minister, Norman Robertson, was gratified that for the first time such conversations "got anywhere." Nevertheless, C. D. Howe warned his friend Beaverbrook that "Berle [is] a difficult man to negotiate with. We were disappointed with the outcome of our talks in Canada, but perhaps the discussion is moving in the right direction." Maybe, the Foreign Office hoped, Berle's "experience in Canada should be very useful to us."[9]

The British too had long anticipated Berle's arrival in London. They had read his bitingly sanctimonious notes and they knew how difficult an adversary he could be. For years they had heard so much about his olympian brilliance and his irascible Anglophobia that British visitors to Washington like Anthony Eden and Richard Law were astonished to discover that this reputed demon was charming. Nevertheless, they were certain that his charm masked his hostility and they wanted to take his measure on their own turf. His opposite number would be Beaverbrook, who "thought Im-

perial Preference the panacea for all ills''—not the sort of Briton to charm
Berle. The Foreign Office armed Beaverbrook with profiles of Berle, in-
cluding a recent advisory telegram from Michael Wright in Washington to
Eden that read:

> It may be helpful in dealing with Berle to bear in mind that he is extremely
> vain of his intellectual attainments, and is susceptible to be being flattered.
> The more personal attention that can be paid to him, the more he is likely
> to respond. He would enormously appreciate being received by yourself
> and the Prime Minister if that is possible. He is less amenable to intellec-
> tual argument or to shock tactics. He is capable of either clever horse-
> dealing or open-handed helpfulness according as the game goes and also
> as he is handled. He is ambitious and feels his future to be at stake in the
> success of the present negotiations.

Beaverbrook's aide, Peter Masefield, interpreted the message to mean that
Berle was "most anxious to return to the United States in triumph with
access to bases," but would settle for at least two of their air freedoms;
"If he goes back without them he will have failed."[10]

The British approached the talks warily. The Colonial Office exhorted
Beaverbrook to "stoutly defend" its imperial interests while *The Economist*
of London admonished all against granting certain air freedoms "without
reciprocal privileges being given." Imperialists wanted Beaverbrook to erect
barriers against American trade in the empire and BOAC wanted to concede
the western hemisphere to America while left alone with its routes in Europe
and to the empire in Asia and Africa. The Americans would have to accept
those terms if they wanted British bases. Yet it was grand self-deception.
"There was no British policy, despite the frantic search . . . to solve all civil
aviation problems," a historian has written. "Its planes and plans mere
paper, its forces divided over monopoly versus competition . . . [,] Britain
had to bargain from weakness."[11]

Indeed, Britain had nothing with which to bargain. Berle saw its bases
as a matter entirely distinct from rules of international civil aviation. The
bases might be necessary evils for America's postwar security, not its commercial success. Otherwise, he detested them as tools of British imperialism,
much as he detested monopolies, cartels, or pools that conferred chosen
instrument privileges upon BOAC or its American counterpart, Pan American. The British deceived themselves if they believed that appeals to Berle's
intellectual vanity would preserve their imperial advantages. While imperialists girded themselves for an imagined confrontation over their bases,
Berle came with conciliatory olive branches, knowing that Britain had little
advantage to yield.

Berle came to London intent upon amicable but firm negotiatoins. Ever
the intellectual, he looked forward to taking the intellectual measure of
"first-rate" Britons. With characteristic determination to guard against

anything that distracted from the business at hand, upon his arrival in London on Sunday, April 2, Berle informed Beaverbrook that he did not wish to be bothered by any social engagements. Nevertheless, it was not the way the British did things. Beaverbrook had made plans for a round of dinner and luncheon engagements and going to the theater; Berle turned down one lunch due to a previous engagement and "didn't seem to be much interested in the theatre." Still, he played the gracious guest and was entertained with all the cordiality Churchill, Eden, Beaverbrook, and Law could muster for an important guest. Upon his departure Beaverbrook presented Berle with a first edition of the *Apologia* of Cardinal Newman and even offered to buy him a cardinal's hat; it was a faux pas inspired by Isaiah Berlin's gossip that Berle secretly took Catholic instruction. Berle accepted the gifts, twitted his hosts for their erroneous intelligence, and presented them with cigars, oranges, and stockings, all precious items in wartime Britain. Significantly, the one social engagement he truly desired was unavailable to him; John Maynard Keynes was ill.[12]

On Monday morning at Gwydyr House, the offices of the Lord Privy Seal, Berle, Warner, and the Embassy's aviation aide, Satterthwaite, sat down to a much-anticipated discussion of postwar aviation with Beaverbrook, Law, Parliamentary Under Secretary of State for Air H. H. Balfour, W. C. G. Cribbett of the Air Ministry, J. H. Le Rougetel of the Foreign Office, and Beaverbrook's aviation aide, Peter Masefield. The British began by asserting their equality, demanding that quotas on U.S.-U.K. flights be evenly divided, 50/50; Berle responded that prior to the war 80 percent of the North Atlantic air traffic had originated in the United States. A stunned Beaverbrook fixed his mind on that figure—repeating "80 per cent" three times. Berle asked that the agenda include discussion of a 1943 Anglo-American agreement that prohibited exclusive or discriminatory trade aviation arrangements—an oblique reference to spheres of influence in aviation; Beaverbrook somewhat uncomfortably agreed. Following lunch, Berle added conciliation to his firmness by defining cabotage to Beaverbrook's surprise and satisfaction as reserving flights between Britain and the colonies to British planes. The Dominions would have their own airlines. "I think that accords with our views," Cribbett observed. Somewhat apologetically Berle explained that national security obliged the United States to include Hawaii, Alaska, Puerto Rico, and Guam as part of its cabotage. When the British again brought forth their 50/50 split of transatlantic traffic, arguing for "equilibrium . . . in order to prevent chaos," Berle allowed that it would not be fair to predict postwar traffic on the basis of prewar figures—an artful reminder that while the United States generated 80 percent of the prewar traffic, it would not press the issue. "At the conference today with the Americans Colonial cabotage was conceded to us," Beaverbrook reported to the Colonial Office later without elation—adding: "While we have had this immense benefit conferred upon us we are being treated very harshly in other respects. Briefly, the Americans seek unrestricted competition."[13]

In order to court favor with Ottawa, both sides took internationalization more seriously than the absent Canadians. Although Beaverbrook later informed the imperialist-dominated Committee on Air Transport (CAT) that "Mr. Berle was indignant at our proposal and had suggested that we must want to break or we would not have put forward the Canadian document," Berle's version of his response to the Canadian plan was "the American group pointed out that in certain essential respects the United States would find difficulty in accepting all of the Canadian proposals"; the minutes reflect Berle's benign interpretation. Yet, Beaverbrook later told C. D. Howe that the Canadian document consumed "two days of difficult and fretful negotiations," half the time Berle spent in London.

> The crux of the matter was that we wanted to set up an International Authority with power to enforce its regulations whereas the Americans wanted an authority with all the concessions but no power. The Americans wanted to increase their overseas airline schedules on a basis of competitive efficiency. We took the view that there must be equilibrium between the total transport capacity and the traffic offering.[14]

Beaverbrook fairly described their opposing positions, but Berle evidently was not hostile to the Canadian proposals (he had every reason not to be). Beaverbrook introduced them in part to confirm British fears that Berle sought to dismantle the British Empire and erect an American empire in its stead and in part to give Britain a program at a time when its own officials could not agree upon one among themselves. Beaverbrook did not like total internationalization, privately telling Berle, "I always favor capital." On the other hand, Berle knew that Congress was not about to give away any American air power to international control. Yet he had assured Ottawa that he would discuss an international rules authority and he dared not offend the Canadians. The British conveniently accused Berle of intransigence, one member of the CAT declaring that "it seemed to him the Americans wanted unrestricted competition with all the advantages they could derive from it at present." That was true, but realists in the Foreign Office also recognized that by accepting internationalization "as the basis for future international discussion *Berle in fact yielded to our point of view.* Whether he will be able to implement such a policy remains to be seen. Meanwhile we can be well content."[15]

Berle and Beaverbrook held a press conference at the end of the discussions and issued a statement that hinted at hidden disagreements by promising further talks without describing concrete results from Berle's visit. While Beaverbrook wanted British officials to be impressed by his tough handling of Berle, he also wanted a public impression of conciliation. And so he told fifty reporters sitting in a charming light green and white room off Whitehall that the British had made concessions. That would have the desired effect of a front-page *New York Times* headline, "British Bow to U.S. on Some Air Issues." Turning aside questions, Beaverbrook graciously insisted that it was his guest's press conference. Berle declared that concessions had been mutual. According to a British reporter, Berle spoke without notes and covered a wide range of topics "crisply, lucidly and without a moment's hesitation," demonstrating "crystal clarity and smiling courtesy, pausing only long enough to light a cigarette. It was a brilliant exposition of an alert mind with a complete mastery of its subject. Every question was answered fully, frankly and with no fumbling for replies." It was "a brilliant lesson on how a conference should be conducted." Still, the absence of details hinted at hidden conflicts. So did Berle's candid comment that there was a "vast difference" in the attitudes of the two countries toward the airplane—the American view being that it was a tool of competitive commerce, the British being that it was an "inherently evil" instrument of war. Although an American reporter childishly accused Berle and Beaverbrook of saying nothing new and then stalked out, the Foreign Office thought "Mr. Berle's remarks were very helpful. . . . The gulf between us and the U.S. government has been bridged (though the bridge is delicate)."[16]

Perhaps fragile was a better word. Even the War Cabinet imperialists realized that Berle was not interested in trading anything for British bases that Amerian dollars had built; he was interested in selling or leasing American transports to be used in free skies. Of all the British fears, one had real substance: Britain could not compete in manufacturing air transport and would be dependent upon American largesse while British manufacturing ability atrophied. Imperialists all believed to a man that the empire which had once been knit together by ships would be maintained after the war by air transports—hopefully British-built and British-owned. Only strict international rules that apportioned to London a gigantic closed market could have satisfied them. Yet it was Berle's duty—and he fairly savored it—to tell them that their day was past, that liberalism would dominate postwar international markets, that the empire would survive for a period after the outbreak of peace if only to keep order in the transition. Without planes or money to build them, the British were powerless in civil aviation negotiations. That made the imperialists dangerous and untrustworthy negotiators who possessed only their recalcitrance as a bargaining device.

Berle did not perceive their intransigence until later. The British knew that they could beguile Berle and other Americans with their intellects—the most available commodities in wartime London. Intellect, Berle believed, could be addressed; certain facts could be agreed upon. In the spring of 1944 the invasion of Western Europe was imminent and the end of the war was in sight. Africa and South America were already available, pacified markets. In London and Washington the race for those markets had begun.

While both capitals agreed on the need for a United Nations conference to write the rules of the race, London hoped that it would not be held until after the 1944 elections when American nationalism had somewhat abated. Then, perhaps, the Americans might be more amenable to strict international rules that apportioned markets. In the meantime, competition had to accomplish what could not be attained by cooperation.

ARISE O ISRAEL

Berle returned from London satisfied with the discussions, lavishly praising his British hosts' hospitality, and "much impressed with Beaverbrook's drive and initiative." Still, he warned the Canadians that the Beaver "showed more enthusiasm for internationalism in practice than an understanding of internationalism in theory"—Berle's way of reminding Canadian liberals that old imperialists do not change their spots and that only liberals were true internationalists. British sophistication impressed Berle, his conciliatory tone surprised them; when he sent a copy of his report on the trip to Beaverbrook, thereby confirming their understandings, Beaverbrook's aviation aide noted with wonder that "Berle has, in fact, accepted even more than we might have hoped."[1]

"You will always be remembered here and we hope you will not forget us," Beaverbrook had told him in a telegram. "Come back soon and do still more and bigger work." But the talks did not change British positions. Questioned about the discussions in the Commons, Churchill declared, "I do not think myself we are in a position to advocate a particular policy at a particular moment." More than ever Britain needed time to build planes and reduce the great American lead in air transports. The talks had revealed how much better prepared for air talks the Americans were than the British; now London wanted no more negotiations. Neither did American nationalists; U.S. lawmakers perceived negotiations with the wily British as furthering London's interests.[2]

Berle sensed that the talks had heightened their rivalry by revealing that the British did not want to compete in open markets with American commercial aviation. The American demand for freedoms inspired London to embark upon a course of surreptitiously capturing aviation markets where it could. On the eve of that great cooperative military venture, D day, Berle heard that Beaverbrook had encouraged a BOAC–Pan American cartel to invade African and South American markets. Accordingly, when the British Embassy asked Berle if the State Department had any reservations about three BOAC planes flying to Brazil via West Africa, Berle responded that he expected a quid pro quo: American service to North Africa. After all, he told Michael Wright, "the British move presented the first major move for expansion of commercial air services since the beginning of the war."[3]

"It seems pretty plain that the field will be open for international aviation . . . before the international arrangements can be completed," Berle warned Hull. If the Americans did not secure British agreements on aviation routes they would have to accept British routes de facto. Berle urged the CAB to free American carriers to seek routes overseas as soon as military circumstances allowed. Four days after D day, Roosevelt, probably at Berle's instigation, alerted senators to the prompt need for an international agreement on civil aviation so that if there was a German collapse, "we should need to have our aviation policy not only fixed but in such shape that we could move out at once."[4]

As Roosevelt and Berle were not swayed by wartime propaganda concerning the "special relationship" of the two English-speaking powers, so imperialists like Beaverbrook were not fond of Americans. According to Beaverbrook's biographer, A. J. P. Taylor, while Churchill might employ sentiment to win American hearts, Beaverbrook "wanted a business relationship in which Great Britain asserted herself as an equal partner and a great power. *He was in the war for Great Britain and her Empire, not for America or for any idealistic cause.*" Beaverbrook did not value highly the sympathies of American Anglophiles. Earlier in 1944 he had told Churchill that "a sound and lasting relationship with the United States" had to be based upon British abilities "to build up our own prestige and safeguard our own inherited interests in the economic as well as the political and military spheres." Beaverbrook expected Americans "to drive a hard bargain and knew that they would respect Great Britain more if the British did the same. Perhaps he misjudged British strength at this time. But those who went about proclaiming British weakness did much to cause it."[5]

In July Beaverbrook traveled to the United States to test American attitudes on oil and civil aviation. Knowing that Berle wanted more aviation discussions, Beaverbrook attempted to wring further concessions from his hosts. In particular, Beaverbrook wanted an American agreement that set terms for other countries, thereby averting an unwieldy international conference that might not tolerate Beaverbrook's passion for dividing the world into British and American spheres of influence. Beaverbrook feared that small countries might "gang up" against the British Empire in self-protection. He wanted to gang up with the Americans *alone*. Since the only alternative to imperialism was internationalization, Beaverbrook raised it anew during lunch with Berle on July 21. Berle did not take it seriously, and accordingly Beaverbrook fell back upon his next position—in Le Rougetel's words, bartering "landing rights in the Middle East for landing rights in the Western Hemisphere." It was a ploy designed to force the Americans into protecting their Good Neighbor Policy and it required concessions to London elsewhere. In order to keep the British talking about aviation, the Americans agreed to discuss routes now before the war in Europe ended.[6]

During his American visit, Beaverbrook played on Berle's aristocratic snobbishness and courted him with some rustic gentility. It was at Beaverbrook's insistence that in late July Berle accepted an invitation to what became "a rather fantastic weekend." Beginning with a small dinner on Friday night at which Berle "enjoyed the desultory talk but was not quite clear what it was all about," the next morning Beaverbrook, Richard Law, and Berle flew to New Brunswick, where they were joined in the woods by C. D. Howe. During a lot of hard drinking ("a comparison of the best whiskey in the world with the best champagne in the world, both of which were flowing around in considerable quantity"), hiking (during which the Beaver waxed upon his Canadian roots), fishing ("the trout were running small; I caught but did not kill"), and lots more desultory talk ("the Beaver was trying to argue Dick Law out of a serious political mistake, namely espousing liberal ideas and supporting imperial privileges, which the Beaver thought, would end his career"), Berle was thoroughly captivated by his aristocratic British host's "shimmering intellectual splendors": "The whole thing from beginning to end was dominated by the abounding bounce, gaiety and endless vitality of Beaverbrook, who seems to have cooked all this up mostly for the fun of it." But what did Beaverbrook really want?

"The Beaver reminded me somewhat of Sunday in Gilbert Chesterton's novel, 'The Man Who Was Thursday,' drawing everyone into a kind of maelstrom of warm-hearted and enthusiastic discussion, below which was a discernible flavor of direct political purpose." Beaverbrook had not gone to Canada for a nostalgic romp in the woods that revived boyhood dreams. He too had aviation in mind. For, as Beaverbrook told London, "I am holding on to Howe. He will support us if his government does not cut loose as they did the last time." However, the ever-intense Berle wanted Beaverbrook to negotiate with him. Attempting an "angle shot," he brought up the subject of aviation with Howe, then Law, and finally on the plane back to Washington, the Beaver himself. BOAC, Berle asserted, was moving out into overseas markets; "there was no dissent from this statement." Nor was there dissent from the proposition that American carriers would not sit still and "an unseemly scramble for considerations, etc.," would ensue before V-E day. The logic of the situation, as Beaverbrook saw it, was either commercial chaos or else Berle would have to satisfy British ambitions for spheres of influence. If the Americans would not accept spheres of influence, the British wanted landing rights in Brazil; the Americans could have landing rights in the Mediterranean and in the Middle East; neither side should prevent the aspirations of the other. Berle took these terms more seriously than did Beaverbrook and Law. When these informal points made on a holiday weekend were discussed in Washington a few days later, the British insisted that they had agreed to nothing. They had only suggested a British invasion of Latin America in the hope that the Americans might defend their interest in Latin America and concede to the British a free hand in Europe and elsewhere.[7]

Beaverbrook returned to London certain that he had manipulated Berle and Howe well, but apprehensive concerning the enormous aviation activity he found in the United States. "Civil aviation is making rapid progress in the United States," Beaverbrook telegraphed from Washington. The Americans spent untold millions of dollars on transports and airfields. "The vision of the future is expansive and far surpasses the outlook of the most optimistic British advocate of civil aviation"—one way of saying that it overwhelmed even Beaverbrook. He was in awe of the way American aircraft factories employed millions of workers to produce thousands of aircraft to be used around the world. With freedom of the skies, the Americans would create a demand for their planes in every market they reached. "I am convinced our only chance is to equip ourselves with British aircraft at the earliest possible moment," Beaverbrook wrote. "A policy of buying American civil aircraft would only confirm the American manufacturing position. . . . If we were to accept American aircraft then the British Aircraft Industry would go to the wall." He concluded that "unless we pursue the policy now of building British transport aircraft promptly and with vigour, Civil Aviation must pass to control of the U.S.A. on the manufacturing and operating basis. Arise O Israel."[8]

Berle, on the other hand—with Allied armies moving upon Germany and financial settlements and the United Nations organization in the works at Dumbarton Oaks—was personally more determined than ever to fulfill his destiny and contribute to history and the making of the peace by getting an aviation agreement before the war ended. In late August he began to press for an international conference on aviation until Hull agreed on September 6 to bring the matter to the president. Beaverbrook, fearing that if London did not talk aviation the Americans would move "out on to civil air routes of the world," reluctantly agreed to an international conference after the American elections in November.[9]

On September 9, Roosevelt approved an American invitation to an international civil aviation conference on November 1. To Berle's great satisfaction, the president hailed it as "another section of the peace settlements" in addition to the Dumbarton Oaks conference to be held in late October. Because Dumbarton Oaks was a Washington conference, Roosevelt preferred that Berle find another site for the aviation conference. Berle suggested Chicago and Roosevelt found the idea of bringing an international conference to the isolationist Midwest appealing. In fact, Berle intended to play upon Midwest nationalism to wring unanimity from the delegates so "that few, if any, countries would care to exclude the United States from its legitimate rights. . . . " That same day Berle sent a telegram to Beaverbrook announcing that the United States would host an International Air Conference within two months, shrewdly adding that Americans would *not* postpone their quest for bilateral routes with countries other than Britain: "We are not contemplating hasty or violent action, but simply cannot be in the position which will prevent us from protecting American interests."[10]

The British had to attend, but Beaverbrook was unhappy about it and bitter. He was not bothered by Berle; "The difference between you and me," Beaverbrook told Minister of Air Archibald Sinclair, "is that you would hold [a] conference without Berle. I would only hold a conference if he comes in." But while Beaverbrook spoke with great bravado about handling Berle, he dreaded an American rush to a conference founded upon a desire to assert and increase America's advantage in civil aviation. On August 26 Beaverbrook had told a War Cabinet meeting, "we have come to the parting of ways. We can either go forward with the Americans or we can stand on our previous policy of international collaboration excluding the United States. The issue involves the whole future of British Civil Aviation." Thus, if he could have his way, Beaverbrook would organize imperial preference in the air independent of any agreement with the Americans.[11]

But he did not get his way. Beaverbrook pleaded with the War Cabinet to seek a postponement of the conference on the grounds that the two sides were in "fundamental disagreement." Britain needed time of organizing the Commonwealth against the Americans and for pursuing an all-out effort to put British transports in the air. Beaverbrook already had Howe's support in Canada for the delay, but Halifax admonished London that any British postponement would lead to American accusations that they were "obstructionists and selfish." Britain could not torpedo a Chicago conference without alienating American opinion.[12]

Since Britain could not escape going to Chicago, Beaverbrook decided to personally shun the conference. If the Americans would not negotiate markets or submit to the control of an international authority, "we must recognize the failure," he told Sinclair. "We should be wrong to think that we can drive them into accepting a regulatory Authority by 'ganging up' the lesser Powers. . . . We should deceive ourselves if we clung to it now." American planes made all negotiations futile. Having resigned from positions before, Beaverbrook now eschewed leading the British delegation to the Chicago conference.[13]

Although Berle had heard rumors that Beaverbrook would resign, it still surprised him when he heard a news broadcast declare that Beaverbrook would not be coming to the conference. In his place would be Lord Philip Swinton, who had held the Air portfolio in the 1930s when it was part of a general scheme for imperial preference. Most recently, Swinton had been in the diplomatic service in West Africa and Berle had had many reports that Swinton was a Colonel Blimp anti-American type. The U.S. air attaché in London reported that the new British policy was "designed to hold back the United States in the air as much and as long as possible in the hope that British aviation will some day be able to meet it. . . . It is probable that England will take a holding and delaying attitude to the limit that can be done without seriously threatening the over-all relations between it and the United States." Although Michael Wright assured him that the personnel change augured no change in policy, Berle, "rather gingerly" expressed his concern that "the British doctrine had now gone in for a closed sky and exclusive arrangements." He correctly suspected that imperialists would control the British delegation in Chicago.[14]

Knowing Berle to be "inclined to think aloud," the Foreign Office dispatched Michael Wright to "draw Berle further into showing on what lines the Americans are thinking and how firmly they are likely to stand on their initial positions." Was an international body feasible? Wright inquired. Yes, if it did not attempt too much. Could an international body regulate routes and frequencies of flight? "The American position is in favor of unlimited frequencies," declared Berle, and from that position he would not budge. But what about an "equitable distribution of frequencies?" asked Wright, looking for the 50/50 split Beaverbrook had sought in London. Berle replied, "If it mean[s] artificially attempting to shift traffic, we [are] against it, lock, stock, and barrel." Besides, he added, under the rules of liberalized trade, the nations of the world should plan their routes and get their planes in the air and the question of frequencies would take care of itself. Finally, he assured Wright that all countries need not fear American discrimination; they would have their share of American planes to fly. It is doubtful that that message comforted Beaverbrook.[15]

Concerned with overall relations with the Americans, the Foreign Office worried that Swinton would clash with Berle. It assigned one of its political aides to Swinton; years later the aide wrote, "Lord Swinton was a fine, fighting, non-highbrow Conservative political leader, with a remarkable political record. He suffered however from the limitation of having no conversation other than business or political reminiscence. [Berle], in contrast, was an extremely able New York radical lawyer, an intellectual who did not repudiate the title and bore a streak of intolerance in his make-up." Nevertheless, went another British characterization, Swinton had "shrewdness and drive" that made him indispensable, even if he was "imperious [and] intolerant of lesser men and with a keen eye to the main chance." Perhaps Swinton lacked Beaverbrook's gregariousness and guile, but it was important to the War Cabinet that he was an imperialist who would follow its instructions well. Indeed, as Swinton defined his task for the War Cabinet, it was to uphold "the interest of the British Empire." As for the four freedoms, about all he agreed with was the right to innocent passage. If he failed to get an even split on frequencies with the United States, then he would demand of the empire preference agreements to counter American strength in bilateral treaties. Reading Swinton's proposed strategy to the War Cabinet, even Masefield was aghast; Swinton would alienate Canada and rupture the Commonwealth. By opposing U.S.

freedom "to carry all the traffic it wishes to fly in American aircraft," Swinton invited a fight at the conference.[16]

It would be a fight Berle could not lose. American air power was awesome. Berle could ignore British bases with certainty that if American planes did not use them after the war those bases would be overgrown with weeds sprouting through the tarmacs. The British simply lacked modern transports of their own manufacture. Without an international agreement, the United States would win landing rights everywhere outside the British Empire through bilateral negotiations. How many countries would refuse to swap their landing rights for modern American planes with their own national markings and the right to land in New York? But Roosevelt and Berle wanted an international agreement as soon as possible because negotiating bilateral treaties with dozens of countries took too long; an international consensus on the rules of air navigation would standardize bilateral agreements. Berle hoped that the Chicago conference, through propaganda about four freedoms and American aviation generosity, would win that consensus and get American planes into foreign airports sooner.

Expecting it to be the climax of his diplomatic career, Berle carefully prepared the ground for maximum support from every direction. He proposed for the U.S. delegation an eclectic group including Senator Owen Brewster of Maine (whom he personally loathed as Juan Trippe's "stooge"), La Guardia (whose postwar career needed a fillip), a businessman, and a woman—even the supernationalistic Clare Boothe Luce. He helped *Fortune* magazine write a story on international aviation that espoused freedom of the air. To disrupt the empire bloc, he wooed the Canadians, demonstrating his sweet reasonableness to Lester Pearson every chance he got. As the conference's host, he invited every member of the United Nations. However, he also invited neutral Ireland and ignored neutral Argentina—a move that angered the British because they feared an antagonistic Ireland and needed Argentine wheat. But the Americans needed air or landing rights in Ireland while Argentina was, Berle quipped, merely "a dagger pointed at the heart of Antarctica."

As for the "lesser powers" whom the British hoped would gang up against the American mammoth, Berle courted them sedulously. Perhaps it was not too different from counting noses in New York City politics. Would the Norwegians vote with the Americans? Perhaps, but the Norwegians waited to see which way the Swedes would go—and who knew how much influence the British had on Stockholm? A Polish delegate said bluntly that his country needed American planes and would support the American position at the conference—although the Russian position would of course exert an influence. With the Danish minister Kauffmann, Berle simply laid out the contrasting British and American positions—and assumed that his would be seconded at Chicago. More discussions like this would follow at the Stevens Hotel.[17]

But one delegation that Berle would not influence was the U.S.S.R.'s; it decided not to come. This was a blow of sorts to him. Having envisioned the conference as his contribution to the making of the postwar world, what could the conference accomplish if one of the great powers did not attend? Politics and economics assured that nobody could afford to ignore Moscow's views. Those views had been sought and would continue to be. Yet, Berle consoled himself, in civil aviation the Russians necessarily were a special case that required separate treatment. Politically the Soviets were important, but location made Russia less important to the United States than Ireland. While Berle may have wished that the Russians were at his conference to add to its prestige and possibly resist British demands for a strong international organization, its recent performance at the Dumbarton Oaks conference suggested that Moscow's perspective was radically different and difficult to conciliate. Moreover, he knew that it would never tolerate American freedoms and had spheres of influence arrangements with the British that could carry over into aviation. He had courted the Soviets and now he had to be satisfied with their decision not to be at Chicago. Berle would have enough trouble trying to reconcile London's position with his own.

The Making of the Peace at Chicago

As Beaverbrook once remarked, "it is not possible to treat civil aviation separately from the general picture." The International Conference on Civil Aviation at Chicago was intended to be, Berle said, "one of a series of conferences which, taken together, constitute the framework of the peace settlements." Although Roosevelt had decreed in 1942 that no one great conference during or after this war would rival that of 1919, he expected that meetings of the Big Three and the specialized conferences at Dumbarton Oaks and at Chicago would establish viable postwar settlements.[1]

Berle had personal goals too—to make his contribution to a durable peace settlement and, in particular, find his place in history as the "Grotius of the Air."[2] But he did not know when he went to Chicago that he had begun the concluding chapter in his career as assistant secretary of state. Washington's turbulent foreign affairs leadership had entered its final war transition. In the last days of the fourth-term campaign, Berle was obviously too busy preparing for Chicago and Roosevelt drew little upon Berle's speechwriting talents. The president himself was visibly a different man—shockingly worn, old, and lacking in the dynamism he once projected so readily. In late August Berle had seen the president and was surprised to find a very tired man: "In older days he would pump so much vitality into everybody present that the effect was like a couple of glasses of champaign [*sic*]. Not so now, though he still is more vigorous than most men who are twenty years younger." Other people likewise commented with amazement at the physical decline of the president; Berle's own rather brief observations also suggest a relationship in decline.[3]

Cordell Hull too had a sense of estrangement from Roosevelt. Complaining to Breckinridge Long in the fall of 1944 that "a rift between him and the President had become real and that his position under these circumstances may not be tenable," Hull refused to make any campaign speeches for Roosevelt's fourth term—a refusal that would have meant dismissal for anyone other than Cordell Hull. Hull too was tired—"tired of intrigue. He was tired of being by-passed. He was tired of being relied upon in public and ignored in private. He was tired of fighting battles which were not appreciated. He was tired of making speeches and holding press interviews—tired of talking and tired of service." After almost twelve tumultuous years, Cordell Hull was tired of being Franklin Roosevelt's secretary of state. With the new year he would be gone from State's leadership, together with Breckinridge Long and Adolf Berle.[4]

Of those who were with FDR in 1932 and survived through 1944, Berle was possibly the man who best interpreted Roosevelt and his foreign policy. With Welles gone and Hull alienated, among the remaining leaders of the State Department Berle best possessed the experience, intellect, and drive to give continuity to Roosevelt's foreign policy without upstaging the president. Berle the braintruster knew Roosevelt's mind and possessed the passion to advance his goals. This is not to imply that that policy was a seamless web which would tear apart without Berle to weave it. For, as the war went on, a consensus among Americans had grown to support that policy. Its principal goal was a durable global prosperity and stability which had eluded the peacemakers of 1918–1919. It would be a *Pax Americana* modeled upon the Good Neighbor Policy and the security arrangements of 1938–1942, and making great amounts of American capital available on liberal credit to the world for reconstruction. But American credit would carry the requirement that the old empires be gradually disbanded and economic spheres of influence be abolished—an emerging liberal internationalism to be supervised by the United Nations. Familiar with the peculiar quality of America's liberal empire and its need for state capitalism at home and abroad, Berle was a major philosopher and architect of the emerging *Pax Americana*.

Its goals were not shared by America's wartime allies. Individually, Britain and Russia could do little to thwart American designs; together they promoted postwar understandings concerning Eastern and Southern Europe which Washington considered inimical to the policy's goals. Moscow and London divided the Old World into spheres of influence that defied self-determination. It angered Berle when he heard Soviet Ambassador Oumansky's comment that the United States should "give its attention most to Western Hemisphere affairs and leave it to the Soviet Union and Great

Britain to attend mostly to European affairs.'' Throughout the war Berle had feared ''Churchill's romantic desire to placate the Soviets'' by encouraging their hegemony over Eastern Europe. Without love for either power, Berle usually gave the Soviets higher marks than the British for including the United States in consultations. He was particularly upset when he heard that the Foreign Office had concluded an air agreement whereby the British bartered rights to land in London for rights to land in Moscow with American planes Washington had given London. While British propaganda celebrated its ''special relationship'' with the United States, British policy sought combination with the Commonwealth and cooperation with the Soviets in order to thwart Roosevelt's anticolonialism.[5]

Moscow was especially mysterious on civil aviation. In the spring of 1944 Joe Grew discussed it with the young Soviet Ambassador, Andrei Gromyko, who did not then seem to understand the issues. Although invited to Washington for aviation discussions with Berle, the Soviets were slow to send their experts. Finally, on May 29, six Soviet Army officers met with Berle in Washington to listen to his explanation of U.S.-U.K. differences on civil aviation—articulated to drive a wedge between London and Moscow. He gave the Soviets his most cordial treatment, even sending flowers to Mrs. Gromyko. Then, in late July, Beaverbrook advised Berle that British talks with the Soviets were filled with misunderstandings. In Moscow's eyes, said Beaverbrook, ''we are all liars.''[6]

The Soviets delivered a civil aviation proposal of their own on August 1, Berle characterizing it as ''a policy of hermetically closed air.'' An American line would terminate in Cairo where Soviet planes would take on American passengers bound for Moscow. Soviet territory would be inviolate to foreign planes, thereby ''flying in the face of both technological and political currents.'' Because the Russians believed there was no such thing as ''innocent passage,'' Berle's vision of flights over Siberia to reach China went aglimmering. Little about the Soviets in 1944 was encouraging. He was angered by the Soviet Army's indifference to the Warsaw uprising against the Germans, ''substantially condemning these people to death.'' Soviet recalcitrance at the Dumbarton Oaks conference in September also bothered him. As the Soviets grew bolder Berle grew concerned about Hull's deteriorating health and escalating rumors that Roosevelt would appoint politicians as new ambassadors; the United States was ''a first-rate power putting up a third-rate act, at a time when Europe would give a great deal if we would take rank and right and decision comparable to our military power.'' Declaring that ''I am rapidly getting to the point where I have had all of this I can take,'' Berle took pen in hand and wrote two policy memos that may have sealed his State Department fate.[7]

The memos dealt with postwar Europe in general and Eastern Europe and the Near East in particular. Tying military power to political power, he began with the assumption that the U.S. Army would be second to the

Soviet Army in continental strength. The Soviets would have governments "in substantial compliance with their desires in Poland, Rumania, Bulgaria, Czechoslovakia, and Hungary." The Soviet demand for "friendly" governments on its borders troubled him: "If it is meant that these governments must not engage in intrigue against the Soviet Union there could be no possible objection; if it is meant that, by subsidizing guerilla or other movements, virtual puppet governments are to be established, a different situation would prevail." He could understand why these countries' foreign policies had to be friendly to the Soviets—as long as they were free to pursue their own economic systems and free from Soviet military control. But Soviet expansionism now threatened Europe and the Middle East. American power and prestige must not be a pawn for any tattered European imperial design when the British, French, Dutch, and Portuguese governments endeavored to restore their empires around the world. America had to define its interests independent of British and Soviet ambitions. Presciently anticipating the cold war events of 1947, Berle warned, "If care is not taken at once we shall find ourselves made jointly responsible for a situation in Greece which in practice is being determined by the Middle Eastern Command and carried out by British propaganda and intelligence officers." He did not oppose all spheres of influence. Seeking "a modification of the ruthlessness of British commercialism and the ruthlessness of Soviet nationalism," Washington should acknowledge that a Soviet sphere of influence in Eastern Europe existed "in somewhat the same fashion" as the American system in the western hemisphere. But Americans should oppose "closed systems" where they could not trade freely. Also, America needed disarmament—confident that its ideas and economic power would prevail while other empires needed force to prevail. Yet, if it had to, imperial America would be unafraid to assert its power.[8]

Berle asserted a few years later that he was pushed out of the State Department because he advocated policies tougher on the Soviets than other policymakers wanted. Those cold war claims appeared to be self-serving by insinuating that State Department survivors led by Acheson were soft. But the actual brunt of his criticism in 1944 fell upon British foreign policy. As Berle saw it then, the real problem was that a State Department faction deferred to the British who courted the Soviets in order to advance the cause of empire—thereby encouraging London to think it could win Washington's endorsement of its deals with Moscow by manipulating Americans such as Hopkins, Stettinius, and Acheson. With Welles gone, only Roosevelt, Hull, and Berle articulated postwar goals consistent with prewar goals—a policy independent of London and greatly preoccupied with the Good Neighbor Policy.

In 1944 Berle sought to implement that policy at the Chicago conference with the more than fifty countries in attendance. Three English-speaking countries defined the conference's issues: Britain, Canada, and the

United States. Lord Swinton, with his experience in colonial affairs, marshalled support from the Empire and the Commonwealth. Berle, with his experience in Latin American affairs, organized the states from south of the Rio Grande, his task made easier by the exclusion of the recalcitrant Argentines. Canada navigated between the British, to whom it was tied by heritage and politics, and the United States, to whom it was tied by economics and geography. All of them desired compromise, but all of them began with inimical positions. Swinton demanded equality of frequencies (number of flights from originating countries), a strong international organization, and no discussion of routes. Berle reacted incredulously and crusaded for "freedoms" which were government grants of privilege. Canada, believing it would be reduced to little more than a corridor between America and Europe, advocated a strong international body and modified its positions to suit American liberalism and British cartelism, enhancing its role of "honest broker" between the predatory Americans and the reactionary British.

The Stevens Hotel on Michigan Avenue facing the lake in the Second City's Loop (it is now the Hilton) was not the most commodious setting for an international conference. Nor is November the gentlest of months in the fabled Windy City—but weather did not have to discomfort the delegates, most of whom seldom ventured out from the Stevens during the five-week conference. One reason it was chosen was that Berle anticipated at most a three-week meeting. Still, "venue" mattered in diplomacy and Berle should have been cognizant of improving diplomatic demeanor through hospitable surroundings that, while not distracting delegates from their tasks, relaxed them between sessions. Diplomatic tempers were not soothed in a hotel where the elevator seemed to take an hour to come or where the wait to use telephones seemed to be a half hour. On the first day many of the delegates swarmed around the desk late into the night awaiting room assignments. The hotel's confusion ineluctably confirmed British aristocrats in their belief that democratic Americans were incapable of giving service. Lord Swinton griped about "chaotic arrangements" at the Stevens which he attributed to the hosts' inadequate planning.[9]

Also inconsistent with good diplomacy was Berle's determination to hold regular press conferences, even though he was the conference's chairman by right of being its host, and by protocol the chairman should not have been overtly partisan. But Berle had Roosevelt's permisison for this in order to marshal American public opinion against the British. Aside from irritating the British and other delegates, the tactic backfired when the antiadministration *Chicago Tribune* distorted developments at every opportunity. Thus, just prior to election day, it ran a front page story accusing Berle of intending to give away U.S. planes and air routes to foreigners without getting anything in return. The Anglophobic *Tribune* even charged Berle with iniquitous subservience to British policy—which must have amazed Lord Swinton. "The only Americans who stand to benefit" from the administration's internationalism, "the World's Greatest Newspaper" declared editorially, "are precisely those little men in spats and their cousins on Long Island whose craving for social recognition outside their own country is their dominant passion."[10]

Aside from *The Tribune,* most delegates and reporters at the conference found amusement in the hotel's bar. Fatigue and stress played important diplomatic roles when sessions sometimes went all night, making sleep the most welcome recreation of all. Berle should have learned something from Beaverbrook about British diplomacy and have made a point of breaking from the scene of discussions. But Berle mourned Beaverbrook's absence and made no effort to elicit good humor from the icy Swinton with a weekend in the country. Rather, his behavior was even more intense than usual—a workaholic who compartmentalized business and pleasure—a trait made all the more unfortunate by the fact that Berle and Swinton instinctively disliked each other. They seldom had lunch or dinner or drinks together. Although Berle usually enjoyed playing the genial and gracious host, he did not seem to care to charm Swinton.

Nor was Swinton the gregarious and puckish intellectual that Beaverbrook was. Also, unlike the Beaver, he was not part of Churchill's circle. Berle felt that the switch from Beaverbrook to the tall, lean-jawed Swinton, whose recent tours in West Africa left him out of touch with recent aviation developments, signaled a British attempt to kill the conference with indifference or intransigence. Moreover, at lunch the first day Swinton told Berle "with great frankness and bluntness" that he would not discuss routes then and that he would seek an equal division of traffic policed by an international body. It was as if there had been no previous talks. And when Swinton delayed further conversation for lack of aviation experts, he suggested deliberate unpreparedness.[11]

Both sides used the first week to cement alliances with smaller countries. Although Berle chafed over "British obstructionist tactics," he welcomed the time to confer with other delegations—seeking landing rights in Ireland, listening to the Czechoslovakian delegates plead for DC-3s, etc. Evidence that the world needed American planes was abundant in Chicago, which unnerved the British. Furthermore, Berle knew that Swinton needed to wring concessions from him but could not return home having alienated and embarrassed the Americans. Thus, Berle was prepared to grant "the prestige point" of an equal number of frequencies, provided that a formula could be devised to allow for increases in traffic—that formula to be known as the "escalator clause." At the end of the first week the British announced that their original position was "a statement of view rather than a defined position," a signal that they were ready to bargain. On the issue of a powerful international authority, Swinton conceded that it would be "consultative" at best. As both sides began to show conciliation, Berle informed

Washington that "the major issues have been met and cracked," forecasting on November 6 agreement on texts in about ten days—"if my analysis is correct." The next day he flew home to New York to vote a fourth time for Franklin Roosevelt for president.[12]

Returning from a whirlwind of activity in New York, Berle held a press conference whose breach of protocol offended both the British and the Canadians. That night, Escott Reid, his young Canadian friend, engaged a tired and nervous Berle in a three-hour round of drinks and dinner. Berle railed against British "malevolence and stupidity." Why had they come to Chicago with the same proposals Beaverbrook had seven months ago? "Lord Swinton was behaving in Chicago as if he were still ruling West Africa." Only Britain's location en route to Europe entitled it to respect. Berle advised Reid that "if the British would not play ball with the United States on air transport, the U.S. could make deals with other countries and leave the British out completely." When Reid protested against that hint of bilateralism, Berle softened and praised Canada's idealism. His pessimism, he explained, was accentuated in part by his recollection that it was twenty-six years to the day since the end of the Great War.[13]

Famed for his own arrogance, Berle despised Swinton's arrogance. At his best Swinton was a tory politician or His Majesty's proconsul in West Africa. In either case Swinton was not a practiced diplomat. As Reid put it, Swinton lacked "that mastery of under-statement which is normally required of diplomatic negotiators." On November 12 they held the first of the ABC (America-Britain-Canada) talks and Reid noted that Swinton "evinced remarkably little knowledge of what he was talking about." Swinton complained that Berle had not given him time to study American proposals and made a comment which caused Berle to snap, "I resent that." Pleading for adjournment, Reid shuttled between Berle and Swinton in an effort to calm them. Berle "was in a raging temper"; Swinton "was in a state of anger equal to Mr. Berle's." Swinton charged that Berle had "double-crossed" him on the topic of discussion for that afternoon (which the Canadians corroborated). Still, Berle professed confidence that a compromise was in the offing and informed Stettinius that he would be able to end the conference on about November 21.[14]

Two days later Berle laid a trap for Swinton. When Swinton took a hard line for fixed frequencies, Berle answered with unlimited frequencies and, "after some pretty heavy argument," switched to the Canadian compromise for an escalator clause. Then he suddenly introduced a "fifth freedom," the right of a transport flying between two points to carry passengers from a point en route to its ultimate destination. Thus, if an American carrier en route to Paris discharged passengers in London, it could take on British passengers bound for Paris. This suggested that the Americans could operate on the London-Paris run in competition with the British and French. Britain's vision of dominating continental traffic would go aglimmering if the Americans had the freedom to carry between countries. Even so, Swinton, having painted himself as intransigent during the frequencies debate and possibly not understanding its consequences, foolishly accepted the fifth freedom and fell into Berle's trap. The British then asked for an adjournment, during which, in Berle's words, they "realized a devastating possibility" that U.S. planes could win traffic on their continental runs and recanted. Having cunningly put Swinton "up against a political stonewall at home," Berle magnanimously compromised on other points. After all, he reasoned, the British and Canadians had approved all five freedoms which gave "American planes [rights] to fly the direct routes we are interested in."[15]

During the next few days the delegates wrote a draft of an agreement in sessions that were "brutal in their length but friendly and cooperative in their nature." A confident Berle held his breath. In London the British War Cabinet debated the fifth freedom and wondered "if they may not be giving up too much." Swinton said he was for it, but the Cabinet was being "sticky." If "the deal has to be re-traded," Berle said, "we shall, of course, be in considerable difficulties." "Short on sleep and stale," Berle took a quiet dinner with a friend on November 17 and went to bed awaiting the reaction in London.[16]

That night Swinton got his instructions from London and showed them to Berle the next day. Berle thought they accepted the general conception of the fifth freedom but tried to "chisel" by allowing an international body to fix rates so that local fares were lower than through fares—meaning that a flight from New York had to charge a higher fare for its London-Paris run than the British or French planes. Even then, London wanted the right to cancel the "fifth freedom" after three years on six months' notice; "I told Lord Swinton there was nothing doing on this one," said Berle. Also, the British infuriated Berle by insisting on all European powers agreeing to the fifth freedom: "If they expected us to go out and get the Soviet Union to agree, this was plainly impossible and they knew it as well as we did. . . . To have a single Balkan or Iberian country capable of stopping the whole crowd of us struck me as absurd." He could not imagine non-Soviet lines flying between Kiev and Moscow and he did not favor self-determination enough to give Portugal a veto on the fifth freedom. Berle was also enraged when the British demanded the right to manufacture civilian air transports (with American money) following V-E day while the United States was prohibited from building them until V-J day: "I told Swinton bluntly that this was an impossible situation and that I wanted nothing of it."[17]

Instead of concluding on the twenty-first, the conference was at a "U.S.-U.K. deadlock." Swinton appeared to have given up on an agreement and the Canadians estimated that the chances were only one in ten that the deadlock would be broken unless Swinton got new instructions from London. Bested by the shrewder and more cunning Berle at every turn, all Swinton had going for him was his stubbornness. The Canadians noted that Berle raised the ante every time he won a point. Had Berle out-smarted himself? The "fifth freedom" was a Pyrrhic victory because it was a totally useless, mischievous ploy that aggravated rather than advanced the American position. While Berle ridiculed the British demand that every European country accept the fifth freedom, the country least likely to ap-prove it, outside of the U.S.S.R., was the United States. In January Roo-sevelt had told Attorney General Francis Biddle that "all intra-state pick-up by foreign aviation corporations should be outlawed"; had the president changed his mind since then? Or had Berle proceeded on his own? In any event, the *Chicago Tribune* was unlikely to approve of British planes com-peting for traffic between Chicago and New York![18]

Berle played another card by breaking off talks with a declaration that he saw no further room for compromise and then calling Stettinius in Wash-ington to request that FDR intercede with a message to Churchill. Of course Berle drafted the message, but it was unmistakably Roosevelt's. "The con-ference is at an impasse because of a square issue between our people and yours," the president told the prime minister. Branding the latest British proposal "a form of strangulation," he warned that "this is as far as I can go." "The limitations now proposed would, I fear, place a dead hand on the use of the great air trade routes," Roosevelt told Churchill. "You don't want that any more than I do."

The message reached London at 2:15 A.M. and all that day the War Cabinet discussed it. The War Cabinet held firm to its instructions to Swin-ton and blamed Berle for injecting new proposals. It decided that "the con-ference should finalise the valuable technical arrangements" already agreed to and adjourn.[19]

November 22 at the conference was a day for funereal speeches that played to the gallery of small countries and "apparently caused consider-able flutterings in the dovecoats." La Guardia, impassionately "speaking for the man in the street," admonished delegates that "the world will be disappointed if we dodge, duck, detour or evade the fundamentals." A Canadian pleaded for "a workable, flexible constitution for an interna-tional air administration." ("Constitution," Berle and Reid had agreed, had more appeal because a "charter" was handed down from above while a constitution was written by equals; that is why the Atlantic Charter was so seldom adhered to.) Delegates from the fifty countries vigorously ap-plauded both. Swinton, intent upon getting out of Chicago as soon as pos-sible, busied himself lining up Commonwealth support against the Cana-dians. Berle, alternately "difficult" and conciliatory, concentrated on playing his hand as Roosevelt's braintruster.[20]

"I am afraid that you do not yet fully appreciate the importance of reaching a satisfactory agreement," Roosevelt told Churchill on November

24. Failure of the conference, he warned, "would seriously affect many other things."

> We are doing our best to meet your lend-lease needs. We will face Congress on that subject in a few weeks and it will not be in a generous mood if it and the people feel that the United Kingdom has not agreed to a generally beneficial air agreement. They will wonder about the chances of our two countries, let alone any others, working together to keep the peace if we cannot even get together on an aviation agreement.

In London, Ambassador John Winant brought the message to Churchill and Churchill correctly called it "pure blackmail." At the least it was tough talk without FDR's usually Dutch uncle sweetness. The PM discussed it with the "shame-faced" Winant who tried to convince him that it "was a friendly message and looked beyond the immediate differences to the larger issues." As Churchill read it aloud to Beaverbrook, Winant knew "that it was not well received." The next move was London's.[21]

"Your aviation message gave me great anxiety," Churchill responded. Implicitly blaming the impasse upon Berle, Churchill threatened that "unless complete agreement is reached I accordingly beg that the Conference should adjourn." He concluded with an eloquent plea for no competition between them: "You will have the world's largest navy. I hope you will have the world's largest air force. You will have the most trade. You already have all the gold. But these things do not worry me because I am confident that the American people under your re-acclaimed leadership will not be given to vainglorious ambitions but rather will be guided by justice and fair play."

However, twelve hours before that Churchillian message to Roosevelt, the PM instructed Swinton to "use damping down and dilatory processes until we communicate with you again"—hinting that London would offer a compromise after Roosevelt had been heard from again. But no compromise was in the works. As Beaverbrook noted, the British position had reverted to its original proposal for a strong international body. "There can be no objection on our part," Beaverbrook commented. "If they accept, all is well. But they won't."[22]

In the midst of all this, Harry Hopkins arrived in Chicago on the twenty-seventh to inform Berle that his "resignation" as assistant secretary of state had been accepted. He would complete the conference and return to Washington for another assignment. It was a cruel blow which, although not publicized then, undercut his position at the conference. Although Roosevelt valued Berle and continued to back him to the hilt at Chicago, the "resignation" undercut Berle at a critical juncture when the British confronted either loss of face or America's wrath. Instead, Berle lost face. Breckinridge Long, no Berle sympathizer, described what Roosevelt had done to Berle as "unpardonable" and "to the detriment of the best interests of the United States and to the dignity and reputation of the head of its delegation to the Conference." Still, Berle had a mission to complete and the realization that it would be his last heightened his intensity, if that was possible. More determined than ever to reduce British imperialism to size and find his own place in history, Berle would not let the British quit the conference. Chicago had become a living hell for Berle (Beatrice Berle never again would go there because of the memories it stirred); he would make it so for them too. He would at least win liberalism in the air.

The hapless Swinton, who did not know the "difference between the atmosphere in the Gulf of Guinea and that of the shores of Lake Michigan," personally represented all Berle detested in British imperialists. Not until almost four weeks after the conference began had Swinton asked Berle to lunch, a discourtesy Berle duly noted. Knowing that the vast majority of the countries there aligned themselves with the United States, Berle pleaded with Roosevelt to resist a British move for "a quiet adjournment" and push instead for a recorded vote that deprived the British of posing "as martyrs trying to protect small nations against us." He wanted to send Swinton home in shame and ignominy. In awe the Canadians marveled at the way Berle "obviously whipped the Latin American nations into line" and noted that Swinton "received a body blow when the smaller European nations began to support the U.S. position." Even Australia and New Zealand, counted in the British camp, now wavered and were evidently confused. Berle bluntly told Swinton that while London could not accept his proposals for greater freedom of the air, he would find out how many states could. He put the American proposals in a document that "states were at liberty to sign or not as they pleased," and then held a press conference that blamed the impasse upon London.[23]

On November 30 Roosevelt responded to Churchill's plea for adjournment: "I am unable to believe that you do not want an agreement at this time. I cannot agree that the answer is to hold everyone back." He repeated generous promises of American planes in return for freedoms that opened British bases—intended as evidence that the United States sought no air monopoly. If the American position was supported among the smaller states, and the Canadians still wanted to broker differences, why did the British want an adjournment without an agreement? "I will give Berle latitude for one more try," he dared Churchill, "if you will give Swinton the same. I know that an agreement can be reached which will be equally beneficial to both our interests and to the world."[24]

The hope of the conference now centered upon whether the British would accept a proposed Canadian compromise. But already Swinton had told London via transatlantic telephone that the Canadian compromise was "irrelevant" and "dead." On his own, Swinton declared, "I turned it down. I turned down anything that was not acceptable." London had not even seen the Canadian compromise, Swinton having dismissed it as "variations of American proposals . . . which would give them the unlimited Fifth Freedom traffic they desired." "Lord Swinton was loath to send the text," Peter Masefield told Beaverbrook, "because he said it was now purely academic and obsolete. . . . He says it is no longer the subject of any interest. . . . The Conference is obviously over."[25]

But it did not have to end on that low note. Beaverbrook called Chicago at midnight on December 1 and was told that "the British delegation recommended standing fast"; Beaverbrook's assurance that London would support his intransigence made Swinton "quite happy . . . confident and resolute." Meanwhile, Churchill told Roosevelt that it was too late for any compromise because negotiations were "too complex and far-reaching in scope" for long-distance decisions. However, Beaverbrook and Churchill then summoned John Winant to tell him that they could have accepted a modified Canadian compromise but, said Beaverbrook, "before they could communicate their decision to Swinton, the conference had adjourned." Winant noted that "Beaverbrook was plainly uncomfortable at this meeting."[26]

Beaverbrook had good reason for discomfort. Swinton had ceased to negotiate, was marshaling empire support behind his move for adjournment and London was afraid to rebuke him, even if it meant offending Roosevelt. Yet Beaverbrook knew that London wanted to give Swinton new instructions for compromise, but what he could not say was that London dared not send them because it knew that the Americans were intercepting their messages to Swinton and tapping the telephones. Years later Masefield would recall that "We got totally confused. We had to cover up and reverse ourselves." Beaverbrook did not give Swinton new instructions or advise him of Roosevelt's interest in the Canadian compromise, *"Nor could he be told with the Americans listening."* London still hoped to bargain around the Canadian compromise and did not want to reveal its flexibility to the Americans. Even Swinton had a hint of the American spying; he later told Beaverbrook that, although he did not show Berle any telegrams from London, "he thought that Mr. Berle was well aware of them. The subject was not pursued any further."

They were correct. Berle had read British cables and knew that the War Cabinet was "on the point of authorizing Swinton to accept the Canadian compromise, but suspended when Swinton reported that the Conference had adjourned. Of course, he had no right to do that. . . . " But Swinton did, correctly believing that his negotiating position had been compromised by American interceptions of telephone and telegraph communications. Therein hangs an irony: the conference's potentially harmonious conclusion was aborted by British knowledge of American spying on its communications—the very messages that might have brought compromise instead of rancor![27]

Nevertheless, in the words of Swinton's aide, "in the end the conference was outwardly a failure and essentially a great success." The conference concluded on December 7 with the election of an Interim Council, plans for a permanent international clearinghouse organization with head-quarters in Montreal, a statement of the five freedoms, and a general convention affirming air rights. Berle packaged the whole thing as separate protocols which states could either sign or ignore; "They could part company while affirming universal solidarity." In essence, states could subscribe to what they wanted and leave the rest. The enunciated principles were more important than whether countries signed the protocols or not because the conference agreed that bilateral treaties could be negotiated and the principles gave the negotiators a guide for agreement. Although the four freedoms were not novel in international air navigation discussions for decades prior to the Chicago conference, Berle's efforts forwarded those accepted principles. Two months later the United States initiated bilateral negotiations with Ireland, to Churchill's enormous consternation. And in February 1946, the United States and the United Kingdom themselves negotiated a bilateral treaty in Bermuda which gave the Americans the freedom of frequencies sought by Berle. (Churchill and the Tories had been turned out of power in 1945.) As sought by the British, the International Civil Aviation Organization (ICAO), based in Montreal, was given nominal power to set rates, subject to the approval of the governments involved. Finally, Britain conceded the "Fifth Freedom," only to have the Americans veto it because they did not want foreign airlines carrying passengers on American routes! It has been written that "what (Britain had been unwilling to grant to every nation in Chicago had been tendered to the United States at Hamilton." Indeed, the Bermuda Agreement of 1946 became the standard for future bilateral agreements. As Berle observed then, it "filled in the gap we could not bridge at Chicago so that the air world seems almost open for international civil aviation."[28]

The conference's real success was mitigated by the rancor of the U.S.-U.K. impasse. Swinton blamed Berle, telling his wife that Berle "is easily the most disagreeable person with whom I have ever negotiated." Following talks with Swinton, Lord Halifax too blamed Berle; "From what I hear," he wrote, "even an archangel would have found it difficult to get further with Berle in the mood he showed at the conference." Berle had been difficult, but some observers in the Foreign Office were less self-righteous about it, perhaps because they knew Swinton too. In any event, the British complained about Berle both because he had been offensive and because he had made the British appear intransigent. Considering that he intended the latter, he succeeded.[29]

In London, Winant blamed Beaverbrook for the "failure" of the conference, without explaining why. Certainly Beaverbrook's decision not to go to Chicago after earlier negotiations with Berle was critical and it did not remove Beaverbrook from policymaking; he was calling the shots in London. Was it to Beaverbrook that Escott Reid obliquely referred in his final report to Ottawa when he blamed "the frustrated ambitions of an influential United Kingdom politician who, having been unable himself to reach an accord with the United States was jealous lest a colleague's efforts be crowned with success"? Berle missed Beaverbrook in Chicago. "I passionately regret that you were not there," Berle told Beaverbrook. "You and I had gone over this ground and Swinton had not."[30]

Escott Reid sympathized with Berle. Perhaps, the Canadian thought as the conference concluded, the news of Berle's dismissal the morning of November 27 had influenced the outcome; "If Berle had felt his position to be secure and particularly if he felt that there was a chance of his getting the Undersecretaryship of State he might even at the last moment have been able to save the conference." Instead, "he played his cards badly" through intemperate attacks on the British. Nor did it help that Berle was quicker than Swinton. "Whenever a new issue was introduced, Swinton would need twenty-four hours before he understood what it meant, and even when Berle was not trying to put over something on him, but was moving with his usual quick mental speed, Swinton would suspect the worst." Swinton gave no evidence of having read the British Foreign Office's personality report on Berle. Reid was amazed that Swinton "showed not the slightest knowledge of Berle's peculiar qualities."[31]

Still, Reid did not buy the notion that the conference was a failure. "The Chicago Conference worked a minor miracle," he wrote. "It failed by a hair's breadth to work a major miracle." The theme was not too different from Berle's address at the closing session of the conference in which he claimed "a notable victory for civilization" because the conference had "put an end to anarchy in the air." Reid now agreed, although he suspected that there would be an attempt made "to saddle Mr. Berle with the responsibility for the so-called failure of the conference." "To make him the scapegoat for the 'failure' of the conference betrays a superficial knowledge of what went on at the conference. A man with less vision and less intellectual and political courage than Mr. Berle would not have aimed so high." In fact, Reid attributed the creation of ICAO, the Canadian goal of a international organization, to Berle. "The Berle formula for creating an effective international regulatory authority with the least possible danger of offending national susceptibilities can be made use of in many fields of international politics and economics," Reid wrote. "It is a statesmanlike contribution to the building of an effective world order."

Berle's diplomacy had been instrumental in bringing the International Civil Aviation Organization, based in Montreal, into existence. Most of the world's countries belong to it, the Soviets having joined it in 1971. Berle's aviation aide in 1944, Edward P. Warner, became a longtime president of the organization.[32] In 1964 Berle was honored as a founder of ICAO. But it was many years before a British writer concluded that "Chicago and its offspring ICAO did provide the starting point for the phenomenal development of world airlines and air travel in peacetime, at a speed which few delegates had conceived possible.'' Berle was not what he aspired to be—the Grotius of the Air—but he advanced considerably the codification of the laws governing international civil aviation. And while the Chicago conference never achieved the historical stature of Dumbarton Oaks or San Francisco, it was part of the framework of peace settlements of World War II. Thus, his was a causative contribution.[33]

8

Brazilian Interlude

*I am more convinced than ever that the only way to get anthing like per-
manent peace is the internationalization of the Good Neighbor Policy.*

> —Berle to Father, June 27, 1945,
> BP-74

To Rio with a Return Ticket

It was not by personal choice that Berle marked his fiftieth birthday in
Rio de Janeiro as United States ambassador to Brazil. A Calvinist sense of
duty brought him there that lovely January 29 summer's day in the southern
hemisphere. In an embassy that was literally falling apart for lack of proper
maintenance—how different from the comfortable mansions he had rented
in Washington—he spent a routine day conferring with American diplomatic and military representatives about Brazilian politics and U.S. relations with Argentina, topics that concerned him for much of the year. Late
in the afternoon he and Beatrice swam at a nearby beach where they watched
a fisherman hauling in his nets and, ever curious and eager for a new experience, swam over and lent the fisherman a hand. Then they returned to
the embassy to dine with his second in command and a visiting businessman. Except for the profuse birthday greetings which were symbolic of his
rank and the Brazilians' affection for the United States, it was a rather
ordinary way to celebrate the occasion.[1]

"I did not want the assignment to Brazil," Berle candidly told a law
school colleague. For a man to whom time, place, position, and purpose
meant so much, a little more than two months ago he had not imagined
that the end of the war would find him thousands of miles from the politics
of Washington. War had made soldiers of everyone. In 1938 he had enlisted
in government service for the duration, or until his services were no longer
desired; while technically free to return to civilian life whenever he chose,
loyalty to country and to president compelled him to remain. Besides, he
enjoyed his proximity to power. He had an appetite for power and had Berle

been offered the secretary's post, we cannot imagine him temporizing over it.

But he never had a chance to replace Hull. Harry Hopkins had made a special trip to Chicago on November 27 to inform the braintruster that the fourth Roosevelt administration had no place for him in Washington. Stettinius would be the new seretary of state and he had the right to choose his own assistants (albeit a right not always accorded to Hull). No one reason can explain why Roosevelt did this. The departure of Welles probably had something to do with it, as well as the influence of Hopkins in the White House. But Roosevelt himself knew Berle best, knew his strengths, uses, and moods, and knew how to use Berle at his best. Now he was dispensable.

Yet it was characteristic of Roosevelt that when he finally brought himself to remove loyal but politically expendable administrators, he offered them service abroad—Berle himself noting in 1939 that "it is an old habit of the President's when he wants to get a man out of the way." The president believed in facilitating a gracious exit, both for loyalty's sake and because he feared the wrath of angry former allies. Nevertheless, Roosevelt's timing had to shock and disappoint Berle, although he maintained his poise and had what Hopkins called a "good and very frank talk" with the bearer of bad tidings. Without hiding his regret, Berle insisted that while the Brazilian post was "one of the most important positions there is, . . . he simply is unwilling to go if it is merely providing him with a nice exit from government. He is quite willing to resign." But Roosevelt, Berle knew, would not let him depart so easily.

Berle wanted more from Roosevelt than a gracious exit and salving words. He delayed giving FDR an answer on the Brazilian post and not even a telegram from the White House pleading for an affirmative response rushed him. Then Berle demanded and got an audience with Caesar, at which Berle disdained a "feather bed" for his departure. He did not need FDR's assurances that Brazil was important to the American system. He wanted to make policy. Roosevelt anticipated Berle's price; the president offered him a "return ticket" from Rio that he could cash in on V-E day. Then he could come back to Washington to brain trust on economic problems that arose during demobilization; was that not what Berle longed to hear? Not really, for Berle was more interested in the Good Neighbor Policy and the upcoming conference of hemisphere governments in Mexico. Not content to be an ordinary envoy, he desired "reasonable liberty of action" to return to Washington periodically. Roosevelt assented to Berle's extraordinary definition of a free-lance ambassadorship; the braintruster had license to take part in the February 1945 conference and to report directly to the president.[2]

Nevertheless, "knowing Washington," he told a friend, "I am pretty clear that this will be the end of [my] governmental adventures for a while at least—I certainly hope so." Even before he left Washington he discovered just how easy it was to be forgotten; he was left off the guest list for FDR's fourth inauguration, an oversight that Sam Rosenman remedied. As important as Brazil was to the American system, throughout his stay there he felt removed from the action in Washington. On the very day that Roosevelt died—thereby taking with him Berle's "return ticket" and accessibility to the White House—the ambassador to Rio wrote mournfully to his brother, "History is not being made much in Brazil."[3]

Berle went to Brazil with his usual sense of self-importance and determination to make history there. Brazil was very important to the Good Neighbor Policy. Before the war the administration feared that the Nazis coveted a foothold in the hemisphere in Rio. During the war Brazil proved to be a valued ally against the Axis, taking the lead among Latin American nations in declaring war on the Axis and even sending troops to fight in Europe—unlike Argentina, a declared neutral that traded with Germany. Brazil was a giant among Latin American nations in terms of area, population, potential wealth, and as a trading partner. Strategically, Brazil was significant for its proximity to Africa and for its location en route to the Argentine market. State Department policy in the war stressed the significance of the Good Neighbor Policy as a model of how a great power dealt cooperatively with undeveloped nations—in contrast to British and European colonialism. It especially cited the example of Brazil in taking its place at Washington's side in war. Brazil's government, a benevolent military dictatorship led by General Getúlio Vargas since 1930, gave Washington some qualms, but it was confident that sometime in the near future Brazilians would restore liberalism and make their country a power in the Americas and a democratic model for the former colonial countries of the world. That was how Roosevelt, Hull, Welles, Berle, and others who would no longer direct American foreign policy after April 12, 1945, saw Brazil.

With little time to do so, Berle prepared himself to be a model ambassador. Already fluent in Spanish, he and Beatrice studied Portuguese and read everything they could find about Brazil. He enjoyed this because he possessed a genuine interest in the Americas based upon his many business and diplomatic experiences of a quarter of a century. He loved the hemisphere, remonstrating with snobs who treated the Americas as inferior civilizations: "It is difficult to make most Americans realize that the South American capitals are great cities, frequently better run than our own; and South American governments have been, in the main, more stable than any European governments (Britain and Scandinavia excepted); that the weakest of them compare favorably with the Balkans, and the best of them turn in a better record than France, Spain and Italy." European civilization, with its record of two cataclysmic wars in the twentieth century, seemed barbarous against the comparative tranquility of Latin America.[4]

Berle's interest in Brazil was enhanced by its exemplary behavior in the

American system. It joined Washington in creating the joint Brazil-United States Defense Commission, a model of military cooperation which enabled Rio to modernize her armed forces to resist the Nazis. Brazil traded strategic materials with the United States, provided bases for American warplanes and ships, diplomatically isolated neutral Argentina from the rest of the Americas, and, in spite of its considerable German and Italian populations, scourged all fifth columnists. With a rapidly growing population, and an area and a rate of development greater than the United States, Brazil's importance could not be minimized. "We shall have to be either generous or imperialistic," Berle declared, "and present history is showing that the generous policy is infinitely the more successful." The United States had to be cautious because Brazil was very sensitive to being exploited by its powerful ally. Early in 1944 Brazilian Ambassador Carlos Martins complained to Berle that while his country's belligerency had caused numerous shortages of materials and the loss of freighters that supplied its European allies, it received less aid from Washington than some of its neighbors. Berle was sympathetic and, in October, he warned Roosevelt that Brazil's shortages threatened its political stability. Moreover, Ambassador to Rio Jefferson Caffery was reassigned to Paris in September, leaving the Brazilians with no high-ranking American to whom they could turn. Even before going to Chicago, Berle had appointed himself Brazil's special pleader in Washington without realizing that it sealed his fate.[5]

After attending the fourth inauguration of Roosevelt and being sworn in as ambassador by Justice Robert Jackson, Berle and his wife left their children in a housekeeper's charge on January 22 and departed for Rio de Janeiro aboard a C-54 military transport carrying their fifty-seven pieces of baggage. They brought much with them because of a warning that the embassy residence lacked the basics for a good kitchen and dining room such as linen and silverware. For two and half days of excited anticipation they flew south via Puerto Rico and Belem on the north coast of Brazil, beholding the magnificent delta of the Amazon River from 10,000 feet at sunset. In Rio, the large embassy, picturesquely located at the foot of the mountain with the Christus Redemptor statue overlooking Rio, lacked many amenities: It reminded Berle of "an Atlantic City hotel in the off season; it will take a carload of stuff to make it warm and intimate." The Berles awoke on their first morning in Rio to find the embassy needed an ambassador less than a plumber to make it livable. Its plumbing was broken and for water they had to dispatch the embassy gardener with a bucket to a spring up the mountain. "So you can imagine yourself in a house about as big as the White House," Berle wrote his children, "camping on the top floor with nothing to wash in!" Days later he marked his birthday, "still struggling with the mechanics of water supply, elevators, telephones, etc." "There is something funny about living in a huge white palace with water coming up in buckets. At this point I would have sold out the whole show for fifteen cents and a free ticket home, but Mummy was wonderful and went at it."[6]

The Berles went at it in a way that Rio had not seen in an American ambassador and his family. Caffery was a bachelor who seldom entertained, but the Berles were eager to meet and receive everyone. Nor did they confine themselves to Rio. Berle made himself more visible throughout Brazil in one year there than any Brazilian could remember of an American ambassador. "The Embassy Palace in Rio is no good whatever unless it means something, says something in relation to the Minas farmer," he later advised a daughter. He traveled everywhere in Brazil determined that Americans had to affect "the lives of little people in obscure places." Berle came loaded with data about Brazil's geography and people, but he was appalled by "the detachment of the Embassy from the life of 98% of the population." Nobody on his staff "could give me even a guess figure about the national income of Brazil." Beatrice asked the wife of the senior aide if she knew the population of Brazil and when the woman replied in the negative Beatrice "asked how long she had been here and on being told about eight months she replied devastatingly 'Then you should know!'"[7]

Berle demanded of himself and other Americans that they be informed of Brazil's politics, economics, or society. His task was to provide his government with intelligence concerning the biggest and richest country in South America and to enhance its economic development and place in the American system. Brazil would someday be a model of liberal capitalism in the hemisphere and a major trading partner with the United States. For that to happen it needed to liberate its people from poverty, exploitation, and autocracy. Analyzing every bit of data he could find, he concluded, "the [social] pyramid is obviously not as horrible and tragic as it is in certain other Latin American countries; but it is bad enough—and, here, unnecessary." He visited a resort and found that "the contrast between the ultra-European luxury of Quitandinha and the squalor just beyond was rather crushing."

"Honored" by the appointment of such a high-ranking American known to be Roosevelt's braintruster, Brazilian newspapers depicted Berle's coming as evidence of Washington's determination to strengthen its close ties with Rio and evidence of Brazil's emerging importance in world affairs. Berle sought to build upon this goodwill and maximize his impact by seeking out Brazil's intellectual and political leadership, even when he felt that his "Portuguese was terrible and must have hurt everybody's ears." He professed openly that Brazil needed liberalized economics and politics. An aide introduced him to a young leftist leader, Carlos Lacerda, "a good honest boy, rather on the poetic side." What is your program, Berle demanded? To rid Brazil of its dictatorship, Lacerda responded. That is not enough, Berle insisted: "was anybody in the street going to be better off?" (Lacerda became a major democratic leader in Brazilian politics over the next two decades.) Berle demanded to know any Brazilian who wanted to improve the lot of all of his people. Briefly meeting the leader of Brazil's outlawed Communist party, Luis Carlos Prestes, only whetted his appetite for more conversation that would enable Berle to know him and Brazil better. He regularly invited the Brazilian intelligentsia to the embassy for evenings of good food and good discussion of the problems of modern government. But he had to be careful not to offend Brazil's military dictatorship. Democracy in Brazil awaited another day. As he told Henry Wallace, who shared Berle's interest in Latin American development, he did not expect to change Brazil right away, but in thirty years it would have a population of 90 million (it was 103 million in 1972) and then "Brazil's friendship will mean much to the United States."[8]

To his disgust, Berle discovered that his predecessor had cannibalized the Rio embassy, taking the best economic and political attachés with him to Paris. Moreover, Washington had not filled consul vacancies. Naively, Berle had been more concerned with advancing his State Department aide, Fletcher Warren, to Ambassador to Nicaragua than taking him to Rio where he might have been of personal service. With only a military attaché, Berle could not accomplish much: "The blunt truth is that we are being carried by the non-Departmental service: Naval, Military, OIAA, FEA, Legal Attache, et cetera." He pleaded with the State Department for embassy help: "This cannot go on." His picture of the State Department, never flattering, now was colored by the view from Rio. "I was on the Personnel Board for some years myself," he groused to a State Department officer, "and from the angle of the field, I hate to think of what I left undone myself. Getting out here is one way of learning." And it confirmed him in his belief that Department officers abroad must know the language of the country where they were posted. "The language of Brazil is Portuguese, and its second language French," he cabled the Department. "Spanish will get you meals at a hotel and the ill will of Brazilians." Rio had only nine foreign officers while Havana, Mexico City, and Buenos Aires had sixteen, nineteen, and fifteen respectively. It would be months before he had all the staff he needed. Was Rio some "outlying post, . . . a minor ripple of larger waves to come"?[9]

He did not like the life of an ambassador. In the wake of an audience with the Brazilian strongman, Getúlio Vargas, Berle commented that he had received "the kindest permission a Chief of State can give: an assurance that any time I wanted to see him he would be available immediately. The older I get, the more I realize that entree to the Chief of staff is the greatest prerogative a man can have. Also, in many ways the most dangerous." He loved the danger of proximity to power and he surely missed it in Rio. For all his cant about knowing the ordinary Brazilian, Berle believed in exercising power; he thrived among an elite few who determined policies and events. He had no stomach for "these infernal ceremonial calls" or the official attention given the American ambassador in Rio. "My principle [*sic*] trouble is to know what to do with 'My Excellency,'" he jocularly told a daughter. He was not against all pomp and circumstance. One of his biggest thrills as ambassador came when the American fleet pulled into Rio harbor. "It is childish," Berle confessed, "but I always get a kick out of the ceremonial of the Star Spangled Banner and men drawn up on deck. You feel about two inches higher when the anthem is played." On a visit by American fliers he was overjoyed on meeting an enlisted man named Foley from the Bronx; he realized that he "was homesick for a New York accent."[10]

But he never doubted the value of Latin America or his Brazilian mission. Here was where America's state capitalism would transform nonindustrial economies into trading partners and allies in a new imperial system. Colonialism's day was past and the era of the Good Neighbor Policy was at hand; its globalization would be the foundation of American foreign policy for decades to come. In early 1945, his assignment to Brazil, FDR's blank check for freewheeling diplomacy, and his former status would make him welcome at the inter-American conference in Mexico, where he would renew both the American System and his policy-making influence.

A GLOBAL GOOD NEIGHBOR?

Berle had been in Rio only a few weeks—interrupted by a side trip to Buenos Aires—when he left for a month of travels to Mexico City and Washington. Only a long and loyal relationship with the president permitted an ambassador such extraordinary license. Perhaps he knew then that it would be his last inter-American conference and the last time he would see Roosevelt. Possibly, too, Berle anticipated that, far from "internationalizing" the Good Neighbor Policy, it would die with its creator unless its supporters fought for it.

Berle expected the Good Neighbor Policy to unify the democratic hemisphere against totalitarian intrusions. However, most of the State Department's new leadership cared less for Latin America's democracy and unity than did Berle. Secretary of State Stettinius had little interest in Latin America and Under Secretary Joe Grew had little knowledge of it. Moreover, Stettinius' assistants, Alger Hiss and Leo Pasvolsky, were more intent upon establishing a world organization that superseded any hemispheric understandings. The only high-ranking official in the Department left to carry the torch for Pan-Americanism was the new assistant secretary, Nelson Rockefeller, former White House coordinator of inter-American affairs. The war had interrupted the 1930s' series of Pan American meetings and the countries to the South felt neglected. In part that inspired plans for a hemispheric conference at Mexico City in February. Invited to a policy meeting in preparation for the conference, Berle used the occasion to push a resolution that would effectively foreclose any world organization's intervention in the hemisphere unless the American states specifically invited it. The stage was set for a State Department conflict at Mexico City in which the globalist Leo Pasvolsky dueled the regionalist Adolf Berle.[1]

The hemisphere had to be made safe for democracy. Berle's trip to Buenos Aires early in February for discussions with Argentine leaders was preparation for debating the Argentine question at Mexico City. The American states who allied themselves with the United States during the war supported the State Department when Hull withheld recognition of Argentina's new military regime. But Hull's decision was not the first time an effort was made to isolate the Argentines. In 1942 the Treasury had tried to freeze Argentine funds in the United States, only to be told by Roosevelt that it was "not in accord with the Good Neighbor Policy." Now the administration despaired of persuading the Argentines of the errors of their fascism and nonrecognition became a part of the Good Neighbor Policy. Received by General Juan D. Perón, whom he considered a Mussolini-like figure, Berle found the Argentine general intent upon convincing him of his regime's legitimacy. Perón assured Berle that Argentina would hold free elections by October and that its army threatened none of its neighbors. Because he doubted the freedom of Perón's planned elections, Berle did not recommend that Washington resume relations. Only truly open elections could free the hemisphere from "militarization . . . [that] constituted itself a continuing danger to the peace of the hemisphere." Whoever ruled in Buenos Aires was a matter of "peace or war in the hemisphere"; the United States should convert the issue from a quarrel between two governments to a question of "Inter-American Public Law" whose enforcement called for collective action by the hemisphere's nations because "a threat to peace from within the hemisphere justifies action."

It was not Perónism that Berle feared; if the United States did not demand free elections in Argentina, he declared *"American popular movements would look increasingly to Moscow"* and thereby threaten the Monroe Doctrine and the hemisphere's collective security. Washington had to push for an "Inter-American Public Law" that made the hemisphere safe for free elections and free enterprise. Open elections in Argentina would guarantee fair elections everywhere in the hemisphere; they would be guarantees against totalitarianism. Disarming Fascist Argentina now would be a precedent for embargoing arms from totalitarians outside the hemisphere later. A tough ideological line toward Fascist Argentina now, he contended, would "command the intellectual respect of the hemisphere, assure the support of the popular parties, and I believe also the support of honest conservative movements." He might have added that it would spare the Americas a lot of grief later.[2]

By way of Belem, Surinam, Panama, and Guatemala, Berle flew in mid-February to Mexico City, where old acquaintances greeted him in the lobby of the Hotel Geneve. He found a conference quite different from previous inter-American gatherings at Lima, Rio, and elsewhere. The leaders of the U.S. delegation were men intent upon putting the hemisphere on a back burner. Stettinius and Pasvolsky considered inter-American hands such as Berle and Ambassador to Mexico George Messersmith "regionalists" who were out of step with the movement for a strong United Nations organization. As Berle defined the division, it was between "the group that thinks entirely globally and knows little about the hemisphere, and the group that thinks about the hemisphere first and global matters second. . . . It is interesting to note that most of these world organization people regard the hemisphere as a positive enemy. . . . They have no hemispheric experience. . . . I do not see that we can or should sacrifice the hard-won liberty of the hemisphere from European disputes and intrigues as a down payment for the right to participate in world organization." While globalists like Pasvolsky would sacrifice an American sphere of influence in the hemisphere for a universal prohibition against hegemonies, the regionalists were intent upon preserving the inter-American framework developed since 1933 within the context of a world organization.[3]

The regionalists prevailed at Mexico City—in part due to the ineptitude of the globalists. As Messersmith observed, Stettinius was incapable of harmonizing differences between the factions because he was "completely beyond his depth. . . . The contrast [with Hull] was really disheartening." Stettinius' "cheerful ignorance remains the amazement of all hands," Berle commented. Even the senators in the delegation were divided between the regionalist Tom Connally of Texas and the globalist Warren Austin of Vermont. The regionalists cheerfully let the South Americans take the lead in pushing resolutions aimed against Argentina. The globalists retorted that by committing the United States to using force against a regional aggressor without a world body's approval, the United Nations would be undermined before it was born. The regionalists retorted that the Monroe Doctrine came first and that Europeans had no business meddling in hemispheric politics. The Latin Americans sided with the regionalists: "The Brazilians want the Monroe Doctrine lock, stock and barrel and make no secret of it," Berle exulted. "The Uruguayans think the British would throw them to the Argentines. The rest of South America simply thinks we don't know what we are doing—and I must say I think they are right."

Berle plunged into the conference with the ease of someone who knew the other delegates better than did the secretary of state. On March 3 the conference adopted the Act of Chapultepec, which guaranteed frontiers and provided for a reorganization of the Pan-American Union which could create a possible "peace-keeping" force of the Americas. Without mentioning Argentina, the Act proclaimed the hemisphere's determination to resist any aggression—a stunning victory for the regionalists. Berle was jubilant and the British Foreign Office attributed much of the conference's result to his labors, admiringly concluding that the Mexico conference "achieved one of its primary objects, namely to enable the American Republics (with the exception of Argentina) to speak with one voice at the San Francisco Conference in April." The Mexico City conference guaranteed that the San Francisco conference would adopt Article 51 of the United Nations Charter, exempting regional confederations from the supremacy of the world organization. Berle was not in San Francisco, but his influence was felt there.[4]

From Mexico City Berle flew with the Brazilian Ambassador, Carlos Martins, to Washington. Having made the most of one part of his agreement with Roosevelt—participation in the Mexico City conference—he sought to cash the other promissory note: access to the president. On March 5 he accompanied Stettinius, the Brazilian foreign minister, Pedro Leão, Velloso, and Martins to the White House for a half-hour conference. "The President is tired and old," Berle noted. "His trip to Yalta obviously aged him a good deal." Yet he was still FDR. Ever the raconteur, he described engagingly what he saw and heard on his recent travels abroad and, for the benefit of Velloso, he spoke warmly of President Vargas' "world point of view." Then the other three retired and Berle remained alone with Roosevelt for a half hour. Berle used the opportunity to reiterate the need for keeping European diplomacy out of the hemisphere. "The President at once cordially agreed," Berle later wrote. "He said that, so far as he could see, Churchill was running things on an 1890 set of ideas." British imperialism was anything but moribund. Wanting to protect the hemisphere from globalism, FDR told Berle that "he had vetoed the sending of Leo Pasvolsky to San Francisco; 'he would get lynched out there.'" The rest of the interview consisted of generalizations that suggested Roosevelt "was obviously unhappy about certain of the settlements he had had to make in Yalta but saw no escape from the situation."[5]

Having cashed Roosevelt's obligations at Mexico City and in Washington, Berle returned to Rio to act as a causative ambassador. He flew to São Paulo to inspect the city and the American Consulate. He sought out his fellow ambassadors, especially those from the Americas. He held press conferences for American and Brazilian reporters. He sought out student leaders at the universities. He met with Jewish refugees who feared deportation as German nationals: "They are right and I will see what I can do about it." His distance from Washington had not made Berle less active or involved in the world. Argentina and the significance of its fascism in a sea of liberalism was on his mind when, on March 30, word arrived that Rockefeller proposed recognizing the military dictatorship if it recognized the Act of Chapultepec. "This in my judgment is a mistake," Berle cabled Rockefeller. Although Rockefeller had the best intentions in the world, he showed his inexperience in dealing with hemisphere politics. Yet, to Berle, it was also symptomatic of a larger lack of perspective in Washington. On Easter Sunday he set his broodings down on paper. Russia wanted not only to dominate Europe but "everything as far west as Egypt including the Suez Canal, the Red Sea, and the Persian Gulf in the Middle East." It was "pretty clear she will want Manchuria, Korea, some ports on the China Sea and a dominant position in Eastern China." While the San Francisco conference would "sound meaningless generalities," the Russians would hold what they could take. In all this the leadership of the State Department would be inert because it was "simply ignorance advised by incompetence."[6]

Then came the worst news. At 6:45 P.M. on April 12, Berle learned that President Roosevelt had died. He canceled a planned dinner and began to receive a steady stream of people coming to the embassy as Brazilians told the American ambassador what the loss of this great man meant to them.

> Through the long watches of the night, I tried to put together the series of pictures since I first saw him in 1918 and came to know him in 1932. The amazing fact was that he had an almost universal interest; there were few fields of knowledge with which he had not contact, many in which he was expert, but in all he had a vivid interest. . . . It is quite accurate to say that nothing human was alien to him.
>
> For that very reason he was tolerant of many things which shocked me: the crude and bitter intrigues of the European powers, often directed against us; the corruption of some of his Tammany friends; the bickering and self-seeking which went on all around him. But more austerity would have prevented him from meeting all of the various conflicting forces, and dealing with each on its own terms instead of on preconceived premises. Looking back over twelve years of almost continuous crisis government, I think he would have been torn to pieces if he had not developed community with each of these forces or groups, and so made himself at all times the principal unifying element. . . .
>
> Many found him puzzling; but this I think was due to their own limitation. He was a friend of nations. . . . So his foreign policy not merely included friendship with other countries, but also friendship with the various classes, expecially the large humbler classes who do not usually find expression in their governments. . . . As a result, no President will ever be able to look at the Presidency again, either in its foreign or its internal implications, as did Presidents before his time.

For days Brazilians stopped Americans on the street to tell them of their sorrow, or called at the embassy to say that they too grieved with Americans. Schools invited Berle to solemn, dignified ceremonies that honored Roosevelt, including a memorial concert consisting of Beethoven's third and fifth symphonies. Nine days after Roosevelt's death, Berle received a parade of about 15,000 led by the Communist leader, Luis Carlos Prestes, who wanted to quietly pay homage to the late American leader. "I never did see a crowd better behaved," Berle thought. "We went onto the balcony, shook hands courteously with Prestes and his friends, stood at attention while the portrait of President Roosevelt and the flags of the United States went by, . . . and that was that!"[7]

Berle had lost a friend, a catalyst for his public service, a powerful man who shared his beliefs and crystallized his ideas, and the only man in Washington who would honor his return ticket. Latin America had lost the author of the Good Neighbor Policy, possibly the only person who could create a hemispheric community. There would be no more leisurely lunches or casual one-hour conversations with the chief executive for Berle. While Truman would be accessible, Berle learned that this president had a strict policy of keeping most visits to an inhospitable fifteen minutes, hardly enough time to develop or exchange ideas. Roosevelt had been a comrade, even if in the last year he relegated Berle to a status that Rexford Tugwell and others had endured before.

No other politician could be Berle's vehicle—both for his quest for power and for his ideas—again. In New York La Guardia played out his third term as mayor, without a party in a political environment decidedly different from that of a decade ago. Berle had once dreamed of a La Guardia presidency; we can imagine the role he imagined for himself. Now it was evident that Berle's return to the States would be a return to private life. Nevertheless, he was still a braintruster. He still could influence policy, as long as cables were transmitted from Rio to Washington—although he conceded that "firing advice by cable is not much fun, and it is still less fun when you say afterwards, 'I told you so.'" Although bereft of FDR's blank check for brain-trusting, he had a Puritan's sense of duty to let few opportunities pass without endeavoring to be causative, to communicate a correct policy.

Just now he was certain that recognition of Buenos Aires was a mistake. He fretted that the floundering Argentine policy would disrupt hemispheric solidarity at the San Francisco conference. The news from San Francisco told how the United States pushed for Argentine admission to the conference and how the Soviets opposed it by reciting past American statements on Buenos Aires. He agreed with Moscow's critique, but its interest in Latin America—while hardly new—worried Berle. The Soviets did not merely concern themselves with those countries contiguous with their own, but promoted their revolution throughout the globe. "If we undertake to oppose this new concept of world empire, the Russians will challenge for the hemisphere." In fact, he believed this was the case already. If the Russians could score propaganda victories on Washington's inconstant Argentine policy and other issues, the Good Neighbor Policy could unravel. The Soviets could promote their revolutions in the hemisphere and the "public law of the hemisphere" as contained in the Act of Chapultepec would become meaningless—along with the Monroe Doctrine itself!

Yet he seemed alone with his visions. The current diplomacy of the State Department was "inept" and lacking in his perception of the Soviet menace or his will to resist it. Perhaps, he consoled himself, he was not being fair and did not see what was really stirring in Washington. But he suspected that "they are not taking our recommendations on anything about the Argentine regime. . . . It makes you pretty tired." He celebrated V-E day in the embassy garden with a reception for the American colony in Rio, feeling it was "wholly anti-climactic in many ways." Berle could not celebrate the conclusion of one war when he suspected that another already was in progress and too few Americans knew it was one for the hemisphere.[8]

END OF A REGIME

Simply put, Berle in 1945 loved Brazil but hated the world. He was happy when he could lose himself in Brazilian matters, traveling about, reveling in the beauties of the country and its people. "I cannot speak too highly of the endless patience and cooperation of the Brazilians," he wrote. Good relations with Brazilians was his most important task and he was impatient with Americans who did not love Brazilians as he did. "For some reason the American colony here simply does not mix with the Brazilians," he remarked. "I cannot make sense of this." Proudly he made the ambassador's residence "one of the few houses where Brazilians and Americans meet."[1]

But the joys and concerns of Brazil could not distract him from the cable traffic that described developments in Europe and brought him anguish. It seemed to him that the Russians had their tentacles everywhere and that the Americans had no leadership anywhere. Encouraged by a British Empire bent upon controlling the Mediterranean, the Soviets expanded their empire westward. The Red Army's conquest of Eastern Europe could not be prevented, but Berle despaired that British imperialists gave it diplomatic support—and in turn found tacit encouragement in the feckless State Department. British and Soviet bloc strength in the United Nations made an American system bloc all the more important. As in 1938–1939, the expansion of a totalitarian system in Europe called for strengthening the American system.

Although he assured President Vargas that Washington "would never go back on the main outlines of the Monroe Doctrine," he ruefully conceded that it had no visible inter-American policy. For Berle, a successful inter-American policy called for exporting liberal capitalism throughout the hemisphere through low-interest credits, quarantining dictatorships such as Argentina's, and demanding free elections throughout the hemisphere. An atmosphere of cooperation and an alliance of mutual interests would reinforce the hemispheric system. But it took America's wealth and leadership to provide the initiative. Yet Washington in 1945 was already forgetting its wartime ally Brazil, and endeavoring to nurture Fascist Argentina. Never one to be limited by the defined duties of a position, in June the meddlesome braintruster headed north to Washington intent upon facilitating economic aid to Brazil and focusing policy toward Latin America.[2]

What he found confirmed his impression that Washington ignored Latin America. Brazilian Ambassador Martins asserted that the United States politically and economically courted neutral Argentina at the expense of its ally Brazil—rushing oil to Argentina while Brazilians desperately pleaded for coal. Berle worked himself into "a right royal rage" when Under Secretary of State Joe Grew told him that he was so busy with European affairs that he had no time for Latin America. The atmosphere in the State Department incensed Berle, what with "everybody trying to get what they wanted and giving Argentina what she wanted." When William Phillips, an old State Department hand, cordially asked Berle how he felt, he unexpectedly got an earful. Phillips smiled and commented that a righteous indignation is the only way to accomplish anything in Washington. Berle took his righteous indignation and Ambassador Martins to President Truman.

On June 13, Berle and Martins, in the presence of Joe Grew (Stettinius did not allow a subordinate to go to the White House unaccompanied by him or his surrogate) used their fifteen minutes with Truman to advise him that Brazil was "greatly shocked and perturbed" by American oil bound for Argentina while its economy awaited a shipment of coal. Berle recalled for Truman's benefit "that during the war Argentine ships had been sailing up and down the coast of Brazil carrying the swastika flag whereas Brazilian shipping had been put into the international pool and had been engaged in fighting the war." Truman agreed with Berle that America's allies came first and said other things that gave Berle "the distinct flash that the entire State Department is due for the skids." Satisfied with Truman, Berle spent the rest of his stay lobbying officials such as Henry Wallace, now secretary of commerce, to remember that during the war Argentine ships had plied the Atlantic "through submarine infested waters with all lights on—without any danger of being sunk, whereas thirty-two Brazilian vessels were sunk because they were on the Allied side."[3]

As Berle saw it, Brazil also needed the New Deal's state capitalism. The United States should export its capital and its raw materials for industry as quickly as possible. Brazilians wanted not only war materials from the United States, but that Washington should "open our markets and sell machinery to purchasers as soon as supplies are ready." Brazil needed the Reconstruction Finance Corporation and Jesse Jones. In Washington Berle discussed American financing of the Brazilian San Francisco Valley irrigation and hydroelectric project and upon his return he toured the valley, telling Brazilian officials that he considered it to be a "Brazilian TVA." Late in July the Berles left Rio for a ten-day flying tour of the Amazon region to personally acquaint themselves with what Brazil needed in order to facilitate its development. The trip itself was a magnificent adventure for the Berles, bringing them into contact with a Brazilian interior seldom seen by Americans. Priests had seen places like Manaos, but now the representative of the president of the United States pumped the hands of everyone in sight, self-consciously trying "to get below the high society in Manaos." He wanted to bring development to Brazil and everywhere he traveled he made notes about communities that needed modern schools, hospitals, or better airports. The experiences on the Brazilian frontier exhilarated him. He ate turtle meat, had brushes with death, once making an unplanned landing in Bolivia, and skidded off the end of the runway into a barbed wire fence in Corumba.[4]

These adventures made him all the more impatient with confused, uncertain, or indifferent policymakers; he knew what had to be done in Latin America. The Good Neighbor Policy had been on target. If anything, it needed to be broadened and, when Latin America became the standard for developing nations, internationalized. In the summer of 1945 Rockefeller was removed as assistant secretary of state, a victim of his own misguided policy toward Argentina. Berle had warned against that policy, but he did not rejoice in the sacking of a man he personally respected. Whatever his mistakes, Rockefeller was a Latin Americanist. "Men who know the hemisphere and love it are few," Berle wrote, "and those who are known by the hemisphere and loved by it are fewer still." September saw Berle in a somber mood. "I have been stewing a good deal recently, he confessed, "and the result of it is not very satisfactory."

In Brazil political circumstances threatened what he hoped was an emerging liberalism. Vargas had promised to hold elections that would restore democracy, but now he seemed to be organizing forces for the retention of his dictatorship. What could Berle do about it? Altruistic foreign aid was one thing and political intervention was another. "American liberal opinion is all for democracy unless the democratic process decides against them [sic]—in which case they are apt to go imperialistic."[5]

Vargas summoned Berle for an audience at the Guanabara Palace at 7 P.M. on Friday, September 28. They discussed the American bases and civil air agreements, both important matters that did not inspire any quarrel. Then the dictator steered the conversation to Argentina and Berle seized the opportunity to remind Vargas that Americans did not approve of dictators. Vargas had promised on September 7 that he would relinquish the presidency, yet Rio was full of gossip about a possible army coup that would reinstate him. Also, a group known as the Queremistas, a coalition of left-wing and right-wing Vargas supporters, wanted him to remain and govern with an elected constituent assembly. Berle knew that the leaders of the Vargas movement were precisely those who had organized the Fascist coup in 1937 that kept Vargas in power and abrogated a previous assurance of a return to democracy. Reminded by Berle of his pledge, Vargas responded that he had given his word to retire and he was tired; he wanted to leave the presidency with the affection and applause of Brazilians, not their hatred or indifference.

At that point Berle pulled out a draft of a speech he intended to give the next day before a luncheon of the government-controlled *Sindicato dos Jornalistas* in Petropolis. In it Berle averred that the United States welcomed Brazil's restoration of a free press and all liberties, and the release of political prisoners. Most of all it hailed the pledge of free elections "by a Government whose word the United States has found inviolable. . . . Americans have not agreed with some who tried to misrepresent straightforward pledges and declarations as insincere, or verbal trickery. . . . We have learned that the only way to be a democracy is to practice democracy." While the speech would have warmed the hearts of American liberals, lecturing Brazilians on the need for elections and a constitution, Berle knew, would "cause a good deal of political comment and in a sense take the Embassy off the pedestal and put it into the firing line." It was blatant intervention in Brazil's internal affairs, yet here was Berle seeking Vargas' blessing for his noblesse oblige. Vargas read the draft and asked only one question: did the Americans disapprove of a constituent assembly? No, Berle answered; they only feared that "hotheads" would defeat Vargas' wise plan to hold elections for a successor to the presidency. Following a brief discussion of Communist intentions, Berle departed amicably with a "sense of a tired, sincere man struggling with many forces, no longer anxious for great power, caught to some extent in the shackles of his past."[6]

The speech elicited a storm of controversy. In Brazil's first open political campaign since 1930, both the Communists and the Fascists attacked Berle for interfering in their country's politics. Nor was the American ambassador to Brazil ignored in the States. A left-wing group in New York, calling itself the Council of Pan American Democracy, demanded through its millionaire spokesman, Frederick V. Field, that Berle be fired for "unwarranted interference in Brazilian internal affairs." The White House had to emphatically deny a New York *Herald Tribune* report that President Truman would recall Berle to explain his intervention. Privately, in the words of that perpetual Washington insider, Tommy Corcoran, the administration thought Berle had "sort of pulled the trigger," which was "all right if you are willing to follow it up, but if you are not willing to follow it up you ought to leave a situation alone." The speech had reflected Berle's policy, not Truman's.[7]

Vargas later claimed that Berle had read the speech to him in such "badly masticated Portuguese" that he could not tell whether the actual speech was the same one he had heard from Berle. However, Berle insisted that Vargas read the copy himself. Vargas had every reason to be unhappy with the speech, for while he told the Queremistas that he would not be a candidate for president, he did little to frustrate reactionaries who conspired against the election of a constituent assembly. Berle considered the sequence of events a "thinly disguised push for a coup d'etat." Indeed, the climax came in late October when Vargas hinted that he would not leave the presidential palace as quietly as he promised: he appointed his brother, Benjamin Vargas, a corruptionist known as "the kiss," to be chief of police of the Federal District. With that news the army moved in and informed Vargas that he was through. Amid the celebrating in Brazil that followed the deposed dictatorship, Brazilians and Americans acclaimed Berle for speaking out at a time when his silence would have been interpreted as "negative but tremendously effective intervention" in Vargas' behalf. Concerned that the army might be rough on civil liberties, Berle himself took "some steps to try to see that the political liberty and rights of the Communist Party are respected." It would not do to liberate only some Brazilians.[8]

Berle justified the army's overthrow of Vargas mostly on the grounds that it averted turmoil which might have jeopardized the safety of American air bases in Brazil. He also told Foreign Minister Velloso that he had bet his career on the Vargas regime's converting itself to democracy, and if Vargas did not follow through Brazil would be in trouble with the United States and "my own position would have been impossible." Berle characterized it as a matter of principle and policy, but Spruille Braden interpreted it differently. The former ambassador to Cuba had been sent to Buenos Aires following American recognition in the spring. His performance there also had been attention-getting, especially when he denounced Argentine fascism publicly, an undiplomatic act which drew hearty approval in the American press. When Truman dropped Rockefeller for, among other things, his Argentine recognition policy, he tabbed Braden as his successor. In late September Braden visited Berle while en route from Buenos Aires to assume his new State Department post. According to Braden, Berle told him, "I want to make a speech in which I, in anticipation of the elections here in Brazil, express a desire that those elections be fair and open and no fraud pulled by the government in those elections, so that Vargas can't put over a fast one the way he always has before." Even though Braden supposedly told Berle that he could not say such things without being guilty of blatant intervention, he helped Berle write the September 29 speech. Braden interpreted Berle's eagerness to give the speech as motivated "a little bit that Adolph [*sic*] wanted to climb on the band-wagon." (Tommy Corcoran encouraged the story that Berle gave it "just to make sure that Spruille Braden didn't get more headlines than he did.) Berle had been much impressed by Braden's actions in Argentina and, Braden quoted Berle, "after much sweating I had come to the conclusion that the only way to have democracy was to have it"—the very expression he used in the speech—"and that the United States was beginning to be expected to express a view," even if it meant intervention in Brazil's affairs. In any event, Berle reasoned that he had not violated Brazil's self-determination because Vargas' dictatorship itself prevented a democratic decision.[9]

"That's more nerve than I even knew Adolf to have," his old friend Ernest Cuneo thought. Undoubtedly the acclaim for Braden's speech in Buenos Aires put steel into Berle's nerve, but Berle had been headed in that direction almost from the day he arrived in Rio. In certain ways the speech was entirely in character for him. Vargas was Brazil's Tammany Hall. "His government is almost as corrupt as Pennsylvania," Berle had told Truman. He disapproved of the regime's graft practices and its infringement upon personal liberties that included censoring telephone calls—even his. While Vargas benefited the masses, and Berle personally liked him, a dictatorship was never democracy. Latin America needed a liberal Brazil and Brazil needed liberal political and economic development. In early September Berle had told Truman that "some in Brazil, and possibly in the United States, suggest that the Embassy here should attack President Vargas as Braden has attacked Perón." However, Berle did not equate the Brazilian dictatorship with Argentine fascism. While Berle practiced "quiet encouragement toward democracy," Truman thought "it would be disastrous to interfere with the internal affairs of Brazil at the present time." Still, Berle recalled that Welles had intervened in Cuban affairs in 1933, as Braden did in Argentina in 1945, and Berle may have to make that decision for Brazil. Convinced that the State Department was "almost shut down," Berle decided that he "had to make our own line of policy as best we could, nobody being there to give us any guidance."[10]

In September, Berle drafted a memo entitled "Economic Assistance and Non-Intervention" in which he denied that the United States possessed the right of intervention in the affairs of any nation dependent upon its economic assistance. However, as sanctioned in the Act of Chapultepec, "breaches of the recognized public law of the hemisphere," gave American nations collectively "a real and solid right of intervention." Every country in the hemisphere had to have a democratic state, democratic being defined as government which "observes the rights of peoples." A coherent American foreign policy for the hemisphere and the world was one which stressed universal political and economic freedoms. Free Brazilian elections, accompanied by liberal doses of American credits, would tell the world that Washington's largesse would be shared only with countries who shared its ideals. His thinking connected hemispheric developments with those in Eastern Europe; thus, he "stewed" unhappily over world opinion, the Soviet threat, and Brazilian politics: "Perpetuation of the dictatorship means absence of democracy. . . . We are being pressed to declare against the continuance of the dictatorship" And so he did.[11]

"All we are trying to do is to reach towards an orderly, peaceful and humane solution of affairs," he wrote. Make no mistake about it, Berle told his sister, Brazilians knew that "Vargas had betrayed the masses." Not merely content to oppose Brazil's dictatorship, he wanted social justice for its people too. He lectured Brazilian businessmen to do "some very serious thinking about improving the condition of the masses, and getting their profits down to [a] reasonable level and prices down to a point where people could buy their goods." He conceded that such tough, patronizing talk put him "in somewhat controversial waters in Brazil as usual." Although it cost him Brazilian friends who were devoted to the dictatorship, Berle assured his daughter that "in these things you cannot go by personalities; we do believe in democracy and the chance of the little people not only to have things for them, but to do things themselves so that they go on growing and making themselves free."[12]

Vargas' fall on October 29 appeared to vindicate him. An interim president was chosen and Brazil then set about the business of organizing an election to find a successor to Vargas. In Washington, Secretary of State James F. Byrnes, having replaced Stettinius, advised President Truman that the new Brazilian government, "committed to carrying out democratic reforms, is solidly entrenched." The Brazilian commitment to "democratic principles as the goal for its political, economic and social development" gratified the United States. In Brazil itself Berle detected an atmosphere of euphoria. A month before Brazilian liberals feared that the dictatorship would block any change; "Today their chins are up and . . . the country seems to have uncovered a new layer of energy and ability and hope." On December 2 Brazil elected a new president and Berle proclaimed himself "delighted with the democratic spectacle. Not even in the United States did I see a cleaner contest." Privately he was uncertain of the new president, General Eurico Dutra, but he was cheered by Brazil's improved prospects. Importantly, he told Fletcher Warren, the United States could return to "the policy of good neighborship and economic cooperation." Indeed, he looked toward "a more enlightened public law of the hemisphere."[13]

"Colonizing Capital"

Many people in Washington and elsewhere had predicted when Berle went to Brazil that he was too freewheeling, arrogant, abrasive, irascible, opinionated, outspoken, and patronizing to be a successful envoy. The Petropolis speech, lecturing Brazilians on democracy, confirmed their worst apprehensions. Moreover, when his announced resignation followed it by a couple of months, detractors could conclude that the difficult Berle had exhausted not only the good will of his host country but the patience of State Department superiors and the president too. Yet all assessments of his brief tenure in Rio were premature.

Berle believed that his paramount duties were to advance his government's interests in Brazil and throughout Latin America consistent with the Good Neighbor Policy and the democratic principles that underlay them. A corollary of this was what Berle called "the public law of the hemisphere," that the Americas had a right to collective action against European powers endeavoring to impose outside ideologies. (He anticipated the Truman Doctrine.) During the war the State Department and the FBI had monitored the activities of Nazis, Communists, and British imperialists in the Americas and Berle included among his duties as ambassador the surveillance of those who espoused ideologies inimical to the hemisphere's liberal capitalism. He knew that such definitions of his duties brought accusations of interventionism or imperialism, but—to his mind—American imperialism was unselfish, something he could not say about British colonialism. American imperialism concerned itself more with free markets than captive colonies. To be sure, the inequitable wealth between the United States and Brazil made it an imperial relationship, but Berle called it a cooperative relationship among political equals because the other country retained its self-determination. An ally like Brazil benefited from the American system through its access to U.S. money, materials, and manufactures. The braintruster hoped to extend this new imperial system throughout the hemisphere.

The British noted in 1942 that Washington showed "an increasing tendency to regard Brazil as a special preserve and to improve their economic position there at our expense." British investments in South America were substantial and London correctly depicted its rivalry with Washington as part of a complex of relations that involved Brazil's rivalry with Argentina for continental supremacy. But America's quest for "a special position" in Rio posed additional problems for London: "In any competition with them in South America we must recognise that it is an area where they are prepared to pay a substantial premium for political prestige." Cooler heads in the Foreign Office counseled that any rivalry with the United States in Brazil and elsewhere in the Americas should not be exaggerated to the point where a clash over markets there caused hard feelings that debilitated the European Grand Alliance. The British line here was not too different from their attitude toward the Soviet Union's quest for freedom of action in Eastern Europe; both American and Soviet spheres of influence buttressed British imperialism elsewhere.[1]

Nevertheless, the Soviet alliance enhanced British colonialism in Africa, Asia, and the Middle East, but the American alliance diminished British markets in noncolonial areas. The Soviets could be bought off with a hegemony over Eastern Europe, but the Americans were anticolonial and could not be bought off with promises of territory—although they always desired more bases. The British did not like economic competition with the Americans because it was inherently unequal—to their disadvantage.[2] Berle's arrival in Brazil inspired British suspicions that their old bête noire was there to develop the American economic empire on that continent—probably to their ultimate exclusion. Indeed, Berle forthrightly told Britain's ambassador to Brazil, Sir Donald Gainer, that Washington intended to keep the hemisphere free of European influences; J. V. Perowne in London's Foreign Office privately jibed, "We, on the other hand, desire that Latin America should continue to be open to *suitable* European influences." Perowne was confident that when the Brazilians encountered Berle's "boorishness, his presence in Rio ought to do U.S. interests more harm than good."[3]

Although wounded by Swinton's rebuff of American air proposals at the Chicago air conference, ("he should be painted bright green and hung up in the House of Lords as an awful warning," he told Gainer), Berle was not interested in pursuing a diplomatic or economic war against the British. The emerging Soviet imperialism worried him more than London's "selfish" efforts to perpetuate a "tired" and anachronistic colonialism. "Britain will have to determine whether she must abandon her position as a world power," he wrote for the benefit of the new secretary of state, James F. Byrnes. Britain had legitimate interests in the Middle East, made more tolerable by apparent Soviet designs in the area, but London could ill afford its aspirations for a commercial aviation fleet and South American markets. Thus, he approached the British ambassador to Rio with great cordiality and Gainer found him "forthcoming on all questions except those relating to Brazil or to United States of America plans in Brazil." While Berle lectured Gainer on Argentina like "a headmaster lecturing a recalcitrant child," Gainer nonetheless found himself curiously drawn to Berle. He found Berle "frank and friendly," but "all too sure of himself. He interested me though I can't say I liked him."[4]

British competition in the hemisphere intimidated Berle less than that of the Soviets or their surrogate Communist parties. The Grand Alliance with Moscow had not inhibited Ambassadors Spruille Braden in Havana and George Messersmith in Mexico City from monitoring Communist activities in the Americas. Attributing the appeal and strength of the indigenous Communist parties to the enormous poverty of the region, local Communists worried Berle only where they were politically dependent on Moscow. He hoped that the dissolution of the Comintern in 1943 signaled a change in Moscow's international ambitions, but the activities of Soviet diplomat Constantine Oumansky, who transferred from Washington to Mexico City that year, suggested otherwise. Berle and Messersmith considered Oumansky a clever troublemaker whose only purpose was espionage and bringing local Communist parties under Moscow's tight control. In early 1945 Oumansky was killed in an airplane crash while, it was believed, en route to El Salvador with aid for an insurrection there.

Most Latin American governments had never recognized the Soviet government; only in response to wartime alliances did Cuba and Mexico recognize Moscow in 1942, but Brazil did not establish relations there until 1945. Brazil lacked a strong Communist party. Cut off from Moscow, the Communists were virtually a Popular Front organization. Vargas repeatedly threatened them with repression or undercut their appeal to the working classes with his own popularity; accordingly, the Communists meekly celebrated the dictator. Berle received regular surveillance reports on them, but it was distinctly dull reading and frequently his agents could not distinguish among liberal intellectuals, philosophical radicals, or Communists subservient to Moscow. Berle's Petropolis speech, which might have inspired bitter Communist denunciations, only brought gentle criticism along with an admonition to the party faithful to "be careful not to attack his character." Their good relations symbolized the weakness of the Communists in Brazil. The Communists supported Vargas and a constituent assembly, thereby allying themselves with the Fascistic Queremistas. When, following the coup, Berle protected them the Communists expressed their gratitude to Berle for his interest. Brazil's Communist party posed no threat to liberal capitalism.[5]

More troublesome to Berle was the fact that the United States frequently sided with what the Left called "colonizing capital." For instance, nothing better symbolized exploitation in a developing nation such as Brazil than the international oil companies. In November Berle observed that "the life of any [American] Ambassador is incomplete without a scrimmage with the international oil people, and my turn has come." Berle resented oil company policy of "charging what the traffic would bear" and reaping profits of 114 percent in Brazil. When Standard Oil suddenly made known that it wished to build a Brazilian refinery to reduce its marketing costs, Berle found Standard's proclaimed concern with consumer prices nothing less than grimly ironic; moreover, it deliberately challenged the government's prohibition against foreign-operated refineries. But Standard got the State Department to instruct Berle to demand that Brazil remove the offending law, even if he had to threaten a loss of American aid if Rio was recalcitrant. But it was Berle who was recalcitrant. When the oil representatives made their case to Berle, "I told them that American capital could be useful in the refining industry in Brazil, but that I did not see how we could invade the sovereignty of Brazil to the extent of telling them they must not put up any refineries unless and until Americans were permitted to have an interest in them." "The Ambassador regrets that he is not in accord with the Department," Berle told Washington. Berle argued that a better case could be made for allowing all companies, foreign and domestic, to operate competitively rather than in a foreign-dominated cartel envisioned by Standard. "Note my dissent and leave me out of it," he told Washington. The Department, he thought, "was getting pretty far off base.'' Brazilians were very nationalistic and for the Department to act as ''colonizing capital's'' partner suggested that it had learned nothing from its experiences with oil companies and nationalism in Mexico.[6]

But the State Department insisted that Berle inform Rio that its own oil monopoly restricted the freedom of American nationals there and that Americans would not accept minority interests in Brazilian refineries. The Department was intent upon making Brazil a precedent for oil policies in Mexico and elsewhere in the Americas. Berle was outraged by this ''really shocking invasion of the sovereignty of Brazil, and a shocking protection of an essentially monopolistic cartel agreement, probably informal, which has had extortionate profits, and has been and is in a position to tax every Brazilian. . . . Having affronted Brazilian independence, wounded her pride, and safeguarded an oppressive cartel, what would prevent a Soviet representative from coming in and offering both to finance and supply with crude oil a Brazilian refining industry? . . . And what would prevent them from campaigning against the United States on the ground that their Embassy was merely an agency of 'colonizing capital?' ''

When the State Department accused Berle of thwarting his own country's interests, Berle vehemently denied that he sympathized with Brazil's restrictions on foreign capital. ''Since Brazil is sovereign country, she has same right to reserve refining industry for Brazilians that California has to prevent Orientals from owning land, or Britain to prevent Americans from owning local aviation business,'' he cabled back. The issues were whether most of the profits would be retained by Brazilians or whether Americans would own and control Brazil's refining industry. He accused the representatives of Standard Oil of conspiring with Gulf Oil to create a U.S. refining cartel that would dominate the Brazilian market. The State Department, through collusion with Standard and Gulf, practiced the ''kind of diplomacy described by Karl Marx and his followers.''

That same day Phil Chalmers at the Brazil desk in the Department called Berle, who guessed that he acted at the behest of the oil division. Still, Berle made it clear to his caller that ''the Brazilians had a right to go into the refining business in their own country and that any effort on our part to oppose such development would be construed by the Brazilians as an unwarranted interference with an internal matter.'' Berle maintained that technically he was not disobeying instructions; he would carry to the Brazilians any message the State Department dared to put in *writing*. He hinted broadly that he might go public with the story about how big oil tried to monopolize Brazil's refineries. After all, he thought, ''The United States is the last great capitalistic country in the world. I should think this sort of monkey-business was forcing the whole situation towards socialism about as fast as could be done. If there ever is a move in the United States anal-

As ambassador to Brazil from 1945 to 1946, Berle tried to involve himself in the life of the country. Here *(above)* he is seen escorting the Brazilian dictator, Getúlio Vargas, for a review of the sailors standing at attention on the ship's deck when the U.S. Navy called at Rio and *(below)* out for a Sunday afternoon of horseback riding with the family (second from left, daughter Beatrice, Dr. Beatrice Bishop Berle, daughter Alice, son Peter). (*Courtesy Dr. Beatrice Bishop Berle and Beatrice Berle Meyerson*)

Following his ambassadorship, Berle took up old causes such as the Henry St. Settlement House, for which he attended fund-raising dinners with its director, Helen Hall *(above)*, and New York's Liberal Party. As chairman of the latter, Berle was both the party's philosopher and liaison to Democratic liberals such as Adlai E. Stevenson *(below)*. *(Courtesy Franklin D. Roosevelt Library and Dr. Beatrice Bishop Berle)*

When John F. Kennedy sought an adviser on Latin American policy, Dean Rusk observed that "all roads lead to Berle." In 1961 he was sworn in as chairman of the president's task force on Latin America with Secretary of State Rusk looking on *(above)*. But Berle proved to be a "difficult personality," and his departure from the administration was viewed as salutary by both him and the president *(below)*. (*Courtesy Dr. Beatrice Bishop Berle and UPI/Bettman Newsphotos*)

In retirement, Berle was always in demand as a historical talisman of the New Deal. Here he appeared on a television program in 1962 remembering FDR on his eightieth birthday, along with Rex Tugwell, Samuel Rosenman, and Herbert Lehman. (*Courtesy Franklin D. Roosevelt Library*) At the same time, along with Luis Muñoz Marín he planned a New Deal for Latin America to keep the southern hemisphere free from Castroism. (*Courtesy Dr. Beatrice Bishop Berle*)

Age made Berle an honored man, whether it was receiving the "Page One" award from New York newspapermen in 1960 along with John L. Lewis *(above)* or receiving an honorary degree from his "intellectual home," Columbia University, in 1963 *(below)*. *(Courtesy Franklin D. Roosevelt Library)*

Great satisfaction and honor came from his role as chairman of the board of trustees of the Twentieth Century Fund. Seated between August Heckscher and Charles P. Taft on the right, Berle presided over a meeting of the "best club" sometime around 1955. On the left is fellow New Dealer Benjamin V. Cohen and fourth from left is long-time vice chairman and former Roosevelt attorney general Francis Biddle. At the extreme right is atomic scientist J. Robert Oppenheimer. (*Courtesy Dr. Beatrice Bishop Berle and Beatrice Berle Meyerson*)

Berle and David E. Lilienthal listening intently at a Twentieth Century Fund meeting in the 1960s. They collaborated often in ventures of state capitalism during the New Deal and devoted their postwar years to articulating the need for liberal developmental policies. (*Courtesy Twentieth Century Fund*)

The Berle "dynasty," A. A. Berle, Jr., Peter A. A. Berle, and A. A. Berle, Sr., had its first three generations in attendance at the Harvard College graduation in 1958. (*Courtesy Dr. Beatrice Bishop Berle and Beatrice Berle Meyerson*)

At a party for his seventy-fifth birthday, eleven-year-old Frederick Adolf Berle Meyerson helped his grandfather blow out the candles while Nobel Prize winner Andre Cournand, Dr. Beatrice Berle, and brother Rudolf Berle looked on. (*Courtesy Dr. Beatrice Bishop Berle and Beatrice Berle Meyerson*)

ogous to the movement of the British Labour party in England, it would pretty nearly put the oil industries at the head of the list for early nationalization. I should think these fellows had better be pretty careful."[7]

The State Department's next ploy was to insist that Brazil's laws contravened that section of the Economic Charter of the Americas adopted in Mexico City setting forth the principle of the free movement of capital. Yes, Berle retorted, but the same charter called for equal access to raw materials—a necessary first step toward refining. Berle pleaded with Chalmers to protect the Department from an embarrassing alignment with the forces of exploitation and when he visited State on December 21, he made his case forcefully enough to win agreement that liberalization of Brazil's laws should precede any push for refinery concessions. In the words of an interested London observer, "Berle appears to have his point."[8]

The episode fascinated the British who believed that all Americans abroad were either Yankee traders or their agents. Moreover, they could not imagine that an ambassador would defy his instructions. In London they speculated that Berle harbored grudges against Standard Oil or backed another oil company for personal reasons. But Gainer agreed with Berle's views that the international oil companies conspired to thwart indigenous Brazilian refining rather than develop it. The representatives of America and Britain in Brazil were in concert on a policy for no exclusive refining concession in Brazil.[9]

By this time Berle had decided to resign as ambassador. When he made this known in early 1946, Rio's diplomatic community buzzed with tales that the noisy Petropolis speech had made him expendable to Brazilians and the quiet fight with the oil cartel had made him expendable to the Americans. He first drafted a letter of resignation on November 26, but there is no evidence that either incident hastened it. During the previous summer Berle had informed Truman of his desire to return to private life and he had gone to Brazil with the understanding that he could come home after V-E day. Truman suggested that Berle might remain at his post beyond V-J day. "I am not a career diplomat," he reminded the president in November. He desired to leave because it was "the fitting time. . . . We have got Brazil onto a democratic basis without violence or bloodshed and she has peace, freedom and a clear opportunity to solve her own problems by men of her choice." (In a later draft he dropped this sentence, it obviously suggesting interventionism.)[10]

As Brazil began a new era, Berle felt the need to begin one himself. He would be fifty-one by the time he departed, "grateful for one of the happiest years Mrs. Berle and I have ever had, among one of the friendliest peoples in the world." He did not leave Rio until February 1946, by which time there were ceremonies, awards, and tokens of appreciation which the

Brazilians bestowed upon the Berles. Few ambassadors figure so prominently in the history of relations between nations as Berle did in the Brazilian-U.S. connection.

But, was it notoriety rather than fame for Berle in Brazil? For the record, Berle wanted to be remembered for having facilitated great quantities of U.S. economic assistance to Brazil during his ambassadorship. He omitted mention of his role in Brazil's transition to an elected government or his resistance to the oil cartel's "colonizing capital." "Regardless of the adverse criticism he invited by his now famous speech in Petropolis," *The New York Times* correspondent in Rio noted, "Mr. Berle is highly esteemed by Brazilians who regard him as a sincere friend of the country." That point was buttressed by President Dutra's visit to the Embassy, the first time a Brazilian head of State had visited any Embassy. But, was the compliment for Berle or for American economic aid?[11]

Perhaps the answer is best given by his old adversaries, the British. Many of the gossipmongers in the Foreign Office were delighted by Berle's "unlamented" departure from Brazil on March 1 and gleefully noted the absence of most of the diplomats and Americans in Brazil when the Berles made their farewells. Nevertheless, Sir Donald Gainer did not share their hostility. Gainer credited Berle with setting a high standard for diplomacy, traveling more and gaining a greater knowledge of Brazil in one year than any other ambassador. Of course, a lot of Berle's activity "created astonishment, admiration, resentment and strong dislike." "If the Petropolis speech is taken into account," Gainer thought, "he probably overstepped diplomatic limits and deserved the criticism that he was intervening in domestic politics." Even so, Berle had weighed the risks and events proved him right. As for Berle's alleged Anglophobia, Gainer wrote:

> Mr. Berle's fundamental beliefs are in the United States brand of democracy, in a hatred for the colonial system, and a general dislike of the British Empire (which however perhaps does not equal his hatred for Russia); this dislike is, however, coupled with a very clear understanding that at the present moment and for some time to come the maintenance and continued existence of the British Empire is a major American interest; thus while not loving us he will support us.

On a personal level, the phlegmatic Gainer did not know what to make of an ebullient Berle. They were of such different temperaments that Gainer could only hope that Berle's successor "will be an easier person to cooperate with and less eccentrically brilliant." He had seen a great deal of Berle and had formed an ambivalent opinion of him: *"He is a curiously unlikeable man for whom I eventually conceived a curiously unreasonable liking."* The message was not lost in London, where a Foreign Office official concluded, "It is significant that Sir D. Gainer shares Mr. Berle's belief that his mission has been successful." Most decisive was Gainer's judgment that "He was no negligible Ambassador and made his influence widely felt though in general he was far more interested in world affairs than in United States/Brazilian affairs." Berle's mission had been successful.[12]

9

Pax Americana and Cold War, 1946-1961

The Western hemisphere is the core of the free world, and the Soviet for-eign affairs officers know it.

—"To the South: A Continent of Problems," *New York Times Magazine,* July 15, 1956, p. 42

"THE REAL LIFE OF THE COUNTRY"

"I wonder what he will now find to do," a British Foreign Officer wrote in February 1946, as Berle departed Brazil. "Mr. Berle is an enigmatic figure, about whose abilities and personal ambition there is little room for doubt," wrote another Whitehall wag. "For the moment I should think he would return to New York business or legal work, but he is almost certain to come into public prominence again before very long though he has few or no real personal friends."[1]

He was in transition. 1946–1947 was Berle's personal "period of re-conversion," a time when he moved physically and emotionally from of-ficialdom with access to power to the uncertainty of a private citizen—a "difficult and unpleasant" experience which "some men break under." He did not break, for he prided himself upon being someone who, like Bernard Baruch, "remains big with or without title." Besides, he was like other Americans who were reconverting from war to peace, from an official life dominated by Washington to what Berle called "the real life of the coun-try"—the mundane tasks of earning a living, making fortunes, and ad-vancing careers. He had witnessed such a process following the last war and believed that postwar Washington was an insipid place because inspired people sought their destinies elsewhere. "The center of gravity is on the street somewhere" and not in Washington, he reassured his despondent children who had played amid famous and powerful dignitaries in wartime

Washington. Washington now was for political men, "who want to be something rather than do something—a laudable ambition but chiefly interesting to themselves." It was not for a braintruster like Berle, not for a man who insisted that a position had to be causative, not for a man with destiny. As in the 1920s, Washington lost its idealism to materialism.[2]

Conscious of place, Berle headed back to New York City. He always preferred the Hudson to the Potomac. Yet he remained ambivalent toward Washington; had not the New Deal's state capitalism made it the center of economic power in America—a power shift which entailed "a national system of planned finance, a national system of welfare, a national system of electric-power distribution, and the rudiments of a national system of industry and agriculture"? But now it was a city for other, lesser men, fixers who enjoyed access to the man at the top in government, men who wanted to make a quick buck instead of being effective policymakers who made history. Again New York suited him well. There he could range far and wide in his political and intellectual activities. A return to New York did not mean exile from public life. On the contrary, New York was still the "imperial city . . . from which music, drama, art, fashion, books, and ideas of all sorts were launched and attained recognition."[3]

He sought to resume activities he had enjoyed in 1932, albeit now enhanced by extended contacts and reputation. He long had claimed that he had so much going for him in New York that only a Calvinist sense of duty to the nation and its president during war justified postponing his return— an assertion which of course belied his appetite for power. His law practice with his brother Rudolf, his teaching at Columbia Law School, his friends in the Liberal party and New York's intellectual circles awaited him. As a braintruster who now lacked a patron for his ideas, he needed to write for the public; he sought a forum that only New York publishing could offer him. There his name commanded attention; there it enjoyed a market as a liberal, intellectual, corporation lawyer, professor, politician, and diplomat.

Always torn between a life of action and one of ideas, in Washington he had been one of the "lords temporal"; in New York he was one of the "lords spiritual." Departing the government was not so bad, Berle assured his friend, David E. Lilienthal, because "one grows in experience, [and] ideas seem more causative than the day-to-day work in the front lines, in which no one in public life is really a free agent." He was a free agent—a lawyer when the case was interesting enough, a law professor at Columbia because he found it intellectually satisfying, and a writer whose ideas found receptive audiences. While he disavowed the need for public life, he found one in New York. Besides his chairmanship of New York's Liberal party, in 1951 he became chairman of the Board of Trustees of the Twentieth Century Fund, which suited his passion for wedding philosophy and history to contemporary social science investigation. Both organizations, along with the Central Intelligence Agency and Radio Free Europe, afforded him with opportunities to brain trust on public matters without necessarily leaving New York. But he could be causative through individual initiative. He made his homes on East 19th Street and in the Berkshires havens to democratic Latin American leaders whose liberalism offended local dictators and even the State Department. In the violent, rapidly changing world of the mid-twentieth century, Berle sought to articulate traditional liberal values in his writings and speeches. The world's turmoil made belief essential: "What Americans want most, need most and (in the form of books) buy most is straight personal philosophy which begins by affirming that there is order in the cosmos and that though the world may blow itself up, individuals can bring themselves and the people they love through the storm, and can build communities somewhat more or less immune from fear as they do it."[4]

Berle built his orderly community anywhere he could, whether it was in Washington or New York: but he knew that a man had failed if he could not bring his ideals into the home. He did not articulate his beliefs for public audiences alone, for even in Washington and in Rio he had found time to be a conscientious father. But part of the satisfaction he derived from returning to civilian life was spending more time giving direction to his children's lives while they were on the threshhold of adulthood. In the fall of 1946 with Alice, "little Beatrice" and Peter turning seventeen, fifteen, and nine respectively, a return to New York gave him more time to shape their ideas and direct their lives. His injunctions for their personal benefit were consistent with his public commitment to ideas, issues, and status—thereby revealing one who was alternately a democrat and an elitist.

In Berle's life the Social Gospel of his parents had given way to the noblesse oblige of the Gospel of Wealth. The Bishop family legacy gave the Berle children both comfort and a sense of public service. Although the Bishop collection of art and other valuables was mostly liquidated in the 1930s, much of the Bishop wealth was in real estate that remained intact into the 1940s. Occupied by old four- and five-story buildings, several of the Bishop properties stood desirably in a line of expansion for Rockefeller Center at 1210–16 and 1221–27 and 1280–86 Sixth Avenue at 48th and 51st Streets. Rockefeller family interests had coveted the properties since 1929. Beatrice's father had given the Rockefellers a 21-year lease in 1930 and his death in 1935 inspired representatives of the Rockefellers to approach Beatrice's lawyer, A. A. Berle, Jr., who professed indifference to a sale of properties whose rentals netted his wife's estate at least $55,000 per annum. The managers of Rockefeller Center were even more anxious to acquire it because an adjustment clause in the lease inflated the rental, but Berle remained indifferent to a sale until August 1943. It netted the Berles more than $2.3 million, of which daughters Alice and Beatrice received 21.8 percent each in trust until their twenty-first birthdays. Their material security assured, Berle concerned himself with making certain that their lives too were causative.[5]

What Berle told his children and how he reacted to their successes reveals a man of contrasts—the snob who aspired to be a democrat. The children followed the family dynasty in the colleges they chose. Alice chose her grandmother's Oberlin, "Beatty" her mother's Vassar, and Peter his father's Harvard. None of them was as intellectual as their parents; each exhibited interests independent of their parents'. Alice was the most rebellious, surprising her parents by refusing to follow her mother to Vassar, showing an artistic bent at Oberlin and at nineteen marrying Clan Crawford, Jr., son of a prominent Cleveland lawyer. Berle noted that Clan's "intellectual background" differed from Alice's:

> His father represented the best of the stern conservative tradition, with reliance on personal character, individual honesty, and private effort—with which we would agree; but it was likewise opposed to any intervention by government in anything other than the simplest jobs of maintaining order and cleaning the streets. Generally speaking, the group out of which he came believed that we had already got to a highly satisfactory state of affairs and there was not much more that need be done about it. We, of course, have always been living close to the underprivileged, and the masses who never did quite get a break, and have been constantly seeking ways and means to give to everybody a more or less fair share of opportunity. You will find, however, that though the ideologies differ, when it comes to meeting practical issues, it is possible to find a common ground. At all events, I have in my wanderings.

Indeed, his son-in-law's Ohio tory Republicanism did not create any family breaches. In an age and a nation that practiced consensus, a liberal Democrat could find happiness with a conservative Republican because "marriage meant sharing and understanding each other's ideals and way of life." Following Clan's graduation, he and Alice lived for a year in Cleveland where Clan's father had secured a job for him with Dun and Bradstreet; but Berle campaigned for his son-in-law to attend law school. "Law school education is never wasted," he intoned. "It gives one an intellectual background which is priceless when you are dealing with other people."[6] In the spring of 1950 Clan enrolled at the University of Michigan Law School; its dean and some faculty were old Berle acquaintances. Berle urged Alice and Clan to invest her legacy in Ann Arbor real estate; they did and Clan became a leader in zoning practices. Scorning Eastern affectations, Alice settled down to raise three sons, teach art in Ann Arbor schools, and make a reputation for herself locally as an artist. Berle was proud of his eldest daughter's artistic talents and individualism, frequently reinforcing her scorn for the "effete East" with visits that carefully monitored the progress of his Crawford grandchildren.[7]

Beatrice Van Cortlandt Berle favored her namesake and made Phi Beta

Kappa at Vassar. Berle advised her to use Vassar to discover "intellectual activity" that would serve her for life—as well as "making those associations which will lead to your marrying the right man. This last means . . . men who are seriously tackling their professions or careers." He guided her intellectually to be a democrat, even as she assumed her mother's station in the American aristocracy and she used his connections following graduation to get a job in Brazil and in her travels around the world. He anticipated she would marry a Harvard or Princeton man who would enter diplomacy, law, medicine, or business and cut "a wide swath"; "you know the game so I do not comment." But Beatty, like Alice, surprised him; she married Dean Meyerson, a graduate of West Point—who represented a tradition "different than ours" and Berle confessed to "mixed emotions." While he did not envision Beatty as an army wife, he consoled himself that "she could go a great deal farther and fare a great deal worse: this is a young man of modest background with first-rate character, kindly instincts, a good record in West Point and a strong decision to do something with his life." She too had three sons, including Adolf Augustus Berle Meyerson, maintained a lively interest in Brazil and Latin America, and settled into a life that mostly kept her in the Washington she knew as a teenager.[8]

But from an early age the daughters understood that their endeavors mattered less than Peter's. Both their grandfather and father considered it of great importance to perpetuate their name and fame through an heir. Peter A. A. Berle got special attention; he carried on the dynasty. Berle hiked, fished, skied, gardened, and climbed mountains with Peter. Although Berle gave Alice and Beatty the same attention when possible, their formative years mostly had been Berle's frenetic years in the State Department. Now Berle had more time to devote to Peter. Handsome, strong, and athletic, Peter grew to six feet, unexpectedly tall for a Berle, and flourished with the rugged activity his father encouraged. At Harvard he played freshman football, although he was not good enough to win a letter; he graduated with a major in economics and was worthy of a fellowship to Oxford. He did not attempt to capitalize on the Berle name with his father's friends on the Harvard faculty, Arthur Schlesinger, Jr., John Kenneth Galbraith, and Seymour Harris. Like his father, Peter was serious and disliked frivolity. "You ask why a collection of school boys just getting to college enjoy getting plastered," Berle wrote to his son. "For the life of me I can not say. On the one or two juvenile occasions when I got plastered I do not recall that it was fun. There have been times since, in a violent career, when getting plastered at least might have had its advantages—but even then the relief was momentary." Berle stressed that college was for developing intellectual interests and for making lifetime associations. Although the right people were not of any particular race or religion, Berle expected Peter to discover that Harvard men "who have some conception of gentility, either traditional or acquired, are likely to be the most interesting." Once when he felt it incumbent upon him to give Peter fatherly advice for coping with their mid-twentieth-century world, Berle divided mankind into altruistic and commercial persuaders, telling Peter "to be careful about altruistic persuaders too. Probably nobody was more altruistic than the Communist Trotsky or the Spanish Inquisition in its day. Fundamentally, no persuader ought to have 'power.' He ought to have a respectable platform." Berle wanted Peter to be wary of certain charismatic radicals while espousing his respectable liberal platform.

As Peter approached graduation in 1958, his father counseled him on paths to be taken and goals to be gained. Given his interests, Peter could do graduate work in economics, go to business school, or go to law school. The first might lead to an academic or government career; the second, Berle cautioned, might trap him in a corporate bureaucracy. Needless to say, Berle favored law school. The possibilities for public service were greater for a lawyer, especially for a man with the "safety" of an inheritance: "you can make changes and take chances that men without that background can not." He suggested that Peter study law at Yale or the University of California: "Harvard is too damned technical. My own professorship at Columbia probably excludes Columbia." But first Peter entered the air force and became engaged to Lila Field Wilde, a great-great granddaughter of Commodore Vanderbilt—"though it should not be held against her," Berle cracked. It was a match that delighted him: given her genealogy and her family background in the Berkshires, "this is very much an engagement of county aristocracy," he declared. After a year in air force intelligence in Southeast Asia, Peter and Lila were married, May 30, 1960, at Lenox. It was a poignant moment for Berle.

> I came back to our farm. I ought to have been as happy as they and wasn't. I went to look at Peter's room and could only think that now there was nothing to do but dismantle it—he would never come back. His first big trout on the wall, his .22 rifle, a handful of odd souvenirs, the Harvard shingle, the little trophies from childhood to young manhood, all had meaning. There were no longer the children of the house in that homestead. The void was great and I was 65 years old.
>
> And yet I know this happened when Priam sent Hector off to the wars and that if it had not happened life would have been unhappy. This is simply one of the great moments of life like birth and death, honorable and natural and not accomplished without pain.[9]

"I feel lonely," he complained when Albert Spalding, his "last contemporary intimate friend," died. A loving man could not fail to know pain with the passage of time and friends. It was a side of Berle that few people saw. Co-workers and the public saw a crusty or prickly man, but others knew a more vulnerable man. Age and his removal from courts of power made him even more of an intellectual. He created his own salon of New York intellectuals whose brilliance was demonstrated in artistic, literary, and political accomplishments or pretensions. They looked to him to be brilliant and profound. A Berle book was brilliant—his friends at Harvard said so in *The New York Times Book Review* and *The Times'* daily critic Charles Poore, a frequent dinner guest, hailed books like *The Twentieth Century Capitalist Revolution* as a "landmark of political and economic thought" (it is "badly over-titled," Berle thought, exhibiting a penchant for self-criticism and not taking himself too seriously). Manhattan and Cambridge intellectual circles in the 1950s were villages where everyone knew everyone worth knowing and nobody dared offend. Berle had to be his own toughest critic—describing his speeches as either "ponderous" or "banal," an article or book as "a dud shell" or a "potboiler on foreign policy."[10]

He relished irony and mischief. Jim Farley, who harbored hopes for a political comeback in 1952, once asked Berle to brain trust and write a speech for him. Flattered by an old enemy in need of his assistance, Berle gave it his best effort and succeeded so well that he delighted in the deception when the old politician attracted esteem as an eloquent orator. Berle gleefully reworked Farley's speech for various occasions, including the receipt of an honorary law degree from Long Island University; "We'll break him into the Ivy League yet," Berle chortled. During one public occasion he himself saluted Farley as a great orator—"bad manners but I could not resist," he chastised himself.[11]

He belonged to that exclusive fraternity of old New Dealers, which persistently brought him maudlin respect and veneration. Inevitably editors and writers sought to discover what old New Dealers did in the years since FDR and noticed Berle. But Berle usually resisted capitalizing on public curiosity about the New Deal or FDR by writing his memoirs or a history of the New Deal; he left that to Moley, Tugwell, and Rosenman. Strangely, he did not like the exercise of vanity implicit in memoirs. Although he publicly flattered Rexford Tugwell's biography of FDR, he confided to his diary, "It is an excellent biography of Rex Tugwell." But he was not at all shy about allowing historians to use his diary and he always intended to have it published in some form.[12]

Many of the old New Dealers were his enemies and those animosities did not mellow with age. Frankfurter and his circle remained anathema—Frankfurter growing more venerable with Supreme Court seniority and Acheson dominant in the Truman State Department. "They hated me at the beginning, in the middle, and at the end," Berle wrote. "They still do." He was not paranoid; they did loathe him. But he courted their hate and certainly returned it. It led them into strange "intellectual politics." For instance, in 1953 he accepted an invitation to review *The Holmes-Laski Letters* in order to settle an old score with that Frankfurter acolyte Harold Laski on the front page of *The New York Times Book Review*—even if Laski was already dead. The review was a masterpiece of subtlety, Berle inferring that Laski had been little more than a sycophantic liar whose parlor socialism betrayed liberalism. Frankfurther and his group returned the favor in 1957 by victimizing Alpheus Thomas Mason's biography of Harlan Fiske Stone; both Stone and Mason had been Berle's friends and Stone had been a Frankfurter detractor on the Supreme Court. These intellectuals were not genteel.[13]

Of all his roles Berle may have taken that as braintrusting soothsayer most seriously. He was an impressario of the future, constantly sponsoring its investigation at the Twentieth Century Fund and with other liberal think tanks. "Tell me where we will be twenty years from now and what the problems will be," Nelson Rockefeller said in commissioning one of his study groups in the 1950s. "I told him that no sane man would take an assignment like that. He said that was why he had asked me. I agreed to do the job." No Machiavelli could refuse a Prince. For the rest of his life he played at being somebody's braintruster. The older he grew the fewer were his opportunities for action and the more he was certain that in the long run ideas mattered more than action. "Machiavelli would not, and could not have written 'The Prince' had he not been Undersecretary of State of Florence," but Machiavelli would be remembered only for his tome. Berle likewise wanted to put his experiences and observations to paper. He would write about power if he could not wield it.[14]

When Dwight Eisenhower left Columbia's presidency for the political hustings in 1952, Berle urged his collegues to consider a successor who came from "an essential scholarly field of wide application, with a reasonable gift for human relations. The broadest field of intellectual scope is, of course, philosophy; probably the next to that is the field of history." As he grew older he repeated this theme with regularity; the world needed philosophers, historians, and braintrusters—a directorate of intellectuals to guide mankind to a more rational future.

He found his directorate in the followers of the French educator and entrepreneur Gaston Berger, founder of the "Prospective" school of philosophy. Through mutual friends such as Edouard Morot-Sir and André Cournand, Berle met Berger and enjoyed long discussions of high philosophy. Berger rejected postwar existentialism and counseled that man must not surrender himself to passivity and victimization by contemporary turmoil. Rather, man should shape the future and determine "what he wills it to be." Man had to master and use the social sciences and technology. As director of higher education in the French Ministry of Education, Berger gathered about him industrialists, academicians, and government officials who sought to guide the nation to the future. However, ideas being more important than a position, Berger left the government to establish a journal and a think tank to propagate the Prospective faith, before dying in an automobile accident in 1960. Nevertheless, the young technocrats of the Fifth Republic carried on Berger's dreams—proof that ideas from above could transcend disruptions from below. For the Prospective school was a corporate elite intent upon ordering the pluralism of a democratic age without suffering the totalitarian dictatorship of the proletariat. And in America the Prospective school found a kindred spirit in the aging braintruster, Adolf Berle.[15]

Liberalism Without FDR

On a warm, sunny day in late June 1947, Berle went to the Riverdale home of his friend La Guardia. In the little garden in back of his house they chatted about the state of the Union and liberalism and Congress ("anybody who was a member of the 80th Congress is guilty of something until he proves he had an alibi"). The Little Flower was recovering from an operation, but his mind was on foreign affairs and other concerns that made him one of the truly heroic figures of twentieth-century American politics. For three decades he had been the best of independent liberalism. But now, although nobody told him so, he was fighting for his life. Late in the afternoon his doctor arrived to administer an injection. Then Berle and the doctor rode downtown together and Berle asked him the obvious question: "Off the record, probably three or four months," came the reply. That was optimistic; La Guardia died less than two months later of cancer of the pancreas. "So a generation passes and I am getting old myself," Berle observed at fifty-two.[1]

La Guardia's passing made Berle a political orphan. He and Roosevelt had been Berle's political mentors, but now both were gone. So too were Berle's ties to political organizations. Accustomed to fighting for "lone hands and lost causes" in politics, even political mavericks like La Guardia and Berle needed a party. For twenty years Berle had had a political hegira from a nominal Republicanism to Fusionism, to Liberalism, to ALPism, before necessity compelled him to join the Democratic party in the late 1930s. But now the Democracy was the party of Truman and O'Dwyer—not his kind of people at all. So Berle gravitated back to the Liberal party.

These Liberals were not really his kind of people either. Unlike La Guardia's aristocratic Fusionists, these Liberals were mostly garment workers—the International Ladies Garment Workers Union of David Dubinsky, a predominantly Jewish trade union in quest of a political coalition with a liberal Democratic party. Berle was their Protestant lawyer front man whom, they hoped, would lure independent-minded professionals into coalition with them. The Liberal party was reformist, Social Democratic, and anti-Communist. "I became its chairman in 1947 partly because of my very anti-Communist record," Berle later wrote. They had spun off from the pro-Soviet factions of the American Labor Party in 1944 to give New York liberals an alternative to the corrupt Tammany Hall leadership of New York

Democrats, the reactionary big business types in the Republican party, and the ALP's Reds. Their platform sought to preserve and extend the social gains of the New Deal era while isolating and then destroying the ALP. Berle's New Deal credentials served their purposes and he needed them to give him a political home and the company of crusaders.[2]

Liberalism without FDR awaited definition. Berle eloquently invented causes and goals while defending the social gains of the thirties. He espoused liberalism's fundamentals, self-determination of all nations and government intervention in the economy to protect the disadvantaged and advance opportunity. He espoused humane capitalistic planning and denounced conspiracies to impose a Soviet America that would subordinate national self-determination to the will of Moscow. He preferred state capitalism that preserved individualism rather than imposing a dictatorship of the proletariat. He believed that the corporation could be an instrument of social democracy if it followed the wishes of its stockholders and if their numbers were sufficiently broadened through prosperity and investment to include all classes of Americans. Large unions and the judicious investment of their pensions presented exciting opportunities for democratizing capitalism. The unions broadened the Liberals' political bases and their pension systems broadened economic involvements, democratizing big corporations by making them responsive to these organized shareholders and making the unions owners and operators of great enterprises. Perhaps he exaggerated these developments and their potential, but more than ever he believed that America enhanced prosperity through a spreading of wealth and work. It was a halfway house between "colonizing capital" and totalitarianism, and it seemed to work. Politically, Berle believed in the Liberal party's mission: compel Democrats to nominate liberals whom the Liberals could endorse or face Liberal party opposition that would likely elect Republicans.

"Last night I accepted the Chairmanship of the Liberal Party," Berle recorded on May 12, 1947. He conceded that it might seem to others a "foolish" act because the party was a pitifully weak political organization. It was not even a third party to the Republicans and Democrats in New York; the Roosevelt candidacy in 1944 won 436,000 votes on the ALP line and only 329,000 on the Liberal line. A Liberal party convention needed only a Manhattan high school auditorium. Berle likened his chairmanship of such a superfluous organization to "being elected Chief Engineer of a vacuum cleaner." Yet he eschewed mainstream party politics and forsook Democratic honors that might have included "occasional plush appointments from the State Department, and [allowed him to] grow old with dignity and leisure." It was the right decision because intellectually, he believed, the Liberals had a "clear monopoly" on relevant ideas: "The Labor Party cannot have an idea unless it is okayed by the Communists. Neither the Democrats nor the Republicans have any ideas at all. We have to draft the program."

Berle the braintruster drafted the Liberals' program and performed as their ideological spokesman. He did not hunker after political office either for himself or other Liberals because, he insisted, the political "wilderness has some attractions." There he would be joined by other reformers to rally against the Democrats' "crooked, bossed government" or the Republican fat cats under whom "the poorest pay [for government] while the richest go scot-free." The Democrats were not his class of people. They promised the masses much and principally delivered patronage. Without FDR, the Democrats were not as progressive and had less need of a braintruster. The Liberals were issue- and program-minded, lacking in any patronage to distribute and disdaining party discipline that made patronage a reward. Berle's role called for him to be more than a back-room ideologue but, though he railed mightily against politics, he secretly enjoyed the hustings. He had known "a thrill in being in the game instead of merely looking at it from the outside," he once told his son. With the Liberals he still had a say on who got elected in New York, although he had no illusions concerning its hazards. Politics, he knew, "damages the ego out of all proportion to the results ordinarily attained; also the end of politics is invariably tragedy." Still, he confessed that "campaigning is a favorite amusement of mine. It has in it (when done on a large scale) the combined qualities of having a ticket in a lottery, listening to great music, being at a Revival meeting, and joining the Army, and it does for America something of what carnival does for Brazil." It was in his blood. "I have lived the life of the court," he reminded B. M. Baruch, "and I am glad to take the field again."[3]

He lusted for the audience which the Liberals bestowed upon him. He had been a vital part of New York and national electoral politics since 1932 and, although he haughtily maintained that electoral politics "ill accords with the detached status of the State Department," during the war he had played the game as he had before—in the back rooms. New York politics had taken some strange turns in 1942 when the party of FDR found itself captive to a conservative Democratic candidate for Governor backed by an embittered Jim Farley. Berle himself briefly considered running for governor on the ALP ticket. He almost preferred to see the Republican candidate, Thomas E. Dewey, elected rather than the conservative Democrat.[4]

Berle and La Guardia had helped launch Dewey's career in 1936 when they had secured Dewey's appointment as a racketsbusting special assistant district attorney in New York County, encouraging him to get all the "publicity as you can." Berle and La Guardia brought Dewey together with the Republican leader, Kenneth Simpson, for Dewey's race for district attorney in 1937. Even then they knew that Dewey was pompously arrogant and ambitious to be governor. Yet, in 1942 Berle and La Guardia backed an ALP candidate for governor, knowing it assured victory for the Republican Dewey.[5]

The 1944 campaign was bitterly ironic for Berle. Dewey won the Republican presidential nomination and during that campaign he pointed to a single sentence from Berle's TNEC testimony of 1939 as an example of how the New Deal sought to turn America Communist by owning all its property. Berle hardly figured in the campaign except for Dewey's slur that Berle was a New Dealer who would communize America. By this time Berle, La Guardia, and Dubinsky had abandoned the ALP to its Communist leadership, taking the garment workers and other liberals with them to form the Liberal party of New York. Berle's lack of speechwriting and speechmaking for Roosevelt was testimony to his remoteness from the White House inner circle now commanded by Harry Hopkins. Yet, in the confusion of wartime gossip and image making, Dewey made Berle out to be the quintessential "New Deal Communist." It was a harbinger of postwar redbaiting.[6]

Of course Berle had been a longtime anti-Communist and saw nothing wrong with baiting the Reds in the ALP. They were disloyal to the United States and subservient to Moscow. They disavowed American democracy for totalitarianism. After the war he had watched with misgivings the advance of the Soviets into middle Europe and the West's uncertain response. He hoped to formulate a liberal anti-Communist policy as effectively outside the State Department as within it. Familiarity with the anti-Communist activities of the International Ladies Garment Workers Union here and in Italy convinced him that its Liberal party was a suitable vehicle for channeling debate into Social Democratic directions. In 1947 he implored the United States to normalize relations with Italy as soon as possible, a position that complemented the ILGWU's covert activities there in behalf of the Social Democratic unions and parties. A few months after resuming private activity in New York, he told a Liberal party convention to ally with Democrats to resist communism in America. The anti-Communist theme was a staple of his rhetoric. The Democratic party should not "hedge or pussyfoot on the issue of communism," he told the Affiliated Young Democrats. Berle insisted that he wanted cooperation with the Soviets but "Soviet propagandists and the Soviet imperialist policy are repeatedly diminishing that hope"; moreover, the ALP wanted slavishness to Moscow on foreign policy. He assured Truman that the Communists in the ALP were "being isolated" and commended his firing of Henry Wallace as secretary of commerce for being "simply naive about foreign policy." He was certain that most Americans were "gravitating toward the center. They are discarding in their own minds the [Robert A.] Tafts on the one hand and the [William Z.] Fosters on the other."[7]

He had returned from Brazil with a case of Potomac fever. Having been an insider for a dozen years, he did not relish life outside the court. Moreover, political exile in New York offended his senses of destiny and mission. He was too young for history to be made without him, particularly when events abroad confronted his eighteenth-century faith in an orderly uni-

verse. To a degree the Liberal party chairmanship gave him a needed political outlet, a vehicle for power, and an opportunity for anti-Communist
brain-trusting. The selection of Berle for that post signaled a stepped-up
drive against Communists in the ALP and right-wing antilabor legislation
in Congress. Liberals put Democrats on notice that Roosevelt's party must
offer disaffected Democrats a liberal alternative to the ALP Communists
or the "fuzzy-heads" in Henry Wallace's progressive movement. Berle endorsed the Truman Doctrine as an extension of Roosevelt's policies and
initiated visits to Truman in July 1947 and January 1948, for the purpose
of coordinating Liberal strategy with the White House—telling reporters
that Communists were behind Wallace and assuring the president that the
Liberals endorsed his veto of the Taft-Hartley bill.[8]

"We will work with existing parties when they adopt liberal measures
and when they join in putting forward men with the capacity for liberal
leadership," Berle told the press during the 1948 campaign. It was the cor-
nerstone of Liberal strategy: Agree with us on the issues and we will give
your liberal candidates another line on the ballot and a few hundred thousand more votes. Labor-minded Liberals, Berle declared, wanted to abolish
a proletariat rather than seek its dictatorship. Liberals opposed Henry Wallace's Progressive party candidacy for president because he was a front for
Communists who sought Soviet appeasement. "The country is swinging
your way," Berle assured the embattled Truman. Relations with Truman
were cordial enough, but at the local level Berle sought Bronx boss Ed
Flynn's agreement to back a mutual candidate in a special judgeship election and was told that the Democratic party was *the* liberal party. Did Flynn
feel that the Liberals should go out of business, Berle asked? Yes, the Bronx
Democratic boss replied.[9]

"The real objective here is to see whether eventually we can take over
the intellectual direction of the Democratic Party in New York," Berle averred. However, to accomplish that, he had to mollify some Liberals who
could not abide Truman and others who were "wild for Eisenhower." One
disappointed Liberal who had wanted to be Truman's secretary of labor
bolted the party and wound up endorsing Dewey that fall; even Liberals
liked political office, Berle notwithstanding. (Nevertheless, Berle made at
least one attempt to secure a federal position for a Liberal worker for Truman). But Berle was loyal to Truman, even as he remained politically remote. Truman had earned Liberal support when he called a special session
of Congress to fight inflation and to desegregate the armed forces. In September Berle formally delivered the Liberal party's endorsement at the
White House. Privately Berle was not so foolish as to expect Truman to
win: "The real stake here is not the Presidency, but the ability to make the
Democratic Party into the thing it ought to have been"—i.e., *liberal*.[10]

Later, a cold analysis of election results showed that Truman ran behind his ticket in New York, thereby confirming for Berle that Liberal strat-

egy had triumphed because its support of the president had, as intended, made the difference. But Liberals still could not expect patronage; they merely looked forward to cordial presidential messages for their dinners and their yearbooks—good public relations for both Liberals and Truman. In fact, however, Berle was unhappy with Truman's choice of Frankfurter's buddy, Dean Acheson, as secretary of state in 1949 and the White House was unhappy with Berle's accusation that Acheson had had Communists on his State Department staff and was soft on the Soviets in 1944. They were his enemies and Berle remained a Washington outsider. Still, the election confirmed Berle's conviction that while third party candidacies did not win elections, the Liberals could become the Democrats' ideological masters. They could compel the Democrats to be more sympathetic to labor at home and more anti-Communist abroad. Significantly, too, in 1949 the ALP was as dead politically as Wallace's Progressive party. Now the Liberals were New York's third party. But the Democrats still had to be convinced that they could not win without the Liberals.[11]

In the Liberal party Berle mattered less than the interests of the unions that composed it; Dubinsky came closest to calling the shots. When Berle piously insisted that Liberals would not attach themselves to a "Democratic hack who would be a servant to the machine," he did not speak for Liberals who wanted power in the Democratic Party no matter how they obtained it. As the 1949 mayoralty contest approached, Berle threatened to run himself rather than endorse a bossed Democrat. He probably was not serious about running and the Liberals certainly did not encourage him. Once again Berle and other white collar Liberals explored Fusion (at Samuel Seabury's office again) with the Republicans. For a time, negotiations on a mayoral candidate were stalemated, although they agreed on Democrat Frank Hogan for district attorney of Manhattan County—Berle punning that Hogan "was more Flynned against than Flynning." When the Democrats renominated William O'Dwyer for mayor, the GOP joined the Liberals behind Newbold Morris—who proved to be a sacrificial lamb; the Republicans were more interested in electing John Foster Dulles in a special Senate race against liberal Democrat Herbert Lehman. However, when Lehman won with a margin that came from his Liberal line, Berle fairly crowded with vindication; it was "balance-of-power with a vengeance."[12]

Wielding the balance of power between the major parties was the Liberals' sole raison d'être. In New York, Berle reasoned, "to drop out of the Liberal Party would mean handing the field over to [Vito] Marcantonio and the pro-Communists—and the state to the Republicans." But Marcantonio and the ALP were in almost total eclipse in 1950 and Berle envisioned himself masterminding a liberal seizure of the Democratic party, much as Hubert Humphrey had accomplished in Minnesota. "I still have a little to say, though not much, about who gets elected in the state of New York," he assured Jesse Jones. Berle and the Liberals stayed to the left of the Democrats, reminding them that New Yorkers wanted a permanent Fair Employment Practices Commission, civil rights laws, laws protecting labor, public housing, and public power laws, and good government. Caught up with liberalism, Berle sought a place for a Negro on the board of trustees of a New York Savings Bank, secured Haiti's "determinative" vote for United Nations partition of Palestine and creation of a Jewish state, and lobbied for Senate approval of the United Nations Convention against Genocide. All of them were good causes that reminded people that Berle still wielded clout.[13]

As chairman of the Liberal party, Berle mostly found candidates for races rather than minding its ideological purity. In 1951 the Liberals ran Rudolph Halley, who had won nationwide fame for his dogmatic pursuit of corruption in government while counsel for the Kefauver Senate Committee investigating the connections between racketeers and government, for president of the City Council. Berle dared to hope that Halley might even be another La Guardia. Although Halley was ambitious, the Democrats would not touch him after his committee had tainted urban Democratic leaders. The major parties chose weak candidates to oppose Halley and, in a light vote, Halley won. It was the most significant victory Liberals ever enjoyed alone. But Berle was less than elated, partly because Halley still was an unknown quantity and partly because the office itself was inconsequential. However, if Halley proved worthy, he might be the next mayor.[14]

Meanwhile, Berle grew increasingly alienated from the Truman administration. Although Liberals warmly supported his intervention in the Korean War and most other cold war initiatives, Truman mostly ignored them. Moreover, the Truman scandals outraged Berle. Reviewing *Mr. President,* a collection of Truman's writings, Berle noted that the Missourian's distaste for "professional liberals" and his fondness for political bosses put him at odds with the thirty-second president of the United States. Also, he privately berated the Truman administration for its inaction elsewhere in Asia and in Latin America. With Acheson in charge of foreign policy, he expected nothing but disaster. Ernest Cuneo once told him that Secretary of Defense Louis Johnson had proposed that Berle be made under secretary, but Acheson vetoed it; "All things considered, I think Acheson did me a service," Berle commented.[15]

But it was time for a change in the White House. Berle anticipated the election of 1952 with certainty that "no candidate could carry New York State without the support of the Liberal Party, unless Taft were the Republican nominee." The Democratic one-party rule of New York was corrupt and the voters "look to us," Berle assured Governor Adlai E. Stevenson of Illinois. Liking Stevenson's intellectual diffidence and apparent liberal independence, he urged the Illinoisan to seek the Democratic nomination. Thanking Berle for his political advice, Stevenson insisted that he was only a candidate to succeed himself, not Truman.[16]

Stevenson's demurrer actually suited Berle well because his top candidate for president was the Democratic senator from Illinois, Paul H. Douglas—"the one Democrat of great experience who could run without being burdened by the miserable record of ingrown political machines and bureaucratic corruption," Berle averred. Formerly an economics professor at the University of Chicago and a supporter of socialist Norman Thomas for president, Douglas' record as an anti-Communist intellectual and liberal reformer suited Berle perfectly, perhaps because they were so similar. (They even agreed on Dean Acheson.) But Douglas was committed to the candidacy of another corruption-fighter, Senator Estes Kefauver of Tennessee, chairman of the Senate Committee Rudolph Halley had served as counsel. Berle had met Kefauver recently and while Kefauver had flattered him, Douglas remained his first choice. Other New York Liberals wanted Averell Harriman, but a consensus was building for Stevenson.[17]

Upon landing in Chicago on July 22 to witness the Democratic Convention, Berle immediatley headed for Paul Douglas' apartment on the South Side. But Douglas discouraged his support by telling Berle that an "avalanche" for Stevenson was in motion. Accordingly, Berle called Stevenson to congratulate him and urged Kefauver for vice-president upon a reluctant Stevenson. Stevenson's "masterpiece" of an acceptance speech enhanced Berle's growing admiration for the Illinois governor: "It was great comfort to have a literate man talking again. The contrast between his talk and the line of slush Truman handed out was painful."[18]

Berle wanted very much to play braintruster again. When Stevenson courted New York Liberals by suggesting that Berle and Dubinsky would figure prominently in the campaign, Berle eagerly sought to press upon Stevenson his views on foreign affairs. He fretted that the nominee might surround himself with others less politically savvy or attuned to the public interest than he. In September Stevenson invited him to join Stevenson's brain trust, submitting drafts of speeches through Stevenson's Raymond Moley, Arthur Schlesinger, Jr. The more he knew Stevenson, the more he found a man who was "likable and liked." Measuring his politicians against Roosevelt and La Guardia, Berle most appreciated Stevenson's intellect— "a clearer gift of analysis than Roosevelt" but lacking in La Guardia's "tremendous, blazing power of communication." But Berle never really got close to Stevenson. In fact, the Liberals proved politically troublesome to Stevenson in New York because in the senatorial race they ran an independent candidate against a Democrat. Also, Berle did not help Stevenson by declaring that "the Democratic Party does not exist in the Bronx, only the Flynn party." Stevenson lost New York to Eisenhower by a sizable majority, but Liberal vote totals left Berle confident that they could control the Democratic choice for mayor in 1953.[19]

But a suitably Liberal candidate was not in evidence. Although Halley wanted to run for mayor, Berle now considered him too weak and vain— certainly not a La Guardia; he preferred a liberal Republican such as Jacob

Javits or Nelson Rockefeller, or an old friend like David E. Lilienthal. However, Republican candidates troubled Liberals, while Rockefeller and Lilienthal had never run for anything. "We had best nominate Halley and be done with it," a dejected Berle decided after eight months in quest of an alternative: "He can develop into a La Guardia—he can also develop into a tumbleweed." This was not politics as Berle liked it; the Democratic bosses were running Robert F. Wagner, Jr., on the basis of his late father's name as a great U.S. senator, and the Republicans were running a sacrificial lamb. It was an unhappy campaign while he wildly accused both parties of being in the grip of "the criminal underworld." Wagner won the mayoralty with only a plurality and Halley was destined for obscurity and an early death. Berle told Dubinsky that this would be his last campaign.[20]

At least, Dubinsky exulted in May 1954, the Liberals had "virtually eliminated the ALP from the political scene." That was important to Berle, but he was unhappy because the Democratic party was not yet reformed. Democratic boss Carmine DeSapio wanted to "exchange ideas" with Berle, but Berle wondered toward what purpose? Democrats persistently challenged Liberals to justify their independent ways. The Liberals divided among themselves as to whether they should call it quits and infiltrate the Democrats, or continue independently without hope of electoral growth or anything but rubber-stamping liberal Democrats. Fortunately, the Democrats nominated an ample supply of certifiable liberals and the Liberal party endorsed Averell Harriman for governor in 1954. Berle plumped for the entire Democratic ticket that year because he had "little use for the general Republican point of view." (An enraged New York County Republican chairman assailed the Liberals as the "most totalitarian" party in the country.) Once more the Liberals provided the margin of victory for a Democratic candidate, but who could say with certainty that those votes would not have gone to Harriman anyway?[21]

Berle felt politically superfluous. His name had currency in foreign affairs and symbolism as a New Dealer, but the real clout in the Liberal party lay with the ILGWU. Dubinsky always made the big decisions in consultation with others. And Berle had no influence with Democrats, most of whom considered him an arrogant troublemaker. Berle did not "find anything to be excited about" in Harriman as a governor or a candidate for president. Liberals were better off when Democrats lost. In July 1955, Berle retired as the Liberals' "intellectual leader" and they honored him with a dinner. Even without a title he remained a part of the Liberals' forlorn inner circle.[22]

Still yearning to be a president's braintruster again, Berle signed on as a charter member of Adlai Stevenson for president in 1956. The state organization for Stevenson was headed by Thomas Finletter, whom Berle distrusted for being ambitious. Insisting that their endorsement was imperative for a Democratic victory, Berle and the Liberal leaders trooped to Chicago in August to tell Democrats in convention there that Stevenson was their man too. The Illinoisan consulted them on the vice-presidency—Kefauver, this time. He also included Berle in his brain trust again. But Berle expected Stevenson to lose once more to the popular Eisenhower and the outcome did not shock him.[23]

Nor did it disappoint him. The Eisenhower administration presented Berle with a small irony: "Believe it or not, I have more personal friends [in the new administration] that I had in the Truman Administration though they represent other ideas and other thinking." His comments betrayed how few friends he had had in the Truman administration. He mused that he "could have a great deal better time in the State Department now than I did when my own friends were in control. There is nothing like having contact with both ends." Nelson Rockefeller in the Department of Health, Education and Welfare, Allen Dulles in the CIA, and C. D. Jackson in the White House were the extent of his acquaintances in the Eisenhower administration, although he might have included his neighbor on East 19th Street, Attorney General Herbert Brownell, on that list. Dulles and Jackson always gave Berle a courteous ear and they indeed involved him in foreign affairs in several ways during the fifties. But Berle's involvement was almost clandestine and his influence was severely limited. He did not like the big business types who inhabited the Republican administration; history had cycles and he considered Eisenhower the near equivalent of Coolidge. What did a general know about economics, politics, or governing?[24]

Nelson Rockefeller was Berle's idea of a Republican who was also a liberal and, at the same time, his personal friend. He liked Rockefeller's sense of noblesse oblige. In the 1950s Rockefeller generously put his money to work by endowing task force studies of capital formation or foreign affairs. Berle frequently brain trusted for the task forces and wrote papers for Rockefeller, for which he was compensated. In 1952 Rockefeller turned a little house he owned on 54th Street, behind the Museum of Modern Art, into a comfortable meeting place for his personal brain trust—Wallace Harrison, Beardsley Ruml, and others. "This ought to be fun," Berle enthused, as the intellectuals tackled great ideas over tea and Dubonnet and then washed the dishes. They would, as Berle put it, provide "some intellectual and philosophical direction . . . to the burden of empire."

As early as 1952 Rockefeller nursed an ambition to run for governor of New York. His departure from the Eisenhower administration in late 1955 gave him more time to plan a political career that would be enhanced by a personal fortune in Standard Oil shares which had quadrupled in value since the war. In 1956 he and Berle began "to cast a part for him in the next few years." From these discussions came the Rockefeller Brothers Fund, panels of intellectuals who brain trusted options for American foreign policy at mid-century, administered by the president of the Rockefeller Foundation, Dean Rusk, and coordinated by a Harvard professor, Henry Kissinger.[25]

On July 8, 1958, in the wake of considerable fanfare surrounding the

Rockefeller Report, Rockefeller announced his candidacy for the Republican nomination for governor. Months before, Berle had urged Rockefeller not to run. In the midst of the second Eisenhower recession, everyone expected Republicans to lose at the polls, which made Rockefeller confident of at least winning the nomination. Also, Berle said, he could not support his friend because "I could not change my party loyalties any more than he could." That was alright, Rockefeller assured him; he wanted nothing to disrupt their friendship. At Rockefeller's birthday party ("in the Medician style," Berle observed) the band struck "Happy Days Are Here Again," FDR's anthem; "I was seeing ghosts," Berle wrote.

Despite a sense of loyalty to the party of Franklin Roosevelt, Berle preferred Rockefeller who consulted him, to Harriman who did not. The Liberals endorsed Harriman, but that did not prevent Berle from publicly praising Rockefeller as a liberal person. Rockefeller upset Harriman and "a warm personal friend now takes a position of national leadership," Berle wrote the day after Rockefeller's victory. "Personal considerations will always have to yield to political necessities, and they should." A month later he had the governor-elect and his wife, Tod, to dinner, a relationship he then enjoyed with no other national political figure. Rockefeller was neither Roosevelt nor La Guardia, but it was good to be brain trusting again for a potential president.[26]

POLICING COMMUNISTS

Political fashion caught up with Berle following World War II as others discovered the Soviet imperialism that had been evident to him since 1941. But that only encouraged a sterile political debate concerning how it had been allowed to happen that American foreign policy tolerated half of Europe to fall under Moscow's hegemony. Opportunistic politicians and intellectuals ascribed Soviet successes to an exhausted and dying Roosevelt who, weakened at Yalta and surrounded by duplicitous State Department officials such as Alger Hiss, gave away too much. Berle knew that was nonsense, but the Hiss case contributed measurably to those charges. It began in 1948 when a journalist and former Communist, Whittaker Chambers, accused Hiss of being a Communist spy as early as 1935. Hiss was eventually convicted of perjury, which satisfied many people who wanted to believe that the wartime State Department was honeycombed with subversives who compromised American policy toward the Soviets. In 1950 Senator Joseph R. McCarthy of Wisconsin asserted that he possessed evidence of Communists still working in the State Department. "McCarthyism" describes the unsubstantiated charges of communism that recklessly besmirched reputations of innocent people. Although he deplored McCarthy, Adolf Berle was the link between Chambers and McCarthyism.

Asked why he had not reported the Communist underground sooner, Chambers replied that he had told Berle of it in 1939. On the advice of anti-Soviet emigré Isaac Don Levine, Chambers had gone to the White House to tell Roosevelt, only to be told by presidential secretary Marvin McIntyre to take it to Berle, who then administered State Department intelligence. On an August evening the day after Germany invaded Poland, Berle listened to Chambers rattle off the names of Communists or former Communists in the government, "a singularly unpleasant job." Russian espionage in the United States did not surprise him; even friendly governments spied upon each other and Berle was not surprised by anything the Soviets did after they had signed a friendship pact with Hitler. Nor was he surprised that Communists or former Communists worked in the government during the 1930s. However, none of this was cause for shouting Chambers' charges in the streets. For reasons he never felt he needed to give, Berle did nothing with Chambers' information until he turned it over to the FBI in 1941 for an investigation of Chambers' charges. While Chambers' list surfaced in the State Department in 1943 again, nothing was done until Chambers showed up once more in 1948 to repeat his charges to the House Committee on Un-American Activities (HUAC).[1]

Berle feared both the Communists and their possible loss of civil liberties. Along with Morris Ernst, in 1948 he opposed legislation that would outlaw the Communist party "because it is both unnecessary and ineffective." Rather than drive Communists underground, he preferred to have them operate visibly in the political system through vehicles such as the ALP. But Berle also argued that while teachers had a right as private citizens to freedom of speech, that did not include the right to advocate "totalitarian doctrine" in the classroom: "I will be everlastingly damned if I don't see why we shouldn't have a pure food and drug bill for politics as well as we do for food. What goes into people's heads is just as important as what goes into their stomachs." Then, lest he be accused of thought control, he added that he feared only advocates of "a foreign political group not ideology. If a man wants to advocate communism as an American he is entitled to. Ideas are free." It was not easy to be both liberal and to legislate against totalitarianism.[2]

In August Berle went before the HUAC to explain why he had waited a couple of years to turn Chambers's information over to the FBI. It was a curious performance. With only three hours' preparation and no time for refreshing his memory by consulting his diary for recorded impressions of Chambers' 1939 visit, Berle's testimony was vague and confused. He insisted that the men Chambers named as spies were no more than a group of Communist sympathizers intent upon organizing a Marxist study group in the State Department. Although Chambers had named names, Berle did not attach any great significance to them; some were already out of government. Was he suspicious of Hiss? Berle said he was "worried" about

Hiss—confessing to "a prejudice here so that you can discount whatever I say here." With that he digressed on how there had been in 1944 a conflict with "Mr. Acheson's group . . . with Mr. Hiss as his principal assistant" over cooperation with the Russians, Hiss taking "what we would call today the pro-Russian point of view." That worried him, Berle said, although it did not suggest Hiss was subversive: "I say that in Mr. Hiss' defense, although I got trimmed in that fight, and, as a result, went to Brazil, and that ended my diplomatic career. I mention that, because I did have a biased view." Since Hiss was Acheson's executive assistant, Berle said that he asked Dean Acheson about Hiss: "Acheson said that he had known the family and he could vouch for them absolutely." So could Felix Frankfurter.[3]

Nevertheless, Berle maintained that Hiss himself was unimportant. Policing Communist espionage in the State Department was less important than a struggle over policy toward Russia. What was more significant than Hiss, he explained to Arthur Schlesinger, Jr., was that "some of us estimated that the Russian policy would be about what it has proved [to be], and pressed for a clear-cut plan as to how to meet the resulting problem." But, in the fight over policy, "practically everyone with experience in foreign affairs was eliminated from policy-making; and the failing President was left almost alone." Berle wanted Americans to keep in mind the overall foreign policy rather than witch hunting for a suspected Communist in the Department. He wanted to avoid Red-baiting, intending his testimony to be a "sedative," he told Jerome Frank; "it is hard to get sanity into a supercharged atmosphere. It seems that the great question was not whether there was treason to the United States, but whether Alger Hiss goes to heaven when he dies—and I cannot contribute anything to that decision." He dismissed the importance of spying: "Espionage even between allies is not unusual among great powers." Ethics and ideas mattered; policies mattered; Hiss did not: Of consequence was "changing the course of a long and powerful movement." Hiss worried him less than arming Americans with liberal principles with which to fight a long war against communism.[4]

Berle had minimized Hiss' alleged espionage in 1939 for the same reasons he minimized it in 1948: "All of this may make some noise but is not really important." It was trivial compared to policies that contained the Russians. Another reason for his inaction in 1939 was his concern for the rights of radicals in a time of crisis. The night before Chambers visited him in 1939, he had dined with Roger Baldwin—an old friend, leader of the American Civil Liberties Union, and an antitotalitarian—and they discussed "the effect of the German-Russian alliance on the soft-headed American liberals." Although many American liberals treated Communists as left-liberals, Berle never differentiated much between the totalitarianism of Nazis and that of Communists; the Nazi-Soviet Pact, Nazi-Soviet collaboration on espionage, and Communist calls for American nonintervention all confirmed that both were intent upon the destruction of liberalism. He reacted with wry amusement to Chambers' information by observing that Jews who had spied for the Russians would now be "furious to find that they are, in substance, working for the Gestapo." But that was a problem for their consciences. Surveillance, Berle believed, not prosecutions, was sufficient for dealing with them.[5]

His argument that what really mattered was not any alleged espionage but the appeasement of Soviet ambitions by Hiss' friends in the State Department found no sympathy on either the Right or the Left. The Right condemned Berle for trivializing Hiss' possible espionage and exculpating Roosevelt. The Left assailed him for being a premature anti-Communist. And even liberals in the center deplored his assault against Acheson. Berle's 1948 portrait of 1944's State Department divisions over policy toward the Russians discomforted liberals and inadvertently provided the Right with ammunition that liberals were soft on Soviet expansion and subversion.[6]

Berle's best possible scenario for the election of 1948 called for Truman to win and then remove a discredited Dean Acheson from the State Department. Once the elections were past, Berle insisted that while the idea that Communists "were going to take over the United States Government was childish" and a Communist or a fellow traveler had a right to civil liberties as an American citizen, the government nevertheless had "a right to know the connections, record and the loyalties of the men who work in it." Appearing in December before a special Federal Grand Jury investigating espionage, he repeated his charge that Hiss was part of a pro-Soviet faction in the State Department headed by Dean Acheson who opposed Berle's "get tough" policy.[7]

To Berle's enormous disappointment, upon the resignation of George C. Marshall, Truman nominated Acheson for secretary of state. The headlines told the story:

Policy Fight Posed
Confirmation of Acheson Likely to Raise Issues of
   Hiss-Chambers Row
Berle Rift Is Recalled

At his Senate confirmation hearings, Acheson was compelled to deny that he appeased the Soviets. "The things I read about myself as an appeaser seem to me so incredible that I cannot believe that even disinterested malevolence could think them up," Acheson told the senators. Before a room packed with reporters and curious spectators, the secretary-designate declared, "Mr. Berle's memory has gone badly astray." Well-prepared from his own files and those of the State Department, Acheson recalled that his 1944 conversation with Berle concerning Hiss really was about Alger's brother Donald who worked under Acheson; Alger did not even work for Acheson. According to Acheson, he then questioned Donald Hiss about whether he had had any associations that would embarrass Acheson, and

Donald Hiss assured him that he had not. As for a conflict over policy toward the Soviets, Acheson maintained "I had no dispute with Mr. Berle of any sort about anything in the fall or summer or other time of 1944." Berle himself attempted to defuse any controversy by sending a telegram which was read into the record. Denying that he opposed Acheson for secretary of state, Berle said that they had had their differences on Russian policy then, but "the matter was one on which honest men could differ, and I have never felt that divergence on this question reflected on the competence or loyalty of men who went along with the policy then adopted." The telegram must have left Acheson furious: Acceding to Acheson's appointment as secretary of state, Berle reiterated charges that, by opposing Berle's hard line, Acheson had been soft on the Russians. And privately Berle continued to rate Acheson as "a rather less intelligent Neville Chamberlain."[8]

Berle did not alter the tenor of his attack on Acheson and Acheson and Frankfurter remained loyal to Alger Hiss as a member of their group. As Hiss' troubles mounted in 1949, Acheson was "anxious about Alger." So was Frankfurter, who feared that it would be recalled that he had secured Hiss' first government position with the Agricultural Adjustment Administration. Berle discomforted Frankfurther and Acheson in 1949, and no doubt he would have liked to block Acheson's appointment without hurting the State Department, but any effort to inflict greater damage upon his old enemies failed. Acheson would be remembered as secretary of state for his containment of the Soviet Union policies—Berle attributing those policies to Acheson's opportunistic "sponsorship of movements which he had been bitterly and actively opposing in 1944 and 1945 when they might have saved much blood and tears."[9]

Berle indirectly and inadvertently encouraged the charges of Communist subversion of the State Department that followed. His own contempt for the State Department suggested its culpability for Soviet successes in Eastern Europe and China. But Berle also deplored McCarthy and his imitators and their impact upon the Foreign Service. "The real complaint," Berle told Fletcher Warren, "is that behind McCarthy there has gathered a fanatical minority like that which supported Father Coughlin in earlier times." In late 1953, the counsel for the Jenner committee called Berle to testify whether Harry Dexter White was a Russian spy. Berle replied that he had no knowledge of White and that he did not much care. White was dead and it was evident that the White case was merely more "noise." "So far as I personally am concerned," he later told his daughter, "they could go on investigating Communist infiltration and espionage until Kingdom come. These people were my bitter enemies and probably contributed as much as anything (outside of my own faults) to my not having been a historic figure in the last few years. There were Soviet spies and there was Communist infiltration. Taken together, it made a little trouble and probably did not vary greatly the course of affairs. . . . But directing the whole course of American politics in 1954 to examination of the mistakes of 1944 gets us absolutely nowhere."[10]

McCarthyism hit close to home when J. Robert Oppenheimer, a member of the Twentieth Century Fund's Board of Trustees, was declared a security risk by the Eisenhower administration in 1954. One member of the Fund's board urged Berle to arrange for the scientist's quiet resignation, but Berle refused. "I don't see that the verdict on Robert Oppenheimer is anything discreditable to him anyhow," Berle thought, "still less that it makes him unworthy. . . . The A.E.C. [Atomic Energy Commission] might decide that he was not a perfect choice for a policy-making position with the government but that should not preclude us from thinking that he could be of great service to the Fund." He did not turn his back on Robert Oppenheimer. Nine years later Oppenheimer was given the Enrico Fermi award for service and Berle took it as a sign that "we are back on a better track." Berle was an anti-Communist liberal, but he never subscribed to the absurdity of McCarthyism.[11]

THE FOREIGN POLICY ESTABLISHMENT

In the 1960s the media discovered an American foreign policy establishment—an elite unobtrusively directing the fortunes of empire in war and peace. The elite, composed of bankers, businessmen, and Wall Street and Washington lawyers, conspired over luncheons at the Century Club in Manhattan, at the Metropolitan Club in Washington, and at Council on Foreign Relations seminars in its Harold Pratt House at Park Avenue and 68th Street, to weave arrangements and understandings that made a coherent imperial strategy. For a half century right-wing populists and Marxists, inspired by the Great War, believed in the efficacy of the establishment's manipulations; following the Second World War, British journalists, fascinated by the shift of the imperial center from London to Washington and New York, eagerly sought to identify an American elite similar to the one that had directed Britain's eroded empire. American establishmentarians were Ivy League in education, centrist and anti-Communist in their politics, liberal in their social attitudes—but hardly a monolith. In truth, multiple establishment networks overlapped and even rivaled each other. Adolf Berle belonged to one such establishment network—which also made him a foreign policy pariah to others.[1]

In the cold war Berle was persona non grata to most men who made U.S. foreign policy. He had left the State Department in 1946, telling President Truman and reporters that the Department directed foreign policy from a "series of watertight compartments" better suited to Ed Stettinius' business administration than practical foreign policy administration. Whatever the truth of his remarks, they did not endear Berle to his former colleagues. He had had a reputation for being "difficult" and neither his tenure nor his departure as ambassador to Brazil changed that. Still, he expected to be an outsider in any State Department where Dean Acheson was under secretary or secretary. Acheson the Anglophile embraced Soviet containment because the British no longer could handle the Mediterranean alone and no longer needed a Soviet alliance that infringed upon their imperial turf. Of course, Berle had warned of the Soviet empire long before it was in British interests to do so and therefore fashionable, but that did not qualify him to run U.S. foreign policy.[2]

Berle knew that the Yalta myth—that an ill, befuddled, and dying Roosevelt conceded too much to the Soviets and therefore unintentionally enhanced the Soviet hegemony—was a calumny and distortion of history. It suited the Roosevelt-haters, who were so diverse as to include American right-wingers who detested FDR for his New Deal and his internationalism as well as the British and American Anglophiles such as Acheson who deplored FDR's arrogance in presumptuously usurping London's interests. Clearly, the Soviet empire began in the Baltic states, which the British in 1940–1941 expediently approved in hopes of a Soviet alliance. Throughout the war the British sedulously pursued separate arrangements with the Soviets—as an old-time empire aiding a parvenu empire against the outrageous anticolonial liberalism of the Americans. To Berle, history had its ironies and none was greater than that of the old anti-Bolshevik Winston Churchill promoting deals with Stalin in order to enhance a Soviet empire that would justify the continued existence of the British Empire. By Yalta Stalin dealt from a position of strength that owed less to FDR's weak health than to the strength of the Red Army and his knowledge that British imperialism feared American imperialism more than it feared Soviet imperialism. In 1945 Churchill realized that he had underestimated the Soviets and that the Americans had to recoup British fortunes. To an extent, that was the mission Acheson and Truman zealously embraced in 1947.

Berle was skeptical about the policies promoted by these belated opponents of Soviet imperialism and rated the globalism and Atlanticism of the Acheson "crowd" as myopic. Berle too believed that Europe was of prime importance, but, "regionalist" that he was, he put Latin America on a par with Europe, while the Atlanticists treated anything south of Missouri as unworthy of their concern. Nevertheless, in 1947–1948 he applauded the Truman Doctrine and the Marshall Plan as policies that would have been implemented earlier if it had not been for the opposition of the people who now invoked them. Still, he lamented that the State Department typically was reactive instead of pursuing long-range policies—tending to "only rig up an opposition" instead of devising "a universal solvent." Thus, the Soviets frequently trapped the Americans who barely knew how to define national interests, much less unflinchingly apply them. In particular,

Berle wanted a global Good Neighbor Policy that organized a community of liberal nations opposed to Soviet totalitarianism. When the Atlanticists decided that a military alliance (NATO) logically followed the Marshall Plan, Berle demurred, arguing that "the whole language of military alliance is out of date"; he preferred collective security within the United Nations.[3]

Communist successes in Czechoslovakia in 1948 and China in 1949, and the Soviet explosion of an atomic bomb, changed Berle's mind about the need for military alliances. Always capable of apocalyptic thoughts, the events of 1949 allowed him to imagine the worst. Bereft of the sources of intelligence he had depended upon for nearly a decade, he now relied upon his own reading of the newspapers and his own informed imagination. At mid-century, it seemed to him that "now, five years after the greatest military victory in history, we are less safe than we were in 1940." Accustomed to thinking in terms of broad geopolitical strategy since 1919, he saw few areas of the globe safe from the threat of the Soviet Army and its surrogates.

> Specifically, our Russian antagonists now have most of Asia and there is little to stop them from getting the rest. They are going to work on the archipelagoes all the way from Japan to Indonesia; we shall be fortuante if two years from now we are not desperately trying to keep a foothold in the Philippines. We could be philosophic about this perhaps if it did not mean an unassailable Russian flank stretching towards the Aleutians, from which, with submarines and long-range aircraft, they could make trouble for us all the way from Alaska to Oregon.

In 1950 he told a Liberal party forum that the western Pacific would likely "prove the balancing factor, tipping the scales for or against the Russian domination of the world." The United States "must be once more the strong champion of freedom for the Pacific and Asiatic peoples . . . in maintaining their independent life . . . against Russian imperialism." Then the North Korean Communists invaded South Korea and Berle rushed to endorse Truman's response to this aggression.[4]

As was his habit, Berle put his alarmist thoughts into memoranda for those few Washington officials who still gave him a hearing—such as Louis Johnson in Defense and Robert Hooker in State. "Fighting the usual sensation of bitterness" that he did not occupy center stage at a critical time and did not not have access to power—that Acheson and his cronies denied Berle his place in history—he nevertheless endeavored to anticipate "the next phase" in the cold war. The United States had "a 50-50 chance of escaping World War III," he told Johnson; "I think the Russians plan a simultaneous move to the Persian Gulf and into the Balkans, aiming across the Mediterranean, which will leave very little alternative" to a military response. Berle forecast that the Russians would employ their surrogates throughout the globe in "local" wars until they compelled the West to resort to an all-out conflagration. If the West lost the ideological struggle it might have to "rely on force alone. This is the tragic circumstance of our diplomatic failure in Asia." Although he applauded Truman for mobilizing the collective security mechanism of the United Nations to resist aggression in Korea, when the war was two years old he urged the president to seek a truce in Korea in order to confront other instances of Soviet aggression. Certain that the Korean engagement had passed its climax, Berle expected "a real bad time somewhere else."[5]

He cultivated ties with influential Europeans and Latin Americans, some of whom were exiles bent upon a return to power in their native lands. In the State Department he had worked with European refugees to overthrow fascism in their homelands; after the war they worked to overthrow communism. Their experiences during the resistance to Fascist totalitarianism had prepared them to organize against Communist totalitarianism. In both cases the informal exile networks found official assistance in their quest to return to a liberated homeland. Just as the Office of War Information (OWI) and the Office of Strategic Services (OSS) had used exiles for propaganda and intelligence operations against the Nazis, so too did the CIA employ fugitives from "the captive countries" for propaganda and intelligence against the Communist hegemony. The CIA covertly sponsored a National Commitee for a Free Europe (NCFE) that created Radio Free Europe (RFE)—ostensibly private coordination of the American and emigré messages to the captive homelands of Eastern Europe or the threatened countries of Western Europe. It also sponsored a College of Free Europe at Strasbourg, France, to educate an elite that would one day roll back the Iron Curtain. Berle worked for both.

The initiative for Radio Free Europe came in 1949 from State Department chief policy planner, George Kennan, who asked Joe Grew to come out of retirement and recruit a private group to create the NCFE and organize Radio Free Europe. The original membership of the NCFE included Dwight D. Eisenhower, Mark Etheridge, Allen Dulles, Fred Dolbeare, Royall Tyler, and Berle. Except for Eisenhower, these men virtually made it a reunion of Americans whose experiences went back to the Paris Peace Conference in 1919. The fiction of voluntarism was deemed necessary because, in the words of a CIA official, "It was thought important to keep intact the cadre of [Eastern European] democratic leaders who had escaped and provide them with some way of communicating with their own people in order to keep alive the hope of eventual freedom." Also, such plans virtually subverted governments with whom the United States maintained diplomatic relations and it was deemed preferable to have private citizens carry on such operations from New York instead of Washington offices. Accustomed to inter-Allied espionage during the war, Berle was unconcerned by any apparent breach of diplomatic protocol. The Russians surely knew that RFE was a government operation; before long Berle heard that RFE was infiltrated by Soviet agents: "We might either throw out the intruders, or possibly keep them and watch them." Espionage was neither a cause for outrage or excitement.[6]

The old hands among RFE administrators, like its leader and former head of the Foreign Nationalities branch of OSS, DeWitt Poole, were no strangers to many of the European emigrés who broadcast to the East. However, veterans of the hot war knew that dealings with the emigrés were hazardous because, Berle noted, "the exile leaders were so divided among themselves on ideological lines, and the different political groups were so prone to infighting, that a tower of Babel would be erected if they were left to their own devices." From his own experiences Berle knew that "whenever a European country is occupied by a foreign power, its politics are automatically transferred to the foreign-language communities in the United States." Thus, Sudeten Germans could not have a civil conversation with Slovakians and Rumanian monarchists insisted that all anti-Communists had to accept the deposed king's leadership. Nationhood did not come easily to Central and Eastern Europeans, even in exile.[7]

RFE floundered until 1951 when Washington decided that the Russians' full-scale political-psychological warfare required something more than Voice of America. Allen Dulles went to the CIA as its chief of operations and Poole was succeeded by C. D. Jackson, a tall, handsome, and exuberant Time Incorporated exeuctive who had served as deputy chief of the Psychological Warfare Branch of OWI. Jackson and Berle soon became mutual admirers—a fortuitous circumstance when Jackson became in 1952 an Eisenhower braintruster. Berle worked closely with Jackson, Allen Dulles, and others as a member of NCFE's board, giving almost half of his time to help steer RFE through its crises in the early 1950s.[8]

RFE's goal was the liberalization of Communist Europe, which squared with Berle's faith that totalitarianism defied the "order of the universe." "There is no harm in dreaming" of the day when "Eastern Europe is opened up," Berle believed. That goal was a modestly realistic one compared to that of "liberation" which obsessed Republican orators. Yet the obstacles Berle encountered made him wonder if he only engaged in self-delusion. For one, the Western Europeans doubted that RFE could accomplish anything without them. Both the French and the British accused RFE of duplicating their work. "This is something like the two tramps on the railroad," Berle thought: "one proposes to buy the railroad but the other refuses to sell." Because RFE located its transmitters in Munich, the Germans insisted that eventually the two Germanies would have to be reunited, an idea that appalled many Westerners who feared a united, revanchist Germany pushing east and embroiling them in World War III. The Truman administration left it to the imaginations and experiences of Grew, Allen Dulles, Jackson, and Chip Bohlen to work out abstract designs for a free Eastern Europe. Sometimes, as they planned the reconstruction of a free and capitalist Eastern Europe, Berle could convince himself that it would be reality within a few years. Other times he doubted they would reap dividends soon: "If the Soviet Union were only a power-system, we could wait it out—these things break up in a surprising short time—but dogma, however bad, does not break up so quickly."[9] In late 1952, NCFE, in coordination with the incoming Eisenhower administration, sought a "dynamic plan" with which, in Berle's words, to "push the Russians back rather nearer their original quarters." Eisenhower made Jackson a political advisor and Allen Dulles took charge of the CIA. Along with other NCFE "alumni" in the State and Defense Departments, Berle mused, it seemed "to be taking over the Eisenhower Government."[10]

In Berle's scheme of things, RFE's "little sister" was the College of Free Europe in Strasbourg. There, young fugitives from the Iron Curtain countries learned "the great intellectual traditions and cultural heritage of the Iron Curtain countries" from exiled scholars. Launched in 1951 under NCFE's auspices with a front-page fanfare in *The New York Times* and a five-year provisional charter from the New York State Board of Regents, the College's American offices recruited both emigré faculty and emigré students for the Strasbourg campus. From there would come the future leaders of a liberated Eastern Europe, to fill political vacuums when the Communist regimes fell with liberal values learned at Strasbourg. Berle gave the college his special attention, both because it suited him intellectually and because few esteemed it as much as he did. But, within a few years it became evident that youths from Eastern Europe were more intent upon becoming Americans than fighting Russian tanks with liberal ideas. For that matter, recruiting faculty was no easy chore; anyone who staffed the place, Berle told the dean of the Collège de l'Europe Libre, had to be a blend "of a philosopher and a missionary to understandingly paint a philosophical ideal for the students. . . . Men who can do that, however, are hard to find, as you and I know every well." Berle found few such idealists. (The first president Berle hired had been fired from a presidency at another college; his tenure proved "catastrophic," obliging Berle to invent the title of chancellor as a device for removing him. Columbia then gave him an honorary degree.) As chairman of the board and its most committed trustee, Berle struggled for funds to keep it alive—to no avail.[11]

In 1953, with Nelson Rockefeller again in the State Department, Dulles in the CIA, and Jackson in the White House, Berle enjoyed telephone access to the Republican administration on foreign policy—greater access than he had had for the six years of the previous Democratic administration. To his great pleasure, he was used in a number of informal ways such as arranging credits for the Brazilian government. Significantly, too, with "liberation" on GOP tongues, Berle sensed that American policy toward Europe among his NCFE friends had changed from a defensive to an "activist line." With Western European unity developing apace, Berle optimistically believed that "this time at least we will not leave an empire adrift again, as we did after Versailles."[12]

Berle wanted to jettison some of his volunteer NCFE duties, but one death and several resignations left its ranks of experienced diplomats and intelligence officers depleted. He believed RFE's propaganda activities were important because "the currents that we let loose can have results whose extent is literally incalculable [and] if we make any major mistakes a great many people can get killed or sentenced to death in concentration camps." After all, the stakes were nothing less than an end to the Russian hegemony over Eastern Europe. Encouraged by its intelligence from the East, the Eisenhower administration grew cocky and by mid-1954 Berle himself thought that RFE could "force changes in the governments and the policies both in Czechoslovakia and Hungary. The question now is how best to use the power." To avoid bloodshed Berle hoped to obtain a settlement on Czechoslovakia and Hungary similar to the neutralization of Austria. But as turmoil brewed in Eastern Europe, RFE suffered from its own inner turmoil over what it should be telling Eastern Europe and how to get the message across.[13]

In regular contact with Allen Dulles, Cord Meyer, and others in the CIA, in 1956 Berle and the NCFE felt that it had made considerable progress. At the behest of Jackson, RFE sent propaganda balloons east, producing consternation among Communists. "The time has come when they ought to raise with the Russians and satellites the whole question of having an Iron Curtain at all," Berle thought. Moreover, the CIA had acquired Soviet Premier Nikita Khrushchev's speech to the Twentieth Party Congress in which he denounced Stalin's crimes; RFE leaked it to the world—stirring all of Europe, including the Communist countries. "The mid-European revolution is getting up steam," he exulted. But while Berle took heart from all this apparent momentum, he groused to Adlai Stevenson about a lack of real leadership in RFE's daily operations, comparing Western strategy in the cold war to "a bunch of separate grocery stores trying to compete with a well-organized chain store organization." Liberals like Chester Bowles cheered Berle for lamenting in the pages of *The New Leader* "the crying need for clear definition of what our foreign policy is supposed to accomplish."[14]

The big test for that policy came that autumn. Following June riots in Poland, Wladyslaw Gomulka became prime minister and fashioned a compromise whereby the Russians withdrew from Poland in return for Polish reaffirmation of its ties with the Soviets. Visions of "a Titoist Poland" that eventually would have free elections danced in Berle's mind. Then, in October, Hungary exploded in revolution. With riots in the streets of Budapest, the Russians appeared to withdraw their armies and give in to Hungarian demands. Anxiously watching events, Berle and RFE wondered how it could influence the outcome. He exhorted New York workers to "light a bonfire that will not go out until every last Russian soldier is out of Hungary." And then came news that the Russian army had returned to Budapest in full force. While Berle wanted to believe that Russian brutality in crushing the Hungarian revolution was a Pyrrhic victory for freedom, he suspected that once more Soviet military might was restoring order to its own universe. "Russian difficulties in Hungary and Poland bought us a little time, and some political advantages," he told Jackson. "And, obviously, we ought to be doing anything we can to assist the struggling Poles and Hungarians. This time, their battle is ours." But, with the Soviets threatening Western Europe with atomic war, Eisenhower's response to the Hungarian tragedy had to be restrained. While not clear as to what it could have done, Berle wished for a stronger response from the Eisenhower administration.[15]

"I feel like a heel being safe in New York while the ideas we have been propagating have engaged the lives of so many men," Berle wrote in the midst of the Hungaran uprising. In December, Budapest's Communist paper blamed Berle personally for the revolution. In Washington, an internal debate erupted as to whether the RFE had acted as an agent provocateur. Although Berle could not prove that RFE incited the rebellion, he himself was "not dead sure" it had not. Had America's "very existence" as a free society provoked the revolution? He did not want to go to war for Hungary, but in the back of his mind he felt the administration "might have thrown some solid shot into the United Nations' debates and at least declared where we stood."

In any event, the Hungarian revolution demonstrated that American policy had to be redrawn to persuade the Soviets that the United States intended to stay in Europe indefinitely. He explored the possiblity of an RFE declaration of aims that resembled an updated Wilsonian Fourteen Points, and suggested giving RFE a government imprimatur that would have made him an official again in the making of American policy. Even without an administration portfolio he seemed to get more attention—as when the head of the Austrian delegation to the United Nations, Bruno Kreisky, invited him to lunch in October 1957, indicating to Berle that "as the prestige of the Eisenhower Administration drops, [Europeans] feel around for opposition men in foreign affairs." Had he not been recently a foreign policy advisor to Adlai Stevenson? In the end Berle felt that the Hungarian revolution proved that Washington could never withdraw its armies from Europe.[16]

However, another consequence of the Hungarian revolution was the phasing out the Collège de l'Europe Libre at Strasbourg. Berle envisioned the College as giving all Europe, east and west, a philosophical unity. But, between the Communists who occupied Eastern Europe and the monarchists who sulked and conspired in the west, liberalism seemed to have very little future east of the Elbe. The College would not inculcate liberal values in a new generation of European leaders if its very existence depended upon Berle alone to recruit its faculty and students. For a brief moment the Hungarian revolution promised to provide it with more recruits, Berle announcing scholarship grants for up to five hundred young Hungarian refugees. But, in 1957 Berle admitted that the College was "under fire" (he did not say from whom) and plagued by aging leadership. He conceded that it was a small institution that would likely get smaller in future generations. In its brief history it had had only about 1,000 students. But in 1958 it ran its last summer session; "something got done though not as much as I had hoped," Berle solemnly wrote.[17]

The complaint that American policy was "all wrong" was heard more frequently in New York and Washington. Although remedies differed with the complainer, Berle concurred. Foreign policy under Eisenhower had become hydra-headed between the State Department and the CIA, with the White House sometimes giving it even a third head. Nelson Rockefeller, in an effort to give the country a clearer picture of foreign policy and make foreign affairs a tighter affair, used the Rockefeller Brothers Fund to organize a panel of "outstanding Americans to consider operating concepts and a consistent pattern for the future." The corporate body was chaired by former Assistant Secretary of State Dean Rusk with Harvard University professor Henry Kissinger as coordinator—two aspiring secretaries of state. It devised panels populated by academics and the business and labor elite who developed and sold a foreign policy consensus that predictably called for greater centralization of policymaking in the government. The Rockefeller brain trust invited Berle to join, suggesting to him that the Republicans needed a bipartisan foreign policy to overcome their false starts and failures and were using Nelson Rockefeller to broaden their base of support.

Excitedly, Berle set down some postulates as guidelines for the Rockefeller panels:

> There is need of an accepted political philosophy in the conduct of American foreign affairs. It is needed most importantly for its own sake—to hold Americans and to provide a criterion for policies. This is a separate question.
>
> But such a philosophy is also essential (1) as a co-efficient of American military power, and (2) as an organizing principle of requisite international economic cooperation.

Berle collaborated with Kissinger in the writing of the overall report which was a few years in the making. In general, he used the panels to press for greater American attention to the Americas south of the Rio Grande. Considering that Rusk had been Truman's assistant secretary of state for Far Eastern Affairs and Kissinger had little interest in Latin America, it remained to be seen what influence he would have. Yet, for the most part, he looked upon the Rockefeller experience as an intellectual exercise that probably would have little translation into actual policy—only to discover that the Republican nominee for president in 1960, Richard Nixon, had turned to Kissinger for foreign policy coordination, as Kennedy would turn to Rusk in 1961 to be his secretary of state. Berle would not be ignored by the next president.[18]

SELF-DETERMINATION FOR GUATEMALA

The problem, according to Berle, was that Truman had ignored the Americas.[1] In 1949 Berle believed that "we have simply forgotten about Latin America which is sliding back to the 20's. . . . Sheer neglect and ignorance endanger our position in South America and the Caribbean." Latin America needed its own Marshall Plan in order to get trade with the region on a sounder basis. He had not forgotten Constantine Oumansky's mission in 1944–1945 and was certain that the Soviets intrigued to increase their presence in the hemisphere. The United States at its peril allowed leftists to lead the drive for democracy in the hemisphere.[2]

The New York foreign policy establishment paid Latin America greater attention than did Washington. From time to time, beginning in late 1946, the Council on Foreign Relations (CFR) held seminars led by scholars such as Frank Tannenbaum at the Harold Pratt House on topics such as industrialization in Latin America. These gatherings were mostly academic in character, although the participants were movers and shakers in Latin American trade and diplomacy. Their business ties in the region excited their interests. Berle too held a retainer from the American Molasses Company, which remained prominent in the Caribbean sugar trade, and served on its Board of Directors; he also arranged loans for countries such as Haiti with New York banks.[3]

Berle was a familiar figure among the liberal elites of Latin America, traveling frequently through the region on trips that were part business, part pleasure, and partly for his own intelligence of the area. Never trusting the State Department to give the hemisphere the attention he thought it deserved, Berle performed as his own roving ambassador and pursued his own policy for the Americas. Berle attributed much of the region's poverty to its authoritarian regimes. The dominance of Cuba by Batista and Nicaragua by the Somozas encouraged corruption and monopolies of the worst sort. He worried over the hemisphere's residue of fascism, as evidenced by Perónism in Argentina and Vargas' return to power in Brazil. And he excoriated Americans such as Franklin D. Roosevelt, Jr. ("that ineffable ass," Berle called him), who profited by representing Dominican dictator Trujillo in Washington. On his own Berle cultivated several aspiring Latin politicians such as Luis Manuel de Bayle, brother-in-law to Anastasio Somoza, the Nicaraguan dictator, and Aldhemar de Barros, a Brazilian populist whom Berle hoped would become either a Huey Long or a Fiorello La Guardia of that country. He did not really like either man, but he considered their proximity to power useful for American policy.[4]

On the other hand he genuinely liked social democrats such as José "Pepe" Figueres of Costa Rica, Rómulo Betancourt of Venezuela, and Ramón Villeda Morales of Honduras. They were the liberal hopes of Latin America. Liberal democracy needed positive programs and Berle had been espousing social and economic reforms for the Americas since the 1930s. For example, Berle wanted to tie the Caribbean nations into a common market with the United States that would buttress liberal governments in the hemisphere—a variation of his proposal for a raw materials cartel during the early days of World War II. Also, he continued to push schemes for injecting large quantities of American capital into Latin American economies through an inter-American bank. In these ways Washington could implement what Berle called the public law of the hemisphere by linking hemispheric governments economically and opening Latin American political systems. Liberal capitalism was incompatible with authoritarian political systems. As he told the Council on Foreign Relations in 1948, the Americas had no place for undemocratic regimes. "It is evident that no community of nations can operate if there is complete disparity of internal objectives and ideals," Berle wrote. "For this reason, *inter-American doctrine already prohibits, as dangerous to common peace, the establishment of 'totalitarian' governments, left or right. Clearly there is a wide field of interpretation here; but the basic doctrine is nevertheless concurred in by all American countries.* Hemispheric application of these basic minima is recognized as a legitimate subject *qualifying the ban against 'intervention.'*"

Berle believed that the Americas had to be made safe for democracy. The Roosevelt administration had erected a hemispheric consensus through treaties running from Lima in 1938 to Mexico City in 1945, stipulating that liberalism would be the order of the day. Any breach of that consensus justified intervention by American states acting in concert. The authoritarian regimes of Perón in Argentina, Vargas in Brazil, Somoza in Nicaragua, or Trujillo in the Dominican Republic, stifled liberal capitalism and economic growth in their countries. But Americans in the cold war era were too concerned with Eurasia to promote a liberal policy toward the hemisphere. In 1948–1949—goaded by Spruille Braden, Rockefeller, Berle, and other Latin Americanists—the CFR debated hemispheric policy and found it easier to articulate liberalism than to apply it to the hemisphere. Many in the establishment did not care what the politics of a regime were as long as they did business with it—thus confirming Berle's suspicion that American bankers and industrialists frequently were too tolerant of Latin dictators. Exasperated after listening to a group of American businessmen discuss foreign affairs in 1946, Berle wrote: "I am no friend of Russian imperialism; but by the time they got through, I was about to run up the Hammer and Sickle myself. That is the devil of this whole business. Apparently you must choose between a popular revolution already battered by Russian imperialists and well-dressed black reaction; I do not see that the little people will get a break either way." While Washington ignored rising poverty in the Americas and the caudillos perpetuated and profited by it, Berle sought indigenous alternatives to both the Communists and the corruptionists.[5]

The only things that drew Washington's attention to the hemisphere were Communist activity and evidence of Moscow's interest in it. Thus, the United States suddenly discovered communism in Guatemala. In June 1952, Berle knew that Washington had evidence "that the communist cell has gotten control of the Guatemalan government and as usual is doing some things that have to be done, and a great many other things that are tremendously dangerous." The government of Jacobo Arbenz Guzman, the duly elected president of Guatemala, was bent upon land reform that threatened the American-owned United Fruit Company's economic hegemony. Was Arbenz a reformer or a revolutionary? Spruille Braden branded Arbenz a Communist, but Berle considered Braden too much of an "extreme rightist" to be fair to Arbenz. On the other hand, he believed what his intelligence sources told him about Communist penetration of Guatemala.[6]

In the midst of Stevenson's 1952 campaign for president, Miguel A. Magaña of El Salvador gave Berle evidence that the Guatemalan regime had imported Czechoslovak arms, that its communism was "hardly even disguised" and that it constituted a "clear-cut intervention by a foreign power, in this case the Soviet Union." Although Berle believed that Guatemalan social reforms were needed, Arbenz's actions simply disguised "a Russian-controlled dictatorship" that violated his cherished public law of the hemisphere. Berle wanted Washington to invoke the Act of Chapultepec and the Treaty of Rio against the Guatemalan regime, thereby allowing it to organize an intervention to overthrow Arbenz. If it did not, Berle feared that the Nicaraguan and Honduran dictatorships would be toppled next, like dominos, leaving the United States not knowing "where to go next to construct a government." In December Berle used the occasion of a telephone call from Allen Dulles to urge that Washington send observers to Guatemala City for a first-hand report. But, whether it did or not, he wanted to check the situation out himself.[7]

Believing that "in Latin America personal contact is the whole story," Berle went to Central America for a week in March 1953. In Nicaragua he dined with the American ambassador, a North Dakota politician, and was horrified to discover that "nobody at the Embassy speaks Spanish; they rely on their Nicaraguan clerks. . . . We might as well have been in Fargo."

(His former State Department aide, a Spanish-speaking Texan, Fletcher Warren, had been a previous ambassador to Managua.) Somoza's "corruption and libertinism" was openly discussed in Managua, even by members of Nicaragua's hierarchy. It especially disgusted Berle that Somoza owned monopolies in most Nicaraguan industries. Listening to the Somoza clan denounce José "Pepe" Figueres, the president of Costa Rica, as a Communist, Berle was skeptical. He changed his itinerary and the next day flew to San José where he found an "amazing" difference: "a thriving, up and coming little country, trim and well-kept as Latin American countries go" in sharp contrast to "the relatively down-at-heel condition" in Managua. On the recommendation of a mutual friend of theirs in New York, Berle called on Figueres and soon they were immersed in discussions that continued off and on for years to come. Figueres was a true liberal, agreeing with Berle that "a Kremlin-Communist government in this hemisphere was impossible." Was Arbenz of Guatemala a Communist? No, Figueres considered Arbenz a weak leader who now was a dupe of Communists but could be induced to expel them from his government. Only when that failed would force against the Guatemalan be justified. However, even then unilateral U.S. military intervention in the Americas was "out of the picture." Figueres thought that Costa Rica could organize El Salvador and Honduras against Guatemalan radicalism, but he could not work with corrupt Nicaragua; "He could not forget that Somoza had sent his troops into Costa Rica in 1948."[8]

Figueres was important to Berle—a national leader who represented all he sought in Latin America, something between the black reaction of dictators and the Reds of revolution. Slightly-built and even shorter than Berle, Figueres had everything Berle liked in a politician, regardless of nationality: enormous charisma, courage, and intellect—a liberal romantic. The son of a Spanish physician, Figueres was born in Costa Rica in 1906. As a youth he demonstrated a stubborn persistence and an individuality that defied social conventions. Rebelling against his teachers in high school, Figueres struck out for Boston to study electrical engineering at MIT, but quit that and spent the next four years educating himself in social philosophy in the public libraries of Boston and New York. He returned to Costa Rica and, using his father's money, bought a run-down farm thirty-five miles from San José which he called "La Lucha"—"the struggle." It took years of struggle to become a prosperous farmer-businessman who owned the country's largest rope and bag factory. Figueres wanted to bring roads and electricity to his impoverished country for its economic development. His advocacy of reforms earned him the affectionate title, "Don Pepe," although he endeavored to avoid paternalism in his relations with the *campesinos*. Like Berle, he was anti-Communist because he envisioned a social revolution of the center. Early in the 1940s Figueres entered politics and even joined a multinational group, the Caribbean Legion, that dedicated itself to overthrowing Caribbean dictators. Through the Legion he allied himself with President Juan José Arevalo of Guatemala, who, in 1948, gave Figueres arms to overthrow a Costa Rican regime that owed its existence to a disputed election and drew its support from both Communists and Somoza of Nicaragua. Figueres' army triumphed in a forty-day war that cost 2,000 lives. Having given assurances that he would not hoard power for himself, Figueres stepped aside in 1949—but not before he nationalized the banks and disbanded the army. He spent the next four years organizing a political party, with which he constitutionally won the presidency. In that time Arevalo was succeeded as Guatemala's president by Arbenz. The State Department was certain that Arbenz was a Communist, but it reserved judgment on Figueres. "He fit no easy ideological categories," Walter LaFeber has written. But Berle knew his man.[9]

"I am very much impressed with Figueres," Berle wrote in his diary. "He looks to me like a first-rate, level-headed anti-communist liberal." Not only was Figueres a businessman and a politician, he was an intellectual with whom Berle could discuss the writings of Alfred North Whitehead, André Gide, and the state of liberalism in a commercial society. Also, Figueres grounded his liberalism upon years of political struggle against reactionaries and Communists alike. The practical Figueres knew, Berle noted, that "politics is not all saving your soul but of getting viable arrangements—even if your soul suffers as a result." But at the same time the braintruster romanticized Figueres as "a philosopher, rather than a politican, a man of delicate sensibility."

In the midst of America's McCarthyite hysteria, Berle did not want anyone to mistake Figueres' liberalism for radicalism. When Figueres came to the United States in May as the prospective president of Costa Rica, Berle introduced him to C. D. Jackson at the White House, Tom Braden at the CIA, and United Fruit executives at the Century Club in New York. Figueres startled the latter with the revelation that United Fruit's publicity director in San José was a Red fellow-traveler; United Fruit had thought Figueres was a fellow-traveler when he told it to help improve living conditions in Costa Rica and expect local protection of property only if it respected local rights. As for Guatemala, Figueres forecast that either Arbenz would change his course or else its army would dispose of him.[10]

Figueres advocated government intervention in the economy to guarantee minimum security and maximum prosperity, delighting Berle with evidence that state capitalism could work in Latin America without Somoza's corruption. Figueres defined liberalism to include anticommunism. Costa Rica had outlawed the Communist party (it removed the prohibition in 1970). He "is the most interesting personality Central America has to offer," Berle enthused to Allen Dulles. He was heartened by Figueres' faith in a regional solution to the Guatemalan situation that avoided American intervention. But "nonintervention" also meant that Americans could accuse a Communist government of violating the hemisphere, or isolate a corrupt government, Berle advised the CFR discussion group on Political Unrest in Latin America. After all, a Communist government in the hemisphere was less of a product of internal circumstances than it was an external tool of Moscow. The Americas expected the United States to lead "in backing a political tide which will force the Guatemalan government either to exclude its Communists, or to change."[11]

In May 1954, President Figueres urgently invited Berle to Costa Rica for some discussions. Within a few days Berle joined his "spiritual companion" on his plantation in a high valley just over the continental divide and listened to Figueres describe how Somoza had accused him recently of trying to assassinate the Nicaraguan dictator. In retaliation Somoza threatened to invade Costa Rica, possibly assisted by United Fruit, against which Figueres had a small police force with 1898 rifles—while the American ambassador (a former Grace Line official) had departed for the United States, leaving Figueres to wonder if that was a "green light" for Somoza. Berle contacted the American chargé d'affaires in San José and Allen Dulles, who assured him that Washington did not conspire against Figueres and that it would not allow Somoza to overturn Costa Rican democracy.[12]

Meanwhile, the real drama was being played out in Guatemala. From an antigovernment source Berle heard that the Communists there were using torture and assassination against their opposition; from the CIA he learned that a shipment of arms from Poland had landed in Guatemala and the guns were being distributed to peasants rather than the army. However, he also heard that forces were being organized in Honduras for a strike against the Arbenz regime. Expecting a "Guatemalan revolt" that summer, Berle described for *The New York Times Magazine* the Communist threat to Latin America, hinting darkly that "It will take more than diplomatic machinery and action to meet the issue now tendered." In June Figueres called Berle to report that he had worked out an agreement with United Fruit which, Berle said, "battens down one hatch"—meaning that United Fruit concessions in Costa Rica were intended to build an opposition to Guatemala in the region. But Berle was not privy to CIA plans and could only guess that CIA money bankrolled outside opposition to Arbenz, which he "thought proper under the circumstances." When a Guatemalan "revolt" erupted in June, and the Arbenz government resigned and fled, Berle's speculations were barely more informed than any newspaper's. When Arbenz took his accusation of U.S. intervention in Guatemala to the United Nations, Berle was pleased that the president of the Security Council, a Brazilian who had fought for regionalism at Chapultepec, ruled it out of order on the grounds that the Organization of American States (OAS) had primary jurisdiction.[13]

The Guatemalan intervention succeeded,[14] but the Americas did not appreciate it. "As you know, the reaction throughout Latin America has been bad,'' wrote Figueres. ''Intervention is considered a worse evil than communism. Especially since intervention is never applied to foster a democratic cause. . . . We now face an alarming difference in political climate between the two Americas: the South is not aware of the imminence of world conflict, while the North is hysterical about it.'' Figueres hoped that the United States would espouse democracy and avoid appearing as the ''ally of tyranny and political vandalism.'' Berle conceded that ''We eliminated a Communist regime—at the expense of having antagonized half the hemisphere.'' He was troubled that Mexico sympathized with the deposed Arbenz.[15]

How could the United States make Central America safe for liberals without intervention? The strongest alternative to caudillos like Somoza was Marxism. The Somozas branded Figueres' liberalism as only a variant of communism and John Foster Dulles' State Department was sadly inclined to believe the dictators. In late August Berle visited ''Don Pepe'' in Costa Rica again, discussing how to get rid of Somoza and how to organize Latin liberals into a political alliance which might liberalize their economies. Berle was certain that Don Pepe and other Latin liberals would demonstrate that ''Marxism belongs in a museum, not in a political movement'' if they adopted the New Deal and Puerto Rico as their models. In November Berle brought Luis Muñoz Marín together with Pepe Figueres. With military dictators ruling in thirteen of twenty Latin American countries, liberals were lonely men in need of each other's aid against both the dictators and the Communists.

But Somoza thwarted Berle's design. Labeling all his Nicaraguan opponents as ''communists,'' Somoza again threatened Figueres; but this time Colombia, Ecuador, Uruguay, and other Latin governments stood with Costa Rica. Importantly, Washington too supported Figueres in the OAS against Somoza. Berle was jubilant that ''the peace machinery we put together at Chapultepec and later embodied in the Treaty of Rio de Janeiro seems to have worked.'' The threat of aggression in the Americas had been met with regional collective security.

When Somoza again threatened war against Costa Rica in early 1955, Berle forecast that someday Nicaragua might have to choose between Somoza or Marxism, and he himself could not abide the Somoza dictatorship. The State Department and the CIA, wanting all non-Communists to unite, asked Berle to bring Somoza and Figueres together for a handshake at their borders—a proposal Berle found ''rather naive.'' Berle played the good soldier and tried to persuade the incredulous Figueres that shaking hands with the corrupt dictator who sought to kill him would bring peace to America's backyard and allow Washington to concentrate on more important Asian quarrels. Berle saw the Somoza-Figueres clashes as ideological struggles between a liberal and a right-wing dictator, but most Americans, he conceded, saw nothing but a personality squabble between non-Communists. Mediating between them was "in some ways the most foolish job I have tackled yet." The Costa Rican wanted to cooperate with his friend, but "the idea of shaking hands with Somoza was obviously not palatable to Figueres: . . . this would be a betrayal of the democratic leadership of the continent." So Berle tried to convince Figueres that a handshake with Somoza only represented "normalization rather than conciliation" and that Figueres was not abandoning his democratic principles. Having no faith in Somoza's word, Figueres considered it a political kiss of death. How could he shake Somoza's hand while the dictator's troops were shooting at Costa Ricans? The problem with the State Department, Berle thought, partly lay with John Foster Dulles who saw the world as bipolar and whose "instructions are flat: do nothing to offend the dictators; they are the only people we can depend on." Thus, Figueres the democrat had to placate Somoza the dictator. When Samuel Eliot Morison commented that Dulles was "the worst Secretary of State since Bryan," Berle retorted, "he's the worst—period." If only Washington realized that a "real difficulty lay in Managua."[16]

Not wanting to offend Figueres, Berle bowed out of the dispute. Despite Dulles, Berle believed that Latin America was "turning against military dictatorship and back to something like democracy." When Argentina toppled Perón later in 1955 Berle was certain that it heralded a growing liberalism along the lines of Costa Rican, Uruguayan, Bolivian, or Puerto Rican models. U.S. businessmen and liberals ought to ally themselves with the Democratic left in the Americas against the dictators of Nicaragua, Colombia, Venezuela, and the Dominican Republic—or the region would see further Marxist threats. But Latin-American reactionaries held firm, an American Embassy official in Bogota describing how the Rojas Pinilla dictatorship machine-gunned a liberal student demonstration, calling the students Communists. And when, in 1956, Figueres gave the ousted democratic leader of Venezuela, Rómulo Betancourt, political asylum, the State Department expressed its displeasure because it feared antagonizing the Venezuelan dictator, Pérez Jiménez. Figueres was outraged: U.S. foreign policy under John Foster Dulles was morally indifferent; Latin-American democrats had to consider whether Washington was "too insensitive to be a safe ally." Berle conceded that CFR policy discussions were rendered useless when leaders like Dulles turned a deaf ear to the foreign policy establishment. Didn't anyone worry that U.S. aid to Latin America was less than one-half of 1 percent of all foreign aid? Did anyone care that Washington supported dictators like Trujillo and Somoza who were nothing but cruel parodies of democracy? He wanted Americans to know that the specter of Marxism in the hemisphere was real and that their neighbors to the south only wanted the "dignity of man" and a stable society in which all people participated.[17]

The CIA sought Berle's help in late August 1956, when Ramón Villeda

Morales, the elected president on Honduras, was expelled from his country by a military coup. It feared that Morales might think that Washington was behind his overthrow unless some respected American liberal could convince him otherwise. (It also feared that rumors of his being a Communist might be true.) Berle invited Morales to New York as a guest of Miss Frances Grant and the Inter-American Association for Democracy and Freedom, an organization that included such American social democrats as Roger Baldwin and Norman Thomas and specialized in contacts with social democratic leaders throughout Latin America. (Berle picked up the tab.) This proved fortunate, for the dictatorship which succeeded Morales proved quite unstable and by January it was gone and Morales again was elected president. Although the CIA again insisted that it had nothing to do with Honduran developments, Berle thought it just had "generally spread the good word and thus probably assisted."[18]

Democracy seemed to be on the rise in Latin America throughout the 1950s. Berle took heart in 1957 that the Guatemalan regime of Castillo Armas struggled to give that country a democratic government and that in Central America the State Department now had some intelligent and professional officers who did not see Red in every local liberal. In February a satisfied Berle toured El Salvador, Honduras, Guatemala, and Costa Rica. Also, he noted a liberal swell in Venezuela and Colombia. Still, he was troubled that Nicaragua remained in Somoza's grasp and an obstacle to his dream of a liberal common market of Central American countries. And he did not know what to make of a revolutionary movement in the hills of Cuba led by a young man named Fidel Castro—although he wished for peaceful change there. Castro did not worry him too much because successful Latin rebels seldom had much staying power. Still, he dreaded turmoil in Cuba. "Anti-intervention is all right up to a point," Berle commented in 1957. "But we are responsible for keeping order in the hemisphere quite aside from the proprieties, and a rather bolder policy in that regard seems indicated." He welcomed a change in Cuba's government, but he also viewed any revolution as a harbinger of either communism or disorder.[19]

SELF-DETERMINATION FOR CUBA

"Salute is due William Appleman Williams for a brilliant book on foreign affairs, gladly given despite profound disagreement by this reviewer with many of his statements and with some of his conclusions," Berle wrote in *The New York Times Book Review* early in 1959 of *The Tragedy of American Diplomacy.* "His insights into the past are provocative. His attempt to grapple with a vast problem is courageous and essential. His present work must be regarded with respect, despite disagreement."

Berle's disagreement with the young Marxist historian at the University of Wisconsin might have been anticipated, but he sought a dialogue with Williams even if he found some things about the book to be "very wrong." On the positive side Berle concurred that "that our policy does not accommodate to revolutionary changes elsewhere in the world. Emphatically he is right in believing the planned use of international resources through international machinery is now essential, discarding nationalist approaches and working with social systems different from our own." He conceded the reality of American economic imperialism. On the other hand, Williams dwelled at length upon American foreign policy problems without acknowledging Soviet faults. Berle did not quarrel with Williams' characterization of an "American empire," having used it himself long before historians like Williams made it fashionable. However, they each used it in different ways—Berle to describe a historic process by which any country achieves and extends its political power, Williams to describe a historic process in which a capitalist power must capture markets in order to grow. "Economics is not the only element in foreign affairs," Berle assured his readers. "Some of his sweeping historical assertions are mistaken." He especially resented Williams interchangeable use of the words, "colonialism" and "imperialism," evidence that Williams confused "mere expansion of economic influence . . . with real 'colonialism.'" At the least, it was imprecise and misleading.

Only six weeks before the appearance of Berle's review, on New Year's Day, 1959, Fidel Castro marched into Havana; at the heart of their "honest" disagreement was U.S. nonrecognition of the Cuban Revolution. While reviewer and historian both wanted a more rational order for the world, Berle assailed Williams' "Open Door for Revolutions" as "uncritical nonsense." He asserted that Williams "really wants an 'open door' for revolutions he likes" whereas Berle bracketed revolutions with wars—"sometimes necessary or unavoidable, always wasteful, sometimes productive, sometimes starkly evil, often unpredictable." While Williams was right that the State Department usually recoiled in horror from any change in government, Berle thought that Williams simplified the American response to Cuba and the Soviet role there and ignored a Soviet quest for empire. In general, Williams just never faulted the Soviets for any cold war clash.[1]

Williams attracted Berle because he possessed a philosophy of history—albeit an erroneous one—and he seemed "to have possibilities." Thus, when an invitation came late in 1959 to give a lecture on the Madison campus and meet Williams' students in a seminar, Berle eagerly accepted. Williams later recalled Berle talking candidly with his seminar for two hours before concluding eloquently that "either we build a true and brilliant community in the Western Hemisphere—or we go under." In 1960 he invited Williams to the Inter-American Conference for Democracy and Freedom in Venezuela, which Williams was unable to attend. And then the two men resumed their disparate ways. In time Berle viewed Williams and his acolytes as dangerously anti-American and he turned erratically hostile toward them. "If they could be induced to separate their historic view from their infernal ideological preoccupation, they would be extremely able and extremely useful," he wrote. "My guess is we shall hear quite a bit from them in any event because they have the inherent capacity to do effective work. . . . The cold war has now entered this hemisphere and I am pretty clear this group will either intentionally or unintentionally find itself mixed up in the intellectual aspect of it." For his part, Williams rated Berle as "one of the most astute and rigorous minds seeking to resolve the Tragedy of American Diplomacy in a creative manner. . . . But Castro so provoked and frightened Berle that he was unable . . . even to interpret the Cuban crisis within the limits of his formerly sophisticated expansionism."[2]

At the heart of their disagreement was Berle's view of Castro as a Soviet agent who violated the "public law of the hemisphere." The Cuban revolution occurred at a time when Berle began to feel that Latin American liberals were gaining an upper hand over the dictators. Nicaragua's Somoza was assassinated in 1956 and, although his sons replaced him, more favorable changes portended in the suicide of Vargas in Brazil, the overthrow of Perón of Argentina, and the fall of dictators in Colombia, Venezuela, Peru, and Haiti. Liberal regimes now held sway in Colombia, Venezuela, Costa Rica, and Honduras—"a fairly good galaxy of governments composed of exiles who at one time had few friends except Beatrice and me," Berle wrote. If the State Department ceased flirting with the dictators, it was possible that Latin America would one day see the sort of political and economic cooperation envisioned in the Good Neighbor Policy. But Castro made Berle apprehensive. Even before he seized power Berle suspected that Castro might be anti-American when Castro's brother Raul kidnapped thirty American sailors near the base at Guantanamo Bay and threatened to hold them until the United States stopped shipping arms to Batista—an incident that was resolved when the CIA and the State Department prevailed upon Berle to ask Figueres and Rómulo Betancourt to use their influence as leaders of the democratic Left with Castro. Everyone knew Batista was evil, but Berle found Castro a "puzzle" and in April 1958, he concluded, "there are probably potential tyrants on both sides." In early 1959 Berle waited to hear word from Havana of an impending election that signaled Castro was more than another caudillo. In January and February 1959, liberals wondered about the way in which Castro used anti-Americanism to unite his faction-ridden regime. Liberals hoped that a democratic Castro would establish good relations with Muñoz Marín and turn U.S. policy against dictators like Batista, but, during a visit to Venezuela, Castro called Puerto Rico a "perfumed colony" of the United States. Anti-Americanism did not endear Castro to Berle.[3]

In late March Pepe Figueres visited Cuba. He anticipated a warm reception as one of the few Latin American leaders to aid Castro's revolution with arms. Also, nine months before, Figueres had told a congressional House hearing on U.S. Latin American policy that, speaking as an American friend, by siding with dictators Washington had alienated Latin American democrats with its hypocrisy. "If you talk human dignity to Russia, why do you hesitate so much to talk human dignity to the Dominican Republic?" he dramatically asked. "When American boys have been dying, your mourning has been our mourning. When *our* people die, you speak of investments. Then you wonder why we spit." After Castro came to power Figueres refused to join Americans in outcries against the executions of "war criminals" in Havana. Now, committed to democratic revolution against dictators, Figueres went to Cuba wanting to discuss with Castro his coolness toward the Inter-American Regional Organization of Labor (ORIT), a rivalry between groups preparing to invade Nicaragua from Cuba and Costa Rica, and how to coordinate efforts to topple Trujillo in the Dominican Republic. But a few days passed without Figueres having a moment alone with Castro and he grew impatient.

Invited to speak at a mass meeting, but asked not to mention Puerto Rico, Figueres—wearing an overseas cap and khaki pants and khaki shirt to symoblize his own fight against tyranny—congratulated the Cubans on their revolution and called upon them to align themselves with other democratic governments in the hemisphere. Then, in the words of his biographer, "Figueres presumed too much [and] proceeded to give a lecture." In particular, he lectured the Cubans on the need for friendship with the United States, only to be interrupted when a Castro supporter siezed the microphone to exclaim, "We cannot be with the Americans who are today oppressing us!" Figueres was allowed to finish his speech, but Castro followed Figueres by denouncing hemispheric democratic leaders as "agents of American imperialism." While Castro conceded that his guest had aided the Cuban revolution, Figueres the landowner was no revolutionary because he had left the social structure of Costa Rica intact. The incident heralded a break between the democratic Left and the Cuban revolution. For Berle, it served "to crystallize Latin American partisanship with breath-taking speed." The bipolar cold war had arrived in the western hemisphere.[4]

1959 was a year of perceived crises in Latin America. While the democratic Left worried that a communist group from Cuba would overthrow the Somozas before a democratic invasion could do the job, Berle tried to have the United States persuade the Nicaraguan dictator to go quietly into the night, warning Allen Dulles that "if the Castro boys get loose in Central America, we shall be in a bloody ruckus." The administration got the message and, although it would not admit it, cooled noticeably toward the hemisphere autocrats in order to deflect charges it was a nest of "dictator lovers." But State Department political appointees in Central America rallied to Somoza as an indispensable American friend; without American military aid, they feared "Nicaragua will end up in the Commie camp." At a "supersecret" gathering in San Salvador in April 1959, a group of them clashed with career officers in demanding that Washington protect Somoza from Castro and all rebels—including liberals.

Fearing bloodshed and abhorring American protection of the dictator, Berle conferred with Luis Manuel de Bayle, whom he believed to be the liberal of the Somoza family. De Bayle hinted that Somoza might be willing to leave Nicaragua if he could take his personal fortune—estimated at *only* forty million by the American ambassador in Managua. Berle flew to Costa Rica where he conferred with Figueres and Nicaraguan exiles. They asked Berle for his views: "I said no outsider had any right to advise other men what they should do; they were risking their lives where I was quite safe and comfortable. I said that I earnestly hoped to get a peaceful solution." The next day, April 15, Berle and Figueres met with Whiting Willauer, American ambassador to Honduras, who arrived "very much in his cups." Willauer related his version of the American diplomatic corps meeting in San Salvador and insisted that the U.S. Navy would protect Somoza and he personally warned Figueres, "If you start anything, I will bump you off." Figueres and Berle left the drunken Willauer, Berle uncharacteristically muttering a few infantry expletives.

Increasingly it seemed to Berle that Nicaragua's immediate future was revolution or "the rotting Somoza dynasty," whose end will be "something terrible." He cursed Washington for having "the brains of a clam and the capacity of a clam in these matters." Feeling desperate, he called a contact in the CIA, Colonel J. C. King, and pleaded with him to "encourage the Somoza dictatorship to dicker out a peaceful conclusion with all possible speed." King agreed, but by himself what could he do? Meanwhile Castro arrested non-Communist Nicaraguan exiles in Cuba; it reminded Berle of Communist politics in New York during the late 1930s—"right and left extremists combining to paralyze liberal groups and then fight it out among themselves." Now, to Berle's discomfort, a reactionary U.S. policy allowed Castro to lead the opposition to the Nicaragua corrupt dictatorship. On May 1 he urged Cord Meyer and two other CIA men to have the United States withdraw its military mission from Nicaragua "so that Somoza does not think the United States is guaranteeing him in power." Also, he brought Luis Manuel de Bayle and Pepe Figueres together in New York for talks on how and when Somoza might be eased out, but two weeks later a discouraged Berle admitted that, "the States Department seems totally unwilling to act."[5]

Berle insisted to himself that he did "not mind the Cubans having a social revolution" and only resented their anti-American hysteria, but he was upset when Castro expropriated American sugar fields without fair compensation, a blow to the American Molasses Company, of which he was chairman of the Board of Directors. Additionally, reports that Castro executed opponents of his regime reminded Berle of "the Terror of the French Revolution." Yet he anticipated that in about a year Castro would be eliminated because "people will be tired of getting killed after a while." Until then he expected Castro to continue "fomenting little revolutions all around the Caribbean" while "the United States seems not to know what it is doing." That seemed confirmed when, in March 1960, his CIA contacts informed Berle that Castro would soon receive Soviet arms for his adventures in Central America. Alarmed, Berle now asserted that *"the doctrine of non-intervention does not apply when any defense of the hemisphere is involved."* In truth, the doctrine of nonintervention had been breached by the CIA in Guatemala and even Pepe Figueres scorned it. The hemisphere was up for grabs.[6]

To counter the Castro threat, in April 1960 Frances Grant organized the Inter-American Conference for Democracy and Freedom of 200 liberal leaders in Venezuela. The conference excluded Fascists and Communists and adopted resolutions condemning dictatorships in the Dominican Republic, Nicaragua, Haiti, and Paraguay. That much suited Berle, but it disheartened him that so many of the conferees admired Fidel Castro. The conference narrowly defeated a resolution branding communism as antidemocratic, although it later adopted a resolution that listed Communism among the many forms of tyranny and assailed the Communist countries of Eastern Europe. Still, Latin-American liberals were not prepared to write Castro off as a Communist puppet of Moscow—even if Berle was. Following the conference, the democratic Left seemed irrelevant to Berle.[7]

At a Liberal party dinner in June 1960, Cuba was on Berle's mind when he found himself seated near John F. Kennedy, the front-runner for the Democratic presidential nomination. While Berle advised the Massachusetts senator that the cold war had infiltrated hemispheric affairs, Kennedy listened intently and then complimented Berle on his recent article in *The Reporter* on Latin America, expressing the hope that Berle's services on Latin American affairs would be available if he won the nomination. The 1960 campaign had not yet involved Berle. He preferred Stevenson ("but I wonder whether he is really the right man") or Chester Bowles (who backed Kennedy), considered the other contenders "self-limiting" and months ago wrote Kennedy off as having "gone about as far as he can." Turning a deaf ear to blandishments from the Stevenson, Kennedy, and Lyndon Johnson camps to use his name ("intellectuals climbing on bandwagons look stupid"), Berle wanted only to support the nominee of the convention. Kennedy flattered and impressed him, but Berle did not expect "great leadership" from him; nonetheless, Archibald Cox's invitation to outline a Latin-American policy for Kennedy was too tempting for an old braintruster to refuse.[8]

"For all practical purposes, Cuba is just as much a Communist satellite as Hungary or North Korea," Berle thought. "For the time being the island republic has been converted into not only a spearhead of Soviet and Chinese propaganda but also a potential base for Soviet and Chinese power.'' From that base "direct aggression against the rest of Latin America" would go forward with Cuba serving as "a supply depot" for Soviet arms to be used against the "dying backward dictatorship" of Nicaragua and other Central American governments. Through their control of Cuba the Soviets threatened the security of the United States. However, under the 1947 Rio treaty the American states could reduce the threat by interdicting the flow of arms into the region as Roosevelt had thwarted Axis arms from entering the hemisphere in 1942. "This is not a breach of the nonintervention principle," Berle maintained. "What I am suggesting is not intervention but defense" against totalitarian intrusions by the American states under the 1945 Act of Chapultepec. Moreover, with Southeast Asia also threatened by Communists, now was the time to act before Americans found themselves "pretty much limited to North America and the waning allegiance of Western Europe. The climax can not be too far off.''[9]

A sense of panic concerning Latin America permeated intelligence reports. Colonel King, his CIA contact, forecast more insurgencies in the Caribbean and Figueres told Berle "that much of Latin America is lost: the combination of hotheads with quietly organized Communists waiting to take over may be invincible." A Soviet vow to defend Castro with their missiles brought an Eisenhower promise of U.S. economic aid to Latin America, a tactic Berle considered "ghastly" only because "Latin America will thank Castro for that—not Eisenhower." A longtime advocate of a "Marshall Plan for Latin America," Berle now began to turn to military solutions to avert "a growing catastrophe in foreign affairs." The United States had to "behave like a great power" in its defense of the hemisphere, he told the press.

And he was eager to be Kennedy's advisor on Latin American affairs—if "it was not too late." Following Kennedy's election, Berle worried about being "left out" of the new Democratic administration, professing that "my vanity would be wounded—but my relief would be extremely great." However, in the afternoon of November 25, Ted Sorenson, Kennedy's aide, called: would Berle head a small task force on Latin America to recommend policy before the inauguration? Of course he would, wishing only that the assignment had come ten years before when he possessed more energy than he had at sixty-five.[10]

On December 7 Berle convened the task force, which included Sorenson aide Richard Goodwin, professors Arthur Whitaker, Robert Alexander, and Lincoln Gordon, and Muñoz Marín's aides, Teodoro Moscoso and Arturo Morales-Carrión. Like 1933, it was a time of crisis for the braintruster, only now Castro threatened instead of the Great Depression. Mindful that "this is the best time to get done those more difficult and controversial items which must be done," Berle pushed the task force to prescribe action for the administration's first sixty days. Those recommendations assured him a prominent place in Kennedy's Latin American policymaking. He disdained trial balloons floated by the Kennedy people that he would be assistant secretary of state for Latin American affairs. He did not expect to be secretary of state, but he was too old for second-level positions, he told Goodwin; he wanted a "first-string job or none." With no little hubris, he demanded that the new administration create a position suitable to his interests and his ego: undersecretary of state for inter-American affairs, "thus ending stepchild status of this area in US policy."

Acting for the task force on December 18, Berle sent Sorenson a telegram with several specific proposals that underscored its essential message: "Area now major and active cold war theatre with outcome in serious doubt. Continued inaction may entail grave risk." The first proposal was for the under secretaryship, followed by recommendations for increased economic aid to the region; a concerted effort by the CIA and Defense Department, with the aid of Colombia and Venezuela, to choke off arms sent from Cuba to other Latin countries; stabilization of prices of Latin American commodities; the removal of the American Ambassador to Nicaragua and his replacement with a negotiator for Somoza's departure; and a presidential representative's unpublicized trip to Colombia and Venezuela to coordinate propaganda and other activities against the Communists and Castro. Otherwise, it omitted mention of direct action against Castro. Privately, he urged the American Molasses Company to boycott Cuban molasses.[11]

At a morning meeting in the Carlisle Hotel on January 6, Berle gave Kennedy and Sorenson "the guts of it," a synopsis of the task force's report. The meeting lasted an hour and a half, longer than he expected. Kennedy listened, while Sorenson complimented Berle on his "hard-hitting" recommendations. The task force report principally reflected Berle's thinking if only because the group had had but a few meetings. On Cuba Berle separated his comments from the task force's, stressing a defense of the hemisphere on a multilateral basis. Kennedy's response to the program seemed sympathetic, even on the matter of an under secretary of state for inter-American affairs.

Two days later secretary of state-designate Dean Rusk informed him that, in Latin American affairs, all roads led to Berle. Berle did not feign modesty, for he believed that his fame in the area entitled him to be Kennedy's braintruster on the republics to the south. Neither did he hide his disappointment when Rusk offered him the post of American representative to OAS—a post so "peripheral. . . . There was nothing in it." Rusk, willing to accommodate Berle's desire for access to Kennedy, tacked and suggested a special position such as "Ambassador at Large" or "Presidential Assistant" on Latin American affairs. But Berle wanted an under secretaryship and not "any third-rate titles," that locked him out of the State

Department—for he remembered Nelson Rockefeller's troubles as "Co-ordinator" under FDR. Ten days later Rusk called to say that they still wanted Berle in the administration, but they knew not where.[12]

Two days before Kennedy's inauguration Rusk asked Berle if it "would be thinkable" to make FDR, Jr., assistant secretary of state for Latin American affairs. Aghast, Berle replied that "it would be fatal," that liberals in the region had not forgotten that young Roosevelt had accepted a retainer from the Dominican dictator, Trujillo. If Kennedy hoped to avoid association with dictators, he would have to find something else for Roosevelt or someone else for Latin American affairs. On this, Berle's word amounted to a veto. The next morning he had a breakfast meeting with Dean Rusk in Washington, during which Rusk offered Berle the amorphous position of chairman of an interdepartmental task force on Latin America. It was defined as an emergency policy-making position that gave Berle direct access to the president and freedom to represent the United States in Latin America. Berle accepted it on the condition that "some fanfare" accompany the announcement to put him and Latin America in the public spotlight. Several days later Berle moved into a State Department office a few doors away from Rusk's—sixteen years after he had been forced out of the Department.

Greeted by the younger men like a long-lost friend upon his return to the Department, Berle sensed vindication. Their flattery reminded him of the epigram, "Praise is the product of present power." The source of his present power was his knowledge of Latin America: "We have better information on the national situation in these countries at 70 Pine Street [his law offices] than they do." But Latin American policy was not big enough to hold the eclectic Berle and he immodestly wished for influence "over some other things too." Soon the old braintruster was rewriting State Department suggestions for the president's state of the union message. By the end of the month his task force consisted of State Department Counselor Theodore C. Achilles, acting assistant secretary of state for inter-American affairs Thomas Mann, deputy assistant secretary of defense for international security affairs William Bundy, and consultant Lincoln Gordon, along with Arturo Morales-Carrión, the first Puerto Rican to hold a State Department post. Administration publicity pointedly made Berle a symbol of Kennedy's continuity with Roosevelt's Good Neighbor Policy. But the hoopla masked uncertain policies and responsibilities toward Latin America.[13]

If the younger people there had not heard the stories of the "difficult" Berle of 1938–1946, they now had their own stories. Troubled by Berle's vanity and independence of its bureaucracy, the Department did not know how to handle his edict that his *policy* group would not involve itself in *operational* matters. His "hazy" distinction of policy and operations perplexed everyone and could not long endure.[14]

"I never did think it was a good idea to try to divorce operations from policy," Tom Mann later declared; "I don't think it's very good administration; I don't think they're divisable." Lincoln Gordon was even more emphatic: "The Task Force was a weird administrative device, a totally unsuccessful one. . . . Friction was built into the arrangement." Arthur Schlesinger charitably characterized it as "a somewhat ambiguous appointment . . . [and] not an altogether satisfactory arrangement." Responsibility for Kennedy's Latin American policy lay with an abrasive, single-minded theorist, a "loner" who neither had nor sought operational power. It had unintended consequences. As long as Berle perched somewhere between the State Department and the White House, nobody wanted to be assistant secretary of state for Latin American affairs. Mann, a holdover from the Eisenhower years, took the embassy in Mexico City rather than remain in Washington with Berle. Moreover, several others declined Mann's vacated position because of Berle. His braintruster status, it was felt, encouraged bureaucratic chaos and ironically helped impede his policy recommendations.[15]

"Whatever your job in Washington, power in Washington is seized by conquest," Berle believed. But Berle distinguished power over policy from power over bureaucracy. The former satisfied his quest. Resigning as chairman of the Board of Directors of the American Molasses Company—lest that position suggest any conflict of interest with his policy recommendations on Cuba—Berle plunged into the task of an "agonizing appraisal of the Cuban situation." Through February a series of meetings discussed policy toward Cuba, Berle stressing that success required collaboration with other Caribbean countries. Believing that diplomacy in Latin America called for the personal touch, Berle went south later in the month.[16]

In Caracas and Bogota he found that Presidents Rómulo Betancourt and Lleras Camargo agreed with him concerning the threat that Castro posed, but neither wanted to lead a Latin movement against Cuba. Camargo suggested that the key to any collective action was Brazil, whose new president, Jânio Quadros, "was a mystery." Berle hastened to Rio and then to its new capital, Brasilia. With American Ambassador John Moors Cabot present, there ensued a "frank" Berle-Quadros dialogue. Quadros wanted to discuss Brazil's economic problems, insisting that $100 million in U.S. aid was insufficient for Brazil's needs—much as he had told Arthur Schlesinger and George McGovern who had preceded Berle by a couple of weeks. Berle "let it go at that" and steered the conversation to the Caribbean situation. Quadros insisted that Brazil's economic problems made its participation in collective action against Cuba impossible. Berle countered testily that "foreign affairs would not always give the luxury of time," admonishing Quadros that Washington might feel compelled to take unilateral action and he hoped that if it came to that the United States could count upon Brazil's sympathy. As Berle departed, a reporter asked if he would look favorably upon a Cuban offer to have its dispute with the United States mediated and he answered that it was not a problem of two countries but a hemisphere-wide concern. Later that day Quadros announced that President Tito of Communist Yugoslavia had accepted an invitation to visit Brazil, a development Berle interpreted correctly as a signal that Brazil intended to follow a "neutralist" cold war policy. Two days later *The New York Times* reported, "U.S.-Brazil Talks Close in Discord over Cuba Issue." But there also was discord among the Americans, Cabot later asserting that Berle had been "tactless" in handling Quadros, and Berle taking exception to Cabot's feckless quip to reporters upon leaving Quadros, "we did not throw bricks at each other." With *The Times'* stories "doing great harm around town," Berle could only think, "If I get out of this with a whole skin, I shall be lucky." However, the Brazilian press rallied to Berle's side and assailed Quadros for an uncharacteristically cold reception of an old friend of Brazil; also, a Brazilian diplomat hastened to bring Berle conciliatory words from his government; finally, Kennedy gave Berle a "kindly reserved, unflustered" welcome—a manner "so opposite to that of Roosevelt that I have to hold on to myself."[17]

But he had failed to win support for collective action against Castro. In Berle's mind, and apparently in Kennedy's, the Cuban threat to Latin America called for prompt American action. Goodwin drafted a Kennedy speech on economic aid to Latin America and the old braintruster was impressed by its call for the Alliance for Progress, a long-range "Marshall Plan" program of economic aid for Latin America—much as Berle had advocated years ago. The task force outlined the Alliance in February and it was unveiled on March 13 as liberalism's answer to Castroism.[18]

That was not all the administration planned. Two days before it announced the Alliance for Progress, Berle attended a high-level White House meeting with the president, diplomatic and military leaders, and the CIA. It discussed an American-sponsored invasion of Cuba by expatriate Cubans to throttle Castroism at its source, a "now-or-never choice." Actually, Kennedy had no real choice: The CIA had been training Cubans in Guatemala for an assault on their homeland since the latter days of the Eisenhower administration and, as Allen Dulles put it, if the United States called off the operation, the Cuban expatriates would tell Latin America that Kennedy suffered a failure of nerve. Such a message would encourage Communists to attempt similar revolutions elsewhere. Schlesinger later wrote, "The contingency had thus become a reality." All Kennedy could do was limit U.S. involvement so as not to offend Latin America.[19]

"My own feeling is crystallizing," Berle reflected after the meeting. "Sooner or later we are going to have to meet the Cuban question head on and *it ceases to be a matter of diplomacy and is rapidly getting to be one of force.* I think we had best precipitate the climax. I can't see that it will be infinitely less if we wait and we ought to have the battle on our ground instead of theirs but it will be frightening when it comes." His meeting with the chimerical Quadros convinced Berle once again that the Good Neighbor Policy was moribund—and buried with it was World War II's collective security arrangements for the hemisphere and America's special relationship with Brazil. Through Castro the Russians had breached and divided the hemisphere; without Brazil collective action in the hemisphere would fail. As if to underline this thinking, on the day the White House approved military action against Cuba, Quadros announced the appointment of a roving ambassador to the Eastern bloc countries and proclaimed a new "independent" foreign policy for Brazil. In Berle's mind, Latin America could be no more neutral now than it could have been in 1942 or Eastern Europe could be in the cold war.[20]

Berle may have known about the CIA's plans for the overthrow of Castro before he joined the administration. They were not an open secret in the administration until early February, but Berle was in frequent communication with J. C. King, who directed CIA operations in the hemisphere. Also, his travels through Central America had alerted him to unusual activity there. Two days before the inauguration he breakfasted with Pepe Figueres and found himself wondering what Figueres knew about anti-Castro Cubans who were "seeking and I assume getting help from the United States." A story had appeared in the newspapers about them. "The training field at Guatemala reported in the papers was accurately described," Berle thought, suggesting his own familiarity with it. Later that day he met with an automobile workers union official and four former Cuban union leaders who complained that the CIA foisted old Batista army men upon them in their fight against Castro. The next day Colonel King called to inquire if Berle could give him some time during the next few months for "negotiating some sort of political structure for the countries that are wobbly" and threatened by Castroism. Berle might have wondered if King really had Cuba in mind. On January 10 the Brazilian ambassador to the United Nations commented that "Castro would have to be stopped by force eventually; that the Americans would have to use the Marines; it is too bad they hadn't done it earlier." Berle responded that Latin America wanted the United States to stop Castro and to criticize it for doing so: "I thought the President should say that if the Cubans were waiting for invasion, they would have to wait for a long time, and offer to send some coffee over to the boys in the trenches." Two months after that flippant remark Berle approved an invasion of Cuba.[21]

Two weeks after the inauguration, the State Department began to circulate a daily bulletin on Cuba to other departments. Reports flowed in that Russian and Czech arms and technicians were arriving in Havana. On February 8 and 17 Berle attended White House meetings on Cuba that deferred a military decision on Cuba. During his trip to South America he had hinted to Quadros and others that Washington had a military solution to the Cuban problem. Indeed, some U.S. military men believed that Berle had breached security by sounding out Betancourt, Camargo, and Quadros on collective action. Cabot, who had sat in on the Quadros meeting, was "pretty sure Berle didn't mention the invasion, no, but he rather strongly intimated that something had to be done about Cuba." Indeed, he did believe that action against Castro was imperative. He worried that it was still "difficult to make anyone see how dangerous the hemisphere situation is." Didn't people realize that in Berlin and Cuba Kennedy confronted more dangerous crises during his first sixty days than any president since Lincoln—and that included FDR? Didn't people realize that the situation in Latin America in 1961 was similar to that in Europe in 1947?[22]

Now committed wholeheartedly to a military solution to Castroism, Berle yielded nothing to intelligence and military men in terms of toughness. Perhaps he surprised officials who expected a soft egghead intellectual. But he had experienced the dangers of Latin America; Figueres, Betancourt, and other social democatic leaders lived with bodyguards in daily fear of their lives from attacks by both right- and left-wingers. Convinced that "Cuba had become a Communist satellite, without formal declaration of that fact being made," and that Castro had "openly declared his intention to export his revolution in all ways," Berle wanted a military showdown as quickly as possible. Schlesinger analyzed his complex friend well:

> For Berle, with all his ardor for democracy and development, comprehended also, in another part of his nature, the shadowy world of intrigue, conspiracy and violence. He had an extensive knowledge of communist movements and a vivid apprehension of communist dangers. He was therefore able to give the new social initiatives an edge of "toughness" which, while it was kept strictly separate from the Alliance for Progress, was still able to protect the idea of the Alliance from those for whom anti-communism was the only issue (as well as in time to protect the operations of the Alliance from the communists who sought to destroy it).[23]

Nobody in the administration was to the left of Berle on Latin America nor to the right of him on anticommunism. He was vitriolically hostile to any liberal who opposed a military solution to Castroism. A great power had to be a great power in its own sphere of influence. At a critical April 4 meeting at the State Department, discussion focused on the argument of Senator J. William Fulbright of Arkansas that, despite Cuba's independent foreign policy, "The Castro regime is a thorn in the flesh; but it is not a dagger in the heart." Invited to the meeting, Fulbright brought Kennedy a memorandum that counseled patience. When he spoke to the assembled officials, Fulbright was eloquent, but Berle was unmoved. To him Fulbright's performance was more evidence that "politicians and intellectuals wished to hide behind cloudy unrealities. The doctrine of 'non-intervention' was used as an excuse for not facing the savage fact that high intentions, good words and even good deeds would not stop Cold War activities carried on with agitation, money, bought demonstrations, and surreptitious organization of guerrillas with arms." As he had said before, the time had come when the United States "instead of acting covertly [had to] act as a great Power." The collective security of the hemisphere—Berle's work since 1938—was at stake. Thus, when the president asked the participants individually what they thought of Fulbright's impassioned analysis, Berle began by composing an intellectual's rebuttal to an intellectual senator, but Kennedy cut him off, demanding a brief reply. Berle's words flashed across the room: "I say, 'let 'er rip!' "[24]

His next role, with Arthur Schlesinger, Jr., called for him to tell the Cuban Revolutionary Council, the exile organization, that it could not expect U.S. military support in its landing. "I had difficulty with this," Berle later wrote, "but the President had made known his decision and we had no further discussion on the point." "We'll take you to the beaches," Berle informed Cuban leader José Miró Cardona when the Cuban inquired incredulously if there would be no further U.S. military assistance. (Miró later claimed that Berle had promised him 15,000 men.) The point was hammered home during lunch at the Century Club. Berle and Schlesinger wanted the Cubans to know that this was their operation—that it depended solely upon Cubans hitting the beaches to inspire an uprising of Cubans all across the island. Cubans had to determine their own destiny. Although Berle privately wished for some demonstration of American force and power, that was not to be. However, he felt that Americans ought to be as aroused to support the anti-Castro Cubans as they had supported Castro against Batista. "There can be no double standard in these matters."[25]

When the battle went against the anti-Castro Cubans at the Bay of Pigs, Kennedy ordered Berle and Schlesinger to fly to Florida to carry word of the disaster to Miró. "I can think of happier missions," Berle wryly said. It was an anguished assignment that virtually concluded Berle's service to Kennedy. With Schlesinger, the only person in the White House inner circle to express doubts about the expedition, Berle drafted a statement for Kennedy hailing the men who fought at the Bay of Pigs as "revolutionaries [who] saw their revolution betrayed by another." When Lleras Camargo offered to assist the United States in extricating itself from the debacle, he contacted Berle and it was through Berle that Kennedy asked the Colombians to request humane treatment for any Cuban prisoners.[26]

The denouement came on May 5 before an administration group of inquiry consisting of Attorney General Robert F. Kennedy, Admiral Arleigh Burke, Allen Dulles, and General Maxwell Taylor. Berle's answers concerning his role in planning the Bay of Pigs operation repeated testimony by previous witnesses and defended the political correctness of the operation; he was not an objective witness. Asked in conclusion to assess Latin-American reaction to the Bay of Pigs, Berle asserted that "They're slowly coming our way. . . . Slowly the people are realizing that they have to choose between the Communist intrusion and the United States, and it seems to be developing favorably for us."

The reply suggested an end to collective action and, as Berle learned from his friend Pepe Figueres, Latin America could not be expected to go along with Washington. Figueres was dining with Berle and Schlesinger when he learned that the anti-Castro Cubans were on the beaches. Figueres supported intervention against Castro, provided that it was consistent with the principle of ridding the hemisphere of *all* dictators, not just Castro. In this instance, he expected "a Dunkirk," Figueres told Schlesinger. Why had he not been consulted? "How can we have an alliance," he said, almost bitterly, "if even our friends will not believe that we can be trusted with secrets. I may disagree with something, but I still can be trusted with secrets." Berle had given up on collective action in the hemisphere in favor of unilateral intervention. Figueres saw it not merely as a defeat of U.S. policy, but of Latin America's democratic Left. His point, which Berle was familiar with, was that if Kennedy attacked Trujillo first, the United States could rally the democratic forces of the hemisphere. An attack against Castro now demonstrated that the United States tolerated right-wing-dictators but not left-wing dictators.

The military disaster could have been avoided only by Kennedy, but the political disaster belonged to Berle as much as anyone. Despite his advocacy of and experience in seeking Latin American cooperation for a defense of the hemisphere against totalitarianism, at this critical time he had opted for a unilateral operation; in his view, imperial Washington had the right and the duty to behave as a great power in cleansing its sphere of an alien influence. For that matter, he was reluctant about consulting even anti-Castro Cubans—asserting, at a March conference, when it was suggested that more Cubans be brought into the planning for military action against Castro, that "we have no time for consulting the Cubans on this." Imperial America would not be deterred from its mission by any of its clients. At the May 5 inquiry the braintruster responded to a question concerning future policy by emphatically asserting that policy should be the province of the president and a brain trust of two or three men—a cold war Chiefs of Staff. Either he did not understand Figueres' point concerning consultation or he did not care to understand it. He had sounded out other Latin American countries and, not satisfied with their responses, felt even more that Washington must take action with or without their approval.[27]

Later Pepe Figueres wrote Berle, "Cheer up! We'll win." "I still believe in freedom along with social progress," Berle responded. Together they would rally the social democrats of the hemisphere. But Berle did not need an office in Washington for that mission and he was anxious to return to New York. Yet he stayed to honor his commitment of six months. It would have satisfied all if he left, but he remained the administration's spokesman on Latin America until July. Then he found deserved retirement.[28]

10

The Lessons of Liberalism

It is a far cry from Versailles to the present. Strangely, the course has been circular. I think we are arriving at a state of affairs surprisingly like that which prevailed in 1910 or 1912. I can only hope that 1914 will not follow. I can see no escape, now, from a policy of American military strength. The League of Nations lasted twenty years after Versailles. The United Nations, after twenty years, is almost impotent. We just may be able to resurrect the United Nations—but while doing so can not indulge illusions or confide in innocent pacifism. Our children will perhaps repeat our careers—all the way from Paris in 1919 around the full cycle. I wish I thought history would not (more or less) repeat itself.

—to Samuel Eliot Morison,
April 30, 1965, BP-87

There is order in the cosmos and if you can not apprehend it, then you make one inside of your head.

—Diary, November 30, 1961

SELF-DETERMINATION IN THE SIXTIES

As 1961 came to a close Berle knew that it had been a painfully disappointing year. "In terms of personal life and the progress of the children, prosperity, and all external family matters, it could not have been happier," Berle reasoned. But what should have been a year of triumphant adventures in the public arena had been a failure. His Puritan mind did not permit personal satisfactions when his own measure of success was the state of the world and his ability to improve it: "The diabolic pounding of international affairs, accompanied by enough knowledge of them to know what is involved, has made it [a year] of cognate agonies. . . . To get out with as few wounds as I did was probably the best that could be hoped for."

He did not shift the onus for his tragedy to anyone else. "The expedition into the government was both a mistake and a failure. A mistake because I did not bargain for the position of power consistent with the responsibility assumed. Or at least the degree of responsibility attributed to me." He was not the architect of U.S. policy in Latin America because, mindful of his nebulous role in the State Department, he had deferred to its secretary, Dean Rusk, using him as an intermediary with the White House—only to find Rusk was a good man but a weak leader. Rusk was a significant barrier to action and Berle could not circumvent Rusk, as he had Hull, because he lacked the personal relationship with Kennedy that he had had with Roosevelt. He was not Kennedy's braintruster—although Berle liked to believe that had it only been "the President and me," the ultimate corporate brain trust, he and Kennedy "probably would have made effective action." Instead, Berle and Kennedy were captive to a Cuban policy that was not of their making.

"It is not difficult to damn the Bay of Pigs operation," a historian has written. "The path is well-marked and well-trod." Berle conceded that it had been a "fiasco," albeit not for reasons of its immorality, illegality, and stupidity, as has been charged. Berle considered it a failure because of its timidity. Fear of inciting anti-Americanism abroad by appearing to be an aggressor had limited the operation's success. Still, Berle insisted that it was consistent with international law and historical policy; "indeed [it] was a fulfillment of a debt we had undertaken to protect the hemisphere against aggression." Part of the problem, as Berle saw it, was that so few people remembered the network of treaties protecting the hemisphere from totalitarian intervention, dating from the late thirties when the threat came from Nazi aggression through 1947 when the hemisphere established a "public law" against all totalitarian intrusions. Those treaties ordained a hemispheric order between 1933 and 1947 that climaxed with the treaties of Chapultepec and Rio de Janeiro—the equivalent of a Truman Doctrine for the Americas. Article 51 of the U.N. Charter had been a world guarantee of that hemispheric order. For Walter Lippmann or other Europeanists, or historians who would base their critiques upon them, not to see this was "ignorance [matched] only by their self-assurance."

More than ever Berle believed that "the Cuban action which rates as a fiasco was probably one of the few intelligent things we did." Berle's first premise designated Cuba as a Soviet military base to be used in Moscow's war against the United States in its own hemisphere. From that premise it followed that Washington could not intervene in Cuba's internal affairs, for Cubans no longer determined them; they were not Soviet surrogates. The Soviet presence in Cuba gave the United States the right and duty to defend Latin America—unilaterally and militarily, if need be—in order to keep the hemispheric community free from totalitarianism. That analysis pointed the way to future U.S. military action in Latin America. A unilateral fight to keep the Americas free from foreign totalitarianism was legal, moral, wise, and required by the historical lessons of empire. If a great power was unwilling to perform its role, it was not a great power and smaller nations would look to another power to assure their self-determination.

Soviet subversion of Latin America was ineluctable. The dictators would fail and the United States would confront other Castros. What then? The prospect filled Berle with despair only because of American ignorance of the threat and institutional ineffectiveness in combating it. American non-intervention was a useless principle when the Soviets intervened ideologically with indigenous surrogates. Collective security was moribund when foolish politicians like Quadros convinced themselves that an "independent" foreign policy was possible. Even the State Department was "unready, inefficient, even in its own way corrupt," if only because it allowed itself to be limited by people like Fulbright and Quadros. He did not criticize Kennedy, for "it takes about a year for a President to take control of his own machinery." At least the administration had initiated the Alliance for Progress, the long-overdue Marshall Plan for Latin America. Yet he sensed it would ultimately fail because it was "nothing more than a platform" and required leadership in both Washington and the capitals of the Americas that was absent.

And now, at the conclusion of 1961, he was once more a private citizen, his political career again at an end. Again, he would turn to writing about his vision of world developments and his philosophy of history. And yet he yearned to be a man of action, for "being vindicated by history is cold comfort. . . . [Writing] counts for nothing if the essential integrity of the American system is not preserved."[1]

The hemisphere lacked ideological cohesion and the State Department lacked ideological consistency. Thus, when in May President Duvalier of Haiti declared himself reelected for another term without the pretense of a vote—and invited the United States to send a representative to his "inauguration"—Berle argued to no avail that to do so was "a moral mistake of the first order and will plague everyone. It comes pretty close to being the last surrender of principle to expediency that has yet been done." Under Secretary Chester Bowles brushed aside Berle's protests because he feared that to antagonize Duvalier would encourage anti-Americanism or even communism in Haiti. The incident was an object lesson in how the dictators manipulated U.S. fears of communism as an alternative to them.[2]

He knew that within the administration the failures of U.S. Latin America policy had been laid at his doorstep. A bold administration would have jettisoned Berle as soon as he refused a position for reasons of ego or made unreasonable distinctions between policy and operations. Instead, it tolerated drift in policy implementation because nobody wanted to be assistant secretary of state for Latin American affairs while Berle was an ill-defined "task force" hovering between the State Department and the White House. All this was bruited about openly. Thus, when the Dominican dictator Trujillo was assassinated that spring, the administration had to circumvent Berle by giving a Bowles deputy (Rusk and Kennedy were in Paris) charge of American contingency planning because it involved operations, not policy. Berle did not see himself as a fifth wheel to the wagon; rather, he attributed the problem to a policy conflict "very like the division we had in 1944." Again, he believed, the tough opponents of Russian imperialism were being pushed out of the Department by appeasers. That was a gross self-deception. Had Berle wanted to remain at State all he had to say was that he wanted to be assistant secretary of state for Latin American affairs! (This assumes that the White House and Rusk still could not refuse him; his incessant complaints about State's bureaucracy had earned him a reputation as an irascible and egotistical old bird who was difficult to work with—or, as *The New York Times* correspondent Tad Szulc would put it, his "overwhelming personality . . . was a contributing factor in Mr. Berle's departure from government.") But then he would have lost his fight to be under secretary of state for inter-American affairs, as well as bruising his ego by accepting a position beneath what he felt his experience entitled him. Somehow the example of John Quincy Adams' career in the House of Representatives following his presidency eluded Berle. Instead he told himself that "Obviously if we are going to let Latin America go [Communist] with sweet phrases, I had best be somewhere else." Although Berle privately castigated one diplomat who resigned for not wanting "to do something about the situation," he himself prepared to abdicate. If he could not be under secretary, he would go home to New York.

Both Berle and Kennedy needed a face-saving departure for him. Meeting with Berle on July 7, the president praised his "dedication and sacrifice in the public interest" and Berle told Kennedy that he "would defend the Cuban adventure even as it came out," to which Kennedy grinned wryly and said that Berle would have "trouble in court proving its success." A few days later Berle performed one more time as the grand old man of Latin American affairs at a press briefing: "No President since Roosevelt has had the same vivid and direct interest in [Latin America] than Kennedy," he intoned. His major contribution to this administration had been as an historical talisman.[3]

"Destiny has taken a rain-check instead of giving me an honorable discharge," he reassured himself; he departed "with a sense of personal defeat" only because at sixty-six he could not stomach bureaucratic battles. He was certain that within a couple of years he would be in a position of influence and again be making history. A year later he was even more remote from power and he took consolation in the conviction that he did not really desire another public office, although he would not refuse one either. "But I think that my forward career will be intellectual rather than political and maybe it is better that way," he told himself. "The six months in Washington last year left me wondering whether I could stand the gaff when every decision may cost thousands of lives. Twenty years ago it was easy." Retaining his enthusiasm for policymaking without accountability, he reconstituted the "East 19th Street crowd" of Latin American democrats that gave activists such as Figueres and Betancourt the benefit of his brain-trusting. The hemisphere's liberals still had no more prominent friend in the United States; yet, at times even Berle enjoyed greater honor in San José and Caracas than in Washington. However, within a few years a request from the CIA to confer with him inspired the reflection, "As I conclude my seventieth year, I find that I still have zest for these adventures."[4]

He always made himself available for policy briefings, advice, speeches, reviews, and articles on Latin America. (Richard Goodwin touched base with him prior to departing for the Punta del Este conference of 1962.) Fearing that Americans and the State Department were too distracted by crises in Southeast Asia or over Berlin to give events south of the border their due, Berle wrote and spoke reminders that the hemisphere was a cold war hot spot meriting attention.[5]

He summarized much of his knowledge and perspective of the region in a small book, *Latin America—Diplomacy and Reality*, which the Council on Foreign Relations published in 1962. It was a sober yet sanguine appraisal of events written with an awareness that some of his comments might antagonize the Latins; but he addressed them honestly as equals. In the judgment of *The New York Times'* specialist on Latin America, Tad Szulc, it was "a highly provocative and thoughtful policy book, possibly the most significant currently available study of the United States–Latin American relationship." He noted that Berle "rather ruthlessly but clearly" minimized the importance of internal events in Castro's Cuba as opposed to how Moscow used Havana as a launching pad for subverting other Latin American states. Szulc concurred with Berle's point that Washington lacked an effective organization to implement the Alliance for Progress and deal with the problems that gave communism its opening wedge, although he hinted that Berle himself was not the man to straighten it out. Szulc agreed with Berle's plea for "enlightened free enterprise" in the region, combined with American tolerance of countries that may develop indigenous Socialist political and eoncomic systems that respect the rights of its citizens and its neighbors.[6]

But the private Berle was less optimistic than apocalyptic. Although Latin America was unstable and a hotbed of anti-Americanism for as long as he could remember, now—like the State Department policymakers he criticized—he tended to treat every blowup in the region as either Communist-inspired or made-to-order for Communist ambitions. This made him more amenable to manipulation by the dictators. He knew that anti-Americanism was historically fashionable among Latin American youths and intellectuals (it was three decades since he and Sumner Welles had confronted anti-American students in Havana), but now he depicted them as "crypto-Communists," a favorite epithet that entered his vocabulary. Anti-Americanism was the work of Communists. Even a movement to make the University of Puerto Rico (of which he was a member of the board and privileged to travel there regularly) more Latin American was "probably Communist-inspired."[7]

Berle saw the Cuban Missile Crisis as an opportunity for the Kennedy administration to exhibit the resolve it lacked at the Bay of Pigs. Initially he applauded Kennedy's response and heaped derision upon those who feared that the administration courted nuclear war. "I never was fonder in my life of Art. 51 in the Charter of the United Nations," he wrote of the section that took hemispheric defense out of the purview of the world body. He publicly boasted that Soviet imperialism in the hemisphere had now "reached its farthest point with Cuba and would . . . recede." But he fretted that the American response to the crisis was "a half-done job" because it left a Russian presence in Cuba and his "frightened" mind envisioned a Cuban strike against Venezuela or Guatemala. Increasingly he viewed Kennedy as a Neville Chamberlain whose administration verged on "disintegration."[8]

Never before a friend of Latin dictators, Berle now preferred Somoza of Nicaragua to chaos or Castro. Much of his liberal platform for Central America remained intact, including a common market that would make the region safe for democracy and cheap capital that would develop its economy and infrastructure. But the corrupt Somoza of Nicaragua made a mockery of it; a Central American common market would reinforce the dictator's monopolies and American capital would find its way into his family's Swiss bank accounts. Berle hoped to persuade Somoza to abdicate before revolution or intervention forced him out and left Nicaragua in turmoil. Representing "nobody but myself," although he kept the State Department informed, in February 1962, he visited the leaders of Mexico, Guatemala (where right-wing leaders resisted land reform and considered "that the last three Popes were Communists"), Costa Rica (where he discussed the ongoing problem of peacefully deposing its troublesome neighbor, Somoza), Honduras (where the liberal Ramón Villeda Morales boasted of improvements in his country's infrastructure), and Nicaragua (where even the opposition party was "reactionary.") Yet, the Somozas held all Nicaragua hostage and Berle ruefully agreed with them that "None of us could afford the luxury of civil war in Central America. We should have Castro in it in no time."[9]

The message from Managua, that liberals like Berle were captive to anti-Communism, was not lost elsewhere in Central America. In 1963 Villeda Morales was overthrown by a Honduran army coup which Berle believed was abetted by Nicaraguan and Guatemalan army officers. Months later the Honduran junta held an election and shrewdly invited the Berles and Frances Grant to witness it as official observers. Berle went, knowing that his presence would legitimize the coup. "It is axiomatic that you can never win an election against a military government—and this one proved it," he wrote. "It was a beautiful exercise on how to steal an election." Yet he counseled Morales not to wage a fight against the regime lest a conflict inspire "steady infiltration from the Cuban side." Liberals had to acquiesce to the stolen election even if it left the Communists to lead the resistance against military government while "the moderates are slowly squeezed to pieces."[10]

He took considerable solace from Venezuela's "socially progressive democracy" which withstood Castro's war of terrorism against it to remain the most liberal government in Latin America: "Backing the Betancourt government was one of the [most successful] contributions I made to the Kennedy Administration," Berle exulted in late 1963. Betancourt "not only beat off the Communists, . . . but the democratic left has made some brilliant progress in Venezuela." Nevertheless, democracy and order were not synonymous. Betancourt's liberals exasperated him because they would not give diplomatic recognition to anti-Communist "governments [that] did not occur by election." The Venezuelans were "still doctrinaire."[11]

He no longer shared the Venezuelan liberals' dread of military rule in the hemisphere, a product of their experience under the Pérez Jiménez dictatorship. Berle now welcomed military coups if they averted the chaos that Communists exploited. U.S. support of Latin American dictators was justified by the Communist threat: "Economic reconstruction and social reform do not, by themselves, stop Skoda bullets or foreign-organized guerrillas. Peoples do not have free choices under those conditions. Conquest, not reform, is the present purpose of our imperialist antagonists."[12]

Liberals like Berle no longer trusted elections. After all, elections had not spared Brazil from foolish leadership and the threat of chaos. He detested Jânio Quadros' attempt at evenhandedness in foreign policy and João Goulart's flirtation with left-wingers in Brazil. He welcomed the army's intrusions into Brazilian politics because, he told Henry Kissinger, "When democracy can not preserve order, it is lost." Enormous poverty still made Brazil a tinderbox, and he lectured a Brazilian friend that his country had to tax its rich, pay its workers well, and educate the masses in order to achieve social progress.[13]

The Brazilian politician closest to his heart was Carlos Lacerda, whom Berle had known in 1945 as a "young leftist leader." In 1961 Lacerda was the governor of Guanabara, the province surrounding Rio, and one of the most skillful manipulators of Brazilian public opinion, ambitious for Brazil's presidency and hardly the romantic Berle knew as a young man. In some ways he was the La Guardia of Brazil—tough, puritanical, progressive, and an effective administrator.[14]

Berle once asked Lacerda what he thought U.S. policy toward Brazil should be; the Brazilian responded that Washington's humanitarian and national interests required that the United States expect Rio to follow America's lead. In 1964 when President Goulart threatened to throw the country into civil war and become a "Cuban ally," Lacerda conspired with the Brazilian army to oust Goulart. In 1965 Berle visited Brazil for the first time in four years and was impressed with its development. He was certain that if the shrewd Lacerda could be elected president ("But [I] better not intervene in Brazilian politics"), he could mitigate any appeal from the Left. In any event, Berle rated economic development and stabilization as more important to Brazil than electoral democracy.[15]

A Brazilian once accused him of being "interested only in the Caribbean"; Berle did not deny it. Not only was it his first passion, but he saw it as paramount to U.S. strategic interests. Had not his career in foreign affairs begun in the Dominican Republic because of America's concern in 1918 for its strategic defense against Germany? That concern now shaped his attitudes toward the Russian intrusion into the area. To the accusation that America only valued the region for economic exploitation, he responded, "We could look elsewhere for our supply of raw materials and tropical products; we can not look elsewhere for the geography of a modern defense." American security in the area long since outweighed his dislike for military intervention that smacked of colonialism. With the odious dictatorship of Trujillo gone, he worried about chaos and then communism ruling the Dominican Republic. Although chiefly motivated by U.S. ideological and security factors, a personal interest contributed to his attitudes: his chairmanship of the Board of Directors of the American Molasses Company (later the Sucrest Corporation) and its purchases of Dominican sugar. In 1962 the largest sugar producer in the Dominican Republic was the government itself, a fact Berle could live with, even when increased wages in the cane fields compelled higher sugar prices. When Sucrest bought sugar directly from President Juan Bosch of the Dominican Republic, it marked, Berle wrote, "the first purchase in years when no bribe is involved."[16]

But in 1963 two events brought Berle back full circle to the Dominican Republic: the military, fearful of a Communist takeover, expelled the weak Bosch; and then Kennedy was assassinated. Still hankering for a top policymaking post on Latin American affairs, Berle moved to ingratiate himself with the new president, using close friends of Lyndon Johnson such as Abe Fortas, Jim Rowe, and Tom Mann, now under secretary of state.[17]

None of them—least of all Mann, whose memory of the debacle of 1961 was fresh—would give Berle the first-rank position he craved, but it was Rowe who saw that Berle could be Johnson's historical talisman for the price of a twenty-minute conversation with the president. After all, if President Johnson wanted to create an image of himself as another FDR, what better way to enhance that "deliberate identification with Roosevelt" than by "buttering up" an old New Dealer like the 69-year-old Berle? Rowe knew that "like everyone else, he does like to 'advise' Presidents." Mann, who valued Berle's endorsement of policy in Latin America, agreed. Berle got an audience at the White House and performed to everyone's expectations: "I was immensely impressed," he declared. "We have, I think, a new Roosevelt in the making."[18]

Encouraged by this attention, Berle went with Beatrice to the Dominican Republic in June 1964, to build up his policymaking credentials. The country was now in the hands of a ruling triumvirate headed by Donald Reid Cabral who, conscious that his government was illegitimate and unrecognized by the United States, lavished the Berles with royal attention. Wanting to establish his liberal credentials with Berle, Reid Cabral "rather wistfully" asked him if there was some way he could meet Muñoz Marín. What Berle perhaps did not know then was that Bosch, who was Muñoz Marín's guest in Puerto Rico, was agitating for a return and Reid Cabral hoped to persuade Muñoz Marín to expel the popular Bosch far from the Dominican Republic. Berle assured Reid Cabral that he would see what could be done. Berle did not see Muñoz Marín until December and then found him "despondent" over the political situation in the Dominican Republic. The fact was, as Muñoz Marín and the CIA informed Berle, Reid Cabral had no political base—while the deposed Bosch came closest of any Dominican, other than an old Trujillo cohort, to having a strong popular following. To head off a resurgence of the Trujillo crowd in an upcoming election, the CIA and the American ambassador to Santo Domingo, W. Tapley Bennett, asked Berle to negotiate Bosch's support of Reid Cabral— "a good trick if you can do it," Bennett confessed. But, Berle apparently did nothing.[19]

"Like Owen Wister's 'Virginian,' I have had a past and intend to make a lot more," Berle answered Lyndon Johnson's birthday telegram on the occasion of his seventieth birthday. He savored Johnson's praise as a braintruster to four presidents preceding him (Eisenhower and possibly Truman would have been surprised to learn that Berle had advised them). On April 24, the Dominican Republic blew up in a civil war. On April 28, with bloodshed on the rise in Santo Domingo, President Johnson gave the order to land American troops in order to save American lives. A lot of Berle's past suddenly caught up with him.[20]

Berle justified the Dominican landing as "a measure not of intervention but of defense." If Johnson "had not acted, Castro-mounted operations would have taken over Santo Domingo in a relatively short time." Although he argued the case for intervention in the pages of *The Reporter,* he was unhappy with himself. "I have been seeing ghosts," he said, a favorite remark when it seemed to him that history repeated itself. He had opposed the American occupation of the Dominican Republic that ended in 1924 and wanted no occupation now. Yet, certain that Communists were at work in Santo Domingo (as were Americans there), he believed that had Johnson not acted as he did the Communists would have emerged the victors out of the chaos of Santo Domingo. Then Cuba and the Russians would have moved in and controlled the Caribbean. He bitterly scorned "all good little intellectuals and good little liberals mightily aided by Communist propaganda [who] are damning the President." On May 27 Johnson invited Berle to the White House for what Berle called "the Red Carpet treatment." Cynicism aside, it was the first time he had had lunch alone with a president since 1944 and when LBJ thanked Berle for the *Reporter* article and explained his perspective of the Dominican situation, Berle "told him that he was dead right."[21]

To put it mildly, he was flattered that Johnson had asked for his advice. "To enter history again, however modestly, is I suppose a compliment," he thought. "History is implacably reaching in my direction—though the stakes for good or evil especially for evil are greater perhaps than they have ever been in human history." However, at seventy he no longer had the stomach for life-or-death decisions, although "it is clear that I know more about the Dominican Republic than most of the people operating there." He drafted a memorandum and sent it to Johnson. On June 3 he attended a dinner celebrating the fifteenth anniversay of the founding of the Inter-American Committee for Democracy and Freedom at which the guest of honor was Rómulo Betancourt. To his horror, his liberal friend Betancourt castigated the American action as a mistake and the dinner, instead of celebrating democracy in the hemisphere, erupted into a debate over whether Washington's intervention undermined Dominican democracy. Further confounding Berle was Pepe Figueres' agreement with Betancourt. Berle found himself at odds with the men he venerated most in Latin America and its most prominent liberals.

"Life is odd," Berle reflected.

> I began in the Dominican Republic—under an American occupation which I disliked—in 1918. In a sort of spiral trajectory, I am coming towards the end of my life once more working on the Dominican Republic, this time defending an occupation. Then, any American was an enemy in Latin America until the contrary was proved. It may work out this way again, and it makes me unhappy.
>
> But the difference is obvious. Now a great hostile power is squarely planted in the Caribbean—namely Cuba. The alleged revolutions in every case are used by that power to establish a position in which eventually they plan to attack the United States. At this point the locus of power becomes important. The incapacity of the Latin Americans to govern themselves, let alone take a hand in world politics, compels the United States to take care of itself and . . . the Latin Americans however much they dislike it.[22]

Forty-seven years after he had advocated the Dominican Republic's self-determination from an American hegemony, Adolf Berle concluded that Latin America was not prepared for freedom.

"A FRANK AND CONSTRUCTIVE IMPERIALISM"

As Berle discussed the Dominican Republic situation with Johnson, the president "brought up a submerged iceberg." The "iceberg" was the Vietnam War, hardly a submerged topic for a White House conversation in the spring of 1965. With congressional authority to defend the Republic of Vietnam against insurgents and infiltrating Communist troops from the North, and thousands of American troops on their way to Southeast Asia and American bombers striking deeper into North Vietnam—Berle was not startled by Vietnam's sudden intrusion in their discussion of America's Caribbean security. In his mind, as in the president's, Southeast Asia and Latin America were inextricably linked. As Berle remarked, "It was clear that he saw—as I did—two icebergs (possibly three) slowly converging with the possibility of all-out war as a result."[1]

Johnson never doubted Berle's enthusiasm for repelling the Communists in Southeast Asia. At a Liberal party dinner marking his seventieth birthday the month before, Berle had pleaded for support of Johnson's policies in Southeast Asia, warning that if America appeased the Communists in East Asia, within two years Chinese armies would be "moving all over Asia" and critics of Johnson's policies would reverse themselves and be "crying for all-out American entry into a full-scale Asian war." The calendar read 1965 but Berle recalled 1938: now the aggressors were the Soviet Union, Cuba, and the People's Republic of China; now the victims were the Dominican Republic and South Vietnam; now, if he and Johnson prevailed, appeasement would not find its Munich and the aggressors would be repelled. If they failed, mankind was "in the penumbra of what would be World War III." Johnson knew that Berle spoke his language.[2]

But some of Berle's best friends wanted no part of an American intervention. Liberal friends such as J. K. Galbraith, Arthur Schlesinger, Jr., Roger Baldwin, and any number of intellectuals considered the American escalation in Vietnam a horrible blunder. Disagreement over the war strained friendships. Liberal comrades who had venerated Berle for leading and sharing past struggles in behalf of liberalism now parted company with Berle over the war in Southeast Asia. They spoke out against the war while Berle defended it. At the same time other liberals such as *Reporter* editor-publisher Max Ascoli stood with Johnson and Berle. Sadly, the struggle in Asia bred conflict in America.[3]

Vietnam did not torment Berle personally as the Dominican Republic intervention did. Knowing very little about Asia or America's historical role there, he applied strategic principles that were unencumbered by historical irony. After all, one did not have to know Asia to despise aggression or know that American interests somehow were at stake there. In Berle's experience America had resisted Japanese imperialism in the 1930s, North Korean aggression in 1950, and now he equated Communist aggression against South Vietnam in the 1960s with those earlier conflicts. For that matter, he linked the opposition of A. A. Berle, Sr., to American imperialism in the Philippines to his own opposition to North Vietnamese imperialism; nobody had a right to occupy another country. Moreover, Berle believed that the brutality of Communist expansion in Asia made the old imperialisms comparatively benign. After all, European imperialism had occupied Asia without attempting to destroy its culture; but Communist imperialism was truly revolutionary. Distinctions between these imperialisms had to be made so that the oppressed knew America as a foe of hegemony. In 1952 he had counseled Adlai Stevenson that "In Indochina as elsewhere, the problem is to make the Western World the best friend of *legitimate* anticolonial nationalism. We did this in the Philippines and Indonesia, and appreciably in India. It could be done in Indochina. This could be made major policy, both for us and for Western Europe." The world had to be made aware that Communist anti-colonialism was illegitimate because it was a proxy of Soviet and Chinese imperialism.[4]

The successful Communist revolution in China, its entry into the Korean War on the side of North Korean aggressors against the United Nations forces, and the withdrawal of French colonialism from Indochina allowed Berle to depict America's role in Southeast Asia as part of a crusade against both colonialism and communism. In 1952 Berle opposed any all-out U.S. participation in France's Indochina war because, although it would have the merit of militarily draining both Russia and China, it would "not compensate for American sacrifices and tends to bind China to the Soviet Union." On the other hand he also opposed both French and American withdrawal because "independence for Indochina is equivalent to transferring the area to Communist China." Although the United States, through its military aid to the French, paid for almost 80 percent of the French war in 1954, he considered the French cause hopeless because the Indochinese people did not support them. Nevertheless, Washington had to persevere in its support of Paris because the war placed it "in a better moral position than would unsuccessful defense of the French empire, or failure to move at all." Indeed, the French defeat in Vietnam and the country's temporary partition deprived Washington of the luxury of a surrogate's resistance and sapped Berle's determination to have America abstain from direct intervention. "In Southeast Asia now," he told a daughter, "we either have to have allies or be prepared to put a great many more Americans into uniforms and on to battlefields than we ought to have to do." While he deprecated the foreign policy leadership of John Foster Dulles, he did not seem to appreciate how much his own policy suggestions dovetailed with those of Eisenhower's secretary of state.[5]

In 1960 Peter Berle served in Indochina with army intelligence and became a major source of information on the war for his father. While Peter encouraged Berle's certainty that the insurgent Viet Minh were agents of the Chinese, he also cautioned his father that Saigon's leadership was "cruel and corrupt; not easily distinguishable from the enemies they are fighting." Berle sent Peter with that message to Schlesinger in the Kennedy White House and told himself, "It looks to me like a lost cause there." Berle paid

Vietnam slight attention at the time because Castro was loose in the Americas and he considered Asia a strategic concern of lesser importance than Latin America. Failure in Southeast Asia would be tragic, but failure in the hemisphere would be catastrophic. "An American can imagine a world in which Southeast Asia is Communist or Communist-dominated," he told Peter. "A world in which Latin America is Communist-dominated, however, would be something quite else." Tired of making distinctions among American interests, European colonialism, and Communist imperialism, and disappointed in the determination of Asians and Latin Americans to resist communism, Berle wondered if "a frank and constructive imperialism in some ways would be more viable than an attempt to claim that incompetent nations can reorganize themselves."

Additionally, part of the problem lay with the mixed signals American liberals gave those "incompetent nations." According to Berle, many of his fellow liberals were not tough enough to endorse a "constructive imperialism" because they wanted "to say 'nice kitty' to pro-Communist forces" and had not faced up to the facts that Communist regimes "kill more than, or as many, people as wars." Communist wars had to be met with American wars; Communist force had to be met with American force. The old liberalism no longer worked: "The United States in dealing with the new countries is mainly indulging a set of myths self created." If smaller nations were as determined to govern their destinies as was the United States determined to have them do so, Berle could profess his old liberalism. Yet liberalism seemed to thrive better in Europe than in Asia or Latin America. He took pains to comfort a Lithuanian fugitive from communism with the affirmation that "the world is slowly returning to self-determination of peoples, and the very confusion in which it is [in] now suggests that in the not too distant future self-determination may once more become a dominant principle in international situations"; but he was not so optimistic where the developing nations were concerned. The West would have to fight to keep the freed colonial peoples free from communism. In the atmosphere of détente that followed the Cuban Missile Crisis, he warned that although the Russians were "increasingly divorced from the headship of the Communist world," they were becoming "increasingly imperialistic. Not by the ideological route but by straight classical armed—and intrigues—action."[6]

Action required reaction and Berle welcomed Johnson's determination to hold the line in Vietnam. Without it all of East Asia, "from Japan to Malaysia," would fall to the Communists: "Never mind how we got here— here is where we are." (However, during the American landing in the Dominican Republic he made a point that might have applied to the American forces in Vietnam: "*Anyone can put troops into a place but it takes a political genius to deal with the ensuing situation and get them out.*") When the American bombing of North Vietnam instigated "teach-ins" against the war on university campuses across America, Berle grimly asserted that many of them were "pretty plainly Communist organized," adding, "Not that all these people are Communists. But the Communist propaganda seems to be able to coopt an adequate number of adherents chiefly drawn from the intellectual world." To him they were the same intellectuals who wanted peace with Hitler in 1938, disengagement from Greece in 1946, and hands off Cuba in 1961: "Practically all of them are as sincere as could be. . . . They never raise a cry in opposition to any Communist aggression. Because of the McCarthy affair, it is unfashionable to suggest Communist influence." Berle dared to be unfashionable in linking antiwar "holy innocents" to the Communists, but he eschewed alliance with the right-wing extremists who endorsed the war. In June 1965, he and Max Ascoli "considered that we were rapidly becoming the last survivors of evolutionary democracy." Neither reactionary conservatives nor left-wing liberals, they might have considered themselves neoliberals or neoconservatives.[7]

For Berle the campus had been an island of intellectual integrity; now it was a hotbed of hostility. No longer were genteel differences of opinion on Southeast Asia possible. "Teach-Ins were conceived in sin," Berle asserted. "They really amount to Communist and pro-Communist demonstrations in universities, in which the real Communists, the crypto-Communists, and the fellow travellers join to belabor America, particularly about Vietnam and the Dominican Republic." Invited by his old friend Escott Reid to confront the devils in debate at Toronto University, Berle went out of a sense of moral duty that required him to defend an America that only defended peoples unable to defend themselves against Chinese and Cuban aggression. In keeping this faith he wanted the White House to know it. When the president resumed bombings following a pause that did not bring fruitful negotiations, Berle hastened to express his "complete confidence" in that decision. The president had to use force, even if "American intellectual opinion declines to face the consequences of non-action." Johnson's handling of the war, he wrote in *The New York Times* and in *Newsday,* "was that of a big man," even if it left him "vulnerable to attack by misguided idealists." He stridently affirmed Johnson's policies in the Dominican Republic and in Vietnam. Americans had to trust the president and his intelligence sources while eschewing "stereotypes, simplistic attitudes, biased appeals, and some pure fiction." With intervention in such distant places as the Dominican Republic and Vietnam, was intervention a policy by itself? During the Middle East war of 1967 an enraged Max Ascoli called Berle to complain that "Johnson was almost criminal and weak in not landing some force and otherwise getting into the picture." Berle did not seem to go that far.[8]

Johnson's announcement in 1968 that he would not run again agitated Berle because he expected Communists to use the nine-month lame-duck period to precipitate crises "from Vietnam to Venezuela." He suspected that Johnson's decision would be interpreted as an American defeat and a retreat from power. Proud of his country's effort in Vietnam, he wanted no part of antiwar Democrats who, like Bobby Kennedy, sought to negotiate with the Viet Cong; yet, he was still enough of a liberal Democrat to disdain prowar Republicans "with a reactionary flavor." He railed privately against Arthur Schlesinger, Jr., whose support for Bobby Kennedy he saw as evidence of a lust for power; "Schlesinger is slowly being derailed from a top flight historian to a petty politician. . . . The combination of some power and a great deal of publicity forced on a man does strange things to him unless he has enormous tensile strength."

But when Schlesinger sent Berle a wire of congratulations of his seventy-third birthday, Berle responded graciously and initiated a dialogue that summed up some of what divided liberals:

> For God's sake stop thinking of Vietnam as the whole affair. It is a big detail indeed—but only a detail in a huge picture whose climax will probably come in the Mediterranean in the not too distant future. At the moment the whole periphery is in motion from North Korea to Guatemala—and "Fortress America" may well be an imposed policy. For, one must admit, the Roosevelt policy—the world organized into regional, cooperative and determinative groups and governed by the United Nations—has pretty decisively failed. The problem is what the price of constructing the next form of order will be since some form will certainly emerge.

Schlesinger answered him in kind:

> I entirely agree with you that Vietnam is not "the whole affair." Surely this admonition should be addressed to the administration, not to me! It is the administration which has brilliantly succeeded in locking up in Vietnam not only 40 per cent of our combat-ready divisions, more than 50 per cent of our air power and more than a third of our naval power but also our international reputation for political sanity and human decency. It is precisely because I believe that the Mediterranean—and Latin America—are a good deal more crucial to our security than Vietnam that I am against the Vietnam obsession. So long as we invest as much attention, talent, energy and armament in Vietnam as we are doing now, we inevitably invite problems in other parts of the world more vital to our national safety.[9]

The Tet offensive of early 1968 eroded some of Berle's confidence in himself and in the policy Johnson set. "I never felt less relevant," Berle wrote. "In most national crises I have had something to do. Here I don't because I don't know what ought to be advocated. The Vietnam war is going badly—of course, *we ought to get out but the problem is how to do it.*" He kept strangely silent concerning most of 1968's tumultuous developments. The Democratic campaign to succeed Johnson, the assassinations of Martin Luther King, Jr., and Robert Kennedy, and the election of Richard Nixon drew no comment from him. The seizures of buildings at Columbia by antiwar demonstrators sickened him and he was sure that they were directed from Moscow. On June 4 he was among the 500 university officials and guests who filled the Cathedral of St. John the Divine for Columbia's commencement amid "an atmosphere of tension" (they anticipated antiwar demonstrations) to see his old friend, David Dubinsky, receive an honorary degree. Historian Richard Hofstadter delivered the commencement address and afterwards Berle wrote on the cover of the program, "Dick Hofstadter made a bad speech. Affirmation not apology is called for when attack is made."

Actually, Hofstadter had affirmed the university "committed to certain basic values of freedom, rationality, inquiry, discussion, and to its own internal order . . . because in this age of rather overwhelming organizations and collectivities, the university is singular in being a collectivity that serves as a citadel of intellectual individualism." Hofstadter had eloquently asserted the principle that a university should be free from all political intimidation; Berle could not have complained against his defense of liberal inquiry. However, Hofstadter attributed the current siege against the university to "the escalation of this cruel and misconceived venture in Vietnam [which] has done more than any other thing to inflame our students, to undermine their belief in the legitimacy of our normal political processes, and to convince them that violence is the order of the day. I share their horror at this war, and I consider that the deep alienation it has inflicted on young Americans who would otherwise be well disposed toward their country is one of the staggering unaccountable costs of the Vietnam undertaking." While young radicals did not want to hear Hofstadter's defense of their iniquitous university, that old radical, Adolf Berle, demanded an affirmation of the war that stirred their fear and loathing.[10]

The campus no longer gave Berle intellectual solace. In the spring of 1969 he vituperatively described an antiwar strike at Harvard as directed by "a small group of organizers working primarily as political warfare agents for Maoist Communism." In a speech at Teachers College, Columbia, he charged that campus demonstrations were the conspiracies of Maoist and Trotskyite students and their "allies in the American intellectual community." This liberal intellectual no longer liked liberals or intellectuals. In 1970 more campus disruptions shook America, one of them forcing cancellation of a speech Berle was to make at a State University of New York campus. "I am more unhappy about the state of the world," he told his diary.[11]

While he did not comment upon Richard Nixon's election as president, he took apparent satisfaction from the fact that Nixon solicited foreign policy advice from Nelson Rockefeller and made Rockefeller's éminence grise, Henry Kissinger, his adviser on national security affairs. Berle rushed forward with his own advice for Kissinger on Latin America, calling for cooperation in the hemisphere on defense and economics. While no country should have communism imposed upon it, he said, the "social structure of every Latin American country is its own affair. If the people of a country decide to be Communist, that is their business." This, of course, was consistent with his old faith in self-determination, for he was certain that no country would opt willingly for communism. Where it existed, communism had to be, as in Cuba—or Vietnam—imposed from outside. A year later he agreed with Nelson Rockefeller "that governments actually there and in power ought to be recognized whether we like them or not." Self-determination still burned strong in the heart of Adolf Berle. But the United States never would recognize Castro even as it recognized Somoza.[12]

THE BEST CLUB

Perhaps nothing else during these troubled times gave Berle more satisfaction than his chairmanship of the Board of Trustees of the Twentieth Century Fund. He saw in the Fund his last great quest to be a powerful braintruster—a "causative" intellectual making history, with its trustees as his own select band of intellectual adventurers and aristocrats. Although he came to the TCF when it was already mature, Berle shaped its work to reflect his interests. In it he sought to "influence American development toward a more effectively just civilization" and influence America's policy toward the world; but the Fund for him took on increasing cosmic importance when he sought to convert it into a vehicle for discovering the essence of power itself.

Founded in 1919 as the Cooperative League by a triumvirate of Wilsonian liberal New England businessmen—E. A. Filene, Henry S. Dennison, and John Fahey—it sought to humanize international liberal capitalism through grants to community organizations. With Filene's department store wealth, idealism, and leadership, the Fund gave initial grants to the League of Women Voters, credit unions, the International Labour Office, and to Bryn Mawr College to study "industrial history and labor development." As Berle chronicled it, "even in its earliest days the Fund required an intellectual as well as ameliorative approach." However, its goals shifted when in 1928 Filene made Evans Clark, a *New York Times* writer with a scholarly interest in economic subjects, its executive director. Clark wanted to study economic development and publish significant findings. Filene, who was president of the Fund until he died in 1937, was tolerantly skeptical toward intellectuals. Preferring the Fund's "next steps forward" to be more ameliorative work, Filene agreed that "whatever problems the Board of Trustees sees fit to study and to grant money for research in—is all right with me. But I want to get those facts out to the people—I want our work to have an impact. We don't want a lot of books put out to stand and gather dust on library shelves. We want to help people *act,* to help them solve problems in a democratic way." He preferred intelligent self-determination to external intellectual manipulation.[1]

However, the scholarly approach pretty well defines the Fund's work today and makes it unique among foundations—most of which did not then exist. It employs social scientists and journalists to study social concerns and disseminate their findings. The director administers its projects but, unlike most other foundations, the director and his staff do not initiate them alone. Principally because of Berle, TCF trustees are expected to be intellectually and socially involved. In his day they competed to be the Fund's policymakers. Since its low eight-figure endowment could not support the massive projects of the Rockefeller and Ford Foundations, the TCF, with Berle leading the way, aimed to become the brain trust among foundations. He constituted its Board of Trustees as an informal think tank before there were formal think tanks. It sought studies that would be "causative"—having an impact upon other policymakers and policy. Although the trustees and Berle liked to think that they explored problems of the future not yet imagined by businessmen and politicians, most of the time they tackled contemporary concerns, struggling to keep one step ahead of the rest of the policy-making crowd.

The TCF did little publishing prior to the New Deal. Berle later claimed that the New Deal inspired the "intellectualization of politics," thereby making the Fund's studies important to Washington in such areas as the regulation of capital markets. The TCF proved that scholarship could be causative and that scholars could be practical fellows. Berle himself was evidence of this and certainly his presence in the New Deal's brain trust facilitated the Fund's earliest interest in him. First contacted by the Fund in December 1932, concerning projects that could "influence business and government policies," Berle signed on in 1934 as a member of a Fund committee investigating "the effects of large corporations on American economic life"—a "task force" before the term found widespread usage. Berle quickly manifested a passion for putting social science inquiry into the largest humanistic dimensions possible, once complaining that the committee's project director may be the best statistician and classical economist available, but the task force really required "an imaginative philosopher." Months later the trustees invited Berle to become one of their number. He remained a member until his death.[2]

The TCF's three founders were still decisive voices in its activities, along with Newton D. Baker, Woodrow Wilson's secretary of war; writer Bruce Bliven; James G. McDonald, chairman of the board of the Foreign Policy Association; and Roscoe Pound, dean of the Harvard Law School. Liberal lawyers, journalists, and academics dominated the board—politicians and businessmen having little time for its wide-ranging activities. A trustee was expected to look upon its meetings as an intellectually stimulating and significant civic duty. The trustees (Berle made it a board of eight; it grew to twenty-two), he later pontificated, had to have broad philosophical outlooks as they "were chosen because they were aware of and sensitive to social problems—the very problems likely to become 'issues' in campaigns, or to precipitate crises in government operations." Of course, nobody savored board meetings as much as did Berle. David E. Lilienthal enjoyed the intellectual bantering of his fellow trustees, but sometimes wondered "whether the time could not be better spent in some other way"; there was "something college facultyish" about their activity. Yet in these sessions Berle expected the trustees to compete with him as intellectual dilettantes and social prophets who integrated the life of the mind with their secular leadership. And for most of them, including Lilienthal, it was enjoyable and rewarding.[3]

In almost any collective, Berle was a powerful if not a dominant voice. Upon his return from Brazil in 1946, he was even more determined to pursue the "causative" ideas the Fund propounded. At the time the trustees were in their periodic quandary as to the Fund's purpose and direction, a circumstance made to order for Berle's leadership. Thus, in late 1948 the trustees debated an updated declaration of its mission, which began:

> The basic aim of the Twentieth Century Fund is to promote higher living standards, more security and greater freedom for the people of the United States and of the world, primarily through improvements in the economic and social order. The Fund's approach is that of the social engineer who assembles and considers all the available information on a problem and then makes the best possible plan for action that time permits.

His colleagues were well-suited to Berle's kind of "intellectual adventuring." "We should put our money where no one else will go," declared sociologist Robert S. Lynd, and seconded by former attorney general Francis Biddle. (Both men had been nominated for the board in 1937 by Berle.) As one of the "few pools of free money," the Fund had an obligation to study why the United States with all its wealth had "failed so lamentably" to meet the needs of its population, Lynd maintained. Berle, who frequently competed with Lynd in demanding "intellectual risk-taking," was not then about to turn down a radical study.

As part of America's policy establishment, the trustees could not decide whether they should be principally communicating with other elites or the masses. During the war they had sponsored six books by Stuart Chase, a journalist who specialized in popularizing economics. His books sold so well as to raise some questions about their scholarliness. In 1947 the Fund again attracted considerable attention with the publication of *America's Needs and Resources*, a study directed by economist J. Frederic Dewhurst. In later years Berle liked to believe that the Fund facilitated the study of economics "on its way to becoming a true science," but Lynd charged—

unfairly, even he conceded—that subjects were being chosen "on the basis of possible book sales." While the trustees agreed that they wanted to plan from above, at issue was what should be planned, how to do it, and who to tell.[4]

In November 1950, upon the death of John Fahey, the trustees elected Berle their chairman, a position he held until he died two decades later. In 1952 Berle put his universalist stamp on the Fund's operations. Arguing that the TCF's pioneering work in economics research had been "well plowed" by larger foundations, Berle proclaimed that "the failure of the twentieth century to establish any great hypothesis comparable to the theories of Adam Smith and Marx" now challenged the Fund. Of course, that was Berle's personal intellectual mission, but he had nominated trustees who could discuss it with him. They now included new trustees such as David E. Lilienthal, atomic physicist J. Robert Oppenheimer, and New Dealer Benjamin Cohen—liberal braintrusters who shared Berle's grand vision. Although Lilienthal doubted that "large amounts of money [could] buy ideas," he too wanted studies less devoted to "facts" and more global in their concern for the "deeper relevance [of] what kind of a society we now have" and anticipating "new directions."[5]

Berle disliked specialization in the social sciences. Sociology was for him a gobbledygook of data that merely buttressed obvious or bland generalizations. Political science was "a kind of a curious bastard thing now with the whole study of the way election opinions are made and polls and this sort of thing." Lacking a "theory to prove or disprove," political scientists were "really thinking primarily in the technique of political process and not in any abstract thinking at all." Without a synthesis "this technique is going nowhere." On the other hand, historians were bound by the "sheer paralysis" of a tradition "that an accurate tale, well told, is an end in itself, and the fact that it signifies nothing is no cause for complaint. My own guess would be that the historians furnish, in large measure, the raw material and case material making possible the construction of Political Science." Berle blamed both political scientists and historians for skirting a synthesis that might inform their particularist studies. However, his attack on the social sciences brought Berle into conflict with the TCF's director, Evans Clark.

Soon after his installation as chairman, Berle asserted that social science research was important of course, but he wanted the Fund to do something of even greater universal significance. In particular, he demanded that the Fund support the work of political theorist Franz Neumann in writing a book on the nature of power and political institutions. Neumann was the author of *Behemoth: The Structure and Practice of National Socialism* (1942), a refugee from Nazi Germany who studied social democracy and totalitarianism. Neumann's Institute of Social Research, affiliated with Columbia, "had set itself the task of elaborating a theoretical conception which was capable of comprehending the economic, political, and cultural institutions of modern society as a specific historical structure from which the *prospective* trends of development could be derived.'' The endeavor to anticipate political trends and guide them also dovetailed with Berle's fascination with Gaston Berger and the French *Prospective* school of philosophy. For Neumann, political theory was, in the words of Herbert Marcuse, "an indispensable weapon in the struggle for a better world." Berle heartily agreed.[6]

But Clark, believing that "a book by an outsider in the realm of political theory was very far indeed from the kind of factual research by Fund staffs on national problems which is the Fund's purpose and its well-tested function," and having devoted twenty-three years of his life to the Fund's empirical work, vehemently opposed the Neumann project. It was "highly speculative in nature," Clark argued, and "seriously threatens the Fund's future" by sowing "confusion and hard feeling" among the trustees. Clark invoked the hallowed memory of "E. A." [Filene], reminding Berle that the Fund believed in documentation and practical goals for its projects. Clark and Berle "were at swords' point" and an aide to the director accused the chairman of being "irresponsible."[7] Although Robert Lynd thought Neumann was "the most sophisticated social scientist I know," Clark and the staff prevailed, the trustees deciding that such work was too "vague and fuzzy." When Dennison, the last of the founding fathers, died in 1952, Clark abdicated the directorship for a place on the Board of Trustees. He was succeeded by J. Frederic Dewhurst, who had been the Fund's economist since 1933. Dewhurst lasted for only a year and was followed as director by August Heckscher, a Berle acolyte.[8]

Berle pressed his argument in 1953. Praising its past intellectual efforts, he questioned whether the TCF's current projects had "any discernible causative effect" or merely defined "the problems of yesterday." While the Fund's passion for economic studies was praiseworthy, modern economics did not lack academics, government agencies, and private institutions to study it. Rather, the Fund should attempt "great hypotheses in economics or in social organization" and commission someone to describe the "order or design in the cosmos." From the Fund's staff came a riposte that obviously the person best able to articulate the great hypothesis desired by Berle was Berle himself.[9]

At issue here was the nature, use, and impact of Fund studies. While the Fund studied the pluralism of American society, Berle wanted corporate planning by an elite to guide the society along lines described by Fund policymakers. He wanted to make political results. For instance, Berle pointed with pride to special research on problems such as studies of the securities market in 1935 or the economy of Turkey in 1949 which influenced government policies. Did the Fund's output point to a usable synthesis? A special committee of trustees consisting of Ben Cohen, architect Wallace Harrison, and New York *Herald Tribune* editorial writer August Heckscher investigated the question and its report, composed by Heckscher, noted that the Fund's studies indeed articulated a central theme, i.e., "The workability of capitalism; the scope of intelligent foresight in dealing with economic resources; the international character of the economy; the underlying similarity of interest between capital and labor." Thus, fund studies affirmed liberalism's "inarticulate premises."

However, speaking for the TCF's empiricists, Fred Dewhurst doubted "whether the validity of these premises can be established by rigorous scientific tests." Robert Lynd joined in to insist that the Fund reconsider "the assumptions of the liberal tradition" that buttressed the Fund's work and reevaluate "the historial doctrine of pluralism in democracy as to its relevance to contemporary wide differences in size and resources of organized interest groups; and, related to the preceding, an analysis of present systems of political representation in terms of their adequacy for the needs of our present mass society." Lynd agreed with Berle on the need for big questions, but the thrust of his queries tested Berle's liberal assumptions. At a 1954 trustees meeting, Robert Oppenheimer tried to dichotomize the debate into a "search for basic truths" versus a "search for solutions," insisting that only "inter-disciplinary studies can be useful for certain purposes, but will not produce a theory of society." Berle brushed aside Oppenheimer's charge that his quest for a synthesis was at cross purposes with the Fund's historical work, asserting that the board had recognized "the need for bold thinking and the large and significant project." Later in the 1950s the TCF would support Calvin B. Hoover's theoretical study, *The Economy, Liberty, and the State,* a book Berle deemed the "happiest" of TCF studies. Yet it is doubtful that Hoover's book wholly satisfied him. The ultimate book on power indeed awaited Berle's hand.[10]

Likening a trustees meeting to a Quaker meeting, Berle frequently would initiate discussion by intoning that he had "a concern." Since his principal concern was for "some generalization which, even if tentative, would stimulate new theories toward new action," in late 1960 the trustees acquiesced and voted $10,000 toward discovering a modern de Tocqueville who could describe a twentieth-century consensus. It is not clear what, if anything, became of that search.[11]

All of the trustees had pet concerns which they promoted with appeals to their colleagues' hearts as well as intellects. These appeals constantly raised the question of how the Fund should be spending its money. It was an old debate at the TCF. Should it continue its scholarly course? No, said attorney Robert Szold, former counsel for Filene, the Fund, and now vice-president of the Good Will Fund, which also owed its existence to Filene money. Szold charged in 1960 that the trustees had distorted Filene's original ameliorative purpose for the Fund: "The Fund became exactly what E. A. had tried to avoid—a book publisher." Books were alright if they dealt with local concerns such as uses of pension funds and group health insurance, not academic concerns such as the political problems of Greece and Brazil. (However, Szold may have had a personal grievance against Berle and the Fund that went back to the Trustees' refusal to subscribe money and collaborate with the Good Will Fund on projects it deemed socially useful.) Legally, the trustees could spend TCF money anyway they saw fit to do so. Ethically, they had to interpret Filene's legacy, whether it was ameliorative as Szold interpreted it, empirical as Clark wanted it, or prophetic as Berle sought it.[12]

Their concerns changed with the times. In the 1930s and 1940s the Twentieth Century Fund did timely studies on the American political economy. However, the cold war brought an additional focus on defense and international concerns. The TCF published studies on modern Greece, Turkey, Brazil, Costa Rica, and Honduras (it is not difficult to discern Berle's influence here). Otherwise, the books on the stock exchanges, antitrust policies, and fiscal policy brought old concerns up to date. The 1960s saw more books on areas overseas—Western Europe, Latin America, Africa, and Asia. But the TCF also became more eclectic, publishing a book on urban America, leisure time, nuclear power, arms reduction, farm problems, American poverty, legislative reapportionment, crime, and finally, in 1966, its first work on race in American life.[13]

The projects reflected the trustees' worldview. By tradition, Filene, Berle, and their fellow trustees were committed planners. The Fund's postwar milestone, *America's Needs and Resources,* was a rebuttal to a post–New Deal reaction against planning and left wing forecasts of capitalist chaos. Even though Berle maintained that they took no positions "on the doctrinal side," they were left-liberals. In 1949 Berle pushed for a Fund study of British socialist economic planning because he expected it to show Americans how the British example might be emulated.

Berle did not always prevail in debates, but he usually persisted and won his point. Thus, when the Fund rejected a proposal to study the Costa Rican economy, Berle revived it with a plea that "it would be tragic" not to undertake "a pilot survey of first importance"; the board unanimously reversed itself. However, when Berle tried in 1951 to get TCF publication of a Stuart Chase book on Puerto Rico, several trustees brought him up short by pointing out that Chase seldom lacked a publisher. Berle was surprisingly weak on economic topics because he did not keep abreast of the literature of economics and was not "enough of a technician in the field" to judge modern econometric proposals. "Who in the world knows about this?" he once asked Evans Clark in 1953. "Wesley Mitchell is dead." In 1960 economist Arthur Burns dismissed a proposal depicting twenty-first-century economics which Berle liked very much as "fantasy."

Of course, Berle was not the only special pleader in the TCF. When Ben Cohen and Charles Taft pushed for a study of the American middle class, sociologist Robert Lynd killed it by disdainfully denouncing it as "primarily a journalistic effort rather than a scientific study." The trustees craved relevance, searching for "wide-angle approaches" that anticipated future concerns, rather than familiar issues that had been "talked to death." Thus, Robert Oppenheimer pushed for disarmament, August Heckscher for leisure time, Ben Cohen for desegregation of Southern schools. But it was easier to discover a timely issue than to find "the right man" to study it.[14]

They seldom kept far ahead of public concerns and the crises of the 1960s exploded upon a Twentieth Century Fund struggling to be current. Racial problems had seemed distant from the Fund's headquarters on fashionable East 70th Street, but early in the decade the trustees supported a proposal by a young Columbia law professor Michael Sovern, to study discrimination in hiring and listened, with some misgivings, to a new trustee from Atlanta, Morris Abram, advocate an examination of the economic costs of racial discrimination to the South. Although they rejected a 1962 proposal for a study of violence and nonviolence in America, they were impressed with the would-be project director, Staughton Lynd. In 1964 J. K. Galbraith campaigned for a study of unemployment, James P. Mitchell promoted "an examination of the Negro problem in its entirety," and Robert Oppenheimer wondered why the Fund had not studied the institution of the press. They turned down Henry Kissinger's request for a grant to write a book on changing theories of international relations because he "probably would not have difficulty in getting it financed elsewhere." As the Vietnam War escalated through 1965–1966, the board endorsed a proposal to study American policy in Southeast Asia since 1945, Galbraith voting against it because he had "reservations about the kind of policy recommendations the study might produce." In 1967 the trustees considered a conference to study "Extremism and the Nation's Electorate." Campus demonstrations had made them apprehensive that they were out of touch with youth; Berle and Galbraith urged the staff to find younger project directors. Galbraith and Rowe wanted the staff to tell the project director of a study of the military "to bring into the study people not connected with the Establishment." In 1968 the board voted $25,000 "for explorations by the staff in two areas: ways of establishing communication with young scholars, especially those outside of major universities; and ways of helping Negroes to take constructive steps toward establishing their racial identity." Within two weeks Martin Luther King's assassination gave the latter greater urgency and brought forth a proposal for a "Black Academy of Arts and Letters." The trustees applauded it, the only caveat coming from Jim Rowe who suspected that the Academy would not escape control by "militants." He need not have worried. They voted $50,000 to establish the Academy, providing that the Fund's contribution would decline after two years and then, in Berle's words, it would "travel independently." Soon the Academy was launched on an undistinguished career and years later the TCF's director would wonder what had become of it.[15]

Many of the proposals of the late 1960s fell into the always dreaded "frothy," "glib," or "superficial" categories so that board discussions grew more vituperative. A proposal recommended by the staff to study "American Corporatism" was attacked by Berle as "impressionistic" and by Ben Cohen as "abstract and jargon-ridden." Only Hodding Carter III made a case for the radical study, pointing out that "if jargon-filled prose were the criterion for rejecting a proposal, he would have voted against several of the preceding proposals." At Galbraith's urgings not to "close its doors to radical scholars," the TCF voted to support a study of "Capitalism and Underdevelopment in India and Pakistan" by Marxist economists. Berle endorsed the study for its scholarly merits, not its perspective. Yet, he was troubled by the shallowness of recent proposals. The trend suggested "that the present program forsook the deep approach, which is mostly appreciated by scholars, for the more general approach, which is more useful to the public." Berle's favored audience for Fund studies always was a policy-making aristocracy.[16]

Although the Fund in principle did not make grants to individuals for their research (it contracted their research), it did in fact make grants. Berle was a frequent proponent of special grants. Intellectuals were dearest to his heart, especially those intellectuals whose work he enjoyed and who now had no support. He wished to be, like a European prince of past centuries, a benefactor of geniuses in the arts and letters. Any trustee had discretion to advocate spending the TCF's money on almost anything and Chairman Berle made the most of his influence. In 1951 he brought to the Fund's attention the fact that declining enrollments at colleges and universities during the Korean War were leading to layoffs of young scholars with serious consequences posed for social science research. That year the Fund made special grants of $5,000 each to eighteen private liberal arts colleges, to be administered by the Social Science Research Council, which received $10,000 for its services. The grants advanced the research of, among others, Joseph H. Parks at Birmingham-Southern College, St. Clair Drake at Roosevelt College, and Kermit Gordon and James MacGregor Burns at Williams College.[17]

But Berle especially preferred elderly scholars. Thus, the French philosopher Jacques Maritain received a grant in 1955 so that "the old man does not starve to death in the streets of Paris or New York." Berle ridiculed any suggestion that such grants were not a legitimate activity for a Foundation and in 1964 it voted another grant to a terminally ill James T. Shotwell. But, when Arthur Schlesinger raised the possibility of a grant to Leon Henderson to aid the old New Dealer in getting his papers in order for the archives, or to improverished novelist James T. Farrell, Berle thought that "out of our usual beat" and the board ruled that "grants to individuals, except in the most exceptional cases, could not be justified as part of the Fund's program." Grants also went to Berle's favorite groups. The Fund decided in 1961 to sponsor a Conference with the Centre d'Etudes Prospectives of France, a French philosophical group of which Berle was the principal American adherent. By 1965, however, it tightened up policies and rejected two Berle requests for grants to the arts.[18] Certain institutions merited special attention. The New School for Social Research, the National Bureau of Economic Research, and the Lawyers' Committee for Civil Rights, were among those institutions qualifying for Fund grants. In 1967 the Fund, mindful of its tax-exempt status, initiated the practice of voluntary grants of $10,000 (later increased to $25,000) to the City of New York in honor of the municipal services that benefited it.[19]

By the 1960s almost all of the trustees owed their places on the board to a nomination by Berle. It was his intellectual salon where a couple of times a year about sixteen to twenty-two men of letters and power gathered to enjoy each other's intellectual company. "This particular group combines as wide a body of experience in public affairs and international matters as any group of similar size in the country," Berle told Adlai Stevenson upon inviting the two-time Democratic nominee for president to be a member in 1958 (he declined). "We like also to think that the Twentieth Century Board is the best club in America."[20] He celebrated its "best club" status; August Heckscher called it "a joke he liked to repeat; it had a serious meaning for him." Berle truly believed that the board combined intellectualism and power. Yet he suspected that "the best club" suffered from an excess of respectability that prevented it from assuming "the right side of some controversy." Nevertheless, he did little to lessen its respectability.[21]

As Berle told J. K. Galbraith in 1960, "It may not be wholly accidental that, in general, the Trustees represent not only the economic thinking of the Roosevelt Adminstration but many of the intellectuals who are active with Kennedy now. It is not, therefore, an ivory tower job." In 1963 he fairly gloated that the board "somehow succeeds in maintaining extrapolitical connections without really trying." Indeed, Berle was proud that most of its members were men who had enjoyed power or were tabbed as "not necessarily men who have made their mark, but those who have shown unusual promise." Galbraith and Morris Abram had been tabbed as men on the make who could bridge the gap between the New Deal and the New Frontier. Abram of Atlanta was known as a fighter for civil rights and against Georgia's beknighted county unit system, and knew he appealed to Berle "for precisely the reasons that I did not fit in the power centers of my own region." Indeed, Berle had great expectations for Abram. In 1965 an FBI man came to check with Berle on Abram, and Berle hoped it was for the purpose of a nomination for solicitor general: "If so, the Twentieth

Century Fund will keep up its reputation for connections with the United States government," he thought.[22]

The trustees esteemed themselves as "a remarkable group of men, as able and as diverse as you will find in a long day."[23] But the composition of the board was a persistent concern. It was too homogeneous. In 1950 Dennison had worried that it was "weak on businessmen," but Henry Ford II and Nelson Rockefeller had declined to join it. Few businessmen had either the time or the interest in its activities. Most politicians too were either not cerebral enough or could not find the time to attend meetings. When Berle became chairman in 1951, several vacancies on the board existed as a result of resignations by men such as Chester Bowles, Robert M. La Follette, Jr., and Paul G. Hoffman, who pleaded that they lacked the time. They were replaced by Lilienthal, Oppenheimer, Senator Paul Douglas (who resigned in 1953), businessmen Herman Steinkraus and Edmund Orgill, journalists Erwin Canham and August Heckscher, Rockefeller architect Wallace Harrison, and New Deal lawyer James Rowe. In 1957 its advancing age began causing unease on the board, and in 1958–1959 it added Abram, economist Arthur Burns, and historian Arthur Schlesinger, Jr. In 1963 the trustees elected to their numbers two Berle friends: editors George-Henri Martin of Geneva, Switzerland, and Lawrence Miller of Pittsfield, Massachusetts. In 1964–1965 it added Congressman Jonathan Bingham, academic Don Price, and the redoubtable Luis Muñoz Marín.[24]

Considerations of religion, race, geography, or gender seldom entered discussions of prospective trustees, although Berle admitted in 1956 that he was bothered by the fact "that there is not, so far as I know, a single Catholic on the Board." But religion was not important to "a bunch of free thinkers like us," he told a prominent Catholic.[25] In 1960 a trustee suggested inviting a woman to become a member, but nothing came of that for some years. In 1965 August Heckscher noted that the board lacked anyone from west of Cincinnati. More than ever the twenty-two trustees fretted about their advancing average age at a time when the president of the United States was younger than most of them and the country was decidedly youth conscious. Yet the elders disdained any voluntary retirement from the Board.[26] By 1968 they felt compelled to search for possible black and/or women members. Insisting that he himself "did not favor a Negro for the sake of getting a Negro or a woman just to get a woman," Berle nonetheless was "glad to recommend Patricia Roberts Harris, who just happened to be a Negro woman." (For her Berle omitted his usual reference to the board as a "club"; it was just a "company of intellectual adventurers.") Her nomination balanced that of liberal Mississippi newsman Hodding Carter III. When Berle pushed 55-year-old David B. Truman for the board, a few members wonderd what became of the youth movement.[27]

Besides influencing its choice of projects and trustees, Berle actively oversaw the Fund's financial operations and the selection of its directors. He had been its treasurer for three years prior to becoming chairman of the Board of Trustees. In the post he nurtured the Fund's portfolio—then largely 180,000 shares of Federated Stores common stock, the successor to Filene's Department Store. Beginning in the recession of 1949 the TCF began to diversify the portfolio in order to protect its income during bad times on Wall Street. Berle soon reported that the Fund may be "sailing so close to the wind" that the trustees would be obliged to draw on its capital. Although Filene had said in 1934 that as far as he was concerned the Fund could spend all its capital in pursuit of liberal goals, Berle and the trustees did not preside over their intellectual empire to liquidate it; they were determined to perpetuate the Twentieth Century Fund to the twenty-first century. Therefore, the board granted additional financial authority to Chairman Berle, Treasurer H. Christian Sonne, and Director Evans Clark while Standard and Poor's served as investment counsel. The sell-off of Federated proceeded apace and the Fund's capital grew from $9.5 million to $12 million during 1954–1955 and reached $25 million in 1961. The TCF entered the New York City real estate market when the Fund lost its lease on offices in the McGraw-Hill building, compelling it to buy and renovate a town house on East 70th Street for its headquarters.[28]

The director ran the daily affairs of the Fund and Berle put his stamp upon the post after Fred Dewhurst resigned. He wanted New York *Herald Tribune* editorial writer August Heckscher, a trustee since 1951 and a man who shared Berle's aristocratic passions for the arts, French philosophers, and liberalism—among other things. At first Heckscher was reluctant to leave the newspaper, but a change in publishers changed Heckscher's mind. However, could a trustee simultaneously be director? Clark did not become a trustee until he resigned as director and so Heckscher resigned as a trustee, but in 1960 the board decided there was no conflict of interest and invited Heckscher to be trustee again. Heckscher also maintained a lively involvement in the arts as a contributor to public television programming and as special consultant on the arts to President Kennedy. Early in 1967 Mayor John Lindsay of New York asked Heckscher to be his administrator on recreation and cultural affairs and commissioner of parks; again Berle searched for a director.[29]

Believing that a journalist was broad-gauged enough to be the TCF's director, Berle proffered it to Anthony Lewis of *The New York Times*—who declined it. However, *The Times'* editorial writer M. J. Rossant was receptive. What attracted Berle to Rossant were articles he had written on national economic policies and the discovery that Rossant had studied philosophy at Swarthmore which he followed with graduate work at the London School of Economics—a strong eclectic background. He did not mind it when Rossant stipulated that as director he would want partial control of Fund investment policies. However, "a difficulty" was introduced when

Arthur Schlesinger reported that the former chairman of President Johnson's Council of Economic Advisors, Walter Heller, had a "very low opinion" of some of the things Rossant had written. Berle dismissed that as normal tensions between government people and the press and pushed for Rossant's approval by the board.[30]

In a world where the second intellectual institution dearest to Berle's heart, Columbia University, was under attack, Berle could not countenance instability in the Twentieth Century Fund. Yet Rossant wanted to make changes and Berle wanted to show that he was amenable to them. Rossant recommended that the TCF become more aggressive in its investments because Wall Street wisdom considered its portfolio excessively cautious among foundations. Some of the trustees treated this as a slur on their handling of the portfolio, but Berle agreed that a growth-minded policy to keep pace with inflation was in order. Also, Rossant pressed to redirect the Fund's research through task force studies on contemporary social problems and retained Theodore Draper as a consultant. Then he proposed that instead of being its own publisher, the Fund should contract its studies with existing scholarly and commercial presses—thereby reaping royalties without the expenses of publishing. More than ever the Fund strayed from Berle's concept of developing a philosophy for the times.[31]

All of these changes generated controversy in Berle's club, but nothing like that engendered by Rossant's report in early 1970 appraising the changes during his three-year tenure. In the words of Augie Heckscher, it was a "tendentious and self-righteous attack on the leadership of the Fund"— meaning himself and Berle. Although recognition was given the fact that Rossant then labored under personal difficulties, trustees like Schlesinger pointed to Rossant's tone of "smug self-satisfaction" as disruptive of the Fund's collegiality. A committee of three trustees began to consider Rossant's removal, although Jim Rowe counseled proceeding with caution.[32]

Matters did not improve later in the year when Rossant opposed a grant to Heckscher on the grounds that legally a trustee could not be a project director. Also, an errant announcement that Rossant would be a consultant to a mutual fund set off another row among the trustees before Rossant assured them that it was all a mistake. It had to be unsettling to Berle that his most precious possession seemed to be getting away from him.[33]

THE FRUSTRATIONS OF *POWER* AND LIBERALISM

In the spring of 1966 the Columbia Law School announced the retirement of Adolf A. Berle. Berle had taught corporation law at Columbia, with time off for forays into government service, since 1927. He thought of Columbia as his "intellectual home," where he blended the study of law and the social sciences. Two years before, at sixty-eight, Columbia had tried to add an "emeritus" to his professorship, but then he had insisted upon continued teaching responsibilties. Now, however, the university's trustees applied their rules; he was past seventy, the mandatory retirement age. Columbia had already conferred an honorary degree upon him and the *Law Review* had dedicated an issue to him. It was a time of reflection for him. Uncertain about what remained intellectually and maudlin over the passing of an era, he nonetheless asserted he was without fear for his future. "It will not be difficult to fill up next year, so retirement does not mean the usual vegetation while waiting to die that it does for some men," he thought. Berle was giving up the first part of his triple life—"professor at Columbia, practitioner of law, and of foreign affairs." Activity was one thing and being causative was another. At seventy-two, "I can not expect any more rendezvous with history and can only take out my frustrations in writing books." But he was apprehensive that intellectually too he was beyond making a contribution. He knew that his "real problem is whether at this point one's thinking remains significant. There is always a sneaking fear that one has said everything one has to say."[1]

He had known the importance of being Berle. He wrote—it was not hard to find something to say; it was not hard to find a publisher—Harcourt, Brace if it was a book, *The Reporter* or *The New York Times Magazine* if it was an article. Always prolific, his output during the previous decade was tremendous—as if to demonstrate that time had not dulled his pen and that what he had to say was as original and timely as ever. He still had great energy and, though now afflicted with diabetes, he still chain-smoked and his health was relatively good. Except for his graying hair, his appearance, with his straight, spare frame, suggested a man who aged well. Of course, neither the need for money or activity compelled Berle to write. He had much to keep him busy: a law practice, membership on the Boards of Directors of Sucrest Corporation and Nationwide Insurance, a broad spectrum of political and social activity, and the chairmanship of the Board of Trustees of his beloved Twentieth Century Fund. But his writings were his personal monument, both in his time and in history. He mostly wrote about the economic changes that had occurred in his lifetime, but foreign affairs was never far from his mind. Berle addressed those concerns in the eight books and the dozens of articles that appeared under his name since 1955.

Economic power had not changed since Berle and Means had described it in 1932. In his writings of the 1960s, Berle restated himself with an acuity of perspective as well as an ease and grace of expression that gave his essays on economic power a freshness that cloaked any repetition. (He even brought out a revised edition of *The Modern Corporation and Private Property* in 1968.) His arguments were not new, just restated with updated data; now his tone was affirming, if not downright celebratory. Although economic power probably transformed itself from concentration to diffusion, the basic issue of control remained. No longer 200, now 500 or 600 corporations owned about two-thirds of the country's assets, fulfilling his prophecy of increasing concentration and making the control of those corporations a continuing concern. Although Berle considered corporate managers a "self-perpetuating oligarchy," because he was more confident of management's increasing awareness of its social responsibility, he was optimistic about the future of economic democracy in a capitalist society.[2] Also, the income tax was "a steady force eroding this concentration" of wealth; "the American economic republic, though it has not socialized wealth, has gone a substantial distance toward socializing income." Real ownership of the corporation had evolved into the hands of broadly subscribed pension funds which were "'socializing' property without a revolution," thereby creating a real "peoples' capitalism." Moreover, American pluralism was stronger than ever and corporation managers deferred to the "spiritual" authority of law, seeking legitimacy, responsibility, and accountability for their temporal power from the public. Finally, although the rhetoric of freedom and individualism governed American lives, their economic collectives (corporations) bowed to federal planning through regulation. Paradoxically, the system had tendencies to both concentration and democratization. Berle's apocalyptic perspective of 1932 seemed to have given way to an apologia in the 1950s. He seemed more embarrassed by reminders of his "alarmist" attitudes of 1932 than by his current euphoria.[3]

He had not graduated to Pollyanna status, but he had a need now to affirm what his generation had accomplished. After all, he wrote, "Age has one privilege: while preoccupied with the troubles of the moment, one can look back and see how far we have come." The New Deal had saved American capitalism. Unlike Tugwell, Berle did not call it "Roosevelt's Revolution." Great change had occurred, but it could not have been a revolution because it sought to preserve essentials; it sought better management and leadership of an economy that had been poorly managed. Amid the turmoil and uncertainty that racked America during his eighth decade, Berle wanted succeeding generations to appreciate that his generation had made technical adjustments to correct old problems that resulted from free markets shibboleths. "We New Dealers, Keynesians, and social economists got the country started towards a way of unexampled prosperity and more distribution than any society has ever known," he wrote an old friend. "We do not readily accept the thesis that all this is rotten and ought to be destroyed—especially when the talk comes from the principal beneficiaries of our work. We know it is not perfect and that the conquest of poverty and distress, now limited more or less to 15% of the population, can be achieved, but not by wrecking the productive machinery of the country." He could not join a "chorus of despair" because he fervently believed that America's resources exceeded its problems.[4]

However, his optimism for American economic power was offset by his morbidity on the prospects for sustainting America's global political power. The Kremlin was an implacable foe bent upon world domination through subversion, conquest, and totalitarianism. Once Berle had been confident that America's ideological system, if properly explained by Berle the social prophet, would overwhelm European imperialism or totalitarianism. But relentless Soviet imperialism and its successful penetration of the western hemisphere shook him. Added to that was the fact that Americans had failed to appreciate the importance of the Good Neighbor Policy and what it meant to sustain an American system. Too few Americans recognized that "the Communist power bloc intends the destruction of the United States" through its activities in the Americas. Only he knew how both American indifference and Castro had undermined the American hemispheric system that prevailed between 1933 and 1947. Yet, as he came to realize that, not only was the system moribund but so was hope for its revival, Berle became more anxious for a stand somewhere against Communist aggression; the failure at the Bay of Pigs made the fight for Vietnam more supportable.[5]

The enormous dissent over Vietnam shook his confidence in liberals and intellectuals; nobody but Berle and his cohorts understood the seriousness of the global threat. A persistent theme of his during 1951–1971 was the inability of Westerners, especially Americans, to philosophically understand power. Americans had fashioned an empire without truly comprehending it. Power for Americans was elusively intangible. Paradoxically, elites understood power but needed to have it explained, which was why Berle attempted through the Twentieth Century Fund to subsidize a political theorist to develop a synthesis of power that could be understood by intellectuals. Thus, he asserted power in the Fund in order to describe and explain it to all informed people. Alas, not even the men of the Best Club appreciated its significance. Even if the task had been conferred upon Franz Neumann, that would not have satisfied Berle, any more than the Calvin Hoover book satisfied him. Interpreting power was his concern, his mission, his destiny. With political power closed to him, only the vastness and complexity of the project excited Berle—even as it daunted him. He always wrote about it. *The Modern Corporation and Private Property* had been about economic power, social power, and political power. In 1954 he updated its themes of corporate power in a book based upon lectures entitled *The 20th Century Capitalist Revolution*. (Its title must have been the inspiration of its publisher because Berle felt it was inaccurate.) Berle was an essayist and tended to be preachy and didactic without much leavening humor, but in 1959 he published *Power Without Property: A New Development in American Political Economy,* probably the best thing he had done since *The Modern Corporation*. It is a relatively brief book of less than 200 pages, marked by some of the best writing of his late period. The ideas are sharply etched, and while they are not new to readers of Berle, they are presented with a lawyerly directness of argument free from the poetic flights he sometimes took. In many ways it was the ultimate book on power he had sought in meetings of the Twentieth Century Fund trustees. However, probably because it dealt primarily with economic power, it did not satisfy Berle. He lusted for a big philosophical, comprehensive tome on power to crown his career.

He began a book on power early in 1960, "but made heavy weather of it." He put it aside and did not return to the project until after he witnessed again first-hand the frustrations of power with Kennedy. Setting for himself the goals of being the Plato and the Machiavelli of his era, he was both awed and enthralled by the task.[6]

He spoke of writing this great book as if he had never written about power before; of course, it was his obsession. Writing articles for *The New York Times Magazine* analyzing the concentration or diffusion of American economic power was almost second nature to him.[7] His fame as a New Deal braintruster gave him an authority for those articles and he also capitalized on his credentials as chairman of Kennedy's task force on Latin America with writings on the hemispheric struggle. In 1962 he simultaneously attempted two books: one on American power in Latin America and the other on the American economic power system. The respectful critical response to the first pleased him. But the writing of the second was arduous and required heavy editing ("1 have never had a manuscript edited before"). Writing both for posterity and his contemporaries, vanity made him an eager reader of his reviews. His friend, Charles Poore, the daily critic of *The New York Times,* celebrated this book as he did with each new book of his, but Berle's own trepidations concerning *The American Economic Republic* were confirmed when Harvard economist Seymour Harris expressed reservations in *The New York Times Book Review.* Berle attributed its "moderate success with the usual 10,000–15,000 copies" to the fact that his "optimism is not popular this year." He wondered if he had anything new to contribute to the world of ideas, if he could ever write that great tome on power.[8]

Still, he swallowed his disappointment over the cool reception for *The American Economic Republic* when his editor, William Jovanovich, encouraged him to write that major work on power. But it was arduous and Berle lamented that he was "continuously finding difficulty in making such ideas as I have on the point stand up, arrange themselves in squads and march in decent formation." In other words, he had difficulty with organization, even brevity. Of course, the key to Berle's amorphous project was his definition of power itself; could he define it differently from the way he already had? Now he murkily depicted power as something "elementary" which "shares with love the distinction of being the oldest emotional force in the history of man." The nebulousness of his thinking was revealed in a published essay that began, "Power is elusive. It is at once absolutely necessary and absolutely feared. By turns it is deified and damned." How could he write a book about power when he defined it as elusive?⁹

At this stage of his life the easy way out would have been to write an autobiography or his memoirs that by concrete example suggested a definition and description of power through his associations with Roosevelt, La Guardia, and other powerful figures—thereby also assuring himself a place in the literature of the New Deal as his old brain trust comrade Rexford Tugwell did in several books on his few years with Roosevelt. However, as Berle told Tugwell, not only did he "vaguely feel it would be better if someone else writes about us than if we write about ourselves," but he was "not yet ready to be ticketed and laid away" without endeavoring to make more history through his writings. Additionally, he rejected a plea from Tugwell's biographer, Bernard Sternsher, to cooperate on a Berle biography, and advised Arthur Schlesinger, Jr., that "there is too much going on now to live in the past." Never one to run away from his history, Berle seemed afraid of something in his past. His ideas on foreign policy and other things had changed, even if he seemed to rewrite the same book on economic and political power. Once, preparing for a visit from a biographer of La Guardia, he sifted through passages from his diaries and later he disgustedly wrote, "As I look at them and myself in them, I do not particularly like that young man." But he did not say what it was in that young man that offended him. He just refused to write about him, except for generalizations. And, only after he wrote his epic work on power did he consider editing and publishing his diary.¹⁰

He had begun to doubt the value of intellectual activity. In 1960 he left a Twentieth Century Fund meeting that discussed proposed projects "worried about this institution; despite the brilliance of conversation, I am wondering whether the research is not getting to be a bit sterile." Aside from the never-ending pursuit of his destiny, another motivation for writing a book on power was that the state of intellectuals in the mid-sixties depressed him. Because he believed that they did not comprehend the facets of American power, he accused intellectuals of contributing to national disintegration in the mid-1960s by "fooling around with any kind of authoritarianism which presents itself" rather than offering the moral leadership needed by a democracy. Amid what Berle considered decay, "We have no doctrine of power which could be interposed instead—assuming we would want to do it." So he would offer one, if he could.

Again he launched his mission in 1964, and again he brooded about whether he could really write an essay "in which theory, fact and forecast must be mingled in about equal degree." He was "having the deuce of a time" trying to avert getting "lost in several cognate labrinthes" and "to keep it choate on one track and incisive enough so that it does not fall away in a 'large demonstration of words.'" His first duty was to clarity and he agonized over whether he simultaneously could "write a poem, a novel, a study in psychology, a study in political science and a study in history." At the same time he wrote a sixtieth anniversary history of The Twentieth Century Fund, *Leaning Against the Dawn,* a hymn of praise for his fellow "argonauts" on the Board of Trustees. It was a poetic history, Berle injecting the most florid prose he was capable of: "So there will always be adventurous groups of men who seek not only to relieve present evils but also to foresee future perils, searching out ways to prevent their arising, or in any case conquer them when they appear. In longer vision, men will carry on the work of discovering intellectual tools and philosophic principles, in the hope of enlarging the capacity of generations yet unborn to confront conditions and dangers no dawn has yet revealed."

That out of the way, his book on power would be his last great adventure. Could he be Goethe, Machiavelli, and Max Weber all rolled into Berle? "But unless that is done, the job is not well done." He could not compromise intellectually because it "ought to be a classic or not written." So he persisted through 1967, consoling himself that it was "a difficult book to finish." His moods toward it alternately soared ("I am sure [it] will be a classic to end all classics") and soured ("I am sorry—I should like to get the damn thing into print.") He feared failure. "In my own intellectual adventures, attempt to impress one's trade-mark on the product is a limiting and paralyzing process," he once told the head of the Rockefeller Foundation; and he added, "Failure to have it impressed is, of course, maddening; but one gets over that." He did not get over failure, but he pressed on anyway, sustained both by his courage and ego. Long ago he had discovered that writing may bring disappointment, but it was better to confront an audience than be silent. Perhaps the frustrations of his father made him push on. Perhaps the compulsiveness of grandfather Wright kept him writing in the twilight of his life. He apologized to himself for the delay because time was running out on him. In late 1969 it came out in print.[11]

With it he realized his worst fears. "It is scarcely possible to deny that *Power* has not been a resounding success," he conceded. *The New York Times Book Review* put it in the hands of a young political science professor at Smith College, Philip Green, who used the book as a touchstone for how corporate liberalism fared in times when a "new left" was ascendant. Anticipating a vigorous defense of corporate liberalism by one of its leading exponents—a "public servant and political economist extraordinary, who more than any other American has attempted to perform the task of demythifying the old pre-New Deal order and rationalizing its successor . . . with a series of what were once, at least, startling propositions"—Green professed disappointment in *Power.* It was "self-indulgent, . . . bloated, twice as long as it ought to be, marred by pointless pseudo-platonic dialogues among Greek gods, by diatribes against potential political opponents and by constant reference to anecdote or sheer personal prejudice to illustrate broad historical and theoretical statements that require considerably more than that in way of validation." Green was essentially correct. It had 568 pages of text alone; it was diffuse, rambling, and inconsistent—lacking in the tightness that had made *Power Without Property* a real gem, even if it was Berle updated. But, as Green observed, Berle on economic power was at his "analytical best." However, Berle's discussion of political power was "mostly sophisticated gossip" that gave "little direction to our thinking." The "classic" was an unwieldy mélange of his old ideas and his current trepidations. Chastised by this penultimate effort and experience, on his seventy-fifth birthday Adolf Berle pondered "what to do with an obviously diminuendo in range of possibilities not to mention energy and activities during [my] remaining active years."[12]

He always had tried to make his future more exciting than his past, but in the 1960s the public was more curious about his past. More than three decades after the fact he was still "a business theorist" and a braintruster for Franklin Delano Roosevelt and the New Deal. It was his fame. If he would be remembered for anything, it was for what he did in 1932. Every so often a reporter called upon him at his Wall Street office at 70 Pine Street to find out how the world looked to an old New Dealer. Berle enjoyed the attention, although he was uneasy about interviews sounding "like an obituary. I don't feel in the least funereal." Nonetheless, his life took an elegiac tone. On the anniversary of FDR's eightieth birthday he found himself with Sam Rosenman and Rexford Tugwell reminiscing on television about when they dreamed the New Deal thirty years before. Later that year Eleanor Roosevelt died and he shared a pew at Hyde Park with Henry Wallace, Jim Farley, and Henry Morgenthau, all of them old and white-haired, "visibly going over the horizon line which divides politics and history."

He was history. His adventures were not in politics but at the Twentieth Century Fund and in his writings. He enjoyed being revered for his history; it suggested he had been causative after all. Many things gave him great gratification. He was a principal speaker at Montreal to commemorate the twentieth anniversary of the International Civil Aviation Organization, of which he was a founder as president of the Chicago conference of 1944. The election of his tall, handsome son Peter, an attorney in Manhattan, to the New York State Assembly as a Democrat in 1970 was an accomplishment he could not equal. Within days of that triumph, Berle announced at a Board of Trustees meeting of the Twentieth Century Fund that he would resign the following year after thirty-six years as a member and nearly twenty as its chairman. Then, almost on cue, Ben Cohen nominated Peter Berle for a board vacancy, remarking that given the younger Berle's achievements, his relationship to the chairman "could hardly be held against him." With a quick second from Arthur Schlesinger, that motion was approved unanimously and Berle thanked the trustees, beaming as he commented that "hereditary associations are supposed to be bad," but he "did not so consider them." His beloved Fund now had a Berle dynasty, a principal interest to him at times of unremitting sorrow concerning the state of the world.[13]

Personal satisfactions were all he had in his waning years. "The United States at the moment is not a happy country," he told an old friend living abroad in 1970. The country was in turmoil, some called it revolution, over the protracted war in Vietnam; but, as Berle remarked, "this revolution has no joy in it." University campuses were seized by students and even young professors in the spring of 1970: "I am more unhappy about the state of the world," Berle wrote. What seemed to bother him most was the increasing absence of intellect and the emerging dominance of nihilism in American culture. The New Left could not "articulate any ideas of the civilization it wants or where it is going." Worse, its materialism permeated even high culture. "It upset me a good deal," he remarked concerning a performance of Gounod's *Faust* at Lincoln Center. It "shattered" him because the production denied any religious or philosophical content in the opera, as if the human drama was not about good and evil: "Gounod of course could not have composed Faust if he had not believed in the Lord Almighty as well as the Devil. How else explain the Devil?" What had become of the love of God in America? Or even the love of man? When a new magazine sought to increase its circulation by polling several notables on nominees for "The Most Hated Man," Berle replied to its query, "I have the same emotion for Hatred that I have for leprosy, syphillis, gangrene and other degenerative diseases. So I nominate *Avant-Garde* and its editor who propose to sell Hatred for profit." What had happened to the world? "New York is not a pleasant or even very inspiring place now," he told a grandson. "It was when I was your age—which is why I have lived here. Today I am not so sure. Its radicals are nasty, its conditions increasingly difficult, its artistic expression confused." (He urged the young man to study history.) Even his obituary had him complaining bitterly that "the New Left has embarked on a calculated campaign to discredit F.D.R. and downgrade his accomplishments—and those of us who worked with him." He found solace in his family during those ebbing years when the world went wrong. As he wrote in 1963, "If it were not for Beatrice and her endless warm contacts, I think life would be rather grim."[14]

Both the world and Berle had changed. Once he had believed that a middle ground in economics and politics would triumph over polarities; now he mostly saw polarities. Once he believed that the American and the Soviet political economies would evolve into administrative systems that more closely resembled each other; now he only saw totalitarianism contradicted by democracy. Once he had envisioned a world of competitive empires in foreign affairs; now he saw only two—American and Soviet. Once he believed that the former empire would be sustained through cooperative arrangements modeled upon the Good Neighbor Policy; now he believed that only through American military strength—even if it meant intervention and occupation—could the United States resist encroachments by the Soviet empire. Once he believed that American corporations in certain industries ought to consolidate under regulation; now he still did—but competition and deregulation were ascendant fads. Once he believed that a welfare state which extended benefits and eliminated unemployment was inevitable, as was economic stabilization; now he found himself espousing such liberal concepts at a time when tolerance for inflation and unemployment made a mockery of the welfare state. He was still a corporate liberal, but between fashionable leftists and fashionable conservatives, Berle was anachronistic.

*   *   *

Berle died on February 17, 1971, of a coronary seizure, perhaps induced by his diabetes. A memorial service was held for him on February 22 in St. Paul's Chapel at Columbia University. He was laid to rest in a small country graveyard within walking distance of his Konkapot farm in the Berkshires. On his tombstone is his name, his dates, and a quote from Job 40:7,

> *Gird up thy loins now like a man;*
> *I will demand of thee, and declare thou unto Me.*

*   *   *

Few are the men who do not seem to outlive their times, and Berle was no exception. The years of his life incorporated enormous social, political, and economic changes which Berle anticipated, adapted to, and failed to do so. Classifying people by "groups," he knew he belonged to a generation of mugwumpish aristocrats, a class caught between the prehensile bourgeoisie and the increasing consciousness of the proletariat, between the corporation "collective" and the militant union. His response to the "status revolution" was an assertion of conscientious progressivism and a romantic national interest. "The Progressive Leaders were the spiritual sons of the Mugwumps," Richard Hofstadter wrote more than three decades ago, "but they were sons who dropped much of the ideological baggage of their parents."

> Where the Mugwumps had been committed to aristocracy, in spirit if not in their formal theories of government, the Progressives spoke of returning government to the people; and where the Mugwumps had clung desperately to liberal economics and the cliches of laissez faire, the Progressives were prepared to make use of state intervention wherever it suited their purposes. The Mugwumps had lacked a consistent and substantial support among the public at large. The Progressives had a rabid and almost enthusiastic following.[15]

Berle was both mugwump and progressive long after their heydays were past. That he survived and thrived is partly due to his ability to find charismatic politicos who also espoused those values (Roosevelt and La Guardia). He adapted to changing social conditions. For Berle came to terms with both the status revolution into which he was born and the organizational revolution that swept America from his youth through his early manhood. And, in a sense he transcended both and endeavored to carry them to a new, undefined stage. Self-consciously part of an emerging generation in 1919, Berle was junior to another group that had begun to wield power. They were Wilsonian liberals, Wilsonian because they espoused ideas associated with President Wilson and liberal because they promoted the self-determination of nations and individuals. Historian Robert Wiebe portrayed Herbert Hoover and Bernard Baruch as leaders of that senior generation: "These men started with the scheme they saw about them. They had no vested interest in its origins. Fresh to the task, they longed for an opportunity to build, to integrate, to supervise a much improved version of what they could watch operating directly at hand. The future would for a time belong to them."[16]

Their time lasted thirteen years; 1932 marked a transition to another era and, significantly, it marked the emergence of Roosevelt, La Guardia, and their braintruster Berle. Berle's last chapter of *The Modern Corporation and Private Property* is triumphantly prophetic, despite the rest of the book's mugwumpish hostility to plutocratic economic organizaiton and concentration, because it opportunistically points the way to the next stage of development: state capitalism. It was a theme Berle pounded away at throughout the Great Depression and one that marked him as a brilliant, profound, and radical thinker. The enterprise of World War II partially fulfilled that vision of massive public investment. Thus, call the new stage and its vision New Deal liberalism, urban liberalism, interest group liberalism, corporate liberalism, or whatever you will, it took America through the turbulent mid-twentieth century before reaction reared its head in the form of rhetorical left- and right-wing revolutions during 1965–1975. That this stage endured as long as it did is in part a tribute to Berle's propagandistic brain-trusting. (And, even in his relatively small way as a political activist for La Guardia and the Liberal party, Berle helped integrate organized labor into the political system.) Through his writings and speeches, for himself and others, Berle ideologically assimilated the earlier regulatory and administrative phases to enable Americans to better accommodate themselves to greater government roles in investment and services which marked the heyday of liberalism.

From its zenith in the 1960s to these times, Americans had no ideological guideposts except either for a murky Marxism or a confused conservatism. The latter had to prevail over the former because it is atavistically a part of the American tradition of individualism, even if its advocates ignore the fact that they repeal the American tradition of community. Deregulation and debureaucratization have been dominant themes in the American political economy since Berle's death. Berle the mugwump would like them, but Berle the progressive and the liberal would have considered them too antique to be relevant to the reality of a modern global political economy. Berle the liberal was conservatively concerned with stability and order. The expansion of the state had been necessary as an expression of America's determination to enhance individualism against "princes of plutocracy." Government could not be alien to the people unless its practitioners grew arrogant and indifferent to their constituencies; and anyone who has dealt with a local public body such as a board of education knows that it is as capable of haughtiness as any bureau or agency in Washington. Government, as idealized by Berle and his milieu, was community. Berle saw the Reconstruction Finance Corporation (as well as the Tennessee Valley Authority) as the fullest expression of opportunity blended with nationalism because it invested in both individual and community enterprise. More than anything else it facilitated the transition to a mixed national economy that facilitated the boom of the 1940s and 1950s, even as it became mired in the greed of the mixed economy. Considerating the fiscal breakdown of the 1980s, it is not surprising that a shrewd investment banker such as Felix Rohatyn wants to revive it.[17]

Few people could better imagine how to innovate the mechanics for marshalling economic power than Berle. No wonder Roosevelt and La Guardia found him so valuable to have around, even if he was sometimes so troublesome as to make FDR ponder whether he was worth it. But economic administration was tedious and Berle lusted for a less localized public arena. New York City and even Washington were hubs of empire, but not empires in themselves. Berle always thought big. State capitalism was America's engine, but also vital for the empire. Together with liberalism, American power necessitated an empire for world peace and order. Thus, the heyday of state capitalism ineluctably was the heyday of the American empire. To his intellectual credit, Berle seldom fudged concerning the reality of America's overseas interests; they were imperial. In fact, he advocated empire as the logical mode of maintaining world order and stability until such time as there would be a democratic world government. Thus, empire was a necessary transition to that millenium.

But in a democratic age the mention of empire had to be disguised under the rhetoric of popular rights. In his time Berle was one of the few figures in public life to use the word, although not even Berle dared to use it in public discourse. Yet his memos concerning the Good Neighbor Policy were candid about the policy's twentieth-century technique of devising a modern, cooperative, liberal empire. In one of the overlooked but significant sections of *Power*, he asks "Is Empire Avoidable?" (to be answered in the negative, along with his earlier question, "Can Statist Economics Be Avoided?"). Berle defined empire in contemporary terms as the ability of a great power to impose its will whether through force of arms or economics upon weaker nations and he concluded that great powers will be imperial and that small countries, contrary to his earlier Wilsonian idealism, will be their victims: "Neither great nor small powers have free choice in the matter." But empires were not all bad and, reminiscent of his conclusions concerning the United States in the Dominican Republic more than forty-five years before, the experience could be altruistic. In any case, "until world government arrives, the need is to make the inevitable empires 'good.'" That, he argued, was the essence of American foreign policy, "translation of nineteenth-century conceptions of empire into co-operative arrangements in which a minimum of control and a maximum of co-operative effort are achieved for all the inhabitants of the region." Of course, his perspective was born of experience: "That was the conception of Roosevelt's Good Neighbor policy as it evolved during his regime. . . . " Thus, the dominant need for empire was to avoid "international chaos" and "move toward an effective system of world order. . . . Absent a world government, the great nations, to the extent of their capacity, will create some sort of order."[18]

"I am unhappy at some of the conclusions reached in this chapter." he wrote. "This does not release me, as a student, from obligation to state them. In international analysis, blinking reality is inexcusable." The braintruster was the empire's ideologist, but his confined and cautious vision of a hemispheric empire had been globalized by others after 1945. While never abandoning the primacy of the Americas, Berle easily accepted globalization. Liberal ideology demanded it. The goose-stepping threat of Fascist totalitarianism had given way to the goose-stepping threat of Communist totalitarianism. Soviet totalitarianism and imperialism were graver threats to liberalism than fascism had been. Berle's tragedy was not in his anticommunism, for he had no more reason to apologize for that than for his antifascism. Rather, his tragedy lay in allowing Castro's capture of Cuba to warrant, in his mind, the ill-fated adventure in Vietnam. The universalism of liberalism had blinked reality. How could he equate Roosevelt's imperial conception of a Good Neighbor Policy with President Lyndon Johnson's outline of co-operative development for the Mekong Delta and River of Southeast Asia? To do so was not only Berle's error of vision, but that of liberalism as well and it deprived America of the very order intended by liberals. Nonintervention or even withdrawal would have been a retreat from empire, but it might have preserved order in America by allowing the nation to establish greater priorities. Perhaps the young man Berle knew in the Dominican Republic and in Paris, 1918–1919, would have approved that policy. But the much older man of the Bay of Pigs and the Dominican landing of the 1960s did not. In retrospect, the effort in Vietnam probably inspired more chaos and uncertainty of purpose than its supporters such as Berle ever imagined. It should not have been the last chapter to the brain-truster's causative story.[19]

Notes

ABBREVIATIONS USED IN NOTES

Diary Diary of Adolf A. Berle, Berle Papers
BP Berle Papers

BBB Beatrice Bishop Berle

FDR Franklin D. Roosevelt
HST Harry S. Truman
JFK John F. Kennedy
LBJ Lyndon B. Johnson

NTR Beatrice Bishop Berle and Travis Jacobs, *Navigating the Rapids, 1918–1971: From the Papers of Adolf A. Berle* (New York, 1973).

COHC Columbia University Oral History Collection

TCF Twentieth Century Fund

From the Roosevelt Library, Hyde Park, New York:
PSF President's Secretary Files
PPF President's Personal Files
OF Official Files
MR Map Room Files

From the Truman Library, Independence, Missouri:
CFTL Confidential File
PSFTL President's Secretary File
OFTL Official File

From the Public Record Office, Kew, England:
FO Foreign Office Papers
CAB War Cabinet Papers

From the John F. Kennedy Library, Boston, Massachusetts:
OHJFK   Oral History

From the National Archives, Washington, D.C.:
RG   Record Group

CHAPTER 1   A CAUSATIVE LIFE

The School in the Home

1. Interview with Lina Berle, May 17, 1983; John McCarten, "Atlas with Ideas," *New Yorker,* January 23, 1943, p. 22; Berle, COHC, p. 3.
2. A. A. Berle, Sr., "William T. Harris—Pragmatic Hegelian," *Journal of Philosophy,* 45 (February 26, 1948), 121–33; interview with Lina Berle.
3. A. A. Berle to G. F. Wright, January 5, 1912, Wright Papers, Box 22.
4. William J. Morison, "George Frederick Wright," *Dictionary of Scientific Biography* (New York, 1976), vol. 14, pp. 516–18; Morison, "George Frederick Wright: In Defense of Darwinism and Fundamentalism, 1838–1921," unpublished doctoral dissertation, Vanderbilt University, 1971.
5. G. Frederick Wright, *Story of My Life and Work* (Oberlin, OH, 1916); Berle to W. B. Inglee, June 25, 1937, BP-25; to George B. Hatfield, September 22, 1944, to Mrs. M. E. Hall, January 25, 1943, BP-36; interview with Alice Crawford, June 17, 1986.
6. Lina Berle interview; A. A. Berle, "The Christian Ministry: A Pragmatic Life," *Bibliotheca Sacra: A Theological Quarterly,* 64 (October 1907), 738–63; "The Rout of the Theological Schools," ibid. (July 1907), 566–87; "The Education of a Minister," ibid. (April 1907), 283–98; Berle, COHC, p. 9.
7. A. A. Berle, "Universities and Social Advance," *Bibliotheca Sacra: A Theological Quarterly,* 65 (April 1908), 306–30; "Professor Moore on Ministeral Training," ibid. (July 1908), 445–51; "The Theologian of the Future," ibid., 68 (January 1911), 13–33; "The Christian Church and Democracy," ibid., 70 (January 1913), 40–55.
8. Lina Berle interview; Arthur Mann, *Yankee Reformers in the Urban Age: Social Reform in Boston 1880–1900* (New York, 1966), p. 17.
9. Berle, COHC, pp. 7–8; Melvin I. Urofsky and David W. Levy, eds., *Letters of Louis D. Brandeis* (Albany, NY, 1971), vol. II, pp. 91–92, 105, 161, vol. III, pp. 36–37.
10. Berle, William T. Harris," p. 133; McCarten, "Atlas with Ideas," p. 26; Lina Berle interview; H. Addington Bruce, "New Ideas in Child Training," *Journal of Education,* 74 (September 21, 1911), 292–93; Berle, "The Montessori Method and the Home," ibid., 77 (May 1, 1913), 484–86; A. A. Berle, *The School in the Home* (New York, 1914).
11. Kathleen Montour, "William James Sidis, The Broken Twig," *American Psychologist* (April 1977), 265–79; H. A. Bruce, "New Ideas in Child Training" *Journal of Education,* 74 (1911), 292–94, *American Magazine* (July 1911), 286–94; A. A. Berle to G. F. Wright, November 3, 1911, Wright Papers, Box 22.

12. A. A. Berle to G. F. Wright, January 5, 1912, Wright Papers; Berle to Oswald Garrison Villard, November 19, 1917, Villard Papers.

13. Lina Wright Berle, *George Eliot and Thomas Hardy: A Contrast* (New York, 1917), pp. 2–7, 12–14, 167–73; Lina Berle interview; Berle, Sr., to Oswald Garrison Villard, November 21, 1917, Villard Papers; to Berle, Jr., May 22, 1918, Mother to Berle, Jr., May 14, 1918, Lina Berle to Berle, Jr., April 27, 1918, BP-2.

14. Beatrice Bishop Berle, *A Life in Two Worlds* (New York, 1983), pp. 82, 88; interview with Beatrice Meyerson, November 20, 1984.

15. A. A. Berle to Oswald Garrison Villard, March 8, October 15, 22, 1926, October 15, 1927, Villard to Berle, October 19, 1927, Berle to Villard, March 23, 30, September 29, 1928, Villard Papers; Dr. Berle to "Ado," September 10, 1934, undated [1935], BP-5.

16. A. A. Berle to Oswald Garrison Villard, October 24, 1938, November 10, 1939, March 15, 1939, Villard Papers.

17. Dr. Berle to Berle, September 10, 1934, March 18, 1935, BP-5; Stephen Wise to Berle, January 16, Berle to Wise, January 19, 1939, BP-12; Emanuel Celler to Berle, October 5, 1943, BP-30; "Strange to Relate," by Rabbi Philip R. Alstat, clipping, BP-33.

18. Berle, *Studies in the Law of Corporation Finance* (New York, 1928), p. iii; Berle to Father, April 9, 1928, Mother to Berle, October 8, 1932, BP-5.

19. Berle to President Roosevelt, February 12, 1940, PSF 94.

20. Interview with Beatrice Bishop Berle, July 7, 1982; Beatrice Berle, *A Life in Two Worlds,* p. 89; Mother to Berle, January 25, 1939, July 7, 1937, BP-5; Alice Crawford interview, June 17, 1986.

21. Mother to Berle, January 29, 1938, BP-25, January 25, 1939, BP-5.

22. Mother to Berle, June 1, 1937, BP-25, September 4, [1938], BP-5, August 10, 1938, BP-25, June 5, 1932, BP-5, July 1, 1937, BP-25.

Harvard Prodigy

1. Harvard College Transcript; on Lippmann at Harvard, see Ronald Steel, *Walter Lippmann and the American Century* (Boston, 1980), pp. 12–22; Berle to Raymond S. Wilkins, March 29, 1965, to Dexter Perkins, January 14, 1955, BP-105.

2. Berle to Peter Berle, December 9, 1954, January 7, May 26, 1955, Berle to Alice Berle Crawford, November 23, 1955, BP-82; Lina Berle interview; Bruce, "New Ideas in Child Training"; Berle, "Follies of 1810," Houghton Library, Harvard University; Berle, COHC, pp. 9–13, 24–26.

3. Lina Berle interview; Beatrice Bishop Berle, *A Life in Two Worlds* (New York, 1983), p. 119; McCarten, "Atlas with Ideas," pp. 23–24; interview with Peter Berle, May 16, 1983; William O. Douglas, *Go East, Young Man* (New York, 1974), pp. 368–69; Berle, COHC, pp. 17, 133.

4. H. N. Hirsch, *The Enigma of Felix Frankfurter* (New York, 1981), pp. 5–6.

5. Berle, COHC, pp. 18, 21, 70–74, 80; A. L. Todd, *Justice on Trial* (Chicago, 1964), p. 211.

CHAPTER 2   OLD EMPIRES AND NEW

Self-Determination for the Dominican Republic

1. Berle, COHC, p. 31.
2. Ibid., pp. 31, 75–76, 81–83.
3. Adjutant general memo for the secretary of war, February 20, Rounds to Berle, March 8, Admiral H. S. Knapp letter, March 8, Berle to Mother, March 8, 1918, BP-2.
4. Berle, COHC, p. 83; an excellent work on the Dominican affair is Bruce J. Calder, *The Impact of Intervention: The Dominican Republic During the U.S. Occupation of 1916–1924* (Austin, TX, 1984).
5. Berle, COHC, p. 31; Calder, *Impact of Intervention,* pp. 102, 106.
6. Berle, COHC, pp. 85–88; Berle to Father, April 17, 1918, BP-2; Berle, "The Dominicans," *Survey,* 47 (October 8, 1921), 41; on the Dominican guerrilla war, see Calder, *Impact of Intervention,* pp. 133–52.
7. Berle to Ralph S. Rounds, May 13, Rounds to Berle, June 28, Berle to Admiral H. S. Knapp, May 31, Colonels R. H. Van Deman and John M. Dunn to Berle, May 29, 1918, BP-3.
8. Beatrice Bishop Berle, *A Life in Two Worlds* (New York, 1983), pp. 229–30.
9. Berle, "Santo Domingo," *Survey,* 45 (January 1, 1921), 510; "Habilitating Haiti," ibid., 46 (June 25, 1921), 433; Beatrice Bishop Berle, *A Life in Two Worlds,* p. 68.

The Russian Section in Paris

1. Berle, COHC, pp. 32–35; Berle Diary, November 27, December 7, 1918, BP-1.
2. Berle Diary, December 8, 12, 1918, BP-1.
3. Berle Diary, December 14, 1918, BP-1.
4. Berle, COHC, pp. 35–39; Berle to Father, February 17, Berle memo to Mr. Herter, February 17, 1918, BP-2; Berle to Colonel House, February 17, 1918, House Papers-12; on Pettit, see Arno J. Mayer, *Politics and Diplomacy of Peacemaking* (New York, 1967), p. 466.
5. Berle Diary, March 5; Berle memo to the Informal Russian Committee, March 10, "The Informal Russian Committee," [ca. March 15], 1919, BP-1; also, see Waldo H. Heinrichs, Jr., *American Ambassador: Joseph Grew and the Development of the United States Diplomatic Tradition* (New York, 1979), pp. 35–44.
6. Memo, the Russian Section to Mr. Herter, March 30, Berle memo, "American Economic Intervention in Russia," Berle memo to Mr. Herter, March 28, 1919, BP-1.
7. Berle to Mimi, April 7, to Mother, April 8, 1919, BP-2.
8. Berle memo of a conversation between Bullitt, Morison, and myself, April 19, R. H. Lord memo to Vance McCormick, April 22, Berle to Father, May 6, 1919, BP-1.
9. Count Axel Gustaffson Oxenstierna, Swedish statesman and diplomat between 1612 and 1654, advocate of a cautious foreign policy abroad and reforms at home, whose son was a Swedish representative at the Peace of Westphalia.

10. Berle, COHC, p. 41–63, 65; Mayer, *Politics and Diplomacy,* pp. 799–801; Arthur Schlesinger, Jr., *The Crisis of the Old Order, 1919–1933* (Boston, 1957), pp. 12–14; Berle to Father, May 6, to Lina, May 8, to Mother, May 25, 1919, BP-2; "Personal," May 8, May 10, May 14, 1919, BP-2; to Upton Sinclair, December 27, 1939, BP-49.
11. Berle to Father, to Mother, May 25, 1919, BP-2; memo to Joseph C. Grew, May 15, Grew to Berle, May 20, June 16, memo, "Relief from Duty with the Commission," June 17, memo, "Possible American Policy towards Russia," original emphasis, June 19, Grew to Berle, June 25, 1919, BP-1; Berle, COHC, p. 64.

Global Self-Determination

1. Berle to Chester D. Rowton, February 15, 1937, to Ralph Henry Van Deman, January 17, 1952, BP-10 and 84.
2. Berle, "Modern Legal Profession," *Encyclopedia of the Social Sciences*, vol. 9 cember 1, 1919, William B. Graham to Berle, February 7, 1922, BP-3.
3. William B. Graham to Berle, January 24, Berle to Graham, January 27, 1922, H. H. Pfeil to Berle, March 13, 1923, BP-3.
4. Berle to Philander C. Knox, undated (1919), to O. G. Villard, August 11, 1919, BP-1; Berle "The Latest Allied-American Dealing with Lenin," *Nation,* 109 (August 9, 1919), 170–71; Berle memo concerning the American Policy toward Russia, BP-2; Berle to secretary of state, February 7, 1920, BP-3.
5. A. A. Berle, "Some Popular American Fallacies Refuted," an address delivered before Oberlin College, February 22, 1900, and "Democracy, Imperialism and Christianity," address at the annual meeting of the N. E. Anti-Imperialist League, November 30, 1901.
6. Berle, "Our Undeclared War," *New Republic,* 23 (June 16, 1920), 92–94; Berle "The Russian Hunger," *Survey,* 46 (August 1, 1921), 562–63.
7. Berle, "Bread and Guns," *Survey,* 47 (1921–1922), 269–70, 361–62, 195–96, 723, 754–56.
8. Berle to John Bassett Moore, August 2, 1932, BP-2; Berle, "The League at the Crossroads," *Survey,* 45 (November 27, 1920), 327; Berle, "A Junior League of Nations," ibid., February 5, 1921, 655–56; Beatrice Bishop Berle, *A Life in Two Worlds,* pp. 121–22.

CHAPTER 3 SOCIAL AND LEGAL REFORMER

Self-Determination on Henry Street and in Santa Fe

1. On the settlement houses in the 1920s, see Clarke A. Chambers, *Seedtime of Reform: American Social Service and Social Action, 1918–1933* (Minneapolis, 1963).
2. Irving Howe, *World of Our Fathers* (New York, 1976), p. 94.
3. Lillian D. Wald to Berle, October 6, 1922, June 12, 1923, Berle to Wald, June 13, to Palmer Canfield, June 23, 1923, Georgiana Sherman to Berle, April 24, 1923, BP-3. Also, see ledger marked "Financial Accounts, 1921–1925," Lillian D. Wald Papers, Box 54, Columbia University Library.

4. Arthur Schlesinger, Jr., *The Crisis of the Old Order* (Boston, 1957), pp. 23–25; Henry Street Board of Governors, BP-3.

5. Berle, "Essentials of Community Life," "Henry Street," BP-2; Beatrice Bishop Berle, *A Life in Two Worlds* (New York, 1983), pp. 73–74; Berle, "Self-Determining New York," *New Republic,* 30 (May 17, 1922), 340–42.

6. Clarke A. Chambers, "Paul Underwood Kellogg," in John A. Garraty, ed., *Dictionary of American Biography,* Supp. 6, 1956–1960 (New York, 1980), pp. 329–30; Chambers, *Paul U. Kellogg and the 'Survey'* (Minneapolis, 1971); Kellogg to Berle, January 22, 1921, BP-2.

7. Berle to Kellogg, December 11, 1922, November 22, 1924, Kellogg to Berle, November 4, 1924, Berle to Kellogg, October 19, Kellogg to Berle, October 23, 1925, Berle to Kellogg, March 25, 1927, Beulah Amidon to Berle, February 7, July 17, 1930, Survey Associates Papers, Boxes 13 and 54.

8. Kenneth Roy Philp, "John Collier and the American Indian," unpublished doctoral dissertation, Michigan State University, 1968, pp. 1–28; John Collier, *From Every Zenith: A Memoir* (Denver, 1963), pp. 124–35.

9. Lawrence C. Kelly, *The Assault on Assimilation: John Collier and the Origins of Indian Policy Reform* (Albuquerque, 1983), p. xxv; Collier, Luhan, and Lawrence quoted in Philp, "John Collier," pp. 51, 6, 3; Collier to Berle, undated, BP-1.

10. Most of these elitiest liberals were unaware of any racial slurs. One liberal lady told a "darkey" story to make a point and Berle himself used the expression "nigger in the woodpile."

11. Berle on Walker in *Studies in the Law of Corporation Finance* (Chicago, 1928), p. 178n; Elizabeth Shipley Sergeant to Margaret McKittrick, May 26, 1923, Collier Papers, Box 13; Berle, COHC, pp. 100–101.

12. Kelly, *Assault on Assimilation,* pp. 280–81; Berle to John Collier, June 9, Collier telegram to Berle, June 4, Collier to Berle, July 5, 1923, BP-1; Elizabeth Shipley Sergeant to Stella M. Atwood, June 23, Atwood to Sergeant, July 21, 1923, Collier Papers, Box 13.

13. Berle to Roger Baldwin, June 19, 1923, BP-1.

14. Berle Diary, July 31, August 1, 2, 3, 7, 8, 10, 1923, BP-2; on Mabel Dodge Luhan and the pueblos, see Lois Palken Rudnick, *Mabel Dodge Luhan: New Woman, New Worlds* (Albuquerque, 1984), pp. 176–82.

15. Berle Diary, August 11, 13, 14, 15, 16, 17, 18, 20, 1923, BP-2.

16. Berle Diary, August 21, 22, 23, 24, 25, 26, 28, 1923, BP-2; Stella M. Atwood to Berle, September 17, 1923, BP-1; Alice Corbin Henderson to Elizabeth Shipley Sergeant, October 1, Margaret McKittrick to Sergeant, October 2, 1923, Berle to Sergeant, March 27, 1923, Collier Papers, Box 13.

17. Berle Diary, August 28, 1923; Mary Austin to Berle, October 1, Stella M. Atwood to Berle, September 28, John Collier to Berle, October 6, 1923, BP-1; Roberts Walker to E. S. Sergeant, January 31, 1924, Collier Papers, Box 13; Philp, "John Collier," pp. 33–37.

18. Roberts Walker to E. S. Sergeant, January 31, Berle to Sergeant, February 4, Howard S. Gans to Sergeant, February 7, Berle to Sergeant, February 15, March 6, 12, 27, July 10, 1924, Collier Papers, Box 13; L. R. Paulin to Berle, June 21, 1924, BP-1; Berle, COHC, pp. 100–111.

A Corporation Lawyer

1. Copy, Reginald Heber Smith to William Nelson, June 30, 1922, BP-3; on Smith, see Jerrold S. Auerbach, *Unequal Justice: Lawyers and Social Change in Modern America* (New York, 1976), pp. 59–62.
2. Berle, "Modern Legal Profession," *Encyclopedia of the Social Sciences*, vol. 9 (New York, 1933), pp. 341–42, "an eminently quotable example of the outspokenly critical attacks on the profession from within." Richard L. Abel, "The Sociology of American Lawyers," *Law and Policy Quarterly,* 2 (1980), 339.
3. Andrew Ten Eyck to Berle, November 14, December 7, 1923, Tax Returns for 1924 and 1925, BP-3; Berle, COHC, p. 112; Auerbach, *Unequal Justice,* p. 142; Auerbach and Eugene Bardach, "'Born to an Era of Insecurity': Career Patterns of Law Review Editors, 1918–1941," *American Journal of Legal History,* 17 (1973), 4.
4. Berle, COHC, pp. 91–100; Berle, "How Labor Could Control," *New Republic,* 28 (September 7, 1921), 37–39; Berle to Henry Yankowich, January 19, 1928, BP-12.
5. Berle to Harry E. Stone, October 23, 1934, BP-11.
6. John McCarten, "Atlas with Ideas," *New Yorker,* January 23, 1943, p. 24.
7. Obituary in *New York Times,* March 31, November 20, 21, 22, 23, 24, 1935, March 8, April 6, 7, 8, 9, 24, VII, p. 23, April 26, 27, 28, November 6, VII, p. 32, November 15, 16, 1938, May 1, 10, 11, 1938, May 9, 10, 23, 24, 1940, January 30, 1941, December 1, 2, 1945, December 8, 9, 1945.
8. Beatrice Bishop Berle, *A Life in Two Worlds* (New York, 1983), pp. 28–29.
9. Berle to Father, June 7, 1928, BP-5; *New York Times,* January 9, 1936, May 24, 1938, October 12, 1939; Beatrice Bishop Berle, *A Life in Two Worlds,* p. 140.
10. Mother to Berle, August 10, 1938, BP-25; Beatrice Bishop Berle, *A Life in Two Worlds,* p. 136.

Berle Without Means

1. Berle, "The Expansion of American Administrative Law," *Harvard Law Review,* 30 (1917), 430. On the development of administrative law, see Jerrold S. Auerbach, *Unequal Justice: Lawyers and Social Change in Modern America* (New York, 1976), p. 221.
2. Edward H. Warren to Berle, October 3, Berle to Warren, October 5, 1921, BP-3; Berle to Norman A. Adler, April 14, 1932, BP-12; for a bibliography of Berle's published works, see *Columbia Law Review,* 64 (December 1964), pp. 1373–76.
3. Berle, COHC, p. 114–19.
4. Berle to Thomas A. Lund, March 7, 1967, BP-87; Berle, COHC, pp. 113–19, 138–41; The Staff of the Foundation for Research in Legal History under the direction of Julius Goebel, Jr., *A History of the School of Law Columbia University* (New York, 1955), pp. 299–305, 316–17.
5. Alfred S. Eichner, "Gardiner C. Means," in David L. Sills, ed., *International Encyclopedia of the Social Sciences: Biographical Supplement,* vol. 18 (New

York, 1979), pp. 532–34; interview with Gardiner C. Means and Caroline Ware, November 27, 1984.

6. Goebel, *School of Law Columbia,* pp. 299–305; James E. Simon, *Independent Journey: The Life of William O. Douglas* (New York, 1980), pp. 92–99; Berle to Hessel E. Yntema, March 7, 1929, BP-12, to Joseph V. Kline, April 25, 1932, BP-8; also see Laura Kalman, *Legal Realism at Yale, 1927–1960* (Chapel Hill, NC, 1986).

7. William Z. Ripley, *Main Street and Wall Street* (New York, 1927), pp. 47n, 53, 60n, 92n, 92–93, 122n, 131, 133n; "William Zebina Ripley," *Dictionary of American Biography:* Suppl. 3 (New York, 1973), pp. 632–33; *New York Times,* January 22, 1927; Berle, COHC, pp. 126–31.

8. Means-Ware interview; Berle, "The Next American Revolution," BP-2; Berle, "How Labor Could Control," *New Republic,* 28 (September 7, 1921), 37–39; Berle, "Non-Cumulative Preferred Stock," *Columbia Law Review,* 23 (1923), 358–67; Berle, "Problems of Non-Par Stock," ibid., 25 (1925), 43–63.

9. Berle, "Non-Voting Stock and 'Bankers' Control'" *Harvard Law Review,* 39 (April 1926), 673–93; Berle, "Participating Preferred Stock," *Columbia Law Review,* 26 (1926), 303–17.

10. Berle, "Convertible Bonds and Stock Purchase Warrants," *Yale Law Journal,* 36 (1927), 649–66; Berle, "Publicity of Accounts and Directors' Purchases of Stocks," *Michigan Law Review* 25 (1927), 827–38; Berle, "Subsidiary Corporations and Credit Manipulation," *Harvard Law Review,* 41 (1928), 874–93.

11. Berle, *Studies in the Law of Corporation Finance* (New York, 1928), pp. v, 36–39, 21–22.

12. Berle to H. Thomas Austern, February 15, 1929, BP-8; to Carl B. Robbins, February 15, 1928, BP-10; David E. Lilienthal to Berle, June 26, Berle to Lilienthal, June 29, 1929, BP-9, Lilienthal Papers, Box 49.

13. Wickersham to Berle, May 15, 1928, Berle to Cornelius W. Wickersham, June 1, 1928, BP-12; Berle, COHC, pp. 127–28; Callaghan and Company to the Deans of all the Commerce Schools, November 5, 1928, Berle file, Baker Library, Harvard University.

14. Berle, *Cases and Materials in the Law of Corporation Finance* (Chicago, 1930); Berle to Father, February 28, 1929, BP-5; to James C. Stephens, April 24, 1929, BP-11; Berle to Alfred W. Bingham, May 8, 1929, BP-12.

15. Berle to Walter Lippmann, May 6, 1929, BP-9, Lippmann Papers, Box 4; Berle, "Historical Inheritance of American Corporations," *Social Meaning of Legal Concepts,* New York University School of Law, no. 3 (1929), pp. 210–11.

16. Berle, "Promoters' Stock in Subsidiary Corporations," *Columbia Law Review,* 29 (1929), 35, 40–42; "Compensation of Bankers and Promoters through Stock Profits," *Harvard Law Review,* 42 (1929), 748, 758–60, 764–65.

The Making of The Modern Corporation

1. Berle to Stephen G. Williams, April 24, 1929, BP-12, emphasis added; Berle to David E. Lilienthal, June 29, 1929, Lilienthal Papers, Box 49. Also, see Berle to James C. Stephens, April 24, 1929, BP-11.

2. Berle, assisted by Gardiner C. Means, "Corporations and the Public Investor," *American Economic Review,* 20 (March 1930), 54–71.

3. Berle, "The Organization of the Law of Corporation Finance," *Tennessee Law Review,* 9 (April 1931), 125–45, emphasis in last sentence added.
4. Berle to William Z. Ripley, March 21, 1931, BP-10; Berle, "Liability for Stock Market Manipulation," *Columbia Law Review,* 31 (1931), 264–79.
5. Berle to George W. Anderson, December 16, 1931, BP-4.
6. Berle to Hermann R. Habicht, November 19, 1930, BP-8.
7. Means-Ware interview.

The Modern Corporation *in History*

1. Thomas Gale Moore, "Introduction: Corporations and Private Property," George J. Stigler and Claire Friedland, "The Literature of Economics," Douglas C. North, "Comment of Stigler and Friedland," *Journal of Law and Economics* 26 (2) (June 1983), 235, 241, 271.
2. New York *Herald Tribune,* February 19, 1933; Frank to Berle, to Frankfurter, December 15, 1932, Frank Papers, Boxes 1 and 3; *Yale Law Journal,* 42 (1933), 989.
3. Ernest Gruening, "Capitalist Confiscation," *Nation,* February 1, 1933, p. 116; Stuart Chase, "Ticker Tapeworms," *New Republic,* January 25, 1933, p. 299; Harry W. Laidler, "The New Ownership," *Survey Graphic,* 22 (June 1933), pp. 330–31.
4. *Liggett Co. et al.* v. *Lee,* 288 U.S. 517; *Time,* April 24, 1933, p. 14; *Sutter v. Groen and Groen,* U.S. Court of Appeals for the Seventh Circuit, 687 F.2d 197; Richard H. Pells, *Radical Visions and American Dreams: Culture and Social Thought in the Depression Years* (New York, 1973), pp. 69–70.
5. John Kenneth Galbraith, *A Life in Our Times* (Boston, 1981), p. 362; Berle Diary, November 17, 1953; Walter Werner, "Management, Stock Market and Corporate Reform: Berle and Means Reconsidered," *Columbia Law Review,* 77 (1977), 399, 397, 408.
6. E.g., Berle, *The Twentieth Century Capitalist Revolution* (New York, 1959), *Economic Power and the Free Society* (New York, 1957), *Power Without Property* (New York, 1959), foreword to Edward S. Mason, ed., *The Corporation in Modern Society* (Cambridge, MA, 1960).
7. Michael Harrington, *The Twilight of Capitalism* (New York, 1976), p. 198; Rick Tilman, "Apology and Ambiguity: Adolf Berle on Corporate Power," *Journal of Economic Issues,* 8 (March 1974), 111–26; Jeffrey Lustig, *Corporate Liberalism: The Origins of Modern American Political Theory* (Berkeley, CA, 1982), pp. 1–35.
8. "Conference on Corporation Law and Finance," December 7, 1951, University of Chicago Law School.

The Marx of the Shareholder Class

1. BBB Diary, September 12, 1934; Berle to Glenn S. Allen, Jr., July 25, 1939, BP-27.
2. Berle to Ellery Sedgwick, July 13, 1932, BP-11; Berle and Means, *The Modern*

Corporation and Private Property (New York, 1932), p. ix; Berle, *Power Without Property* (New York, 1959), pp. 19–20.

3. Berle and Means, *Modern Corporation,* pp. vi-viii; Berle to George W. Anderson, October 17, 1932, BP-4; Berle, "Review of Objectives," November 1, 1953, TCF.

4. Gilbert H. Montague to Berle, April 19, 1932, BP-9; Beulah Amidon memo, September 8, 1938, Survey Associates Papers, Box 54.

5. Berle, *The Twentieth Century Capitalist Revolution* (New York, 1954), p. 169; Joseph L. Weiner, "The Berle-Dodd Dialogue on the Concept of the Corporation, *Columbia Law Review,* 64 (1964), 1458–67; Berle, "Corporate Powers as Powers in Trust," *Harvard Law Review,* 44 (1931), 1049–74.

6. E. Merrick Dodd, "For Whom Are Corporate Managers Trustees?" and Berle, "For Whom Corporate Managers *Are* Trustees: A Note," *Harvard Law Review,* 45 (1932), 1145–63, 1365–72, emphasis added.

7. Herbert Croly to Berle, March 27, 1922, BP-2; Beatrice Bishop Berle, *A Life in Two Worlds* (New York, 1983), p. 109; Berle, "How Labor Could Control," *New Republic* 28 (September 7, 1921), 37–39; "The Next American Revolution," BP-2.

8. NTR, pp. 21–22; David E. Lilienthal, *Journals: Venturesome Years 1950–1955,* vol. III (New York, 1966), pp. 618–19; Frank to Frankfurter, December 29, 1932, Frank Papers, Box 3, emphasis added.

CHAPTER 4   ROOSEVELT AND LA GUARDIA

Adventurous Minds

1. Samuel I. Rosenman, *Working with Roosevelt* (New York, 1952), pp. 56–58; Frank Freidel, *FDR: The Triumph* (Boston, 1956), pp. 261–63; Ernest K. Lindley, "War on the Brains Trust," *Scribner's Magazine* (November 1933), 258; Samuel B. Hand, *Counsel and Advise: A Political Biography of Samuel I. Rosenman* (New York, 1979), pp. 58–61.

2. Raymond Moley, *After Seven Years* (New York, 1939), pp. 1–9; Moley, *The First New Deal* (New York, 1966), pp. 11–15; R. G. Tugwell, *The Brains Trust* (New York, 1968), pp. 9–10; Elliot A. Rosen, *Hoover, Roosevelt, and the Brains Trust* (New York, 1977), pp. 113–14, 126–29.

3. Rosen, *Hoover, Roosevelt,* pp. 151–96; Tugwell, *Brains Trust,* pp. 12–40; Moley, *After Seven Years,* pp. 14–18.

4. Moley, *After Seven Years,* pp. 3, 18. On their memories of Columbia before Roosevelt, see Moley, *Realities and Illusions, 1886–1931: Autobiography* (New York, 1980), pp. 152–64; Tugwell, *To the Lesser Heights of Morningside: A Memoir* (Philadelphia, 1982), pp. 141–77, 185–87, 200–203, 241–43.

5. Berle et al. to Newton D. Baker, April 1932, BP-15; David E. Lilienthal, *Journals: The TVA Years 1939–1945* (New York, 1964), pp. 30–31.

6. Berle to Charles Evans Hughes, November 17, 1919, BP-2, to Henry Cabot Lodge, September 14, 17, December 9, 1920, Lodge to Berle, September 15, December 10, 1920, BP-3, John C. Clark to Berle, November 27, 1920, July 26, 1921, BP-2, to W. H. Van Benschoten, May 11, 1921, BP-3.

7. Berle to Bruce Bliven, October 6, 1928, BP-4; also, see Arthur Schlesinger, Jr., *The Crisis of the Old Order, 1919–1933* (Boston, 1957), pp. 286–88.
8. Lilienthal to Berle, February 13, Berle to Lilienthal, February 15, Berle to Lilienthal, February 24, 1932, Lilienthal Papers, Box 55.
9. Berle to Lilienthal, letter and memo, March 14, Lilienthal to Berle, March 29, Berle to Lilienthal, March 31, Lilienthal to Berle, April 4, 1932, Berle to Lilienthal, July 13, 22, August 2, 1932, Lilienthal Papers, Box 55; Berle to Edwin J. Marshall, April 11, 1932, BP-9.
10. Berle to E. J. Marshall, October 23, 1931, BP-9.
11. Berle to Elisha Friedman, April 20, 1932, BP-7, to Ordway Tead and Lewis Gannett, March 4, 1932, BP-11 and BP-7, to Hermann Habicht, February 13, 1932, BP-8, to Louis Brandeis, February 19, 1932, BP-5.
12. Berle to Louis M. Faulkner, May 16, BP-7, to Nicholas Murray Butler, October 4, 1932, BP-5; Beatrice Bishop Berle and Travis Beal Jacobs, *Navigating the Rapids 1918–1971: From the Papers of Adolf A. Berle* (New York, 1973), pp. 31–51.
13. Jordan A. Schwarz, *The Speculator: Bernard M. Baruch in Washington 1917–1965* (Chapel Hill, NC, 1981), pp. 260–70; John Kennedy Ohl, *Hugh S. Johnson and the New Deal* (DeKalb, IL, 1985), pp. 85–90; Rosen, Hoover, Roosevelt, p. 115; John Kenneth Galbraith, *A Life in Our Times* (Boston, 1981), p. 290; Lindley, "War on the Brains Trust," p. 260.
14. See essay on Frankfurter marked "Louis Rittenberg Univ. Jew. Encycl." in BP-34 and Rittenberg to Berle, December 31, 1940, BP-46.
15. Berle memo, August 5, Berle to Frankfurter, August 6, Frankfurter to Berle, August 8, Berle to Frankfurter, August 10, Frankfurter to Berle, August 11, 1932, BP-15; Michael E. Parrish, *Felix Frankfurter and His Times: The Reform Years* (New York, 1982), pp. 204–12.
16. Schwarz, *Speculator: Bernard M. Baruch,* pp. 265, 269; Edmund Wilson, *The Thirties* (New York, 1980), p. 339; Berle memos to Franklin D. Roosevelt, July 20, August 1, 2, 5, BP-16, August 10, 15, 1932, BP-15, Roosevelt to Berle, August 16, 1932, BP-16.
17. BBB Diary, September 1932, October 6, 1932; Frankfurter to FDR, September 9, to Berle, September 23, 1932, PPF 140; Berle to Moley, September 19, 1932, Moley Papers, Box 5; Berle to FDR, August 17, BP-16, to Frankfurter, September 21, BP-15, to W. Z. Ripley, September 21, 1932, BP-10.
18. Elliot Roosevelt, ed., *The Public Papers and Addresses of Franklin D. Roosevelt,* vol. I (New York, 1938), pp. 742–56; BBB Diary, September 1932, October 6, 1932.
19. Lindley, "War on the Brains Trust," p. 265; Schlesinger, *Crisis,* p. 425; Richard Hofstadter, *Great Issues in American History,* vol. II (New York, 1958), p. 343; Rexford G. Tugwell, *The Democratic Roosevelt* (Garden City, NY, 1957), p. 246.
20. Berle to Nicholas Murray Butler, September 29, October 4, to Raymond Moley, September 30, October 17, 1932, BP-15; to F. E. Richter, October 24, 1932, BP-10; Berle to Roosevelt, October 10, 1932, PPF 140; BBB Diary, October 6, 16, 1932; Journals, October 13, 1932, Lilienthal Papers.
21. Berle memo, November 3, 1932, BP-15; Berle to Roosevelt, October 24, Roosevelt to Berle, October 28, 1932, BP-16; BBB Diary, October 16, 1932.

New Dealer

1. Berle to George W. Anderson, November 14, 1932, BP-4.
2. Berle memo, November 7, 1932, BP-15; Berle to George W. Anderson, November 14, 1932, BP-4.
3. Moley Diary, February 8, 1933; Tugwell Diary, February 10, 1933.
4. Berle to James G. McDonald, November 10, 1932, BP-15; to John Hanna, November 9, 16, 1932, BP-8, emphasis added.
5. Frank Freidel, *FDR: Launching the New Deal* (Boston, 1973), p. 73; Berle memo to R. M., November 10, 1932, BP-15.
6. Berle to John Hanna, November 9, 1932, BP-8; to George W. Anderson, November 14, BP-4; to Raymond Moley, November 23, 1932, Moley Papers, Box 5; memo to Roosevelt, December 2, 1932, BP-16; to Moley, November 28, 1932, BP-15.
7. Berle to G. W. Anderson, November 14, 1932, BP-4.
8. Berle to H. E. Ellsworth, November 28, December 2, 1932, BP-7.
9. Berle, "The Trend of the Turn," *Saturday Review of Literature,* 9 (April 15, 1933), pp. 533–35.
10. Michael E. Parrish, *Felix Frankfurter and His Times: The Reform Years* (New York, 1982), pp. 206–7; Berle to G. W. Anderson, November 14, 1932, BP-4; Moley Diary, January 11, 1933; Berle to Bernard Baruch, January 11, 1933, Baruch Papers; Berle to Jerome Frank, January 25, 1933, Frank Papers, Boxes 1 and 3.
11. Berle to James Harvey Rogers, February 7, 1933, Rogers Papers, Box 20; *New York Times,* February 24, 1933; Freidel, *Launching the New Deal,* pp. 175–95; Berle to Charles Fay, November 2, 1935, BP-7.
12. Memo of the Treasury Conference, BP-17; Berle to Jesse Jones, August 16, 1933, BP-19; *New York Times,* October 18, 21, 1933; Thomas Lamont to Berle, March 8, 1933, Lamont Papers; Freidel, *Launching the New Deal,* pp. 219–220.
13. Kenneth S. Davis, *FDR: The New York Years 1928–1933* (New York, 1985), pp. 276–77.
14. Raymond Moley, *After Seven Years* (New York, 1939), pp. 149–50; James P. Warburg, COHC, pp. 149–50; Berle, NTR, p. 84; BBB Diary, March 18, 1933.
15. *New York Times,* April 13, May 26, 1933; Freidel, *Launching the New Deal,* pp. 413–16; Berle to David E. Lilienthal, April 15, 1933, Lilienthal Papers, Box 55; April 18, 1933, PPF 1306; Berle memo, April 24, 1933, BP-15.
16. NTR, pp. 86–87, 90–91; Berle to George Foster Peabody, June 15, 1933, BP-19; *New York Times, VIII,* June 4, 1933; Berle, "High Finance: Master or Servant," *Yale Review,* 23 (Autumn 1933), 42; Michael E. Parrish, *Securities Regulation and the New Deal* (New Haven, CN, 1970), p. 190.
17. *New York Times,* June 11, 27, 1933; Berle to Brandeis, February 19, 1932, BP-5; Berle, "A High Road for Business," *Scribner's Magazine,* 93 (June 1933), 325–32; Berle, "What's Behind the Recovery Laws," ibid., 94 (September 1933), 129–35; BBB Diary, September 12, 1934.
18. Berle, "The Social Economics of the New Deal," *New York Times Magazine,* October 29, 1933, pp. 4–5; *New York Times,* November 1, 1933; V. M. memo for Thomas W. Lamont, November 3, 1933, Lamont Papers.
19. Mary Ross to Berle, July 27, August 2, 1933, Survey Associates Papers, Box

54; Berle to Jerome Frank, July 14, Lee Pressman to Frank, August 12, Pressman to Berle, August 15, 24, 1933, Frank Papers, Box 10.

20. *New York Times,* July 20, August 5, 17, 30, 31, September 1, 1933; Berle to Jesse Jones, August 31, 1933, BP-19; John Dickinson to Berle, September 25, October 10, 1933, BP-22; E. B. Schwulst to Berle, July 29, 1933, BP-11.

The Last Chamberlain

1. Berle to Raymond Moley, November 28, 1932, BP-15; Lowell M. Limpus and Burr Leyson, *This Man La Guardia* (New York, 1938); William Manners, *Patience and Fortitude: Fiorello La Guardia* (New York, 1976); Lawrence Elliott, *Little Flower* (New York, 1983); Ernest Cuneo, *Life with Fiorello* (New York, 1955), pp. 186–87.

2. La Guardia telegram to Berle, May 13, La Guardia to Berle, November 16, BP-8; Berle memo to Roosevelt, December 2, 1932, BP-16; Howard Zinn, *La Guardia in Congress* (Ithaca, NY, 1958), pp. 255–56; Arthur Mann, *La Guardia: A Fighter Against His Times, 1882–1933* (Philadelphia, 1959), pp. 323–26.

3. Berle to Samuel I. Rosenman, to Raymond Moley, September 30, 1932, BP-10 and 15; Berle to Harold R. Medina, October 17, 1932, BP-9; Cuneo, *Life with Fiorello,* pp. 187–88.

4. Herbert Mitgang, *The Man Who Rode the Tiger: The Life and Times of Judge Samuel Seabury* (Philadelphia, 1963), pp. 316–20; Robert A. Caro, *The Power Broker: Robert Moses and the Fall of New York* (New York, 1975), pp. 348–56; Arthur Mann, *La Guardia Comes to Power 1933* (Philadelphia, 1965), pp. 67–87.

5. Mitgang, *Man Who Rode the Tiger,* p. 319; August Heckscher, *When La Guardia Was Mayor* (New York, 1978), p. 26; Mann, *La Guardia Comes to Power,* p. 159; Charles Garrett, *The La Guardia Years* (New Brunswick, NJ, 1961), pp. 98–103; Paul J. Kern, "Fiorello H. La Guardia," in J. T. Salter, ed., *The American Politician* (Chapel Hill, NC, 1938), pp. 3–46.

6. Mann, *La Guardia Comes to Power,* pp. 90–121; *New York Times,* July 19, August 6, 1933; Berle to Roosevelt, August 19, 1933, BP-10, September 24, October 21, 1933, PSF; NTR, pp. 88–89.

7. Berle to Bernard M. Baruch, December 18, 1933, Baruch Papers.

8. La Guardia quoted in Heckscher, *When La Guardia Was Mayor,* p. 152.

9. La Guardia memos, April 23, December 4, 1934, December 6, 1935, November 21, 1935, La Guardia Papers, Box 3, folder 1, Box 22, folder 22.

10. Robert Moses, *Public Works: A Dangerous Trade* (New York, 1970), p. 848; Berle to Stuart Godwin, March 11, 1937, BP-7. On Faulkner, see Berle to Kidder, Peabody and Co., March 24, 1936, BP-7, to Ellwood N. Rabenold, September 17, 1936, BP-10.

11. *New York Times,* January 7, 8, 1934; Garrett, *The La Guardia Years,* pp. 143–44.

12. Berle to Roosevelt, January 9, Roosevelt to Berle, January 13, 1934, BP-10, PPF 1306; La Guardia memo, January 29, 1934, La Guardia Papers, Box 3, folder 1.

13. *New York Times,* February 2, 4, 9, 10, 17, March 2, 11, May 11, 1934; Heckscher, *When La Guardia Was Mayor,* pp. 37–47; Caro, *The Power Broker,* pp. 376–77.

14. *New York Times,* January 16, December 6, 1934; Berle to Lillian D. Wald, December 7, 1934, BP-12; Berle to Roosevelt, July 16 ("not sent—hold as memo"), July 25, October 23, 1934, BP-10, PPF 1306.
15. Berle to Samuel Seabury, August 3, 1934, BP-11; Mitgang, *Man Who Rode the Tiger,* pp. 328–39.
16. Berle to Roosevelt, March 1, 3, 15, Roosevelt to Berle, March 2, 1934, BP-10, PPF 1306; Caro, *The Power Broker,* pp. 426–28.
17. Berle to Roosevelt, October 2, 1934, BP-10; *New York Times,* October 4, 19, 30, November 1, 1934; Berle to Roosevelt, October 23, November 8, 1934, BP-10, PPF 1306.
18. *New York Times,* January 3, April 23, 24, 1935; Berle memo to La Guardia, February 4, 1936, La Guardia Papers, Box 39, folder 11; Berle to S. M. Stroock, August 26, 1935, BP-11.
19. *New York Times,* February 20, September 6, 12, 13, 14, 28, October 26, November 2, 1935, January 3, 1936; Paul Windels, COHC, pp. 116–18; Garrett, *The La Guardia Years,* pp. 210–19.
20. Berle to Lillian D. Wald, February 18, 1936, BP-12; *New York Times,* March 12, 1936; Berle to La Guardia, March 10, 1936, La Guardia Papers, Box 39, folder 11; David E. Lilienthal, *Journals: The TVA Years 1939–1945* (New York, 1964), p. 57, NRT, pp. 111–12; Berle to La Guardia, June 9, 1936, BP-25.
21. *New York Times,* November 29, 30, 1938; R. A. Lazarus, COHC, pp. 239–42.
22. *New York Times,* July 19, 1936; Stephen Early memo for the president, July 18, McIntyre telegram to Early, July 21, 1936, PPF 1376; Garrett, *The La Guardia Years,* p. 258.
23. *New York Times,* August 14, 1936; Heckscher, *When La Guardia Was Mayor,* p. 138; David Dubinsky and A. H. Raskin, *David Dubinsky: A Life With Labor* (New York, 1977), pp. 269–70.
24. Berle to Sumner Welles, August 6, 1937, BP-26.
25. *New York Times,* November 7, 1936, January 15, April 18, May 27, September 26, November 3, 1937; Berle Diary, August 3, 17, November 8, 10, 1937; Berle to George S. Van Schaick, to Hugh S. Robertson, November 17, 1936, BP-26 and 25.
26. Berle to Lillian D. Wald, July 30, 1937, BP-12; copy, A. A. Berle, Sr., to Mr. Buxton, November 5, 1937, PPF 3924; Berle to Father, June 16, 1953, BP-81; Berle to James Harvey Rogers, January 14, 1937, BP-10 and Rogers Papers, Box 32.
27. *New York Times,* December 7, 31, 1937; Berle to La Guardia December 6, 10, 1937, La Guardia Papers, Box 53, folder 4; Berle memo to La Guardia, November 10, 1937, BP-25; Berle Diary, May 26, August 5, September 14, 17, October 13, 15, 19, 28, November 29, December 2, 10, 30, 31, 1937, January 10, 1938.

A Cabin in Washington

1. Berle, "The Way of an American," *Survey Graphic,* 25 (November 1936), 597; "The Lost Art of Economics," *Virginia Quarterly Review,* 14 (Summer 1938), 328.

2. On New York intellectuals in the 1930s, see Nathan Glazer, "New York Intellectual—Up from Revolution," *New York Times Book Review,* February 26, 1984, p. 1.

3. Berle, "Business and Government: Toward a Common Ground," *Scribner's Magazine,* 96 (November 1934), 257–65; "U.S.A., Incorporated," *Saturday Review of Literature,* September 21, 1935, pp. 11–12.

4, *New York Times,* January 7, October 19, 1934; Berle, "The Law and the Social Revolution," *Survey Graphic,* 22 (December 1933), 593–95; "Private Business and Public Opinion," *Scribner's Magazine,* 95 (February 1934), 84.

5. Moley to Tugwell, June 15, 1934, Moley Papers, Box 55; Berle to FDR, April 23, FDR to Berle, April 30, 1934, BP-10.

6. Brandeis to Berle, June 7, July 17, Berle to Brandeis, July 11, 26, 1934, Memo, August 3, 1934, BP-5; FDR to Berle, August 7, 1934, Berle to FDR, September 12, 13, 17, November 17, 1934, BP-10; FDR to Morgenthau, October 5, Oliphant to McIntyre, December 3, 1934, PPF 1306.

7. *New York Times,* May 29, June 23, 1935; Berle to Frederick L. Allen, October 19, to Charles D. Williams, September 5, 1935, BP-4 and 12.

8. Berle to Robert La Follette, April 27, 1936, BP-8; Berle, "Revenue and Progress," *Survey Graphic,* 24 (October 1935), 469–73; "Redistributing the National Income," *Yale Review,* 26 (1937), 741–59.

9. Frank to Frankfurter, January 21, 1936, Frank Papers, Box 12; Frankfurter to Frank, June 10, 1935, Frankfurter Papers, Box 55; Berle, "The Way of an American," *Survey Graphic,* 25 (November 1936), p. 597; La Follette to FDR, January 29, 1936, PPF 1306.

10. Berle to James M. Landis, February 16, 28, Landis to Berle, February 25, 1934, BP-22; *New York Times,* September 27, 28, 1934; Berle to Richard Whitney, July 6, Whitney to Berle, September 27, October 8, 1934, BP-12 and 23; Berle to FDR, August 14, FDR to Berle, August 15, 1934, BP-10.

11. Berle to FDR, February 4, 1937, PSF 94; Berle to Douglas, January 26, September 23, November 5, "not sent," 1937, BP-25 and 7; Berle to Peter Nehemkis, November 10, 1937, BP-10.

12. *New York Times,* December 11, 1937; also, see James F. Simon, *Independent Journey* (New York, 1980), pp. 162–75; Michael E. Parrish, *Securities Regulation and the New Deal* (New Haven, CN, 1970), pp. 216–17.

13. Berle to FDR, March 3, May 18, FDR to Berle, March 10, May 24, 1934, BP-10; Tugwell Diary, April 13, May 19, 1934; *The Secret Diary of Harold L. Ickes: The First Thousand Days* (New York, 1953), p. 693.

14. Berle to Rexford G. Tugwell, November 15, Tugwell to Berle, November 16, 1939, Tugwell Papers, Box 1; Horace N. Gilbert to Berle, October 29, to FDR, November 2, FDR to Berle, November 6, 1935, BP-10, PPF 1306.

15. NTR, pp. 110–11, 115; Berle to Charles Taussig, July 8, Taussig to Berle, November 21, 27, Berle to Taussig, December 1, 1936, Taussig Papers, Box 21; on the struggle between planners and atomizers, see Arthur Schlesinger, Jr., *The Politics of Upheaval* (Boston, 1960), pp. 220–41, 385–408.

16. Berle to FDR, February 4, 1937, BP-26; M.A.L. memo to FDR, February 9, FDR memo to McIntyre, February 11, 1937, PSF 94, PPF 1306; Berle Diary, March 4, 1937.

17. Berle Diary, April 26, 29, August 5, September 14, 17, October 13, 19, 28, 29,

November 1, 8, 17, 29, December 2, 10, 13, 1937; Beatrice Bishop Berle, *A Life in Two Worlds* (New York, 1983), p. 15; Rudolf Berle memo in Berle Diary, January 1938; FDR to Berle, September 4, 1937, BP-10, PPF 1306.

18. Berle to R. A. Gordon, September 30, 1936, to Ralph E. Flanders, July 21, 1937, BP-7, to Rufus Tucker, February 13, 1937, BP-11, memo re sit-down strikes, March 22, 1937, BP-5; *New York Times,* February 7, section 4, March 23, 1937.

19. Memos, December 24, 30, 1937, Tugwell Papers, Box 30; Memo, December 23, 1937, BP-9; Lamont to Berle, December 14, 28, 1937, Lamont Papers, BP-25; Ellis W. Hawley, *The New Deal and the Problem of Monopoly* (Princeton, 1966), pp. 392–93; Berle Diary, December 24, 27, 29, 30, 1937.

20. *New York Times,* January 14, 15, 16, 1938; memo for FDR, Tugwell Papers, Box 30; Berle Diary, January 17, 19, 25, February 7, 1938; Berle to Lamont, March 1, 1938, BP-9; Hawley, "The Corporate Ideal as Liberal Philosophy in the New Deal," in Wilbur Cohen, *The Roosevelt New Deal* (Austin, TX, 1986), pp. 95–96.

CHAPTER 5   IMPERIAL VISIONS, 1938–1941

Six Months in 1938

1. Robert Moses, *Public Works: A Dangerous Trade* (New York, 1970), p. 849.
2. Washington *Star,* April 29, 1934; *New York Times,* April 24, 25, 1934; R. A. Lazarus, COHC, pp. 296–97; "Washington Merry-Go-Round," New York *Daily Mirror,* January 24, 1938.
3. New York *Daily Mirror,* January 24, 27, February 2, 11, 1938; Berle Diary, January 24, 1938; John McCarten, "Atlas with Ideas," *New Yorker,* January 16, 1943, p. 22.
4. Clipping, Rodney Dutcher column, February 21, 1938, Hornbeck Papers, Box 26; New York *Herald Tribune,* February 15, 1938; Hull to FDR, January 25, 1938, PSF 94.
5. Berle to Jerome Frank, June 7, 1938, Frank Papers, Box 22; to Paul Kellogg, May 19, 1938, Survey Associates Papers, Box 54; to FDR, January 28, February 1, 1938, BP-27; Berle Diary, February 10, 11, 16, 18, 21, 1938.
6. Otto C. Wierum to Berle, April 29, Berle to Wierum, April 30, Wierum to Berle, May 6, 1937, BP-12.
7. Berle to Editor, New York *Herald Tribune,* April 2, 1937, BP-25; to Maury Maverick, January 2, 1936, to E. J. Marshall, November 14, 1934, BP-9; to W. Z. Ripley, February 15, 1934, August 5, 1936, BP-10; to Paul Kellogg, January 6, 1936, Kellogg to Berle, January 14, 1935, Survey Associates Papers, Box 54.
8. Berle to David E. Lilienthal, December 14, to Carl I. Wheat, December 6, 1934, to C. L. Richey, January 31, 1935, BP-9 and 12.
9. James Harvey Rogers to Berle, February 14, March 11, Berle to Rogers, February 18, 1936, Rogers Papers, Box 29; to Young B. Smith, November 7, 1934, BP-11.
10. William O. Douglas, *Go East, Young Man* (New York, 1974), p. 368; Alvin

Johnson to Berle, October 25, 1937, BP-25; Berle Diary, April 13, 1934, Tugwell Diary, May 5, 1935; R. Walton Moore to William C. Bullitt, April 26, 1940, Moore Papers, Box 3; For Berle on William O. Douglas, see Berle, COHC, pp. 141–44.

11. *New York Times,* February 10, 1938.

12. R. C. Lindsay to Viscount Halifax, March 7, 1938, FO 371/21527.

13. On Jones and the RFC, see Jesse H. Jones with Edward Angly, *Fifty Billion Dollars* (New York, 1951) and James Stuart Olson's forthcoming history of the RFC during the New Deal, *Saving Capitalism.*

14. Berle memo, March 9, 1938, BP-55; E. W. Hawley, *The New Deal and the Problem of Monopoly* (Princeton, 1966), p. 321; Paul Mallon clipping, un-dated, BP-56; Louis Faulkner to Berle, March 24, 1938, BP-27; Berle to FDR, "re: Capital Credit Banks," March 24, 1938, PSF 94; Moffat Diary, August 10, 1938.

15. Berle to FDR, August 16, 1938, PSF 94; Berle memo, April 5, 1938, BP-66; Berle memo to FDR, April 18, FDR memo for Morgenthau, May 13, 1938, PPF 1306; Hawley, *New Deal and Monopoly,* pp. 413–14; H. B. Elliston in *Christian Science Monitor,* August 31, 1938; *New York Times,* August 19, 20, 1938.

16. Berle Diary, June 30, 1938; Berle memo to FDR, September 2, 1938, BP-66.

17. Berle memos, March 15, 20, 1938, BP-68 and 66; Berle memos, June 1, August 15, 16, PSF 94; O. D. Skelton memos for Mackenzie King, August 17, 19, 1938, King Papers, vol. 210, folder 1992.

18. Berle Diary, March 19, May 26, 1938.

19. See Foreign Policy Association correspondence, BP-7; Berle to Sumner Welles, October 3, 1932, BP-16; Hudson Strode, *The Pageant of Cuba* (New York, 1934), pp. 318–21; Berle to Hudson Strode, December 17, 1934, to Roy W. Howard, April 24, 1936, BP-11.

20. Berle to Taussig, December 1, 1936, September 21, 1937, Taussig Papers, Box 21; Robert Dallek, *Franklin D. Roosevelt and American Foreign Policy, 1932–1945* (New York, 1979), pp. 132–34; Irwin F. Gellman, *Good Neighbor Diplomacy: United States Policies in Latin America 193–1945* (New York, 1979), pp. 61–68.

21. On U.S. appeasement, see C. A. MacDonald, *The United States, Britain and Appeasement* (Baltimore, 1981), pp. 64–65, 76, 87–88, 95–96, 107; Arnold A. Offner, *American Appeasement: United States Foreign Policy and Germany, 1933–1938* (Baltimore, 1969).

22. Berle memo to FDR, September 1, 1938, PSF 94; Berle to Paul Kellogg, June 13, 1938, Survey Associates Papers, Box 54.

23. Berle to FDR, September 1, 1938, PSF 94; Moffat Diary, September 17 and 18, 1938.

24. Berle Diary, July 9, 1938; Martin Weil, *A Pretty Good Club* (New York, 1978), p. 78; Hugh De Santis, *The Diplomacy of Silence* (Chicago, 1979), pp. 13–15, 19–21, 25–26; R. C. Lindsay to Viscount Halifax, September 3, 1938, FO 371/21528; "Subject: Conversations . . . July 1937," Messersmith Papers.

25. Berle Diary, March 26, September 14, 1938; Moffat Diary, August 29, 1938; *Washington Star,* September 8, 1938.

26. Beulah Amidon to Berle, September 15, Berle to Amidon, September 21, 1938,

Survey Associates Papers, Box 54; Berle Diary, September 19, 1938; Joseph Alsop and Robert Kintner, *American White Paper* (New York, 1940), pp. 7–8.

Death Watch

1. R. C. Lindsay to Viscount Halifax, March 10, 1939, FO 371/22754; New York *Herald Tribune,* January 13, 1939.
2. Berle to James Harvey Rogers, October 28, 1938, Rogers Papers, Box 37; NTR, p. 190; Berle memo, November 4, 1938, BP-55; Mother to Berle, November 6, 1938, BP-5; Berle to Nicholas Murray Butler, October 11, 1940, BP-30.
3. George S. Messersmith to D. N. Heineman, November 7, 1938, Messersmith Papers; Berle memo for FDR, November 19, 1938, PSF 94; *New York Times,* New York *Herald Tribune,* November 21, 1938.
4. Berle Diary, January 10, 1939; Alsop and Kintner, *American White Paper,* p. 22; *New York Times,* December 28, 1938, January 10, 1939; Lee Pressman, COHC, pp. 129–30.
5. *New York Times,* December 1, 4, 1938; Cordell Hull, *The Memoirs of Cordell Hull* (New York, 1948), pp. 601–11; Gellman, *Good Neighbor Diplomacy,* pp. 74–79; Berle Diary, January 10, 1939.
6. Berle quoted in Alsop and Kintner, *American White Paper,* p. 21; *Washington Post,* March 7, 1939; Berle, "After Lima," *Yale Review,* 28 (March 1939), 449–71; Berle to Winthrop Murray Crane, April 15, to Frank P. Corrigan, May 8, 1939, BP-31; R. C. Lindsay to Viscount Halifax, March 10, 1939, FO 371/22754.
7. Gellman, *Good Neighbor Diplomacy,* pp. 50–54; Berle Diary, March 23, 26, 1938; Conversations, March 28, 30 (2), Sumner Welles memo to Larry Duggan, March 30, 1938, RG 59, 812.6363/3337–8, 3320, 3322.
8. Messersmith to D. M. Heineman, November 7, 1938, Messersmith Papers; Berle Diary, December 14, November 28, 1939; Berle memo to Welles, April 17, 1939, RG 59, 812.00 Revolutions/468.
9. Berle memo, November 4, 1938, BP-55; Berle quoted in Alsop and Kintner, p. 16; Berle Diary, April 15, 1939, with attached April 14 letter to Hitler showing authorship of paragraphs; Alsop and Kintner, *American White Paper,* pp. 35–38; Berle memo to FDR, April 18, 1939, BP-66; Berle Diary, April 20, 1938.
10. Berle memos to FDR, April 24, June 3 "not sent," 1939, BP-66; *New York Times,* May 4, June 25, 1938.
11. Berle Diary, August 17, 18, 22, 24, 26, 28, September 1, 1939; *Time,* September 4, 1939, p. 10; Robert Sherrod to Berle, August 30, 31, 1939, BP-48; Alsop and Kintner, *American White Paper,* pp. 54, 66–67.
12. Berle Diary, September 4, 1939.

The Pax Americana *in 1940*

1. Berle to Beulah Amidon, September 25, 1939, BP-46; Berle Diary, September 21, 1939; *New York Times,* December 6, 1939, February 25, 1940; Berle, "Should We Turn to 'Isolationism'?—No, Says Berle," *New York Times Magazine,* January 14, 1940; Henry Wallace, COHC, p. 966; Berle Diary, March 29, 1940.

2. Berle to William Hard, March 1, 1940, BP-36; Berle Diary, May 10, 1940; Berle memo to FDR, March 21, 1940, BP-67; Berle to George Messersmith, March 25, 1940, BP-43.

3. Berle Diary, November 17, December 5, 8, 11, 19, 1939, January 12, 16, 22, 25, February 16, 28, 1940; James Rowe to FDR, January 24, 1940, PSF 148; John Morton Blum, *From the Morgenthau Diaries: Years of Urgency, 1938–1941* (Boston, 1965), p. 57; David Rees, *Harry Dexter White* (New York, 1973), p. 104; Gellman, *Good Neighbor Diplomacy,* pp. 157–62.

4. Berle Diary, May 9, 14, 31, June 10, 13, 1940; Berle to Elbert D. Thomas, June 6, 1940, BP-50.

5. *New York Times,* June 23, 1940; Berle Diary, December 5, 1939, January 16, 1940; "United States plans a cartel for all the Americas," Lothian to Viscount Halifax, June 28, 1940, FO 371/24210; Gellman, *Good Neighbor Diplomacy,* pp. 93–94.

6. Frank R. Kent in the *Baltimore Sun,* January 30, 1941; interview with Beatrice Berle, July 7, 1982.

7. Joseph W. Alsop to "Alec," February 26, 1940, Alsop Papers, Box 2; draft memo 818, April 1940, Reid Papers, vol. 5, folder 3; R. Walton Moore to William C. Bullitt, April 26, 1940, Moore Papers, Box 3; Berle Diary, April 23, 1940.

8. Long Diary, April 27, May 10, 13, December 29, 1940.

9. Long Diary, December 18, 20, 21, 1939; Paul Appleby, COHC, pp. 318; Martin Weil, *A Pretty Good Club* (New York, 1978), pp. 112–13; Dean Acheson, *Present at the Creation* (New York, 1969), pp. 12, 13.

10. Moffat Diary, April 13–14, 1940; Long Diary, April 23, March 23, 1940; Berle Diary, March 18, June 13, 1940.

Braintruster for a Third Term

1. Interview with James H. Rowe, Jr., December 30, 1982; also, see Berle Diary, March 26, 1938.

2. Berle to Nathan D. Lobell, February 16, 1939, "not sent," BP-9; Moley quoted in Ellis Hawley, *The New Deal and the Problem of Monopoly* (Princeton, 1966), p. 417; Berle Diary, July 16, 1938.

3. Herbert Stein, *The Fiscal Revolution in America* (Chicago, 1969), pp. 167–68.

4. Berle Diary, December 11, 1939; Berle to Jerome Frank, March 10, 1939, Frank Papers, Box 22; Berle to Nathan D. Lobell, February 16, 1939, "not sent," to R. A. Gordon, May 1, 1939, BP-9 and 35.

5. Berle to Arthur C. Holden, December 8, 1938, to Lauchlin Currie, May 26, 1939, to Louis H. Bean, February 4, 1939, BP-37, 31, and 5; Berle *New Directions in the New World* (New York, 1940), pp. 100–101, 124–25.

6. Berle to Peter Nehemkis, February 3, 8, 1939, BP-71; Jerome Frank to Berle, February 22, 25, Berle to Frank, to FDR, February 23, April 4, 1939, BP-7 and 66; Alsop and Kintner in *Washington Star,* February 11, 1939; Frank to William O. Douglas, March 17, 1939, Frank Papers, Box 25.

7. Berle to Lobell, February 16, 1939, "not sent," BP-9; Nehemkis to Berle, May 5, Berle memos, May 10, 12, 1939, BP-71.

8. Frank to Berle, to Nehemkis, May 22, 1939, Frank Papers, Box 22; Berle memo

to FDR, May 10, to Currie, May 26, 1939, BP-47 and 31; to Dennison, May 20, 1939, BP-43; *New York Times,* May 24, June 4, 1939.

9. *Washington Post,* May 28, 1939; Beulah Amidon to Berle, June 20, 1939, Survey Associates Papers, Box 54; Filene to Berle, June 15, 1939, H. W. Conde to Berle, May 29, Berle to Conde, May 31, 1931, BP-71; *New York Times,* May 25, 26, 29, June 11, 1939; Berle to Fred I. Kent, August 5, 1939, BP-51.

10. Homer Jones to Berle, June 1, Berle to Jones, June 2, to Merwin K. Hart, August 3, 1939 [emphasis added], BP-71; Stein, *The Fiscal Revolution,* p. 121; Raymond Moley, "Economic Totalitarianism," *Newsweek,* June 12, 1939, p. 56.

11. Berle to Marquis Childs, February 26, 1940, BP-30. On economic thinking of the time, see Stein, *Presidential Economics* (New York, 1984), pp. 62-84; Stein, *The Fiscal Revolution,* pp. 131-68; Jordan A. Schwarz, *The Speculator: Bernard M. Baruch in Washington, 1917-1965* (Chapel Hill, NC, 1981), pp. 329-88, 401-8.

12. *New York Times,* September 17, 1939; Rexford Tugwell to Berle, November 14, Berle to Tugwell, November 15, 1939, BP-51, Tugwell Papers, Box 1; Tugwell Diary, November 17, 1939, July 30, 1940.

13. Berle Diary, July 16, 1938; George Messersmith to Charles C. Burlingham, July 13, 1939, Messersmith Papers.

14. Berle to Fiorello H. La Guardia, June 6, 1939, BP-38; Berle Diary, June 12, 1939; Berle to Wilbur Cortes Abbott, July 31, 1939, BP-27; Berle Diary, August 16, 1939; Berle memo to FDR, August 14, 1939, BP-66; Berle Diary, August 18, October 31, November 15, 1939.

15. Berle memos to FDR, April 8, July 18, 1940, PSF 94; *New York Times,* April 14, 1940; Berle Diary, April 30, May 9, July 1, 1940; Long Diary, July 12, 28, 1940; Tugwell Diary, July 30, 1940.

16. Berle Diary, November 4, October 9, 11, 17, 25, 1940; interview with Ernest Cuneo, May 5, 1984.

"Neutrality Does Not Imply Impartiality"

1. David Reynolds, *The Creation of the Anglo-American Alliance 1937-41: A Study in Competitive Co-Operation* (Chapel Hill, NC, 1981), p. 181; Long Diary, February 7, 1941; Moffat Diary, February 3, 4, 5, 1941; Berle Diary, February 6, 1941.

2. *Washington Times-Herald,* October 23, 1940; Berle memo to Welles, October 23, Welles to Berle, October 24, 1940, BP-73; Berle Diary, May 8, December 28, 1940; Moffat Diary, September 25, 1939, November 24-27, October 6-10, 1940, January 31, 1941.

3. Moore to William Bullitt, April 26, 1940, Moore Papers, Box 3; Long Diary, December 29, 1940, January 13, February 15, 17, 1941; Moffat Diary, April 13-14, 1940; Berle Diary, February 17, 1941.

4. Moffat Diary, November 24-27, 1940, April 3, January 31, 1941; Long Diary, April 17, 1941; Berle Diary, October 24, 1941.

5. Berle Diary, November 28, 1939, October 10, 1940, February 11, 14, 17, March 5, 13, 14, 16, 1941; Moffat Diary, February 5, 1941; Berle memos, "Fund Freez-

ing," February 17, "The Internal Problem," February 24, Berle to Hull, "hold," June 2, 1941, BP-57; "Berle, April 8, 1941," Alsop Papers, Box 32; Blum, *Years of Urgency,* pp. 326–37.

6. Berle Diary, May 24, 5, August 2, 28, 1940; Long Diary, June 13, 1940; Berle memo to Welles, July 8, 1940, BP-57; Gellman, *Good Neighbor Diplomacy,* pp. 98–100; *New York Times,* August 4, 1940, section IV.

7. Long Diary, August 31, 1940; Berle Diary, September 2, October 10, 13, 15, December 1, 1940, February 24, 1941; Moffat Diary, October 6–10, 1940; Berle, "Peace Without Empire," "Common Defense and Common Welfare," *Survey Graphic,* 30 (March, May 1941), 103–8, 281–83; Reynolds, *Anglo-American Alliance,* pp. 95–155.

8. Berle memo, January 11, to Lauchlin Currie, February 10, 1941, BP-67; Moffat Diary, April 7–9, 1941; Long Diary, February 7, 1941; Berle Diary, February 13, 1941; Clapper Diary, February 18, 1941.

9. Moffat Diary, March 31, 1941; Berle Diary, March 13, 1941.

10. Berle Diary, March 5, May 26, June 19, 1941; Moffat Diary, June 23, 26, 1941.

Canadian Capers

1. J. L. Granatstein, *Canada's War: The Politics of the Mackenzie King Government, 1939–1945* (Toronto, 1975), pp. 19–20; Berle Diary, September 6, 8, 11, 1939.

2. M. F. Hepburn to W. L. Mackenzie King, January 16, 1937, memo for Fyle, October 3, 1939, King Papers, vol. 210, folder 1993; copy, F. P. Walsh memo to FDR, February 15, 1938, BP-68; *New York Times,* February 24, 1939; Berle Diary, March 16, October 16, 1939, Olds memo to FDR, October 16, 1939 in Berle Diary.

3. Berle Memo, October 16, 1939, BP-66; Berle Diary, October 31, December 26, 1939, January 4, 1940; King Diary, December 21, 1939, King Papers, vol. 210, folder 1993; Christie to Hull, Berle memo, December 26, 1939, Hull to Christie, January 3, 1940, RG 59, 711.42157 SA 29/1640; *New York Times,* January 4, 5, 7, 1940.

4. Berle Diary, January 7, 8, 9, 31, May 2, 25, 1940; L. W. Brockington memo to King, March 8, 1940, O. D. Skelton memo, May 2, 1940, King Papers, vol. 350, folder 3788, vol. 330, folder 3504.

5. Loring C. Christie to O. D. Skelton, August 12, 22, Skelton memo to King, September 11, King to Christie, September 14, Christie to King, September 16, 17, October 10, 11, 1940, King Papers, vol. 403, folder 88; Berle Diary, September 9, October 3, 9, 10, 14, 1940.

6. Berle Diary, December 3, 5, 1940, February 10, 1941; *New York Times,* December 6, 1940, January 4, 24, 1941; Moffat Diary, December 11, 1940, January 4, 1941; Berle to Charles Eliasson, December 28, 1940, BP-68; Meeting, January 3 and 4, 1941, Reid Papers, vol. 5, folder 1; Berle to FDR, January 6, 1941, BP-67.

7. Clipping, *Montreal Gazette,* January 7, 1941, King Papers, vol. 404, folder 89; *New York Times,* January 11, 1941; Berle Diary, February 1, 5, 1941; Moffat Diary, January 24, 29, 31, February 1, 6, 1941.

8. Moffat Diary, February 6, 13, 18, March 9, 11, 1941; Hickerson memo to Berle, March 11, Berle memo to FDR, March 12, 1941, BP-68; Berle Diary, March 12, 1941.
9. Berle Diary, March 16, 1941.
10. Moffat Diary, March 17, 1941; Berle Diary, March 18, 19, 1941; Moffat Diary, March 18, 1941.
11. Berle memo to FDR, March 12, 1941, BP-67; Berle, "Great Lakes–St. Lawrence Waterway Project," *Vital Speeches,* 7 (July 1, 1941), 565–66; Moffat Diary, April 2, 1941; Berle Diary, June 5, 19, July 23, August 2, 1941; *New York Times,* June 18, 1941; Berle to Fred S. Keiser, August 11, 1941, BP-68.
12. Berle Diary, June 12, 1940; Granatstein, *Canada's War,* p. 126; Hutchison memo, June 12, 1940, King Papers, vol. 400, folder 73.
13. M. M. Mahoney to O. D. Skelton, June 14, Skelton to Mackenzie King, June 16, 1940, King Papers, vol. 400, folder 75; Keenleyside quoted in Granatstein, *Canada's War,* p. 127.
14. Granatstein, *Canada's War,* pp. 132–37; Berle Diary, November 26, 1940; Moffat Diary, November 24–27, December 11, 1940; H. L. Keenleyside memo, "The Integration of War Industry in Canada and the United States," December 27, 1940, King Papers, vol. 350, folder 3788.
15. Granatstein, *Canada's War,* pp. 145–46; Escott Reid to H. L. Keenleyside, January 13, Keenleyside to Reid, January 15, 1941, External Affairs Papers, file 1497–40.
16. Aide-mémoire, March 17, McCarthy to King, March 18, Keenleyside memo, March 18, External Affairs Papers, file 1497–40; Roberton to King, March 19, King to Canadian High Commissioner, March 21, 1941, King Papers, vol. 348, folder 3773; Berle Diary, March 18, 19, 1941; Moffat Diary, March 18, 1941.
17. Berle memo for Hull and Welles, April 19, 1941, BP-60; statement, April 20, 1941, King Papers, vol. 350, folder 3788; *New York Times,* April 21, 1941; Granatstein, *Canada's War,* pp. 137–47; Moffat Diary, April 21, 25, June 2, 23, 1941; Berle Diary, April 25, June 5, July 15, 1941.

Ideological Politics

1. Isaac Don Levine to Berle, December 7, 1934, BP-8; Berle to Luigi Antonini, February 6, 1939, BP-4; Berle Diary, January 31, April 2, 1939.
2. Berle Diary, September 4, 13, 30, 1939; Berle memo to FDR, September 18, 1939, PSF 94; Long Diary, October 5, 11, 1939.
3. See Robert Sobel, *The Origins of Interventionism: The United States and the Russo-Finnish War* (New York, 1960) and Travis Beal Jacobs, *America and the Winter War, 1939–1940* (New York, 1981).
4. Berle Diary, November 15, December 5, 1939, February 12, March, 3, April 30, May 3, 1940; Memo of conversation, January 25, 1940, BP-64; FDR memo to Berle, January 27, Berle memos to FDR, January 30, February 20, 1940, PSF 94, BP-67; Moffat Diary, December 28, 1939, April 30, 1940.
5. Berle Diary, September 28, 1940; *New York Times,* September 29, 1940; Berle to Frank Oliver, October 3, 1940, BP-44.
6. Berle Diary, December 28, 1939, February 14, April 23, 1940; *New York Times,* April 11, 1940; Berle to FDR, May 27, to Paul Kellogg, February 26, 1940, BP-38.

7. *New York Times,* October 5, 1936; Berle to Alex Rose, to David Dubinsky, to Luigi Antonini, August 17, Dubinsky to Berle, August 23, 1939, BP-47, 33 and 28; Berle Diary, October 16, 1939.

8. Berle to David Dubinsky, October 17, 1939, telegram, Dubinsky to Berle, February 2, letter, Berle to Dubinsky, February 2, 1940, BP-33; Berle Diary, February 1, April 5, 1940; on the ALP, see Harvey Klehr, *The Heyday of American Communism* (New York, 1984), pp. 265–69, 403–4.

9. Klehr, *Heyday of American Communism,* p. 323; Paul Kellogg to Berle, April 16, 1940, Survey Associates Papers, Box 54; Berle Diary, October 31, 1939, April 5, 30, 1940.

10. Jerold S. Auerbach, *Unequal Justice* (New York, 1976), pp. 198–204; Executive Board Minutes, February 10, 1939, National Lawyers Guild Papers; Ferdinand Pecora, "Democracy and the Legal Profession," *National Lawyers Guild Quarterly,* 2 (April 1939), pp. 6–7; Morris L. Ernst, *The Best Is Yet* (New York, 1945), pp. 51–52.

11. Janet Stevenson, *The Undiminished Man: Robert Kennedy* (Berkeley, CA, 1980), pp. 128, 131–33; Nathan Margold to John Gutknecht, May 29, memo to Berle, May 29, Berle to Gutknecht, June 3, to Leo J. Neeson, July 9, 1940, BP-44; *New York Times,* June 6, 1940; Mark Sullivan in the *Washington Post,* June 22, 1940.

12. Berle Diary, November 4, October 9, 11, 17, 25, 1940; Cuneo interview.

13. Berle to David Dubinsky, November 13, 1940, BP-33; to Harry W. Laidler, November 16, 1940, BP-38; Berle speech, "The Defense Program and Democratic Progress," BP-46.

14. Berle Diary, December 7, April 23, 5, 1940, February 28, 1941; clipping, "Who Is Harold Moskovit and What Are the Affiliated Young Democrats Up To," BP-63; Berle to Samuel Seabury, July 28, 1941, BP-48.

15. Harold Moskovit to Berle, April 3, 9, 14, May 1, 10, June 2, 9, 16, November 17, telegram, June 16, Berle to Moskovit, April 17, May 26, 1941, BP-63.

16. August Heckscher, *When La Guardia Was Mayor* (New York, 1978), pp. 288–90, 303–4; Berle Diary, November 29, 1940, February 16, 20, 1941.

17. Berle Diary, July 17, 1941; *New York World-Telegram,* February 19, March 15, 1941; *New York Times,* February 21, May 23, 24, 25, 27, 1941; Tugwell Diary, April 16, 1941; Berle to Raymond Schwartz, July 4, 1941, BP-48.

18. Charles Garrett, *The La Guardia Years* (New Brunswick, NJ, 1961), pp. 268–73; Heckscher, *When La Guardia Was Mayor,* pp. 303–13; Berle Diary, July 23, November 3, 1941; *New York Times,* October 3, 4, 31, 1941; Morris L. Ernst to La Guardia, October 7, telegram, Ernst to Berle, November 1, Berle to Eugene Early, November 9, 1941, BP-33.

19. Berle Diary, memo of conversation, January 21, September 19, 1941; Ickes Diary, June 28, 1941; *New York World-Telegram,* March 15, 1941; Berle to FDR, November 5, 1941, BP-67.

A Temporary Confluence of Interest

1. Berle to FDR, July 8, memo to Sumner Welles, July 7, memo to Harry Hopkins, July 7, memo, "Economic Post-War Commitments," July 9, 1941, BP-54; Moffat Diary, July 14, 1941; Clapper Diary, October 19, 1941.

2. Berle Diary, July 11, 17, 23, 31, August 1, 2, 1941; Reynolds, *Anglo-American*

Alliance, pp. 256–57; Berle memo to FDR, July 17, memos, August 1, 2, 1941, BP-54; Berle memo to Hull, August 4, 1941, BP-58; Moffat Diary, July 14, September 19–23, 1941.

3. *New York Times,* August 9, 1941.
4. Berle Diary, April 9, 20, June 3, memo, September 7, 1940, April 15, September 23, 1941; Long Diary, April 9, 10, 11, 23, 24, 26, 1940; Moffat Diary, April 27–28, 1940; Berle memo to FDR, February 7, 1941, BP-67; press releases, April 10, 14, 1941, Berle to Mrs. Roosevelt, July 24, 1941, BP-57 and 47.
5. A. D. Marris minute, July 15, Nevile Butler to David Scott, July 17, T. North Whitehead minute, August 1, 1941, FO 371/29261, his emphasis; also, see Berle Diary, July 31, 1941.
6. Berle memo to Hull, September 15, 1941, BP-54; Reynolds, *Anglo-American Alliance,* p. 219, emphasis added; on British-Soviet plans for Eastern Europe, see Albert Resis, "Spheres of Influence in Soviet Wartime Diplomacy," *Journal of Modern History,* 53 (September 1981), 417–39.
7. Board of Economic Operations minutes, October 16, 14, 21, November 6, December 4, 1941, BP-56; Berle Diary, September 25, October 24, November 18, 1941; Berle memo to Hull, October 14, 1941, BP-58.
8. Berle Diary, October 24, July 30, July 31, August 2, Berle memos to Welles, July 11 and 30, memo to Harry Hopkins, July 30, 1941; Berle to Morris L. Ernst, October 22, to J. T. Craps, Jr., October 10, 1941, BP-33 and 31.
9. Berle Diary, November 7, 1940. For an excellent introduction to American intelligence prior to 1939, see Thomas F. Troy, *Donovan and the CIA; A History of the Establishment of the Central Intelligence Agency* (Frederick, MD, 1981), pp. 1–16.
10. "Random notes on intelligence and investigating services," "Request of President Roosevelt and Secretary of State Hull that I coordinate the activities of the investigating agencies of our government," Messersmith Papers.
11. Berle Diary, September 2, 18, 22, 1939, March 12, 18, 27, 28, 29, April 25, May 8, 16, 1940; Berle memo to FDR, September 22, 1939, to Captain Schuirman, March 19, 1940, BP-66 and 48; Ickes Diary, September 23, 1939; Long Diary, April 4, May 8, 1940.
12. Stanley E. Hilton, *Hitler's Secret War in South America, 1939–1945* (Baton Rouge, LA, 1981), pp. 192–96.
13. Berle to Welles, October 18, 1939, RG 59, 821.105/73; Berle Diary, May 31, June 1, 3, 11, August 27, October 17, 29, November 9, 27, 1940, February 7, 12, 1941; Long Diary, June 8, 11, October 4, 7, 1940; Berle to General Miles, June 24, 1940, BP-43; Troy, *Donovan and the CIA,* pp. 16–18.
14. Berle Diary, February 7, 25, 1941.
15. Berle to Welles, February 10, 20, July 28, Carter to Berle [ca. May], June 18, December 31, Berle memo, June 9, memo to John Blandford, June 9, 1941, BP-57; to Frederick Lyon, July 5, 1945, BP-75; Boxes 122–39, PSF; Wayne Cole, *Roosevelt and the Isolationists, 1932–45* (Lincoln, NE, 1983), p. 461.
16. Berle memo to Lowell Mellett, October 29, 1940, Mellett Papers, Box 2; Berle Diary, August 28, December 7, 1940, Troy, *Donovan and the CIA,* pp. 80–82; Hilton, *Hilter's Secret War,* pp. 197–200; Bradley F. Smith, *The Shadow Warriors: O.S.S. and the Origins of the C.I.A.* (New York, 1983), pp. 28–30.
17. Smith, *Shadow Warriors,* pp. 63–64; Berle Diary, February 7, September 18,

memo to Welles, September 27, memo, September 3, 1941; Nelson Rockefeller to Berle, April 3, July 17, 1941, BP-57; Troy, *Donovan and the CIA,* pp. 83, 94, 100–104, 111; Berle to Hull, September 3, to FDR, October 9, 1941, BP-58 and 67; Hilton, *Hitler's Secret War,* pp. 201–2.

18. Roosevelt quoted in Anthony Cave Brown, *Wild Bill Donovan: The Last Hero* (New York, 1982), p. 191.
19. Berle Diary, July 23, August 13, 1941; Christopher Thorne, *Allies of a Kind: The United States, Britain, and the War Against Japan, 1941–1945* (London, 1978), p. 240; Clapper Diary, November 18, 1941; Berle to Joseph C. Grew, November 18, 1941, BP-35.
20. Berle Diary, November 27, December 1, 1941.
21. Berle Diary, December 8, 10, 13, 1941; Berle to Fletcher Warren, December 10, 1941, BP-52; Frederick B. Lyon to Warren, December 12, 1941, Warren Papers; John Toland, *The Rising Sun: The Decline and Fall of the Japanese Empire* (New York, 1970), p. 259.

CHAPTER 6   A LIBERAL'S WAR

Empires

1. Escott Reid to Norman Robertson, December 6, 1944, "not sent," "Results," December 14, 1944, Reid Papers, vol. 5, folder 6.
2. Interview with Peter Berle, May 16, 1983; H. G. Nicholas, ed., *Washington Despatches 1941–1945: Weekley Political Reports from the British Embassy* (Chicago, 1981), p. 475; Berle Diary, February 13, 1941, February 24, 1942; Berle to Edward S. Mason, May 9, 1944, BP-43.
3. Berle Diary, April 18, 1940, September 13, 1939; R. C. Lindsay to Viscount Halifax, August 4, 1939, "Records of Leading Personalities in the United States," FO 371/22834; memo of conversation, September 14, 1939, BP-64.
4. Berle Diary, September 22, 1939.
5. Berle memo to Hickerson, November 16, 1939, RG 59, FW 300.11 (39)/253; draft, aide mémoire, January 12, memo of conversation, January 12, 1940, BP-64; Berle Diary, February 2, March 5, 1940.
6. Sir Frederick Whyte to John Balfour, March 16, 27, 1940, FO 371/24237.
7. David Reynolds, *The Creation of the Anglo-American Alliance: A Study in Competitive Co-operation* (Chapel Hill, NC, 1982), pp. 67–68, 69, 69–72, 80–82; Moffat Diary, April 13–14, 1940; Morgenthau-Farley conversation, December 14, 1939, Morgenthau Diaries, vol. 229, p. 5; Henry Wallace, COHC, pp. 924–25.
8. "Record of Leading Personalities in the United States," R. C. Lindsay to Viscount Halifax, August 4, 1939, FO 371/22834.
9. Observer quoted in Reynolds, *Anglo-American Alliance,* p. 89; Nicholas, *Washington Despatches 1941–1945* (1981), p. xvii; confidential report by the Washington Chancery, July 25, 1943, note by Mr. Isaiah Berlin for Mr. Gore-Booth of the Washington Chancery, September 4, 1943, Beaverbrook Papers, file D/237.

10. Confidential report compiled by the Washington Chancery, July 25, 1943, Beaverbrook Papers, file D/237; Frankfurter Diary, January 6, 1943; *New York Times,* February 21, 1942; "Speech by Mr. Berle in Alabama," FO 371/30707; Berle Diary, October 27, December 4, 1942, January 4, 1943.
11. Frankfurter Diary, January 6, 24, 1943; Isaiah Berlin, *Personal Impressions* (New York, 1981), pp. 86, 89; Louis Rittenberg to Berle, December 31, 1940, "Felix Frankfurter," undated, BP-46 and 34.
12. Nicholas, *Washington Despatches 1941–1945,* pp. 38–39; Christopher Thorne, *Allies of a Kind: The United States, Britain, and the War Against Japan, 1941–1945* (London, 1978), pp. 139–42; Moffat Diary, April 13, 1942; Berle Diary, February 24, 1942; Berle to Julian S. Huxley, March 2, 1942, BP-18.
13. Berle Diary, January 24, 1942; "U.S. Economic Policy in Latin America," "Conflict of U.S. and British trade influences in Latin America," "Feelings in the State Department . . . ," "Anglo-U.S. interests . . . ," "Position of the U.S. and Great Britain in Latin America," FO 371/30516.
14. Berle memo to Hull, November 26, 1942, BP-58; personal memo, "The bases of the present war," ca. 1943, BP-65; Berle to Richard Law, October 20, 1942, BP-40.
15. Halifax to Berle, January 6, 16, Berle to Halifax, January 14, 18, 1943, BP-36; Berle to Richard Law, February 1, Law to Berle, March 11, 1943, BP-40; Berle to Anthony Eden, June 18, 1943, BP-33; Berle Diary, June 19, memos of conversation with Richard Law, June 8, 1943.
16. Berle to Alfred C. Lane, July 16, 1943, BP-40; memo, May 28, 1943, Pasvolsky Papers, Box 7; Berle, "Both dreamers and Diplomats Are Needed," *Vital Speeches,* 10 (December 15, 1943), p. 150; *New York Times,* May 14, 1944; "Address by Mr. Berle . . . ," FO 371/38606.
17. On Soviet diplomacy, see Vojtech Mastny, *Russia's Road to the Cold War* (New York, 1979), pp. 37–72 passim; Berle Diary, February 1, 5, 1942.
18. Moffat Diary, March 2–4, 1942; Berle to Alfred C. Lane, March 7, 1942, BP-40; Roosevelt quoted in Berle Diary, March 28, 1942; Churchill quoted in Mastny, *Russia's Road to the Cold War,* pp. 44–45; on the Atlantic Charter, see Robert Dallek, *Franklin D. Roosevelt and American Foreign Policy, 1932–1945* (New York, 1979), pp. 281–85, 337–38.
19. Berle Diary, March 28, April 3, 4, 27, 30, June 20, 1942; Berle memo to Sumner Welles, April 3, Welles memo to Berle, April 4, 1942, BP-73.
20. I. F. Stone, "U.S. Officials Defied FDR," PM, September 28, 1942; Berle to John M. Coffee, October 6, to Cordell Hull, June 27, 1942, BP-31 and 58; Berle Diary, July 4, 21, 29, 1942, September 18, 1943; Ickes Diary, October 18, 1942, emphasis added; Berle to Helen Rogers Reid, November 3, 1942, BP-46.
21. Berle Diary, November 28, 1942, February 2, March 5, 1943; *New York Times,* April 5, 7, 1943; Nicholas, *Washington Despatches 1941–1945,* p. 175, 167.
22. Berle Diary, August 5, 1943; Berle memo, September 6, 1943, BP-65; Stanley Hornbeck to Berle, September 14, 1943, Hornbeck Papers, Box 27.
23. Berle Diary, September 13, 18, 1943; Drew Pearson to Berle, September 28, Berle to Pearson, October 2, 1943, "not sent," BP-45; Berle to Charles A. Davila, September 17, 1943, BP-32; *New York Times,* September 19, 1943; Berle to Hull, January 7, to Stettinius, February 21, 1944, BP-59 and 70.

The Riddle of the State Department

1. Berle Diary, January 24, 1942. For an excellent description of the background for the Pan American policy and the personalities involved, see Irwin F. Gellman, *Good Neighbor Diplomacy: United States Policies in Latin America 1933–1945* (Baltimore, 1979), and pp. 120–26 on the Hull-Welles rupture.
2. Berle Diary, March 5, 1940.
3. Berle Diary, September 15, 1940; Gellman, *Good Neighbor Diplomacy,* pp. 176–78; Ickes Diary, December 7, 1941.
4. Ted Morgan, *FDR: A Biography* (New York, 1985), pp. 677–86; Ickes Diary, June 28, December 7, 1941; Tugwell Diary, July 12, 1941; Henry A. Wallace, COHC, March 31, 1942, p. 1468; Long Diary, September 11, 12, 1942, August 29, 1943; Gellman, *Good Neighbor Policy,* p. 178.
5. Moffat Diary, July 14, September 19–23, 1941; Long Diary, August 11, September 1, 1941; Berle to Edwin J. Marshall, September 30, 1941, BP-42.
6. Berle Diary, December 1, 1941; Moffat Diary, December 1–4, 1941; Berle to Hull, December 15, 1941, BP-58; Long Diary, January 13, 1942; Berle Diary, February 1, 5, March 5, 1942; Moffat Diary, March 2–4, 1942.
7. Long Diary, May 9, June 20, 28, 1942; Berle Diary, June 24, 27, July 25, 1942; Armstrong story in Frankfurter Diary, June 3, 1943; Morgan, *FDR: A Biography,* p. 679.
8. Long Diary, November 18, 1942, February 16, August 29, 1943; John Morton Blum, *From the Morgenthau Diaries: Years of War 1941–1945* (New York, 1967), pp. 172–73; Berle Diary, November 25, 1942, January 4, 1943; Jonathan Daniels, *White House Witness, 1942–1945* (Garden City, NY, 1975), pp. 174–75, 192–193; Nicholas, *Washington Despatches,* pp. 231–32; Gellman, *Good Neighbor Diplomacy,* pp. 178–79; Morgan, *FDR: A Biography,* pp. 682–84.
9. *New York Times,* August 6, 29, 1943; Pearson clipping in Long Diary, August 29, September 4, 7, 1943; Berle Diary, September 1, 18, 1943; L. B. Pearson to N. A. Robertson, September 28, 1943, Pearson Papers, vol. 3, folder 6; Nicholas, *Washington Despatches,* p. 254.
10. Long Diary, September 26, 1943; Hornbeck autobiography, 1942–1944, Hornbeck Papers; Halifax to Foreign Office, January 23, 1944, FO 371/38538 emphasis added; Berle Diary, January 18, 1944; Halifax to Eden, March 15, 1944, FO 371/38540, emphasis added.

An American Liberal and the Jews

1. Copy, Ralph Ingersoll to Felix Frankfurter, February 28, 1941, Feis Papers, Box 34; Tabitha Petran and William Walton, "Berle Does Better in Theory Than in Practice," *PM,* February 12, 1941.
2. Copy, Morris L. Ernst to Ralph Ingersoll, February 13, Sylvia Ashton to Ernst, undated, Berle to Ernst, February 27, 1941, BP-33; Berle Diary, March 4, 1941. Also, see Berle to Nathan Lobell, February 20, to James M. Mead, February 24, 1941, BP-41 and 43.
3. Herbert Feis to Felix Frankfurter, February 26, 28, Frankfurter to Ralph Ingersoll, February 27, Ingersoll to Frankfurter, February 28, Frankfurter to Feis, March 6, Feis to Frankfurter, March 12, 1941, Feis Papers, Box 34.

4. Berle to Raymond M. Schwartz, February 13, 1941, BP-48.
5. David S. Wyman, *The Abandonment of the Jews: America and the Holocaust, 1941–1945* (New York, 1984), p. 190.
6. Jerome Frank, "Red-White-and-Blue-Herring," *Saturday Evening Post,* December 6, 1941, pp. 9–10; Jordan Schwarz, *The Speculator: Bernard M. Baruch in Washington 1917–1965* (Chapel Hill, NC, 1981), p. 564; also see Frank to Frankfurter, December 7, 8, Frankfurter to Frank, December 8, 9, 1941, Frank Papers, Box 3.
7. Berle to Walter A. White, May 27, 1942, BP-52; Berle, "The Challenge of Color," *Survey Graphic* (November 1942), pp. 506–8; Berle speech to Joint Annual Meeting of the National Association of Jewish Social Welfare, etc., May 20, 1944, Cleveland, Ohio.
8. Berle to Annette V. Marshall, June 19, 1941, BP-42; to William G. Mulligan, March 31, 1942, BP-44; to Clemencia Hand, February 26, 1936, BP-11; Berle Diary, October 31, 1939; Berle to Chase Mellen, Jr., November 21, 1939, BP-43; memo to Mayor La Guardia, November 10, 1937, BP-25.
9. Robert Jerome Glennon, *The Iconoclast as Reformer: Jerome Frank's Impact on American Law* (Ithaca, NY, 1985), pp. 78–79; Jerold S. Auerbach, *Unequal Justice: Lawyers and Social Change in America* (New York, 1976), pp. 184–88.
10. Summary of Invitation Conference, New York, October 18–19, 1941, BP-47; Quoted in Saul S. Friedman, *No Haven for the Oppressed: United States Policy Toward Jewish Refugees, 1938–1945* (New York, 1973), p. 134 and in Wyman, *Abandonment of the Jews,* p. 74; Berle Diary, January 13, 1943; Berle to Frances Perkins, January 26, 1943, BP-45.
11. Berle, Sr., to Oswald Garrison Villard, March 15, 1939, Villard Papers; Emanuel Celler to Berle, October 5, Berle to Celler, October 6, "hold," 1943, BP-30; Henry Epstein to Berle, April 24, 1944, BP-33; Glennon, *Iconoclast as Reformer,* p. 31.
12. Berle memo of conversation, April 28, Alling memo of conversation, April 28, 1939, RG 59, 811.607 New York, 1939/1557–8; Berle Diary, November 1, 1938, May 25, 26, 1939.
13. Berle Diary, December 19, 1939, September 11, 23, October 10, 1940, February 25, 1941; Berle memo to FDR, March 18, 1940, PSF 94; Berle memo to General Watson, April 28, 1941, PPF 601; Berle to Norman H. Davis, October 5, 1940, BP-32; Berle memo to Sumner Welles, July 23, 1942, BP-73.
14. Berle memos to Hull, March 24, 29, April 20, 1943, BP-58, to Welles, February 8, March 9, 1943, BP-73; Berle to Robert H. Jackson, September 20, 1940, BP-38; *New York Times,* October 2, 1943; Jacob Billikopf to Berle, May 9, Berle to Billikopf, May 22, 1944, BP-29.

A Ganglion of Complexes

1. Robert Bendiner, *The Riddle of the State Department* (New York, 1942), pp. 180, 175.
2. Berle to Beatrice V. C. Berle, July 18, 1951, BP-81; H. G. Nicholas, ed., *Wash-*

ington Despatches 1941–1945 (Chicago, 1981), p. 142; Dean Acheson, *Present at the Creation* (New York, 1969), pp. 14–15; David E. Lilienthal, *Journals: Unfinished Business, 1968–1981* (New York, 1983), p. 90.

3. Moffat Diary, March 2–4, 1942; C. C. Burlingham to Felix Frankfurter, October 2, February 3, 1942, Frankfurter Papers, Box 35; Morgenthau Diaries, October 12, 1942, vol. 578, pp. 86A–86H.
4. James P. Warburg, COHC, p. 234; Henry A. Wallace, COHC, pp. 1767–68, 2063–64; Berle memo to FDR, May 31, FDR memo to Berle, June 1, 1940, BP-67, PSF 94.
5. Bendiner, *Riddle of the State Department,* p. 174; Berle Diary, July 9, 1938, February 9, 16, September 11, 1940; Ickes Diary, February 11, 1940, November 23, 1941; Ickes to FDR, February 2, Berle memo to FDR, February 10, 1940, PSF 75; Berle to Edwin J. Marshall, September 15, 1941, BP-42.
6. Samuel I. Rosenman to Berle, September 13, 1943, BP-47; C. C. Burlingham to Felix Frankfurter, October 26, 1942, Frankfurter Papers, Box, 35.
7. Moffat Diary, November 15, 1939; Berle Diary, November 17, 1939; Beatrice Bishop Berle, *A Life in Two Worlds* (New York, 1983), pp. 147–50, 153–55; Henry A. Wallace, COHC, pp. 2063–64; interview with Fletcher Warren, February 28, 1983.
8. Morris L. Ernst to Adolf A. Berle, October 19, 1943, Berle to Ernst, October 21, 1943, BP-33; Confidential report compiled by the Washington Chancery, July 25, 1943, Beaverbrook Papers, file D/237 and Michael Wright's report, FO 371/36439; Henry Wallace, COHC, p. 3277.
9. Berle Diary, July 1, 1940, February 14, 1941, February 24, 1940; Berle, "The Place of the University in a Modern Democracy," *Vital Speeches,* 7 (December 15, 1940), 151; also, see *New Directions in the New World* (New York, 1940), pp. 126–41.
10. Berle to Charles C. Burlingham, March 1, 1940, BP-30; Berle Diary, October 14, 1940, May 6, 1942.
11. Berle Diary, September 19, 1940; Paul Blanshard, *Personal and Controversial* (Boston, 1973), p. 177; Berle to Morris L. Ernst, October 21, 1943, BP-33; Henry A. Wallace, COHC, p. 1766.
12. Colleague quoted in Henry A. Wallace, COHC, p. 3277; R. C. Lindsay to Viscount Halifax, August 16, 1939, FO 371/22834 and September 3, 1938, FO 371/21528; Samuel I. Rosenman, COHC, pp. 113–14.
13. "Most secret," Halifax to FO, March 31, 1944, Beaverbrook Papers, file D/237; Michael Wright to Nevile M. Butler, March 25, 1944, FO 371/38606; Wright to Foreign Office, undated, FO 371/36439; Henry Wallace, COHC, p. 1766.
14. Confidential report by the Washington Chancery, July 25, 1943, Beaverbrook Papers, file D/237; James A. Farley, COHC, p. 94; Berle to Beulah Ratliff, October 17, 1946, Survey Associates Papers, Box 54; James P. Warburg, COHC, p. 235.
15. *Washington Star,* April 29, 1934; note by Mr. E. Baring, March 30, 1944, Beaverbrook Papers, file D/237; R. C. Lindsay to Viscount Halifax, September 3, 1938, FO 371/2158; Jonathan Daniels, *White House Witness, 1942–1945* (Garden City, NY, 1975), p. 225; *Time,* August 29, 1938, p. 41.

16. Berle Diary, October 31, December 15, 1939; interview with Ernst Cuneo, May 5, 1984; Berle Diary, June 20, 1942; Berle to D'Arcy Edmondson, June 29, 1953, BP-82; Berle memo to Edward Stettinius, February 28, 1944, BP-70.

17. R. G. Tugwell to Berle, November 1, 1939, Tugwell Papers, Box 1; Berle Diary, December 15, 1939; Viner to Berle, August 12, Berle to Jacob Viner, August 14, 25, 1942, Viner Papers, Box 50.

"And What Shall We Do Then?"

1. John Morton Blum, *The Price of Vision: The Diary of Henry A. Wallace 1942–1946* (Boston, 1973), p. 144; Wallace, COHC, pp. 1764–67.

2. Quoted in *New York Times,* September 25, 1941; Berle, "And What Shall We Do Then?" *Fortune,* 24 (October 1941), 124.

3. Memo, "The bases of the present war, the mechanism of a progressively developing victory and of a peace based thereon," ca. March, 1942, BP-37.

4. Harry C. Hawkins memo to Berle's subcommittee, April 1, Bean memos to Stone, June 9, 13, 17, 1942, Bean Papers, Box 25; Berle Diary, May 19, 1942; Henry A. Wallace, COHC, p. 1768; Berle to Henry A. Wallace, September 24, 1942, BP-51.

5. Meeting at the Treasury, July 11, 1942, Pasvolsky Papers, Box 1; Louis H. Bean to Stone and Lowenthal, July 25, 1942, Bean Papers, Box 25; Richard N. Gardner, *Sterling-Dollar Diplomacy* (Boston, 1969), pp. 71–100; Blum, *Years of War,* pp. 228–40.

6. Berle memo, Post-War Economic Mechanisms, July 31, Bean to Stone and Lowenthal, August 1, 4, 17, 24, Bean to Milo Perkins, August 24, 1942, Bean Papers, Box 25; Berle memo, August 18, 1942, BP-70; Berle to Hull, August 24, September 28, 1942, BP-58.

7. Memo, November 10, 1942, Wrong Papers, vol. 4, folder 23; Berle Diary, September 10, 1942.

8. Berle, "The Realist Base of American Foreign Policy," *Vital Speeches,* 9 (November 1, 1942), 53–56; Berle Diary, October 6, November 26, 27, 1942; Blum, *Years of War,* p. 236; Berle Memo, November 19, 1942, BP-58; Notes on meeting, November 20, 1942, Bean Papers, Box 25.

9. Minutes, December 4, 1942, January 8, 1943, Bean to Milo Perkins, December 8, 1942, Bean Papers, Box 25; Berle Diary, December 1, 8, 1942, January 26, 1943; Berle to Hull, December 8, 1942, January 11, 1943, BP-58; David Rees, *Harry Dexter White: A Study in Paradox* (New York, 1973), pp. 137–53.

10. Berle to Sam Rosenman, February 11, 1943, Rosenman Papers, Box 1; Berle Diary, memo of conversation, February 16, 1943; Berle to Harry D. White, February 19, March 6, 1943, BP-52; Rees, *Harry Dexter White,* p. 149.

11. Berle Diary, memos of conversations, March 20, 12, 1943.

12. Berle Diary, March 15, 23, [2], 24 [2], June 8, 17, 1943; Lloyd C. Gardner, *Economic Aspects of New Deal Diplomacy* (Madison, WI, 1964), pp. 285–87; Blum, *Years of War,* pp. 238–40; Rees, pp. 149–53; Richard Gardner, *Sterling-Dollar Diplomacy,* pp. 95–100; Berle to Hull, July 7, September 14, 1943, BP-58; Berle Diary, September 16, 1943, August 28, 1944.

CHAPTER 7   AIR POWER

"Internationalization or Americanization"

1. Berle Diary, January 2, 1943.
2. On Trippe and Pan American Airways, see Marylin Bender and Selig Altschul, *The Chosen Instrument: Juan Trippe and Pan Am* (New York, 1982), pp. 9–368, passim; Berle Diary, October 14, 1940, March 5, 1941; Berle to Walter F. George, December 16, 1942, BP-55.
3. Norman A. Robertson memo to MacKenzie King, December 12, 1941, King Papers, vol. 240, folder 2411; Berle Diary, January 1, 1942; Moffat Diary, April 4–11, June 10, 1942; Berle Diary, memo of conversation with Norman Robertson, June 10, 1942.
4. Copy, L. W. Pogue, "Freedom of the Air," June 22, 1942, Berle to Pogue, July 3, 30, 1942, BP-54 and 45; memo on Lissitzyn, July 13, 1942, Hornbeck Papers, Box 27.
5. Henry A. Wallace, COHC, August 23, 1942, p. 1798; Berle to L. Welch Pogue, December 31, 1942, BP-45; Berle Diary, Berle memo to Hull, August 26, 1942, "hold,"; Berle memo, September 2, "file for record only," to Hull, September 24, "hold," to Welles, November 18, 1942, BP-58 and 73.
6. Berle Diary, November 21, 1942; minutes of State Department Economic Subcommittee, December 4, 1942, Bean Papers, Box 25; Berle memo to Welles, January 9, 1943, BP-73; Berle Diary, memos, January 15, 19, 1943; *London Times* editorial, February 6, 1943, in FO 371/36431.
7. Bender and Altschul, *Chosen Instrument,* pp. 374–76; *Washington Star,* February 15, 1943; H. G. Nicholas, ed., *Washington Despatches 1941–1945: Weekly Political Reports from the British Embassy* (Chicago, 1981), pp. 152–53; "Postwar Aviation," February 18, 1943, FO 371/36431; copy, Matthews to Hull, February 12, 1943, BP-54.
8. Hornbeck to Berle, February 20, 1943, Hornbeck Papers, Box 27; Berle Diary, February 18, 1943; "Post-war Aviation," February 18, 1943, FO 371/36431; Pogue to Berle, March 2, Berle to Pogue, March 11, to FDR, March 12, on Aviation Policy, March 24, 1943, BP-54.
9. Le Rougetel minute, Wright to Eden, June 9, 1943, FO 371/36436.
10. Copy, War Cabinet discussion, June 22, 1943, King Papers, vol. 235, folder 2294; John Andrew Miller, "Air Diplomacy: The Chicago Civil Aviation Conference of 1944 in Anglo-American Relations and Postwar Planning," unpublished doctoral dissertation, Yale University, 1971.
11. "Post-war Civil Aviation," August 7, 1943, FO 371/36439; "Confidential Report by Washington Chancery," July 25, 1943, Beaverbrook Papers, file D/237; Robertson to King, July 28, Churchill to King, August 3, Escott Reid comments, September 14, 1943, King Papers, vol. 238, folder 2294.
12. Berle Diary, memos of conversations, February 9, 16, March 20, April 2, 1943; Berle memo to Welles et al., March 29, 1943, BP-73.
13. Robertson memos to King, April 21, May 2, Escott Reid memo to King, April 5, W. A. Riddell to Robertson, May 25, Robertson memo to King, May 29,

Reid memo for the War Committee, June 17, Reid memo, June 21, 1943, King Papers, vol. 235, folder 2294.

14. Berle Diary, memo, June 8, 1943; "Post-war Civil Aviation," FO 371/36436; *Observer,* June 13, 1943, Beaverbrook Papers, file D/237; Berle Diary, June 15, June 17, 1943; Berle to Hull, July 9, 1943, BP-58; "Post-war Civil Aviation," June 21, 1943, FO 371/36437; Berle to Paul T. David, July 21, 1943, BP-55.

15. Berle memo to Hull, April 30, 1943, memo to be included with the minutes of the Aviation Committee, May 26, 1943, BP-54; memo for meeting re aviation of June 4, 1943, draft, "Main Heads of Aviation Policy," June 19, 1943, BP-55; to Pat McCarran, June 23, 1943, BP-42.

16. Pearson quoted in Norman A. Robertson to C. D. Howe, September 21, 1943, Howe Papers, vol. 100, folder 22; Berle Diary, memo of conversation, September 28, 1943; H. H. Wrong to C. D. Howe, October 1, to King, October 8, Robertson memo to King, October 14, 1943, King Papers, vol. 235, folder 2294.

17. Biddle Diary, January 14, 1944; Berle Diary, memo of conversation, November 11, 1943; Berle memo draft, August 30, 1943, memo, August 31, 1943, BP-55; Berle to Alvin Hanson, September 16, 1943, BP-36; to L. Welch Pogue, November 5, 1943, BP-45; memo to Hull and Stettinius, November 18, 1943, BP-58.

18. Extract from Sir R. Campbell to Eden, September 27, 1943, Beaverbrook Papers, file D/237; Berle Diary, memo of conversation, January 1, 1944; Beaverbrook to C. D. Howe, November 18, Howe to Beaverbrook, November 20, to Robertson, November 22, 1943, Howe Papers, vol. 100, folder 24.

19. Berle Diary, memo of conversation, December 18, 1943; Berle memo to Hull and Stettinius, November 26, 1943, BP-55; Robertson memos for King, November 20, December 28, 1943, King Papers, vol. 235, folder 2294.

20. Berle Diary, January 10, 1944.

Mr. Berle Goes to London

1. John Colville, *Winston Churchill and His Inner Circle* (New York, 1981), pp. 89, 96.

2. Colville, *The Fringes of Power: 10 Downing Street Diaries 1939–1955* (New York, 1985), p. 476, 564, his emphasis; excerpts from Hansard, January 19, 1944, King Papers, vol. 235, folder 2294.

3. Masefield, "The President on Civil Aviation Policy," January 25, Eden to Beaverbrook, January 29, February 9, Beaverbrook to Eden, February 1, 11, "not sent," 1941, "Points Raised at the Meeting," February 4, Sinclair to Beaverbrook, February 7, 1944, Beaverbrook Papers, file D/241.

4. Berle to Hull, January 28, to FDR, February 3, 12, 1944, BP-59 and 67; Berle Diary, Berle to Hull, February 3, 23, Memos of conversation, February 9, 14, 15, 21, 23, 28, March 2, 3, 4, 6, 7, 8, 1944; to John G. Winant, February 14, 1944, BP-53; Berle Diary, February 22, 1944.

5. Robertson to King, January 29, February 23, 1944, King Papers, vol. 235, folder 2294; "Canadian Reactions on Conference," February 26, 1944, Beaverbrook

Papers, file D/237; "Post-war Civil Aviation," March 3, 1944, FO 371/42556; Minutes of C.A.T. meeting, March 2, 1944, FO 371/42557.

6. "Post-war Civil Aviation," March 8 and 21, 1944, FO 371/42557-8; "Conference, Foreign Office Opinion, March 11, 1944, Beaverbrook Papers, file D/237; Berle Diary, March 10, 13, 15, 1944; copy, Hull to FDR, March 11, 1944, BP-67; copies, Pearson to King, March 8, 9, 13, 15, 16, Howe Papers, vol. 100, folder 21.

7. Le Rougetel minute, March 16, Richard Law, "Talks on Civil Aviation," March 22, Beaverbrook to Law, March 29, minutes, March 30, 1944, FO 371/42558; Robertson memo to King, March 25, 1944, King Papers, vol. 235, folder 2294.

8. Berle Diary, copy, Berle memo to FDR, March 21; copies, Pearson to King, March 27, J. R. Baldwin, "General Comment," March 27, King to London, April 1, 1944, Howe Papers, vol. 100, folder 21.

9. C. D. Howe to Beaverbrook, April 11, 1944, Beaverbrook Papers, file D/161; "Post-war Civil Aviation," April 2, 1944, FO 371/42559; Miller, *Air Diplomacy,* pp. 151-54; Robertson quoted in *Foreign Relations,* 1944, vol. II, pp. 430-31.

10. Colville, *Winston Churchill,* p. 93; Masefield to Balfour, telegram, Halifax to Eden, P.G.M. [Philip Masefield], "Mr. Berle," March 31, 1944, Beaverbrook Papers, file D/237.

11. Eden to Beaverbrook, Oliver Stanley to Beaverbrook, March 30, 1944, Beaverbrook Papers, file D/237; *Economist* quoted in *New York Times,* April 2, 1944; Miller, Air Diplomacy, p. 145.

12. "Conversation between Lord Beaverbrook and Mr. Berle . . . ," Beaverbrook Papers, file D/151; Berle to Mrs. Winston Spencer Churchill, to Eden, to Beaverbrook, to Law, April 8, to Keynes, April 6, 1944, BP-63; Law to Berle, April 7, BP-40; A. J. P. Taylor, *Beaverbrook* (London, 1972), p. 557.

13. Informal Discussions, April 3, 1944, BP-63; Beaverbrook to Oliver Stanley, April 3, 1944, Beaverbrook Papers, file D/238.

14. Beaverbrook telegrams to Howe, April 5, 7, 1944, Howe Papers, vol. 100, folder 24.

15. Informal Discussions, April 6, 1944, BP-63; C.A.T. minutes, April 6, 1944, Beaverbrook Papers, file D/238; "Civil Aviation," April 8, extract from War Cabinet, April 7, 1944, FO 371/42559; minutes, Informal Discussions, April 4, 5, 6, Report on Air Conversations, April 19, 1944, BP-63.

16. *New York Times,* April 8, 9, 1944; *Times* of London, April 10, 1944; excerpts from *Sunday Dispatch* and *Sunday Express,* BP-33; *Time,* April 17, 1944, p. 22; "Post-war Civil Aviation," April 12, 18, 1944, FO 371/42559.

Arise O Israel

1. Copy, Lester Pearson to MacKenzie King, April 14, 1944, Howe Papers, vol. 100, folder 21; *Foreign Relations,* 1944, vol. II, p. 442; P.G.M. [Philip Masefield], "Berle telegram," April 20, 1944, Beaverbrook Papers, file D/238.

2. *Foreign Relations,* 1944, vol. II, pp. 444, 459, 469-70, 471-74, 477-81; *New York Times,* May 12, 16, 17, 1944; Beaverbrook to Berle, May 16, Berle to

Beaverbrook, May 19, 1944; Beaverbrook Papers, file D/151; Hull to Senators Clark and Bailey, May 24, 1944, BP-55.

3. Berle Diary, May 13, 1944, memos of conversation, May 27, June 3, 23, 1944.

4. Berle memo to Hull and Grew, May 30, 1944, BP-59; Berle to L. Welch Pogue, May 31, June 2, 3, 1944, BP-45; Berle Diary, memo of conversation, June 10, 1944.

5. Taylor, *Beaverbrook,* pp. 439, 555–56, emphasis added; "Berle's opinions," June 29, 1944, Beaverbrook Papers, file D/243.

6. Berle Diary, memo of conversation, July 21, 1944; Le Rougetel to Minister of State, July 24, 1944, Beaverbrook Papers, file D/243; Berle Diary, July 26, 1944; copy, L. B. Pearson to N. A. Robertson, July 28, [2] 1944, Howe Papers, vol. 100, folder 21.

7. Berle Diary, July 30, 31, 1944; memos of conversations, August 4, 9, in *Foreign Relations,* 1944, vol. II, pp. 522–23, 526–27, telegram, August 16, 1944, pp. 530–31.

8. Beaverbrook to CAT Committee, August 2, 4, 11, Beaverbrook to Ralph Assheton, August 26, Assheton to Beaverbrook, August 31, 1944, Beaverbrook Papers, file D/243.

9. Berle to Hull, August 31, September 4, 1944, BP-55; copy, Dominion Affairs to King, Howe Papers, August 22, 1944, vol. 100, folder 21; Berle to Beaverbrook, August 21, Beaverbrook to Berle, August 29, September 1, 1944, *Foreign Relations,* 1944, vol. II, pp. 531–532, 533–37.

10. Berle to Beaverbrook, September 9, 1944, *Foreign Relations,* 1944, vol. II, pp. 535–37.

11. Beaverbrook to Archibald Sinclair, August 26, 1944, Beaverbrook Papers, file D/243; Civil Air Conversations in the United States, August 26, 1944, CAB 66/54; International Air Conference, September 19, 1944, CAB 66/55.

12. *Foreign Relations,* 1944, vol. II, pp. 540–41; Air Conference, September 23, 1944, CAB 66/55; Howe to Beaverbrook, August 29, 1944, Howe Papers, vol. 100, folder 24; "Halifax's telegram," August 30, "Berle's views," August 31, Beaverbrook to Halifax, September 3, 1944, Beaverbrook Papers, files D/243–244.

13. Beaverbrook to C. D. Howe, September 19, 1944, Howe Papers, vol. 100, folder 24; Masefield, "International Conference," September 15, 18, Beaverbrook to Archibald Sinclair, September 18, 25, 1944, Beaverbrook Papers, file D/244.

14. *Foreign Relations,* 1944, vol. II, pp. 549–55; Berle Diary, memo of conversation, October 9, 1944; Berle to Beaverbrook, October 12, 1944, BP-55; on Swinton, see J. A. Cross, *Lord Swinton* (New York, 1982).

15. Copy, Halifax to FO, October 3, 1944, Beaverbrook Papers, file D/244; Berle Diary, memo of conversation, October 21, 1944; Halifax to FO, October 22, 1944; Masefield, "Berle Speaks Again," October 22, 1944, Beaverbrook Papers, file D/244.

16. Paul Gore-Booth, *With Great and True Respect* (London, 1974), p. 131; Colville, *The Fringes of Power,* p. 769; "Civil Aviation—Chicago Conference," October 25, 1944, [2], CAB 66/56; Masefield, "Lord Swinton's Minute to the Prime Minister," October 25, 1944, Beaverbrook Papers, file D/244.

17. Berle memos to Hull, September 19, 21, 1944, BP-55; Janet McEnany to Berle, August 30, 1944, BP-42; Berle Diary, memo of conversation, September 8, 1944;

copy, Pearson to King, September 8, 1944, Howe Papers, vol. 100, folder 21; *Foreign Relations,* 1944, vol. II, pp. 557, 559–60, 567.

The Making of the Peace at Chicago

1. Beaverbrook to Richard Law, May 25, 1944, Beaverbrook Papers, file D/242; Berle Diary, Berle memo on International Aviation Conference, September 16, 1944; *Foreign Relations,* 1944, vol. II, p. 536.
2. Hugo Grotius (1583–1645), Dutch jurist and humanist, generally regarded as the founder of international law, which he derived from reading the Bible and classical history and propounded in a text intended to make war more humane and prohibitive among nations.
3. Berle Diary, August 24, 1944.
4. Long Diary, September 26, October 18, 1944.
5. Berle to Beaverbrook, June 29, 1944, Beaverbrook Papers, file D/242; Berle, June 8, 1944, Hornbeck Papers, Box 27; Berle Diary, June 9, 23, 30, July 3, 6, memos of conversations, July 21, 24, 1944; copy, Dominion Affairs to King, July 8, 1944, Howe Papers, vol. 100, folder 21.
6. Conversations with Andrei Gromyko, March 29, 31, April 29, 1944, Grew Papers; "Post-war Civil Aviation," April 4, 1944, FO 371/42558; A. Gromyko to Berle, April 6, copy, Grew to Gromyko, April 15, 1944, BP-36; Berle Diary, May 29, July 21, 24, 1944.
7. Berle Diary, July 28, August 29, September 23, October 21, 1944; memo to Hull, August 2, 1944, BP-59; Berle to L. Welch Pogue, Pogue to Berle, August 3, 1944, BP-55; Beaverbrook in New York, August 11, 1944, Beaverbrook Papers, file D/243.
8. Berle memos, "Principle Problems in Europe," September 26, 1944, "U. S. Policy toward Eastern Europe and the Near East," October 14, 1944, BP-70.
9. Copy, Lord Swinton to Sir Edward Bridges, November 1, 1944, Beaverbrook Papers, file D/245.
10. *Chicago Tribune,* November 4, 5, 7, 13, 27, 28, 1944.
11. Berle Diary, November 1, 3, 1944; copy, Swinton to Bridges, November 1, 1944, Beaverbrook Papers, file D/245.
12. Berle Diary, November 3, 6, 9, 1944.
13. Reid memo, November 11, 1944, Reid Papers, vol. 5, folder 6; also, see Berle to Fletcher Warren, November 11, 1944, BP-52.
14. Gore-Booth, *With Great Truth and Respect,* pp. 131–32; Escott Reid to N. A. Robertson, November 12, 1944, Reid Papers, vol. 5, folder 6; Berle to Stettinius, November 11, 1944, BP-59.
15. Richard Law to Beaverbrook, November 8, 1944, Beaverbrook Papers, file D/245; memo by the Secretary of State for Air, November 8, 1944, CAB 66/57; Berle Diary, November 11, 14, 1944.
16. Berle Diary, November 15, 17, 1944; *New York Times,* November 16, 1944; Bender and Altschul, *Chosen Instrument,* p. 388.
17. Berle Diary, November 18, 1944.
18. J. R. Baldwin to Howe, November 21, 1944, Howe Papers, vol. 99, folder 19; Biddle Diary, January 14, 1944; Reid to Robertson, November 21, 1944, Reid Papers, vol. 5, folder 6.

19. Berle Diary, Stettinius memo to Grace Tully, FDR to Churchill, November 21, 1944; Churchill to FDR, November 22, 1944, CAB 66/58, MR 32.

20. *New York Times,* November 23, 1944; Reid memo, November 11, 1944, J. R. Baldwin to A. D. P. Heeney, November 23, 1944, Reid Papers, vol. 5, folder 6; Berle Diary, November 26, 1944; Swinton to Howe, November 23, 1944, Howe Papers, vol. 99, folder 19; Swinton to E. Bridges, November 22, 1944, FO 371/42588.

21. FDR to Churchill, November 24, Winant to FDR, November 26, 1944, MR 32, 20; Colville, *The Fringes of Power,* p. 528; Warren F. Kimball, ed., *Churchill and Roosevelt: The Complete Correspondence,* vol. III (Princeton, NJ, 1984), pp. 402, 404–8.

22. Kimball, *Churchill and Roosevelt,* pp. 819–21; Churchill to FDR, November 28, 1944, MR 32, 20, Beaverbrook to Churchill, November 25, 30, 1944, Beaverbrook Papers, file D/245; Swinton to E. Bridges, November 25, 26, 1944, FO 371/42589; Churchill to Swinton, November 28, 1944, CAB 66/58.

23. Long Diary, July 1, 1945; Berle Diary, November 27, 1944; Robertson memo for King, November 29, 1944, King Papers, vol. 235, folder 2294; Berle to FDR, November 29, 1944, MR 20 and 32; J. R. Baldwin to Howe, November 28, 1944, Howe Papers, vol. 99, folder 19; Swinton to Bridges, November 29, 1944, FO 371/42591.

24. Admiral Leahy to FDR, FDR to Churchill, November 30, 1944, MR 32 and 20; Kimball, *Churchill and Roosevelt,* pp. 424–25.

25. Telephone conversation between Lord Swinton and Mr. Hildred, Masefield to Beaverbrook, November 30, Cribbett to Hildred, December 3, 1944, Masefield, "The Chicago Conference," Beaverbrook Papers, files D/240 and D/246.

26. Conversation between Lord Beaverbrook and Sir Arthur Street, Lord Beaverbrook's telephone conversation with Lord Swinton, December 1, 1944, Beaverbrook Papers, file D/240; Churchill to FDR, December 1, Winant to FDR and Stettinus, December 1, 1944, MR 20 and 32; Kimball, *Churchill and Roosevelt,* p. 427.

27. Masefield in Anthony Sampson, *Empires of the Sky* (New York, 1984), p. 68; Masefield to Beaverbrook, emphasis added, November 30, 1944, Lord Beaverbrook's telephone conversation with Lord Swinton, December 1, 1944, Beaverbrook Papers, file D/240; Berle Diary, December 1, 1944.

28. Gore-Booth, *With Great Truth,* p. 132; Bender and Altschul, *Chosen Instrument,* p. 392, 396–98; *New York Times,* December 6, 8, 1944; *Time,* December 11, 1944, p. 77; Churchill to FDR, January 27, March 6, FDR to Churchill, March 7, Grew to FDR, January 30, 1945, MR 32; Berle to Ralph Damon, March 6, 1946, BP-82.

29. Swinton in Cross, *Lord Swinton,* p. 248; Copy, Halifax to Richard Law, December 12, 1944, Beaverbrook Papers, file D/246; "Publicity at International Conferences," December 31, 1944, FO 371/44609.

30. Winant to FDR, December 2, 1944, MR 20; "Results," December 14, 1944, Reid Papers, vol. 5, folder 6; Berle to Beaverbrook, December 30, 1944, BP-59.

31. Escott Reid to Norman A. Robertson, December 6, 1944, "not sent," vol. 5, folder 6; also, see J. R. Baldwin to C. D. Howe, November 30, 1944, Howe Papers, vol. 99, folder 19.

32. T. P. Wright, "Edward P. Warner: An Appreciation," *Journal of the Royal Aeronautical Society, LXII* (October 1958), 691–703, in Warner Papers.
33. Address, December 7, 1944, BP-59; "Results," December 12, 1944, Reid Papers, vol. 5, folder 6; Sampson, *Empires of the Sky,* p. 71; Edward Warner, "The Chicago Air Conference: Accomplishments and Unfinished Business," *Foreign Affairs* (April 1945), 24–34.

CHAPTER 8   BRAZILIAN INTERLUDE

To Rio with a Return Ticket

1. Berle Diary, January 30, 31, 1945.
2. Berle Diary, October 31, 1939; Hopkins telegram to FDR, November 28, 1944, MR 20; Berle Diary, FDR telegram to Berle, November 29, Berle to FDR, December 3, 1944; Berle Diary, December 21, 28, 1945; *New York Times,* December 22, 24, 1944, January 11, 1945.
3. Berle to Edwin W. Patterson, January 11, 1945, BP-56; Rosenman memo to General Watson, January 17, 1945, Rosenman Papers, Box 1; Berle to Rudolf P. Berle, April 12, 1945, BP-74.
4. Berle to Louis Finkelstein, February 11, 1943, to Nathan Straus, September 12, 1940, to Alan J. Lowrey, July 28, 1941, BP-134, 49 and 41.
5. Berle quoted in *New York Times,* August 26, 1942; Berle to Wallace E. Pratt, August 24, 1942, memo to Hull, August 24, 1943, BP-45; Berle Diary, Berle memo of conversation, January 6, memo to FDR, October 11, 1944.
6. Berle Diary, January 20, 22, 23, 24, 29, 1945; copy, Harold S. Tewell to Randolph Harrison, Jr., January 6, 1945, BP-77; Berle to Charles Taussig, February 5, to Stettinius, January 26, 29, to Alice, Beatrice and Peter, January 26, 1945, BP-77 and 74.
7. Berle to "Beatty," July 18, 1951, BP-81; Berle Diary, January 25, 26, April 18, 1945; Sir D. Gainer to J. V. Perowne. February 15, 1945, FO 371/44818.
8. *New York Times,* January 12, 15, 1945; State Department memo, December 20, 1944, BP-76; Carleton S. Smith to Berle, February 3, Berle to Charles Taussig, February 5, 1945, BP-77; Berle Diary, January 30, February 4, 9, March 24, April 18, 21, 1945; Henry Wallace, COHC, June 13, 1945, p. 3918.
9. Berle to FDR, March 14, BP-76, Nathaniel P. Davis, April 24, to Julius C. Holmes, May 3, 1945, BP-75; to James F. Byrnes, July 3, 1945, BP-74; Berle Diary, April 4, copy of telegram to Stettinius and Rockefeller, April 5, 1945.
10. Berle Diary, January 30, February 8, March 24, April 6, May 3, 1945; Berle to Beatrice, February 6, 1945, BP-81.

A Global Good Neighbor?

1. *Foreign Relations of the United States,* 1945, vol. IX, pp. 50–52; Irwin F. Gellman, *Good Neighbor Diplomacy: United States Policies in Latin America 1933–1945* (Baltimore, 1979), pp. 198–202.
2. Gellman, *Good Neighbor Diplomacy,* p. 197; Berle Diary, May 14, 1942, February 7, 12, 1945, memo to Rockefeller, February 9, 1945, emphasis added.

3. Berle Diary, February 13, 14, 16, 17, 18, 19, 20, 21, 27, March 6, 1945, memos of conversations, February 12, 15, 1945; D. Gainer to Foreign Office, February 14, 1945, FO 371/44685; *New York Times,* February 16, 18, 1945.

4. "Inadequacies of Stettinius as Secretary of State," no. 2027, Messersmith Papers; Berle Diary, February 27, March 1, 6, 14, 21, 1945; Gellman, *Good Neighbor Diplomacy,* pp. 204–9; "Mexico City Conference," March 5, 1945, FO 371/45015; Nelson Rockefeller to Adolf Berle, March 13, 1945, BP-77; *New York Times,* March 5, 1945.

5. Berle Diary, March 14, 1945.

6. Berle Diary, April 11, March 30, April 1, 5, 24, 1945.

7. Berle Diary, April 12, 13, 21, 24, May 5, 7, 1945; Berle to Alice, April 25, to Father, April 16, 1945, BP-74.

8. See Berle to Father, April 16, 1945, Berle to Truman, April 17, 1945, CFTL, BP-77; D. V. Kelly to A. Eden, April 27, 1945, FO 371/44686; Berle Diary, April 17, 1942, April 24, May 1, April 28, May 1, 2, 7, 8, 1945.

End of a Regime

1. Berle Diary, July 8, May 11, 15, 1945.

2. Berle Diary, May 12, 15, June 1, 1945, Memo of conversation, May 24, 1945.

3. Alberto Queiroz to Berle, May 31, Berle to Queiroz, June 2, 1945, BP-74; Berle Diary, June 8, 11, 12, 1945; memo of conversation, June 13, 1945, Grew Papers; The President's Appointments, Wednesday, June 13, 1945, Henry Wallace, COHC, June 13, 1945, p. 3917.

4. *New York Times,* March 29, July 4, 29, August 15, 17, 1945; Berle Diary, July 15, July 28–August 7, 1945.

5. Berle Diary, September 3, 20, 1945.

6. Berle Diary, September 29, October 1, 1945; Berle to Truman, October 1, 1945, BP-74, 77, PSFTL.

7. Berle Diary, October 4, 1945; *New York Times,* October 3, 19, December 4, 1945; *New York Herald Tribune,* December 2, 1945; Ernest Cuneo–Tom Corcoran conversation, October 31, 1945, PSFTL; Braden to Berle, December 5, Berle to Chalmers, December 11, 1945, BP-74, 75.

8. Thomas E. Skidmore, *Politics in Brazil, 1930–1964* (New York, 1967), pp. 51–53, 349n; John W. F. Dulles, *Vargas of Brazil* (Austin, TX, 1967), pp. 270–74, 283–84; Berle Diary, October 3, 30, 1945; *New York Times,* November 9, 1945; also, see Berle telegram to State, October 30, 1945, CFTL.

9. On Rockefeller's fall, see Philip Chalmers to Berle, August 31, 1945, BP-75; Dulles, *Vargas of Brazil,* p. 269; Berle Diary, October 6, 1945; Ernest Cuneo–Tom Corcoran conversation, October 31, 1945, PSFTL; Spruille Braden, COHC, pp. 2133–35; Berle Diary, September 20, 23, 1945.

10. Ernest Cuneo–Tom Corcoran conversation, October 31, 1945, PSFTL; Berle to Truman, September 4, Truman to Berle, August 24, 1945, BP-77, OFTL; Truman to Berle, September 13, 1945, CFTL, BP-77; Berle to State, September 3, to Fletcher Warren, September 10, 1945, BP-74 and 77.

11. "Memorandum: Economic Assistance and Non-Intervention," September 15, 1945, BP-75; Berle Diary, copy of telegram, Berle to State, September 18, 20, 1945.

12. Berle to Anna N. Brock, October 25, 1945, BP-74; memo of conversation, October 5, 1945, BP-76; Berle to Alice, November 5, to Lina, November 6, 1945, BP-74.

13. James F. Byrnes memo to Truman, November 9, Truman to Berle, November 9, 1945, CFTL; Berle to Philip Chalmers, November 14, 1945, BP-75; *New York Times,* December 4, 1945; Berle to Philip Chalmers, December 5, to Fletcher Warren, November 6, 1945, BP-75 and 77.

"Colonizing Capital"

1. "Conflict of United States and British trade interests in Latin America," May 15, 1942, FO 371/30516; copy, British "Memo respecting the Anglo-United States-Brazilian Triangle," July 15, 1942, King Papers, vol. 300, folder 3089.

2. On British conflicts with Berle, see "Proposed British Air Service to South America," June 6, 1944, FO 371/42600; Berle Diary, November 8, 1943; "Brazilian External Debt," November 11, 1943, FO 371/33664-5; "Mr. Berle's Aspersions on Mr. Phillimore's Character," February 2, 1944, FO 371/37836.

3. "Attitude of the United States to the results of the Mexico City Conference," April 10, 1945, FO 371/45017, original emphasis.

4. Berle quoted in Gainer to Perowne, July 13, 1945, FO 371/50254; "United States Representation in Brazil," March 2, 1945, FO 371/44818; Berle to James F. Byrnes, July 3, 1944, BP-74; Gainer on Berle, January 30, Gainer to Perowne, February 15, 1945, FO 371/44818.

5. Berle memo to Mr. Clegg, July 7, 1945, July 7, Luis Carlos Prestes to Berle, August 21, Berle to Prestes, August 24, Heber M. Clegg memo to Berle, October 24, 1945, BP-76; Berle memo to James F. Byrnes, October 23, November 5, 1945, BP-74; Berle Diary, November 3, 1945, February 13, 21, 1946.

6. Berle to Philip O. Chalmers, August 21, 1945, BP-75; Berle Diary, November 24, memo, November 16, Byrnes cable to Berle, November 10, Berle cables to Byrnes, November 13 [2], 14, 17, Berle cable to Braden, November 17, 1945, Berle memo to DuWayne Clark, September 27, 1945, BP-76.

7. Berle Diary, November 24, December 7, Byrnes cable to Berle, November 19, Berle cable to Byrnes, November 23, cable to Braden, November 27, Brynes cable to Berle, November 30, 1945; copy, State memo of telephone conversation, November 23, 1945, BP-76.

8. Berle Diary, December 7, Berle cable to Byrnes, December 4 [2], 1945; Berle to Philip O. Chalmers, December 5, 1945, BP-75; NTR, pp. 563-64; R. H. Hadow to Donald Gainer, December 21, 1945, FO 371/52077; also, see John D. Wirth, *The Politics of Brazilian Development 1930-1954* (Stanford, CA, 1970), p. 162.

9. Berle Diary, Berle cable to Byrnes, November 26, 1945; D. St. Clair Gainer to R. H. Hadow, January 4, 1946, "Brazil-U.S. Relations: Oil interests in Brazil," January 25, 1946, FO 371/52077; "Brazil-U.S. Relations: Mr. Berle," March 1, 1946, FO 371/51904.

10. Berle to Truman, November 26, December 3, 1945, BP-77.

11. Truman to Berle, February 20, 1946, BP-77; Berle Diary, February 8, 11, 21, 1946; *New York Times,* December 16, 1945, January 9, February 1, 5, 9, 1946; Woodward memo to Connelly, December 27, 1945, Woodward memo to M. C. Latta, February 7, 1946, OFTL; Berle Diary, press release, February 8, 1946.

12. "Brazil-U.S. Relations: Mr. Berle," D. Gainer to Ernest Bevin, February 14, 1946, FO 371/51904, emphasis added.

CHAPTER 9   *PAX AMERICANA* AND COLD WAR, 1946–1961

"The Real Life of the Country"

1. "Resignation of Mr. Berle," February 12, 1946, FO 371/51904.
2. Berle Diary, February 5, 1953; Berle to Bernard M. Baruch, October 25, 1954, to Alice, April 25, 1946, to Beatty, December 8, 1948, BP-81; Berle to Jesse Jones, October 27, 1954, BP-83.
3. Berle, "How Long Will New York Wait?" *Reporter,* September 8, 1955, p. 14.
4. Berle to David E. Lilienthal, November 29, 1949, Lilienthal Papers, Box 142; to Alfred Starratt, April 12, 1954, BP-84.
5. See "Bishop Property Lease and General" and "Bishop Lease Purchase from Mrs. Berle 1943" folders in Rockefeller Papers; *New York Times,* August 4, 5, 8, 1943, section viii.
6. Beatrice Bishop Berle, *A Life in Two Worlds: Autobiography* (New York, 1983), pp. 184–87; Berle to Alice, October 20, 1947, August 4, September 12, November 15, 1949, BP-81 and 82.
7. Berle Diary, May 4, 1950, July 12, 1951, May 15, July 1, 1952, September 30, 1954, November 23, 1955, March 13, 1957, October 2, 1958; interview with Alice Crawford, June 17, 1986.
8. Beatrice Bishop Berle, *A Life in Two Worlds,* p. 194; Berle to "Beattie," October 4, 1949, March 5, July 12, 1951, March 18, June 11, July 31, 1952, to Alice, June 11, 1953, BP-81 and 82; Berle Diary, September 12, 1951; interview with Beatrice Meyerson, November 20, 1984.
9. Berle to Peter, September 28, October 6, 21, November 4, 1954, December 7, 1955, December 4, 1956, May 15, 1957, February 13, 24, 1958, BP-81; Berle to J. K. Galbriath, June 13, 23, September 17, 1958, Berle Diary, December 9, 1958, July 6, 15, 22, 1959, May 30, 1960.
10. Berle Diary, October 2, 1953, July 25, 1947, October 21, 1954; *New York Times,* October 21, 1950; May 16, 1957, September 12, 1959, also see *New York Times Book Review,* September 24, 1954, May 19, 1957, September 6, 1959.
11. Berle Diary, February 9, June 11, December 23, 1954, May 4, 1956, May 8, October 11, 1957.
12. See Cabell Phillips, "The New Dealers—Where Are They Now?" and Richard and Daz Harkness, "Where Are Those Rampaging New Dealers?" *New York Times Magazine,* September 29, 1946, May 22, 1960; Berle Diary, October 2, 1953, June 15, 1956, January 3, 9, October 3, 1957.
13. Berle to "Mimi," January 3, 1949, BP-82; *New York Times Book Review,* March 15, 1953; Berle Diary, June 20, 1957, Alpheus Thomas Mason to Berle, June 27, 1957.
14. Berle Diary, April 4, 1956, December 27, 1958, January 20, 1959, Berle to James Perkins, February 11, 1959.
15. Berle to Dean Rusk, January 7, 1960, BP-96; Berle Diary, June 6, 1957, Berle to James W. Angell, November 20, 1952; see André Cournand and Maurice

Levy, eds., *Shaping the Future: Gaston Berger and the Concept of Prospective* (New York, 1973).

Liberalism Without FDR

1. Berle Diary, July 25, 1947; *New York Times,* September 21, 1947.
2. Berle Diary, April 4, 1956; Berle to Morris B. Abram, February 23, 1955, BP-138; on Dubinsky and the ILGWU, see David Dubinsky and A. H. Raskin, *David Dubinsky: A Life with Labor* (New York, 1977), and Max D. Danish, *The World of David Dubinsky* (Cleveland, 1957).
3. Berle Diary, May 13, 1947, July 16, 1953; Berle to Peter, November 17, 4, 1954, to Alice, November 7, 1956, BP-81 and 82; Berle to B. M. Baruch, May 15, 1947, Baruch Papers, Selected Correspondence.
4. Berle Diary, July 21, April 29, May 2, July 21, 25, August 14, 22, 24, 1942; *New York Times,* May 24, 25, July 23, 24, 1942; Harold R. Moskovit to Berle, June 2, 1942, BP-63; Owen D. Young to Berle, June 20, 1942, BP-64; Berle memos to FDR, June 19, 24, July 8, 1942, PSF 94.
5. Berle to Beulah Amidon Ratliff, August 13, 1936, Survey Associates Papers, Box 54; Berle to Thomas E. Dewey, August 13, 1936, BP-11; Richard N. Smith, *Thomas E. Dewey and His Times* (New York, 1982), pp. 229–31; Berle Diary, August 12, 17, October 21, 1937.
6. *New York Times,* October 8, 10, 15, 16, 18, 28, 31, 1944; Berle to FDR, October 12, 1944, BP-67.
7. *New York Times,* May 22, 1946, February 10, May 1, 1947, June 15, 22, October 22, 1946; Berle to Truman, October 1, 1946, CFTL; Berle to William A. Wieland, October 9, 1946, BP-85; Berle Diary, November 6, 1946.
8. *New York Times,* May 5, 12, 13, June 18, 21, July 9, 20, 21, 24, 1947; Berle Diary, June 13, July 9, 20, 1947, January 19, 1948; telegrams, Berle to Truman, June 30, Matthew Connelly to Berle, July 2, 1947, January 8, 1948, Appointments, July 8, 1947, January 13, 1948, PSFTL.
9. Berle and Joseph V. O'Leary to Truman, September 11, October 1, 24, Truman to Berle, September 22, October 9, 28, 1947, PSFTL; *New York Times,* September 27, 28, November 6, December 17, 31, 1947, January 14, February 16, May 13, 1948; Berle Diary, January 19 [2], 1948.
10. Berle to Louis E. Johnson, April 12, to Alice, October 4, 1948, BP-83; *New York Times,* April 18, July 22, September 17, 3, 1948; Berle Diary, July 28, 1948; Berle speech to State Convention of Americans for Democratic Action, April 3, Dean Alfange to Berle, September 17, 1,948, Dubinsky Papers, Box 149, file 3a, ILGWU.
11. Telegram, Berle to Truman, November 3, 1948, PSFTL 200; *New York Times,* January 8, 14, 1949; PSFTL 2640; Berle Diary, memo, "The Liberal Party: 1948–1949 Position," December 1, Berle to J. Howard McGrath, November 18, 1948; Berle to Hugh K. Frederick, Jr., January 24, 1949, BP-97.
12. Berle Diary, June 1, 13, July 7, 12, 21, August 5, November 9, 10, 1949, Berle to C. C. Burlingham, August 4, 1949; *New York Times,* May 26, June 1, 7, 30, October 6, 8, 1949; Berle telegram to Oscar Chapman, April 27, 1950, Chapman Papers.
13. Berle to Oscar L. Chapman, November 15, to Jesse H. Jones, December 28,

1949, to Raymond Pace Alexander, November 3, 1947, BP-81 and 83; to the Editor of the *New York Times,* BP-91; Berle Diary, November 28, 1947.

14. *New York Times,* May 28, June 26, December 9, 1951; Berle to Father, June 27, to Beatrice, November 7, 1951, BP-81; Berle Diary, July 18, September 12, November 1, 7, 1951.
15. See White House correspondence with Berle and Liberal party, PSFTL 2640; Berle telegram to Truman, June 28, 1950, PSFTL 471-B; *New York Times Book Review,* March 23, 1952; Berle Diary, January 21, 1953, April 6, 1951.
16. Berle to Adlai E. Stevenson, March 26, April 3, 14, 1952, Stevenson Papers, Box 263.
17. Berle Diary, May 27, June 12, July 1, 15, 16, 17, 28, 1952, Berle to Paul H. Douglas, May 21, 27, Douglas to Berle, May 26, Estes Kefauver to Berle, August 1, 1952; Berle to Beatrice, June 11, to Father, July 1, 1952, BP-81; *New York Times,* June 12, July 1, 1952.
18. Berle Diary, July 28, 1952; Berle to Paul Douglas, August 5, 1952, BP-82.
19. Berle Diary, July 29, 31, September 22, 24, 1952; *New York Herald Tribune,* July 30, 1952; *New York Times,* September 23, October 23, 31, November 3, 5, 1952; Berle to Stevenson, July 29, October 1, November 7, 1952, Stevenson Papers, Box 263; Berle to Alice, November 14, 1952, BP-82.
20. Berle Diary, November 7, 12, December 3, 1952, February 11, 26, April 10, 23, May 13, 21, 29, June 2, 10, 18, 24, 26, July 1, 16, 24, September 22, October 2, 30, November 4, 1953; *New York Times,* April 27, 30, June 18, July 6, September 9, October 2, 5, 8, 13, 1953.
21. *New York Times,* May 27, September 24, November 7, 1954, May 7, 26, 1955; Berle Diary, May 28, June 11, September 23, November 3, 1954.
22. Berle Diary, November 9, 17, 1954, July 7, 13, January 3, 1955; Berle to Alice, November 17, 1954, BP-82; *New York Times,* July 8, 13, 1955.
23. *New York Times,* April 26, August 15, September 13, 1956; Berle to Stevenson, February 8, March 23, June 19, Stevenson to Berle, June 15, 1956, Stevenson Papers, Box 426; to Mimi, February 6, 1956, BP-82; Berle Diary, May 4, June 19, August 12–13, September 24, 1956; Ben Davidson, COHC, p. 388.
24. Berle to Fletcher Warren, April 7, 1953, Warren Papers; to Alice, February 17, 1953, BP-82; Berle Diary, December 30, 1954.
25. Berle Diary, October 15, 1948, March 20, December 8, 1952, February 11, 1953, April 4, May 17, 1956, March 27, 1957; Nelson A. Rockefeller to Berle, January 6, June 8, Berle to Rockefeller, June 13, 1950, May 29, 1953, BP-183; Berle to Fletcher Warren, October 3, 1951, Warren Papers.
26. Berle Diary, June 6, 1957, January 17, February 26, June 10, July 8, August 27, September 3, November 3, 5, November 24, December 8, December 29, 1958; *New York Times,* November 3, 1958.

Policing Communists

1. Athan G. Theoharis, "Unanswered Questions: Chambers, Nixon, the FBI and the Hiss Case," in Theoharis, ed., *Beyond the Hiss Case: The FBI, Congress, and the Cold War* (Philadelphia, 1982), pp. 246–308.
2. Berle to Alice, January 16, 1948, BP-81; "Memo of testimony, February 11,

1948," Berle to Orlo M. Brees, May 27, to Christopher Emmet, July 28, 1948, BP-97; *New York Times,* February 12, March 14, Mary 19, 1948.

3. *New York Times,* August 4, September 1, 2, 24, October 15, 1948.

4. Berle to John McDowell, September 3, to Arthur Schlesinger, Jr., September 29, to Jacob Billikopf, August 17, 1948, BP-97, to Gilberto Freyre, January 25, 1949, BP-82; Berle Diary, September 3, 1948; Berle to Frank, September 9, 1948, Frank Papers, Boxes 1 and 3.

5. Berle Diary, September 1, 4, 1939, August 9, 18, 1948, March 18, 1952.

6. Alistair Cooke, *A Generation on Trial: U.S.A.* v. *Alger Hiss* (New York, 1950); Whittaker Chambers, *Witness* (New York, 1952); John Cabot Smith, *Alger Hiss: The True Story* (New York, 1976); Allen Weinstein, *Perjury: The Hiss-Chambers Case* (New York, 1978); Edith Tiger, ed., *In Re Alger Hiss* (New York, 1979).

7. Berle to Beatty, December 8, 1948, BP-81; *New York Times,* December 15, 1948.

8. *New York Times,* January 8, 14, 1949; Dean Acheson, *Present at the Creation: My Years in the State Department* (New York, 1969), pp. 251–53; David S. McLellan, *Dean Acheson: The State Department Years* (New York, 1976), pp. 138–39; Berle Diary, January 15, 1951; see Acheson Papers on Berle and Hiss.

9. Dean Acheson to Felix Frankfurter, July 8, 1949, Frankfurter Papers; Jerome Frank to Felix Frankfurter, August 20, 1949, Frank Papers, Box 53, with Frankfurter writing in margins; Frankfurter to Frank, June 6, 1933, Frank Papers, Box 12.

10. Berle to Fletcher Warren, April 7, 1953, Warren Papers; Berle Diary, May 29, November 11, 1953, February 27, 1954; Berle to Alice, November 23, 1954, BP-82.

11. *New York Times,* September 24, October 24, 1954; Berle Diary, June 7, 16, July 1, 1954, February 1, 1956; Berle to J. Robert Oppenheimer, April 13, 1954, April 16, 1963, Oppenheimer Papers.

The Foreign Policy Establishment

1. See Godfrey Hodgson, *America in Our Time* (New York, 1976), pp. 111–33; Robert D. Schulzinger, *The Wise Men of Foreign Affairs: The History of the Council of Foreign Relations* (New York, 1984); Priscilla M. Roberts, "The American 'Eastern Establishment' and Foreign Affairs," SHAFR Newsletter, XIV and XV, pp. 9–28, 8–19.

2. *New York Times,* March 13, 1946; Berle to Walter Laves, March 25, to Truman, October 1, 1946, BP-97 and 98; Berle Diary, August 9, 1948, January 12, 1949; Berle to Alice, April 21, to Herbert Cummings, August 5, 1947, BP-81; Lilienthal to Berle, September 30, 1949, Lilienthal Papers, Box 121.

3. Berle to Fletcher Warren, April 21, 1949, Warren Papers; Berle memo to Louis E. Johnson, April 13, 1948, BP-83.

4. Berle to Jesse H. Jones, December 28, 1949, BP-83; *New York Times,* March 4, June 29, 1950; also, see Berle Diary, May 12, 1949, Berle to Louis Johnson, March 13, April 3, 1950, BP-98.

5. Berle to Louis Johnson, July 12, to Alice, July 17, 1950, BP-98 and 82; *New*

York Times, September 4, 1950, December 10, 1951; Berle Diary, March 1, 1951; Berle to Truman, December 15, 1950, PSFTL; Berle to Hugh Frederick, June 25, August 31, 1951, BP-82.

6. Cord Meyer, *Facing Reality: From World Federalism to the CIA* (New York, 1980), pp. 110–11; Robert T. Holt, *Radio Free Europe* (Minneapolis, 1958), p. 10; Blanche Wiesen Cook, *The Declassified Eisenhower* (Garden City, NY, 1981), pp. 126–28; Berle to R. H. Van Deman, January 17, 1952, BP-84; Berle Diary, August 13, 1952, August 10, 1951.

7. Berle to Louis Johnson, July 12, 1950, BP-98; Berle Diary, July 5, 1949, January 15, 16, February 21, March 8, 22, April 6, 12, 1951, February 15, 1954, April 25, 1955.

8. Berle to Allen Dulles, May 11, Dulles to Berle, May 28, 1951, Dulles Papers, Box 55; Meyer, *Facing Reality,* p. 112; Irving Dilliard, "Charles Douglas Jackson," DAB, Supplement Seven 1961–1965, pp. 383–85; Cook, *The Declassified Eisenhower,* pp. 122–25.

9. Berle Diary, November 9, 1951, November 28, "conversation with Joseph Retinger, December 1," December 2, March 18, April 3, May 12, June 12, August 5, 1952, February 13, 1953, "Excerpts from S.P. letter dated October 26, 1952"; *New York Times,* February 15, 1953.

10. Berle Diary, November 17, 20, December 8, 1952, January 16, 23, 1953; Berle to Allen Dulles, February 9, Dulles to Berle, February 13, 1953, Dulles Papers, Boxes 55 and 61.

11. Berle to Adlai E. Stevenson, July 29, 1952, Stevenson Papers, Box 263; *New York Times,* June 2, 1950, July 23, 1951; Berle Diary, April 9, September 12, 1951, September 22, 1952, November 1, 1954; Berle to Malcolm Davis, September 19, 1952, BP-82; also, see NCFE file in Rockefeller Papers.

12. Berle Diary, January 30, February 5, July 16, 20, 21, 1951; Berle Diary, February 24, June 24, July 1, 1953; Berle to Fletcher Warren, April 7, September 17, 1953, Warren Papers.

13. Berle Diary, December 21, 1953, February 9, June 7, July 1, December 30, 1954, March 4, 8, 10, 1955; Allen Dulles to Berle, January 10, May 10, Berle to Dulles, April 25, 1955, Dulles Papers, Box 66; C. D. Jackson to Berle, December 9, 1955, BP-83.

14. Cook, *The Declassified Eisenhower,* pp. 196–202; Berle Diary, March 6, 8, April 4, August 2, 1956; Berle to Adlai Stevenson, June 29, 1956, Stevenson Papers, Box 426; Bowles to Berle, July 13, 1956, Bowles Papers, Box 123.

15. Berle Diary, October 22, 25, 30, 31, November 5, 14, 1956; *New York Times,* November 3, 1956; Stephen E. Ambrose with Richard H. Immerman, *Ike's Spies: Eisenhower and the Espionage Establishment* (Garden City, NY, 1981), pp. 235–40; Cook, *The Declassified Eisenhower,* pp. 203–5; Meyer, *Facing Reality,* pp. 123–30.

16. Berle Diary, October 31, December 5, 1956, January 3, 7, April 30, October 22, 31, 1957.

17. Berle to Nelson Rockefeller, January 3, 1954, BP-84; Berle Diary, December 30, 1954, January 1, 1955, August 28, 1957, August 25, 1958; *New York Times,* November 15, 1956; Berle to Frederick Lyon, August 28, 1957, BP-83.

18. Berle Diary, January 3, 9, May 8, October 3, November 13, 1957, June 8, 1959,

May 17, July 25, 1960; Nelson A. Rockefeller to Berle, September 18, October 31, 1956, Berle memo, November 21, 1956, statement, June 24, 1959, Special Studies Project, Berle folders, 1956-1957, 1958-1959, Rockefeller Papers.

Self-Determination for Guatemala

1. On Truman, see David Green, "The Cold War Comes to Latin America," in Barton Bernstein, ed., *Politics and Policies of the Truman Administration* (Chicago, 1970), pp. 149-95; David Green, *The Containment of Latin America* (Chicago, 1971), pp. 237-97; Richard Immerman, *The CIA in Guatemala* (Austin, TX, 1982), pp. 7-13.
2. Berle to Sumner Welles, June 24, September 14, Welles to Berle, June 27, 1949, BP-84; Berle Diary, October 11, 1950; Berle to Spruille Braden, March 15, April 16, 1946, BP-97.
3. "Industrialization in Latin America," November 18, 1946, and other Council on Foreign Relations material in BP-103; on American Molasses and Haiti, see Berle to Hermann Habicht, April 7, 1948, to Spruille Braden, November 23, 1946, BP-97 and 82.
4. Berle Diary, July 12, 1948, July 28, June 18, October 22, November 7, 1952.
5. Berle, CFR memo. October 11, 1948, BP-103, emphasis added; Berle Diary, December 9, 1946, June 2, 1949; also, on the CFR meeting, see Walter LaFeber, *Inevitable Revolutions: The United States in Central America* (New York, 1984), pp. 103-4.
6. Berle Diary, June 18, 23, 1952; on Guatemala, see Immerman, *The CIA in Guatemala,* pp. 20-126; Stephen Schlesinger and Stephen Kinzer, *Bitter Fruit: The Untold Story of the American Coup in Guatemala* (Garden City, NY, 1982), pp. 25-97; LaFeber, *Inevitable Revolutions,* pp. 111-26; Berle quoted on Braden in Immerman, *The CIA in Guatemala,* p. 126; Cook, *The Declassified Eisenhower,* pp. 218-33.
7. Berle Diary, October 17, December 2, 8, 1952, Berle to Arthur Schlesinger, October 17, 1952; Immerman, *The CIA in Guatemala,* pp. 128-29; Berle to Alice, February 17, 1953, BP-82.
8. Berle Diary, Berle to John C. McClintock, May 20, 1953, April 1, memo of conversation with Jose Figueres, March 31, 1953.
9. Charles Ameringer, *Don Pepe* (Albuquerque, NM, 1978), pp. 1-143, passim; Ameringer, *The Democratic Left in Exile* (Coral Gables, FL, 1974), pp. 72-87; John Patrick Bell, *Crisis in Costa Rica: The 1948 Revolution* (Austin, TX, 1971); Robert Alexander, *Prophets of the Revolution* (New York, 1962), pp. 144-73; La Feber, *Inevitable Revolutions,* p. 105.
10. Berle to Nelson Rockefeller, April 14, 1953, BP-84; Berle Diary, April 1, May 25, 1953, May 10, 1954.
11. Immerman, *The CIA in Guatemala,* pp. 130-31; Berle Diary, memo to Figueres, May 12, 1953; Berle to Allen Dulles, April 8, 1953, Dulles Papers, Box 66; Berle memo for CFR, May 15, 1953, BP-103; John A. Peeler, *Latin American Democracies,* (Chapel Hill, NC, 1985), pp. 30-31, 71-75.
12. Berle Diary, May 10, 17, 1954, Berle to Figueres, May 19; to Dulles, May 19, Dulles to Berle, May 27, 1954, Dulles Papers, Box 66.

13. Berle Diary, May 14, 28, June 7, 16, 21, 22, 28, July 1, 2, 1954; Berle, "Communist Thunder to the South," *New York Times Magazine,* July 4, 1954, p. 8; Ameringer, *Don Pepe,* pp. 129, 143.
14. See Immerman, *The CIA in Guatemala,* pp. 133–86; Schlesinger and Kinzer, *Bitter Fruit,* pp. 99–226; Cook, *The Declassified Eisenhower,* pp. 239–92; Ambrose with Immerman, *Ike's Spies,* pp. 215–234; David Atlee Phillips, *The Night Watch* (New York, 1977), pp. 30–54; LaFeber, *Inevitable Revolutions,* pp. 111–126.
15. Berle Diary, July 19, 20, 29, 1954, Jose Figueres to Berle, July 11, Berle to Figueres, July 19, 1954.
16. Berle Diary, September 9, November 20, 21, 26, 29, December 1, 1954, January 8, 10, 11, 12, 14, 17, 25, 29, 30, February 1, 7, 8, 9, 1955, to Rockefeller, January 12, 1955; Berle to Antonio Espinoso, September 9, 1954, BP-82; Morison to Berle, July 16, 1964, BP-87.
17. Berle Diary, March 23, 1955, January 6, 10, February 24, 1956; Jose Figueres to Berle, August 17, 1955, BP-82; Berle, *The New York Times Magazine,* October 16, 1955, p. 22, July 15, 1956, p. 7; Berle to Lyman Bryson, February 28, 1956, BP-103; *New York Times,* April 8, 1956.
18. Berle Diary, August 27, September 24, October 22, November 19, 1956, January 30, April 8, November 13, 1957, Frank Wissner to Berle, August 27, Berle to Villeda Morales, August 27, November 19, Frances Grant to Peggy Poole, October 1, 1956; Ameringer, *The Democratic Left in Exile,* pp. 49–50, 227–28.
19. Berle Diary, January 30, March 11, May 10, June 6, August 28, November 25, 1957; Berle to Luis Muñoz Marín, May 9, 1957, BP-83.

Self-Determination for Cuba

1. Berle, "A Few Questions for the Diplomatic Pouch," *New York Times Book Review,* February 15, 1959, p. 3.
2. Berle Diary, December 9, 1959, Berle to Kenneth W. Thompson, October 28, 1960; William A. Williams to Berle, March 28, Berle to Williams, March 30, 1960, BP-105; William Appleman Williams, *The Tragedy of American Diplomacy,* second revised and enlarged edition (New York, 1972), p. 105.
3. Berle Diary, November 25, 1957, July 9, October 16, December 9, 1958, January 30, February 5, 1959; Berle to Arthur Schlesinger, Jr., April 16, 1958, BP-84; Ameringer, *Don Pepe,* pp. 150, 152.
4. Philip W. Bonsal, *Cuba, Castro, and the United States* (Pittsburgh, 1971), pp. 53–54; Ameringer, *Don Pepe,* pp. 144–57; Berle, "Latin America: The Hidden Revolution," *Reporter,* May 28, 1959, pp. 17–20; Berle Diary, March 24, March 25, April 1, 3, 13, 1959.
5. *New York Times,* April 13, 20, 1959; Willauer Cuban Diary, April 10, 11, 12, 13, May 15, June 4, 1959; Berle Diary, April 8, 12, 13, 15, 17, 20, May 1, 2, 4, 6, 7, 8, 13, 29, June 6, 15, 16, 1959, June 23, 1960; Ameringer, *Don Pepe,* pp. 159–61.
6. Berle to William C. Wieland, August 24, 1959, BP-92; Berle Diary, October 26, 1959, February 2, 15, 17, 26, March 1, 18, June 27, 1960, emphasis added.
7. Berle Diary, April 23, 1960; Frances Grant to Berle, June 14, Berle to Grant, June 16, 1960, "Second Inter-American Conference for Democracy and Free-

dom," BP-106; Robert J. Alexander, *Romulo Betancourt and the Transformation of Venezuela* (New Brunswick, NJ, 1982), pp. 550–51; Ameringer, *Don Pepe,* p. 298, n. 102.

8. Berle Diary, June 23, 1960, December 7, 1959, February 15, June 16, 22, July 8, 14, 1960; Berle to Chester Bowles, December 28, 1959, Bowles to Berle, January 8, 1960, Bowles Papers, Box 203.

9. Berle, "The Communist Invasion of Latin America," *Reporter,* July 7, 1960, pp. 23–25; Berle Diary, July 11, 1960.

10. Berle Diary, July 12, 21, September 22, October 4, 18, 25, November 4, 10, 25, 1960, Berle to Bayless Manning, July 19, 1960; *New York Times,* October 26, 1960; Chester Bowles to Berle, November 18, 1960, Bowles Papers, Box 203.

11. Berle Diary, December 7, 17–18, 20, 15, 1960; Theodore Sorenson to Berle, December 6, Berle to Lincoln Gordon, December 9, telegram Berle to Sorenson, December 18, 1960, BP-94.

12. Berle Diary, January 6, 8, 17, 1961; Berle to Richard Goodwin, January 9, to Teodoro Moscoso, January 10, 1961, BP-94; Lincoln Gordon, OHJFK, p. 6; interview with Robert Alexander, April 4, 1986; John Bartlow Martin, *U.S. Policy in the Caribbean* (Boulder, CO, 1978), pp. 50–51.

13. Berle Diary, January 18, 24, 26, 1961; *New York Times,* February 1, 1961.

14. George R. Marotta memo to McGeorge Bundy, February 3, 1961, National Security Papers, Box 215; Chester Bowles, *Promises to Keep: My Years in Public Life 1941–1969* (New York, 1971), p. 311.

15. Thomas C. Mann, OHJFK, pp. 3, 6; Lincoln Gordon, OHJFK, pp. 11–15; Bonsal, *Castro, Cuba,* p. 179; Arthur Schlesinger, Jr., *A Thousand Days: John F. Kennedy in the White House* (Boston, 1965), pp. 182–84, 190.

16. Berle Diary, January 30, February 8, 10, 16, 1961; Berle to Frank C. Staples, February 6, 1961, BP-85.

17. Schlesinger, *A Thousand Days,* pp. 170–71; Berle Diary, February 27, March 1, 2, 6, 7, 22, 28, 1961, A. S. Jr. to Adolf, handwritten, undated; John Moors Cabot, OHJFK, pp. 4–5; *New York Times,* March 3, 4, 7, 8, 10, 1961.

18. Berle Diary, March 8, 9, 1961; Schlesinger, *A Thousand Days,* pp. 191–94.

19. Schlesinger, *A Thousand Days,* pp. 225–28.

20. *New York Times,* March 12, 1961; *Time,* March 14, 1961; Berle Diary, March 11, 12, 1961, emphasis added, March 22, 28, May 3, 1961.

21. Schlesinger, *A Thousand Days,* pp. 225–26, 168–76; Berle Diary, January 10, 18, 19, 24, 1961.

22. George R. Marotta to McGeorge Bundy, February 3, 1961, National Security Papers, Box 215; Berle Diary, February 8, 10, March 2, 6, 8, 28, 1961; John Moors Cabot, OHJFK, p. 4; *Operation Zapata: The "Ultrasensitive" Report and Testimony of the Board of Inquiry on the Bay of Pigs* (Frederick, MD, 1981), pp. 65, 83, 264.

23. *New York Times,* April 13, 1961; Berle Diary, May 3, 1961; Schlesinger, *A Thousand Days,* p. 190.

24. Schlesinger, *A Thousand Days,* pp. 235–36; Peter Wyden, *Bay of Pigs: The Untold Story* (New York, 1979), pp. 146–47; Berle Diary, May 3, 1961.

25. Schlesinger, *A Thousand Days,* pp. 243–48; Wyden, *Bay of Pigs,* pp. 161, 166–68; Berle Diary, May 3, 1961; *Operation Zapata,* pp. 355–56.

26. Schlesinger, *A Thousand Days,* pp. 260–66; Wyden, *Bay of Pigs,* pp. 271,

290–92; handwritten draft, April 19, copy, Rusk telegram to Amembassy Bogota, April 21, 1961, Cuba (Berle) file, Schlesinger Papers, Box 5; Berle Diary, Schlesinger to Berle, April 21, 1961.

27. Ameringer, pp. 180–81; Schlesinger, *A Thousand Days,* p. 157; Wyden, *Bay of Pigs,* p. 115; Berle Diary, May 5, 1961; *Operation Zapata,* pp. 83, 226–31.
28. Figueres to Berle, May 5, Berle to Figueres, May 9, 31, 1961, BP-85.

CHAPTER 10   THE LESSONS OF LIBERALISM

Self-Determination in the Sixties

1. Berle Diary, December 29, 1961; Richard E. Welch, Jr., *Response to Revolution: The United States and the Cuban Revolution* (Chapel Hill, NC, 1985), pp. 86, 85. Also see Welch, "Lippmann, Berle, and the U.S. Response to the Cuban Revolution," *Diplomatic History,* 6 (Spring 1982), 125–43.
2. Berle Diary, May 11, 15, 17, 23, 25, 26, June 13, 16, 1961; Berle to Peter, May 16, to José Figueres, May 31, 1961, BP-85; Chester Bowles memo to Berle, May 25, 1961, Bowles Papers, Box 299.
3. *New York Times,* May 21, 28, July 8, 1961, *New York Times Book Review,* October 14, 1962, p. 1; *Washington Post,* July 10, 1961; Berle Diary, May 31, June 5, 12, 17–19, July 7, Kennedy to Berle, July 7, State Department Transcript, July 11, 1961; Berle to Wayne Morse, June 23, 1961, BP-85.
4. Berle Diary, July 21, 1961, November 7, 1962, January 8, 1965.
5. Berle Diary, January 25, 1962; *New York Times,* March 22, July 27, 1962; Berle, "Are We 'Ignoring' Latin America?" *New York Times Magazine,* November 24, 1963, p. 26; "When They Shout, 'Yanqui, No!'" ibid., January 26, 1964, p. 9.
6. Tad Szulc, "So Cuba's Red Fire May Not Spread," *New York Times Book Review,* October 14, 1962, p. 1.
7. Berle Diary, May 22, November 22, 1962, November 30, 1961, January 10, 1963, October 1, 1962, Berle to Robert F. Woodward, September 1, 1961; Berle, "Our Role in Latin America," *Reporter,* 25 (November 23, 1961), pp. 30–33.
8. Berle, "It Had to be Faced," *Reporter,* 27 (November 8, 1962), 28–29; Berle Diary, October 23, 24, 26, 29, November 2, December 4, 1962, March 12, 26, 1963.
9. Berle Diary, December 6, 1961, January 25, March 14, 1962; Berle to Richard Goodwin, April 18, 1962, BP-93.
10. Berle Diary, May 15, 1962, January 13, 1966, April 6, 24, September 25, 1962, January 8, May 11, 1964, February 13, 1965; Berle to Jose Figueres, March 26, 1962, BP-93; Charles D. Ameringer, *Don Pepe* (Albuquerque, NM, 1978), p. 215; interview with Frances Grant, June 6, 1986.
11. Berle to Rómulo Betancourt, September 20, 1963, telegram, March 10, 1964, BP-86; Berle Diary, March 27, 1964, September 19, December 3, 6, 12–13, 1963, April 15, 1964, Berle to Arthur Schlesinger, Jr., September 29, 1964, November 4, 1964.
12. Berle to Hermann Habicht, January 4, to David Mandel, June 3, 1963, BP-87 and 93; Berle, "Latin America," *Reporter,* 26 (January 4, 1962), pp. 7–8.

13. Berle to Henry Kissinger, September 21, 1962, to Drault Ernanny de Mello e Silva, May 4, 1965, BP-93.
14. On Lacerda, see Thomas E. Skidmore, *Politics in Brazil, 1930–1964* (New York, 1967), passim.
15. Berle Diary, April 17, 1945, October 19, 1961, January 19, 1962, April 2, 15, May 18, June 2, 9, 19, December 1, 1964, September 21, 1965; *New York Times,* April 7, 1964; Berle, "As the Dust Settles in Brazil," *Reporter,* 30 (April 23, 1964), pp. 27–28.
16. Berle to William R. Kintner, February 18, 1963, BP-103; Berle Diary, December 11, October 26, 1961, January 19, May 1, 10, 1962, March 21, April 22, 1963; on sugar in 1962, see John Bartlow Martin, *Overtaken by Events: The Dominican Crisis from the Fall of Trujillo to the Civil War* (New York, 1966), pp. 161–77.
17. Berle Diary, December 3, Berle to Abe Fortas, December 3, 1963, to James Rowe, December 16, 1963, May 14, 1964, to Lyndon Johnson, December 16, 1963, May 14, 1964, to Thomas A. Mann, December 16, Johnson to Berle, December 18, 19, 1963, November 4, 1964, Mann to Berle, May 28, 1964.
18. James Rowe memo to LBJ, May 26, Rowe memo to Walter Jenkins, May 26, Jack Valenti memo to Thomas Mann, May 30, Mann memo to Valenti, June 3, Douglass Cater to Berle, September 14, 1964, Appointment file, Berle file, LBJ Papers, Box 7; Berle to Rowe, July 15, 1964, BP-88.
19. Berle Diary, June 19, 21, 22, 23, 24, 25, 26, 27, 28, December 13, 1964, January 8, 18, 1965; Berle to Jose Figueres, July 1, 1964, BP-86; to Donald Reid Cabral, July 1, 1964, BP-88.
20. LBJ to August Heckscher, January 28, Berle to LBJ, February 1, 1965, Berle file, LBJ Papers; on the intervention, see John Bartlow Martin, *U.S. Policy in the Caribbean* (Boulder, CO, 1978), pp. 640–94 and Piero Gleijeses, *The Dominican Crisis: The 1965 Constitutionalist Revolt and American Intervention* (Baltimore, 1978), passim.
21. Berle to Luis Manuel de bayle, May 13, 1965, BP-86; to Douglas Cater, May 24, 1965, BP-97; Berle Diary, May 25, 28, June 4, 1965; Berle telegram to Jack Valenti, May 27, 1965, Berle file, Berle to LBJ, June 3, 1965, ND19/CO62, LBJ Papers.
22. Berle Diary, May 25, 28, June 4, 1965; Robert J. Alexander, *Rumulo Betancourt and the Transformation of Venezuela* (New Brunswick, NJ, 1982), pp. 591–92; Ameringer, *Don Pepe,* pp. 221–26.

"A Frank and Constructive Imperialism"

1. Berle Diary, May 28, 1965.
2. *New York Times,* April 11, 1965; Berle Diary, May 28, 1965.
3. Berle to Kenneth Galbraith, May 6, 1966, BP-87; on Roger Baldwin, see his memo, September 23, 1965, BP-86; Berle to Jose Figueres, December 28, 1965, January 12, 1966, to Romulo Betancourt, January 12, February 2, 1966, Betancourt to Berle, November 29, 1967, BP-86.
4. Berle memo, "Indochina Policy," October 27, 1952, Stevenson Papers, Box 263, emphasis added.

5. Ibid.; Berle to Alice Crawford, May 28, 1954, BP-82; Berle Diary, May 28, 1954.

6. Interview with Peter Berle, May 16, 1983; Berle Diary, May 22, 1960, October 2, 1961, November 6, 1964, Berle to Josef Kajeckas, September 5, 1961; Berle to Peter, May 16, 1961, BP-85; Berle, "Dialogue? Yes—Concessions? Beware!" *New York Times Magazine,* October 20, 1963, pp. 9ff.

7. Berle Diary, January 25, May 25, February 9, March 11, 31, April 7, June 4–7, 1965, emphasis added.

8. Berle Diary, October 8, 1965, February 1, 9, 1966, January 16, June 6, 1967, December 4, 1967, Berle to LBJ, February 2, 1966; to Jose Figueres, February 1, 1966, BP-86; *New York Times,* October 10, 1965, January 14, 1967; "The Man on the Spot," *New York Times Book Review,* November 20, 1966, p. 3, *Newsday,* November 22, 1967.

9. Berle Diary, April 1, 1968, May 19, June 22, 1966; Berle to Max Steenberghe, April 1, to John Scott, May 20, Berle to Arthur Schlesinger, Jr., January 29, Schlesinger to Berle, February 2, 1968, BP-88.

10. Berle Diary, March 21, June 4, 1968; *New York Times,* June 5, 1968, emphasis added.

11. Berle Diary, April 18, 1969, April 6, 1970; *New York Times,* July 17, 1969; Berle to Max Ascoli, June 16, 1969, BP-86.

12. Berle to Henry Kissinger, December 4, 1968, January 13, 1969, BP-87; *New York Times,* January 16, 1969; Berle to Nelson Rockefeller, January 6, 1970, BP-88.

The Best Club

1. Berle, *Leaning Against the Dawn* (New York, 1969), pp. 17–24; "Fact and Faces: The Story of The Twentieth Century Fund, May 20, 1946," TCF.

2. Samuel L. Kuhn to Berle, December 20, 1932, Evans Clark to Berle, August 24, 1933, August 1, September 24, 1934, Berle to Clark, August 3, September 26, 1934, BP-11; John H. Fahey to Berle, February 21, 1935, BP-7.

3. David E. Lilienthal, *Journals: The Venturesome Years 1950–1955* (New York, 1966), pp. 172; Berle, *Leaning Against the Dawn,* p. 29.

4. Executive Committee Meeting, December 3, 1948, "Objectives and Policies," January 19, 1949, Trustees Meetings, March 25, 1949, February, May 12, 1950, Evans Clark to Berle, October 9, 1952, TCF; Berle, *Leaning Against the Dawn,* pp. 32–36, 41–42, 46–48, 102–103.

5. Minutes, Special Meeting of Board of Trustees, June 5, 1951; Lilienthal, *Venturesome Years,* pp. 172–73.

6. See Herbert Marcuse preface to Franz Neumann, *The Democratic and the Authoritarian State: Essays in Political and Legal Theory* (Glencoe, IL, 1957), pp. vii-ix, emphasis added.

7. Charles Dollard memo, March 29, Thomas Carskadon to Dollard, March 30, 1951, John Gardner memo, December 15, 1952, Carnegie Corporation Papers; Telephone Conversation Between AA Berle and EC—November 13, 1951, Berle memo to Evans Clark, November 21, 1951, TCF.

8. Minutes, Trustees Meeting, March 21–22, 1952, Evans Clark to Berle, March 26, 1952, TCF; Lilienthal, *Venturesome Years,* p. 617.

9. Berle to Francis Biddle, April 24, 1953, TCF, BP-125; Berle memo, "Review

of Objectives," November 1, 1953, emphasis added, SNW memo to JFD, July 29, 1953, TCF.

10. August Heckscher memo, "Interim Report: On Future Directions for Fund Research," March 10, 1954, TCF; copy, J. Fredric Dewhurst to August Heckscher, September 9, 1954, BP-125; Trustees Meetings, March 19, 1954, March 24-25, 1955, TCF; Berle, *Leaning Against the Dawn,* p. 49.

11. Special Meeting of the Board of Trustees, December 6, 1957, Heckscher memo to the Board of Trustees. November, 1960, Trustees Meetings, May 6, 1960, April 26, 1963, Special Meetings of the Board of Trustees, December 2, 1960, December 1, 1961, TCF.

12. Interview with Szold, June 6, 1960, Oral History folder, Minutes, Trustees Meetings, March 21-22, 1952, March 2-3, 1951, Berle to Francis Biddle, April 19, 1951, Special Meeting of Board of Trustees, June 5, 1951, TCF.

13. For a list of Twentieth Century Fund publications through 1968, see Berle, *Leaning Against the Dawn,* pp. 107-13.

14. Berle to Clark, December 30, 1948, Clark conversations with Berle, April 7, 1949, February 27, 1953, TCF; Trustees Meetings, March 25-26, 1949, February 10, 1950, March 2-3, 1951, March 24-25, 1953, November 30, 1956, April 11, November 13-14, 1958, April 24, December 4, 1959, April 19, 1960, TCF.

15. Trustees Meetings, May 6, December 2, 1960, December 1, 1961, April 27, 1962, December 13, 1963, May 1, December 4, 1964, November 10, 1966, June 22, 1967, November 17, 1967, March 29, November 8, 1968, March 29, November 7, 1969, TCF.

16. Trustees Meetings, March 28, 1969, May 8, 1970, Fund Policy Projects Committee Meeting, October 24, 1969, TCF.

17. Trustees Meetings, March 2-3, June 5, 1951; Pendleton Herring to Berle, January 3, 1952, TCF.

18. Trustees Meetings, December 1, 1961, December 4, 1964, May 6, 1965, Berle to Frederick Dewhurst, September 9, 1954, TCF; Berle Diary, December 5, May 11, 1964; Berle to Jacques Maritain, to Heckscher, January 27, 1956, March 13, 1964, Schlesinger to Berle, July 3, 1962, BP-126.

19. Trustees Meeting, April 24, 1959, May 7, 1965, April 29, 1966, November 10, 1966, TCF; The Twentieth Century Fund Annual Report 1984, p. 47; Berle to Heckscher, April 2, 1965, BP-127.

20. Berle to Stevenson, April 30, 1958, Stevenson Papers, Box 743.

21. Berle Diary, November 29-30, 1962; John Fahey to David E. Lilienthal, May 29, 1950, TCF; Berle to James P. Mitchell, BP-126; Heckscher in TCF Annual Report 1971; Trustees Meeting, December 1, 1961, TCF; Berle to Luis Muñoz Marín, August 19, 1965, BP-127.

22. Berle to J. K. Galbraith, July 21, 25, 1960, BP-126; Morris Abram, *The Day is Short* (New York, 1982), pp. 121-22; Berle Diary, December 12-13, 1963, December 16, 1964, February 24, 1965.

23. David E. Lilienthal, *Journals: Creativity and Conflict,* (New York, 1976), p. 34.

24. Trustees Meetings, February 10, May 12, 1950, April 12, 1957, April 23-24, 1959, December 2, 1960, April 26, 1963, December 3, 1965, TFC; Berle Diary, April 24, 1963; Berle to Trustees, October 25, Rowe to Berle, November 27, 1962, Heckscher to Berle, November 22, 1963, BP-126.

25. Berle to George C. Schuster, January 27, 1956, BP-126.

26. Trustees Meetings, November 11, 1966, March 29, 1968, March 28, 1969, TCF; Berle to Heckscher, January 16, 1967, BP-128.

27. Berle to Trustees, October 9, 1968, BP-129; Schlesinger to Murray Rossant, January 20, Rowe to Rossant, January 23, Berle to Patricia Roberts Harris, April 3, 1969, BP-130.

28. Trustees Meetings, March 25–26, 1949, March 2–3, June 5, 1951, March 21–22, 1952, October 16, 1952, March 24–25, 1955, April 11, 1958, November 30, 1961, December 1, 1961, August Heckscher to Francis Biddle, November 22, 1961, TCF.

29. Trustees Meeting, March 24–25, 1955, December 2, 1960, May 1, 1964, TCF; Heckscher to Berle, April 12, Berle to Heckscher, April 15, 1955, BP-125; Heckscher to Berle, February 2, March 17, 1967, BP-128; Berle Diary, July 1, 1954, February, 3, 1967.

30. Berle Diary, February 3, 10, 16, April 5, June 6, 22, July 13, 1967, TCF; Executive Committee, February 14, 1967, Trustees Meeting, April 6, 1967, TCF; Berle to Anthony Lewis, April 17, 1967, BP-128; to all Trustees, June 29, 1967, BP-129.

31. Trustees Meetings, March 29, 1968, November 7, 1969, TCF; Executive Committee, November 7, 1968, May 14, 1969, TCF; M. J. Rossant to the Trustees, May 7, to Berle, June 15, copy, to Lawrence K. Miller, October 6, 1969, BP-130.

32. Heckscher to Trustees, March 3, Berle to Heckscher, March 9, to Rowe, March 16, Schlesinger to Berle, March 16, Berle to Schlesinger, March 30, 1970, BP-130.

33. Heckscher to Berle, April 5, October 20, Rowe to Berle, May 22, July 1, copy, Richard E. Burns to Rossant, November 11, Rossant to Berle, November 16, Berle to Abrams, December 15, Schlesinger to Berle, December 21, 1970, Rossant to Berle, January 7, 1971, BP-131.

The Frustrations of Power *and Liberalism*

1. *New York Herald Tribune,* June 23, 1963; Berle Diary, April 26, 1966; Berle to Paul M. Hollister, August 1, 1968, to Margaret E. Newman, January 13, 1966, (1967?), BP-87.

2. Berle, *Economic Power and the Free Society* (New York, 1957); Berle in *New York Times Magazine:* "Marx Was Wrong and So Is Khrushchev," November 1, 1959, pp. 9ff; "Why Our Economy Must Grow Faster," February 7, 1960, pp. 18ff; "Bigness: Curse or Opportunity?" February 18, 1962, pp. 18ff.

3. Berle, *The American Economic Republic,* p. 221; Berle to David E. Lilienthal, November 1, 1966, BP-87.

4. Berle to Margaret E. Newman, January 13, 1966, BP-87; Berle, *American Economic Republic,* pp. 98–99; Berle to Paul M. Hollister, August 1, 1968, BP-87; to Gertrude Dennison, January 6, 1971, BP-68.

5. Berle Diary, December 29, 1961.

6. Berle Diary, February 2, 1960, December 29, 1961.

7. Berle in *New York Times Magazine:* "Unwritten Constitution for Our Economy," April 29, 1962, pp. 7ff; "How Free Shall the 'Free Market' Be?" June

23, 1963, pp. 10ff; Berle, "The Impact of the Corporation on Classical Economic Theory," *Quarterly Journal of Economics,* 79 (February 1965), 25–40.

8. Berle, *Latin America: Diplomacy and Reality* (New York, 1962); *The American Economic Republic* (New York, 1963); Berle Diary, October 13–14, 1962, January 10, December 31, 1963; Seymour Harris, "We Improvised, We Prevailed," *New York Times Book Review,* May 5, 1963, p. 6ff.

9. Berle Diary, May 26, 1964; Berle to Lindsay Rogers, January 6, 1964, BP-88; Berle, "The Coin of Governance," *Reporter,* 30 (June 18, 1964), pp. 48ff.

10. Berle Diary, Rexford G. Tugwell to Berle, March 6, Berle to Tugwell, March 10, 1964; Berle to Bernard Sternsher, May 6, Arthur Schlesinger to Berle, December 9, Berle to Schlesinger, December 14, 1965, BP-88; Berle Diary, March 29, 1960.

11. Berle Diary, April 13, 1960, October 1, 1964, April 7, October 7, 1965, January 5, 1966, June 22, 1967, October 2, 1968; Berle to William Jovanovich, March 9, 1965, Berle to Paul M. Hollister, August 1, 1968, BP-87; to Dean Rusk, January 7, 1960, BP-96; Berle, *Leaning Against the Dawn,* p. 105.

12. Berle Diary, January 29, 1970; Philip Green, "America's Ends and Means—A Disappointing Analysis," *New York Times Book Review,* November 3, 1969, pp. 8ff.

13. Berle Diary, February 1, November 10, 1962, June 22, 1965, November 4, 1970; *New York Herald Tribune,* June 23, 1963; *New York World-Telegram and Sun,* January 29, 1965; Trustees Meeting, November 6, 1970, TCF.

14. Berle to Hermann Habicht, May 7, 1970, BP-87, to Alice Crawford, April 7, 1970, BP-86; Berle Diary, March 26, April 6, March 26, 1970; Berle to Leonard Lyons, September 17, 1969, BP-87, to Peter Crawford, February 24, 1969, BP-86; *New York Times,* February 17, 1971; Berle Diary, December 31, 1963.

15. Richard Hofstadter, *The Age of Reform* (New York, 1955), pp. 167–68.

16. Robert H. Wiebe, *The Search for Order, 1877–1920* (New York, 1967), p. 303.

17. Felix Rohatyn, *The Twenty-Year Century: Essays on Economics and Public Finance* (New York, 1983).

18. Berle, *Power* (New York 1969), pp. 469–505, passim.

19. Ibid., pp. 470, 504.

Bibliography
of Unpublished Sources

MANUSCRIPT COLLECTIONS

Dean G. Acheson Papers, Harry S. Truman Library
Joseph Alsop Papers, Library of Congress
Hamilton Fish Armstrong Papers, Mudd Library, Princeton University
Bernard M. Baruch Papers, Mudd Library, Princeton University
Louis Bean Papers, Franklin D. Roosevelt Library
Lord Beaverbrook Papers, House of Lords Archives, London, England
Adolf A. Berle Papers, Diary, Franklin D. Roosevelt Library
Berle File, Baker Library, Harvard Business School
Beatrice Bishop Berle Diary, in author's possession
Francis Biddle Papers, Diary, Franklin D. Roosevelt Library
Chester Bowles Papers, Yale University Library
Charles C. Burlingham Papers, Harvard Law School Archives
Arthur F. Burns Papers, Gerald Ford Library
John Moors Cabot Oral History, John F. Kennedy Library
Carnegie Corporation Papers, Carnegie Corporation, New York City
Oscar Chapman Papers, Franklin D. Roosevelt Library
Emanuel Celler, Library of Congress
Raymond Clapper Papers, Diary, Library of Congress
John Collier Papers, Yale University Library
Council on Foreign Relations Papers, Council on Foreign Relations, New York City
Norman Davis Papers, Library of Congress

Department of External Affairs Papers, Department of External Affairs, Ottawa, Canada

William O. Douglas Papers, Library of Congress

David Dubinsky Papers, International Ladies Garment Workers Union Archives

Allen Dulles Papers, Mudd Library, Princeton University

Herbert Feis Papers, Library of Congress

Foreign Office Papers, Public Record Office, Kew, England

Jerome Frank Papers, Yale University Library

Felix Frankfurter Papers, Diary, Library of Congress

Lincoln Gordon Oral History, John F. Kennedy Library

Joseph C. Grew Papers, Houghton Library, Harvard University

Stanley Hornbeck Papers, Hoover Institution, Stanford University

Clarence D. Howe Papers, Public Archives of Canada, Ottawa, Canada

Cordell Hull Papers, Library of Congress

Harold L. Ickes Papers, Diary, Library of Congress

Lyndon Baines Johnson Papers, Lyndon Baines Johnson Library

John F. Kennedy Papers, John F. Kennedy Library

William L. Mackenzie King Papers, Public Archives of Canada, Ottawa, Canada

Fiorello H. La Guardia Papers, New York City Municipal Archives

Thomas Lamont Papers, Baker Library, Harvard University

David E. Lilienthal Papers, Mudd Library, Princeton University

Walter Lippmann Papers, Yale University Library

Breckenridge Long Papers, Diary, Library of Congress

Thomas C. Mann Oral History, John F. Kennedy Library

Vito Marcantonio Papers, New York Public Library

Gardiner C. Means Papers, Franklin D. Roosevelt Library

Lowell Mellett Papers, Franklin D. Roosevelt Library

George Messersmith Papers, University of Delaware Library

Jay Pierrepont Moffat Papers, Diary, Houghton Library, Harvard University

Raymond Moley Papers, Hoover Institution, Stanford University

R. Walton Moore Papers, Franklin D. Roosevelt Library

Henry Morgenthau Papers, Franklin D. Roosevelt Library

National Lawyers Guild Papers, Alexander Meikeljohn Civil Liberties Library, Berkeley, California

National Security Papers, John F. Kennedy Papers

J. Robert Oppenheimer Papers, Mudd Library, Princeton University

Leo Pasvolsky Papers, Library of Congress

Lester B. Pearson Papers, Public Archives of Canada, Ottawa, Canada

L. Welch Pogue Papers, Harry S. Truman Library

Escott Reid Papers, Public Archives of Canada, Ottawa, Canada

Norman A. Robertson Papers, Public Archives of Canada, Ottawa, Canada

Nelson A. Rockefeller Papers, Rockefeller Family Archives

James Harvey Rogers Papers, Yale University Library

Franklin D. Roosevelt Papers, Franklin D. Roosevelt Library

Samuel I. Rosenman Papers, Franklin D. Roosevelt Library

Arthur Schlesinger, Jr., Papers, John F. Kennedy Library

State Department Papers, National Archives

Adlai E. Stevenson Papers, Mudd Library, Princeton University

Survey Associates Papers, Social Welfare History Archives Center, University of Minnesota

Charles Taussig Papers, Franklin D. Roosevelt Library

Harry Truman Papers, Harry S. Truman Library

Rexford Guy Tugwell Papers, Franklin D. Roosevelt Library

Twentieth Century Fund Papers, Twentieth Century Fund

Oswald Garrison Villard Papers, Houghton Library, Harvard University

Jacob Viner Papers, Mudd Library, Princeton University

Lillian D. Wald Papers, New York Public Library

————, Columbia University Library

War Cabinet Papers, Public Record Office, Kew, England

Caroline Ware Papers, Franklin D. Roosevelt Library

Edward Warner Papers, International Civil Aviation Organization Library, Montreal, Canada

Fletcher Warren Papers, East Texas State University Library

Harry Dexter White Papers, Mudd Library, Princeton University

Whiting Willauer Papers, Mudd Library, Princeton University

George Frederick Wright Papers, Oberlin College

Hume Wrong Papers, Public Archives of Canada, Ottawa, Canada

DOCTORAL DISSERTATIONS

Erb, Claude Curtis. "Nelson Rockefeller and United States–Latin American Relations, 1940–1945." Clark University, 1982.

Kelso, Quinten Allen. "The Dominican Crisis of 1965: A New Appraisal." University of Colorado at Boulder, 1982.

Miller, John Andrew. "Air Diplomacy: The Chicago Civil Aviation Conference of 1944 in Anglo-American Wartime Relations and Postwar Planning." Yale University, 1971.

Morison, William J. "George Frederick Wright: In Defense of Darwinism and Fundamentalism, 1838–1921." Vanderbilt University, 1971.

Philp, Kenneth Roy. "John Collier and the American Indian, 1920–1945." Michigan State University, 1968.

Schifter, Jacobo. "Origins of the Cold War in Central America: A Study of Diplomatic Relations between Costa Rica and the United States (1940–1949)." Columbia University, 1983.

Index

Income tax, 107, 365
Independent, The, 4
India, 172, 177, 208, 224, 359
Indian Bureau, 42
Indian Welfare Committee, of the General
Federation of Women's Clubs, 40–41,
44
Indochina, 172–73
Indonesia, 346
Inflation, 76, 79–80, 86, 292, 372
Influenza, 28–29
Ingersoll, Ralph, 194–95
Inside traders, 53
Institute of Social Research, 354–55
Intelligence operations, 31–32, 169–73,
180*n,* 299
Inter-American Association for Democ-
racy and Freedom, 320
Inter-American Bank, 131–32, 213, 313
Inter-American Committee for Democracy
and Freedom, 344
Inter-American Conference for Democ-
racy and Freedom, 321, 325
Inter-American Regional Organization of
Labor (ORIT), 323
International Civil Aviation Organization
(ICAO), 251–53, 370
International Labour Office, 351
International Ladies Garment Workers
Union (ILGWU), 102, 158, 159, 288,
291, 296
International Monetary Fund (IMF), 213
Interstate Commerce Act, 83
Interstate Commerce Commission (ICC),
137
Ireland, 238, 239, 244, 251
Is Capitalism Doomed? (Dennis), 74
Italy, 12, 256, 291
fascist, 128, 129, 156

J. P. Morgan & Company, 193
Jackson, Andrew, 100
Jackson, C. D., 297, 307–10, 316
Jackson, Robert, 112, 113, 140, 141, 160,
257
James, William, 5, 13, 16
Japan, 28, 110, 127, 129, 130, 191, 345,
347
and Anti-Comintern Pact, 122
Pearl Harbor attack by, 173–74
Soviet pact with, 157
threat from, 172–73
Javits, Jacob, 295–96
Jervey, Huger W., 51
Jeunesse Radicale, 29–30
Jews, 8–12, 19, 168, 301
Berle's attitude toward, 194–98
and Palestine, 198–200

Johns Hopkins University, 52
Johnson, Alvin, 118
Johnson, Hugh, 75, 76, 106–108
Johnson, Louis, 294, 305
Johnson, Lyndon B., 325
Berle advises on Latin America, 342–44
and Vietnam War, 345, 348–49, 375
Johnson, Tom, 71
Joint Economic Committee (U.S.–Can-
ada), 155
Jones, Jesse, 88, 103, 119, 131, 139, 142,
168, 267, 293
Jovanovich, William, 367
Juliana, Princess, 151

Kauffmann, Henrik, 165, 166, 238
Keenleyside, H. L., 153–55
Kefauver, Estes, 294, 295, 297
Kellogg, Paul U., 40
Kennan, George, 306
Kennedy, John F., 312, 360, 362, 367
assassination of, 342
Berle advises on Latin America, 325–38,
341, 346
Berle's opinion of, 340
Berle's relationship with, 336
Kennedy, Joseph P., 106, 128, 143
Kennedy, Robert F., 333, 349
Kenney, Robert, 160
Kerensky, Alexander, 158
Kern, Paul H., 92
Kerr, Sir Philip, 178
Keynes, John Maynard, 62–63, 107, 118–
20, 136, 137, 140, 216, 217, 229
Economic Consequences of the Peace,
32, 74
European reconstruction plan of, 212–
15
General Theory, 119
and Paris Peace Conference, 29, 30, 32
Khalid, Prince, 199
Khrushchev, Nikita, 309
Kieran, James, 75
King, J. C., 324, 326, 331
King, Mackenzie, 121, 148–55
King, Martin Luther, Jr., 349, 358
Kintner, Robert, 124, 133–34
Kissinger, Henry, 297, 311–12, 341, 350,
358
Knapp, H. S., 20
Knox, Philander C., 32
Kolchak, Aleksandr Vasiliyevich, 27, 30
Korea, 264; *see also* North Korea; South
Korea
Korean War, 294, 305–306, 345, 346, 359
Kreisky, Bruno, 310
Krock, Arthur, 113, 190, 192
Kurusu, Saburo, 172